P9-CEC-677

| | |
|---|---|
| **Fall 1974** | The Provisional Irish Republican Army launched a bombing campaign in England. |
| **1975–1979** | The communist Khmer Rouge killed up to 2 million Cambodians through executions, starvation, exhaustion, and torture. |
| **December 1975** | Terrorist Carlos the Jackal and his comrades seized 70 hostages at an OPEC ministers' meeting in Vienna, Austria. |
| **July 4, 1976** | Israeli commandos attacked an airport in Entebbe, Uganda, to rescue 103 hostages after an Air France Airbus hijacking by Palestinian and West German terrorists. |
| **September 5, 1977** | The German Red Army Faction kidnapped industrialist Hanns-Martin Schleyer, whose body was later found in the trunk of a car. |
| **October 1977** | West German commandos attacked an airport in Mogadishu, Somalia, to rescue hostages taken when a Lufthansa Boeing 737 was hijacked by Palestinian supporters of Red Army Faction prisoners held in West German prisons. |
| **1978–1995** | During a 17-year FBI manhunt, Theodore Kaczynski, also known as the Unabomber, killed 3 people and injured 22 in a series of bombings. |
| **March 16, 1978** | Former Italian Prime Minister Aldo Moro was kidnapped in Rome by the Red Brigade. Moro's body was later found in the trunk of a parked car. |
| **December 1979** | The Soviet Army invaded Afghanistan. Fighting alongside the Afghani resistance were thousands of "Afghan Arabs," including Osama bin Laden. |
| **1980s** | Colombian drug cartels killed hundreds of public officials, including police officers, judges, presidential candidates, and criminal justice employees. |
| **May 1981** | A Brinks armored car was robbed in Nyack, New York, by former members of the Weather Underground Organization, Students for a Democratic Society, Black Panther Party, the Republic of New Africa, and the Black Liberation Army. |
| **April 1983** | A neo-Nazi group calling itself the Order initiated a campaign of violence, hoping to foment a race war in the United States. |
| **December 16, 1983** | The Provisional Irish Republican Army bombed Harrods Department Store in London. |
| **June 1985** | Hijackers belonging to Lebanon's Hezbollah hijacked TWA Flight 847, taking it on a high-profile and media-intensive odyssey around the Mediterranean. |
| **December 27, 1985** | The Abu Nidal Organization carried out simultaneous attacks at the Rome and Vienna airports. |
| **November 1987** | Operatives from North Korea bombed a Korean Air Lines flight, killing more than 100 people. |
| **1994** | Marauding Hutu and Tutsi militias in Rwanda committed genocide against civilians of these ethnic groups, leaving more than 500,000 dead. |
| **March 1995** | The Japanese religious cult Aum Shinrikyo⁻ released sarin nerve gas into the Tokyo subway system. Twelve people died, and thousands were injured. |
| **April 19, 1995** | The Alfred P. Murrah Federal Building was bombed in Oklahoma City, Oklahoma, by rightist extremists. |
| **January 1996** | Yehiya Ayyash, Hamas's expert bomb maker, known as the Engineer, was assassinated when his cell phone exploded next to his ear as he was using it. |
| **January 1997** | A bomb was detonated in Atlanta, Georgia, at a family health clinic that provided abortion services. A second bomb was detonated soon thereafter. |
| **January 16, 1997** | Two bombs exploded at an abortion clinic in Sandy Springs, Georgia. The Army of God was suspected. |
| **August 7, 1998** | Two car bombs exploded at the U.S. embassies in Nairobi, Kenya, and Dar es Salaam, Tanzania, killing more than 250 and wounding about 5,000. |
| **September 8 and 13, 1999** | Bombs destroyed two Moscow apartment complexes, killing hundreds. Chechen terrorists carried out the attacks. |
| **September 11, 2001** | Terrorists hijacked four airliners. Two of the planes were crashed into the twin towers of the World Trade Center in New York City, causing them to collapse. One plane was crashed into the Army section of the Pentagon building. The final plane crashed into rural Pennsylvania. |
| **Late 2001** | Letters containing anthrax were sent through the U.S. postal system in the New York and Washington, DC, areas. |
| **June 18, 2002** | A 22-year-old Hamas terrorist detonated the 69th suicide bomb in 21 months. During that period, 547 Israelis and 1,712 Palestinians were killed. The terrorist's family proudly referred to him as a "martyr." |
| **October 12, 2002** | A large bomb exploded in a pub in Kuta, on the Indonesian island of Bali. As patrons and others rushed into the street, a more powerful second bomb hidden inside a van was detonated; 202 people were killed and 209 were injured. |
| **May 12, 2003** | Three housing compounds for expatriate workers in Riyadh, Saudi Arabia, were bombed. Dozens were killed and about 140 were injured. |
| **October 23-26, 2003** | Chechen terrorists took more than 700 people hostage in a Moscow theater. After special forces troops pumped anesthetic gas into the theater and attacked, all of the hostage takers were killed, as were 129 of the hostages. |
| **March 11, 2004** | Ten bombs were detonated on several commuter trains in Madrid, Spain, killing 191 people and wounding more than 1,500. |
| **September 1–3, 2004** | Heavily armed Chechen terrorists seized a school in Beslan, North Ossetia, taking 1,200 hostages. As explosives were detonated and special forces retook the school, more than 330 people were killed, most of them schoolchildren. |
| **November 2, 2004** | A Dutch citizen of Moroccan descent murdered filmmaker Theo van Gogh. The assailant shot his victim repeatedly on a busy Amsterdam street and then slit his throat. van Gogh had been a critic of Islam. |

# Understanding TERRORISM

## EDITION 5

http://study.sagepub.com/martin5e

# The open-access Student Study Site includes the following:

- Mobile-friendly **eFlashcards** reinforce understanding of key terms and concepts that have been outlined in the chapters.

- Mobile-friendly **web quizzes** allow for independent assessment of progress made in learning course material.

- EXCLUSIVE! Access to selected full-text **SAGE journal articles** that have been carefully selected for each chapter. Each article supports and expands on the concepts presented in the chapter. This feature also provides questions to focus and guide student interpretation. Combine cutting-edge academic journal scholarship with the topics in your course for a robust classroom experience.

- Carefully selected, web-based **video resources** feature relevant interviews, lectures, personal stories, inquiries, and other content for use in independent or classroom-based explorations of key topics.

- **Original Video** feature interviews with the author and and provide contemporary examples that relate back to the chapter content.

# UNDERSTANDING
# **TERRORISM**

## 5TH EDITION

This book is dedicated to Sarah, Jonathan, Lauren, Jamie, Lark, Mimi, Margot, and Eric.

*Be not the slave of your own past. Plunge into the sublime seas, dive deep and swim far, so you shall come back with self-respect, with new power, with an advanced experience that shall explain and overlook the old.*

—Ralph Waldo Emerson

# UNDERSTANDING TERRORISM

*Challenges, Perspectives, and Issues*

5TH EDITION

## GUS MARTIN

*California State University, Dominguez Hills*

Los Angeles | London | New Delhi
Singapore | Washington DC | Boston

Los Angeles | London | New Delhi
Singapore | Washington DC | Boston

FOR INFORMATION:

SAGE Publications, Inc.

2455 Teller Road

Thousand Oaks, California 91320

E-mail: order@sagepub.com

SAGE Publications Ltd.

1 Oliver's Yard

55 City Road

London EC1Y 1SP

United Kingdom

SAGE Publications India Pvt. Ltd.

B 1/I 1 Mohan Cooperative Industrial Area

Mathura Road, New Delhi 110 044

India

SAGE Publications Asia-Pacific Pte. Ltd.

33 Pekin Street #02-01

Far East Square

Singapore 048763

Acquisitions Editor:   Jerry Westby

Editorial Assistant:   Laura Kirkhuff

Production Editor:   David C. Felts

Copy Editor:   Talia Greenberg

Typesetter:   C&M Digitals (P) Ltd.

Proofreader:   Sarah J. Duffy

Indexer:   Mary Mortensen

Cover Designer:   Scott Van Atta

Marketing Manager:   Terra Schultz

Copyright © 2016 by SAGE Publications, Inc.

All rights reserved. No part of this book may be reproduced or utilized in any form or by any means, electronic or mechanical, including photocopying, recording, or by any information storage and retrieval system, without permission in writing from the publisher.

Printed in the United States of America

A catalog record of this book is available from the Library of Congress.

ISBN 978-1-4833-7898-5 (pbk.)

This book is printed on acid-free paper.

SUSTAINABLE FORESTRY INITIATIVE

Certified Chain of Custody
Promoting Sustainable Forestry
www.sfiprogram.org
SFI-01268

SFI label applies to text stock

15 16 17 18 19 10 9 8 7 6 5 4 3 2 1

# Brief Contents

*Note:* **Appendix: Historical Examples**, which presents a more extensive version of the timeline printed in the front and back of this book, is available on the companion study site at **http://study.sagepub.com/martin5e.**

# Detailed Contents

# Part III. The Terrorist Trade and Counterterrorism   265

## 10.  Tools of the Trade: Tactics and Targets of Terrorists   266

## 11.  The Information Battleground: Terrorist Violence and the Role of the Media   303

*Note:* **Appendix: Historical Examples**, which presents a more extensive version of the time line printed in the front and back of this book, is available on the companion study site at **http://study.sagepub.com/martin5e**.

# About the Author

**C. Augustus "Gus" Martin** is associate vice president for human resources management at California State University, Dominguez Hills, where he regularly teaches a course on the subject of terrorism and extremism. He has also served as acting associate dean of the College of Business Administration and Public Policy, associate vice president for faculty affairs, and chair of the Department of Public Administration and Public Policy. He began his academic career as a member of the faculty of the Graduate School of Public and International Affairs, University of Pittsburgh, where he was an Administration of Justice professor. His current research and professional interests are terrorism and extremism, homeland security, administration of justice, and juvenile justice.

Dr. Martin is author of several books on the subjects of terrorism and homeland security, including *Understanding Homeland Security* (SAGE Publications, 2014); *The SAGE Encyclopedia of Terrorism,* Second Edition (SAGE Publications, 2011); *Terrorism and Homeland Security* (SAGE Publications, 2011); *Essentials of Terrorism: Concepts and Controversies* (SAGE Publications, 2011); and *The New Era of Terrorism: Selected Readings* (SAGE Publications, 2004). He is also author of *Juvenile Justice: Process and Systems* (SAGE Publications, 2005).

Prior to joining academia, Dr. Martin served as managing attorney for the Fair Housing Partnership of Greater Pittsburgh, where he was also director of a program created under a federal consent decree to desegregate public and assisted housing. He was also Special Counsel to the Attorney General of the U.S. Virgin Islands on the island of St. Thomas. As Special Counsel he occupied a personal and confidential position in the central office of the Department of Justice; sat as hearing officer for disciplinary hearings and departmental grievances; served as chair of the drug policy committee; served as liaison to the intergovernmental Law Enforcement Coordinating Committee as well as to the Narcotics Strike Force; and provided daily legal and policy advice to the Attorney General. Prior to serving as Special Counsel, he was a "floor" legislative assistant to Congressman Charles B. Rangel of New York. As legislative assistant, he researched, evaluated, and drafted legislation in areas of foreign policy, foreign aid, human rights, housing, education, social services, and poverty. He also drafted House floor statements, *Congressional Record* inserts, press releases, and news articles, and composed speeches, briefing materials, and legislative correspondence.

# Acknowledgments

I am indebted for the support and encouragement of many people in bringing this venture to completion, with special appreciation given to the very professional and expert attention given to this project by the editorial group at SAGE. Without their patient professionalism and constructive criticism, this project would not have attained the comprehensiveness and completeness that was its underlying objective from the beginning.

Thanks are extended to colleagues who shared their expert advice and suggestions for crafting this volume. Deep appreciation is also given to the panel of peer reviewers assembled by the very able editors and staff of SAGE Publications during several rounds of review. The insightful, constructive comments and critical analysis of the following reviewers were truly invaluable:

Gregory Allen Sr.
*Bellevue University*

Ronda Blevins
*Roane State Community College*

Matthew Costello
*Arkansas State University*

David DiBari
*Adams State University*

Marcie Goodman
*University of Utah*

Shannon Hankouse
*Tarleton State University*

Anthony Offret
*Pima College*

Filiz Otucu
*Plymouth State University*

Shawn Schwaner
*Miami-Dade College*

Finally, I thank my wife and children for their constant support, encouragement, and humor during the course of this project.

# Introduction and Rationale

**W**elcome to the fifth edition of *Understanding Terrorism: Challenges, Perspectives, and Issues*. This edition has been revised in several respects to enhance the educational quality of the study of terrorism. In the same spirit as the first four editions, *Understanding Terrorism, Fifth Edition* is a comprehensive textbook for students and professionals who wish to explore the phenomenon of modern terrorist violence. Readers who fully engage themselves in the recommended course of instruction offered in the pages that follow will acquire a solid foundation for understanding the nature of terrorism. Readers will also discover that their facility for critically assessing terrorism in general—and terrorist incidents in particular—will be greatly improved.

At the outset, it is important to understand that the study of terrorism is, first and foremost, a study in human behavior. It is an investigation of highly volatile human interaction. Courses that investigate terrorism must therefore review the events, ideas, motivations, theories, and histories that result in terrorist violence. None of these factors can be discussed in isolation from one another if the reader wishes to develop a facility for critically evaluating the nature of terrorism. Thus, the study of terrorism is one of the most multidisciplinary subjects in the social sciences. It is also one of the most dynamic subjects.

This book is designed to be a primary resource for university students and professionals who require fundamental expertise in understanding terrorist violence. The content of *Understanding Terrorism: Challenges, Perspectives, and Issues, Fifth Edition* is directed to academic and professional courses of instruction whose subject areas include terrorism, homeland security, international security, criminal justice administration, political conflict, armed conflict, and social environments. It can be incorporated into classes and seminars covering security studies, the administration of justice, the sociology of terrorism, conflict resolution, political theory, and other instruction in the social sciences. The intended level of instruction is undergraduate and master's-level university students, as well as professionals who require instruction in understanding terrorism.

No prerequisites are specifically recommended, but grounding in one of the following disciplines would be helpful: political science, government, administration of justice, sociology, history, or philosophy.

## ❖ Course Overview and Pedagogy

*Understanding Terrorism: Challenges, Perspectives, and Issues, Fifth Edition* introduces readers to terrorism in the contemporary era, focusing on the post–World War II period as its primary emphasis. It is a review of nations, movements, and individuals who have engaged in what many people would define as terrorist violence. It is also a review of the many kinds of terrorism that have existed in the postwar era. Of most importance, a serious exploration will be made of the underlying causes of terrorism—for example, extremist ideologies, religious intolerance, and traumatic episodes in the lives of nations and people.

The pedagogical approach of *Understanding Terrorism: Challenges, Perspectives, and Issues, Fifth Edition* is designed to stimulate critical thinking by readers. Students, professionals, and instructors will find that each chapter follows a sequence of instruction that builds on previous chapters and thus incrementally enhances the reader's knowledge of each topic. Chapters incorporate the following features:

- **Opening Viewpoints.** At the beginning of each chapter, Opening Viewpoints present relevant examples of theories and themes discussed in each chapter and serve as "reality checks" for readers.
- **Chapter Introduction.** Each chapter is introduced by an overview of the subject under investigation. The introduction provides perspective for the incorporation of each chapter's topic into the broader themes of the textbook.
- **Chapter Perspectives.** Chapters incorporate focused presentations of perspectives that explore people, events, organizations, and movements that are relevant to the subject matter of each chapter.
- **Chapter Summary.** A concluding discussion recapitulates the main themes of each chapter and introduces the subject matter of the following chapter.
- **Discussion Boxes.** Discussion Boxes present provocative information and pose challenging questions to stimulate critical thinking and further debate.
- **Key Terms and Concepts.** Important terms and ideas introduced in each chapter are listed for review and discussion. These Key Terms and Concepts are further explored and defined in the book's glossary.
- **Recommended Websites and Web Exercises.** Web exercises at the ends of chapters have been designed for students, professionals, and instructors to explore and discuss information found on the Internet.
- **Recommended Readings.** Suggested readings are listed at the end of each chapter for further information or research on each topic.

## ❖ Companion Study Site

SAGE has dedicated a companion study site for *Understanding Terrorism: Challenges, Perspectives, and Issues, Fifth Edition* at **http://study.sagepub.com/martin5e**. This companion website enables readers to better master the course and book material and provides instructors with additional resources for enriching the quality of their course of instruction.

## ❖ Chapter Guide

This volume is organized into four thematic units, each consisting of several chapters. An appendix and a glossary are included after the substantive chapters.

### Part I. Terrorism: A Conceptual Review

The first section of the book is a comprehensive discussion of definitions of terrorism and the root causes of violent political extremism. Readers develop comprehensive, contextual, and critical skills for defining terrorism and for understanding the many causes of terrorist behavior.

#### Chapter 1. Terrorism: First Impressions

The introductory chapter presents an introduction to modern terrorism and extremism. This chapter begins with an overview of basic concepts that are developed in later chapters. It continues with a discussion of conceptual considerations of terrorist violence such as the significance of symbolism and the Just War doctrine. The discussion also explores historical perspectives and criminal skill.

### Chapter 2. The Nature of the Beast: Defining Terrorism

The definitional discussion in this chapter investigates the reasons underlying why certain groups, movements, and individuals are labeled as terrorists or freedom fighters. The characteristics of extremism are defined and investigated in this chapter. Terrorism is discussed at length by sampling official definitions, reviewing the American context, and summarizing several types of terrorism. Readers are introduced to several perspectives of terrorism that are relevant for definitional discussions.

### Chapter 3. Beginnings: The Causes of Terrorism

Readers become familiar with central factors in the personal and group histories of individuals and groups who become associated with terrorism. The motives of extremists and several explanations of terrorism are explored, including sociological explanations, psychological explanations, and acts of political will. The morality of political violence is also discussed. An important discussion probes the degree to which a fresh generation of new terrorists is being forged in reaction to how the post–September 11, 2001, war on terrorism has been conducted by the West and its allies.

## Part II. The Terrorists

Part II educates readers about the many manifestations of terrorism by developing skills to critically assess and understand historical and modern examples of political violence. In particular, state- and dissident-initiated terrorism are discussed, compared, and contrasted. Readers also develop the facility to distinguish religious, ideological, and international terrorism, and the emerging environments of gender-selective and criminal dissident terrorism.

### Chapter 4. Terror From Above: Terrorism by the State

This chapter investigates state-initiated repression and terror. A state terrorism paradigm is offered to explain state sponsorship of terrorism. A detailed discussion explores terrorism as foreign policy and terrorism as domestic policy. Important examples of state terrorism include the deployment of death squads in Latin America and the link between Janjaweed fighters and the government in Sudan.

### Chapter 5. Terror From Below: Terrorism by Dissidents

This chapter critically evaluates terrorism emanating from dissident movements. A dissident terrorism paradigm is offered to explore the different typologies of dissident terrorism, and dissident terror in the era of the New Terrorism is investigated. The discussion includes the problems of antistate dissident terrorism and communal terrorism. Important examples of dissident terrorism include the modern use of child soldiers by extremists and Chechen terrorism against Russia.

### Chapter 6. Violence in the Name of the Faith: Religious Terrorism

In this chapter, the historical and modern origins and quality of religious terrorism are evaluated. The purpose of this presentation is to engender critical discussion on the subject of religious terrorism and to develop a contextual perspective on the modern era of religious terrorism. Because religious terrorism has become so prominent in the modern era, it is important for readers to investigate the different manifestations of religious violence and to understand the contexts of regional case studies.

### Chapter 7. Violent Ideologies: Terrorism From the Left and Right

The nature of ideological political violence is investigated in this chapter, which compares and contrasts radical and reactionary ideological tendencies, identifies the causes of left-wing and right-wing terrorism, and explores the qualities of ideological violence. Because both ideological poles were inextricably entwined during the 20th century, and adherents continue to be active in the 21st century, it is important for readers to grasp the importance of the ideologies of class struggle, national liberation, order, and race. This chapter also discusses regional examples of ideological terrorism. Unlike the other chapters, this discussion presents two Discussion Boxes, one each for the left and right.

### Chapter 8. Terrorist Spillovers: International Terrorism

This chapter logically concludes the presentation of common terrorist environments prior to the discussion of emerging environments. In this chapter, recent and historical examples of international terrorism are discussed. Our discussion about this subject defines what is meant by *international terrorism* and explores the reasons for terrorist spillovers. The phenomenon of international terrorist networks is discussed, as is the concept of "stateless revolutionaries." In this regard, readers evaluate newly emerging threats from movements and networks that have adapted the Al-Qa'ida example as a prototypical model.

### Chapter 9. Emerging Terrorist Environments: Gender-Selective Political Violence and Criminal Dissident Terrorism

This chapter incorporates two examples of emerging terrorist environments. The purpose of this chapter is to stimulate critical thinking among readers on the questions of gender-focused political violence and the nexus between criminal enterprises and terrorist violence. The discussion of gender-selective terrorist violence against women begins with an overview of political violence specifically targeted against women and men. This introduction orients readers to an emerging recognition that many terrorist environments direct their violence specifically against enemy women or men. The discussion investigates gender-selective state-sponsored and dissident-sponsored terrorism. The section on criminal dissident terrorism distinguishes political violence conducted by traditional criminal enterprises from that of violent criminal-political enterprises and discusses regional case studies of criminal dissident terrorism.

## Part III. The Terrorist Trade and Counterterrorism

Part III discusses the "nuts and bolts" of the terrorist trade, including the informational war that is waged between adversaries and the role of the mass media. Readers explore how the applications of the concepts of "propaganda by deed" and "armed propaganda" have been a historically common feature of extremist violence. With the availability of high-yield weaponry in the arsenals of terrorists and the globalization of information, it is important for readers to grasp the significance of the terrorist trade in the modern world. Readers will also investigate the case of terrorism in the United States.

### Chapter 10. Tools of the Trade: Tactics and Targets of Terrorists

This chapter investigates the methodology of terrorism. Terrorist objectives, methods, and targets are analyzed at length, as is the question of whether terrorism is "effective." Recent data and examples identify new challenges in the new era of terrorism, including examples of the use of the Internet and social networking media to post incidents and communiqués, and the plausible threat from cyberterrorism.

### Chapter 11. The Information Battleground: Terrorist Violence and the Role of the Media

The centrality of the media and mass communications in the modern era of political violence is investigated and evaluated. The chapter first discusses the nature of mass communications and reporting within the context of terrorist environments. An investigation is made of the war of manipulation for favorable media coverage. In particular, readers assess the manipulation of information technologies and the media by modern terrorists, including the utility of extremist manipulation of social networking media. A discussion is also presented on the efficacy of regulating the media.

### Chapter 12. The American Case: Terrorism in the United States

The case of the United States presents an overview of terrorism in postwar America. It probes the background to political violence from the left and right and presents a detailed discussion of leftist and rightist terrorism in the United States. The chapter also evaluates international terrorism and prospects for violence emanating from modern extremists on the left and right and from religious extremism.

## Part IV. Securing the Homeland

Part IV presents studies of counterterrorism and the concept of homeland security. Readers investigate counterterrorist options and the homeland security environment from both theoretical and organizational perspectives. Projections for political violence in the future are also explored.

### Chapter 13. Counterterrorism: The Options

This chapter explores counterterrorist options and security measures. Several categories of responses are assessed: the use of force, repressive operations other than war, conciliatory operations other than war, and legalistic responses. Contemporary controversies are explored, such as the status and treatment of captured suspects.

### Chapter 14. A New Era: Homeland Security

This chapter explores the concept of homeland security in Europe and the United States. Readers are challenged to critically assess options, trends, and other factors that shape the homeland security bureaucracy. The missions of agencies are explained and assessed. The role of intelligence agencies is assessed within the context of homeland security. The case of the United States is explored within the contexts of the reorganization of homeland security bureaucracies and the legal foundations for counterterrorist policies. Civil liberties controversies stemming from the application of homeland security laws and policies are presented and discussed. The final discussion examines achieving security when liberal democracies are beset by threats to national security.

### Chapter 15. What Next? The Future of Terrorism

Readers are challenged to critically assess trends and other factors that can be used to project the near future of terrorism. In particular, this chapter presents fresh discussions and data. New issues and likely scenarios are offered for the near future of ideological terrorism, religious terrorism, international terrorism, political violence against women, and criminal dissident terrorism.

**SAGE** was founded in 1965 by Sara Miller McCune to support the dissemination of usable knowledge by publishing innovative and high-quality research and teaching content. Today, we publish more than 750 journals, including those of more than 300 learned societies, more than 800 new books per year, and a growing range of library products including archives, data, case studies, reports, conference highlights, and video. SAGE remains majority-owned by our founder, and after Sara's lifetime will become owned by a charitable trust that secures our continued independence.

Los Angeles | London | Washington DC | New Delhi | Singapore | Boston

# PART I

# Terrorism

## *A Conceptual Review*

The Pentagon on the morning of September 11, 2001.

Stocktrek Images/Getty Images

# Terrorism

## *First Impressions*

## CHAPTER 1

### OPENING VIEWPOINT: THE IDEOLOGY OF AL-QA'IDA

Prior to his death in May 2011, Osama bin Laden established Al-Qa'ida as an international network that came to symbolize the globalization of terrorism in the 21st century. The network is perceived by many to represent a quintessential model for small groups of like-minded revolutionaries who wish to wage transnational insurgencies against strong adversaries. Although Al-Qa'ida certainly exists as a loose network of relatively independent cells, it has also evolved into an idea—an ideology and a fighting strategy—that has been embraced by sympathetic revolutionaries throughout the world. What is the ideology of Al-Qa'ida? Why did a network of religious revolutionaries evolve into a potent symbol of global resistance against its enemies? Which underlying commonalities appeal to motivated Islamist activists?

Al-Qa'ida leaders such as the late Osama bin Laden and his successor as leader Ayman al-Zawahiri consistently released public pronouncements of their goals, often by delivering audio and video communiqués to international news agencies such as Al Jazeera in Qatar. Based on these communiqués, the following principles frame the ideology of Al-Qa'ida:[a]

- The struggle is a clash of civilizations. Holy war is a religious duty and necessary for the salvation of one's soul and the defense of the Muslim nation.
- Only two sides exist, and there is no middle ground in this apocalyptic conflict between Islam and the forces of evil.

Western and Muslim nations that do not share Al-Qa'ida's vision of true Islam are enemies.
- Violence in a defensive war on behalf of Islam is the only course of action. There cannot be peace with the West.
- Because this is a just war, many of the theological and legal restrictions on the use of force by Muslims do not apply.
- Because U.S. and Western power is based on their economies, mounting large-scale mass casualty attacks that focus on economic targets is a primary goal.
- Islamic governments that cooperate with the West and do not adopt strict Islamic law are apostasies and must be violently overthrown.
- Israel is an illegitimate nation and must be destroyed.

These principles have become a rallying ideology for Islamist extremists who have few, if any, ties to Al-Qa'ida. Thus, the war on terrorism is not solely a conflict against an organization but also a conflict against a belief system.

### Note

a. Adapted from Office of the U.S. Department of State, Coordinator of Counterterrorism. *Country Reports on Terrorism 2013*. Washington, DC: U.S. Department of State, 2014.

Terrorism has been a dark feature of human behavior since the dawn of recorded history. Great leaders have been assassinated, groups and individuals have committed acts of incredible violence, and entire cities and nations have been put to the sword—all in the name of defending a greater good. Terrorism, however defined, has always challenged the stability of societies and the peace of mind of everyday people. In the modern era, the impact of terrorism—that is, its ability to terrorize—is not limited to the specific locales or regions where the terrorists strike. In the age of television, the Internet, satellite communications, and global news coverage, graphic images of terrorist incidents are broadcast instantaneously into the homes of hundreds of millions of people. Terrorist groups understand the power of these images, and they manipulate them to their advantage as much as they can. Terrorist states also fully appreciate the power of instantaneous information, and so they try to control the "spin" on reports of their behavior. In many respects, the 21st century is an era of globalized terrorism.

Some acts of political violence are clearly acts of terrorism. Most people would agree that politically motivated planting of bombs in marketplaces, massacres of enemy civilians, and the routine use of torture by governments are terrorist acts. As we begin our study of terrorism, we will encounter many definitional gray areas. Depending on which side of the ideological, racial, religious, or national fence one sits on, political violence can be interpreted either as an act of unmitigated terrorist barbarity or as freedom fighting and national liberation. These gray areas will be explored in the chapters that follow.

**September 11, 2001: The Dawn of a New Era.** The death of Al-Qa'ida leader Osama bin Laden in May 2011 occurred prior to the 10th commemoration of the September 11, 2001, terrorist attacks on the U.S. homeland. The attacks were seen by many as a turning point in the history of political violence. In the aftermath of these attacks, journalists, scholars, and national leaders repeatedly described the emergence of a new international terrorist environment. It was argued that within this new environment, terrorists were now quite capable of using—and very willing to use—weapons of mass destruction to inflict unprecedented casualties and destruction on enemy targets. These attacks seemed to confirm warnings from experts during the 1990s that a New Terrorism,[1] using "asymmetrical" methods, would characterize the terrorist environment in the new millennium.[2] (Asymmetrical warfare is discussed further in Chapters 8 and 10.)

Several questions about this new environment have arisen:

❖ **Photo 1.1**
Osama bin Laden. From the U.S. Federal Bureau of Investigation most-wanted terrorists website. Bin Laden was killed during a raid by a U.S. naval Special Forces unit in Abbottabad, Pakistan, on May 2, 2011.

U.S. Federal Bureau of Investigation

- How has the new terrorist environment affected traditional terrorist profiles?

- How has traditional terrorism been affected by the collapse of revolutionary Marxism?

- What is the likely impact of "stateless" international terrorism?

Readers will notice that these questions focus on terrorist *groups* and *movements*. However, it is very important to understand that terrorist *states* were responsible for untold millions of deaths during the 20th century. In addition, genocidal fighting between *communal groups* claimed the lives of many millions more. Our exploration of terrorism, therefore, requires us to consider every facet of political violence, from low-intensity campaigns by terrorist gangs to high-intensity campaigns by terrorist governments and genocidal paramilitaries.

---

[1]See Laqueur, Walter. *The New Terrorism: Fanaticism and the Arms of Mass Destruction.* New York: Oxford University Press, 1999.

[2]For a discussion on "urban legends" that have arisen in the post-9/11 environment, see Krueger, Alan B. "5 Myths About Terrorism." *Washington Post,* September 11, 2007.

This chapter is a general introduction to the subject of terrorism. It is an overview—a first glance—of basic concepts that will be developed in later discussions. The following themes are introduced here and will be explored in much greater detail in subsequent chapters:

- First Considerations
- Conceptual Considerations: Understanding Political Violence
- The Past as Prologue: Historical Perspectives on Terrorism
- Terrorism and Criminal Skill: Three Cases From the Modern Era

## ❖ First Considerations

At the outset, readers must develop a basic understanding of several issues underlying the study of terrorism. These issues are ongoing topics of research and debate among scholars, government officials, the media, and social activists, and all of them will be explored in detail in later chapters. The discussion here introduces the following:

- An Overview of Extremism and Terrorism
- Terrorism at First Glance
- Sources of Extremism and Terrorism

### An Overview of Extremism and Terrorism

**Extremism** is a quality that is "radical in opinion, especially in political matters; ultra; advanced."[3] It is characterized by intolerance toward opposing interests and divergent opinions, and it is the primary catalyst and motivation for terrorist behavior. Extremists who cross the line to become terrorists always develop noble arguments to rationalize and justify acts of violence directed against enemy nations, people, religions, or other interests.

Extremism is a radical expression of one's political values. Both the *content* of one's beliefs and the *style* in which one expresses those beliefs are basic elements for defining extremism. Laird Wilcox summed up this quality as follows:

> Extremism is more an issue of style than of content. . . . Most people can hold radical or unorthodox views and still entertain them in a more or less reasonable, rational, and non-dogmatic manner. On the other hand, I have met people whose views are fairly close to the political mainstream but were presented in a shrill, uncompromising, bullying, and distinctly authoritarian manner.[4]

Thus, a fundamental definitional issue for extremism is *how* one expresses an idea, in addition to the question of *which* belief one acts upon. Both elements—style and content—are important for our investigation of fringe beliefs and terrorist behavior.

Extremism is a precursor to terrorism—it is an overarching belief system terrorists use to justify their violent behavior. Extremism is characterized by what a person's beliefs are as well as how a person expresses his or her beliefs. Thus, no matter how offensive or reprehensible one's thoughts or words are, they are not by themselves acts of terrorism. Only those who violently act out their extremist beliefs are terrorists.

---

[3]*Webster's New Twentieth-Century Dictionary of the English Language, Unabridged.* 2nd ed. New York: Publishers Guild, 1966.

[4]Wilcox, Laird. "What Is Extremism? Style and Tactics Matter More Than Goals." In *American Extremists: Militias, Supremacists, Klansmen, Communists, and Others,* edited by John George and Laird Wilcox. Amherst, NY: Prometheus, 1996, p. 54.

**Terrorism** would not, from a layperson's point of view, seem to be a difficult concept to define. Most people likely hold an instinctive understanding that terrorism is

- politically motivated violence,
- usually directed against **soft targets** (i.e., civilian and administrative government targets), and
- with an intention to affect (terrorize) a target audience.

This instinctive understanding would also hold that terrorism is a criminal, unfair, or otherwise illegitimate use of force. Laypersons might presume that this is an easily understood concept, but defining terrorism is *not* such a simple process. Experts have for some time grappled with designing (and agreeing on) clear definitions of terrorism; the issue has, in fact, been at the center of an ongoing debate. The result of this debate is a remarkable variety of approaches and definitions. Walter Laqueur noted that "more than a hundred definitions have been offered," including several of his own.[5] Even within the U.S. government, different agencies apply several definitions. These definitional problems are explored further in the next chapter.

## Terrorism at First Glance

The modern era of terrorism is primarily (though not exclusively) a conflict between adversaries who on one side are waging a self-described war on terrorism and on the other side are waging a self-described holy war in defense of their religion. It is an active confrontation, as evidenced by the fact that the incidence of significant terrorist attacks often spikes to serious levels. For example, the number of terrorist incidents worldwide has repeatedly spiked and declined, as reported by the U.S. Department of State's Office of the Coordinator of Counterterrorism (Bureau of Counterterrorism):[6]

Spencer Platt/Getty Images News/Getty Images

❖ **Photo 1.2**
Hijacked United Airlines Flight 175 from Boston crashes into the south tower of the World Trade Center and explodes at 9:03 a.m. on September 11, 2001, in New York City.

- 11,023 in 2005
- 14,443 in 2006
- 14,415 in 2007
- 11,663 in 2008
- 10,968 in 2009
- 11,641 in 2010
- 10,283 in 2011
- 6,771 in 2012
- 9,707 in 2013

Although such trends are disturbing, it is critical for one to keep these facts in perspective because the modern terrorist environment is in no manner a unique circumstance in human history.

---

[5]Laqueur, *The New Terrorism*, p. 5.

[6]Office of the Coordinator for Counterterrorism. *Country Reports on Terrorism, 2011*. Washington, DC: U.S. Department of State, 2012; Office of the Coordinator for Counterterrorism, *Country Reports on Terrorism, 2012*. Washington, DC: U.S. Department of State, 2013; and Bureau of Counterterrorism, *Country Reports on Terrorism, 2013*. Washington, DC: U.S. Department of State, 2014. In these reports, incidents are limited to attacks against noncombatant targets. Statistical data are derived from the "Annex of Statistical Information" appended to the *Country Reports*.

It will become clear in the following pages that the history of terrorist behavior extends into antiquity and that common themes and concepts span the ages. State terrorism, dissident terrorism, and other types of political violence are found in all periods of human civilization. It will also become clear to readers that many common *justifications*—rooted in basic beliefs—have been used to rationalize terrorist violence throughout history. For example, the following concepts hold true regardless of the contexts of history, culture, or region:

- Those who practice revolutionary violence and state repression always claim to champion noble causes and values.
- Policies that advocate extreme violence always cite righteous goals to justify their behavior—such as the need to defend a religious faith or defend the human rights of a people.
- The perpetrators of violent acts uniformly maintain that they are freedom fighters (in the case of revolutionaries) or the champions of law and social order (in the case of governments).

## Sources of Extremism and Terrorism

The underlying causes of terrorism have also been the subject of extensive discussion, debate, and research. This is perhaps because the study of the sources of terrorism spans many disciplines—including sociology, psychology, criminology, and political science. The causes of terrorism will be explored in detail in Chapter 3. For now, a general model will serve as a starting point for developing our understanding of which factors lead to terrorist violence. To begin, we must understand that

> political violence, including terrorism, has systemic origins that can be ameliorated. Social and economic pressures, frustrated political aspirations, and in a more proximate sense, the personal experiences of terrorists and their relations, all contribute to the terrorist reservoir.[7]

Nehemia Friedland designed "a convenient framework for the analysis of the antecedents of political terrorism," outlined as follows:

> First, terrorism is a group phenomenon . . . perpetrated by organized groups whose members have a clear group identity—national, religious or ideological. . . . Second, political terrorism has its roots in intergroup conflict. . . . Third, "insurgent terrorism," unlike "state terrorism," . . . is a "strategy of the weak."[8]

One should appreciate that these issues continue to be a source of intensive debate. Nevertheless, working definitions have been adopted as a matter of logical necessity. Let us presume for now that terrorist acts are grounded in extremist beliefs that arise from group identity, intergroup conflict, and a chosen strategy.[9]

## ❖ Conceptual Considerations: Understanding Political Violence

The term *terrorism* has acquired a decidedly pejorative meaning in the modern era, so that few if any states or groups who espouse political violence ever refer to themselves as terrorists. Nevertheless,

---

[7]Lesser, Ian O. "Countering the New Terrorism: Implications for Strategy." In *Countering the New Terrorism,* edited by Ian O. Lesser, Bruce Hoffman, John Arquilla, David Ronfeldt, and Michele Zanini. Santa Monica, CA: RAND, 1999, p. 127.

[8]Friedland, Nehemia. "Becoming a Terrorist: Social and Individual Antecedents." In *Terrorism: Roots, Impact, Responses,* edited by Lawrence Howard. New York: Praeger, 1992, p. 82.

[9]See also Nicholson, Marc E. "An Essay on Terrorism." *American Diplomacy* 8, no. 3 (2003).

these same states and groups can be unabashedly extremist in their beliefs or violent in their behavior. They often invoke—and manipulate—images of a malevolent threat or unjust conditions to justify their actions. The question is whether these justifications are morally satisfactory (and thereby validate extremist violence) or whether terrorism is inherently wrong.

## The Significance of Symbolism

**Symbolism** is a central feature of terrorism. Most terrorist targets at some level symbolize the righteousness of the terrorists' cause and the evil of the opponent they are fighting. Symbolism can be used to rationalize acts of extreme violence and can be manipulated to fit any number of targets into the category of an enemy interest. Terrorists are also very mindful of their image and skillfully conduct public relations and propa-

U.S. Federal Bureau of Investigation

❖ **Photo 1.3**

Fazul Abdullah Mohammed. Photographs from the U.S. Federal Bureau of Investigation most-wanted terrorists website. Mohammed was killed at a checkpoint in Somalia on June 8, 2011. He was believed to be the mastermind behind the 1998 bombings of the U.S. embassies in Nairobi, Kenya, and Dar es Salaam, Tanzania.

ganda campaigns to "package" themselves. Modern terrorists and their supporters have become quite adept at crafting symbolic meaning from acts of violence.

Symbolism can create abstract ideological linkages between terrorists and their victims. This process was seen during the wave of kidnappings by Latin American leftists during the 1970s, when terrorists seized civilian business executives and diplomats who the kidnappers said symbolized capitalism and exploitation. Symbolic targets can also represent enemy social or political establishments, as in the Irish Republican Army's (IRA's) assassination of Lord Louis Mountbatten (the uncle of Prince Philip Mountbatten, husband of Queen Elizabeth II) in 1979 and the IRA's attempted assassination of Prime Minister Margaret Thatcher in 1984. In some cases, entire groups of people can be symbolically labeled and slaughtered, as during the genocides of the Nazi Holocaust (pseudo-racial), in the killing fields of Cambodia (social and political), in Rwanda (ethnic and social), and in the Darfur region of Sudan (racial).

## Political Violence: *Mala Prohibita* or *Mala in Se?*

It is helpful to use two concepts from the field of criminal justice administration. In criminal law, the terms *mala prohibita* and *mala in se*[10] are applied to behaviors that society defines as deviant acts. They represent concepts that are very useful for the study of terrorism.

- *Mala prohibita* acts are "crimes that are made illegal by legislation."[11] These acts are illegal because society has declared them to be wrong; they are not *inherently* immoral, wicked, or evil. Examples include laws prohibiting gambling and prostitution, which are considered to be moral prohibitions against socially unacceptable behaviors rather than prohibitions of fundamental evils.

- *Mala in se* acts are crimes "that are immoral or wrong in themselves."[12] These acts cannot be justified in civilized society, and they have no acceptable qualities. For example, premeditated murder and forcible rape are *mala in se* crimes. They will never be legalized.

---

[10]"Prohibited wrongs." Singular: *malum prohibitum* and *malum in se*. Black, Henry Campbell. *Black's Law Dictionary.* 4th ed., revised. St. Paul, MN: West, 1968, pp. 1108, 1112.

[11]Rush, George E. *The Dictionary of Criminal Justice.* 5th ed. Guilford, CT: Dushkin/McGraw-Hill, 2002, p. 205.

[12]Ibid., p. 204.

Are terrorist methods fundamentally evil? Perhaps so, because terrorism commonly evokes images of maximum violence against innocent victims carried out in the name of a higher cause. However, is terrorist violence always such a bad thing? Are not some causes worth fighting for? Killing for? Dying for? Is not terrorism simply a matter of one's point of view? Most would agree that basic values such as freedom and liberty are indeed worth fighting for, and sometimes killing or dying for. If so, perhaps "where you stand depends on where you sit." Thus, if the bombs are falling on your head, is it not an act of terrorism? If the bombs are falling on an enemy's head in the name of your freedom, how can it possibly be terrorism?

Conceptually, right and wrong behaviors are not always relative considerations, for many actions are indeed *mala in se*. However, this is not an easy analysis because violence committed by genuinely oppressed people can arguably raise questions of *mala prohibita* as a matter of perspective.

## The Just War Doctrine

The **just war doctrine** is an ideal and a moralistic philosophy. The concept is often used by ideological and religious extremists to justify acts of extreme violence. Throughout history, nations and individuals have gone to war with the belief that their cause was just and their opponents' cause unjust. Similarly, attempts have been made for millennia to write fair and just laws of war and rules of engagement. For example, in the late 19th and early 20th centuries, the Hague Conventions produced at least 21 international agreements on the rules of war.[13]

This is a moral and ethical issue that raises the questions of whether one can ethically attack an opponent, how one can justifiably defend oneself with force, and what types of force are morally acceptable in either context? The just war debate also asks who can morally be defined as an enemy and what kinds of targets it is morally acceptable to attack. In this regard, there are two separate components to the concept of just war (which philosophers call the "just war tradition"): the rationale for initiating the war (a war's ends) and the method of warfare (a war's means). Criteria for whether a war is just are divided into *jus ad bellum* (justice of war) and *jus in bello* (justice in war) criteria.[14]

Thus, ***jus in bello*** is correct behavior while waging war, and ***jus ad bellum*** is having the correct conditions for waging war in the first place. These concepts have been debated by philosophers and theologians for centuries. The early Christian philosopher **Saint Augustine** concluded in the 5th century that war is justified to punish injuries inflicted by a nation that has refused to correct wrongs committed by its citizens. The Christian religious tradition, especially the Roman Catholic Church, has devoted a great deal of intellectual effort to clarifying Augustine's concept. Augustine was, of course, referring to warfare between nations and cities, and Church doctrine long held that an attack against state authority was an offense against God.[15] Likewise, the Hague Conventions dealt only with rules of conflict between nations and afforded no legal rights to spies or antistate rebels. Neither system referred to rules of engagement for nonstate or antistate conflicts.

In the modern era, both dissidents and states have adapted the just war tradition to their political environments. Antistate conflict and reprisals by states are commonplace. Dissidents always consider their cause just and their methods proportional to the force used by the agents of their oppressors. They are, in their own minds, freedom fighters waging a just war. As one Hamas fighter said, "Before

---

[13]See Janis, Mark W. *An Introduction to International Law*. 5th ed. New York: Aspen Publishers, 2008.

[14]Stern, Jessica. *The Ultimate Terrorists*. Cambridge, MA: Harvard University Press, 1999, p. 18.

[15]See Hurwood, Bernhardt J. *Society and the Assassin: A Background Book on Political Murder*. New York: Parents' Magazine Press, 1970, pp. 17ff.

I start shooting, I start to concentrate on reading verses of the Koran because the Koran gives me the courage to fight the Israelis."[16]

Antiterrorist reprisals launched by states are also justified as appropriate and proportional applications of force—in this case, as a means to root out bands of terrorists. For example, after three suicide bombers killed or wounded scores of people in Jerusalem and Haifa in December 2001, Israeli Prime Minister Ariel Sharon justified Israeli reprisals by saying,

> A war of terrorism was forced on us [by the terrorists]. . . . If you ask what the aim of this war is, I will tell you. It is the aim of the terrorists . . . to exile us from here. . . . This will not happen.[17]

From the perspective of terrorism and counterterrorism, both dissident and state applications of force are legitimate subjects of just war scrutiny, especially because dissidents usually attack soft civilian targets and state reprisals are usually not directed against standing armies. The following "moral checklist" was published in the American newspaper *The Christian Science Monitor* during the first phase of the war on terrorism begun after the September 11, 2001, terrorist attacks:

- Is it justified to attack states and overturn regimes to get at terrorists?
- Can the U.S. legitimately target political figures like Taliban leader Mullah Mohammad Omar?
- What are U.S. obligations in terms of minimizing civilian casualties?
- What type of force should be used?
- When should U.S. forces take prisoners, rather than killing Afghan troops?
- Is there a plan for peace?[18]

❖ **Photo 1.4**

The war on terrorism. A United States Army soldier on patrol during the post-2003 insurgency phase of the war in Iraq.

U.S. Department of Defense

These questions are generically applicable to all state antiterrorist campaigns, as well as to antistate dissident violence. Rules of war and the just war tradition are the result of many motivations. Some rules and justifications are self-serving, others are pragmatic, and still others are grounded in ethnonationalist or religious traditions. Hence, the just war concept can easily be adapted to justify ethnic, racial, national, and religious extremism in the modern era.

## ❖ The Past as Prologue: Historical Perspectives on Terrorism

It is perhaps natural for each generation to view history narrowly, from within its own political context. Contemporary commentators and laypersons tend to interpret modern events as though they have no historical precedent. However, terrorism is by no means a modern phenomenon; in fact, it has a long history. Nor does terrorism arise in a political vacuum. Let us consider a brief summary of several historical periods to illustrate the global and timeless sweep of terrorist behavior.

---

[16]Jaffar. Interview with Jamil Hamad. "First Person: I Shot an Israeli." *Time*, October 23, 2000.

[17]Sharon, Ariel. "Sharon Vows to Defeat 'War of Terrorism.'" *New York Times*, December 3, 2001.

[18]Tyson, Ann Scott. "Weighing War in Afghanistan on a Moral Scale." *Christian Science Monitor*, October 19, 2001.

## Antiquity

In the ancient world, cases and stories of state repression and political violence were common. Several ancient writers championed **tyrannicide** (the killing of tyrants) as for the greater good of the citizenry and to delight the gods. Some assassins were honored by the public. For example, when the tyrant Hipparchus was assassinated by Aristogeiton and Harmodius, statues were erected to honor them after their executions.[19] Conquerors often set harsh examples by exterminating entire populations or forcing the conquered into exile. An example of this practice is the Babylonian Exile, which followed the conquest of the kingdom of Judea. Babylon's victory resulted in the forced removal of the Judean population to Babylon in 598 and 587 B.C.E. Those in authority also repressed the expression of ideas from individuals whom they deemed dangerous, sometimes violently. In ancient Greece, Athenian authorities sentenced the great philosopher Socrates to death in 399 B.C.E. for allegedly corrupting the city-state's youth and meddling in religious affairs. He drank hemlock and died among his students and followers.

## The Roman Age

During the time of the Roman Empire, the political world was rife with many violent demonstrations of power, which were arguably examples of what we would now call state terrorism. These include the brutal suppression of Spartacus's followers after the Servile War of 73–71 B.C.E., after which the Romans crucified surviving rebels along the Appian Way's route to Rome. **Crucifixion** was used as a form of public execution by Rome for offenses committed against Roman authority, and involved affixing condemned persons to a cross or other wooden platform. The condemned were either nailed through the wrist or hand or tied on the platform; they died by suffocation as their bodies sagged.

Warfare was waged in an equally hard manner, as evidenced by the final conquest of the North African city-state of Carthage in 146 B.C.E. The city was reportedly allowed to burn for 10 days, the rubble was cursed, and salt was symbolically ploughed into the soil to signify that Carthage would forever remain desolate. During another successful campaign in 106 C.E., the Dacian nation (modern Romania) was eliminated, its population was enslaved, and many Dacians perished in gladiatorial games. In other conquered territories, conquest was often accompanied by similar demonstrations of terror, always with the intent to demonstrate that Roman rule would be imposed without mercy against those who did not submit to the authority of the empire.

**Regicide** (the killing of kings) was also common during the Roman age. Perhaps the best-known political incident in ancient Rome was the assassination of Julius Caesar in 44 B.C.E. by rivals in the Senate. Other Roman emperors also met violent fates: Caligula and Galba were killed by the Praetorian Guard in 41 and 68 C.E., respectively; Domitian was stabbed to death in 96 C.E.; a paid gladiator murdered Commodus in 193 C.E.; and Caracalla, Elagabalus, and many other emperors either were assassinated or died suspiciously.[20]

## The Ancient and Medieval Middle East

Cases exist of movements in the ancient and medieval Middle East that used what modern analysts would consider to be terrorist tactics. For example, in *History of the Jewish War*—a seven-volume account of the first Jewish rebellion against Roman occupation (66–73 C.E.)—the historian Flavius Josephus describes how one faction of the rebels, the ***sicarii*** (named after their preferred use of *sica,* or short, curved daggers), attacked both Romans and members of the Jewish establishment.[21]

[19]Laqueur, *The New Terrorism,* p. 10.

[20]An extraordinary and classic history of the Roman Empire is found in Edward Gibbon's great work of literature, *The History of the Decline and Fall of the Roman Empire.* 1909. Reprint, New York: AMS Press, 1974.

[21]For a discussion of the Roman occupation of Judea and the First Jewish Revolt within the broader context of Roman politics, see Grant, Michael. *The Twelve Caesars.* New York: Penguin Classics; revised edition, 2007.

They were masters of guerrilla warfare and the destruction of symbolic property, and belonged to a group known as the **Zealots** (from the Greek *zelos,* meaning ardor or strong spirit), who opposed the Roman occupation of Palestine. The modern term *zealot,* used to describe uncompromising devotion to radical change, is derived from the name of this group. Assassination was a commonly used tactic. Some *sicarii* zealots were present at the siege of Masada, a hilltop fortress that held out against the Romans for 3 years before the defenders committed suicide in 74 c.e. rather than surrender.

Another important historical case, the Assassins in 13th-century Persia, is discussed in Chapter 6. Both the Zealots and Assassins are important historical examples because they continue to inform modern analyses of terrorist violence and motives.

## The Dark Ages: Prelude to Modern Terrorism

During the period from the Assassins (13th century) to the French Revolution (18th century), behavior that would later be considered terrorism was commonly practiced in medieval warfare. In fact, a great deal of medieval conflict involved openly brutal warfare. However, the modern terrorist profile of politically motivated dissidents attempting to change an existing order, or state repression to preserve state hegemony, was uncommon. Nation-states in the modern sense did not exist in medieval Europe, and recurrent warfare was motivated by religious intolerance and political discord between feudal kings and lords. The post-Assassin Middle East also witnessed periodic invasions, discord between leaders, and religious warfare, but not modern-style terrorism. It was not until the rise of the modern nation-state in the mid–17th century that the range of intensity of conflict devolved from open warfare to include behavior the modern era would define as insurgency, guerrilla warfare, and terrorism.

## The French Revolution

During the French Revolution, the word *terrorism* was coined in its modern context by British statesman and philosopher Edmund Burke. He used the word to describe the *régime de la terreur,* commonly known in English as the **Reign of Terror** (June 1793 to July 1794).[22] The Reign of Terror, led by the radical Jacobin-dominated government, is a good example of state terrorism carried out to further the goals of a revolutionary ideology.[23] During the Terror, thousands of opponents to the Jacobin dictatorship—and others merely *perceived* to be enemies of the new revolutionary Republic—were arrested and put on trial before a **Revolutionary Tribunal**. Those found to be enemies of the Republic were beheaded by a new instrument of execution—the guillotine. The guillotine had the capability to execute victims one after the other in assembly-line fashion and was regarded by Jacobins and other revolutionaries at the time as an enlightened and civilized tool of revolutionary justice.[24]

The ferocity of the Reign of Terror is reflected in the number of victims: Between 17,000 and 40,000 persons were executed, and perhaps 200,000 political prisoners died in prisons from disease and starvation.[25] Two incidents illustrate the communal nature of this violence: In Lyon, 700 people were massacred by cannon fire in the town square, and in Nantes, thousands were drowned in the Loire River when the boats in which they were detained were sunk.[26]

---

[22]Burke, a Whig Member of Parliament, was a progressive in his time. He opposed absolutism, poor treatment of the American colonists, and the slave trade. He expressed his opposition to Jacobin extremism in a series of writings, including *Reflections on the French Revolution* and *Letters on a Regicide Peace.*

[23]For a classic account of the Terror, see Loomis, Stanley. *Paris in the Terror: June 1793–July 1794.* Philadelphia: Lippincott, 1964.

[24]A French physician, Joseph Ignace Guillotin, invented the guillotine. He was loyal to the revolution and a deputy to the Estates-General. Guillotin encouraged the use of the beheading machine as a painless, humane, and symbolically revolutionary method of execution.

[25]Griset, Pamala L., and Sue Mahan. *Terrorism in Perspective.* 3rd ed. Thousand Oaks, CA: Sage, 2012, p. 44.

[26]Ibid.

The Revolutionary Tribunal is a symbol of revolutionary justice and state terrorism that has its modern counterparts in 20th-century social upheavals. Recent examples include the **"struggle meetings"** in revolutionary China (public criticism sessions, involving public humiliation and confession) and the *komiteh* (ad hoc "people's committee") of revolutionary Iran.[27]

## CHAPTER PERSPECTIVE 1.1: The Gunpowder Plot of Guy Fawkes

The reign of James I, King of England from 1603 to 1625, took place in the aftermath of a religious upheaval. During the previous century, King Henry VIII (1509–1547) wrested from Parliament the authority to proclaim himself the head of religious affairs in England. King Henry had requested permission from Pope Clement VII to annul his marriage to Catherine of Aragon when she failed to give birth to a male heir to the throne. His intention was to then marry Anne Boleyn. When the Pope refused his request, Henry proclaimed the Church of England and separated the new church from papal authority. The English crown confiscated Catholic Church property and shut down Catholic monasteries. English Catholics who failed to swear allegiance to the crown as supreme head of the church were repressed by Henry and later by Queen Elizabeth I (1558–1603).

When James I was proclaimed king, Guy Fawkes and other conspirators plotted to assassinate him. They meticulously smuggled gunpowder into the Palace of Westminster, intending to blow it up along with King James and any other officials in attendance on the opening day of Parliament. Unfortunately for Fawkes, one of his fellow plotters attempted to send a note to warn his brother-in-law to stay away from Westminster on the appointed day. The note was intercepted, and Fawkes was captured on November 5, 1605, while guarding the store of gunpowder.

Guy Fawkes suffered the English penalty for treason. He was dragged through the streets, hanged until nearly dead, his bowels were drawn from him, and he was cut into quarters—an infamous process known as hanging, drawing, and quartering. Fawkes had known that this would be his fate, so when the noose was placed around his neck he took a running leap, hoping to break his neck. Unfortunately, the rope broke, and the executioner proceeded with the full ordeal.

## Nineteenth-Century Europe: Two Examples From the Left

Modern, left-wing terrorism is not a product of the 20th century. Its ideological ancestry dates to the 19th century, when anarchist and communist philosophers began to advocate the destruction of capitalist and imperial society—what Karl Marx referred to as the "spectre . . . haunting Europe."[28] Some revolutionaries readily encouraged the use of terrorism in the new cause. One theorist, Karl Heinzen in Germany, anticipated the late-20th-century fear that terrorists might obtain weapons of mass destruction when he supported the acquisition of new weapons technologies to utterly destroy the enemies of the people. According to Heinzen, these weapons could include poison gas and new, high-yield explosives.[29]

During the 19th century, several terrorist movements championed the rights of the lower classes. These movements were prototypes for 20th-century groups and grew out of social and political environments that were unique to their countries. To illustrate this point, the following two cases are drawn from early industrial England and the semifeudal Russian context of the late 19th century.

---

[27]For a good discussion about the consolidation of the Chinese Revolution and the Great Proletarian Cultural Revolution that occurred later, see Fairbank, John King. *The Great Chinese Revolution: 1800–1985.* New York: Harper & Row, 1987. For an analysis of the ideology of the Ayatollah Khomeini and the Iranian revolution, see Martin, Vanessa. *Creating an Islamic State: Khomeini and the Making of a New Iran.* London: I. B. Tauris, 2000.

[28]Marx, Karl, and Friedrich Engels. "Manifesto of the Communist Party." In *The Marx-Engels Reader,* edited by Robert C. Tucker. New York: Norton, 1972, p. 335.

[29]Laqueur, *The New Terrorism,* p. 13.

The **Luddites** were English workers in the early 1800s who objected to the social and economic transformations of the Industrial Revolution. Their principal objection was that industrialization threatened their jobs, so they targeted the machinery of the new textile factories. Textile mills and weaving machinery were disrupted and sabotaged. For example, they attacked stocking looms that mass-produced stockings at the expense of skilled stocking weavers who made them by hand.

A mythical figure, Ned Ludd, was the supposed founder of the Luddite movement. The movement was active from 1811 to 1816 and was responsible for sabotaging and destroying wool and cotton mills. The British government eventually suppressed the movement by passing anti-Luddite laws, including establishing the crime of "machine breaking," which was punishable by death. After 17 Luddites were executed in 1813, the movement gradually faded out. Although historians debate whether Luddites clearly fit the profile of terrorists, modern antitechnology activists and terrorists, such as the Unabomber in the United States, are sometimes referred to as neo-Luddites.

**People's Will (Narodnaya Volya)** in Russia was a direct outgrowth of student dissatisfaction with the czarist regime in the late 19th century. Many young Russian university students, some of whom had studied abroad, became imbued with the ideals of anarchism and Marxism. Many of these students became radical reformists who championed the rights of the people, particularly the peasant class. A populist revolutionary society, Land and Liberty (Zemlya Volya), was founded in 1876 with the goal of fomenting a mass peasant uprising by settling radical students among them to raise their class consciousness. After a series of arrests and mass public trials, Land and Liberty split into two factions in 1879. One faction, Black Repartition, kept to the goal of a peasant revolution. The other faction, People's Will, fashioned itself into a conspiratorial terrorist organization.

People's Will members believed that they understood the underlying problems of Russia better than the uneducated masses of people did, and they concluded that they were therefore better able to force government change. This was, in fact, one of the first examples of a revolutionary vanguard strategy. They believed that they could both demoralize the czarist government and expose its weaknesses to the peasantry. People's Will quickly embarked on a terrorist campaign against carefully selected targets. Incidents of terror committed by People's Will members—and other revolutionaries who emulated them—included shootings, knifings, and bombings against government officials. In one successful attack, Czar Alexander II was assassinated by a terrorist bomb on March 1, 1881. The immediate outcome of the terrorist campaign was the installation of a repressive police state in Russia that, although not as efficient as later police states would be in the Soviet Union or Nazi Germany, succeeded in harassing and imprisoning most members of People's Will.

## The Modern Era and the War on Terrorism

It is clear from human history that terrorism is deeply woven into the fabric of social and political conflict. This quality has not changed, and in the modern world, states and targeted populations are challenged by the New Terrorism, which is characterized by the following:

- Loose, cell-based networks with minimal lines of command and control
- Desired acquisition of high-intensity weapons and weapons of mass destruction
- Politically vague, religious, or mystical motivations
- Asymmetrical methods that maximize casualties
- Skillful use of the Internet and manipulation of the media

The New Terrorism should be contrasted with traditional terrorism, which is typically characterized by the following:

- Clearly identifiable organizations or movements
- Use of conventional weapons, usually small arms and explosives

- Explicit grievances championing specific classes or ethnonational groups
- Relatively "surgical" selection of targets

New information technologies and the Internet create unprecedented opportunities for terrorist groups, and violent extremists have become adept at bringing their wars into the homes of literally hundreds of millions of people. Those who specialize in suicide bombings, vehicular bombings, or mass-casualty attacks correctly calculate that carefully selected targets will attract the attention of a global audience. Thus, cycles of violence not only disrupt normal routines; they also produce long periods of global awareness. Such cycles can be devastating. For example, during the winter and spring of 2005, Iraqi suicide bombings increased markedly in intensity and frequency, from 69 in April 2005 (a record rate at that time) to 90 in May.[30] Likewise, sectarian violence in 2014 was a reinvigoration of the sectarian bloodletting that occurred during the U.S.-led occupation of Iraq in the early 2000s.[31] These attacks resulted in many casualties, including hundreds of deaths, and greatly outpaced the previous cycle of car bombings by more than two to one.

All of these threats offer new challenges for policy makers about how to respond to the behavior of terrorist states, groups, and individuals. The war on terrorism, launched in the aftermath of the attacks of September 11, 2001, seemed to herald a new resolve to end terrorism. This has proven to be a difficult task. The war has been fought on many levels, as exemplified by the invasions of Afghanistan and Iraq and the disruption of terrorist cells on several continents. There have been serious terrorist strikes such as those in Madrid, Spain; Bali, Indonesia; London, England; and Sharm el Sheikh, Egypt. In addition, differences arose within the post–September 11 alliance,

| Table 1.1 | Ten Countries With the Most Terrorist Attacks, 2013 | | | | |
|---|---|---|---|---|---|
| Country | Total Attacks | Total Killed | Total Wounded | Average Number Killed per Attack | Average Number Wounded per Attack |
| Iraq | 2,495 | 6,378 | 14,956 | 2.56 | 5.99 |
| Pakistan | 1,920 | 2,315 | 4,989 | 1.21 | 2.60 |
| Afghanistan | 1,144 | 3,111 | 3,717 | 2.72 | 3.25 |
| India | 622 | 405 | 717 | 0.65 | 1.15 |
| Philippines | 450 | 279 | 413 | 0.62 | 0.92 |
| Thailand | 332 | 131 | 398 | 0.39 | 1.20 |
| Nigeria | 300 | 1,817 | 457 | 6.06 | 1.52 |
| Yemen | 295 | 291 | 583 | 0.99 | 1.98 |
| Syria | 212 | 1,074 | 1,773 | 5.07 | 8.36 |
| Somalia | 197 | 408 | 485 | 2.07 | 2.46 |

Source: U.S. Department of State, Office of the Coordinator for Counterterrorism. Country Reports on Terrorism 2013. Washington, DC: U.S. Department of State, 2014.

[30]Williams, Carol J. "Suicide Attacks Rising Rapidly." Los Angeles Times, June 2, 2005.

[31]Rubin, Alissa J., and Rod Nordland. "As Sunnis Die in Iraq, a Cycle Is Restarting." Boston Globe, June 18, 2014.

creating significant strains. It is clear that the war will be a long-term prospect, likely with many unanticipated events. Table 1.1 reports the scale of terrorist violence in 2013 for 10 countries with active terrorist environments.

# ❖ Terrorism and Criminal Skill: Three Cases From the Modern Era

Terrorism is condemned internationally as an illegal use of force and an illegitimate expression of political will. Applying this concept of *illegality,* one can argue that terrorists are criminals and that terrorist attacks require some degree of criminal skill. For example, the radical Islamist network **Al-Qa'ida** set up an elaborate financial system to sustain its activities. This financial system included secret bank accounts, front companies, offshore bank accounts, and charities.[32] Al-Qa'ida is an example of a stateless movement that became a self-sustaining revolutionary network. It is also an example of a sophisticated transnational criminal enterprise.

Terrorist attacks involve different degrees of criminal skill. The following cases are examples of the wide range of sophistication found in incidents of political violence. All three cases are short illustrations of the criminal skill of the following individual extremists:

- Anders Breivik, a Norwegian right-wing extremist who detonated a lethal bomb in Oslo and went on a killing spree at a youth camp in July 2011

- Ted Kaczynski, also known as the Unabomber, who was famous for sending mail bombs to his victims and who eluded capture for 18 years, from 1978 to 1996

- Ramzi Yousef, an international terrorist who was the mastermind behind the first World Trade Center bombing in February 1993

## Case 1: Anders Breivik

Many terrorist incidents are the acts of individual extremists who simply embark on killing sprees, using a relatively *low degree* of criminal sophistication. For example, domestic "lone wolf" attacks in Europe and the United States have usually been ideological or racially motivated killing sprees committed by individual extremists who are often neo-fascists, neo-Nazis, or racial supremacists.[33] One of these attacks occurred on July 22, 2011, in and around Oslo, Norway, when a right-wing extremist murdered nearly 80 people.

**Anders Breivik**, a self-professed right-wing ideologue, detonated a car bomb in the government district of Oslo and methodically shot to death dozens of victims at a Norwegian Labor Party youth summer camp on the island of Utøya. His victims were government workers, bystanders, and teenage residents of the camp. The sequence of Breivik's assault occurred as follows:

- Breivik detonated a car bomb in Oslo's government district using ammonium nitrate and fuel oil (ANFO) explosives. The blast killed eight people and wounded at least a dozen more.

- He next drove nearly 2 hours to a youth summer camp on the island of Utøya. The camp was sponsored by the youth organization of the ruling Norwegian Labor Party, and hundreds of youths were in attendance. Breivik was disguised as a policeman.

---

[32]For an excellent discussion of the financial profile of Al-Qa'ida and affiliates, see Gomez, Juan Miguel del Cid. "A Financial Profile of the Terrorism of Al-Qaeda and Its Affiliates." In *Perspectives on Terrorism* 4, no. 4 (October 2010).

[33]Exceptions to this general profile have occurred in the United States. For example, an Egyptian-born resident of the United States committed a lone wolf attack at Los Angeles International Airport on July 4, 2002. He shot and stabbed several people at the El Al (Israeli airline) counter before being killed by El Al security officers. The assailant killed two people and injured several others.

- When Breivik arrived on the island, he announced that he was a police officer who was following up on the bombing in Oslo. As people gathered around him, he drew his weapons and began shooting.
- Using a carbine and semiautomatic handgun, Breivik methodically shot scores of attendees on Utøya, most of them teenagers. The attack lasted for approximately 90 minutes and ended when police landed on the island and accepted Breivik's surrender.

In August 2012, Breivik was convicted of murdering 77 people and received Norway's maximum sentence of 21 years imprisonment. Under Norwegian law, his incarceration may be extended indefinitely if he is deemed to be a risk to society.

The Breivik case illustrates how the lone wolf scenario involves an individual who believes in a certain ideology but who is not acting on behalf of an organized group. These individuals tend to exhibit a relatively *low degree* of criminal skill while carrying out their assault.

## Case 2: Theodore "Ted" Kaczynski

Using a *medium degree* of criminal sophistication, many terrorists have been able to remain active for long periods of time without being captured by security agents. Some enter into "retirement" during this time, whereas others remain at least sporadically active. An example of the latter profile is **Theodore "Ted" Kaczynski**, popularly known as the **Unabomber**. The term *Unabomber* was derived from the FBI's designation of his case as **UNABOM** during its investigation of his activities.

In May 1978, Kaczynski began constructing and detonating a series of bombs directed against corporations and universities. His usual practice was to send the devices through the mail disguised as business parcels. Examples of his attacks include the following:

- A bomb caught fire inside a mail bag aboard a Boeing 727. It had been rigged with a barometric trigger to explode at a certain altitude.
- A package bomb exploded inside the home of the president of United Airlines, injuring him.
- A letter bomb exploded at Vanderbilt University, injuring a secretary. It had been addressed to the chair of the computer science department.
- A University of California, Berkeley, professor was severely injured when a pipe bomb he found in the faculty room exploded.
- Two University of Michigan scholars were injured when a package bomb exploded at a professor's home. The bomb had been designed to look like a manuscript for a book.
- An antipersonnel bomb exploded in the parking lot behind a computer rental store, killing the store's owner.

During an 18-year period, Ted Kaczynski was responsible for the detonation of more than 15 bombs around the country, killing 3 people and injuring 22 more (some very seriously). He was arrested in his Montana cabin in April 1996. Kaczynski was sentenced in April 1998 to four consecutive life terms plus 30 years.

## Case 3: Ramzi Yousef

Involving a *high degree* of criminal sophistication, some terrorist attacks are the work of individuals who can be described as masters of their criminal enterprise. The following case illustrates this concept.

On February 26, 1993, **Ramzi Yousef** detonated a bomb in a parking garage beneath Tower One of the World Trade Center in New York City. The bomb was a mobile truck bomb that Yousef and an associate had constructed in New Jersey from a converted Ford Econoline van. It was of a fairly simple design but extremely powerful. The detonation occurred as follows:

The critical moment came at 12:17 and 37 seconds. One of the fuses burnt to its end and ignited the gunpowder in an Atlas Rockmaster blasting cap. In a split second the cap exploded with a pressure of around 15,000 lbs per square inch, igniting in turn the first nitro-glycerin container of the bomb, which erupted with a pressure of about 150,000 lbs per square inch—the equivalent of about 10,000 atmospheres. In turn, the nitro-glycerin ignited cardboard boxes containing a witches' brew of urea pellets and sulphuric acid.[34]

U.S. Federal Bureau of Investigation

❖ **Photo 1.5**

Ramzi Yousef, master terrorist and mastermind of the first bombing of the World Trade Center in New York City in 1993.

According to investigators and other officials, Yousef's objective was to topple Tower One onto Tower Two "like a pair of dominoes,"[35] release a cloud of toxic gas, and thus achieve a very high death toll.

Ramzi Yousef, apparently born in Kuwait and reared in Pakistan, was an activist educated in the United Kingdom. His education was interrupted during the Soviet war in Afghanistan, when he apparently "spent several months in Peshawar [Pakistan] in training camps funded by Osama bin Laden learning bomb-making skills."[36] After the war, Yousef returned to school in the United Kingdom and received a Higher National Diploma in computer-aided electrical engineering.

In the summer of 1991, Ramzi Yousef returned to the training camps in Peshawar for additional training in electronics and explosives. He arrived in New York City in September 1992 and shortly thereafter began planning to carry out a significant attack, having selected the World Trade Center as his target. Yousef established contacts with former associates already in the New York area and eventually became close to Muhammed Salameh, who assisted in the construction of the bomb. They purchased chemicals and other bomb-making components, stored them in a rented locker, and assembled the bomb in an apartment in Jersey City. They apparently tested considerably scaled-down versions of the bomb several times. After the attack, Yousef boarded a flight at JFK Airport and flew to Pakistan.

This case is a good example of the technical skill and criminal sophistication of some terrorists. Ramzi Yousef had connections with well-funded terrorists, was a sophisticated bomb maker, knew how to obtain the necessary components in a foreign country, was very adept at evasion, and obviously planned his actions in meticulous detail. As a postscript, Ramzi Yousef remained very active among bin Laden's associates, and his travels within the movement took him far afield, including trips to Thailand and the Philippines. In an example of international law enforcement cooperation, he was eventually captured in Pakistan in February 1995 and sent to the United States to stand trial for the bombing. Yousef was tried, convicted, and sentenced to serve at least 240 years in prison in the "supermaximum" federal prison in Florence, Colorado.

---

[34]Reeve, Simon. *The New Jackals: Ramzi Yousef, Osama bin Laden, and the Future of Terrorism.* Boston: Northeastern University Press, 1999, p. 10.

[35]Comment by Judge Kevin Duffy. *United States of America v. Muhammed A. Salameh et al.,* S593 CR. 180 (KTD).

[36]Reeve, *The New Jackals,* p. 120.

## Chapter Summary

As a first consideration, this chapter introduced readers to an overview of extremism and terrorism, whereby their sources and interrelationship were summarized. Conceptual considerations include the symbolism and criminality of political violence, as well as the concept of the just war. Whether terrorist acts are *mala in se* or *mala prohibita* is often a relative question. Depending on one's perspective, there are gray areas that challenge us to be objective about the true nature of political violence.

Some of the historical and modern attributes of terrorism were also discussed, with a central theme that terrorism is deeply rooted in the human experience. The impact of extremist ideas on human behavior should not be underestimated because there are historical examples of political violence that in some ways parallel modern terrorism. For example, we noted that state terrorism and antistate dissident movements have existed since ancient times.

Most, if not all, nations promote an ideological doctrine to legitimize the power of the state and to convince the people that their systems of belief are worthy of loyalty, sacrifice, and (when necessary) violent defense. Conversely, when a group of people perceives that an alternative ideology or condition should be promoted, revolutionary violence may occur against the defenders of the established rival order. In neither case would those who commit acts of political violence consider themselves to be unjustified in their actions, and they certainly would not label themselves terrorists.

In Chapter 2, readers will be challenged to probe the nature of terrorism more deeply. The discussion will center on the importance of perspective and the question of how to define terrorism.

## Key Terms and Concepts

The following topics are discussed in this chapter and can be found in the glossary:

Al-Qa'ida

Breivik, Anders

crucifixion

dissident

extremism

*jus ad bellum*

*jus in bello*

just war doctrine

Kaczynski, Theodore "Ted" (the Unabomber)

*komiteh*

Luddites

*mala in se*

*mala prohibita*

People's Will (Narodnaya Volya)

regicide

Reign of Terror (régime de la terreur)

Revolutionary Tribunal

Saint Augustine

*sicarii*

soft targets

"struggle meetings"

symbolism

terrorism

total war

tyrannicide

UNABOM

Yousef, Ramzi

Zealots

## Discussion Box: Total War

*This chapter's Discussion Box is intended to stimulate critical debate about the legitimacy of using extreme force against civilian populations.*

Total war is "warfare that uses all possible means of attack, military, scientific, and psychological, against both enemy troops and civilians."[a] It was the prevailing military doctrine applied by combatant nations during the Second World War.

Allied and Axis military planners specifically targeted civilian populations. In the cases of German and Japanese strategists, the war was fought as much against indigenous populations as against opposing armies. The massacres and genocide directed against civilian populations at Auschwitz, Dachau, Warsaw, Lidice, and Nanking and countless other atrocities are a dark legacy of the 20th century.

The estimated number of civilians killed during the war is staggering:[b]

| | |
|---|---|
| Belgium | 90,000 |
| Britain | 70,000 |
| China | 20,000,000 |
| Czechoslovakia | 319,000 |
| France | 391,000 |
| Germany | 2,000,000 |
| Greece | 391,000 |
| Japan | 953,000 |
| Poland | 6,000,000 |
| Soviet Union | 7,700,000 |
| Yugoslavia | 1,400,000 |

An important doctrine of the air war on all sides was to bomb civilian populations, so that the cities of Rotterdam, Coventry, London, Berlin, Dresden, and Tokyo were deliberately attacked. It is estimated that the atomic bombs dropped on Hiroshima and Nagasaki killed, respectively, 70,000 and 35,000 people.[c]

### Discussion Questions

- Are deliberate attacks against civilians legitimate acts of war?

- Were deliberate attacks on civilians during the Second World War acts of terrorism?

- If these attacks were acts of terrorism, were some attacks justifiable acts of terrorism?

- Is there such a thing as justifiable terrorism? Is terrorism *malum in se* or *malum prohibitum*?

- Is the practice of total war by individuals or small and poorly armed groups different from its practice by nations and standing armies? How so or how not?

### Notes

a. *Webster's New Twentieth Century Dictionary of the English Language, Unabridged.* 2nd ed. New York: Publishers Guild, 1966.

b. Mercer, Derrik, ed. *Chronicle of the Second World War.* Essex, UK: Longman Group, 1990, p. 668.

c. Jablonski, Edward. *Flying Fortress.* New York: Doubleday, 1965, p. 285.

## On Your Own

The open-access Student Study Site at **http://study.sagepub.com/martin5e** has a variety of useful study aids, including eFlashcards, quizzes, audio resources, and journal articles. The websites, exercises, and recommended readings listed below are easily accessed on this site as well.

## Recommended Websites

The following websites provide general information about terrorism:

Anti-Defamation League: http://www.adl.org/

Combating Terrorism Center at West Point: http://www.ctc.usma.edu/

Iraq Coalition Casualty Count: http://icasualties.org/

Memorial Institute for the Prevention of Terrorism: http://www.mipt.org/

RAND Corporation: http://www.rand.org/

Southern Poverty Law Center: http://www.splcenter.org/

Terrorism Research Center: http://www.terrorism.com/

Timeline of Terrorism: http://www.timelineofterrorism.com/

## Web Exercise

Using this chapter's recommended websites, conduct an online investigation of organizations that monitor extremist sentiment and terrorist behavior. Compare and contrast these organizations.

1. What are the primary agendas of these organizations?

2. How would you describe the differences between research, government, and social activist organizations?

3. In your opinion, are any of these organizations more comprehensive than other organizations? Less comprehensive?

For an online search of research and monitoring organizations, readers should activate the search engine on their Web browser and enter the following keywords:

"Human Rights Organizations"

"Terrorism Research"

## Recommended Readings

The following publications provide an introduction to terrorism:

Bergen, Peter I. *A Very Long War: The History of the War on Terror and the Battles With Al Qaeda Since 9/11.* New York: Free Press, 2011.

Coll, Steve. *The Bin Ladens: An Arabian Family in the American Century.* New York: Penguin, 2008.

Cronin, Isaac, ed. *Confronting Fear: A History of Terrorism.* New York: Thunder's Mouth Press, 2002.

Farber, David, ed. *What They Think of Us: International Perceptions of the United States Since 9/11.* Princeton, NJ: Princeton University Press, 2007.

Gage, Beverly. *The Day Wall Street Exploded: A Story of America in Its First Age of Terror.* Oxford, UK: Oxford University Press, 2009.

Griset, Pamala L., and Sue Mahan. *Terrorism in Perspective.* 3rd ed. Thousand Oaks, CA: Sage, 2013.

Haberfeld, M.R., and Agostino von Hassel, eds. *A New Understanding of Terrorism: Case Studies, Trajectories, and Lessons Learned.* New York: Springer, 2009.

Heinze, Eric A., and Brent J. Steele, eds. *Ethics, Authority, and War: Non-State Actors and the Just War Tradition.* New York: Palgrave Macmillan, 2009.

Hersh, Seymour M. *Chain of Command: The Road From 9/11 to Abu Ghraib.* New York: HarperCollins, 2004.

Heymann, Phillip B., and Juliette N. Kayyem. *Protecting Liberty in an Age of Terror.* Cambridge, MA: MIT Press, 2005.

Hobsbawm, Eric J. *On Empire: America, War, and Global Supremacy.* New York: Pantheon, 2008.

Hoffman, Bruce. *Inside Terrorism, Revised and Expanded Edition.* New York: Columbia University Press, 2006.

Kaczynski, Theodore. *Technological Slavery: The Collected Writings of Theodore J. Kaczynski, a.k.a. "The Unabomber."* Port Townsend, WA: Feral House, 2010.

Laqueur, Walter, ed. *Voices of Terror: Manifestos, Writings, and Manuals of Al-Qaeda, Hamas, and Other*

*Terrorists From Around the World and Throughout the Ages*. New York: Reed Press, 2004.

National Commission on Terrorist Attacks Upon the United States. *The 9/11 Commission Report*. New York: Norton, 2004.

Reed, Charles, and David Ryall, eds. *The Price of Peace: Just War in the Twenty-First Century*. Cambridge, UK: Cambridge University Press, 2007.

Scheuer, Michael. *Imperial Hubris: Why the West Is Losing the War on Terror*. Washington, DC: Brassey's, 2004.

Scheuer, Michael. *Osama bin Laden*. New York: Oxford University Press, 2011.

Tanner, Stephen. *Afghanistan: A Military History From Alexander the Great to the War Against the Taliban*. Updated edition. New York: Da Capo, 2009.

# The Nature of the Beast

CHAPTER 2

## Defining Terrorism

**Hate crimes** refers to behaviors that are considered to be bias-motivated crimes but that at times seem to fit the definition of acts of terrorism. Hate crimes are a legalistic concept in Western democracies that embody (in the law) a criminological approach to a specific kind of deviant behavior. These laws focus on a specific motive for criminal behavior—crimes that are directed against protected classes of people because of their membership in these protected classes. Thus, hate crimes are officially considered to be a law enforcement issue rather than one of national security.

The separation between hate crimes and terrorism is not always clear because "hate groups at times in their life cycles might resemble gangs and at other times paramilitary organizations or terrorist groups."[a] They represent "another example of small, intense groups that sometimes resort to violence to achieve their goals by committing . . . vigilante terrorism."[b] Among experts, the debate about what is or is not "terrorism" has resulted in a large number of official and unofficial definitions. A similar debate has arisen about how to define hate crimes because "it is difficult to construct an exhaustive definition of the term. . . . Crime—hate crime included—is relative."[c] In fact, there is no agreement on what label to use for behaviors that many people commonly refer to as "hate crimes." For example, in the United States, attacks by white neo-Nazi youths against African Americans, gays, and religious institutions have been referred to with such diverse terms as *hate crime, hate-motivated crime, bias crime, bias-motivated crime,* and *ethno-violence.*[d]

Are hate crimes acts of terrorism? The answer is that not all acts of terrorism are hate crimes, and not all hate crimes are acts of terrorism. For example, dissident terrorists frequently target a state or system with little or no animus against a particular race, religion, or other group. Likewise, state terrorism is often motivated by a perceived need to preserve or reestablish the state's defined vision of social order without targeting a race, religion, or other group. On the other hand, criminal behavior fitting federal or state definitions of hate crimes in the United States can have little or no identifiable political agenda, other than hatred toward a protected class of people.

It is when *political* violence is directed against a particular group—such as a race, religion, nationality, or generalized "undesirable"—that these acts possibly fit the definitions of both hate crimes and terrorism. **Terrorists** often launch attacks against people who symbolize the cause that they oppose. In the United Kingdom, Germany, the United States, and elsewhere, many individuals and groups act out violently to promote an agenda that seeks to "purify" society. These crimes are committed by groups or individuals who are "dealing in the artificial currency of . . . 'imagined communities'—utopian pipe dreams and idealizations of ethnically cleansed communities."[e] For example, after German reunification, "street renegades [demanded] a new *Lebensraum* of a purified Germany whose national essence and coherence will not be weakened and 'contaminated' by ethnic and racial minorities."[f] Their targeted enemies were Turkish, Slavic, and southern European immigrants and "guest workers."

## Notes

a. Barkan, Steven E., and Lynne L. Snowden. *Collective Violence.* Boston: Allyn & Bacon, 2001, p. 105.

b. Ibid., p. 106.

c. Perry, Barbara. *In the Name of Hate: Understanding Hate Crimes.* New York: Routledge, 2001, p. 8.

d. Hamm, Mark S. "Conceptualizing Hate Crime in a Global Context." In *Hate Crime: International Perspectives on Causes and Control*, edited by Mark S. Hamm. Cincinnati, OH: Anderson, 1994, p. 174.

e. Kelly, Robert J., and Jess Maghan. *Hate Crime: The Global Politics of Polarization.* Carbondale: Southern Illinois University Press, 1998, p. 6. Citing Anderson, Benedict. *Imagined Communities: Reflections on the Origin and Spread of Nationalism.* London: New Left, 1983.

f. Ibid., p. 5.

This chapter investigates definitional issues in the study of terrorism. Readers will probe the nuances of these issues and will learn that the truism **"one person's terrorist is another person's freedom fighter"** is a significant factor in the definitional debate. It must be remembered that this debate occurs within a practical and "real-life" framework—in other words, a nontheoretical reality that some political, religious, or ethnonationalist beliefs and behaviors are so reprehensible that they cannot be considered to be mere differences in opinion. Some violent incidents are *mala in se* acts of terrorist violence. For example, the **New Terrorism** is characterized by the threat of weapons of mass destruction, indiscriminate targeting, and intentionally high casualty rates—as occurred in the attacks of September 11, 2001, in the United States; March 11, 2004, in Spain; July 7, 2005, in Great Britain; November 26–29, 2008, in India; and repeated attacks in Iraq and Pakistan. The use of these weapons and tactics against civilians is indefensible, no matter what cause is championed by those who use them.

The definitional debate is evident in the following examples drawn from state-sponsored and dissident terrorist environments:

❖ **Photo 2.1**
A new fascist generation? Youthful racist skinheads in London give the fascist salute.

Leon Morris/Hulton Archive/Getty Images

- **State-Sponsored Terrorist Environments.** The *régime de la terreur* during the French Revolution was an instrument of revolutionary justice, so that terrorism was considered a positive medium used by the defenders of order and liberty. From their perspective, state-sponsored domestic terrorism was both necessary and acceptable to consolidate power and protect liberties won during the revolution. Modern examples of state terrorism such as Nazi Germany and Stalinist Russia also sought to consolidate an ideological vision through internal political violence—a racial new order in Germany and an egalitarian worker's state in the Soviet Union. The methods they used to build the ideological vision resulted in the deaths of many millions of noncombatant civilians, and both the Nazi and Stalinist regimes were by definition quintessential terrorist states.

- **Dissident Terrorist Environments.** The anticolonial and nationalist wars after World War II often pitted indigenous rebels against European colonial powers or ruling local elites. Many of these wars involved the use of terrorism as an instrument of war by both state and dissident forces. During these wars, as well as in subsequent domestic rebellions, the rebels were referred to as freedom fighters by those who favored their cause.[1] The counterpoints to these freedom fighters were the European and American "colonial and imperialist oppressors." Thus, for example, indiscriminate attacks against civilians by rebels in French Indochina and French Algeria were rationalized by many of their supporters as acceptable tactics during wars of liberation by freedom fighters against a colonial oppressor.

---

[1]See Hoffman, Bruce. *Inside Terrorism.* New York: Columbia University Press; revised and enlarged edition, 2006.

The discussion in this chapter will review the following:

- Understanding Extremism: The Foundation of Terrorism
- Defining Terrorism: An Ongoing Debate
- A Definitional Problem: Perspectives on Terrorism
- The Political Violence Matrix

# ❖ Understanding Extremism: The Foundation of Terrorism

An important step toward defining terrorism is to develop an understanding of the sources of terrorism. To identify them, one must first understand the important role of extremism as a primary feature of all terrorist behavior.

Behind each incident of terrorist violence is some deeply held belief system that has motivated the perpetrators. Such systems are, at their core, extremist systems characterized by intolerance. One must keep in mind, however, that though terrorism is a violent expression of these beliefs, it is by no means the only possible manifestation of extremism. On a scale of activist behavior, extremists can engage in such benign expressions as sponsoring debates or publishing newspapers. They might also engage in vandalism and other disruptions of the normal routines of their enemies. Though intrusive and often illegal, these are examples of political expression that cannot be construed as terrorist acts.

Our focus in this and subsequent chapters will be on violent extremist behavior that many people would define as acts of terrorism. First, we must briefly investigate the general characteristics of the extremist foundations of terrorism.

## Defining Extremism

Political extremism refers to taking a political idea to its limits, regardless of unfortunate repercussions, impracticalities, arguments, and feelings to the contrary, and with the intention not only to confront, but to eliminate opposition. . . . Intolerance toward all views other than one's own.[2]

Extremism is a precursor to terrorism—it is an overarching belief system that is used by terrorists to justify their violent behavior. Extremism is characterized by *what* a person's beliefs are as well as *how* a person expresses his or her beliefs. Thus, no matter how offensive or reprehensible one's thoughts or words are, they are not by themselves acts of terrorism. Only persons who *violently* act out their extremist beliefs are labeled terrorists.

Two examples illustrate this point:

First, an example of extremist behavior. Daniel and Philip Berrigan were well-known members of the Roman Catholic pacifist left and were leaders in the antiwar and antinuclear movements in the United States during the 1960s and 1970s. *What* they believed in was an uncompromising commitment to pacifism. *How* they expressed their beliefs was by committing a series of symbolic, and often illegal, protest actions. During one such action on May 17, 1968, they and seven other Catholic men and women entered the Baltimore Selective Service Board; stole Selective Service classification forms; took them outside to a parking lot; and burned several hundred of the documents with a homemade, napalm-like gelled mixture of gasoline and soap flakes. This was certainly extremist behavior, but it falls short of terrorism.[3]

---

[2]Scruton, Roger. *A Dictionary of Political Thought.* New York: Hill & Wang, 1982, p. 164.

[3]For a good biography of the Berrigan brothers, see Polner, Murray, and Jim O'Grady. *Disarmed and Dangerous: The Radical Life and Times of Daniel and Philip Berrigan, Brothers in Religious Faith and Civil Disobedience.* Boulder, CO: Westview, 1998.

Second, an example of extremist speech. The American Knights of the Ku Klux Klan (AK-KKK) were an activist faction of the KKK that operated mostly in the Midwest and East during the 1990s. *What* they believed in was racial supremacy. *How* they expressed their beliefs was by holding a series of rallies at government sites, often county courthouses. They were known for their vitriolic rhetoric. The following remarks were reportedly taken from a speech delivered by the Imperial Wizard of the AK-KKK in March 1998 at a rally held at the county courthouse in Butler, Pennsylvania, near Pittsburgh:

> Take a stand. . . . Join the Klan, stick up for your rights. . . . Only God has the right to create a race—not no black and white, not no nigger, not no Jew. . . . Yes, I will use the word *nigger,* because it is not illegal. . . . We are sick and tired of the government taking your money, and giving food and jobs to the niggers when the white race has to go without! Wake up America.[4]

This language is intentionally racist, hateful, and inflammatory; yet it falls short of advocating violence or revolution. A sympathetic listener might certainly act out against one of the enemy groups identified in the speech, but it reads more like a racist diatribe than a revolutionary manifesto.

## Common Characteristics of Violent Extremists

Scholars and other experts have identified common characteristics exhibited by violent extremists. These characteristics are expressed in different ways, depending on a movement's particular belief system. The following commonalities are summaries of traits identified by these experts and are by no means an exhaustive inventory.[5]

### Intolerance

Intolerance is the hallmark of extremist belief systems and terrorist behavior. The cause is considered to be absolutely just and good, and those who disagree with the cause (or some aspect of the cause) are cast into the category of the opposition. Terrorists affix their opponents with certain negative or derisive labels to set them apart from the extremists' movement. These characterizations are often highly personalized, so that specific individuals are identified who symbolize the opposing belief system or cause. Thus, during the Cold War, the American president was labeled by the pro–United States camp as the "leader of the free world" and by Latin American Marxists as the embodiment of "Yankee imperialism."[6]

### Moral Absolutes

Extremists adopt moral absolutes, so that the distinction between good and evil is clear, as are the lines between the extremists and their opponents. The extremist's belief or cause is a morally correct vision of the world and is used to establish moral superiority over others. Violent extremists thus become morally and ethically pure elites who lead the oppressed masses to freedom. For example, religious terrorists generally believe that their one true faith is superior to all others and that any behavior committed in defense of the faith is fully justifiable.

---

[4]Remarks of Jeff Berry, Imperial Wizard of the American Knights of the Ku Klux Klan, Butler, Pennsylvania, March 1998. Quoted in Weller, Worth H., and Brad Thompson. *Under the Hood: Unmasking the Modern Ku Klux Klan.* North Manchester, IN: DeWitt, 1998, pp. 40–1.

[5]For an excellent list of traits of extremists, see Wilcox, Laird. "What Is Extremism? Style and Tactics Matter More Than Goals." In George, John, and Laird Wilcox, eds. *American Extremists: Militias, Supremacists, Klansmen, Communists, and Others.* Buffalo, NY: Prometheus, 1996, pp. 54ff.

[6]For references to the Cuban perspective, see Kenner, Martin, and James Petras. *Fidel Castro Speaks.* New York: Grove, 1969.

### *Broad Conclusions*

Extremist conclusions are made to simplify the goals of the cause and the nature of the extremist's opponents. These generalizations are not debatable and allow for no exceptions. Evidence for these conclusions is rooted in one's belief system rather than based on objective data. Terrorists often believe these generalizations because in their minds, they simply *must* be true. For example, ethnonationalists frequently categorize all members of their opponent group as having certain broadly negative traits.

### *New Language and Conspiratorial Beliefs*

Language and conspiracies are created to demonize the enemy and set the terrorists apart from those not part of their belief system. Extremists thus become an elite with a hidden agenda and targets of that agenda. For example, some American far-right conspiracy proponents express their anti-Semitic beliefs by using coded references to international bankers or a Zionist-occupied government (ZOG). Neo-Nazi rightists degrade members of non-European races by referring to them as mud people.

## The World of the Extremist

Extremists have a very different—and, at times, fantastic—worldview compared with nonextremists. They set themselves apart as protectors of some truth or as the true heirs of some legacy. For example, racial extremists within the American Patriot movement have argued that nonwhites are "Fourteenth Amendment citizens," and that only

> whites are sovereign citizens whose rights are delineated, not by the government, but rather by a cobbled assortment of historical writings whose meaning is often subject to their fanciful interpretation.[7]

Extremists frequently believe that secret and quasimystical forces are arrayed against them, and that these forces are the cause of worldwide calamities. For example, some bigoted conspiracy believers argue that the Illuminati or international Judaism mysteriously control world banking and the media, or that they run the governments of France and the United States. One conspiracy theory that was widely believed among Islamist extremists in the aftermath of the September 11, 2001, attacks was that Israeli agents were behind the attacks; that 4,000 Jews received telephone calls to evacuate the World Trade Center in New York; and thus, that no Jews were among the victims of the attack.

As in the past, religion is often an underlying impetus for extremist activity. When extremists adopt a religious belief system, their worldview becomes one of a struggle between supernatural forces of good and evil. They view themselves as living a righteous life in a manner that fits with their interpretation of God's will. According to religious extremists, those who do not conform to their belief system are opposed to the one true faith. Those who live according to the accepted belief system are a chosen people, and those who do not are not chosen. These interpretations of how one should behave include elements of the social or political environment that underlies the belief system. For example, Bob Jones University in Greenville, South Carolina, is a fundamentalist Christian university founded in 1927. It once justified its prohibition against interracial dating and marriage as an application of God-mandated truths found in Holy Scripture. Similarly, one student at a Pakistani religious school explained that "Osama [bin Laden]

❖ **Photo 2.2**

Members of the neo-Nazi National Socialist Movement march in Washington, DC, from the Washington Monument to the U.S. Capitol building.

David S. Holloway/Getty Images News/Getty Images

---

[7]Kushner, Harvey W., ed. *The Future of Terrorism: Violence in the New Millennium.* Thousand Oaks, CA: Sage, 1998, pp. 125, 126.

wants to keep Islam pure from the pollution of the infidels. . . . He believes Islam is the way for all the world. He wants to bring Islam to all the world."[8]

Extremists have a very clear sense of mission, purpose, and righteousness. They create a worldview that sets them apart from the rest of society. Thus, extremist beliefs and terrorist behaviors are very logical from the perspective of those who accept the extremists' belief system but illogical from the point of view of those who reject the system.

# ❖ Defining Terrorism: An Ongoing Debate

The effort to formally define terrorism is a critical one because government antiterrorist policy calculations must be based on criteria that determine whether a violent incident is an act of terrorism. Governments and policy makers must piece together the elements of terrorist behavior and demarcate the factors that distinguish terrorism from other forms of conflict.

There is some consensus among experts—but no unanimity—on what kind of violence constitutes an act of terrorism. Governments have developed definitions of terrorism, individual agencies within governments have adopted definitions, private agencies have designed their own definitions, and academic experts have proposed and analyzed dozens of definitional constructs. This lack of unanimity, which exists throughout the public and private sectors, is an accepted reality in the study of political violence.

A significant amount of intellectual energy has been devoted to identifying formal elements of terrorism, as illustrated by Alex Schmid's surveys, which identified more than 100 definitions.[9] Establishing formal definitions can, of course, be complicated by the perspectives of the participants in a terrorist incident, who instinctively differentiate freedom fighters from terrorists, regardless of formal definitions. Another complication is that most definitions focus on political violence perpetrated by dissident groups, even though many governments have practiced terrorism as both domestic and foreign policy.

## Guerrilla Warfare

One important distinction must be kept in mind and understood at the outset: *Terrorism is not synonymous with guerrilla warfare*. The term **guerrilla** ("little war") was developed during the early 19th century, when Napoleon's army fought a long, brutal, and ultimately unsuccessful war in Spain. Unlike the Napoleonic campaigns elsewhere in Europe, which involved conventional armies fighting set-piece battles in accordance with rules of engagement, the war in Spain was a classic unconventional conflict. The Spanish *people,* as opposed to the Spanish *army,* rose in rebellion and resisted the invading French army. They liberated large areas of the Spanish countryside. After years of costly fighting—in which atrocities were common on both sides—the French were driven out. Thus, in contrast to terrorists, the term *guerrilla fighters* refers to

a numerically larger group of armed individuals who operate as a military unit, attack enemy military forces, and seize and hold territory (even if only ephemerally during the daylight hours), while also exercising some form of sovereignty or control over a defined geographical area and its population.[10]

Dozens, if not scores, of examples of guerrilla warfare exist in the modern era. They exhibit the classic strategy of hit-and-run warfare by small mobile units, and many examples exist of

---

[8]Goldberg, Jeffrey. "Inside Jihad U.: The Education of a Holy Warrior." *New York Times Magazine,* June 25, 2000, p. 35.

[9]See Schmid, Alex P., and Albert J. Jongman. *Political Terrorism: A Guide to Actors, Authors, Concepts, Data Bases, Theories, and Literature.* 2nd ed. New Jersey: Transaction Publishers, 2005. The book reports the results of a survey of 100 experts asked for their definitions of terrorism.

[10]Whittaker, David J., ed. *The Terrorism Reader.* 4th ed. New York: Routledge, 2012, p. 8.

successful guerrilla campaigns against numerically and technologically superior adversaries. Guerrilla insurgencies have often been successful in affecting the global political environment. The following are examples of conflicts in the modern era when guerrilla insurgents prevailed against strong adversaries:

- 1940s. Chinese communist guerrillas led by Mao Zedong defeated Chinese nationalists.
- 1950s. Communist-led Viet Minh guerrillas forced French colonial forces to withdraw from Vietnam.
- 1960s–1970s. Numerous guerrilla insurgencies successfully resisted European colonial forces, including anticolonial wars in Africa.
- 1980s. Afghan *mujahideen* guerrillas fought invading Soviet troops for 10 years, eventually prevailing after the Soviet withdrawal.

## A Sampling of Formal Definitions

In Europe, countries that endured terrorist campaigns have written official definitions of terrorism. The British have defined terrorism as "the use or threat, for the purpose of advancing a political, religious or ideological cause, of action which involves serious violence against any person or property."[11] In Germany, terrorism has been described as an "enduringly conducted struggle for political goals, which are intended to be achieved by means of assaults on the life and property of other persons, especially by means of severe crimes."[12] And the European interior ministers note that "terrorism is . . . the use, or the threatened use, by a cohesive group of persons of violence (short of warfare) to effect political aims."[13]

Scholars have also tried their hand at defining terrorism. Terrorism has been described by Gurr as "the use of unexpected violence to intimidate or coerce people in the pursuit of political or social objectives."[14] It was described by Gibbs as "illegal violence or threatened violence against human or nonhuman objects," so long as that violence meets additional criteria such as secretive features and unconventional warfare.[15] Bruce Hoffman wrote,

> We come to appreciate that terrorism is ineluctably political in aims and motives; violent—or, equally important, threatens violence; designed to have far-reaching psychological repercussions beyond the immediate victim or target; conducted by an organization with an identifiable chain of command or conspiratorial structure (whose members wear no uniform or identifying insignia); and perpetrated by a subnational group or non-state entity. We may therefore now attempt to define terrorism as the deliberate creation and exploitation of fear through violence or the threat of violence in the pursuit of change.[16]

To further illustrate the range of definitions, Whittaker lists the following descriptions of terrorism by terrorism experts:[17]

---

[11]Ibid., p. 1.

[12]Office for the Protection of the Constitution. See Whittaker, *The Terrorism Reader*.

[13]Ibid.

[14]Gurr, Ted Robert. "Political Terrorism: Historical Antecedents and Contemporary Trends." In *Violence in America: Protest, Rebellion, Reform,* edited by Ted Robert Gurr. Vol. 2. Newbury Park, CA: Sage, 1989.

[15]Gibbs, J. P. "Conceptualization of Terrorism." *American Sociological Review* 54 (1989): 329. Quoted in Hamm, Mark S., ed. *Hate Crime: International Perspectives on Causes and Control.* Cincinnati, OH: Anderson, 1994, p. 111.

[16]Hoffman, *Inside Terrorism*, p. 43.

[17]Whittaker, *The Terrorism* Reader, p. 8.

- Contributes the illegitimate use of force to achieve a political objective when innocent people are targeted. (Walter Laqueur)
- A strategy of violence designed to promote desired outcomes by instilling fear in the public at large. (Walter Reich)
- The use or threatened use of force designed to bring about political change. (Brian Jenkins)

From this discussion, we can identify the common features of most formal definitions:

- The use of illegal force
- Subnational actors
- Unconventional methods
- Political motives
- Attacks against "soft" civilian and passive military targets
- Acts aimed at purposefully affecting an audience

The emphasis, then, is on terrorists adopting specific types of motives, methods, and targets. One fact readily apparent from these formal definitions is that they focus on terrorist *groups* rather than terrorist *states*. As will be made abundantly clear in Chapter 4, state terrorism has been responsible for many more deaths and much more suffering than has terrorism originating in small bands of terrorists.

## The American Context: Defining Terrorism in the United States

The United States has not adopted a single definition of terrorism as a matter of government policy, instead relying on definitions that are developed from time to time by government agencies. These definitions reflect the United States' traditional law enforcement approach to distinguishing terrorism from more common criminal behavior. The following definitions are a sample of the official approach.

The U.S. Department of Defense defines terrorism as "the unlawful use of violence or threat of violence, often motivated by religious, political, or other ideological beliefs, to instill fear and coerce governments or societies in pursuit of goals that are usually political."[18] The U.S. Code defines terrorism as illegal violence that attempts to "intimidate or coerce a civilian population; . . . influence the policy of a government by intimidation or coercion; or . . . affect the conduct of a government by assassination or kidnapping."[19] The Federal Bureau of Investigation has defined terrorism as "the unlawful use of force or violence against persons or property to intimidate or coerce a Government, the civilian population, or any segment thereof, in furtherance of political or social objectives."[20] The State Department has defined terrorism as "premeditated, politically motivated violence perpetrated against non-combatant targets by subnational groups or clandestine agents."[21]

---

[18]U.S. Department of Defense. *Department of Defense Dictionary of Military and Associated Terms.* Washington, DC, November 8, 2010 (as amended through June 15, 2014). At 266.

[19]18 U.S.C. 3077.

[20]Terrorist Research and Analytical Center, National Security Division, Federal Bureau of Investigation. *Terrorism in the United States 1995.* Washington, DC: U.S. Department of Justice, 1996, p. ii.

[21]Bureau of Counterterrorism. *Country Reports on Terrorism 2013.* Washington, DC: U.S. Department of State, 2014. At Executive Summary.

Using these definitions, common elements can be combined to construct a composite American definition.

Terrorism is a premeditated and unlawful act in which groups or agents of some principle engage in a threatened or actual use of force or violence against human or property targets. These groups or agents engage in this behavior, intending the purposeful intimidation of governments or people to affect policy or behavior, with an underlying political objective.

These elements indicate a fairly narrow and legalistic approach to defining terrorism. When these elements are assigned to individual suspects, they may be labeled and detained as terrorists. Readers, in evaluating the practical policy implications of this approach, should bear in mind that labeling and detaining suspects as terrorists is not without controversy. Some counterterrorist practices have prompted strong debate as a consequence of the post–September 11, 2001, war on terrorism. For example, when enemy soldiers are taken prisoner, they are traditionally afforded legal protections as *prisoners of war*. This is well recognized under international law. During the war on terrorism, many suspected terrorists were designated by the United States as *enemy combatants* and were not afforded the same legal status as prisoners of war. Such practices have been hotly debated among proponents and opponents. These practices and the concomitant civil liberties debate are more fully discussed in Chapter 14. Chapter Perspective 2.1 discusses the ongoing problem of labeling the enemy.

## CHAPTER PERSPECTIVE 2.1: The Problem of Labeling the Enemy in the New Era of Terrorism

When formulating counterterrorist policies, policy makers are challenged by two problems: first, the problem of defining terrorism, and second, the problem of labeling individual suspects. Although defining terrorism can be an exercise in semantics—and is often shaped by subjective political or cultural biases—there are certain fundamental elements that constitute objective definitions. In comparison, using official designations (labels) to confer special status on captured suspects has become a controversial process.

During the post–September 11, 2001, war on terrorism, it became clear to experts and the public that official designations and labels of individual suspected terrorists is a central legal, political, and security issue. Of essential importance is the question of a suspect's official *status* when he or she is taken prisoner.

Depending on one's designated status, certain recognized legal or political protections may or may not be observed by interrogators or others involved in processing specific cases.

According to the protocols of the third Geneva Convention, prisoners who are designated as *prisoners of war* and who are brought to trial must be afforded the same legal rights in the same courts as would soldiers from the country holding them prisoner. Thus, prisoners of war held by the United States would be brought to trial in standard military courts under the Uniform Code of Military Justice and would have the same rights and protections (such as the right to appeal) as all soldiers.

Suspected terrorists have not been designated as prisoners of war. Official and unofficial designations such as *enemy combatants, unlawful combatants,* and *battlefield detainees* have been used by U.S. authorities to differentiate them from prisoners of war. The rationale is that suspected terrorists are not soldiers fighting for a sovereign nation and are therefore ineligible for prisoner-of-war status. When hundreds of prisoners were detained at facilities such as the American base in Guantánamo Bay, Cuba, the United States argued that persons designated as enemy combatants were not subject to the protocols of the Geneva Conventions. Thus, such persons could be held indefinitely, detained in secret, transferred at will, and sent to allied countries for more coercive interrogations. Under enemy combatant status, conditions of confinement in Guantánamo Bay included open-air cells with wooden roofs and chain-link walls. In theory, each case was to be reviewed by special military tribunals, and innocent prisoners would be reclassified as *nonenemy combatants* and released.

Civil liberties and human rights groups disagreed with the special status conferred by the labeling system on prisoners. They argued that basic legal and humanitarian protections should be granted to prisoners regardless of their designation. In June 2008, the United States Supreme Court held that foreign detainees held for years at Guantánamo Bay had the right to appeal to U.S. federal judges to challenge their indefinite imprisonment without charges. At the time of the decision, about 200 foreign detainees had lawsuits pending before federal court in Washington, DC.

In one interesting development, the U.S. Department of Defense conferred *protected persons* status on members of the Iranian Mujahideen-e Khalq Organization (MKO), who were under guard in Iraq by the American military. The MKO is a Marxist movement opposed to the postrevolution regime in Iran. The group was regularly listed on the U.S. Department of State's list of terrorist organizations, and it was responsible for killings of Americans and others in terrorist attacks.

## Types of Terrorism

The basic elements of terrorist environments are uncomplicated, and experts and commentators generally agree on the forms of terrorism found in modern political environments. For example, the following environments have been described by academic experts:

- Barkan and Snowden describe vigilante, insurgent, transnational, and state terrorism.[22]
- Hoffman discusses ethnonationalist/separatist, international, religious, and state-sponsored terrorism.[23]
- While undertaking the task of defining the New Terrorism, Laqueur contextualizes far-rightist, religious, state, "exotic," and criminal terrorism.[24]
- Other experts evaluate narco-terrorism, toxic terrorism, and netwar.[25]

We will explore all of these environments in later chapters within the following contexts:

### State Terrorism

Terrorism "from above" committed by governments against perceived enemies. State terrorism can be directed externally against adversaries in the international domain or internally against domestic enemies.

### Dissident Terrorism

Terrorism "from below" committed by nonstate movements and groups against governments, ethnonational groups, religious groups, and other perceived enemies.

---

[22]Barkan, Steven E., and Lynne L. Snowden. *Collective Violence*. Boston: Allyn & Bacon, 2001.

[23]Hoffman, *Inside Terrorism*.

[24]Laqueur, Walter. *The New Terrorism: Fanaticism and the Arms of Mass Destruction*. New York: Oxford University Press, 1999, p. 230.

[25]Ehrenfeld, Rachel. *Narco Terrorism*. Basic Books, 1990; Tucker, Jonathan B., ed. *Toxic Terror: Assessing Terrorist Use of Chemical and Biological Weapons*. Cambridge, MA: MIT Press, 2000.

### Religious Terrorism

Terrorism motivated by an absolute belief that an otherworldly power has sanctioned—and commanded—the application of terrorist violence for the greater glory of the faith. Religious terrorism is usually conducted in defense of what believers consider to be the one true faith.

### Criminal Terrorism

Terrorism motivated by sheer profit or some amalgam of profit and politics. Traditional organized criminal enterprises (such as the Italian Mafia and the Japanese Yakuza) accumulate profits from criminal activity for personal aggrandizement. Criminal-political enterprises (such as Colombia's FARC and Sri Lanka's Tamil Tigers) accumulated profits to sustain their movement.

### International Terrorism

Terrorism that spills over onto the world's stage. Targets are selected because of their value as symbols of international interests, either within the home country or across state boundaries.

## ❖ A Definitional Problem: Perspectives on Terrorism

It should now be clear that defining terrorism can be an exercise in semantics and context, driven by one's perspective and worldview. Absent definitional guidelines, these perspectives would be merely the subject of personal opinion and academic debate.

Perspective is a central consideration in defining terrorism. Those who oppose an extremist group's violent behavior—and who might be its targets—would naturally consider them terrorists. On the other hand, those who are being championed by the group—and on whose behalf the terrorist war is being fought—often see them as liberation fighters, even when they do not necessarily agree with the methods of the group. Fighters within movements may themselves resist attempts to classify them within Western perspectives. For example, many radical Islamists view themselves as *mujahideen* (holy warriors) or *shaheed* (martyrs), whose motivating ideal is selfless obedience to God's will rather than Western notions of freedom. "The problem is that there exists no precise or widely accepted definition of terrorism."[26] We will consider four perspectives that illustrate this problem:

1. **Four Quotations.** Several well-known statements provide a useful conceptual foundation for understanding the importance of perspective.
2. **Participants in a Terrorist Environment.** People who participate in, or are affected by, terrorist incidents are prone to have very different interpretations of the incident.
3. **Terrorism or Freedom Fighting?** The classification of a group or movement as terrorists or freedom fighters is simply a question of one's perspective.
4. **Extremism or "Mainstreamism"?** Whether extremist behavior can move from the ideological fringes into a nation's or people's mainstream.

## Perspective 1: Four Quotations

Evaluating the following aphorisms critically will help to address difficult moral questions:

---

[26]Riley, Kevin Jack, and Bruce Hoffman. *Domestic Terrorism: A National Assessment of State and Local Preparedness.* Santa Monica, CA: RAND, 1995, p. 2.

### *"One Person's Terrorist Is Another Person's Freedom Fighter"*

Who made this statement is not known; it most likely originated in one form or another in the remote historical past. The concept it embodies is, very simply, perspective. It is a concept that will be applied throughout our examination of terrorist groups, movements, and individuals.

As will become abundantly clear, terrorists never consider themselves the "bad guys" in their struggle for what they would define as freedom. They might admit that they have been *forced* by a powerful and ruthless opponent to adopt terrorist methods, but they see themselves as freedom fighters—or, in the case of radical Islamists, obedient servants of God. Benefactors of terrorists always live with clean hands because they present their championed group as plucky freedom fighters. Likewise, nations that use the technology of war to knowingly attack civilian targets justify their sacrifice as incidental to the greater good of the cause.

This concept will be applied throughout our examination of terrorist groups, movements, and individuals.

### *"One Man Willing to Throw Away His Life Is Enough to Terrorize a Thousand"*

This concept originated with Chinese military philosopher **Wu Ch'i**, who wrote,

Now suppose there is a desperate bandit lurking in the fields and one thousand men set out in pursuit of him. The reason all look for him as they would a wolf is that each one fears that he will arise and harm him. This is the reason one man willing to throw away his life is enough to terrorize a thousand.[27]

These sentences are the likely source for the better-known aphorism, **"kill one man, terrorize a thousand."** Its authorship is undetermined but has been attributed to the leader of the Chinese Revolution, **Mao Zedong**, and to the Chinese military philosopher **Sun Tzu**. Both Wu Ch'i and Sun Tzu are often discussed in conjunction with each other, but Sun Tzu may be a mythical figure. Sun Tzu's book *The Art of War* has become a classic study of warfare. Regardless of who originated these phrases, their simplicity explains the value of a motivated individual who is willing to sacrifice herself or himself when committing an act of violence. They suggest that the selfless application of lethal force—in combination with correct timing, surgical precision, and an unambiguous purpose—is an invaluable weapon of war. It is also an obvious tactic for small, motivated groups who are vastly outnumbered and outgunned by a more powerful adversary.

Abid Katib/Getty Images News/Getty Images

❖ **Photo 2.3**

Indoctrinating the young. A Palestinian boy wearing a Hamas headband attends a pro-Islamist demonstration at a refugee camp in Nuseirat, central Gaza Strip.

### *"Extremism in Defense of Liberty Is No Vice"*

Senator Barry M. Goldwater of Arizona made this statement during his bid for the presidency in 1964. His campaign theme was staunchly conservative and anti-Communist. However, because of the nation's rivalry with the Soviet Union at the time, every major candidate was overtly anti-Communist. Goldwater simply tried to outdo incumbent president Lyndon Johnson, his main rival, on the issue.[28]

---

[27]In Chinese literature and propaganda, *bandit* is often a synonym for *rebel*. Sun Tzu. *The Art of War*. New York: Oxford University Press, 1963, p. 168. Wu Ch'i's comments are cited in the translation.

[28]Within the context of the campaign, Lyndon Johnson's anti-Communist "credentials" were decisively validated during the Gulf of Tonkin crisis in August 1964. The destroyer *USS Maddox* was reported to have been attacked by North Vietnamese torpedo boats off the coast of North Vietnam. American air strikes were launched in reprisal, and Congress almost unanimously passed the Gulf of Tonkin Resolution, which supported President Johnson's use of measures to protect U.S. interests in Vietnam and elsewhere. For a discussion of the incident within the context of the politics at the time, see Kearns, Doris. *Lyndon Johnson and the American Dream*. New York: Harper & Row, 1976, pp. 195ff. For an insider's discussion, see Miller, Merle. *Lyndon: An Oral Biography*. New York: Ballantine, 1980, pp. 465–77.

This aphorism represents an uncompromising belief in the absolute righteousness of a cause. It defines a clear belief in good versus evil and a belief that the end justifies the means. If one simply substitutes *any cause* for the word *liberty,* one can fully understand how the expression lends itself to legitimizing uncompromising devotion to the cause. Terrorists use this reasoning to justify their belief that they are defending their championed interest (be it ideological, racial, religious, or national) against all perceived enemies—whom they view, of course, as evil. Hence, the practice of ethnic cleansing was begun by Serb militias during the 1991–1995 war in Bosnia to forcibly remove Muslims and Croats from villages and towns. This was done in the name of Bosnian Serb security and historical claims to land occupied by others.[29] Bosnian and Croat paramilitaries later practiced ethnic cleansing to create their own ethnically pure enclaves.

### "It Became Necessary to Destroy the Town to Save It"[30]

This quotation has been attributed to a statement by an American officer during the war in Vietnam. When asked why a village thought to be occupied by the enemy had been destroyed, he allegedly replied that American soldiers had destroyed the village to save it.[31] The symbolic logic behind this statement is seductive: If the worst thing that can happen to a village is for it to be occupied by an enemy, then destroying it is a good thing. The village has been denied to the enemy, and it has been saved from the horrors of enemy occupation. The symbolism of the village can be replaced by any number of symbolic values.

Terrorists use this kind of reasoning to justify hardships that they impose not only on a perceived enemy but also on their own championed group. For example, in Chapter 5, readers will be introduced to nihilist dissident terrorists, who are content to wage "revolution for revolution's sake." They have no concrete plan for what kind of society will be built upon the rubble of the old one—their goal is simply to destroy an inherently evil system. To them, anything is better than the existing order. A historical example of this reasoning on an enormous scale is found in the great war between two totalitarian and terrorist states—Germany and the Soviet Union—from July 1941 to May 1945. Both sides used scorched-earth tactics as a matter of policy when their armies retreated, destroying towns, crops, roadways, bridges, factories, and other infrastructure as a way to deny resources to the enemy.

## Perspective 2: Participants in a Terrorist Environment

Motives, methods, and targets of violent extremists are interpreted differently by the **participants in a terrorist environment**. These participants can, and often do, draw their own subjective conclusions about violent political incidents regardless of the accepted formal definitions that have been crafted by officials or experts.

The participants in a terrorist environment adopt a multiplicity of interpretations of political violence. Depending on their role when an incident occurs, these participants often provide different

---

[29]For a discussion of this subject from the cultural perspectives of Bosnian Muslims and Serbs, see Weine, Steven M. *When History Is a Nightmare: Lives and Memories of Ethnic Cleansing in Bosnia-Herzegovina.* New Brunswick, NJ: Rutgers University Press, 1999.

[30]The quote has been more widely reported since the Vietnam War as "we had to destroy the village to save it." See Oberdorfer, Don. *Tet!* Garden City, NY: Doubleday, 1971, pp. 184–5, 332. See also Sheehan, Neil. *A Bright Shining Lie: John Paul Vann and America in Vietnam.* New York: Random House, 1988, p. 719.

[31]Associated Press reporter Peter Arnett attributed the source of the quotation to a U.S. soldier at the city of Ben Tre in South Vietnam during the Tet offensive in 1968. As reported, it was the statement of an officer higher up in the chain of command—a U.S. Army major. Although widely repeated at the time and since the war, only Arnett said he heard the statement at the site, and only Arnett filed the quotation from the Ben Tre visit. The U.S. officer was not identified and has not been identified since the war. See Oberdorfer, *Tet!* and Sheehan, *A Bright Shining Lie.* The U.S. Department of Defense launched an investigation to find the source of the quote. No officer or enlisted man was identified. See Oberdorfer, *Tet!*

assessments of the motives, methods, and targets of violent extremists.[32] Subjective considerations commonly affect how an incident will be interpreted. Adversaries in a terrorist environment view participants as audiences that can be manipulated by effective propaganda or other selective information. In many ways, the hearts and minds of the participants in a terrorist environment can become a virtual battleground.

Typically, the participants in a terrorist environment include the following actors, each of whom may advance different interpretations of an incident:[33]

### The Terrorist

Terrorists are the perpetrators of a politically violent incident. The perspective of the terrorist is that the violent incident is a justifiable act of war against an oppressive opponent. "Insofar as terrorists seek to attract attention, they target the enemy public or uncommitted bystanders."[34] This is a legitimate tactic in their minds because, from their point of view, they are always freedom fighters and never terrorists.

Terrorists seek attention and legitimacy for their cause by engaging in publicity-oriented violence. **Propaganda by the deed**, if properly carried out, will deliver symbolic messages to a target audience and to large segments of an onlooker audience. One message could be, for example, to "show their power preeminently through deeds that embarrass their more powerful opponents."[35] Terrorists also attempt to cast themselves as freedom fighters, soldiers, and martyrs. If successful, their image will be that of a vanguard movement representing the just aspirations of an oppressed people. When this occurs, political and moral pressure can be brought against their adversaries, possibly forcing them to grant concessions to the movement.

### The Supporter

Supporters of terrorists are patrons, in essence persons who provide a supportive environment or apparatus. Supporters will generally refer to the terrorist participants as freedom fighters. Even if supporters disagree with the use of force or with the application of force in a specific incident, they will often rationalize its use as the unfortunate consequence of a just war.

Supporters and patrons of terrorists often help with "spinning" the terrorists' cause and manipulating the reporting of incidents. Supporters with sophisticated informational departments—such as Northern Ireland's Sinn Féin, Lebanon's Hezbollah, or the Palestine Liberation Organization's Fatah—can successfully use the Internet and the media to deliver their message to a wide audience. And in societies with a free press—or with supportive authoritarian regimes—sympathetic reporters and editors might lend a hand in portraying the terrorists as freedom fighters. Supporters will always defend the underlying grievances of the extremists and will often allude to these grievances as the reason for the group's decision to use terrorist methods. For example, in November 2002, an audiotape purportedly from Osama bin Laden was broadcast by Al Jazeera. The speaker paid tribute to those who had carried out a series of attacks in Indonesia, Russia, Kuwait, Jordan, and Yemen, noting that the attacks were "undertaken by the zealous sons of Islam in defense of their religion and in response to the call of their God and prophet, peace be upon him."[36] The key for activist supporters is to convey to the audience the impression that the terrorists' methods are understandable under the

---

[32]For a discussion of the participants in media events, see Weimann, Gabriel, and Conrad Winn. *The Theater of Terror: Mass Media and International Terrorism.* New York: Longman, 1994, p. 104.

[33]Ibid. Weimann and Winn mention the following societal participants in media events: the direct victims, the terrorists, the broadcasting audience, journalists, and governments.

[34]Paletz, David L., and Alex P. Schmid. *Terrorism and the Media.* Newbury Park, CA: Sage, 1992, p. 179.

[35]Gerrits, Robin P. J. M. "Terrorists' Perspectives: Memoirs." In *Terrorism and the Media,* edited by David L. Paletz and Alex P. Schmid. Newbury Park, CA: Sage, 1992, p. 36.

[36]Chandrasekaran, Rajiv. "Purported Bin Laden Tape Lauds Bali, Moscow Attacks." *Washington Post,* November 13, 2002.

circumstances. If they can do this successfully, public opinion "can provide the movement with a feeling of legitimacy."[37]

### The Victim

Victims of political violence, and of warfare, will rarely sympathize with the perpetrators of that violence, regardless of the underlying motive. From their perspective, the perpetrators are little better than terrorists.

Terrorist violence can be used to spin incidents so that they symbolize punishment or chastisement against victims for injustices. From the terrorists' point of view, high-profile attacks that victimize an audience are useful as "wake-up calls" for the victims to understand the underlying grievances of the movement. Although victims do not sympathize with the perpetrators who cause their suffering, terrorists believe that they can become educated, through propaganda, by the deed. Because they are the innocent "collateral damage" of a conflict, victims—with help from political and expert commentators in the media—will often question why they have become caught up in a terrorist environment. This process can theoretically cause public opinion shifts.

### The Target

Targets are usually symbolic. They represent some feature of the enemy and can be either property targets or human targets. As is the case with the victim, human targets will rarely sympathize with the perpetrators.

Targets are selected because they symbolize the interests of the terrorists' adversaries. Of course, attacks on some targets—such as symbolic buildings—frequently risk inflicting casualties on large numbers of people. With the proper symbolic spin, terrorists can achieve "the lowering of the opponent's morale and the boosting of the self-confidence of its own constituency."[38] Terrorists can also garner sympathy, or at least a measure of understanding, if they can successfully use the Internet or the media to disseminate their reasons for selecting the target. Targeted interests engage in an assessment process similar to that of victims and are likewise assisted by media commentators. The difference is that the investigatory process is conducted with the understanding that they have been specifically labeled as an enemy interest. In many circumstances, targeted audiences can have a significant impact on public opinion and government policy.

### The Onlooker

Onlookers are the broad audience to the terrorist incident. They can be directly affected by the incident at the scene of an attack or indirectly affected via modern mass media. The onlooker may sympathize with the perpetrators, revile them, or remain neutral. Depending on the worldview of the onlooker, he or she might actually applaud a specific incident or a general dissident environment. Television is a particularly effective medium for broadening the scope of who is an onlooker. This was evident during the live broadcasts of the attacks on the World Trade Center and Pentagon on September 11, 2001. The Internet has also become a means for broadening the audience for terrorist acts, such as beheadings of hostages, bombings, and other incidents.

Onlookers to terrorist incidents observe the dynamics of the attack, public reactions to the event, and political and media analyses of the incident. They can be directly or indirectly affected by the incident, and the media play a significant role in how the onlooker receives information. Depending on who is successful in the battle for information, the result can be that the onlooker will sympathize with the terrorists' grievances, oppose them, or remain indifferent. If the government engages in repression, and terrorists or their supporters can spin this to their advantage, "one positive effect of repression is that it can supply the movement with new volunteers."[39]

---

[37]Gerrits, "Terrorists' Perspectives," p. 39.

[38]Ibid., p. 38.

[39]Ibid.

### The Analyst

The analyst is an interpreter of the terrorist incident. Analysts are important participants because they create perspectives, interpret incidents, and label the other participants. Analysts can include political leaders, media experts, and academic experts. Very often, the analyst will simply define for the other participants who is—or is not—a terrorist.

Political leaders and the media play strong roles as interpreters of the terrorist incident. The media also play a role in how other (nonmedia) analysts will have their views broadcast to a larger audience. Political leaders, experts, and scholars all rely on the media to promulgate their expert opinions. Aside from contact with these analysts, journalists are prominently—and consistently—in communication with other participants in the terrorist environment. Journalists and other media analysts investigate perspectives, interpret incidents, and have significant input on the labeling process.

Many factors shape the perspectives of terrorists, supporters, victims, targets, onlookers, and analysts. These factors include culture, collective history, individual experiences, and group identity. The same event can be interpreted in a number of ways, causing participants to adopt biased spins on that event. The following factors illustrate this problem:

- *Political associations* of participants can create a sense of identification with either the target group or the defended group. This identification can be either favorable or unfavorable, depending on the political association.

- *Emotional responses* of participants after a terrorist incident can range from horror to joy. This response can shape a participant's opinion of the incident or the extremists' cause.

- *Labeling* of participants can create either a positive or negative impression of an incident or cause. Labeling can range from creating very positive symbolism on behalf of the terrorists to the dehumanization of enemy participants (including civilians).

- *Symbolism* plays an important role in the terrorists' selection of targets. The targets can be inanimate objects that symbolize a government's power or human victims who symbolize an enemy people. Other participants sometimes make value judgments on the incident based on the symbolism of the target, thus asking whether the selected target was legitimate or illegitimate.

## Perspective 3: Terrorism or Freedom Fighting?

The third perspective for understanding terrorism is the question of whether the use of political violence is terrorism or freedom fighting. Members of politically violent organizations will rarely label themselves as terrorists. Instead, they adopt the language of liberation, national identity, religious fervor, and even democracy. Ethnonationalist and religious organizations such as **Hamas (Islamic Resistance Movement)** in the Palestinian Territories, **Liberation Tigers of Tamil Eelam (LTTE)** in Sri Lanka, and the **Provisional Irish Republican Army (Provos)** in the United Kingdom all declared that they are armies fighting on behalf of an oppressed people, and they are viewed by their supporters as **freedom fighters**. Conversely, many Israelis, Sinhalese, and British would label members of these groups as terrorists.

The declarations published by these and other organizations are in the language of liberation and freedom. For example, the Palestinian Information Center explained that

Hamas is an acronym that stands for the Islamic Resistance Movement, a popular national resistance movement which is working to create conditions conducive to emancipating the Palestinian people, delivering them from tyranny, liberating their land from the occupying usurper, and to stand up to the Zionist scheme which is supported by neo-colonist forces. . . . Hamas . . . is part of the Islamic awakening movement and upholds that this awakening is the road which will lead to the liberation of Palestine from the river to the sea. It is also a popular movement in the sense that it is a practical manifestation of a wide popular current that is deeply rooted in the ranks of the Palestinian people and the Islamic nation.[40]

Likewise, the leader of the LTTE delivered the following remarks on November 27, 2001, the LTTE's Heroes' Day:

> The Tamil people want to maintain their national identity and to live in their own lands, in their historically given homeland with peace and dignity. They want to determine their own political and economic life; they want to be on their own. These are the basic political aspirations of the Tamil people. It is neither separatism nor terrorism.[41]

Despite the seemingly noble aspirations embodied in the Hamas and LTTE statements, both conflicts were markedly violent and included many assassinations and terrorist bombings, as well as thousands of deaths. However, as ruthless as the LTTE and Hamas organizations were capable of being, their opponents—the Sri Lankan and Israeli governments, respectively—regularly applied repressive measures against them and their supporters, including physically coercive interrogations, the destruction of homes, and assassinations. This repression fueled fresh support for the rebellions, including the LTTE until it was overrun by the Sri Lankan army.

**Sinn Féin**, the aboveground Irish republican political party that champions the unification of Northern Ireland with the Republic of Ireland, remarked in a statement titled "The Conditions for Peace in Ireland,"

> The root cause of the conflict in Ireland is the denial of democracy, the refusal by the British government to allow the Irish people to exercise their right to national self-determination. The solution to the conflict in Ireland lies in the democratic exercise of that right in the form of national reunification, national independence and sovereignty.[42]

❖ **Photo 2.4**

An Irish Catholic boy holds plastic bullets fired at demonstrators during violent riots in the streets of Londonderry, Northern Ireland.

© Matthew Polak/Sygma/Corbis

Although Sinn Féin participated in the successful brokering of a peace agreement between the Provos and their opponents, it has historically championed many Provo "martyrs" and their common goal of unification.

These cases exemplify the important role of perspective in defining one's champions or opponents and how the absence of a definitional model relegates the debate of terrorism or freedom fighting to one of opposing values and opinions.

## Perspective 4: Extremism or "Mainstreamism"?

The fourth perspective for understanding terrorism is the question of whether political violence always lies at the political fringes of society or whether it is in fact a rational choice of some self-defined mainstream alignment. Members of organizations such as Hamas, the LTTE, and the Provos (prior to the peace accord) readily acknowledge that their methods are extreme but justify them as being proportional to the force used by the agents of their oppressors. In Colombia, the **Revolutionary Armed Forces of Colombia (FARC)** argued that the Colombian government's response to FARC peace initiatives

---

[40]Palestinian Information Center. Hamas website: http://www.palestine-info.com/ (accessed November 30, 2001).

[41]Velupillai Pirapaharan. Tamil Eelam website: http://www.eelam.com/ (accessed November 28, 2001).

[42]Sinn Féin. "Freedom: A Sinn Féin Education Publication." Sinn Féin website: http://sinnfein.ie/ (accessed November 30, 2001).

was to strengthen the quasi-official death squads, the most despicable form of extermination. In this way, they cold-bloodedly annihilated the opposition political parties, union leaders, defenders of human rights, priests, peasant leaders and democratic personalities, among others. . . . From the moment a new agreement was made with President Andres Pastrana to establish the talks at San Vicente del Caguan on Jan. 7, 1999, the savagery grew. No week passed without a massacre, a murder or a forced evacuation, all done in the name of the paramilitaries but planned in the military bases. It is the realization of the imperialist doctrine of internal security.[43]

Governments have also adopted authoritarian measures to counter domestic threats from perceived subversives. They likewise rationalize their behavior as a proportional response to an immediate threat. Numerous cases of this rationalization exist, such as when the Chilean and Argentine armed forces seized power during the 1970s and engaged in widespread violent repression of dissidents. In Argentina, an estimated 30,000 people disappeared during the so-called **Dirty War** waged by its military government from 1976 to 1983. The Chilean and Argentine cases are explored further in Chapter 7.

Thus, from the perspective of many violent groups and governments, extremist beliefs and terrorist methods are logical and necessary. They are considered to be rational and justifiable choices. Such beliefs and methods become mainstreamed within the context of their worldview and political environment, which in their minds offer no alternative to using violence to acquire freedom or to maintain order. Conversely, those who oppose the practitioners of political violence reject their justifications of terrorist methods and disavow the opinion that these methods are morally proportional to the perceived political environment.

## ❖  The Political Violence Matrix

To properly conceptualize modern terrorism, one must understand the qualities and scales of violence that define terrorist violence. The **Political Violence Matrix** is a tool that aids in this conceptualization.

Experts have identified and analyzed many terrorist environments. These environments include state, dissident, religious, ideological, international, and criminal terrorism. One distinguishing feature within each model is the relationship between the *quality of force* used by the terrorists and the *characteristics of the intended target* of the attack. Figure 2.1 depicts how the relationship between quality of force and target characteristics often defines the type of conflict between terrorist and victim.

### Combatants, Noncombatants, and the Use of Force

Definitional and ethical issues are not always clearly drawn when one uses terms such as *combatant target, noncombatant target, discriminate force,* or *indiscriminate force.* Nevertheless, the association of these concepts and how they are applied to one another are instructive references for determining whether a violent incident may be defined as terrorism.

#### Combatant and Noncombatant Targets

The term *combatants* certainly refers to conventional or unconventional adversaries who engage in armed conflict as members of regular military or irregular guerrilla fighting units. The term *noncombatants* obviously includes civilians who have no connection to military or other security forces. There are, however, circumstances in which these definitional lines become blurred. For example, in times of social unrest, civilians can become combatants. This has occurred repeatedly in societies in which communal violence (e.g., civil war) breaks out between members of ethnonational, ideological,

---

[43]Fuerzas Armados Revolucionarias de Colombia. Resistencia page on the FARC website: http://www.contrast.org/mirrors/farc/ (accessed October 11, 2002).

| Figure 2.1 | The Political Violence Matrix |
| --- | --- |

The purpose of the Political Violence Matrix is to create a framework for classifying and conceptualizing political violence. This classification framework is predicated on two factors: **force and intended target**.

When force (whether conventional or unconventional) is used against *combatant* targets, it occurs in a warfare environment. When force is used against *noncombatant* or *passive military* targets, it often characterizes a terrorist environment. Violent environments can be broadly summarized as follows:

- **Total War.** Force is indiscriminately applied to destroy the military targets of an enemy combatant to absolutely destroy them.
- **Total War/Unrestricted Terrorism.** Indiscriminate force is applied against noncombatant targets without restraint, either by a government or by dissidents.
- **Limited War.** Discriminating force is used against a combatant target, either to defeat the enemy or to achieve a more limited political goal.
- **State Repression/Restricted Terrorism.** Discriminating force is directed against noncombatant targets either as a matter of domestic policy or as the selective use of terrorism by dissidents.

The following figure summarizes factors to be considered when evaluating the application of different scales of force against certain types of targets.

| Indiscriminate force, combatant target | Total war (WWII Eastern Front) | Limited war (Korean War) | Discriminate force, combatant target |
| --- | --- | --- | --- |
| Indiscriminate force, noncombatant target | Total war (WWII bombing of cities) | State repression (Argentine "Dirty War") | Discriminate force, noncombatant target |
| | Unrestricted terrorism (Rwandan genocide) | Restricted terrorism (Italian Red Brigade) | |

*Source*: Adapted from Sederberg, Peter C. *Terrorist Myths: Illusion, Rhetoric, and Reality*. Englewood Cliffs, NJ: Prentice Hall, 1989, p. 34.

❖ **Photo 2.5**

A child soldier from the rebel Sudanese Liberation Army in Darfur, Sudan, which fought against government-supported Janjaweed militias.

Alvaro Ybarra Zavala/Edit/Getty Images

or religious groups. Similarly, noncombatants can include off-duty members of the military in nonwarfare environments.[44] They become targets because of their symbolic status.

### Indiscriminate and Discriminate Force

*Indiscriminate force* is the application of force against a target without attempting to limit the level of force or the degree of destruction of the target. *Discriminate force* is a more surgical use of limited force. Indiscriminate force is considered to be acceptable when used against combatants in a warfare environment. However, it is regularly condemned when used in *any* nonwarfare environment, regardless of the characteristics of the victim.[45] There are, however, many circumstances in which adversaries define "warfare environment" differently. When weaker adversaries resort to unconventional methods (including terrorism), they justify these methods by defining them as being necessary during a self-defined state of war. Discriminate force is considered to be a moral use of force when it

[44]For a discussion of the ambiguities about defining combatants and noncombatants, see Sederberg, Peter C. *Terrorist Myths: Illusion, Rhetoric, and Reality.* Englewood Cliffs, NJ: Prentice Hall, 1989, pp. 37–9.

[45] For a discussion of the ambiguities in defining indiscriminate force, see Sederberg, *Terrorist Myths,* pp. 39–40.

is applied against specific targets with the intention to limit so-called collateral damage, or unintended destruction and casualties.

## Chapter Summary

This chapter presented readers with an understanding of the nature of terrorism and probed the definitional debates about the elements of these behaviors. Several fundamental concepts were identified that continue to influence the motives and behaviors of those who support or engage in political violence. It is important to understand the elements that help define terrorism. Common characteristics of the extremist beliefs that underlie terrorist behavior include intolerance, moral absolutes, broad conclusions, and a new language that supports a particular belief system. Literally scores of definitions of terrorism have been offered by laypersons, academics, and policy professionals to describe the elements of terrorist violence. Many of these definitions are value laden and can depend on one's perspective as an actor in a terrorist environment.

The role of perspective is significant in the definitional debate. Terrorists always declare that they are fighters who represent the interests of an oppressed group. They consider themselves to be freedom fighters and justify their violence as a proportional response to the object of their oppression. Their supporters will often "mainstream" the motives of those who violently champion their cause.

In the United States, official definitions have been adopted as a matter of policy. No single definition has been applied across all government agencies, but there is some commonality among their approaches. Commonalities include premeditation, unlawfulness, groups or agents, force or violence, human or property targets, intimidation, and a political objective.

In Chapter 3, readers will investigate the causes of terrorism. The discussion will focus on the motivations of terrorists, explanations of terrorist behavior, and cases in point that illustrate causal factors in the making of a terrorist.

## Key Terms and Concepts

The following topics are discussed in this chapter and can be found in the glossary:

Castro, Fidel

Dirty War

"Extremism in defense of liberty is no vice"

freedom fighters

guerrilla

Hamas (Islamic Resistance Movement)

"It became necessary to destroy the town to save it"

"Kill one man, terrorize a thousand"

Liberation Tigers of Tamil Eelam (LTTE)

Mao Zedong

New Terrorism

"One man willing to throw away his life is enough to terrorize a thousand"

"One person's terrorist is another person's freedom fighter"

participants in a terrorist environment

Political Violence Matrix

propaganda by the deed

Provisional Irish Republican Army (Provos)

Revolutionary Armed Forces of Colombia (FARC)

Sinn Féin

Sun Tzu

terrorists

Wu Ch'i

## Discussion Box: Cold War Revolutionaries

*This chapter's Discussion Box is intended to stimulate critical debate about the role of perspective in labeling those who practice extremist behavior as "freedom fighters" or "terrorists."*

The Cold War between the United States and the Soviet Union lasted from the late 1940s until the fall of the Berlin Wall in 1989. During the roughly 40 years of rivalry, the two superpowers never entered into direct military conflict—at least conventionally. Rather, they supported insurgent and government allies in the developing world (commonly referred to as the "Third World"),[a] who often entered into armed conflict. These conflicts could be ideological or communal in nature. Conflicts were often "proxy wars," wherein the Soviets or Americans sponsored rival insurgent groups (such as in Angola), or "wars of national liberation," which were nationalistic in nature (such as in Vietnam).

The following examples illustrate how Cuba became an important "front" in the Cold War between the United States and the Soviet Union.

### The Cuban Revolution

The American influence in Cuba had been very strong since it granted the country independence in 1902 after defeating the Spanish in the Spanish-American War of 1898. The United States supported a succession of corrupt and repressive governments, the last of which was that of Fulgencio Batista. Batista's government was overthrown in 1959 by a guerrilla army led by **Fidel Castro** and Ernesto "Che" Guevara, an Argentine trained as a physician. Castro's insurgency had begun rather unremarkably, with significant defeats at the Moncada barracks in 1953 and a landing on the southeast coast of Cuba from Mexico in 1956 (when only 15 rebels survived to seek refuge in the Sierra Maestra mountains).

It was Batista's brutal reprisals against urban civilians that eventually drove many Cubans to support Castro's movement. When Batista's army was defeated and demoralized in a rural offensive against the rebels, Castro, his brother Raúl, Guevara, and Camilo Cienfuegos launched a multifront campaign that ended in victory when their units converged on the capital of Havana in January 1959. The revolution had not been a Communist revolution, and the new Cuban government was not initially a Communist government. But by early 1960, Cuba began to receive strong economic and military support from the Soviet Union. Castro and his followers soon declared the revolution to be a Communist one, and the Soviet–American Cold War opened a new and volatile front. American attempts to subvert Castro's regime included the Bay of Pigs invasion in April 1961 and several assassination attempts against Castro.[b] The Soviets and Americans came close to war during the Cuban Missile Crisis in October 1962.

### Cubans in Africa

In the postwar era, dozens of anticolonial and communal insurgencies occurred in Africa. During the 1970s, Africa became a central focus of the rivalry between Soviet- and Western-supported groups and governments. Thousands of Cuban soldiers were sent to several African countries on a mission that Fidel Castro justified as their "internationalist duty." For example, in the 1970s, Cuba sent 20,000 soldiers to Angola, 17,000 to Ethiopia, 500 to Mozambique, 250 to Guinea-Bissau, 250 to Equatorial Guinea, and 125 to Libya.[c]

### Angola

Portugal was the colonial ruler of this southern African country for more than 500 years. Beginning in 1961, guerrillas began conducting raids in northern Angola, committing brutal atrocities that few can argue were not acts of terrorism. Three guerrilla movements eventually drove the Portuguese from Angola and declared independence in November 1975. These were the Front for the Liberation of Angola (FNLA), the National Union for the Total Independence of Angola (UNITA), and the Movement for the Liberation of Angola (MPLA).

In the civil war that broke out after the Portuguese withdrawal, the United States and China supported the FNLA, the Soviets and Cubans supported the MPLA, and the United States and South Africa supported UNITA. The MPLA became the de facto government of Angola. Cuban soldiers were sent to support the MPLA government, the United States and South Africa sent aid to UNITA, and South African and British mercenaries fought with UNITA. The FNLA never achieved much success in the field. Direct foreign support was withdrawn as the Cold War and South African apartheid ended, although the conflict continued through the 1990s. The MPLA finally forced UNITA to end its insurgency when UNITA leader Jonas Savimbi was killed in February 2002.

## Nicaragua

U.S. influence and intervention in Nicaragua were common during most of the 20th century. Its governments had been supported by the United States, and its National Guard (the "Guardia") had been trained by the United States. These pro-American Nicaraguan governments had a long history of corruption and violent repression. Cuban-oriented Marxist guerrillas, the Sandinista National Liberation Front, overthrew the government of Anastasio Somoza in 1979 with Cuban and Soviet assistance.

During much of the next decade, the United States armed, trained, and supported anti-Sandinista guerrillas known as the Contras ("counterrevolutionaries"). This support included clandestine military shipments managed by the U.S. Central Intelligence Agency (CIA), the mining of Managua Harbor, and an illegal arms shipment program managed by Marine Lieutenant Colonel Oliver North.

## Discussion Questions

- Che Guevara is revered by many on the left as a "principled" revolutionary. He believed that a revolutionary "spark" was needed to create revolution throughout Latin America. Guevara was killed in Bolivia trying to prove his theory. Was Che Guevara an internationalist freedom fighter?

- The United States used sabotage to destabilize Cuba's economy and government and plotted to assassinate Fidel Castro. Did the United States engage in state-sponsored terrorism? Compare this to the Soviet Union's support of *its* allies. Is there a difference?

- The Soviet Union sponsored the Cuban troop presence in Africa during the 1970s. The wars in Angola, Ethiopia/Somalia, and Mozambique were particularly bloody. Did the Soviet Union engage in state-sponsored terrorism? Compare this to the United States' support of *its* allies. Is there a difference?

- During the Soviet–United States rivalry in Angola, Jonas Savimbi commanded the pro-Western UNITA army. He was labeled as a freedom fighter by his U.S. patrons. Savimbi never overthrew the MPLA government. Promising efforts to share power after an election in 1992 ended in the resumption of the war when Savimbi refused to acknowledge his electoral defeat, and a 1994 cease-fire collapsed. From the U.S. perspective, has Jonas Savimbi's status as a freedom fighter changed? If so, when and how?

- The Sandinistas overthrew a violent and corrupt government. The Contras were presented by the Reagan administration as an army of freedom fighters battling a totalitarian Communist government. Contra atrocities against civilians were documented. Were the Contras freedom fighters? How do their documented atrocities affect your opinion?

*(Continued)*

(Continued)

**Notes**

a. At the time, the First World was defined as the developed Western democracies; the Second World was the Soviet bloc; and the Third World was the developing world, composed of newly emerging postcolonial nations.

b. At least one plot allegedly proposed using an exploding cigar.

c. See Cross, R. W., ed. *20th Century*. London: Purnell, 1979, p. 2365; and "The OAU and the New Scramble for Africa," pp. 2372–3.

## On Your Own

The open-access Student Study Site at **http://study.sagepub.com/martin5e** has a variety of useful study aids, including eFlashcards, quizzes, audio resources, and journal articles. The websites, exercises, and recommended readings listed below are easily accessed on this site as well.

## Recommended Websites

The following websites illustrate the nature of extremism:

British National Party: http://www.bnp.org.uk/

Council of Conservative Citizens: http://www.cofcc.org/

Earth First! Radical Environmental Journal: http://www.earthfirstjournal.org/

Front National (France): http://www.frontnational.com/

Socialist Party USA: http://www.sp-usa.org/

## Web Exercise

Using this chapter's recommended websites, conduct an online investigation of the fundamental characteristics of extremism.

1. What commonalities can you find in the statements of these groups?

2. Is there anything that strikes you as being particularly extremist?

3. Why or why not?

For an online search of different approaches to defining extremism and terrorism, readers should activate the search engine on their Web browser and enter the following keywords:

"Definitions of Terrorism"

"Extremism"

## Recommended Readings

The following publications provide discussions for defining terrorism and terrorism's underlying extremist motivations:

Carr, Matthew. *The Infernal Machine: A History of Terrorism*. New York: New Press, 2007.

Gerstenfeld, Phyllis B. *Hate Crimes: Causes, Controls, and Controversies*. Thousand Oaks, CA: Sage, 2013.

Hamm, Mark S., ed. *Hate Crime: International Perspectives on Causes and Control*. Cincinnati, OH: Anderson, 1994.

Howard, Lawrence, ed. *Terrorism: Roots, Impact, Responses*. New York: Praeger, 1992.

Kassimeris, George, ed. *Playing Politics With Terrorism: A User's Guide*. New York: Columbia University Press, 2007.

Laqueur, Walter. *The New Terrorism: Fanaticism and the Arms of Mass Destruction*. New York: Oxford University Press, 1999.

Lawrence, Frederick M. *Punishing Hate: Bias Crimes Under American Law*. Cambridge, MA: Harvard University Press, 2002.

Sederberg, Peter C. *Terrorist Myths: Illusion, Rhetoric, and Reality*. Englewood Cliffs, NJ: Prentice Hall, 1989.

# Beginnings

## The Causes of Terrorism

CHAPTER 3

## OPENING VIEWPOINT: THE CASE OF CARLOS

The case of Ilich Ramírez Sánchez, popularly known as **Carlos the Jackal,** is a unique and interesting study of the career of an ideologically motivated revolutionary. Although his example is idiosyncratic, it represents an excellent study of motivations adopted by international ideological revolutionaries.

Sánchez was a Venezuelan-born terrorist who became notorious during the 1970s for his violence on behalf of the Palestinian cause. He became politically conscious at a very young age, his Marxist father having named him after Vladimir Ilich Lenin (Ilich's brothers were named Vladimir and Lenin). His father indoctrinated Sánchez in Marxist ideology and literature, as well as stories of Latin American rebellion, when he was a boy. Sánchez came from a family of revolutionaries, with an uncle who participated in a coup in 1945 and a grandfather who led an army that overthrew the government in 1899. When he was 14, he joined the Venezuelan Communist Youth. He supposedly received guerrilla training in Cuba. Sánchez then attended Patrice Lumumba University in Moscow, but he rejected the Soviets' doctrinaire brand of communism.

It was in Moscow that Sánchez learned about the Popular Front for the Liberation of Palestine (PFLP). He traveled to Beirut, Lebanon, in July 1970 and walked into an office of the PFLP. He was immediately accepted into the fold and began training with the PFLP, apparently in Jordan. Sánchez was given the *nom de guerre* of "Carlos" by Bassam Abu-Sharif, a top official in the PFLP. Later, a reporter for the British newspaper *The Guardian* appended the new *nom de guerre* of "The Jackal," named for the assassin in Frederick Forsyth's novel *The Day of the Jackal*.

Carlos the Jackal was a terrorist-for-hire, apparently retained by Libya, Iraq, Syria, Cuba, the PFLP, Italy's Red Brigades, and Germany's Red Army Faction. He has been suspected of committing dozens of attacks, including assassinations, bombings, skyjackings, kidnappings, and the taking of hostages. Carlos's most stunning operation was the 1975 kidnapping in Vienna of approximately 70 people attending a meeting by the ministers of the powerful Organization of Petroleum Exporting Countries (OPEC). He also carried out a series of bombings in 1982 and 1983, killing 12 people and injuring about 100, in a vain attempt to win the release of a comrade and his girlfriend, Magdalena Kopp.

The Jackal's career was terminated when the government of Sudan "sold" him to France in August 1994. French DST intelligence agents, acting on a tip from the U.S. Central Intelligence Agency (CIA) and in cooperation with Sudanese security officials, seized Carlos from a Khartoum villa where he was recovering from minor testicular surgery. He was sedated in the villa and regained his senses on board a French jet. In 1997, he was prosecuted, convicted, and sentenced to life imprisonment for the 1975 murders of two French counterterrorist operatives and an alleged informer. He received a second life sentence in December 2011 for a 1982–1983 bombing campaign in France that killed 11 people and maimed dozens more. By his own count, Ilich Ramírez Sánchez had personally killed 83 people.

### Notes

a. For an interesting written account of Carlos's career, see Follain, John. *Jackal: The Complete Story of the Legendary Terrorist, Carlos the Jackal.* New York: Arcade, 1998.

b. For an interesting film biography of Carlos's career, see *Carlos.* Dir. Olivier Assayas. Perf. Édgar Ramírez, Alexander Scheer, Alejandro Arroyo. Films en Stock, Egoli Tossel Film, 2010.

This chapter investigates the causes of terrorism. In the following discussion, readers will identify factors that explain why individuals and groups choose to engage in terrorist violence. Readers will also explore and critically assess the sources of ideological belief systems and activism and the reasons such activism sometimes results in terrorist violence. This search for causes requires a critical examination of many possible reasons. For example, is the terrorist option somehow forced on people who have no other alternative? Is terrorism simply one choice from a menu of options? Or is politically motivated violence a pathological manifestation of personal or group dysfunction?

Experts have long struggled to identify the central causes of terrorist violence. The most fundamental conclusion in this regard is that terrorism originates from *many* sources. The final decision by an individual or group to accept a fringe belief or to engage in terrorist behavior is often a complex process. For example, the decision to engage in violence may be the result of the following:

❖ **Photo 3.1**

Ilich Ramírez Sánchez, also known as Carlos the Jackal. He was personally responsible for the deaths of scores of victims.

- Logical choice and political strategy
- Collective rationality
- Lack of opportunity for political participation
- Disaffection within an elite[1]

Keystone/Hulton Archive/Getty Images

It is useful in the beginning of our discussion to identify broad causes of terrorism at the individual and group levels.

At the *individual level,* some experts have distinguished rational, psychological, and cultural origins of terrorism:

Rational terrorists think through their goals and options, making a cost-benefit analysis. . . . Psychological motivation for resorting to terrorism derives from the terrorist's personal dissatisfaction with his/her life and accomplishments. . . . A major cultural determinant of terrorism is the perception of "outsiders" and anticipation of their threat to ethnic group survival.[2]

These factors are only a few of many theoretical sources, but they illustrate the different types of motivations that shape the individual behavior of terrorists.

At the *group level,* terrorism can grow out of an environment of political activism, when a group's goal is to redirect a government's or society's attention toward the grievances of an activist social movement. It can also grow out of dramatic events in the experience of a people or a nation. Although these two sources—social movements and dramatic events—are generalized concepts, it is instructive to briefly review their importance:

- **Social Movements.** Social movements are campaigns that try either to promote change or to preserve something that is perceived to be threatened. Movements involve mass action on behalf of a cause; they are not simply the actions of single individuals who promote their personal political beliefs. Examples of movements include the Irish Catholic civil rights movement of the 1960s in Northern Ireland and the African American civil rights movement in the American South during the same decade. Proponents of this type of movement seek the "moral high ground" as a way to rally sympathy and support for their cause and to bring pressure on

[1]Whittaker, David J., ed. *The Terrorism Reader.* 4th ed. New York: Routledge, 2012, p. 14. Explaining the model developed by Crenshaw, Martha. "The Causes of Terrorism." *Comparative Politics* (July 1981): 381–5.

[2]See Simonsen, Clifford E., and Jeremy R. Spindlove. *Terrorism Today: The Past, the Players, the Future.* 5th ed. Upper Saddle River, NJ: Pearson, 2013, pp. 15–16.

their opponents. In both of these cases, radicalized sentiment grew out of frustration with the slow pace of change and the violent reaction of some of their opponents. The modern era has witnessed many movements that advocate violent resistance.

- **Dramatic Events.** A synonym for this source of terrorism is *traumatic* events. They occur when an individual, a nation, or an ethnonational group suffers from an event that has a traumatizing and lasting effect. At the personal level, children of victims of political violence may grow up to violently oppose their perceived oppressor. This is likely to occur in regions of extended conflict, such as the war between Tamils and Sinhalese in Sri Lanka, "the Troubles" in Northern Ireland, or the Palestinian *intifada*.[3]

At the *national level,* nations may be victims of traumatic events, such as invasions or terrorist attacks that shape their behavior and culture for an extended period of time. For example, the 1979–1989 Soviet invasion and occupation of Afghanistan destabilized the country dramatically, leading to a breakdown in central authority, civil war, and then the rule of the Taliban regime and its alliance with al-Qa'ida. At the ethnonational level, and in the histories of ethnonational groups, massacres, forced migrations, or extended repression can affect them for generations. For example, the Kurds of Iraq, Turkey, Syria, and Iran have suffered from all of these traumas, including being gassed by the Iraqis in the aftermath of the 1991 Gulf War.

Regardless of the specific precipitating cause of a particular terrorist's behavior, the fact that so many individuals, groups, and nations resort to terrorist violence so frequently suggests that common motives and reasons can be found. There are many explanations given for terrorism by scholars and other experts who have devoted a great deal of effort to explaining terrorist behavior. This has not been a simple task because explanatory models consider many factors to account for why a particular group or people chooses to employ terrorism. This calculus includes political history, government policy, contemporary politics, cultural tensions, ideological trends, economic cycles, individual idiosyncrasies, and other variables. Although many terrorist environments exhibit similar characteristics—and groups have historically carried out attacks "in solidarity" with one another—explanations for terrorist activity are not readily transferable across national boundaries.

Finding a single explanation for terrorism is impossible. Nevertheless, experts have identified common characteristics among politically violent groups and individuals. The following discussion summarizes three explanatory categories:

- Political Violence as the Fruit of Injustice
- Political Violence as Strategic Choice
- Moral Justifications for Political Violence

## ❖ Political Violence as the Fruit of Injustice

### Sociological Explanations of Terrorism: Intergroup Conflict and Collective Violence

Sociological explanations generally hold that terrorism is a product of intergroup conflict that results in collective violence. The sociological approach argues that terrorism is a group-based phenomenon that is selected as the only strategy available to a weaker group. From the perspective of an opponent group, "terrorism and other forms of collective violence are often described as 'senseless,' and their participants are often depicted as irrational."[4] However, this is not an entirely complete analysis, because

---

[3]*Intifada* literally means "shaking off."

[4]Barkan, Steven E., and Lynne L. Snowden. *Collective Violence.* Boston: Allyn & Bacon, 2001, p. 6.

if "rational" means goal directed . . . then most collective violence is indeed rational. . . . Their violence is indeed directed at achieving certain, social change–oriented goals, regardless of whether we agree with those goals or with the violent means used to attain them. If "rational" further means sound, wise, and logical, then available evidence indicates that collective violence is rational . . . because it sometimes can help achieve their social goals.[5]

In essence, the disadvantaged group asserts its rights by selecting a methodology—in this case, terrorism—that from the group's perspective is its only viable option. The selection process is based on the insurgent group's perceptions and its analysis of those perceptions. To illustrate this point, the following example describes a hypothetical group's analytical progression toward revolution:

- The perception grows within a particular group that the government or social order is inherently brutal or unfair toward the group.
- Because the system does not allow for meaningful social dissent by the group (in the opinion of group members), it concludes that the only recourse is to oust the existing government or order.
- The group perceives that an opportunity for change is available at a particular point in history. To wait longer would likely mean a lost possibility for revolutionary change.
- After analyzing the contemporary political environment, the group perceives that the government or system possesses inherent weaknesses or "contradictions" (to use a Marxist term).[6] All that is needed is a revolutionary "push" to achieve the group's goals.
- An important ingredient in the group's calculation is the perception that the people are ripe for revolution. What is required is for the group to act as a vanguard to politicize the broader masses and lead them to revolution.

The foregoing analytical progression incorporates two theoretical concepts: structural theory and relative deprivation theory.[7] These theories are summarized below.

### Theoretical Foundations for Sociological Explanations

**Structural theory** has been used in many policy and academic disciplines to identify social conditions (structures) that affect group access to services, equal rights, civil protections, freedom, or other quality-of-life measures. Examples of social structures include government policies, administrative bureaucracies, spatial (geographic) location of the group, the role of security forces, and access to social institutions. Applying this theory to the context of terrorism,

structural theories of revolution emphasize that weaknesses in state structures encourage the potential for revolution. . . . According to this view, a government beset by problems such as economic and military crises is vulnerable to challenges by insurgent forces. . . . Other governments run into trouble when their . . . policies alienate and even anger elites within the society.[8]

---

[5]Ibid., p. 7.

[6]Maoists and Trotskyites in particular cite "contradictions" in the capitalist democracies—for example, the existence of democratic institutions and ideologies of equality existing alongside entrenched poverty, racism, sexism, and so on.

[7]Relative deprivation theory was pioneered by James C. Davies. See Davies, James Chowning. "Toward a Theory of Revolution." *American Sociological Review* 25 (1962): 5–19.

[8]Barkan and Snowden, *Collective Violence*, p. 53. Citing Goldstone, Jack A. "Introduction: The Comparative and Historical Study of Revolutions." In *Revolutions: Theoretical, Comparative, and Historical Studies*, edited by Jack A. Goldstone. San Diego: Harcourt Brace Jovanovich, 1986, pp. 1–17.

The state is the key actor in structural theories of revolution. Its status is the precipitating factor for popular revolutions. Popular discontent, the alienation of elites, and a pervasive crisis are the central ingredients for bringing a society to the brink of revolution.[9]

**Relative deprivation theory** essentially holds that "feelings of deprivation and frustration underlie individual decisions to engage in collective action."[10] According to this theory, when a group's rising expectations are met by sustained repression or second-class status, the group's reaction may include political violence. Their motive for engaging in political violence is their observation that they are *relatively* deprived, vis-à-vis other groups, in an unfair social order. This should be contrasted with **absolute deprivation**, when a group has been deprived of the basic necessities for survival by a government or social order. This condition can also lead to political violence.

One observation must be made about relative deprivation theory: Although it was, and still is, a popular theory among many experts, three shortcomings have been argued:

- Psychological research suggests that aggression happens infrequently when the conditions for relative deprivation are met.
- The theory is more likely to explain individual behavior rather than group behavior.
- Empirical studies have not found an association between relative deprivation and political violence.[11]

Nevertheless, many sociologists and political scientists continue to reference relative deprivation as an explanatory theory when investigating the characteristics and motivations of social movements.

### Cases in Point: Sociological Explanations in an International Context

Examples of movements that are motivated against a government or social order include ethnonationalist movements among Basques in Spain, Irish Catholics in Northern Ireland, Palestinians in Israel, and French Canadians in Quebec. Sociological explanations for these movements are summarized below.

***Basque Nationalism in Spain.*** The Basque region of northern Spain is home to approximately 2.5 million Basques. Nationalism in the region dates to the defeat of Spanish Republicans during the Spanish Civil War of 1936 to 1939. After the war, Francisco Franco's fascist regime suppressed Basque culture, integrated the region into Spain, and banned the Basque language. Spanish culture and language were imposed on the Basque region. Since the late 1950s, Basque nationalists, especially **Basque Fatherland and Liberty (Euskadi Ta Azkatasuna, or ETA)**, have fought for autonomy from Spain and the preservation of their national identity. The Basque cause will be explored further within the context of dissident terrorism.

***Irish Catholic Nationalism in Northern Ireland.*** Irish Catholic nationalism in Northern Ireland dates to the 16th century, when English King James I granted Scottish Protestant settlers land in Ireland, thus beginning a long process of relegating Irish Catholics to second-class status in their own country. Protestant ("Scotch-Irish") and English domination was secured in 1690 at the Battle of the Boyne. Catholic independence was finally won in 1919 and 1920, but the island was formally divided between the independent Irish Republic in the south and the British-administered six-county region of Northern Ireland. Since that time, some Irish Republicans in the north, especially the Provisional Irish Republican Army, have engaged in armed resistance against Protestant and British political domination. They seek union with the southern republic. The Irish Republican cause will be explored further within the contexts of dissident and ideological terrorism.

---

[9]See ibid., p. 33.

[10]Ibid., p. 17.

[11]Discussed in ibid., p. 18.

***Palestinian Nationalism.*** Palestinian nationalism dates to the formal creation of the state of Israel on May 14, 1948. The next day, the Arab League (Lebanon, Egypt, Jordan, and Syria) declared war on Israel. Israel was victorious, and in the subsequent consolidation of power, hundreds of thousands of Palestinians either left Israel or were expelled. Since that time, Palestinian nationalists, especially the Palestine Liberation Organization and Hamas, have fought a guerrilla and terrorist war against Israel to establish a Palestinian state. The Palestinian cause will be explored further within the context of dissident terrorism.

***French Canadian Nationalism.*** French Canadian nationalism is centered in Quebec, where French-descended residents (known as the Québécois) predominate. The French identity in Quebec has always been vigorously protected by Québécois against English domination. Some Québécois are nationalists, seeking greater autonomy or independence from English-speaking Canada. Most French Canadian nationalism has been democratic in expression and has been led by the Parti Québécois. However, a separatist group founded in 1963, known as the Front du Liberation de Québec (FLQ), engaged in a bombing campaign to promote an independent Quebec. Nationalist sentiment increased during the late 1960s when, during a visit by French President Charles de Gaulle in July 1967, he delivered a speech using the now famous phrase "*Vive le Québec libre,*" or "Long live free Quebec."

Table 3.1 summarizes the constituencies and enemies of groups promoting the foregoing causes.

## Psychological Explanations of Terrorism: Rationality and Terrorist Violence

Psychological approaches to explaining terrorism broadly examine the effects of internal psychological dynamics on individual and group behavior. At the outset, it is useful to examine the presumption held by a number of people—experts, policy makers, and

Frederick Hoare/Hulton Archive/Getty Images

❖ **Photo 3.2**

Bloody Sunday (January 30, 1972): A British soldier runs down an Irish Catholic demonstrator during protests and rioting in the city of Londonderry in Northern Ireland. The confrontations resulted in elite paratroopers firing on Catholic civilians. The incident was a seminal event that rallied many Catholics to support the Provisional Irish Republican Army.

| Table 3.1 | Nationalism and Sociological Explanations of Terrorism: Constituencies and Adversaries |
|---|---|

Nationalism is an expression of ethnonational identity. Nationalist activism can range in scale from the promotion of cultural heritage to armed insurrection. Its goals can range from a desire for equal political rights to complete national separation.

Some ethnonational groups have engaged in nationalist activism to preserve their cultural heritage and have opposed what they consider to be national and cultural repression. Within these ethnonational groups, violent extremists have engaged in terrorism.

The following table summarizes the constituencies and adversaries of several nationalist movements that have used terrorism to obtain autonomy from social orders they perceive to have repressed their national and cultural aspirations.

| Group | Activity Profile | |
|---|---|---|
| | Constituency | Adversary |
| Irish Republican Army factions | Northern Irish Catholics | British and Ulster Protestants |
| ETA factions | Spanish Basques | Spaniards |
| Secular and religious Palestinian groups | Palestinians | Israelis |
| FLQ | French-speaking residents of Quebec (Québécois) | English-speaking Canadians |

laypersons—that terrorism is a manifestation of *insanity* or *mental illness,* or that terrorism is the signature of a *lunatic fringe.* This presumption suggests that terrorism is *a priori* (fundamentally) irrational behavior, and that only deranged individuals or deranged collections of people would select terrorist violence as a strategy. Most experts agree that this blanket presumption is incorrect. Although individuals and groups do act out of certain idiosyncratic psychological processes, their behavior is neither insane nor necessarily irrational.

Those who engage in collective violence are, in many respects, "normal" people:

> How rational are the participants in collective violence? Are they sane? Do they really know what they're doing? . . . The available evidence favors rationality. . . . Although some explanations of collective violence stress psychological abnormality among its participants, studies on this issue suggest that in general they're as psychologically normal and rational as the average person.[12]

### Individual-Level Psychological Explanations

Some experts argue that the decision to engage in political violence is frequently an outcome of significant events in individual lives that give rise to antisocial feelings. They actively seek improvement in their environment or desire redress and revenge from the perceived cause of their condition. Very often,

> psychological motivation for terrorism derives from the terrorist's personal dissatisfaction with his life and accomplishments. He finds his raison d'être in dedicated terrorist action. . . . Terrorists tend to project their own antisocial motivations onto others, creating a polarized "we versus they" outlook. They attribute only evil motives to anyone outside their own group. This enables the terrorists to dehumanize their victims and removes any sense of ambiguity from their minds. The resultant clarity of purpose appeals to those who crave violence to relieve their constant anger.[13]

Research has *not* found a pattern of psychopathology among terrorists. In comparing nonviolent and violent activists, studies reported "preliminary impressions . . . that the family backgrounds of terrorists do not differ strikingly from the backgrounds of their politically active counterparts."[14] There is evidence of some psychosocial commonalities among violent activists. For example, research on 250 West German terrorists reported "a high incidence of fragmented families"; "severe conflict, especially with the parents"; conviction in juvenile court; and "a pattern of failure both educationally and vocationally."[15]

### Group-Level Psychological Explanations

In a number of social and political contexts, political violence is a familiar social phenomenon for some people. When this process is combined with "the pronounced need to belong to a group,"[16] individuals can in the end "define their social status by group acceptance." Thus, at the group level,

---

[12]Ibid., p. 8.

[13]Crenshaw, Martha. "The Causes of Terrorism." *Comparative Politics* (July 1981): 381–5.

[14]Post, Jerrold M. "Terrorist Psycho-logic: Terrorist Behavior as a Product of Psychological Forces." In *Origins of Terrorism: Psychologies, Ideologies, Theologies, States of Mind,* edited by Walter Reich. Washington, DC: Woodrow Wilson Center, 1998, p. 9.

[15]Ibid., p. 28. Reporting findings of the Ministry of the Interior, Federal Republic of Germany. *Analysen Zum Terrorismus* 1–4. Darmstadt: Deutscher Verlag, 1981, 1982, 1983, 1984; Jäger, H., G. Schmidtchen, and L. Süllwold, eds., *Analysen Zum Terrorismus 2: Lebenlaufanalysen.* Darmstadt: Deutscher Verlag, 1981; and von Baeyer-Kaette, W., D. Classens, H. Feger, and F. Neidhardt, eds. *Analysen Zum Terrorismus 3: Gruppeprozesse.* Darmstadt: Deutscher Verlag, 1982.

[16]Post, "Terrorist Psycho-logic," p. 28.

another result of psychological motivation is the intensity of group dynamics among terrorists. They tend to demand unanimity and be intolerant of dissent . . . [and] pressure to escalate the frequency and intensity of operations is ever present. . . . Compromise is rejected, and terrorist groups lean towards maximalist positions.[17]

An important outcome of these dynamics is the development of a self-perpetuating cycle of ratio-nalizations of political violence. This occurs because

the psychodynamics also make the announced group goal nearly impossible to achieve. A group that achieves its stated purpose is no longer needed; thus, success threatens the psycho-logical well-being of its members.[18]

### Generalized Psychological Explanations

Psychological explanations are fairly broad approaches to the dynamics of terrorist behavior. Both individual and group theories attempt to generalize reasons for the decision to initiate political violence and the processes that perpetuate such violence. These explanations may be summarized as follows:

- Terrorism is simply a choice among violent and less violent alternatives. It is a rational selection of one methodology over other options.
- Terrorism is a technique to maintain group cohesion and focus. Group solidarity overcomes individualism.
- Terrorism is a necessary process to build the esteem of an oppressed people. Through terror-ism, power is established over others, and the weak become strong. Attention itself becomes self-gratifying.[19]
- Terrorists consider themselves to be an elite vanguard. They are not content to debate the issues because they have found a "truth" that needs no explanation. Action is superior to debate.
- Terrorism provides a means to justify political violence. The targets are depersonalized, and symbolic labels are attached to them. Thus, symbolic buildings become legitimate targets even when occupied by people, and individual victims become symbols of an oppressive system.

**Case: Psychology and the Stockholm Syndrome.** In August 1973, three women and one man were taken hostage by two bank robbers in Stockholm, Sweden. The botched robbery led to a hos-tage crisis that lasted for 6 days. During the crisis, the robbers threatened to kill the four hostages if the authorities tried to rescue them. At the same time, the hostages received treatment from the robbers that they began to think of as kindness and consideration. For example, one hostage was told that he would not be killed, but rather shot in the leg if the police intervened, and that he should play dead. Another hostage, who suffered from claustrophobia, was let out of the bank vault on a rope leash. These were perceived as acts of kindness because the situation was very tense inside the bank:

The hostages were under extended siege by a horde of police seeking opportunities to shoot the robbers, depriving the group of food and other necessities to force their surrender, and poking holes in walls to gas the robbers into submission. The captors often acted as the hos-tages' protectors against the frightening maneuvers by the police.[20]

---

[17]Ibid., p. 20.

[18]Ibid.

[19]For an interesting discussion of the effect of youthfulness on one's decision to engage in political violence, see Benard, Cheryl. "Toy Soldiers: The Youth Factor in the War on Terror." *Current History* (January 2007): 27–30.

[20]Bandura, Albert. "Mechanisms of Moral Disengagement." In *Origins of Terrorism: Psychologies, Ideologies, Theologies, States of Mind,* edited by Walter Reich. Washington, DC: Woodrow Wilson Center, 1998, p. 183.

During the 6-day episode, all of the hostages began to sympathize with the robbers and gradually came to completely identify with them. They eventually denounced the authorities' attempts to free them. After the situation was resolved, the hostages remained loyal to their former captors for months. They refused to testify against them and raised money for their legal defense. One of the female former hostages actually became engaged to one of the robbers. This was, to say the least, surprising behavior. The question is whether this was an isolated phenomenon or whether it is possible for it to occur in other hostage crises.

Experts are divided about whether the **Stockholm syndrome** is a prevalent condition. Those who contend that it can occur and has occurred in other situations argue that the syndrome sets in when a prisoner suffers a psychological shift from captive to sympathizer. In theory, the prisoner will try to keep his or her captor happy in order to stay alive whenever he or she is unable to escape, is isolated, and is threatened with death. This becomes an obsessive identification with what the captor likes and dislikes, and the prisoner eventually begins to sympathize with the captor. The psychological shift theoretically requires 3 or 4 days to set in. An example of the Stockholm syndrome during the kidnapping of newspaper heiress Patricia Hearst is presented in Chapter 12; Hearst was kidnapped by the terrorist group the Symbionese Liberation Army and joined the group after being psychologically and physically tormented for more than 50 days.

### *Summing Up Psychological Explanations*

In essence, then, psychological explanations of terrorist behavior use theories of individual motivations and group dynamics to explicate why people first decide to adopt strategies of political violence and why groups continue their campaigns of violence. Among violent extremists,

it appears that people who are aggressive and action-oriented, and who place greater-than-normal reliance on the psychological mechanisms of externalization and splitting, are disproportionately represented among terrorists.[21]

Pressures to conform to the group, combined with pressures to commit acts of violence, form a powerful psychological drive to carry on in the name of the cause, even when victory is logically impossible. These influences become so prevalent that achieving victory becomes a consideration secondary to the unity of the group.[22] Having said this, it is inadvisable to completely generalize about psychological causes of terrorism because "most terrorists do not demonstrate serious psychopathology," and "there is no single personality type."[23]

Chapter Perspective 3.1 investigates the profiles of two Palestinian nationalists, Leila Khaled and Abu Nidal.

❖ **Photo 3.3**

Palestinian terrorist or freedom fighter? Leila Khaled in a photograph dating from the 1970s.

AFP/Getty Images

## Criminological Explanations of Terrorism: The Path to Political Criminality

Criminological explanations generally hold that terrorism is a product of the same socialization processes that cause individuals to engage in criminal behavior. Such processes explain why individuals become terrorists or criminals and why groups of people establish terrorist or criminal organizations. The criminological approach

---

[21]Post, "Terrorist Psycho-logic," p. 9.

[22]Ibid., pp. 25–42.

[23]Ibid., p. 31.

## CHAPTER PERSPECTIVE 3.1: Profiles of Violent Extremists: Leila Khaled and Abu Nidal

The processes that cause people to become political extremists and terrorists are very idiosyncratic. Individuals adopt extremist beliefs and engage in terrorist behaviors for many of the reasons discussed in this chapter.

A comparison of two revolutionaries championing the Palestinian cause is very useful for critically assessing why nationalists engage in terrorist violence. These are cases that illustrate the origins of the motives and ideologies of politically violent individuals.

### Leila Khaled: Freedom Fighter or Terrorist?

During the early 1970s, **Leila Khaled** was famous both because of her exploits as a Palestinian revolutionary and because she was for a time the best-known airline hijacker in the world.

Khaled was born in Haifa in Palestine. After the Israeli war of independence, she and her family became refugees in a camp in the city of Tyre, Lebanon, when she was a young child. Khaled has said that she was politicized from a very young age and became a committed revolutionary by the time she was 15. Politically, she was influenced by leftist theory. One of her revolutionary heroes was Ernesto "Che" Guevara, whom she considered to be a "true" revolutionary, unlike other Western radicals.

In August 1969, at the age of 23, Leila Khaled hijacked a TWA flight on behalf of the Popular Front for the Liberation of Palestine (PFLP). The purpose of the hijacking was to direct the world's attention to the plight of the Palestinians. It was a successful operation, and she reportedly forced the pilots to fly over her ancestral home of Haifa before turning toward Damascus. In Damascus, the passengers were released into the custody of the Syrians and the plane was blown up. Afterward, a then-famous photograph was taken of her.

In preparation for her next operation (and because the photograph had become a political icon), Khaled underwent plastic surgery in Germany to alter her appearance. She participated in a much larger operation on September 6 and 9, 1970, when the PFLP attempted to hijack five airliners. One of the hijackings failed, one airliner was flown to a runway in Cairo where it was destroyed, and the remaining three airliners were flown to Dawson's Field in Jordan, where they were blown up by the PFLP on September 12. Khaled had been overpowered and captured during one of the failed attempts on September 6—an El Al (the Israeli airline) flight from Amsterdam. She was released on September 28 as part of a brokered deal exchanging Palestinian prisoners for the hostages.

Leila Khaled published her autobiography in 1973, entitled *My People Shall Live: The Autobiography of a Revolutionary*.[a] She eventually settled in Amman, Jordan, and became a member of the Palestinian National Council, the Palestinian parliament. She has never moderated her political beliefs, has always considered herself to be a freedom fighter, and takes pride in being one of the first to use extreme tactics to bring the Palestinians' cause to the world's attention. Khaled considers the progression of Palestinian revolutionary violence—such as the *intifadeh* ("shaking off") uprisings—to be a legitimate means to regain Palestine.

### Abu Nidal: Ruthless Revolutionary

Sabri al-Banna, a Palestinian, adopted the *nom de guerre* of **"Abu Nidal,"** which has become synonymous with his **Abu Nidal Organization** (ANO). He was a radical member of the umbrella Palestine Liberation Organization (PLO) from an early point in its history. Yasir Arafat's nationalist **Al Fatah** organization was the dominant group within the PLO. Unlike the Fatah mainstream, Abu Nidal was a strong advocate of a dissident ideology that was **pan-Arabist,** meaning he believed that national borders in the Arab world were not sacrosanct. Abu Nidal long argued that Al Fatah membership should be open to all Arabs, not just Palestinians. In support of the Palestinian cause, he argued that

*(Continued)*

(Continued)

Palestine must be established as an Arab state. Its borders must stretch from the Jordan River in the east to the Mediterranean Sea. According to pan-Arabism, however, this is only one cause among many in the Arab world.

After the 1973 Yom Kippur war, when invading Arab armies were soundly defeated by Israel, many in the mainstream Al Fatah group argued that a political solution with Israel should be an option. In 1974, Abu Nidal split from Al Fatah and began his "rejectionist" movement to carry on a pan-Arabist armed struggle. He and his followers immediately began engaging in high-profile international terrorist attacks, believing that the war should not be limited to the Middle East. At different periods in his struggle, he successfully solicited sanctuary from Iraq, Libya, and Syria—all of which have practiced pan-Arabist ideologies.

The ANO became one of the most prolific and bloody terrorist organizations in modern history. It carried out attacks in approximately 20 countries and was responsible for killing or injuring about 900 people. The ANO's targets included fellow Arabs, such as the PLO, Arab governments, and moderate Palestinians. Its non-Arab targets included the interests of France, Israel, the United Kingdom, and the United States. Many of these attacks were spectacular, such as an attempted assassination of the Israeli ambassador to Great Britain in June 1982, simultaneous attacks on the Vienna and Rome airports in December 1985, the hijacking of a Pan Am airliner in September 1986, and several assassinations of top PLO officials in several countries. It has been alleged that Abu Nidal collaborated in the 1972 massacre of 11 Israeli athletes by the Black September group at the Munich Olympics.

Abu Nidal remained a dedicated pan-Arabist revolutionary and never renounced his worldwide acts of political violence. His group has several hundred members, a militia in Lebanon, and international resources. The ANO operated under numerous names, including the Al Fatah Revolutionary Council, Arab Revolutionary Council, Arab Revolutionary Brigades, Black September, Black June, and Revolutionary Organization of Socialist Muslims. The group seemingly ended its attacks against Western interests in the late 1980s. The only major attacks attributed to the ANO in the 1990s were the 1991 assassinations of PLO deputy chief Abu Iyad and PLO security chief Abu Hul in Tunis, and the 1994 assassination of the senior Jordanian diplomat Naeb Maaytah in Beirut.

The whereabouts of Abu Nidal were usually speculative, but he relocated to Iraq in December 1998. In August 2002, he was found dead in Iraq of multiple gunshot wounds. The official Iraqi account of Abu Nidal's death was that he committed suicide. Other unofficial accounts suggested that he was shot when Iraqi security agents came to arrest him, dying either of self-inflicted wounds or during a shootout.

### Note

a. Khaled, Leila. *My People Shall Live: The Autobiography of a Revolutionary.* London: Hodder & Stoughton, 1973.

argues that terrorism and crime are explainable within the framework of established theoretical perspectives used to explain criminal deviance.[24]

### Differential Association Theory

Edwin Sutherland described the theory of differential association in his 1939 book, *Principles of Criminology.*[25] Differential association is a process of social learning in which criminals and law-abiding people learn their behavior from associations with others. People imitate or otherwise internalize the

---

[24]Grabosky and Stohl cogently summarize the criminological perspective within the context of four theoretical perspectives. See Grabosky, Peter, and Michael Stohl. *Crime and Terrorism.* Thousand Oaks, CA: Sage, 2010.

[25]Sutherland, Edwin H. *Principles of Criminology.* 3rd ed. Philadelphia: J. B. Lippincott, 1939.

quality of these associations. Criminality—and, by implication, political extremism—are learned behaviors that are acquired from interacting with others who participate in criminal politically activist lifestyles, so that the difference between offenders and nonoffenders lies in individual choices. In other words, offenders and nonoffenders strive for similar goals, but they choose different avenues to achieve those goals. These choices are based on the lessons they take from exposure to certain kinds of life experiences. In particular, those who grow up in criminal or politically polarized milieus will adopt values that can result in crime or political extremism.

Although differential association theory has been criticized for relying on variables that are difficult to operationalize, it remains a potent and influential approach to explaining crime. Its appeal is perhaps grounded in its proposition that all persons possess the same learning processes, which are developed through communicating and interacting with groups of people. The difference between criminals and noncriminals is that they base their choices on different lessons learned from their different experiences. Norms and values are similarly learned, but some people internalize deviant norms and values.

### Anomie and Strain Theories

The great sociologist Emile Durkheim's concept of anomie[26] was applied to criminology during the 1930s by Robert Merton and others, who studied the tension between socially acceptable goals and the means one is permitted by society to use for achieving those goals.[27] Merton's theory focused on the *availability* of goals and means. He posited that the greater society encourages its members to use acceptable means to achieve acceptable goals. For example, in the United States, "acceptable means" include hard work, prudent savings, and higher education. Acceptable goals include comfort, leisure time, social status, and wealth. However, not all members of society have an equal availability of resources to achieve society's recognized goals, thus creating *strain* for these less empowered members. Strain is manifested as a desire to achieve these goals and one's inability to acquire the legitimate means to attain them. In theory, those who do not have access to acceptable means may resort to illegitimate and illicit avenues to achieve their goals. In other words, those without resources and access may become criminals to achieve comfort, leisure, status, and wealth.

The implications of Merton's and his fellow researchers' findings are clear: Lack of opportunity and inequality are central causal factors for crime and, by implication, political extremism. However, anomie and strain theory have been criticized for placing too much emphasis on deviance emanating from the poorer classes and for failing to adequately explain why so many youths and adults who suffer from strain do not turn to crime or political extremism.

### Routine Activity Theory

This theory, first posited by Cohen and Felson,[28] holds that political extremism and criminal behavior require the convergence of three societal elements. The adaptation of this theory to the convergence of extremism and crime is summarized as follows:

- **A steady supply of motivated offenders.** At a fundamental level of analysis, this element holds that the political motivations of terrorists and the profit-based motivations of criminals require observable benefits for individuals. Examples of such benefits may include increased status, greed satisfaction, vengeance, or sheer adventure. Within this framework, the political violence option is an attractive motivation because it provides individuals with an outlet to express their indignation with a sense of glory.

---

[26]See Durkheim, Emile. *Suicide* (J. A. Spaulding & G. Simpson, Trans.). New York: Free Press, 1951; see also Durkheim, Émile. *The Division of Labor in Society* (W. D. Halls, Trans.). New York: Free Press, 1994.

[27]See Merton, Robert K. "Social Structure and Anomie." In *American Sociological Review* 3 (1938); see also Merton, Robert K. *Social Theory and Social Structure* (enlarged ed.). New York: Free Press, 1968.

[28]Cohen, Lawrence, and Marcus Felson. "Social Change and Crime Rate Trends: A Routine Activity Approach." *American Sociological Review* 44, no. 4 (1979): 588–608.

- **The ready availability of attractive victims and targets of opportunity.** This element holds that terrorists and criminals profit from the presence of victims who will provide them with certain benefits. For terrorists, appropriate victims will return maximum symbolic and political effect when they strike. For criminals, appropriate victims and customers will return maximum profit-making opportunities.
- **The presence, or lack thereof, of social guardians.** Examples of guardians include the police, surveillance systems, and social networks. Thus, a critical societal element for the calculus of terrorists and criminals is whether the social or political environment possesses weak guardianship and is, therefore, ripe for exploitation. In this regard, relatively weak antiterrorist or anticrime barriers will create a socio-political vacuum that dedicated terrorists or criminals may perceive as an opportunity for exploitation.

### Radical Criminology

During the 1960s and 1970s, a good deal of theory and research on criminality reflected the political and social discord of the period. Critical theorists challenged previous conventions of criminal causation, arguing that delinquency and criminality were caused by society's inequitable ideological, political, and socioeconomic makeup.[29] Proponents of the emergent radical approach argued that because power and wealth have been unequally distributed, those who have been politically and economically shut out understandably resort to criminal antagonism against the prevailing order. According to radical criminologists, these classes will continue to engage in behavior labeled as criminal until society remedies the plight of the powerless and disenfranchised.

Critical theories similar to radical criminology frequently use Marxist theory to critique the role of capitalist economics in creating socioeconomic inequities.[30] Marxist perspectives on criminology argue that the ruling capitalist classes exploit the labor of the lower classes and co-opt them by convincing them that capitalism is actually beneficial for them.[31] Marxist-oriented radical criminologists hold that ruling elites have used their own interpretations of justice to maintain their status. Hence, the criminal justice system is inherently exploitative and unfair toward criminals who originate from the lower classes. The fact that social minorities and the poor are overrepresented in prisons is explained as a manifestation of the inherent unfairness at the core of the existing capitalist establishment.

Critical theories and Marxist ideological tendencies have been used to explain the role of gender in radical movements. Women have historically been prominently represented in many extremist movements and organizations. Chapter Perspective 3.2 investigates the subject of gender and terrorism by discussing women as terrorists.

## ❖ Political Violence as Strategic Choice

## Making Revolution: Acts of Political Will

An **act of political will** is an effort to force change and consists of strategic choices made by ideologically motivated revolutionaries who pursue victory by sheer force of will.[32] It is a choice, a rational decision from the revolutionaries' perspective, to adopt specific tactics and methodologies to defeat an adversary. These methodologies are instruments of rational strategic choice, wherein terrorism is

---

[29]See Krisberg, B. *Crime and Privilege: Toward a New Criminology.* Englewood Cliffs, NJ: Prentice-Hall, 1975.

[30]See Chambliss, William J., and Robert B. Seidman. *Law, Order and Power.* Reading, MA: Addison-Wesley, 1982.

[31]Ibid.; see also Quinney, Richard. *The Social Reality of Crime.* Boston: Little, Brown, 1970.

[32]For a good discussion of terrorism as a product of strategic choice, see Crenshaw, Martha. "The Logic of Terrorism: Terrorist Behavior as a Product of Strategic Choice." In *Origins of Terrorism: Psychologies, Ideologies, Theologies, States of Mind,* edited by Walter Reich. Washington, DC: Woodrow Wilson Center, 1998, pp. 7–24.

## CHAPTER PERSPECTIVE 3.2: Women as Terrorists

From October 23 to 26, 2003, Chechen terrorists seized approximately 800 hostages in a Moscow theater. The episode ended with the deaths of scores of hostages and all of the terrorists. Russian authorities reported that many of the hostage takers were women who had suicide explosive vests strapped to their bodies. The presence of female suicide bombers was not uncommon within the Chechen resistance movement. As a result, the Russian media dubbed the women among Chechen terrorists "**Black Widows**" because they are allegedly relatives of Chechen men who died in the ongoing war in Chechnya.

How common is terrorism by women? What motivates women to become terrorists? In which environments are female terrorists typically found?[a]

Women have been active in a variety of roles in many violent political movements.[b] Historically, some women held positions of leadership during terrorist campaigns and were well integrated into the command systems and policy decision-making processes in extremist groups. In the modern era, women were central figures in Sri Lanka's Tamil Tigers, Germany's Red Army Faction, Italy's Red Brigades,[c] Spain's Basque ETA, and the Japanese Red Army. During the Palestinian *intifada* against Israel, a number of Palestinian suicide bombers were young women. More commonly, women serve as combatants rather than leaders, or women are recruited to participate as support functionaries, such as finding safe houses and engaging in surveillance.

Regardless of the quality of participation, it is clear that such involvement belies the common presumption that terrorism is an exclusively male preserve. In fact, some of the most committed revolutionaries around the world are women.

The following examples are instructive:

- Prior to the 1917 Bolshevik revolution, Russian women were leading members of violent extremist groups such as People's Will (Narodnaya Volya) and the Social Revolutionary Party.

- Female anarchists such as Emma Goldman in the United States demonstrated that women could be leading revolutionary theorists.

- Leila Khaled became a well-respected and prominent member of the Palestinian nationalist movement after her participation in two airline hijacking incidents.

- During the unrest leading up to the Iranian Revolution in the late 1970s, women participated in numerous antigovernment attacks.

- Gudrun Ensslin, Ulrike Meinhof, and other women were leaders and comrades-in-arms within Germany's Red Army Faction during the 1970s.

- During the 1970s and 1980s, other West European terrorist groups such as France's Direct Action, Italy's Red Brigades, and Belgium's Communist Combat Cells fully integrated women into their ranks.

- Women were leaders in the nihilistic Japanese Red Army during the 1970s and 1980s, and the movement was founded by Shigenobu Fusako.

- During the latter quarter of the 20th century, many Provisional Irish Republican Army (IRA) "soldiers" were women, reflecting the fact that the IRA was a nationalist and mildly socialist movement.

- Women became renowned leaders among Sri Lanka's Tamil Tigers group during the 1990s and thereafter when many male leaders were killed or captured, and female terrorists known as Freedom Birds engaged in many attacks, including numerous suicide bombings.

- Among Chechen rebels, since 2002, young women have been recruited, manipulated, or coerced into becoming suicide fighters, known among Russians as Black Widows.

- Since around 2002, the Al-Aqsa Martyr Brigades unit of the Palestine Liberation Organization has actively recruited and deployed women as suicide bombers.[d]

*(Continued)*

(Continued)

- Female combatants have been found in the ranks of many insurgent groups, such as Colombia's FARC and ELN, India's Naxalites, the Communist Party of Nepal, Peru's Shining Path, and Mexico's Zapatistas.
- In Iraq, the number of female suicide bombers increased markedly from 8 in all of 2007 to more than 20 in the first half of 2008. This was because Iraqi insurgents learned that women were much less likely to be searched or otherwise scrutinized by security forces and could therefore more easily penetrate many levels of security.
- In March 2011 the recruitment of women took an interesting turn when al-Qa'ida published a magazine for women, entitled *al Shamikha* ("The Majestic Woman"). Examples of content include articles on beauty advice and suicide bombing.

Active participation of women is arguably more common among left-wing and nationalist terrorist movements than in right-wing and religious movements. Rightist and religious movements yield some cases of women as terrorists but very few examples of female leaders. One reason for these characteristics is that, on one hand, many leftists adopt ideologies of gender equality and many nationalists readily enlist female fighters for the greater good of the group.[e] On the other hand, right-wing and religious movements often adopt ideologies that relegate women to secondary roles within the group. Among religious movements, ideologies of male dominance and female subordination have been common, so that women rarely participate in attacks, let alone in command systems and policy decision-making processes. Having said

this, the incidence of female suicide bombings increased markedly in some conflicts (especially in Iraq and Israel) because extremists realized that women were less likely to be scrutinized by security forces.

In a particularly disturbing trend, young girls have been recruited as fighters by paramilitary groups, such as the Lord Resistance Army in Uganda and the Revolutionary United Front in Sierra Leone. Some of these "Small Girls Units" were made to participate in the brutalization of local populations.[f]

## Notes

a. For a good discussion of these and other issues, see Talbot, Rhiannon. "Myths in the Representation of Women Terrorists." *Eire-Ireland* 35 (2001): 165–86.
b. For a discussion of the roles of women in terrorist movements, see Talbot, Rhiannon. "The Unexpected Face of Terrorism." *This Is the Northeast,* January 31, 2002.
c. For a good discussion of Italian women in violent organizations, see Jamieson, Alison. "Mafiosi and Terrorists: Italian Women in Violent Organizations." *SAIS Review* (Summer/Fall 2000): 51–64.
d. For interviews with female Al-Aqsa Martyr Brigades volunteers, see Tierney, Michael. "Young, Gifted and Ready to Kill." *The Herald* (Glasgow, UK), August 3, 2002.
e. Bloom, Mia. "Female Suicide Bombers: A Global Trend." *Daedalus* (Winter 2007): 94–102.
f. McKay, Susan. "Girls as 'Weapons of Terror' in Northern Uganda and Sierra Leonean Rebel Fighting Forces." *Studies in Conflict & Terrorism* (April 2005): 385–97.

adopted as an optimal strategy. All that is required for final victory is to possess the political and strategic will to achieve the final goal. The selection of terrorism as a strategic methodology is a process based on the experiences of each insurgent group, so that its selection is the outcome of an evolutionary political progression. Thus,

perhaps because groups are slow to recognize the extent of the limits to action, terrorism is often the last in a sequence of choices. It represents the outcome of a learning process.

Experience in opposition provides radicals with information about the potential consequences of their choices. Terrorism is likely to be a reasonably informed choice among available alternatives, some tried unsuccessfully.[33]

As a result, terrorism is simply a tool, an option, selected by members of the political fringe to achieve their desired goal. Terrorism is a deliberate strategy, and from the perspective of the people employing it, success is ensured so long as their group's political and strategic will remains strong.

The evolution of Marxist revolutionary strategy illustrates the essence of political will. Karl Marx argued that history and human social evolution are inexorable forces that will inevitably end in the triumph of the revolutionary working class. He believed that the prediction of the eventual collapse of capitalism was based on scientific law. However, Vladimir Ilich Lenin understood that capitalism's demise would not come about without a "push" from an organized and disciplined *vanguard organization* such as the Communist Party. This organization would lead the working class to victory. In other words, the political will of the people can make history if they are properly indoctrinated and led.

An important conceptual example will help readers better understand the theory of revolutionary change through acts of political will. It is a strategy known as **people's war**. The context in which it was first developed and applied was the Chinese Revolution.

Mao Zedong led the Communist Red Army to victory during the Chinese Revolution by waging a protracted war—first against Chiang Kai-shek's Nationalists (Kuomintang), then in alliance with the Nationalists against the invading Japanese, and finally driving Chiang's forces from mainland China in 1949. The Red Army prevailed largely because of Mao's military-political doctrine, which emphasized waging an insurgent people's war. His strategy was simple:

- Indoctrinate the army.
- Win over the people.
- Hit, run, and fight forever.

People's war was a strategy born of necessity, originating when the Red Army was nearly annihilated by the Nationalists prior to and during the famous Long March campaign in 1934–1935. During the Long March, the Red Army fought a series of rearguard actions against pursuing Nationalist forces, eventually finding refuge in the northern Shensi province after a reputed 6,000-mile march. After the Long March, while the Red Army was being rested and refitted in Shensi, Mao developed his military doctrine. People's war required protracted warfare (war drawn out over time), fought by an army imbued with an iron ideological will to wear down the enemy.[34]

According to Mao, the Red Army should fight a guerrilla war, with roving bands that would occasionally unite. The war was to be fought by consolidating the countryside and then gradually moving into the towns and cities. Red Army units would avoid conventional battle with the Nationalists, giving ground before superior numbers. Space would be traded for time, and battle would be joined only when the Red Army was tactically superior at a given moment. Thus, an emphasis was placed on avoidance and retreat. In people's war, assassination was perfectly acceptable, and targets included soldiers, government administrators, and civilian collaborators. Government-sponsored programs and events—no matter how beneficial they might be to the people—were to be violently disrupted to show the government's weakness.

A successful people's war required the cooperation and participation of the civilian population, so Mao ordered his soldiers to win their loyalty by treating the people correctly. According to Mao,

The army is powerful because all its members have a conscious discipline; they have come together and they fight not for the private interests of a few individuals or a narrow clique, but

---

[33]Ibid., p. 11.

[34]For a good summary of Mao's political ideology, see Schram, Stuart R. *The Political Thought of Mao Tse-tung*. New York: Praeger, 1974.

for the interests of the broad masses and of the whole nation. The sole purpose of this army is to stand firmly with the Chinese people and to serve them whole-heartedly.[35]

Mao's contribution to modern warfare—and to the concept of political will—was that he deliberately linked his military strategy to his political strategy; they were one and the same. Terrorism was a perfectly acceptable option in this military-political strategy. The combination of ideology, political indoctrination, guerrilla tactics, protracted warfare, and popular support made people's war a very potent strategy. It was an effective synthesis of political will.

Leftist revolutionaries adopted this strategy elsewhere in the world in conflicts that ranged in scale from large insurrections to small bands of rebels. Terrorism was frequently used as a strategic instrument to harass and disrupt adversaries, with the goal of turning the people against them and forcing them to capitulate. In the end, people's war had mixed success. It was sometimes very successful, such as in China and Vietnam, but failed elsewhere, such as in Malaysia and the Philippines.[36]

## Perception and Cultural Disconnect: Adversaries in the War on Terrorism

One final consideration is necessary to fully appreciate modern causes of terrorism. This theory is rooted in the political environment that gave rise to the new era of terrorism.

The concept of "one person's terrorist is another person's freedom fighter" is pertinent to how the behavior of the West, and particularly the behavior of the United States, is perceived around the world. When the September 11 attacks occurred, many Americans and other Westerners saw them as an attack on Western-style civilization. Reasons given for the subsequent U.S.-led war on terrorism included the argument that war was necessary to defend civilization from a new barbarism. From the official American and allied point of view, the war was simply a counteraction against the enemies of democracy and freedom. However, many Muslims had a wholly different perspective.

Most nations and people in the Muslim world expressed shock and sorrow toward the U.S. homeland attacks and the innocent lives that were lost. At the same time, many Middle Eastern analysts interpreted the attacks as part of a generalized reaction against U.S. policies and behavior. Although little official support was expressed for the ideologies of radical Islamists such as Osama bin Laden, analysts decried the perceived imbalance in U.S. Middle Eastern policies, especially toward Israel in comparison to friendly Muslim countries.

Interestingly, many young Muslims are keen to adopt some degree of Western culture, yet remain loyal to the Muslim community. As one student commented,

> Most of us here like it both ways, we like American fashion, American music, American movies, but in the end, we are Muslims. . . . The Holy Prophet said that all Muslims are like one body, and if one part of the body gets injured, then all parts feel that pain. If one Muslim is injured by non-Muslims in Afghanistan, it is the duty of all Muslims of the world to help him.[37]

The argument, then, is that the cause of anti-American and Western sentiment is the *behavior* of those nations—that is, the things that they do rather than their values or culture. In the opening paragraph of his controversial book *Imperial Hubris,* former high-ranking Central Intelligence Agency (CIA) official Michael Scheuer presented the central precept of this argument:

---

[35]Mao Tse-tung. "On Coalition Government." In *Selected Works.* Vol. III. New York: International Publishers, 1954, p. 264.

[36]For a summary discussion of the history of irregular warfare, see Keegan, John, and Richard Holmes. *Soldiers: A History of Men in Battle.* New York: Elisabeth Sifton Books, 1986, pp. 241–58.

[37]Quotation in Ford, Peter. "Why Do They Hate Us?" *Christian Science Monitor,* September 27, 2001.

In America's confrontation with Osama bin Laden, al Qaeda, their allies, and the Islamic world, there lies a startlingly clear example of how loving something intensely can stimulate an equally intense and purposeful hatred of things by which it is threatened. This hatred shapes and informs Muslim reactions to U.S. policies and their execution, and it is impossible to understand the threat America faces until the intensity and pervasiveness of this hatred is recognized.[38]

As religion professor Bruce Lawrence observed, "They hate us because of what we do, and it seems to contradict who we say we are . . . the major issue is that our policy seems to contradict our own basic values."[39] Assuming the plausibility of this theory, terrorists possess ample promise to recruit new fighters from among young Muslims who are incensed by American and Western intervention in their regions and nations.[40] Although such intervention is justified in the West as being fundamentally beneficial to the people of the Middle East, the perception of many local people is to the contrary.[41] Ongoing civilian deaths in Afghanistan resulting from "collateral damage" by drone aircraft and NATO airstrikes precipitated repeated denunciations by Afghan leaders and civilians. Perceptions of incidents in Iraq such as killings of civilians in November 2005 in Haditha by U.S. Marines,[42] as well as in September 2007 in Baghdad by members of the Blackwater Worldwide U.S. security firm,[43] are further examples of how this theory could explain resentment against U.S. and Western policy in the Middle East.

Can Muslim perceptions and Western behaviors be reconciled? What are the prospects for mitigating this source of terrorism in the modern era? Several events portend a continued disconnect between these perceptions and behaviors, at least for the immediate future:

- The American-led occupation of Iraq and the protracted insurgency that arose
- An open-ended presence of Western troops in or near Muslim countries
- Broadcasted images of civilian casualties and other "collateral damage" during military operations
- Broadcasted images and rumors of the mistreatment of prisoners in American-run detention facilities
- Cycles of chronic violence between Israelis and Palestinians and the perception that the United States and the West unfairly favor Israel

In this regard, a July 2007 report by the CIA's National Intelligence Council concluded that the terrorist threat to the U.S. homeland remained high and that Al-Qa'ida remained a potent adversary in the war on terrorism.[44] The 2007 National Intelligence Estimate essentially reiterated the 2004 estimate, which had warned that the war in Iraq created a new training ground for professional terrorists, much as the 1979 to 1989 Soviet war in Afghanistan created an environment that led to the rise of Al-Qa'ida and other international **mujahideen** (Islamic holy warriors).[45] It also projected that veterans of the Iraq

---

[38]Scheuer, Michael (as Anonymous). *Imperial Hubris: Why the West Is Losing the War on Terror.* Washington, DC: Brassey's, 2004, p. 1.

[39]Ibid.

[40]For a discussion of the transference of *jihadi* sentiment to the next generation, see Caryl, Christian. "Iraq's Young Blood." *Newsweek,* January 22, 2007, 22–34.

[41]See Munson, Henry. "Lifting the Veil: Understanding the Roots of Islamic Militancy." *Harvard International Review* (Winter 2004): 20–3.

[42]See White, Josh. "Report on Haditha Condemns Marines." *Washington Post,* April 21, 2007.

[43]See Daragahi, Borzou, and Raheem Salman. "Blackwater Shooting Highlights a U.S., Iraq Culture Clash." *Los Angeles Times,* May 4, 2008.

[44]Office of the Director of National Intelligence. *National Intelligence Estimate: The Terrorist Threat to the U.S. Homeland.* Washington, DC: National Intelligence Council, 2007.

[45]Priest, Dana. "Report Says Iraq Is New Terrorist Training Ground." *Washington Post,* January 14, 2005.

war would disperse after the end of the conflict, thus constituting a new generation of international *mujahideen* who would supplant the first Afghanistan-trained generation of fighters. This is a plausible scenario because many foreigners volunteered to fight in Iraq out of a sense of pan-Islamic solidarity.[46]

## ❖ Moral Justifications for Political Violence

Although not all extremists become terrorists, some do cross the line to engage in terrorist violence. For them, terrorism is a calculated strategy. It is a specifically selected method that is used to further their cause. Significantly,

> the terrorist act is different in that the violence employed is not only in pursuit of some long-range political goal but is designed to have far-reaching psychological repercussions on a particular target audience.[47]

Affecting a target audience is an important reason for political violence. Dissident terrorists—as compared with state terrorists—are small bands of violent subversives who could never defeat a professional army or strong government, so they resort to high-profile acts of violence that have an effect on a large audience. It is instructive to review the basic motives of those who commit acts of terrorist violence. To facilitate readers' critical understanding of the motives of terrorists, the following four motives are reviewed:

- Moral convictions of terrorists
- Simplified definitions of good and evil
- Seeking utopia
- Codes of self-sacrifice

### Moral Convictions of Terrorists

Moral conviction refers to terrorists' unambiguous certainty of the righteousness of their cause; to them, there are no gray areas. The goals and objectives of their movement are considered to be principled beyond reproach and their methods absolutely justifiable. This conviction can arise in several environments, including the following two settings:

In the first, a group of people can conclude that they have been morally wronged and that a powerful, immoral, and evil enemy is arrayed against them. This enemy is considered to be adept at betrayal, exploitation, violence, and repression against the championed group. These conclusions can have some legitimacy, especially when a history of exploitation has been documented. This historical evidence is identified and interpreted as being the source of the group's modern problems. For example, many leftist insurgents in Latin America characterized the United States as an imperialist enemy because of its long history of military intervention, economic penetration, and support for repressive regimes in the region.[48] In fact, U.S. intervention in Central America and the Caribbean was unlike European imperialism elsewhere, because

> [U.S. military] officers shared several convictions about America's tropical empire. They believed the racist canards of their generation that professed the inferiority of Caribbean peoples, and

---

[46]For a profile of one foreign volunteer's experience in Iraq, see Stack, Megan K. "Getting an Education in Jihad." *Los Angeles Times,* December 29, 2004.

[47]Riley, Kevin Jack, and Bruce Hoffman. *Domestic Terrorism: A National Assessment of State and Local Preparedness.* Santa Monica, CA: RAND, 1995, p. 3.

[48]For an analysis of American intervention in Central America and the Caribbean, see Langley, Lester D. *The Banana Wars: United States Intervention in the Caribbean, 1898–1934.* Chicago: Dorsey, 1985.

they acknowledged, though occasionally grudgingly, America's obligation to police what their countrymen called "turbulent little republics." Their role was to inculcate respect for rule in what they saw as unruly societies.[49]

In later generations, native populations who shared this kind of history, and who interpreted it to be part of an ongoing pattern in contemporary times, developed strong resentment against their perceived oppressor—in this case, the United States and the governments it supported. To them, there was no need to question the morality of their cause; it was quite clear.

A second setting in which moral conviction may arise is when a group or a people conclude that it possesses an inherent moral superiority over its enemy. This can be derived from ideological convictions, ethnonational values, or religious beliefs. From this perspective, the cause is virtually holy; in the case of religious beliefs, it *is* holy. A sense of moral "purity" becomes the foundation for the simplification of good and evil. In this setting, extremists decide that no compromise is possible and that terrorism is a legitimate option.

For example, a major crisis began in the Yugoslavian territory of Kosovo in 1998 when heavy fighting broke out between Serb security forces, the **Kosovo Liberation Army**, and the Serb and Albanian communities. The conflict ended when the North Atlantic Treaty Organization (NATO) and Russian troops occupied Kosovo and the Serb security units were withdrawn. The strong Serb bond with Kosovo originated in 1389 when the Serb hero, Prince Lazar, was defeated by the Ottoman Turks in Kosovo. Kosovo had been the center of the medieval Serb empire, and this defeat ended the Serb nation. Over the next 500 years, as the Turks ruled the province, Albanian Muslims migrated into Kosovo and gradually displaced Serb Christians. Nevertheless, Serbs have always had strong ethnonational ties to Kosovo, considering it to be a kind of spiritual homeland. It is at the center of their national identity. Thus, despite the fact that 90% of Kosovo's population was Albanian in 1998, Serbs considered their claim to the territory to be paramount to anyone else's claim. From their perspective, the morality of their position was clear.

The Kosovo case exemplifies how quasi-spiritual bonds to a territory, religion, or history can create strong moral self-righteousness. When this occurs, extremists often conclude that their claim or identity is *naturally* superior to that of opponents, and that terrorist violence is perfectly justifiable.

## Delineating Morality: Simplified Definitions of Good and Evil

Revolutionaries universally conclude that their cause is honorable, their methods are justifiable, and their opponents are representations of implacable evil. They arrive at this conclusion in innumerable ways, often—as in the case of Marxists—after devoting considerable intellectual energy to political analysis. Nevertheless, their final analysis is uncomplicated: *Our cause is just, and the enemy's is unjust.* Once this line has been clearly drawn between good and evil, the methods used in the course of the struggle are justified by the ennobled goals and objectives of the cause.

A good example of the application in practice of simplified delineations of good and evil is found in the influential ***Mini-Manual of the Urban Guerrilla***, written by Brazilian revolutionary **Carlos Marighella**.[50] In this document, Marighella clearly argues that the use of terrorism is necessary against a ruthless enemy. The *Mini-Manual* was read and its strategy implemented by leftist revolutionaries throughout Latin America and Europe. Marighella advocated terrorism as a correct response to the oppression of the Brazilian dictatorship. He wrote,

The accusation of assault or terrorism no longer has the pejorative meaning it used to have. . . . Today to be an assailant or a terrorist is a quality that ennobles any honorable man because it is an act worthy of a revolutionary engaged in armed struggle against the shameful military dictatorship and its monstrosities.[51]

---

[49]Ibid., pp. 7–8.

[50]Marighella's name has been alternatively spelled with one *l* and two *l*s. Marighella himself alternated between spellings.

[51]Marighella, Carlos. *Mini-Manual of the Urban Guerrilla*. Quoted in Mallin, *Terror*, pp. 70–1.

As articulated by Marighella, terrorism is an "ennobling" option if it is applied by a selfless revolutionary against a ruthless dictatorship. This concept is at the heart of modern **urban guerrilla warfare,** which in practice has involved the application of terrorist violence. From this perspective, the use of terrorism is perfectly acceptable because of the nature of the enemy.

One fact is clear: There is a moment of decision among those who choose to rise in rebellion against a perceived oppressor. This moment of decision is a turning point in the lives of individuals, people, and nations.

## Seeking Utopia: Moral Ends Through Violent Means

The book ***Utopia*** was written by the English writer Sir Thomas More in the 16th century. It was a fictional work that described an imaginary island with a society having an ideal political and social system. Countless philosophers, including political and religious writers, have since created their own visions of the perfect society.[52] Terrorists likewise envision some form of utopia, although for many terrorists, this can simply mean the destruction of the existing order. For these **nihilist dissidents**, any system is preferable to the existing one, and its destruction alone is a justifiable goal.

The question is, What kind of utopia do terrorists seek? This depends on their belief system. For example, religious terrorists seek to create a God-inspired society on Earth that reflects the commandments, morality, and values of their religious faith. Political terrorists similarly define their ideal society according to their ideological perspective. A comparison of left-wing and right-wing goals on this point is instructive. *Radical leftists* are future oriented and idealistic, while *reactionary rightists* are nostalgic. Radical leftists seek to reform or destroy an existing system prior to building a new and just society. The existing system is perceived to be unjust, corrupt, and oppressive toward a championed group. In comparison, reactionaries on the right seek to return to a time of past glory, which in their belief system has been lost or usurped by an enemy group or culture. Reactionaries perceive that there is an immediate threat to their value system and special status; their sense of utopia is to consolidate (or recapture) this status.

Regardless of which belief system is adopted by terrorists, they uniformly accept the proposition that the promised good (a utopia) outweighs their present actions, no matter how violent those actions are. The revolution will bring utopia after a period of trial and tribulation, so that the **end justifies the means**. This type of reasoning is particularly common among religious, ethnonationalist, and ideological terrorists.

## Moral Purity: Codes of Self-Sacrifice

Terrorists invariably believe that they are justified in their actions. They have faith in the justness of their cause and live their lives accordingly. Many terrorists consequently adopt **"codes of self-sacrifice"** that are at the root of their everyday lives. They believe that these codes are superior codes of living and that those who follow the code are superior to those who do not. The code accepts a basic truth and applies it to everyday life. This truth usually has a religious, ethnonational, or ideological foundation. Any actions taken within the accepted parameters of these codes—even terrorist actions—are justified, because the code "cleanses" the true believer.

A good example of ideological codes of self-sacrifice is found on the fringe left among the first anarchists. Many anarchists did not simply believe in revolution; they *lived* the revolution. They crafted a lifestyle that was completely consumed by the cause. Among some anarchists, an affinity for death became part of the revolutionary lifestyle. The Russian anarchist Sergei Nechayev wrote in *Revolutionary Catechism,*

---

[52]For an interesting attack against Marxist ideology, see Djilas, Milovan. *The Unperfect Society: Beyond the New Class*. New York: Harcourt, Brace & World, 1969.

The revolutionary is a man committed. He has neither personal interests nor sentiments, attachments, property, nor even a name. Everything in him is subordinated to a single exclusive interest, a single thought, a single passion: the revolution.[53]

A review of codes of self-sacrifice is instructive as a reference point for understanding contemporary terrorism. The following discussion explores examples of 20th-century quasi-mystical and militaristic codes that exemplify how some modern movements inculcated a sense of superiority—and a belief in a higher calling—among their members. The examples are the following:

- Racial Soldiers at War: Germany's Waffen SS
- The New Samurai: Japan's Code of Bushido

### Racial Soldiers at War: Germany's Waffen SS

The **Waffen SS** were the "armed SS" of the German military establishment during World War II. They are to be distinguished from the original SS, who were organized in 1923 as Adolf Hitler's bodyguard unit. The acronym "SS" is derived from *Schutzstaffel*, or "protection squad."

From the late 1920s, membership in the SS was determined by one's racial "purity." Members were to be of "pure" Aryan stock and imbued with unquestioning ideological loyalty to Hitler, Germany, and the Aryan race. Height, weight, and physical fitness requirements were established. Their image was eventually honed to symbolize a disciplined, respectable, and racially pure elite. This was accomplished by conducting racial background checks and purging certain "morally deviant" individuals from the ranks, such as the unemployed, alcoholics, criminals, and homosexuals.

The SS eventually grew into a large and multifaceted organization. Different suborganizations existed within the SS. For example, the Algemeine SS, or "general SS," was a police-like organization and also served as a recruiting pool. Recruits from the Algemeine SS eventually became the first administrators and commanders of SS-run concentration camps. In addition, a Nazi-led "foreign legion" was recruited from Germany's conquered territories to fight for Germany and was placed under Waffen SS command. A surprising number of non-Germans volunteered to serve in these international SS units: From the West, volunteers included an estimated 50,000 Dutch; 40,000 Flemings and Walloons (Belgians); 20,000 French; and 12,000 Danes and Norwegians.[54] Many Western recruits were idealistic anti-Bolshevik fascists who enlisted to fight against the Soviet Union and the spread of Communism.

The German-manned Waffen SS units were a special military organization, organized around mobile *Panzer* and *Panzergrenadier* (armored and armored infantry) units. They were an elite force, receiving the best equipment, recruits, and training. They were also strictly indoctrinated Nazis, or ideological soldiers, so that their training "adhered to the very roots of National Socialist doctrine: the cult of will, the attachment to 'blood and soil,' the scorn of so-called 'inferior' peoples."[55] Their war (especially in the East) became a racial war, and the war against the Russians was often characterized as a racial crusade. In essence,

the consequence of their training was to dehumanize the troops. Ideological indoctrination convinced them that the Russians and other eastern Europeans were *Untermenschen,* or subhuman, who had no place in the National Socialist world.[56]

The Waffen SS committed many atrocities during World War II. For example, in the West during the German invasion of France, an SS unit massacred 100 British soldiers at Paradis-Finistère.

---

[53]Barkan and Snowden, *Collective Violence.*

[54]Masson, Philippe. "The SS: Warders of Hitler's Europe." In *20th Century,* edited by A. J. P. Taylor and J. M. Roberts. London: Purnell Reference Books, 1979, p. 1733.

[55]Ibid., p. 1732.

[56]Ailsby, Christopher. *SS: Hell on the Eastern Front: The Waffen-SS War in Russia 1941–1945.* Oceola, WI: MBI, 1998, p. 19.

During the Normandy campaign, groups of Canadian and British prisoners of war (POWs) were shot.[57] In December 1944, a Waffen SS unit under the command of Jochen Peiper machine-gunned 71 American POWs at Malmédy during the Ardennes campaign (the Battle of the Bulge). On the Eastern Front and in the Balkans, the SS were responsible for killing tens of thousands of military and civilian victims. Behind the front lines, their reprisals against civilians for guerrilla attacks by partisans (resistance fighters) were brutal. For example, during the time of the Normandy invasion in June 1944, Waffen SS troops massacred 642 French civilians at Oradour-sur-Glane.[58] In August 1944, Waffen SS soldiers massacred 560 Italian civilians in the Tuscan village of Sant'Anna di Stazzena during an antipartisan campaign.[59] In both examples, the villages were destroyed.

Although not all Waffen SS soldiers participated in these atrocities, the organization as a whole was condemned because of this behavior. At the war crimes trials in Nuremberg after the war, their unmatched sadism was the main reason why the Nuremberg tribunal condemned the SS *in toto* as a criminal organization after the war.[60]

### The New Samurai: Japan's Code of Bushido

**Bushido**, or "way of the warrior," formed the core of Japanese military philosophy from the late 16th century to the collapse of the Japanese Empire in 1945. Modern Bushido hearkened back to the origins of Japan's code of the **Samurai**. Sometime during the eighth century,[61] the breakdown of central authority motivated Japan's wealthy landowners to establish a feudal system of service that lasted (in principle, if not in fact) until well into the 19th century. Large landowners retained the military services of smaller landowners in times of crisis, resulting in an intricate system of loyalty and service, wherein a master–servant relationship grew, whose bonds were strong and whose loyalties were local and personal:

❖ **Photo 3.4**

Bushido in practice. Using living Chinese prisoners for bayonet practice, Japanese soldiers conduct a bayonet drill during the Rape of Nanking in 1937.

© Bettmann/Corbis

When trouble threatened the servant would follow his master's lead. . . . Supporters of the powerful landowners called themselves "Samurai," which is roughly translatable as "those who serve."[62]

The Samurai became a separate martial class, a kind of nobility, who served their masters with unquestioning devotion. *Bushi* is literally translated as "warrior," so that a Samurai was a specific type of *bushi,* or warrior. Throughout Japanese history, the Samurai were renowned for their bravery, obedience, and discipline. For example, Samurai *bushi* twice repulsed Mongol invasions prepared by the Great Khan, Kublai Khan, in the 13th century. Legend holds that during the second invasion, when the Samurai faced likely defeat despite fanatical resistance, they prayed to the gods for victory. That night, a small cloud appeared, grew in size to become a great storm, and smashed the Mongol fleet. This storm became known as the Divine Wind, or **kamikaze**.[63]

The martial class declined—for many reasons—so that it became almost a social burden by the 17th century. Beginning in that century, a series of philosophers redefined the role of the martial class and rekindled Bushido. They instilled the class with a sense of duty that went beyond martial discipline

[57]Masson, "The SS," p. 1734.

[58]For a discussion of the French commemoration of the massacre, see Farmer, Sarah. *Martyred Village: Commemorating the 1944 Massacre at Oradour-sur-Glane.* Berkeley: University of California Press, 1999.

[59]The SS soldiers were allegedly overcome by a "bloodlust." See Carroll, Rory. "Revelations of Wartime SS Massacre in Tuscany Haunt Former Ruling Party." *The Guardian,* November 27, 1999.

[60]Lee, Martin A. *The Beast Reawakens.* New York: Routledge, 1997, p. 16.

[61]Dating the origins of the code of Bushido and the Samurai is imprecise and must be approximated.

[62]Turnbull, Stephen R. *The Samurai: A Military History.* New York: Macmillan, 1977, p. 15.

[63]Ibid., pp. 84–94.

and required that they set high moral and intellectual examples.[64] It was at this time that modern Bushido began to take shape. By the end of this intellectual rebirth, the Way of the Warrior had become a code of life service. "The main virtues [that Bushido] emphasized are the Samurai's bravery, integrity, loyalty, frugality, stoicism and filial piety."[65] Included in Bushido was a zealous code of honor, wherein self-inflicted death—ideally by *seppuku,* an ancient Samurai ritual of self-disembowelment—was preferable to dishonor. Cowardice was considered to be contemptible. Surrender was unthinkable.

By the 19th century, Bushido was a well-entrenched credo, so much so that during relentless attempts to modernize Japan, a rebellion occurred in 1877; an army of 15,000 traditionalist Samurai refused to accept abolishment of the class and restrictions on the wearing of swords. During World War II, imperial Japanese soldiers were indoctrinated with the martial virtues of Bushido. In practice, enemy soldiers who surrendered to the Japanese were often dehumanized and treated harshly. Conquered civilians, particularly in Korea and China, were brutalized. When faced with defeat, Japanese soldiers would often make suicidal charges into enemy lines rather than surrender. Suicide was also common among imperial troops. Toward the end of the war, thousands of Japanese pilots flew planes packed with explosives on missions to crash into American naval vessels. They were called the kamikaze and were considered—under the code of Bushido—to be the new Divine Wind.

## Understanding Codes of Self-Sacrifice

As demonstrated by the foregoing cases, codes of self-sacrifice are an important explanatory cause for terrorist behavior. Those who participate in movements and organizations similar to the Waffen SS and Bushido adopt belief systems that justify their behavior and absolve them of responsibility for normally unacceptable behavior.

These belief systems "cleanse" participants and offer them a sense of participating in a higher or superior morality.

## Chapter Summary

This chapter introduced readers to theories about the causes of terrorism and presented examples that represent some of the models developed by scholars and other researchers. Individual profiles, group dynamics, political environments, and social processes are at the center of the puzzle of explaining why people and groups adopt fringe beliefs and engage in terrorist behavior. Social movements and dramatic (or "traumatic") events have been identified as two sources of terrorism, with the caveat that they are generalized explanations.

Not all extremists become terrorists, but certainly all terrorists are motivated by extremist beliefs. Motives behind terrorist behavior include a range of factors. One is a moral motivation, which is an unambiguous conviction of the righteousness of one's cause. Terrorists believe that the principles of their movement are unquestionably sound. A second motive is the simplification of notions of good and evil, when terrorists presume that their cause and methods are completely justifiable because their opponents represent inveterate evil. There are no "gray areas" in their struggle. A third factor is the adoption of utopian ideals by terrorists, whereby an idealized end justifies the use of violence. These idealized ends are often very vague concepts, such as Karl Marx's dictatorship of the proletariat. The fourth motive is critical to understanding terrorist behavior: It is the development of codes of self-sacrifice, when an ingrained belief system forms the basis for a terrorist's lifestyle and conduct. Collectively, these factors form a useful theoretical foundation for explaining terrorist motives.

[64]Ibid., p. 282.

[65]Ibid., p. 286.

❖ **Photo 3.5**

AFP/Getty Images

Aircraft explode at Dawson's Field in Jordan during Black September, 1970. The hijackings and intense fighting afterward marked the beginning of a period when international airline hijackings and Palestinian attacks became common events.

Explanations of terrorism also consist of a range of factors. The theory of acts of political will is a rational model in which extremists choose to engage in terrorism as an optimal strategy to force change. Criminological and sociological explanations of terrorism look at intergroup dynamics, particularly social environments and conflict that result in collective violence.

Perception is an important factor in the decision to engage in collective violence. Psychological explanations broadly explain individual motivations and group dynamics. Psychological theories also help to explicate the cohesion of terrorist organizations and why they perpetuate violent behavior even when victory is logically impossible.

One final point should be considered when evaluating the causes of terrorism: When experts build models and develop explanatory theories for politically motivated violence, their conclusions sometimes "reflect the political and social currents of the times in which the scholars writing the theories live."[66] It is plausible that

> to a large degree, the development of theories . . . reflects changing political and intellectual climates. When intellectuals have opposed the collective behavior of their times . . . they have tended to depict the behavior negatively. . . . When scholars have instead supported the collective behavior of their eras . . . they have painted a more positive portrait of both the behavior and the individuals participating in it.[67]

This is not to say that analysts are not trying to be objective or that they are purposefully disingenuous in their analyses. But it is only logical to presume that the development of new explanatory theories will be affected by factors such as new terrorist environments or new ideologies that encourage political violence. The progression of explanations by the social and behavioral sciences in the future will naturally reflect the socio-political environments of the times in which they are developed.

---

[66]Barkan and Snowden, *Collective Violence*, p. 27.

[67]Ibid., pp. 27–8.

## Key Terms and Concepts

The following topics are discussed in this chapter and can be found in the glossary:

absolute deprivation

Abu Nidal Organization

act of political will

Al Fatah

Basque Fatherland and Liberty (Euskadi Ta Azkatasuna, or ETA)

Black September

Black Widows

Bloody Sunday

Bushido

Carlos the Jackal

codes of self-sacrifice

end justifies the means

*intifada*

kamikaze

Khaled, Leila

Kosovo Liberation Army

Marighella, Carlos

*Mini-Manual of the Urban Guerrilla*

*mujahideen*

Nidal, Abu

nihilist dissidents

pan-Arabist

people's war

relative deprivation theory

Samurai

*Schutzstaffel*

Stockholm syndrome

structural theory

*Utopia*

Waffen SS

## Discussion Box: Bloody Sunday and Black September

*This chapter's Discussion Box is intended to stimulate critical debate about seminal incidents in the history of national groups.*

### Bloody Sunday

In the late 1960s, Irish Catholic activists calling themselves the Northern Ireland Civil Rights Association attempted to emulate the African American civil rights movement as a strategy to agitate for equality in Northern Ireland. They thought that the same force of moral conviction would sway British policy to improve the plight of the Catholics. Their demands were similar to those of the American civil rights movement: equal opportunity, better employment, access to housing, and access to education. This ended when mostly peaceful demonstrations gradually became more violent, leading to rioting in the summer of 1969, an environment of generalized unrest, and the deployment of British troops. After 1969, the demonstrations continued, but rioting, fire bombings, and gun battles gradually became a regular feature of strife in Northern Ireland.

On January 30, 1972, elite British paratroopers fired on demonstrators in Londonderry. Thirteen demonstrators were killed. After this incident, many Catholics became radicalized and actively worked to drive out the British. The Irish Republican Army received recruits and widespread support from the Catholic community. In July 1972, the Provos launched a massive bombing spree in central Belfast.

### Black September

When Leila Khaled and her comrades attempted to hijack five airliners on September 6 and 9, 1970, their plan was to fly all of the planes to an abandoned British Royal Air Force (RAF) airfield in Jordan, hold hostages, broker the release of Palestinian prisoners, release the hostages, blow up the planes, and thereby force the world to focus on the plight of the Palestinian people. On September 12, 255 hostages were released from the three planes that landed at Dawson's Field (the RAF base), and 56 were kept to bargain for the release of 7 Palestinian prisoners, including Leila Khaled. The group then blew up the airliners.

Unfortunately for the hijackers, their actions greatly alarmed King Hussein of Jordan. Martial law was declared on September 16, and the incident led to civil war between Palestinian forces and the Jordanian army. Although the Jordanians' operation was precipitated by the destruction of the airliners on Jordanian soil, tensions had been building between the army and Palestinian forces for some time. King Hussein and the Jordanian leadership interpreted this operation as confirmation that radical Palestinian groups had become too powerful and were a threat to Jordanian sovereignty.

On September 19, Hussein asked for diplomatic intervention from Great Britain and the United States when a Syrian column entered Jordan in support of the Palestinians. On September 27, a truce ended the fighting. The outcome of the fighting was a relocation of much of the Palestinian leadership and fighters to its Lebanese bases. The entire incident became known among Palestinians as Black September and was not forgotten by radicals in the Palestinian nationalist movement. One of the most notorious terrorist groups took the name Black September, and the name was also used by Abu Nidal.

### Discussion Questions

- What role do you think these incidents had in precipitating the IRA's and PLO's cycles of violence?

- Were the IRA's and PLO's tactics and targets justifiable responses to these incidents?

*(Continued)*

(Continued)

- What, in your opinion, would have been the outcome in Northern Ireland if the British government had responded peacefully to the Irish Catholics' emulation of the American civil rights movement?

- What, in your opinion, would have been the outcome if the Jordanian government had not responded militarily to the Palestinian presence in Jordan?

- How should the world community have responded to Bloody Sunday and Black September?

## On Your Own

The open-access Student Study Site at **http://study.sagepub.com/martin5e** has a variety of useful study aids, including eFlashcards, quizzes, audio resources, and journal articles. The websites, exercises, and recommended readings listed below are easily accessed on this site as well.

## Recommended Websites

The following websites provide links to examples of the reasons given for political agitation, as explained by activist organizations and movements:

Ejército Zapatista de Liberación Nacional (Mexico): http://www.ezln.org.mx/index.html/

European Federation of Green Parties (Belgium): http://www.europeangreens.org/

Jewish Defense League (United States): http://www.jdl.org.il/

Palestinian Information Center (Palestine/Israel): http://www.palestine-info.co.uk/

Puerto Rican Independence Party (Puerto Rico): http://www.independencia.net/

## Web Exercise

Using this chapter's recommended websites, conduct an online investigation of the causes of extremist agitation and terrorist violence.

1. What issues do these groups consider to have unquestioned merit? What reasons do they give for this quality?

2. What scenarios do you think might cause these groups to engage in direct confrontation or violence?

3. Act as "devil's advocate" and defend one of the causes with which you *disagree*.

For an online search of factors that are commonly cited as causes for terrorist violence, readers should activate the search engine on their Web browser and enter the following keywords:

"Intifada"

"Just War"

# Recommended Readings

The following publications provide discussions about the causes of terrorist behavior:

Crotty, William, ed. *Democratic Development and Political Terrorism: The Global Perspective*. Boston: Northeastern University Press, 2005.

Bloom, Mia. *Bombshell: Women and Terrorism*. Philadelphia: University of Pennsylvania Press, 2011.

Djilas, Milovan. *Memoir of a Revolutionary*. New York: Harcourt Brace Jovanovich, 1973.

Eager, Page Whaley. *From Freedom Fighters to Terrorists: Women and Political Violence*. Burlington, VT: Ashgate, 2008.

Forest, James J. F., ed. *The Making of a Terrorist: Recruitment, Training, and Root Causes*. Westport, CT: Praeger Security International, 2006.

Franks, Jason. *Rethinking the Roots of Terrorism*. New York: Palgrave Macmillan, 2006.

Huntington, Samuel P. *The Clash of Civilizations and the Remaking of World Order*. New York: Touchstone, 1996.

Khaled, Leila. *My People Shall Live: The Autobiography of a Revolutionary*. London: Hodder & Stoughton, 1973.

Martinez, Thomas, and John Guinther. *Brotherhood of Murder*. New York: Simon & Schuster, 1988.

McKelvey, Tara, ed. *One of the Guys: Women as Aggressors and Torturers*. Emeryville, CA: Seal Press, 2007.

Nassar, Jamal R. *Globalization and Terrorism: The Migration of Dreams and Nightmares*, 2nd ed. Lanham, MD: Rowman & Littlefield, 2009.

Ocalan, Abdullah. *Prison Writings: The Roots of Civilization*. London: Pluto, 2007.

Pedahzur, Ami and Arie Perliger. *Jewish Terrorism in Israel*. New York: Columbia University Press, 2009.

Perry, Barbara. *In the Name of Hate: Understanding Hate Crimes*. New York: Routledge, 2001.

Reich, Walter, ed. *Origins of Terrorism: Psychologies, Ideologies, States of Mind*. Washington, DC: Woodrow Wilson Center, 1998.

Shultz, Richard H., and Andrea J. Dew. *Insurgents, Terrorists, and Militias: The Warriors of Contemporary Combat*. New York: Columbia University Press, 2006.

Sjoberg, Laura, and Caron E. Gentry. *Mothers, Monsters, Whores: Women's Violence in Global Politics*. London: Zed Books, 2007.

Skaine, Rosemarie. *Female Suicide Bombers*. Jefferson, NC: McFarland, 2006.

# PART II
# The Terrorists

Ulrike Meinhof and Gudrun Ensslin, prominent members of West Germany's Red Army Faction, also known as the Baader-Meinhof Gang. Both committed suicide in prison.

Keystone/Hulton Archive/Getty Images

# Terror From Above

## CHAPTER 4

## Terrorism by the State

### OPENING VIEWPOINT: STATE TERRORISM AS DOMESTIC AND FOREIGN POLICY

#### State Terrorism as Domestic Policy in Central America

*Honduras* during the early 1980s was a staging area for American-supported Nicaraguan counterrevolutionary guerrillas known as the **Contras**. During this period, the Honduran government vigorously suppressed domestic dissent. The military established torture centers and created a clandestine death squad called **Battalion 3-16**. Battalion 3-16 was allegedly responsible for the disappearances of hundreds of students, unionists, and politicians.

In *El Salvador* during the 1980s, a Marxist revolutionary movement fought to overthrow the United States–backed government. To counter this threat, right-wing death squads worked in conjunction with Salvadoran security services to eliminate government opponents, leftist rebels, and their supporters. ORDEN was a paramilitary and intelligence service that used terror against rural civilians. Another death squad, the White Hand, committed numerous atrocities against civilians.

In *Guatemala*, a brutal civil war and related political violence cost about 200,000 lives, including tens of thousands of "disappeared" people. It was, in part, a racial war waged against Guatemala's Indians, descendants of the ancient Mayas, who made up half the population. The government responded to an insurgency in the Indian-populated countryside with widespread torture, killings, and massacres against Indian villagers. Death squad activity was also widespread. One government campaign, called **Plan Victoria 82**, massacred civilians, destroyed villages, and resettled survivors in zones called "strategic hamlets." Plan Victoria 82 was responsible for thousands of deaths by mid-1982.

#### State Terrorism as Foreign Policy in North Africa and the Middle East

*Libya* was implicated in a number of terrorist incidents during the 1980s, including attacks at the Rome and Vienna airports in 1985, the bombing of the La Belle Discotheque in Berlin in 1986, and the bombing of Pan Am Flight 103 in 1988. Libya was also implicated in providing support for the Popular Front for the Liberation of Palestine–General Command and the Abu Nidal Organization. During this period, Libya sponsored training camps for many terrorist organizations such as Germany's Red Army Faction and the Provisional Irish Republican Army.

*Sudan* supported regional terrorist groups, rebel organizations, and dissident movements throughout North Africa and the Middle East. It provided safe haven for Osama bin Laden's Al-Qa'ida network, the Abu Nidal Organization, Palestine Islamic Jihad, Hamas, and Hezbollah. It also provided support for rebels and opposition groups in Tunisia, Ethiopia, Uganda, and Eritrea.

*Syria* provided safe haven and support for Hezbollah, Palestine Islamic Jihad, Hamas, the Popular Front for the Liberation of Palestine–General Command, and the Abu Nidal Organization. Its decades-long occupation of the Beka'a Valley, which ended in 2005, provided open safe haven for many extremist groups, including Iranian Revolutionary Guards.

**T**his chapter explores the characteristics of terrorism from above—state terrorism—committed by governments and quasi-governmental agencies and personnel against perceived enemies. State terrorism can be directed externally against adversaries in the international domain or internally against domestic enemies. Readers will explore the various types of state terrorism and will acquire an appreciation for the qualities that characterize each state terrorist environment. A state terrorist paradigm will be discussed, and interesting cases will be examined to understand what is meant by *terrorism as foreign policy* and *terrorism as domestic policy.*

Political violence by the state is the most organized and potentially the most far-reaching application of terrorist violence. Because of the many resources available to the state, its ability to commit acts of violence far exceeds in scale the kind of violence perpetrated by antistate dissident terrorists. Only communal dissident terrorism (group-against-group violence) potentially approximates the scale of state-sponsored terror.[1]

Why do governments use terrorism as an instrument of foreign policy? What is the benefit of applying terrorism domestically? How do states justify their involvement in either international or domestic terrorism? The answers to these questions incorporate the following considerations:

- *Internationally,* the state defines its interests in a number of ways, usually within the context of political, economic, or ideological considerations. When promoting or defending these interests, governments can choose to behave unilaterally or cooperatively, and cautiously or aggressively.

- *Domestically,* the state's interests involve the need to maintain internal security and order. When threatened domestically, some regimes react with great vigor and violence.

In both the international and domestic domains, states will choose from a range of overt and covert options.

Terrorism by states is characterized by official government support for policies of violence, repression, and intimidation. This violence and coercion is directed against perceived enemies that the state has determined threaten its interests or security.

Although the perpetrators of state terrorist campaigns are frequently government personnel acting in obedience to directives originating from government officials, those who carry out the violence are also quite often *unofficial* agents who are used and encouraged by the government.

An example illustrating this concept is the violent suppression campaign against the pro-independence movement in the former Indonesian province of East Timor. East Timor comprises the eastern half of the island of Timor, which is located at the southeastern corner of the Indonesian archipelago north-

© Reuters/Corbis

❖ **Photo 4.1**

Libyan leader Muammar el-Qaddafi. Qaddafi's regime provided assistance and safe haven to a number of terrorist groups for two decades before renouncing such support in the early 2000s. He later ordered Libyan security forces and mercenaries to crush opposition during the 2011 "Arab Spring" uprising in Libya; they failed, and Qaddafi was killed during the final phase of the uprising.

west of Australia. East Timor is unique in the region because it was ruled for centuries as a Portuguese colony and its population is predominantly Roman Catholic. Portugal announced in 1975 that it would withdraw in 1978 after occupying the territory for more than 450 years. The Indonesian army invaded East Timor in December 1975 and annexed the territory in 1976. During the turmoil that followed, more than 200,000 Timorese were killed in the fighting or were starved during a famine. At the same time that the Indonesian army committed numerous atrocities—including killing scores of protesters by firing on a pro-democracy protest in November 1991—the government encouraged the operations of pro-Indonesian paramilitaries. The paramilitaries were armed by the government and permitted to wage an extended campaign of terror for nearly two decades against East Timor's pro-independence

---

[1]One communal dissident terrorist incident that approximated state terrorism in sheer scale was the September 11, 2001, Al-Qa'ida attack on the United States.

movement. This violence became particularly brutal in 1999 as the territory moved toward a vote for independence. For example, in April 1999, a paramilitary murdered about 25 people in a churchyard. The long period of violence ended in September 1999, when Indonesia gave control of East Timor to United Nations (UN) peacekeepers. Under UN supervision, East Timor's first presidential elections were held in April 2002, and former resistance leader Xanana Gusmao won in a landslide victory.

The East Timor case illustrates the common strategy of using violent state-sponsored proxies (paramilitaries in this example) as an instrument of official state repression. The rationale behind supporting these paramilitaries is that they can be deployed to violently enforce state authority, while at the same time permit the state to deny responsibility for their behavior. Such "deniability" can be useful for propaganda purposes because the government can officially argue that its paramilitaries represent a spontaneous grassroots reaction against their opponents.

The discussion in this chapter will review the following:

- The State as Terrorist: A State Terrorism Paradigm
- Violence Abroad: Terrorism as Foreign Policy
- Violence at Home: Terrorism as Domestic Policy
- The Problem of Accountability: Monitoring State Terrorism

## ❖ The State as Terrorist: A State Terrorism Paradigm

A **paradigm** is "a pattern, example, or model"[2] that is logically developed to represent a concept. Paradigms represent theoretical concepts that are accepted among experts, and they can be useful for practitioners to design policy agendas. When paradigms change—commonly called a *paradigm shift*—it is often because new environmental factors persuade experts to thoroughly reassess existing theories and assumptions. A dissident terrorism paradigm will be presented in Chapter 5.

Experts and scholars have designed a number of models to describe state terrorism. These constructs have been developed to identify distinctive patterns of state-sponsored terrorist behavior. Experts agree that several models of state involvement in terrorism can be differentiated. For example, one model[3] describes state-level participants in a security environment as including the following:

- *Sponsors* of terrorism, meaning those states that actively promote terrorism and that have been formally designated as "rogue states," or state sponsors, under U.S. law.[4]
- *Enablers* of terrorism, or those states that operate in an environment wherein "being part of the problem means not just failing to cooperate fully in countering terrorism but also doing some things that help enable it to occur."[5]
- *Cooperators* in counterterrorism efforts, including unique security environments wherein "cooperation on counterterrorism is often feasible despite significant disagreements on other subjects."[6]

State terrorism incorporates many types and degrees of violence. The intensity of this violence may range in scale from single acts of coercion to extended campaigns of terrorist violence. Another model describes the scale of violence as including the following:

---

[2]*Webster's New Twentieth Century Dictionary of the English Language, Unabridged.* 2nd ed. New York: Publishers Guild, 1966.

[3]Pillar, Paul R. *Terrorism and U.S. Foreign Policy.* Washington, DC: Brookings Institution, 2001, pp. 157–98.

[4]Ibid., p. 157.

[5]Ibid., p. 178.

[6]Ibid., p. 186.

- In **warfare**, the conventional military forces of a state are marshaled against an enemy. The enemy is either a conventional or guerrilla combatant and may be an internal or external adversary. This is a highly organized and complicated application of state violence.

- In **genocide**, the state applies its resources toward the elimination of a scapegoat group. The basic characteristic of state-sponsored genocidal violence is that it does not differentiate between enemy combatants and enemy civilians; all members of the scapegoat group are considered to be enemies. Like warfare, this is often a highly organized and complicated application of state violence.

- **Assassinations** are selective applications of homicidal state violence, whereby a single person or a specified group of people is designated for elimination. This is a lower-scale application of state violence.

- **Torture** is used by some states as an instrument of intimidation, interrogation, and humiliation. Like assassinations, it is a selective application of state violence directed against a single person or a specified group of people. Although it is often a lower-scale application of state violence, many regimes will make widespread use of torture during states of emergency.[7]

A number of experts consider the quality of violence to be central to the analysis of state terrorism and have drawn distinctions between different types of state coercion. Thus, "some analysts distinguish between oppression and repression. Oppression is essentially a condition of exploitation and deprivation . . . , and repression is action against those who are seen to be threats to the established order."[8]

## Understanding State-Sponsored Terrorism: State Patronage and Assistance

Linkages between regimes and terrorism can range from very clear lines of sponsorship to very murky and indefinable associations. States that are inclined to use terrorism as an instrument of statecraft are often able to control the parameters for their involvement, so that governments can sometimes manage how precisely a movement or an incident can be traced back to its personnel. For example, the Soviet Union established the **Patrice Lumumba Peoples' Friendship University** in Moscow. Named for the martyred Congolese Prime Minister **Patrice Lumumba**, the university recruited students from throughout the developing world. Much of its curriculum was composed of standard higher education courses. However, students also received instruction in Marxist theory, observed firearms demonstrations, and were networked with pro-Soviet "liberation" movements. Patrice Lumumba University was also used by the KGB, the Soviet intelligence service, to recruit students for more intensive training in the intricacies of national liberation and revolution. Many graduates went on to become leaders in a number of extremist movements. Many Palestinian nationalists attended the university, as did the Venezuelan terrorist Ilich Ramírez Sánchez, known as Carlos the Jackal.

Thus, state sponsorship of terrorism is not always a straightforward process. In fact, it is usually a covert, secret policy that allows states to claim "deniability" when accused of sponsoring terrorism. Because of these veiled parameters, a distinction must be made between **state patronage for terrorism** and **state assistance for terrorism**.

As discussed in the next section, the basic characteristic of state patronage is that the state is overtly and directly linked to terrorist behavior. The basic characteristic of state assistance is that the state is tacitly and indirectly linked to terrorist behavior. These are two subtly distinct concepts that are summarized in Table 4.1.

---

[7]Adapted from Iadicola, Peter, and Anson Shupe. *Violence, Inequality, and Human Freedom.* 3rd ed. Lanham, MD: Rowman & Littlefield, 2012.

[8]Sederberg, Peter C. *Terrorist Myths: Illusion, Rhetoric, and Reality.* Englewood Cliffs, NJ: Prentice Hall, 1989, p. 59. Citing Stohl, Michael, and George Lopez. "Introduction." In *The State as Terrorist: The Dynamics of Governmental Violence and Repression,* edited by Michael Stohl and George Lopez. Westport, CT: Greenwood, 1984, p. 77.

| Table 4.1 | State Sponsorship of Terrorism |
|---|---|

State participation in terrorist and extremist behavior can involve either direct or indirect sponsorship and can be conducted in the international or domestic policy domains. State *patronage* refers to relatively direct linkages between a regime and political violence. State *assistance* refers to relatively indirect linkages.

The following table distinguishes state patronage and assistance in the international and domestic policy domains.

| Domain | Type of Sponsorship | |
|---|---|---|
| | *Patronage* | *Assistance* |
| **International** | International violence conducted on government orders | International violence with government encouragement and support |
| | Case: Assassination of former Iranian prime minister Shahpour Bakhtiar in France by Iranian operatives | Case: Pakistani assistance for anti-Indian extremists in Jammu and Kashmir, including the **Jammu Kashmir Liberation Front** |
| **Domestic** | Domestic repression by government personnel | Domestic repression by progovernment extremists |
| | Case: Argentina's "Dirty War" conducted by the military | Case: Violence by rightist paramilitaries in El Salvador during the 1980s civil war |

## State Sponsorship: The Patronage Model

State patronage for terrorism refers to active participation in, and encouragement of, terrorist behavior. Its basic characteristic is that the state, through its agencies and personnel, actively takes part in repression, violence, and terrorism. Thus, state patrons adopt policies that *initiate* terrorism and other subversive activities—including directly arming, training, and providing sanctuary for terrorists.

### State Patronage in Foreign Policy

In the *foreign policy domain,* state patronage for terrorism occurs when a government champions a politically violent movement or group—a proxy—that is operating beyond its borders. Under this model, the state patron will directly assist the proxy in its cause and will continue its support even when the movement or group has become known to commit acts of terrorism or other atrocities. When these revelations occur, patrons typically reply to this information with rationalizations. The patron will

- accept the terrorism as a necessary tactic,
- deny that what occurred should be labeled as terrorism,
- deny that an incident occurred in the first place, or
- issue a blanket and moralistic condemnation of all such violence as unfortunate.

The 1981 to 1988 U.S.-directed guerrilla war against the **Sandinista** regime in Nicaragua incorporated elements of the state patronage model.[9] Although it was not a terrorist war, per se, the United States' proxy did commit human rights violations. It is, therefore, a good case study of state patronage for a proxy that was quite capable of engaging in terrorist behavior.

---

[9]For a good discussion of U.S. policy in Nicaragua, see Walker, Thomas W., ed. *Revolution and Counterrevolution in Nicaragua.* Boulder, CO: Westview, 1991.

In 1979, the U.S.-supported regime of **Anastasio Somoza Debayle** was overthrown after a revolution led by the Sandinistas, a Marxist insurgent group. Beginning in 1981, the Reagan administration began a campaign of destabilization against the Sandinista regime. The most important component of this campaign was U.S. support for anti-Sandinista Nicaraguan counterrevolutionaries, known as the **Contras**. During this time,

> the centerpiece of the Reagan administration's low-intensity-warfare strategy was a program of direct paramilitary attacks. Conducted by a proxy force of exiles supplemented by specially trained U.S. operatives, these operations were, ironically, meant to be the covert side of Reagan's policy. Instead, the so-called contra war became the most notorious symbol of U.S. intervention in Nicaragua.[10]

From December 1981 until July 1983, funding and equipment were secretly funneled by the Central Intelligence Agency (CIA) to build training facilities, sanctuaries, and supply bases for the Contras along the Nicaraguan–Honduran border. Allied personnel from Honduras and Argentina assisted in the effort. From this base camp region, the Contras were able to be trained, supplied, and sent into Nicaragua to conduct guerrilla missions against the Sandinistas. The Contras were sustained by U.S. arms and funding—without this patronage, they would not have been able to operate against the Sandinistas. Unfortunately for the United States, evidence surfaced that implicated the Contras in numerous human rights violations. These allegations were officially dismissed or explained away by the Reagan administration.

### State Patronage in Domestic Policy

In the *domestic policy domain,* state patronage of terrorism occurs when a regime engages in direct, violent repression against a domestic enemy. Under this model, state patronage is characterized by the use of state security personnel in an overt policy of state-sponsored political violence. State patrons typically rationalize policies of repression by arguing that they are necessary to

- suppress a clear and present domestic threat to national security,
- maintain law and order during times of national crisis,
- protect fundamental cultural values that are threatened by subversives, or
- restore stability to governmental institutions that have been shaken, usurped, or damaged by a domestic enemy.

The Syrian government's 1982 suppression of a rebellion by the **Muslim Brotherhood** is a case study of the state patronage model as domestic policy. The Muslim Brotherhood is a transnational Sunni Islamic fundamentalist movement that is very active in several North African and Middle Eastern countries. Beginning in the early 1980s, the Muslim Brotherhood initiated a widespread terrorist campaign against the Syrian government. During its campaign, the movement assassinated hundreds of government personnel, including civilian and security officials. They also assassinated Soviet personnel who were based in Syria as advisers. This phase in the Muslim Brotherhood's history posed significant dissident defiance to secular governments in Syria, Egypt, and elsewhere.

In 1980, a rebellion was launched (and suppressed) in the city of Aleppo. In 1981, the Syrian army and other security units moved in to crush the Muslim Brotherhood in Aleppo and the city of Hama, killing at least 200 people. Syrian President Hafez el-Assad increased security restrictions and made membership in the organization a capital offense. In 1982, another Muslim Brotherhood revolt broke out in Hama. The Syrian regime sent in troops and tanks, backed by artillery, to put down the revolt; they killed approximately 25,000 civilians and destroyed large sections of Hama. Since the suppression of the Hama revolt, the Muslim Brotherhood and other religious fundamentalist groups

---

[10]Kornbluh, Peter. "The U.S. Role in the Counterrevolution." In *Revolution and Counterrevolution in Nicaragua,* edited by Thomas W. Walker. Boulder, CO: Westview, 1991, p. 326.

posed little threat to the Syrian regime, which is a secular government dominated by a faction of the nationalistic **Ba'ath Party**. Nevertheless, when the Ba'athist regime was again challenged by mass protests during the 2011 Arab Spring uprisings, it again deployed the army and other security forces to violently attack centers of protest nationwide, and again assaulted Hama.[11] A civil war ensued, with antigovernment forces initially comprised of a loose coalition of disparate militias, collectively known as the Free Syrian Army. A potent, well-armed Islamist movement eventually rose to challenge both the Free Syrian Army and the Ba'athist government.

## State Sponsorship: The Assistance Model

State assistance for terrorism refers to tacit participation in, and encouragement of, terrorist behavior. Its basic characteristic is that the state, through sympathetic proxies and agents, implicitly takes part in repression, violence, and terrorism. In contrast to state patronage for terrorism, state assisters are less explicit in their sponsorship, and linkages to state policies and personnel are more ambiguous. State assistance includes policies that help sympathetic extremist proxies engage in terrorist violence, whereby the state will *indirectly* arm, train, and provide sanctuary for terrorists.

### State Assistance in Foreign Policy

In the *foreign policy domain,* state assistance for terrorism occurs when a government champions a politically violent proxy that is operating beyond its borders. Under this model, state assistance will indirectly help the proxy in its cause, and the state may or may not continue its support if the movement or group becomes known to commit acts of terrorism or other atrocities. When the proxy's terrorism becomes known, state assisters typically weigh political costs and benefits when crafting a reply to these allegations. The ambiguity that the assister has built into its linkages with the proxy is intended to provide it with the option to claim "deniability" when accused of complicity. The assister can

- deny that a linkage exists between the state and the politically violent movement,
- admit that some support or linkage exists but argue that the incident was a "rogue" operation that was outside the parameters of the relationship,
- admit or deny a linkage but label the alleged perpetrators as "freedom fighters" and assert that their cause is a just one despite unfortunate incidents, or
- blame the movement's adversary for creating an environment that is conducive to, and is the source of, all of the political violence.

The Contra insurgency against the Sandinistas was discussed previously as a case study of the state patronage model—with the caveat that it was not, per se, a terrorist war. The later phases of the war are also good examples of the state assistance model.

Several incidents undermined the U.S. Congress's support for the Reagan administration's policy in Nicaragua. First, "assassination of civilians and wanton acts of terrorism against nonmilitary targets . . . were . . . well recognized within U.S. national security agencies."[12] Second, an alleged CIA "assassination manual" was discovered and made public. Third, the CIA was implicated in the mining of the harbor in the capital city of Managua. In December 1982, Congress passed the **"Boland Amendment,"** which forbade the expenditure of U.S. funds to overthrow the Sandinista government. In mid-1983, Congress appropriated $24 million as the "final" expenditure to support the Contras—after it was spent, the CIA was required to end support for the Contras. In late 1984, a second Boland Amendment forbade all U.S. assistance to the Contras.

---

[11]In Syria and other countries during the Arab Spring protests (particularly Egypt), the Muslim Brotherhood proved to be a participatory faction of the protests rather than at the vanguard of insurgency.

[12]Ibid., p. 331.

These legislative measures were the catalyst for a highly covert effort to continue supplying the Contras. Sources of supply had always included an element of covert transfer of arms for the Contras. For example, Operation Tipped Kettle sought to funnel arms to the Contras that were captured from the Palestine Liberation Organization (PLO) by Israel during Israel's 1982 invasion of Lebanon. Another example was Operation Elephant Herd, which sought to transfer surplus U.S. military equipment to the CIA free of charge, to be distributed to the Contras.[13]

The most effective effort to circumvent the congressional ban was the resupply network set up by Marine Lt. Col. Oliver North, an official of the National Security Council. While the CIA explored obtaining support for the Contras from international sources (primarily allied countries), North and others successfully set up a resupply program that shipped large amounts of arms to the Contras—both in their Honduran base camps and inside Nicaragua itself. This program was intended to wait out congressional opposition to arming the Contras and was successful, because in June 1986, Congress approved $100 million in aid for the Contras. Congressional support for this disbursement was severely shaken when a covert American cargo plane was shot down inside Nicaragua, an American mercenary was captured, and the press published reports about North's operations. The United States was embarrassed in November 1986 when a Lebanese magazine revealed that high-ranking officials in the Reagan administration had secretly agreed to sell arms to Iran. The operation, which was under way in August 1985, involved the sale of arms to Iran in exchange for help from the Iranian government to secure the release of American hostages held by Shi'a terrorists in Lebanon. Profits from the sales (reportedly $30 million) were used to support Nicaraguan Contras in their war against the Sandinista government. This support was managed by National Security Adviser John Poindexter and Lt. Col. Oliver North. This combination of factors—known as the **Iran-Contra scandal**—ended congressional support for the Contra program.

The administration's embarrassment was aggravated by the fact that the United States had previously adopted a get-tough policy against what it deemed to be terrorist states, and Iran had been included in that category. Soon after the American captives were released (apparently as a result of the weapons deal), Lebanese terrorists seized more hostages.

As a postscript to the Contra insurgency, it is instructive to report the economic and human costs of the war:

> Between 1980 and 1989, the total death toll—Nicaraguan military, contra, and civilian—was officially put at 30,865. Tens of thousands more were wounded, orphaned, or left homeless. As of 1987, property destruction from CIA/contra attacks totaled $221.6 million; production losses, $984.5 million. Nicaraguan economists estimated monetary losses due to the trade embargo at $254 million and the loss of development potential from the war at $2.5 billion.[14]

### State Assistance in Domestic Policy

In the *domestic policy domain,* state assistance for terrorism occurs when a regime engages in indirect violent repression against an enemy. Under this model, state assistance is characterized by the use of sympathetic proxies in a policy of state-assisted political violence. The use of proxies can occur in an environment in which the proxy violence coincides with violence by state security personnel. Thus, the overall terrorist environment may include both state patronage (direct repression) and state assistance (indirect repression). The East Timor case discussed at the beginning of this chapter is an example of a repressive environment characterized by both patronage and assistance. State assisters typically rationalize policies of indirect repression by adopting official positions that

- blame an adversary group for the breakdown of order and call on "the people" to assist the government in restoring order,
- argue that the proxy violence is evidence of popular patriotic sentiment to suppress a threat to national security,

---

[13]Ibid., p. 327.

[14]Ibid., pp. 344–5.

- call on all parties to cease hostilities but focus blame for the violence on an adversary group, or
- assure everyone that the government is doing everything in its power to restore law and order but that the regime is unable to immediately end the violence.

The **Great Proletarian Cultural Revolution** in China lasted for 3.5 years, from 1965 to 1969.[15] It is a good example of state assistance for an ideologically extremist movement. Launched by national leader Mao Zedong and the Chinese Communist Party Central Committee, the Cultural Revolution was a mass movement that mobilized the young, postrevolution generation. Its purpose was to eliminate so-called revisionist tendencies in society and create a newly indoctrinated revolutionary generation. The period was marked by widespread upheaval and disorder.

In late 1965 through the summer of 1966, factional rivalries within the leadership of China led to a split between Mao's faction and the "old guard" establishment of the Chinese Communist Party. Members of the establishment were labeled revisionists by the Maoist faction. Mao successfully purged these rivals from the Communist Party, the **People's Liberation Army**, and the government bureaucracy. When this occurred, the pro-Mao Central Committee of the Communist Party launched a full-scale nationwide campaign against revisionism. The Great Proletarian Cultural Revolution had begun.

Maoists mobilized millions of young supporters in the **Red Guards**, who waged an ideological struggle to eliminate the **"Four Olds"**: old ideas, old culture, old customs, and old habits.[16] The Red Guards were the principal purveyors of the Cultural Revolution and were strongly encouraged to attack the Four Olds publicly and with great vigor. This led to widespread turmoil. For example, the Red Guards were deeply anti-intellectual and suppressed "revisionist" ideas. They did so by denouncing teachers and professors, destroying books, banning certain music, and forbidding other "incorrect" cultural influences, so that the Chinese education system collapsed. Also, establishment Communist Party leaders were denounced and purged by the Red Guards in public trials (essentially, public show-trials), which led to massive disruption within the ranks of the party. For approximately 18 months, beginning in early 1967, the Red Guards seized control of key government bureaucracies. Because they were completely inexperienced in government operations, the government ceased to operate effectively.

During this period, the Maoists kept the People's Liberation Army in check, allowing the Red Guards to wage the ideological war against the Four Olds. It was not until violent infighting began between factions within the Red Guards that Mao ordered an end to the Cultural Revolution and deployed the People's Liberation Army to restore order. The chaos of the Cultural Revolution was officially interpreted by the Maoists as promoting revolutionary liberation for a new generation.

## ❖ Violence Abroad: Terrorism as Foreign Policy

During the 20th century, military forces were used by states to pursue policies of aggression, conquest, and cultural or ethnic extermination. The military forces have been used repeatedly as

> agents of state violence in the process of invading a foreign country and engaging in killing the enemy. The major wars of the twentieth century are examples of the tremendous levels of violence inflicted by standing armies.[17]

In the latter half of the 20th century—and especially in the latter quarter of the century—many governments used terrorism as an instrument of foreign policy. As a policy option, state-sponsored

---

[15]See Fairbank, John King. *The Great Chinese Revolution: 1800–1985*. New York: Harper & Row, 1987, pp. 316–41.

[16]Ibid., p. 317.

[17]Iadicola and Shupe, *Violence*, p. 269.

terrorism is a logical option because states cannot always deploy conventional armed forces to achieve strategic objectives. As a practical matter for many governments, it is often logistically, politically, or militarily infeasible to directly confront an adversary. For example, few states can hope to be victorious in a conventional military confrontation with the United States—as was learned by Saddam Hussein's well-entrenched Iraqi army in Kuwait during the Gulf War of 1990 to 1991 and U.S.-led invasion in March to April 2003. Terrorism thus becomes a relatively acceptable alternative for states pursuing an aggressive foreign policy. A report from Israel's International Policy Institute for Counter-Terrorism noted that

> state-sponsored terrorism can achieve strategic ends where the use of conventional armed forces is not practical or effective. The high costs of modern warfare, and concern about non-conventional escalation, as well as the danger of defeat and the unwillingness to appear as the aggressor, have turned terrorism into an efficient, convenient, and generally discrete weapon for attaining state interests in the international realm.[18]

Most state sponsors of terrorism attempt to conceal their involvement. This is a practical policy decision because

> if the sponsorship can be hidden, the violence against one's enemy can be safe and unaccountable. The nation that is the target of the terrorism cannot respond, as it might to a direct attack, unless and until it can develop evidence of its enemy's responsibility. Nor can the domestic opposition object to violent adventures for which its government disclaims responsibility.[19]

Therefore, governments use terrorism and other means of confrontational propaganda because, from their point of view, it is an efficacious method to achieve their strategic objectives. As a practical matter for aggressive regimes, state terrorism in the international domain is advantageous in several respects:

- **State terrorism is inexpensive.** The costs of patronage and assistance for terrorist movements are relatively low. Even poor nations can strike at and injure a prosperous adversary through a single spectacular incident.
- **State terrorism has limited consequences.** State assisters who are clever can distance themselves from culpability for a terrorist incident. They can cover their involvement, disclaim responsibility, and thereby escape possible reprisals or other penalties.
- **State terrorism can be successful.** Weaker states can raise the stakes beyond what a stronger adversary is willing to bear. Aggressor states that wish to remain anonymous can likewise successfully destabilize an adversary through the use of a proxy movement. They can do this through one or more spectacular incidents or by assisting in a campaign of terror.

State patrons and assisters overtly and covertly sponsor many subversive causes. These patrons and assisters have available to them a range of policy options that represent different degrees of state backing. For example, Pakistan and India—both nuclear powers—have been engaged in recurrent confrontation in Kashmir, a large mountainous region on the northern border of India and northeast of Pakistan. Conditions are extremely difficult for the combatants, with much of the fighting conducted at very high altitudes in a harsh climate. Nevertheless, Pakistan has used proxies to combat

---

[18]International Policy Institute for Counter-Terrorism, Herzliya, Israel. Website: http://www.ict.org.il/. Quoted in Whittaker, David J., ed. *The Terrorism Reader.* New York: Routledge, 2001, p. 37.

[19]Heymann, Philip B. *Terrorism and America: A Commonsense Strategy for a Democratic Society.* Cambridge, MA: MIT Press, 1998, p. 66.

Indian forces in Kashmir. Pakistan has also deployed Pakistani veterans from Afghanistan to the front lines. Although the fighting in Kashmir has sometimes been conventional in nature, some Pakistani-supported groups have engaged in terrorist attacks against the Indians.[20]

One study listed the following categories of support as comprising the range of policy options available to states:

- **Ideological Support.** The terrorist organization is provided with political, ideological, or religious indoctrination via agents of the supporting state or is trained by institutions of the sponsoring state.
- **Financial Support.** A terrorist organization requires large sums of money, which are sometimes unavailable through its own independent resources.
- **Military Support.** The state supplies the terrorist organization with a broad range of weapons, provides military training, organizes courses for activists, and so on.
- **Operational Support.** The direct provision of . . . false documents, special weapons, safe havens, etc.
- **Initiating Terrorist Attacks.** The state . . . gives specific instructions concerning attacks, it initiates terrorist activities, and it sets their aims.
- **Direct Involvement in Terrorist Attacks.** The state carries out terrorist attacks . . . using agencies from its own intelligence services and security forces, or through people directly responsible to them.[21]

To simplify matters for the purposes of our discussion, we will discuss the following four policy frameworks. They signify the varied qualities of state-sponsored terrorism in the international domain:

- *Moral support:* Politically sympathetic sponsorship
- *Technical support:* Logistically supportive sponsorship
- *Selective participation:* Episode-specific sponsorship
- *Active participation:* Joint operations

Table 4.2 summarizes each of these policy frameworks by placing them within the context of state patronage and state assistance for terrorism.

As the discussion proceeds through the four policy frameworks, it is important to remember that international state terrorism is not limited to "rogue" states. It has also been used as a covert alternative by democracies. For example,

during the 1960s the French Intelligence Agency hired an international mercenary to assassinate the Moroccan leader Ben Barka. The French Intelligence Agency in 1985 [also] bombed Greenpeace's flag ship in New Zealand, killing one member of its crew.[22]

## Moral Support: Politically Sympathetic Sponsorship

**Politically sympathetic sponsorship** occurs when a government openly embraces the main beliefs and principles of a cause. This embrace can range in scope from political agreement with a movement's

---

[20]For further information, see U.S. Department of State, Bureau of Counterterrorism. *Country Reports on Terrorism 2013.* Washington, DC: U.S. Department of State, 2014.

[21]Ganor, Boaz. "Countering State-Sponsored Terrorism." International Policy Institute for Counter-Terrorism, Herzliya, Israel: http://www.ict.org.il/ (accessed October 14, 2002). Quoted in ibid., pp. 268–9.

[22]Iadicola and Shupe, *Violence,* p. 281.

---

**Table 4.2**   State-Sponsored Terrorism: The Foreign Policy Domain

State participation in terrorism in the international domain can involve several types of backing for championed causes and groups. This backing can range in quality from relatively passive political sympathy to aggressive joint operations.

The following table distinguishes state patronage and assistance within four policy frameworks. Each policy framework—a type of state backing—is summarized within the state sponsorship model that distinguishes between patronage and assistance.

| Type of State Backing | Type of Sponsorship | |
|---|---|---|
| | Patronage | Assistance |
| **Politically sympathetic (moral support)** | Overt political support and encouragement for a championed group's motives or tactics | Implicit political support and encouragement for a championed group's motives or tactics |
| | Case: Official Arab governments' political support for the objectives of the PLO | Case: Iran's ideological connection with Lebanon's Hezbollah |
| **Logistically supportive (technical support)** | Direct state support, such as sanctuary, for a championed cause to the group | The provision of state assistance to a group, such as providing *matériel* (military hardware) |
| | Case: Jordanian facilitation of PLO *fedayeen* bases inside Jordan for raids on Israel prior to Black September | Case: Syria's provision of sanctuary, resupply, and other facilities for extremist movements |
| **Episode-specific (selective participation)** | Direct involvement by government personnel for a specific incident or campaign | The provision of state assistance to a group or movement for a specific goal |
| | Case: Yugoslavia's deployment of Yugoslav army units to Bosnia during the Bosnian civil war | Case: Iran's attempted delivery of 50 tons of munitions to the PLO in January 2002 |
| **Joint operations (active participation)** | Operations carried out by government personnel jointly with its proxy | Indirect state support for a proxy using allied personnel |
| | Case: The American–South Vietnamese "Phoenix Program" during the war in Vietnam | Case: Soviet deployment of Cuban troops to Ethiopia |

motives (but not its tactics) to complete support for both motives and tactics. Such support may be delivered either overtly or covertly. Although politically sympathetic governments act as ideological role models for their championed group, such support is often a means for the state to pursue its own national agenda.

Iran's support for several violent movements in the Middle East represents an unambiguous policy of mentorship for groups that are known to have engaged in acts of terrorism. Iran consistently provided politically sympathetic (as well as logistically supportive) sponsorship for several movements, including Lebanon's Hezbollah, Palestine Islamic Jihad, and Hamas.[23] All of these organizations adopted religious revolutionary ideologies—including strong anti-Israel goals—which created a sense of revolutionary common cause among religious hardliners in Iran.

---

[23]See Alfoneh, Ali. "Iran's Suicide Brigades: Terrorism Resurgent." *Middle East Quarterly* 14, no. 1 (Winter 2007).

## Technical Support: Logistically Supportive Sponsorship

**Logistically supportive sponsorship** occurs when a government provides aid and comfort to a championed cause. This can include directly or indirectly facilitating training, arms resupply, safe houses, or other sanctuary for the movement. These options are relatively "passive" types of support that allow state sponsors of terrorism to promote an aggressive foreign policy agenda but at the same time deny their involvement in terrorist incidents.

An excellent case study of logistically supportive sponsorship is the foreign policy adopted by Syria during the regime of Hafez el-Assad. During his rule (February 1971 to June 2000), Syria fought two wars against Israel, strongly backed the Palestinian cause, occupied the Beka'a Valley in Lebanon, and supported the Lebanese militias Amal and Hezbollah. Assad's regime could certainly be aggressive in the international domain, but despite this activism, Syria was rarely linked directly to terrorist incidents. In fact, "there is no evidence that either Syria or Syrian government officials have been directly involved in the planning or execution of international terrorist attacks since 1986."[24]

Assad was very skillful in creating a covert support network for sympathetic terrorist movements in the region. This policy was strictly one of pragmatism. His regime provided safe haven and extensive logistical support for these movements but cleverly maintained official deniability when an incident occurred. This skillful policy was continued by his son, Bashar el-Assad, after Hafez el-Assad's death.

Syria consistently permitted the presence on its soil of several terrorist organizations, such as Palestine Islamic Jihad and the Popular Front for the Liberation of Palestine–General Command. It also facilitated the presence of the Japanese Red Army, the Abu Nidal Organization, Hamas, and others in the Beka'a Valley and Syria proper. Significantly, both Assad regimes permitted the Iranian Revolutionary Guards Corps presence in the Beka'a Valley and established strong links with Lebanon's Hezbollah.[25] All of these groups were very active in targeting Israeli and Western interests in the Middle East and Europe. Despite this support, the Assad regimes were rarely called to account for their activities.

However, Syria's success as a hidden sponsor was severely shaken in late 2004 and 2005.

In September 2004, Israel demonstrated its intolerance for Syria's policy when the Israelis admitted that their agents were responsible for the assassination of a Hamas military operative, Izz el-Deen al-Sheikh Khalil, in a car bomb attack in the Syrian capital of Damascus.[26] In February 2005, the Syrians were implicated in the assassination of Lebanese billionaire and former prime minister Rafik Hariri when he was killed by a massive bomb in downtown Beirut. Hariri had supported Lebanese opposition to the decades-long presence of Syrian troops in Lebanon and its occupation of the Beka'a Valley. Blame for his assassination was immediately attributed to Syrian agents, even though Syrian President Bashar el-Assad sent condolences to Hariri's family, and his government officially condemned the assassination as "an act of terrorism."[27] An international outcry and massive demonstrations in Lebanon led to the withdrawal of Syrian troops from Lebanon in April 2005 after nearly 30 years of occupation.[28] Lebanese elections in 2005 further diminished Syrian influence when voters turned against pro-Syrian politicians and elected an anti-Syrian majority in Lebanon's parliament. Nevertheless, anti-Syrian leaders continued to be targets of violence, as evidenced by the June 2005 assassinations of Lebanese journalist Samir Kassir and politician George Hawi.

---

[24]Hoffman, Bruce. *Inside Terrorism.* New York: Columbia University Press, 1998, p. 195.

[25]For a discussion of Syria's relationship with Hezbollah, see El-Hokayem, Emile. "Hizballah and Syria: Outgrowing the Proxy Relationship." *The Washington Quarterly* 30, no. 2 (2007): 35–52.

[26]Lynfield, Ben. "Israel Sends Syria Tough Message With Hamas Strike." *Christian Science Monitor,* September 27, 2004.

[27]Blanford, Nicholas. "Bomb Strains Syria-Lebanon Ties." *Christian Science Monitor,* February 15, 2005.

[28]"Syrian Troops Leave Lebanese Soil." *BBC News World Edition,* April 26, 2005.

## Selective Participation: Episode-Specific Sponsorship

**Episode-specific sponsorship** refers to government support for a single incident or series of incidents. For this type of operation, the government will provide as much patronage or assistance as is needed for the terrorist episode. Sometimes members of the proxy will carry out the episode, and at other times agents of the state sponsor will participate in the assault.

One example of episode-specific support was the bombing of **Pan Am Flight 103**, which exploded over Lockerbie, Scotland, on December 21, 1988. Two hundred seventy people were killed, including all 259 passengers and crew and 11 persons on the ground. In November 1991, the United States and Great Britain named two Libyan nationals as the masterminds of the bombing. The men—**Abdel Basset al-Megrahi** and **Lamen Khalifa Fhima**—were alleged to be agents of Libya's **Jamahiriya Security Organization (JSO)**. This was a significant allegation because the JSO was repeatedly implicated in numerous acts of terrorism, including killing political rivals abroad, laying mines in the Red Sea, attacking Western interests in Europe, and providing logistical support and training facilities for terrorists from around the world. Libyan leader **Muammar el-Qaddafi** denied any involvement of the Libyan government or its citizens. Both men were prosecuted in Scotland for the bombing; Megrahi was convicted and sentenced to life imprisonment, and Fhima was acquitted. In August 2009, a Scottish judge released Megrahi and returned him to Libya, citing humanitarian reasons because Megrahi was reportedly terminally ill with prostate cancer.

## Active Participation: Joint Operations

**Joint operations** occur when government personnel jointly carry out campaigns in cooperation with a championed proxy. Close collaboration occurs, with the sponsor providing primary operational support for the campaign. Joint operations often occur during a large-scale and ongoing conflict.

An example of joint operations is the **Phoenix Program**, a campaign conducted during the Vietnam War to disrupt and eliminate the administrative effectiveness of the **Viet Cong**, the communist guerrilla movement recruited from among southern Vietnamese. It was a 3-year program that attacked the infrastructure of the Viet Cong. Both American and allied South Vietnamese squads were to wage the campaign by pooling intelligence information and making lists of persons to be targeted. The targets were intended to be hard-core communist agents and administrators, and they were supposed to be arrested rather than assassinated. In essence, the Phoenix Program was to

> kill, jail, or intimidate into surrender the members of the secret Communist-led government the guerrillas had established in the rural eras of the South. The program . . . resulted in the death or imprisonment of tens of thousands of Vietnamese.[29]

The program was, by some accounts, an initial success. The Viet Cong had suffered severe losses during its 1968 Tet offensive. When the Phoenix Program was launched, it could not adequately protect its cadres, so that many were denounced, arrested, and often killed. In theory, this was supposed to be a program to efficiently root out the communist infrastructure. In practice, although the communists were significantly disrupted, many innocent Vietnamese were swept up in the campaign. Also, "despite the fact that the law provided only for the arrest and detention of the suspects, one-third of the 'neutralized agents' were reported dead."[30] Corruption was rampant among South Vietnamese officials, so that they

> saw the glitter of extortionist gold in the Phoenix Program, blackmailing innocents and taking bribes not to arrest those they should have arrested. In the rush to fill quotas they

---

[29]Sheehan, Neil. *A Bright Shining Lie: John Paul Vann and America in Vietnam.* New York: Random House, 1988, p. 18.

[30]FitzGerald, Frances. *Fire in the Lake: The Vietnamese and the Americans in Vietnam.* New York: Vintage, 1972, p. 549.

posthumously elevated lowly guerrillas killed in skirmishes to the status of VC hamlet and village chiefs. . . . Thousands died or vanished into Saigon's prisons.[31]

Estimates of casualties are that 20,585 Viet Cong were killed and 28,000 captured. It is likely that many of those killed were not Viet Cong members.[32] In the end, the Viet Cong were badly hurt but not eliminated. Unfortunately for the Viet Cong's status as an independent fighting force, after Tet and the Phoenix Program, the North Vietnamese army became the predominant communist fighting force in the South.

Thus, terrorism and sponsorship for subversive movements are methods of statecraft that have been adopted by many types of governments, ranging from stable democracies to aggressive and revolutionary regimes. It is certainly true that democracies are less likely to engage in this type of behavior than are aggressively authoritarian states. However, as suggested by the cases of the Phoenix Program and French intelligence operations, democracies have been known to resort to terrorist methods when operating within certain security or political environments.

Chapter Perspective 4.1 discusses the case of the officially defined threat posed by the authoritarian government of **Saddam Hussein** that precipitated the U.S.-led invasion of Iraq in 2003.

❖ **Photo 4.2**

Scott Peterson/Getty Images News/Getty Images

A typical propaganda portrait commissioned by Iraqi dictator Saddam Hussein. Although Hussein had minimal (if any) ties to Islamist groups such as Al-Qa'ida, his regime did provide support and safe haven to a number of wanted nationalist terrorists such as Abu Nidal.

## CHAPTER PERSPECTIVE 4.1: Calculation or Miscalculation?

### The Threat From Weapons of Mass Destruction and the Iraq Case

One of the most disturbing scenarios involving state-sponsored terrorism is the delivery of weapons of mass destruction (WMDs) to motivated terrorists by an aggressive authoritarian regime. This scenario was the underlying rationale given for the March 2003 invasion of Iraq by the United States and several allies.

In January 2002, U.S. President George W. Bush identified Iraq, Iran, and North Korea as the "**axis of evil**" and promised that the United States "will not permit the world's most dangerous regimes to threaten us with the world's most destructive weapons." In June 2002, President Bush announced during a speech at the U.S. Military Academy at West Point that the United States would engage in preemptive warfare if necessary.

Citing Iraq's known possession of weapons of mass destruction in the recent past and its alleged ties to international terrorist networks, President Bush informed the United Nations in September 2002 that the United States would unilaterally move against Iraq if the UN did not certify that Iraq no longer possessed WMDs. Congress authorized an attack on Iraq in October 2002. UN weapons inspectors returned to Iraq in November 2002. After a 3-month military buildup, Iraq was attacked on March 20, 2003, and Baghdad fell to U.S. troops on April 9, 2003.

The Bush administration had repeatedly argued that Iraq still possessed a significant arsenal of WMDs at the time of the invasion, that Saddam Hussein's regime had close ties to terrorist groups, and that a preemptive war was necessary to prevent the delivery of these weapons to Al-Qa'ida or another network. Although many experts discounted links between Hussein's regime and religious terrorists, it was widely expected that WMDs would be found. Iraq was known to have used chemical weapons against Iranian troops during the Iran–Iraq War of

---

[31]Ibid., p. 733.

[32]Schlagheck, Donna M. "The Superpowers, Foreign Policy, and Terrorism." In *International Terrorism: Characteristics, Causes, Controls,* edited by Charles W. Kegley. New York: St. Martin's, 1990, p. 176.

1980 to 1988 and against Iraqi **Kurds** during the **Anfal Campaign** of 1987.

In actuality, UN inspectors identified no WMDs prior to the 2003 invasion; nor were WMDs found by U.S. officials during the occupation of Iraq. Also, little evidence was uncovered to substantiate allegations of strong ties between Hussein's Iraq and Al-Qa'ida or similar networks. The search for WMDs ended in December 2004, and an inspection report submitted to Congress by U.S. weapons hunter Charles A. Duelfer essentially "contradicted nearly every prewar assertion about Iraq made by Bush administration officials."[a]

Policy makers and experts bear two fundamental questions for critical analysis and debate:

- Did the reasons given for the invasion reflect a plausible threat scenario?
- Was the invasion a well-crafted policy option centered on credible political, military, and intelligence calculations?

**Note**

a. Linzer, Dafna. "Search for Banned Arms in Iraq Ended Last Month." *Washington Post,* January 12, 2005.

## ❖ Violence at Home: Terrorism as Domestic Policy

State terrorism as domestic policy refers to the state's politically motivated application of force inside its own borders. The state's military, law enforcement, and other security institutions are used to suppress perceived threats; these institutions can also be supplemented with assistance from unofficial **paramilitaries** and **death squads**. The purpose of domestically focused terrorism is to demonstrate the supreme power of the government and to intimidate or eliminate the opposition. In environments in which the central government perceives its authority to be seriously threatened, this use of force can be quite extreme.

An example of the latter environment occurred in South Africa during the final years of **apartheid**, the system of racial separation. When confronted by a combination of antiapartheid reformist agitation, mass unrest, and terrorist attacks, the South African government began a covert campaign to root out antiapartheid leaders and supporters. This included government support for the Zulu-based **Inkatha Freedom Party** in its violence against the multiethnic and multiracial **African National Congress (ANC)**. The South African government also assigned security officers to command death squads called **Askaris**, who assassinated ANC members both inside South Africa and in neighboring countries:

These officially sanctioned groups targeted in particular African National Congress members suspected of being dissidents or sympathizers, both black and white. The African National Congress claims that police have been involved in the killings of more than 11,000 people [between 1990 and 1994].[33]

### Legitimizing State Authority

Every type of regime seeks to legitimize its authority and maintain its conception of social order. Governmental legitimization can be enforced in many ways and often depends on the nature of the political environment that exists at a particular point in a nation's history. Some governments legitimize their authority through intimidation and force of arms.

[33]Ibid., p. 267.

Violent state repression against reformers and revolutionaries has been a common occurrence that has been justified by rulers since the dawn of the nation-state. For example, during Europe's Age of Absolutism (at its height in the 17th century), each monarchy's legitimacy was indisputable, and deviations from the law were harshly punished as offenses against the authority of the monarch. In the modern era, repression has been a frequent instrument of domestic policy. As a policy option, state-sponsored domestic terrorism and other forms of coercion have been used to quell dissent, restore order, eliminate political opponents, and scapegoat demographic populations.

State authority is legitimized and enforced with varying degrees of restraint. Stable democracies with strong constitutional traditions will usually enforce state authority with measured restraint. Regimes with weak constitutional traditions, or those that are in a period of national crisis, will often enforce state authority with little or no restraint. Examples of state domestic authority can be summarized as follows:

- *Democracy* is a system of elected government wherein authority is theoretically delegated from the people to elected leaders. Under this model, a strong constitution grants authority for elected leaders to govern the people and manage the affairs of government. The power of the state is clearly delimited.

- *Authoritarianism* is a system of government in which authority and power emanate from the state and are not delegated from the people to elected leaders. Law, order, and state authority are emphasized. Authoritarian regimes can have elected leaders, but they have authoritarian power and often rule for indefinite periods of time. Constitutions do not have enough authority to prohibit abuses by the state.

- *Totalitarianism* is a system of total governmental regulation. All national authority originates from the government, which enforces its own vision of an ordered society.

| Table 4.3 | State Domestic Authority |
|---|---|

Several models can be constructed that illustrate the manner in which state authority is imposed and the degree of coercion that is used to enforce governmental authority. Sources of state authority differ depending on which model of authority characterizes each regime.

| Models of State Authority | Sources of State Authority | | Examples of Authority Models |
|---|---|---|---|
| | *Legitimization of Authority* | *Center of Authority* | |
| **Democracy** | Secondary role of security institutions; strong constitution and rule of law | Government with constrained authority | United States Western Europe Japan |
| **Authoritarianism** | Central role of official security institutions; strong constitution possible | Government with minimally constrained authority | Egypt Myanmar (Burma) Syria |
| **Totalitarianism** | Central role of official security institutions | Government with unconstrained authority | China North Korea Taliban Regime |
| **Crazy states** | Central roles of official and unofficial security institutions | Government with unconstrained authority, or unconstrained paramilitaries, or both | Liberia Somalia Uganda under Idi Amin |

- *Crazy states*[34] are those whose behavior is not rational; in such states, the people live at the whim of the regime or a dominant group. Some **crazy states** have little or no central authority and are ravaged by warlords or militias. Other crazy states have capricious, impulsive, and violent regimes in power that act out with impunity.

Table 4.3 illustrates these models of domestic state authority by summarizing sources of state authority and giving examples of these environments.

## State Domestic Authority

The following discussion is a domestic state terrorist model adapted from one originally designed by Peter C. Sederberg.[35] It defines and differentiates broad categories of domestic state terrorism

**Table 4.4    State-Sponsored Terrorism: The Domestic Policy Domain**

State participation in terrorism in the domestic domain can involve several types of support for championed causes and groups. This support can range in quality from relatively passive encouragement of vigilante political violence to unrestrained genocidal violence.
  The following table distinguishes state patronage and assistance within four policy frameworks.

| Type of State Support | Type of Sponsorship | |
| --- | --- | --- |
| | Patronage | Assistance |
| **Vigilante** | Members of the security forces unofficially participate in the repression of undesirables. | Members of the security forces unofficially provide support for the repression of undesirables. |
| | Case: Social cleansing in Colombia by security personnel | Case: Social cleansing in Colombia by civilian vigilante groups and paramilitaries |
| **Overt official** | The state openly deploys its security forces to violently assert its authority. | The state openly provides support for progovernment political violence. |
| | Case: China's suppression of the **Tiananmen Square** demonstrations | Case: Indonesian army's support for anti-independence gangs in East Timor |
| **Covert official** | The state clandestinely uses its security forces to violently assert its authority. | The state clandestinely provides support for progovernment political violence. |
| | Case: South Africa's assignment of security personnel to eliminate ANC members and supporters | Case: South African security agencies' support for anti-ANC Askari death squads |
| **Genocidal** | The resources of the state are deployed to eliminate or culturally suppress a people, religion, or other demographic group. | The state provides support for the elimination or cultural suppression of a people, religion, or other demographic group. |
| | Case: Iraq's anti-Kurd Anfal Campaign | Case: Anti-Semitic pogroms by the Black Hundreds in Czarist Russia |

[34]Dror, Yehezkel. *Crazy States: A Counterconventional Strategic Problem.* New York: Kraus, Milwood, 1980.

[35]Sederberg, *Terrorist Myths.*

that are useful for critically analyzing the motives and behaviors of terrorist regimes. They signify the varied qualities of state-sponsored terrorism directed against perceived domestic enemies:

- *Unofficial repression:* Vigilante domestic state terrorism
- *Repression as policy:* Official domestic state terrorism
- *Mass repression:* Genocidal domestic state terrorism

Table 4.4 summarizes these policy frameworks by placing them within the context of state patronage and state assistance for terrorism.

## Unofficial Repression: Vigilante Domestic State Terrorism

Vigilante terrorism is political violence that is perpetrated by nongovernmental groups and individuals. These groups can receive unofficial support from agents of the state.

Why do regimes encourage vigilante violence? What are the benefits of such support? From the perspective of the state, what are the values that are being safeguarded by the vigilantes? Vigilante violence committed on behalf of a regime is motivated by the perceived need to defend a demographic group or cultural establishment. The overall goal of **vigilante state terrorism** is to violently preserve the preferred order. In a classic terrorist rationalization process, the end of an orderly society justifies the means of extreme violence.

The vigilante terrorists, sometimes alongside members of the state security establishment, unofficially wage a violent suppression campaign against an adversarial group or movement. This type of suppression campaign occurs when civilians and members of the state's security forces perceive that the state is threatened. This perception can occur in warlike environments or when an established order is challenged by an alternative social movement or ideology. Civilians and members of the security establishment who participate in vigilante violence adhere to a code of duty and behavior similar to those discussed in Chapter 3, so that they believe their actions are absolutely justifiable.

Nongovernmental vigilantes often organize themselves into paramilitaries and operate as death squads. Death squads have committed many documented massacres and atrocities, including assassinations, massacres, disappearances, and random terrorist attacks. One incident reported by Amnesty International illustrates the style of terrorism perpetrated by paramilitaries:

In February [2000], 200 paramilitary gunmen raided the village of El Salado, Bolivar department [Colombia], killing 36 people, including a six-year-old child. Many victims were tied to a table in the village sports field and subjected to torture, including rape, before being stabbed or shot dead. Others were killed in the village church. During the three-day attack, military and police units stationed nearby made no effort to intervene.[36]

The case of Latin American death squads is discussed further below.

Interestingly, some scholars have linked paramilitary activity in Latin America to U.S. training programs during its Cold War rivalry with the Soviet Union. In this regard, it has been argued that

the death squad made its appearance in ten different Latin America countries in the 1960s and 1970s, all of them recipients of U.S. military and police aid and training, which stressed counterinsurgency and unconventional warfare against subversion from the Kennedy Era onward. In a number of countries . . . death squads appeared immediately following a major U.S. intervention.[37]

---

[36]Amnesty International. "Colombia." In *Amnesty International Report 2001*. London: Amnesty International Secretariat, 2001.

[37]Herman, Edward, and Gerry O'Sullivan. *The Terrorism Industry.* New York: Pantheon, 1989, p. 37. Quoted in Iadicola and Shupe, *Violence,* p. 271.

## Repression as Policy: Official Domestic State Terrorism

State-sponsored repression and political violence were practiced regularly during the 20th century. Many regimes deliberately adopted domestic terrorism as a matter of official policy, and directives ordering government operatives to engage in violent domestic repression frequently originated with ranking government officials.

Why do regimes resort to official policies of domestic violence? What are the benefits of such programs? From the perspective of the state, who are the people that deserve this kind of violent repression? The goals of **official state terrorism** are to preserve an existing order and to maintain state authority through demonstrations of state power. Regimes that officially selected violent repression as a policy choice rationalized their behavior as a legitimate method to protect the state from an internal threat. Two manifestations of official state terrorism in the domestic domain must be distinguished: overt and covert official state terrorism.

*Overt official state terrorism* refers to the visible application of state-sponsored political violence. It is a policy of unconcealed and explicit repression directed against a domestic enemy. Overt official terrorism has been commonly practiced in totalitarian societies, such as Stalinist Russia, Nazi Germany, Khmer Rouge Cambodia, and Taliban Afghanistan. In the modern era, governments continue to use extreme measures to suppress domestic challenges to their authority. For example, in 2013 the Syrian government used chemical weapons to attack regions held by insurgent forces near Damascus. Approximately 1,400 people were killed; most were civilians, including hundreds of children.

*Covert official state terrorism* refers to the secretive application of state-sponsored political violence. In contrast to overt state terrorism, it is a policy of concealed and implicit repression directed against a domestic enemy. Covert official terrorism has been commonly practiced in countries with extensive secret police services, such as President Hafez el-Assad's Syria, President Saddam Hussein's Iraq, General Augusto Pinochet's Chile, and Argentina during the Dirty War. The case of **Shah Mohammad Reza Pahlavi**'s Iran further illustrates how covert official terrorism is implemented.

Iran during the regime of Shah Mohammad Reza Pahlavi is a model for the convergence of state-sponsored policies of overt and covert terrorism. The shah, who ruled Iran from 1953 to 1979, considered himself to be the *Shahanshah,* or King of Kings. His reign hearkened back to the ancient kings of Persia, his authority was unquestioned, and dissent was impermissible. The shah regularly used his army and security services to suppress dissidents. His secret police, **SAVAK**, were particularly efficient and ruthless. The army was used to quell demonstrations and other public forms of dissent, frequently firing on protestors to

Popperfoto/Getty Images

❖ **Photo 4.3**

Soviet leader Joseph Stalin poses with a Russian family in a propaganda photograph. Stalin's totalitarian regime brutally purged and killed many thousands of ideological rivals and sent millions of members of ethnonational groups into internal exile. Millions of others died during famines and in work camps.

disperse crowds. In one incident in 1963, as many as 6,000 people were killed by the army and SAVAK.[38] The shah strongly relied on SAVAK's extensive intelligence network to root out potential dissidents and opposition groups. It was permitted to imprison people with virtual impunity, with an estimated annual average of political prisoners reaching 100,000.[39] SAVAK was extremely harsh toward persons detained in its own special prisons, and its torture methods were renowned for their brutality. Despite the shah's extensive system of repression, he could not defeat a popular uprising in 1978, notwithstanding the deaths of thousands of Iranians at the hands of the army and SAVAK. Shah Pahlavi was deposed and forced into exile in 1979 after an Islamic revolution inspired by the **Ayatollah Ruhollah Khomeini**.

Official state terrorism is not always directed against subversive elements. It is sometimes conducted to "cleanse" society of an undesirable social group. These groups are perceived to be purveyors of a decadent lifestyle or immoral values, or are seen as otherwise unproductive drains on society. Chapter Perspective 4.2 discusses how extremist regimes have solved this problem by engaging in so-called **social cleansing** and **ethnic cleansing**.

---

[38]Iadicola and Shupe, *Violence,* p. 271.

[39]Ibid.

## CHAPTER PERSPECTIVE 4.2: Cleansing Society

Among the euphemisms used by propagandists to characterize state-initiated domestic terrorism, perhaps the most commonly applied term is that of "cleansing" society. Conceptually, an image is constructed that depicts an undesirable group as little more than a virus or bacterium that has poisoned society. The removal of this group is considered to be a necessary remedy for the survival of the existing social order.

This imagery has been invoked repeatedly by extremist regimes. An example from Fascist Italy illustrates this point:

"Terror? Never," Mussolini insisted, demurely dismissing such intimidation as "simply . . . social hygiene, taking those individuals out of circulation like a doctor would take out a bacillus."[a]

For society to solve its problems, the bacterium represented by the group must be removed. Acceptance of this characterization makes domestic terrorism palatable to many extremist regimes. The following "cleansing" programs include examples of recent uses of this imagery.

### Social Cleansing

*Social cleansing* refers to the elimination of undesirable social elements. These undesirable elements are considered to be blights on society and can include street children, prostitutes, drug addicts, criminals, homeless people, transvestites, and homosexuals. In Colombia, undesirable social elements are commonly referred to as *disposables*.

Social cleansing has occurred in a number of countries. The term was probably coined in Latin America, where social cleansing took on the attributes of vigilante state domestic terrorism in Brazil, Guatemala, Colombia, and elsewhere. Participants in cleansing campaigns have included members of the police and death squads. In societies where social cleansing has occurred, the "disposables" have been killed, beaten, and violently intimidated.

### Ethnic Cleansing

The term *ethnic cleansing* was coined during the war in Bosnia in the former Yugoslavia. It refers to the expulsion of an ethnonational group from a geographic region as a means to create an ethnically "pure" society. During the war in Bosnia, Serb soldiers and paramilitaries initiated a cycle of ethnic cleansing. They officially and systematically expelled, killed, raped, and otherwise intimidated Bosnian Muslims to create Serb-only districts. The most intensive campaigns of Serb-initiated ethnic cleansing in Bosnia occurred in 1992 and 1993. As the war progressed, Croats and Bosnians also engaged in ethnic cleansing, so that there were periods during the war in which all three groups "cleansed" areas populated by members of the other groups.

Since the war in Bosnia, the term has become widely used to describe present and past campaigns to systematically and violently remove ethnonational groups from geographic regions.

a. Hoffman, Bruce. *Inside Terrorism*. New York: Columbia University Press, 1998. p. 24. Quoting Laqueur, Walter. *The Age of Terrorism*. Boston: Little, Brown, 1987, p. 66.

## Mass Repression: Genocidal Domestic State Terrorism

The word *genocide* was first used by Raphael Lemkin in 1943 and first appeared in print in his influential book *Axis Rule in Occupied Europe,* published in 1944.[40] It is derived from the Greek word *genos,* meaning race or tribe, and the Latin-derived suffix *cide,* meaning killing. Genocide is, first and foremost, generally defined as the elimination of a group as a matter of state policy, or communal dissident violence by one group against another.

[40]Lemkin, Raphael. *Axis Rule in Occupied Europe: Laws of Occupation, Analysis of Government, Proposals for Redress.* Washington, DC: Carnegie Endowment for International Peace, 1944. Chapter 9 of Lemkin's book discussed genocide in detail.

Whether perpetrated at the state or communal level, genocide is considered by the world community to be an unacceptable social policy and an immoral application of force. Genocide has been regarded as a crime under international law since 1946, when the General Assembly of the United Nations adopted Resolution 96(I). In 1948, the General Assembly adopted the Convention on the Prevention and Punishment of the Crime of Genocide. Under Article 2 of the convention, genocide is formally defined as follows:

Any of the following acts committed with intent to destroy, in whole or in part, a national, ethnic, racial or religious group, such as:

a. Killing members of the group;
b. Causing serious bodily or mental harm to members of the group;
c. Deliberately inflicting on the group conditions of life calculated to bring about its physical destruction in whole or in part;
d. Imposing measures intended to prevent births within the group;
e. Forcibly transferring children of the group to another group.[41]

Why do regimes resort to genocidal policies against their fellow domestic civilians? What are the benefits to a regime of eliminating a particular group? From the perspective of the state, why do some groups deserve to be eliminated? One practical reason for terrorist regimes is that scapegoating a defined enemy is a useful strategy to rally the nation behind the ruling government. The goal is to enhance the authority and legitimacy of the regime by targeting internal enemies for genocidal violence.

States have available to them, and frequently marshal, an enormous amount of resources for use against an undesired group. These resources can include the military, security services, civilian paramilitaries, legal systems, private industry, social institutions, and propaganda resources. When the decision is made to eliminate or culturally destroy a group, state resources can be brought to bear with devastating efficiency.

Jehangir Gazdar/Woodfin Camp/ TIME & LIFE Images/Getty Images

❖ **Photo 4.4**

The killing fields. Skulls are displayed of victims of Cambodia's genocidal Khmer Rouge regime. The Khmer Rouge waged a campaign of domestic terrorism that claimed the lives of at least one million Cambodians.

**Genocidal state terrorism** occurs, then, when the resources of a nation are mobilized to eliminate a targeted group. The group can be a cultural minority—such as a racial, religious, or ethnic population—or the group can be a designated segment of society—such as believers in a banned ideology or a socioeconomically unacceptable group. When ideological or socioeconomic groups are singled out for elimination, the resulting terrorist environment is one in which members of the same ethnic or religious group commit genocide against fellow members, a practice that is known as **auto-genocide** (self-genocide).

Unlike vigilante and official state terrorism, the scale of violence during campaigns of state-sponsored genocidal terrorism can be virtually unlimited. In some cases, no check at all is placed on the use of violence against an adversary group, with the result that the targeted group may suffer casualties in the many thousands or millions.

One important distinction must be understood: The elimination of a group does not necessarily require its physical extermination. The state's goal might also be to destroy a culture. This can be accomplished through forced population removals or prohibitions against practicing religious, linguistic, or other measures of cultural identification. In fact, the original deliberations that crafted the legal definition of genocide recognized that genocide was much more than physical extermination. Because of the policies of the Nazi regime, it was considered necessary to design a new conceptual category for certain types of state-sponsored practices. It was agreed that

---

[41]Quoted in von Glahn, Gerhard. *Law Among Nations: An Introduction to Public International Law.* 5th ed. New York: Macmillan, 1986, pp. 303–4.

genocide . . . went beyond the killing of people: it covered such related acts as the practice of [forced] abortion, sterilization, artificial infection, the working of people to death in special labor camps, and the separation of families or of sexes in order to depopulate specific areas. . . . These activities . . . had to be regarded as criminal in intent as well as in execution.[42]

Most cases of state genocide are not examples of a precipitous policy whereby the security services or paramilitaries are suddenly unleashed against a targeted group. More commonly, the methodology and purpose behind genocidal policies require a coordinated series of events, perhaps in phases over months or years. During these phases, cultural or other measures of identification can be suppressed in a number of ways—perhaps with the ultimate goal of physical extermination.

Table 4.5 identifies several examples of state-sponsored genocidal campaigns directed against domestic groups.

## Case in Point: Death Squads in Latin America

State terrorism in Latin America has come primarily from two sources: government security forces and right-wing paramilitaries—commonly called "death squads" (*esquadrón muerte*). Death squads have been defined as

| Table 4.5 | State-Initiated Genocide |
| --- | --- |

Genocidal state terrorism is directed against populations within countries that the state declares to be undesirable. When this occurs, governments and extremist regimes have designed policies of elimination that can include cultural destruction, mass resettlement, violent intimidation, or complete extermination. Historically, state-initiated genocide is not an uncommon policy selection.

As summarized in the following table, state-initiated genocide has occurred in every region of the world.

| Country | Activity Profile | | |
| --- | --- | --- | --- |
| | Incident | Target Group | Outcome |
| **Rwanda** | Rwandan President Habyarimana assassinated | Tutsis and Hutu moderates | Genocidal violence; approximately 500,000 people killed by Rwandan army and Hutu militants |
| **Cambodia** | Victory on the battlefield by the Khmer Rouge; imposition of a new regime | City dwellers, educated people, upper class, Buddhists, fellow Khmer Rouge | The Killing Fields; up to 2 million deaths |
| **Bosnia** | The breakup of Yugoslavia and Serb resistance to the declarations of independence by Slovenia, Croatia, and Bosnia | Muslims living in territory claimed by Serbs | Ethnic cleansing assisted by Serbia, population removals, massacres, systematic rape, and cultural destruction |
| **Germany** | Racially motivated genocide by the Nazi regime | German Jews | The Holocaust; deaths of most of Germany's Jewish population |
| **United States** | Conquering the frontier and 19th-century frontier wars | Native Americans | Annihilation of some tribes; resettlement of others on reservations |

---

[42]Ibid., p. 303.

clandestine and usually irregular organizations, often paramilitary in nature, which carry out extrajudicial executions and other violent acts (torture, rape, arson, bombing, etc.) against clearly defined individuals or groups of people. . . . [I]n the rare case where an insurgent group forms them, death squads operate with the overt support, complicity, or acquiescence of government, or at least some parts of it.[43]

Government-initiated and paramilitary sources of right-wing terrorism are not clearly separable because there is frequently some degree of linkage between the two. Death squads have historically been covertly sanctioned by governments or agents of the government, and government personnel have covertly operated with rightist terrorists. Death squads have had a measure of independence, but connections with government security apparatuses have been repeatedly discovered.

Case studies from four countries are explored below. They summarize the environments that gave rise to paramilitary activity, as well as types of linkages between governments and death squads.

### Colombia

Colombia is a country with a long history of communal strife, military coups, and revolutions. During the latter decades of the 20th century, it became a country beset by armed insurgencies on the left, paramilitary death squads on the right, a weak central government, and the problems of being the world's principal supplier of cocaine. Colombia has been home to death squads since Marxist guerrillas began attacking the interests of rich property owners—and the owners themselves—in the 1960s and 1970s. Guerrillas also extorted money from the owners. In the 1980s, wealthy landowners hired private security units to defend their landholdings. This protective mission became more aggressive as Marxist rebellion spread.

***Colombian Death Squads.*** Security units hired by wealthy landowners gradually began operating as counterinsurgency paramilitaries, often fighting in units numbering several hundred. The paramilitaries also engaged in what can only be described as terrorist attacks against suspected Marxists and their sympathizers. It was not uncommon for these squads to commit atrocities to frighten peasants from helping members of rebel groups. The progression from security units to right-wing death squads included the use of these groups not only by wealthy property owners but also by *narcotraficantes* (drug traffickers). The *narcotraficantes* wished to pacify drug-producing regions by driving away Marxist guerrillas and intimidating local residents. The most prominent paramilitary was the **United Self-Defense Forces of Colombia (AUC)**. Colombian security forces evidently encouraged death squad activity by the AUC and other groups, although the relationship was not entirely cooperative. Under government pressure, the AUC agreed to a ceremonial stand-down and disarmament in July 2005.

### Argentina

Early in the 20th century, Argentina was a dynamic country with a thriving economy. Culturally, it has long been a Europeanized country, with significant waves of immigration from Italy, the United Kingdom, Germany, and elsewhere. In the 1960s and 1970s, Argentina was beleaguered by an unstable economy, political turmoil, and an ever-weakening central government. This eventually led to a military coup d'état in 1976.

***Argentine Anticommunist Alliance.*** Prior to the 1976 coup d'état, Jose Lopez Rega, an adviser to President Juan Peron, organized the **Argentine Anticommunist Alliance (Triple-A)**. Rega was a right-wing terrorist and arguably a Nazi-style fascist. The death squad was responsible for numerous acts of violence against leftists, human rights organizers, students, and others. Some of its clandestine operatives were members of the Argentine security apparatus. After the 1976 coup and the institutionalization of Argentina's Dirty War, Triple-A was integrated into the Argentine state terrorist apparatus.

---

[43]Campbell, Bruce B. "Death Squads: Definition, Problems, and Historical Context." In *Death Squads in Global Perspective: Murder With Deniability,* edited by Bruce B. Campbell and Arthur D. Brenner. New York: St. Martin's, 2000, pp. 1–2.

❖ **Photo 4.5**

The Guardia on patrol. Salvadoran troops patrol a village during the brutal civil war in the 1980s. The Guardia and rightist death squads were responsible for thousands of civilian deaths.

Max Schneider/Hulton Archive/Getty Images

## El Salvador

Business executives and wealthy landowners have traditionally built close ties to security and intelligence agencies in El Salvador. The National Guard (Guardia Nacional), founded in 1910, was used repeatedly to suppress peasant organizations. During the 1970s, three leftist guerrilla movements were organized, and by 1980, at least five groups were operational. They formed the Farabundo Martí National Liberation Front. At the same time, student and labor activism spread. The right wing responded violently.

**ORDEN.** During the late 1960s, army general José Alberto Medrano organized a paramilitary counterinsurgency group known as ORDEN ("Order"). Originally affiliated with the National Guard, ORDEN was used to root out unionists, student activists, communists, and other leftists. It evolved into a ruthless death squad. During the Salvadoran civil war, "the military and right-wing terrorists killed approximately 30,000 civilians to stop spreading revolution"[44] in 1980 and 1981 alone. On March 24, 1980, Catholic Archbishop Oscar Romero was assassinated by right-wing terrorists while celebrating mass.

### Honduras

During the late 1970s, attempted land reforms had been only marginally successful, and unrest spread among poor peasants. Some leftists organized themselves into revolutionary groups, including the Morazan Honduran Liberation Front. The army, which had positioned itself to be the true center of power, encouraged a right-wing reaction against leftists. It also supported the U.S.-backed Nicaraguan counterrevolutionary guerrillas based in Honduras. Right-wing paramilitaries were formed and supported by the government. During the 1980s, hundreds of civilians were killed by these death squads. One unit, **Battalion 3-16**, had been directly organized by the Honduran military.

| Table 4.6 | Vigilante Terrorism: The Case of the Paramilitaries |
| --- | --- |

Paramilitaries are armed nongovernmental groups or gangs. Progovernment paramilitaries generally consider themselves to be the defenders of an established order that is under attack from a dangerously subversive counterorder. Some paramilitaries are well armed and receive direct official support from government personnel. Others are semi-independent vigilante groups.

Reactionary right-wing paramilitaries in Latin America have been implicated in numerous atrocities, including massacres and assassinations. The following table summarizes several of these groups.

| Paramilitary Group | Benefactor | Target |
| --- | --- | --- |
| **United Self-Defense Groups (AUC)** | Colombian security services, Colombian landholders | Marxist FARC rebels and suspected supporters |
| **Civil Patrols (CAP)** | Guatemalan security services, Guatemalan landholders | Marxist rebels and suspected supporters |
| **Chiapas Paramilitaries** | Possibly Mexican security force members; Mexican landholders | Zapatistas and suspected supporters |
| **Argentine Anti-Communist Alliance (Triple-A)** | Argentine security services | Leftists |

[44]LaFeber, Walter. *Inevitable Revolutions: The United States in Central America.* New York: Norton, 1984, p. 10.

Table 4.6 identifies several paramilitaries that have operated in Latin America with the support of government security services.

# ❖ The Problem of Accountability: Monitoring State Terrorism

The incidence of state-sponsored terrorism is monitored by public and private organizations. These organizations compile data and publish annual reports on domestic and international state terrorism. They also perform a "watchdog" function and are resources for collecting data on the characteristics of state terrorism. These agencies provide useful standards for identifying and defining terrorist behavior by governments.

In the *international policy domain,* the U.S. Department of State regularly compiles a list of Designated State Sponsors of Terrorism. This list reports official U.S. designations of specified regimes, and it includes an annual list of countries that the Department of State defines as state terrorist sponsors. The following comments from the Department of State's official *Country Reports on Terrorism 2012* summarize the status of designated countries on the list.[45]

*Iran* was again considered by the State Department to remain "the most active state sponsor of terrorism" from previous years and also "remained the principal supporter of groups that are implacably opposed to the Middle East Peace Process." According to the State Department, Iran

> increased its terrorist-related activity, including attacks or attempted attacks in India, Thailand, Georgia, and Kenya. Iran provided financial, material, and logistical support for terrorist and militant groups in the Middle East and Central Asia. Iran used the Islamic Revolutionary Guard Corps–Qods Force (IRGC-QF) and militant groups to implement foreign policy goals, provide cover for intelligence operations, and stir up instability in the Middle East."[46]

In addition, Iran's Islamic Revolutionary Guard Corps and Ministry of Intelligence and Security are "the regime's primary mechanism for cultivating and supporting terrorists abroad."

*Syria* "continued its political support to a variety of terrorist groups affecting the stability of the region and beyond, even amid significant internal unrest. Syria provided political and weapons support to Lebanese Hizballah and continued to allow Iran to re-arm the terrorist organization." In addition, "President Assad continued to express public support for Palestinian terrorist groups as elements of the resistance against Israel. Damascus provided safe haven in Syria for exiled individuals, although the Palestinian groups were subject to the same level of insecurity as the rest of the Syrian population and fighting has fractured their alliances with the Syrian regime."

*Cuba* "was trying to distance itself from Basque Fatherland and Liberty (ETA) members living on the island by employing tactics such as not providing services including travel documents to some of them. The Government of Cuba continued to provide safe haven to approximately two dozen ETA members." Cuba also "continued to harbor fugitives wanted in the United States. The Cuban government also provided support such as housing, food ration books, and medical care for these individuals."

Regarding *Sudan,* though still on the designated list, "Sudanese officials regularly discussed counterterrorism issues with U.S. counterparts in 2012 and were generally responsive to international community concerns about counterterrorism efforts. Sudan remained a cooperative counterterrorism partner on certain issues, including al-Qa'ida (AQ)–linked terrorism, and the outlook

---

[45]U.S. Department of State, Office of the Coordinator for Counterterrorism. *Country Reports on Terrorism 2013.* Washington, DC: U.S. Department of State, 2014.

[46]Ibid.

for continued cooperation on those issues remained somewhat positive." However, "hard-line Sudanese officials continued to express resentment and distrust over actions by the United States and questioned the benefits of continued cooperation. Their assessment reflected disappointment that Sudan's cooperation on counterterrorism, as well as the Sudanese government's decision to allow for the successful referendum on Southern independence leading to an independent Republic of South Sudan in July 2011, have not resulted in Sudan's removal from the list of state sponsors of terrorism."

The State Department's list includes countries that have significantly reduced their involvement in terrorism, such as Sudan and Cuba. However, the list of designated sponsors is dynamic and the designation is sometimes removed, as indicated by the examples of North Korea, Libya, and Iraq:

- *North Korea* had been a perennial member on the list. For example, North Korea was at one time quite active in attacking South Korean interests. In November 1987, North Korean operatives destroyed **Korean Airlines Flight 858**, which exploded over Myanmar (Burma). The North Korean government has since renounced its sponsorship of terrorism and was removed from the list in 2008.

- *Libya,* which had been on the list for 27 years, was removed in 2006. Western nations and international organizations eased sanctions when Libya announced in December 2003 that it would destroy weapons of mass destruction and certain missiles. Libya had engaged in documented cases of international terrorism, both directly and through the use of proxies. However, Libya's renunciation of support for dissident groups and its cooperation with the world community during the 2000s led to its removal from the list in 2006.

- *Iraq,* which had also been perennially designated on the list of state sponsors, was removed in October 2004 in the aftermath of the U.S.-led invasion and overthrow of the regime of Saddam Hussein.

In the *domestic policy domain,* several private agencies monitor political abuses by governments and have catalogued examples of state-sponsored domestic terrorism. These organizations usually refer to these abuses as "human rights violations." One such group, **Human Rights Watch**, was founded in 1978.[47] Human Rights Watch actively monitors the status of human rights throughout the world and maintains field offices in closely monitored countries. It reports in detail on government-sponsored and internecine violations of human rights. Another organization, **Amnesty International**, was founded in 1961. In 1983, Amnesty International published a special report on political killings by governments, which described government political killings as

> unlawful and deliberate killings of persons by reasons of their real or imputed political beliefs or activities, religion, other conscientiously held beliefs, ethnic origin, sex, colour or language, carried out by order of a government with its complicity.[48]

Both Human Rights Watch and Amnesty International promote publicity campaigns from time to time to highlight specific human rights issues. The purpose of these campaigns is to focus the world's attention on particularly urgent human rights issues.

All of these approaches to the analysis of state terrorism are useful for evaluating different types of state-sponsored political violence.

---

[47]The organization was originally called Helsinki Watch. Its Western Hemisphere branch is called Americas Watch.

[48]Amnesty International. *Political Killings by Government.* London: Amnesty International, 1983. Quoted in Iadicola and Shupe, *Violence,* p. 255.

# Chapter Summary

This chapter introduced readers to the "terror from above" that characterizes state-sponsored terrorism. Readers were provided with an understanding of the nature of state terrorism. The purpose of this discussion was to identify and define several state terrorist environments, to differentiate state terrorism in the foreign and domestic policy domains, and to provide cases in point of these concepts.

The state terrorism paradigm identified several approaches that are used by experts to define and describe state terrorism. Included in this discussion was a comparison of the underlying characteristics of the state patronage and state assistance models of terrorism. The patronage model was characterized by situations whereby regimes act as active sponsors of, and direct participants in, terrorism. Under the assistance model, regimes tacitly participate in violent extremist behavior and indirectly sponsor terrorism.

The discussion of state terrorism as foreign policy applied a model that categorized terrorism in the foreign domain as politically sympathetic, logistically supportive, episode specific, or joint operations. Each of these categories described different aspects in the scale of support and directness of involvement by state sponsors. Several examples were provided to clarify the behavioral distinctions of these categories.

In the domestic policy domain, several models of state domestic authority and legitimacy were identified and summarized. The sources of authority and centers of power were contrasted in these models. These models were democracy, authoritarianism, totalitarianism, and crazy states. Because the methodologies of state domestic terrorism differ from case to case, several models provide a useful approach to understanding the characteristics of a particular terrorist environment. These models were vigilante, overt official, covert official, and genocidal state domestic terrorism.

Readers were introduced to public and private agencies that monitor state terrorism. The U.S. Department of State's list of sponsors of state terrorism is a useful compilation of information about states that are active in the foreign policy domain. Human Rights Watch and Amnesty International are private activist organizations that have extensive databases on state terrorism in the domestic policy domain.

In Chapter 5, readers will be introduced to dissident terrorist environments and examples of "terrorism from below" conducted by nongovernmental dissident movements. The discussion will present a dissident terrorism paradigm that will be applied in a similar manner as the state terrorism paradigm. Cases in point will be presented to explain the causes and contexts of dissident terrorist behavior.

# Key Terms and Concepts

The following topics are discussed in this chapter and can be found in the glossary:

African National Congress (ANC)

al-Megrahi, Abdel Basset

Amnesty International

Anfal Campaign

apartheid

Argentine Anticommunist Alliance (Triple-A)

Askaris

assassinations

auto-genocide

"axis of evil"

Ba'ath Party

Battalion 3-16

"blacklisted"

"Boland Amendment"

Contras

crazy state

death squads

el-Qaddafi, Muammar

episode-specific sponsorship

ethnic cleansing

Fhima, Lamen Khalifa

"Four Olds"

genocidal state terrorism

genocide

Great Proletarian Cultural Revolution

House Un-American Activities Committee

Human Rights Watch

Hussein, Saddam

Inkatha Freedom Party

Iran-Contra scandal

Jamahiriya Security Organization (JSO)

Jammu Kashmir Liberation Front

joint operations

Khomeini, Ayatollah Ruhollah

Korean Airlines Flight 858

Kurds

logistically supportive sponsorship

Lumumba, Patrice

McCarthy, Senator Joseph

Muslim Brotherhood

Northern Ireland

official state terrorism

ORDEN

Pahlavi, Shah Mohammad Reza

Palmer, Alexander Mitchell

Palmer Raids

Pan Am Flight 103

paradigm

paramilitaries

Patrice Lumumba Peoples' Friendship University

People's Liberation Army

Phoenix Program

Plan Victoria 82

politically sympathetic sponsorship

Red Guards

"Red Scares"

Sandinistas

SAVAK

social cleansing

Somoza Debayle, Anastasio

state assistance for terrorism

state patronage for terrorism

Tiananmen Square

torture

United Self-Defense Forces of Colombia (AUC)

Viet Cong

vigilante state terrorism

warfare

# Discussion Box: Authoritarianism and Democracy

*This chapter's Discussion Box is intended to stimulate critical debate about the application of authoritarian methods by democratic governments and the justifications used by these governments for such methods.*

Democracies are constrained by strong constitutions from summarily violating the rights of their citizens. Most democracies have due process requirements in place when security services wish to engage in surveillance, search premises, seize evidence, or detain suspects. However, when confronted by serious security challenges, democracies have resorted to authoritarian security measures. Germany, Italy, France, the United Kingdom, and the United States have all adopted aggressive policies to suppress perceived threats to national security.

For example:

In the **United States**, periodic anti-Communist "**Red Scares**" occurred when national leaders reacted to the perceived threat of Communist subversion. Government officials reacted by adopting authoritarian measures to end the perceived threats. The first Red Scare occurred after the founding of the Communist Party–USA in 1919, and a series of letter bombs were intercepted. President Woodrow Wilson allowed Attorney General **Alexander Mitchell Palmer** to conduct a series of raids—the so-called **Palmer Raids**—against Communist and other leftist radical groups. Offices of these groups were shut down, leaders were arrested and put on trial, and hundreds were deported.

A second Red Scare occurred in the 1930s. This scare resulted in the creation of the **House Un-American Activities Committee** and the passage of the Smith Act in 1940, which made advocacy of the violent overthrow of the government a federal crime. In the late 1940s, Communists were prosecuted, and high-profile investigations were made of people such as Alger Hiss.

A third Red Scare occurred in the 1950s, when Senator **Joseph McCarthy** of Wisconsin held a series of hearings to expose Communist infiltration in government, industry, and Hollywood. Hundreds of careers were ruined, and many people were "**blacklisted**," meaning that they were barred from obtaining employment.

In **Northern Ireland**, the British government has periodically passed legislation to combat terrorism by the IRA. These laws granted British forces authoritarian powers in Northern Ireland. One such law was the 1973 Northern Ireland Emergency Provisions Act, which provided the military with sweeping powers to temporarily arrest and detain people and to search homes in Northern Ireland without warrants. Under the act, the army detained hundreds of people and searched more than 250,000 homes. This sweep was actually fairly successful, in that thousands of weapons were found and seized.

## Discussion Questions

- Are authoritarian methods morally compatible with democratic principles and institutions?

- Under what circumstances are authoritarian policies justifiable and necessary, even in democracies with strong constitutional traditions?

- The postwar Red Scare investigations in the United States have been labeled by many as "witch hunts." Were these investigations nevertheless justifiable, considering the external threat from the Soviet Union?

- The British security services detained hundreds of innocent people and searched the homes of many thousands of non-IRA members. Considering the threat from the IRA, were these inconveniences nevertheless justifiable?

- Assume for a moment that some security environments justify the use of authoritarian measures by democracies. What kind of "watchdog" checks and balances are needed to ensure that democracies do not move toward permanent authoritarianism?

## On Your Own

The open-access Student Study Site at **http://study.sagepub.com/martin5e** has a variety of useful study aids, including eFlashcards, quizzes, audio resources, and journal articles. The websites, exercises, and recommended readings listed below are easily accessed on this site as well.

## Recommended Websites

The following websites are links to international organizations that provide information about countries and human rights conditions:

Amnesty International: http://www.amnesty.org/

CIA World Factbook: https://www.cia.gov/library/publications/the-world-factbook/

Doctors of the World: http://www.doctorsoftheworld.org.uk/

Human Rights Watch: http://www.hrw.org/

Médecins Sans Frontières (Doctors Without Borders): http://www.doctorswithoutborders.org/

## Web Exercise

Using this chapter's recommended websites, conduct an online investigation of state terrorism.

1. Are there certain governmental or institutional profiles that distinguish repressive regimes from nonrepressive regimes?

2. Read the mission statements of the monitoring organizations. Do they reflect objective and professionally credible approaches for monitoring the behavior of states?

3. In your opinion, how effective are these organizations?

For an online search of state terrorism, readers should activate the search engine on their Web browser and enter the following keywords:

"State Terrorism"

"Terrorist States"

## Recommended Readings

The following publications provide discussions on state-sponsored terrorism:

Bullock, Alan. *Hitler: A Study in Tyranny*. New York: Harper, 1958.

Byman, Daniel. *Deadly Connections: States That Sponsor Terrorism*. New York: Cambridge University Press, 2005.

Dror, Yehezkel. *Crazy States: A Counterconventional Strategic Problem*. New York: Kraus, Milwood, 1980.

Goren, Roberta, and Jillian Becker, eds. *The Soviet Union and Terrorism*. London: Allen & Unwin, 1984.

Mann, Michael. *The Dark Side of Democracy: Explaining Ethnic Cleansing*. New York: Cambridge University Press, 2005.

McSherry, J. Patrice. *Predatory States: Operation Condor and Covert War in Latin America*. Lanham, MD: Rowman & Littlefield, 2005.

O'Sullivan, Meghan L. *Shrewd Sanctions: Statecraft and State Sponsors of Terrorism*. Washington, DC: Brookings Institution, 2003.

Stohl, Michael, and George Lopez, eds. *The State as Terrorist: The Dynamics of Governmental Violence and Repression*. Westport, CT: Greenwood, 1984.

Tucker, Robert C. *Stalin in Power: The Revolution From Above, 1928–1941*. New York: Norton, 1990.

Wright, Thomas C. *State Terrorism in Latin America: Chile, Argentina, and International Human Rights*. Lanham, MD: Rowman & Littlefield, 2007.

## CHAPTER 5

# Terror From Below

## *Terrorism by Dissidents*

### OPENING VIEWPOINT: THE TUPAMAROS

Uruguay is situated on the southeast Atlantic coast of South America. Although poor economic conditions led to labor unrest in the late 1950s, Uruguay, unlike many Latin American countries, had a political tradition of liberal democracy. It was, in fact, the most politically progressive country in South America. When militant unionists demonstrated in the capital city of Montevideo in 1962, a confrontation with the police led the government to denounce the labor activists as Marxists and revolutionaries. Out of this confrontation, the National Liberation Movement—better known as the **Tupamaros**—was formed. They named themselves after Tupac Amaru, the greatest Incan leader to resist the Spanish *conquistadores*, who was executed in 1572.

The Tupamaros were young, idealistic, middle-class rebels. Their enemy was the Uruguayan "oligarchy," and their constituency was the Uruguayan people. They styled themselves as Marxists and sought to redirect government priorities to redistribute wealth and political power to the working class. They sought broad-based public support from among the urban workers and unionists and had a fairly large and active cadre of aboveground supporters. Early in their movement, the Tupamaros realized that they could not directly confront the Uruguayan security forces, so they adopted Carlos Marighella's strategy of waging an "urban guerrilla," or terrorist, war with the immediate objective of forcing the government to adopt repressive measures, thereby causing the general population to rise up in revolt.

The Tupamaros operated widely in Montevideo, received worldwide media attention, and are the only urban rebel movement to have come close to establishing "liberated zones" inside a major city. About 2,000 fighters were counted at the peak of their war. In the beginning, Tupamaro targets were selective, and they refrained from indiscriminate bombings or shootings. They robbed banks, exploded bombs, and kidnapped prominent Uruguayans for ransom. Later, they began to kill security officers and assassinate officials. In 1972, the Tupamaros kidnapped Sir Geoffrey Jackson, the British ambassador to Uruguay, holding him prisoner in a "people's prison" for 8 months. When the British Foreign Office refused to negotiate for his release, the Tupamaros seemed to be at a loss about what to do—killing Jackson or releasing him without a ransom would accomplish nothing. They finally released him when 100 Tupamaros dramatically escaped from prison during a riot.

As anticipated, the Uruguayan government did respond harshly—but not with the outcome theorized by Marighella. When the police could not contain the Tupamaros, they resorted to the systematic use of torture as a way to intimidate supporters and eliminate Tupamaro cells. Beatings, rapes, electric shocks, sleep deprivation, murder, and other methods were applied to extract information about Tupamaro operatives and sympathizers. They were successful, and mass arrests followed. When aboveground Tupamaro supporters failed to win any appreciable support at the election polls and the labor unionists whom they had championed refused to support them, the Tupamaros were eventually wiped out. Interestingly, popular support for government repression of the Tupamaros was widespread among Uruguayans.

The legacy of the Tupamaros was significant. They became a model for other armed dissidents in the 1960s and 1970s. Many young rebels in Latin America adopted their urban-based application of Marighella's strategy. Outside of Latin America, the Red Army Faction in West Germany, the Irish Republican Army in Northern Ireland, and Weather Underground in the United States all imitated the Tupamaros.

In the end, however, they were unable to accomplish any of the goals they fought for in Uruguay. In fact, their campaign was responsible for temporarily destroying democracy in the only country in Latin America that had never experienced a repressive dictatorship.

This chapter discusses the characteristics of terrorism from below—**dissident terrorism**—committed by nonstate movements and groups against governments, ethnonational groups, religious groups, and other perceived enemies. Readers will probe the different types of dissident terrorism and develop an understanding of the qualities that differentiate each dissident terrorist environment. A dissident terrorist paradigm will be discussed, and cases in point will be applied to illustrate what is meant by **antistate terrorism** and **communal terrorism**.

Political violence by nonstate actors has long been viewed as a necessary evil by those who are sympathetic to their cause. Revolutionaries, terrorists, and assassins have historically justified their deeds as indispensable tactics that are necessary to defend a higher cause. The methods used to defend the higher cause can range in intensity from large-scale "wars of national liberation"—such as the many anticolonial wars of the 20th century—to individual assassins who strike down enemies of their cause. In the United States, for example, when Confederate sympathizer John Wilkes Booth assassinated President Abraham Lincoln during a play at Ford's Theater in Washington, DC, he leaped from Lincoln's balcony to the stage after shouting, "*Sic semper tyrannis*!" ("Thus always to tyrants!").

❖ **Photo 5.1**

The assassination of American President Abraham Lincoln by Confederate sympathizer John Wilkes Booth.

© Corbis

The U.S. Department of State publishes an annual report that identifies and describes an official list of foreign terrorist organizations. Table 5.1 reproduces a typical list of these organizations.

Why do people take up arms against governments and social systems? What weapons are available to the weak when they make the decision to confront the strong? Do the ends of

| **Table 5.1** | Foreign Terrorist Organizations, 2013 |
| --- | --- |

*Terrorist Groups*

Title 22 of the U.S. Code, Section 2656f, which requires the Department of State to provide an annual report to Congress on terrorism, requires the report to include, inter alia, information on terrorist groups, as well as umbrella groups under which any terrorist group falls, known to be responsible for the kidnapping or death of any U.S. citizen during the preceding 5 years; groups known to be financed by state sponsors of terrorism about which Congress was notified during the past year in accordance with Section 6(j) of the Export Administration Act; and any other known international terrorist group that the Secretary of State determines should be the subject of the report. The list of designated foreign terrorist organizations (FTOs) for 2013 follows:

*U.S. Government Designated Foreign Terrorist Organizations*

Abdallah Azzam Brigades (AAB)
Abu Nidal Organization (ANO)
Abu Sayyaf Group (ASG)
Al-Aqsa Martyrs Brigade (AAMB)
Ansar al-Dine (AAD)
Ansar al-Islam (AAI)
Army of Islam (AOI)
Asbat al-Ansar (AAA)
Aum Shinrikyo (AUM)
Basque Fatherland and Liberty (ETA)
Boko Haram (BH)

Communist Party of Philippines/New People's Army (CPP/NPA)
Continuity Irish Republican Army (CIRA)
Gama'a al-Islamiyya (IG)
Hamas
Haqqani Network (HQN)
Harakat ul-Jihad-i-Islami (HUJI)
Harakat ul-Jihad-i-Islami/Bangladesh (HUJI-B)
Harakat ul-Mujahideen (HUM)
Hizballah
Indian Mujahedeen (IM)
Islamic Jihad Union (IJU)
Islamic Movement of Uzbekistan (IMU)
Jama'atu Ansarul Muslimina Fi Biladis-Sudan (Ansaru)
Jaish-e-Mohammed (JEM)
Jemaah Ansharut Tauhid (JAT)
Jemaah Islamiya (JI)
Jundallah
Kahane Chai
Kata'ib Hizballah (KH)
Kurdistan Workers' Party (PKK)
Lashkar e-Tayyiba
Lashkar i Jhangvi (LJ)
Liberation Tigers of Tamil Eelam (LTTE)
Libyan Islamic Fighting Group (LIFG)
Al-Mulathamun Battalion (AMB)
National Liberation Army (ELN)
Palestine Islamic Jihad–Shaqaqi Faction (PIJ)
Palestine Liberation Front–Abu Abbas Faction (PLF)
Popular Front for the Liberation of Palestine (PFLP)
Popular Front for the Liberation of Palestine–General Command (PFLP-GC)
Al-Qa'ida (AQ)
Al-Qa'ida in the Arabian Peninsula (AQAP)
Al-Qa'ida in Iraq (AQI)
Al-Qa'ida in the Islamic Maghreb (AQIM)
Real IRA (RIRA)
Revolutionary Armed Forces of Colombia (FARC)
Revolutionary Organization 17 November (17N)
Revolutionary People's Liberation Party/Front (DHKP/C)
Revolutionary Struggle (RS)
Al-Shabaab (AS)
Shining Path (SL)
Tehrik-e Taliban Pakistan (TTP)
United Self-Defense Forces of Colombia (AUC)

*Source:* U.S. Department of State, Office of the Coordinator for Counterterrorism. *Country Reports on Terrorism 2013.* Washington, DC: U.S. Department of State, 2014.

antistate dissident rebels justify their chosen means? State repression and exploitation are frequently cited as grievances to explain why nonstate actors resort to political violence. These grievances are often ignored by state officials, who refuse to act until they are forced to do so.

An example illustrating this grievance-related concept is the rebellion in Mexico waged by rebels calling themselves the **Zapatista National Liberation Front** (Ejercito Zapatista de Liberación Nacional). The Zapatistas were leftists who championed the cause of Indians native to Mexico's Chiapas state, where starvation and disease were endemic and where the government had long supported large landowners in their exploitation of poor Indian peasants. In January 1994, the Zapatistas began attacking Mexican army troops and police stations in Chiapas. During this initial campaign, approximately 145 people were killed before the rebels retreated into the jungle to continue the conflict. A low-intensity guerrilla insurgency continued, with the government gradually agreeing to address the grievances of all of Mexico's 10 million Indians. By 2001, the Zapatistas had evolved into an aboveground political movement lobbying for the civil rights of Mexico's Indians and poor peasants. A key reason for the Zapatistas' success was their ability to adopt a Robin Hood image for their movement and thereby garner support from many Mexicans.

The discussion in this chapter will review the following:

- The Rebel as Terrorist: A Dissident Terrorism Paradigm
- Warring Against the State: Antistate Dissident Terrorism
- Warring Against a People: Communal Terrorism
- Operational Shifts: Dissidents and the New Terrorism

## ❖ The Rebel as Terrorist: A Dissident Terrorism Paradigm

Remember from Chapter 4 that a paradigm is "a pattern, example, or model"[1] that is logically developed to represent a concept. Policy experts and academics have designed a number of models that define dissident terrorism. For example, one model places dissident terrorism into a larger framework of "three generalized categories of political action"[2] that include the following:

- **Revolutionary Terrorism:** The threat or use of political violence aimed at effecting complete revolutionary change.
- **Subrevolutionary Terrorism:** The threat or use of political violence aimed at effecting various changes in a particular political system (but not aimed at abolishing it).
- **Establishment Terrorism:** The threat or use of political violence by an established political system against internal or external opposition[3]

Other models develop specific types of dissident terrorism, such as *single-issue, separatist,* and *social revolutionary* terrorism.[4] Likewise, *insurgent* terrorism has been defined as violence "directed by private groups against public authorities [that] aims at bringing about radical political change."[5] One comprehensive definition of "nonstate domestic" terrorism describes it as "illegal violence or threatened violence directed against human or nonhuman objects,"[6] conducted under the following five conditions, assuming that the violence

- was undertaken with a view to maintaining a putative norm in at least one particular territorial unit . . .
- had secretive, furtive, and/or clandestine features that were expected by the participant to conceal their personal identity . . .

[1]*Webster's New Twentieth Century Dictionary of the English Language, Unabridged.* 2nd ed. New York: Publishers Guild, 1966.

[2]Whittaker, David J., ed. *The Terrorism Reader.* New York: Routledge, 2001, p. 33.

[3]Schultz, Richard. "Conceptualizing Political Terrorism." *Journal of International Affairs* 32 (1978): 1, 7–15. Quoted in Whittaker, *The Terrorism Reader,* 2001.

[4]Barkan, Steven E., and Lynne L. Snowden. *Collective Violence.* Boston: Allyn & Bacon, 2001, p. 70.

[5]Gurr, Ted Robert. "Political Terrorism: Historical Antecedents and Contemporary Trends." In *Violence in America: Protest, Rebellion, Reform,* edited by Ted Robert Gurr. Vol. 2. Newbury Park, CA: Sage, 1989, p. 204.

[6]Gibbs, J. P. "Conceptualization of Terrorism." *American Sociological Review* 54 (1989): 329–40.

- was not undertaken to further the permanent defense of some area . . .
- was not conventional warfare . . .
- was perceived by the participants as contributing to the normative putative goal . . . by inculcating fear of violence in persons other than the immediate target of the actual or threatened violence and/or by publicizing some cause.[7]

To simplify our analysis, the discussion here presents a dissident terrorist model adapted from one designed by Peter C. Sederberg.[8] It defines and differentiates broad categories of dissident terrorism that are useful for critically analyzing terrorist motives and behaviors. Although each category—**revolutionary**, **nihilist**, and **nationalist dissident terrorism**—is specifically defined for the purposes of our discussion, one should keep in mind that the same terms are applied by experts in many different contexts. A fourth category, **criminal dissident terrorism**, is discussed in Chapter 9.

## Revolutionary Dissident Terrorism: A Clear World Vision

The goals of revolutionary dissidents are to destroy an existing order through armed conflict and to build a relatively well-designed new society. This vision for a new society can be the result of nationalist aspirations, religious principles, ideological dogma, or some other goals.

Revolutionaries view the existing order as regressive, corrupt, and oppressive; their envisioned new order will be progressive, honest, and just. Revolutionary dissident terrorists are not necessarily trying to create a separate national identity; they are activists seeking to build a new society on the rubble of an existing one. Many Marxist revolutionaries, for example, have a general vision of a Communist Party–led egalitarian classless society with centralized economic planning. Many Islamist revolutionaries also have a grand vision—that of a spiritually pure culture that is justly based on the application of *shari'a,* or God's law. The latter case is exemplified by the Hezbollah (Party of God) organization in Lebanon, which is actively agitating for its own vision of a spiritually pure Lebanon; to that end, Hezbollah has its own political movement, armed militia, and social services. Various factions of the Muslim Brotherhood also advocate a rather clear program.

As a practical matter, revolutionary dissidents are often outnumbered and outgunned by the established order. Their only hope for victory is to wage an unconventional war to destabilize the central authority. Terrorism thus becomes a pragmatic tactical option to disrupt government administration and symbolically demonstrates the weakness of the existing regime.

Good case studies for the selection of terrorism as a legitimate tactic are found in the Marxist revolutionary movements in Latin America during the 1950s to the 1980s. For example, during the Cuban Revolution, which began in 1956, rebels operating in rural areas waged classic hit-and-run guerrilla warfare against the Batista government's security forces. Fidel Castro and Ernesto "Che" Guevara led these rural units. In urban areas, however, terrorist attacks were commonly carried out by the rebels, who successfully disrupted government administration and thereby undermined public confidence in Batista's ability to govern. This model was repeated throughout Latin America by Marxist revolutionaries (usually unsuccessfully), so that urban terrorism became a widespread phenomenon in many countries during this period. Carlos Marighella, the Brazilian revolutionary and author of the *Mini-Manual of the Urban Guerrilla,* detailed the logic of urban terrorism in the Latin American context.[9]

---

[7]Hamm, Mark S., ed. *Hate Crime: International Perspectives on Causes and Control.* Cincinnati, OH: Anderson and Academy of Criminal Justice Sciences, 1994, p. 178. Citing Gibbs, "Conceptualization."

[8]Sederberg, Peter C. *Terrorist Myths: Illusion, Rhetoric, and Reality.* Englewood Cliffs, NJ: Prentice Hall, 1989.

[9]The *Mini-Manual* is reprinted in Mallin, Jay, ed. *Terror and Urban Guerrillas: A Study of Tactics and Documents.* Coral Gables, FL: University of Miami Press, 1971, pp. 70–115.

## Nihilist Dissident Terrorism.
## Revolution for the Sake of Revolution

**Nihilism** was a 19th-century Russian philosophical movement of young dissenters who believed that only scientific truth could end ignorance. They believed that religion, nationalism, and traditional values (especially family values) were at the root of ignorance. Nihilists had no vision for a future society, asserting only that the existing society was intolerable. Nihilism was, at its core, a completely negative and critical philosophy. The original nihilists were not necessarily revolutionaries, but many anarchists (including Petr Kropotkin and Sergei Nechayev) adapted basic nihilist philosophy to anarchist activism.

Modern nihilist dissidents exhibit a similar disdain for the existing social order but offer no clear alternative for the aftermath of its destruction. The goal of modern nihilists is to destroy the existing order through armed conflict, with little forethought given to the configuration of the new society; victory is defined simply as the destruction of the old society. Nihilist dissidents, like revolutionary dissidents, define the existing order as regressive, corrupt, and oppressive. Unlike revolutionaries, nihilists believe that virtually anything is better than the current establishment, so that destruction of the establishment alone becomes the ultimate goal. Many modern nihilists do have a vague goal of "justice," but they offer no clear vision for building a just society other than destroying the existing social order.

Because nihilist dissidents have no clear postrevolution societal design, they have been relegated to the political fringes of society. They have never been able to lead broad-based revolutionary uprisings among the people and have never been able to mount sustained guerrilla campaigns against conventional security forces. Thus, the only armed alternative among hard-core nihilists has been to resort to terrorism. Examples of modern nihilist dissident terrorists include the leftist **Red Brigades** in Italy and **Weather Underground Organization** in the United States, each of which had only a vaguely Marxist model for postrevolutionary society. These cases are discussed in Chapters 7 and 13, respectively. Another example is the Palestinian terrorist Abu Nidal, who had no postrevolution vision. Arguably, Osama bin Laden's Al-Qa'ida network fits the nihilist dissident model because "from the moment it was established during the chaos of the Afghan war, the aim of Al-Qa'ida was to support, both militarily and financially, oppressed Muslims around the world."[10]

Although Al-Qa'ida has a generalized goal of defending Islam and fomenting a pan-Islamic revival, the group offers no specific model for how the postrevolution world would be shaped, and its long-term goals are not clearly defined.

## Nationalist Dissident Terrorism:
## The Aspirations of a People

Nationalist dissidents champion the national aspirations of groups of people who are distinguished by their cultural, religious, ethnic, or racial heritage. The championed people generally live in an environment in which their interests are subordinate to the interests of another group or a national regime. The goal of nationalist dissidents is to mobilize a particular demographic group against another group or government. They are motivated by the desire for some degree of national autonomy, such as democratic political integration, regional self-governance, or complete national independence.

Nationalist sentiment has been commonplace—particularly during the 19th and 20th centuries—and can arise in many social or political environments. For example, the championed group may be a minority living among a majority group, such as the Kurds in Turkey and Iraq.[11] Or it may be a majority national group living in a region that is politically dominated by the government of another ethnic group, such as the domination of Tibet by the Chinese. The group may be a minority with a

---

[10]Reeve, Simon. *The New Jackals: Ramzi Yousef, Osama bin Laden, and the Future of Terrorism*. Boston: Northeastern University Press, 1999, p. 170.

[11]See Raghavan, Sudarsan. "Kurdish Guerrillas Remain Resolute." *Washington Post*, November 11, 2007.

separate cultural and linguistic identity, such as the French Canadians in Quebec. Some national groups have a distinct cultural, ethnic, and regional identity that exists within the borders of several countries, such as the Kurds, whose Kurdistan region is divided among Iran, Iraq, Turkey, and Syria.

Keystone/Hulton Archive/Getty Images

❖ **Photo 5.2**

The Irish Republican Army (IRA) at work. A photograph of members of the Provisional IRA as they conduct training exercises and a demonstration.

Although many nationalist dissident factions incorporate ideological or religious agendas into their movements, the core component of their activism is their ethnonational or other identity. For instance, not all Vietnamese nationalists were communists. Those who were led by Ho Chi Minh certainly were communists, but their wars against the Japanese, French, Americans, and South Vietnamese were ultimately fought to unify Vietnam. Likewise, Muslim rebels in the Southwest Asia Kashmir region have fought a long *jihad* or holy war against India with the support of Pakistan, but their underlying goal is regional independence from India rather than solidarity with international Islamists.

Many nationalist dissidents have used terrorism to achieve their goals. This has often been a practical option because their opponents have overwhelming military and political superiority and would quickly defeat them during a guerrilla or conventional conflict. An example of this type of strategy is that adopted by the **Provisional Irish Republican Army (Provos)** in Northern Ireland. In other contexts, the armed opposition must operate in urban areas, which always favor the dominant group or regime because of the impossibility of maneuver, the concentration of security forces, and sometimes the lack of mainstream support from the championed group. An example of this type of environment is the Basque Fatherland and Liberty (ETA) organization in northern Spain. These

are logical operational policies, because for nationalists, "the basic strategy is to raise the costs to the enemy occupiers until they withdraw."[12]

Chapter Perspective 5.1 explores the case of Chechen terrorism in Russia. The Chechen Republic is located in the Caucasus region of the Russian Federation. Also known as Chechnya, it has a long history of opposition to Russian rule that dates to the 18th century. In the modern era, the region has been at war since 1994.

## CHAPTER PERSPECTIVE 5.1: Chechen Terrorism in Russia

During the pending collapse of the Soviet Union, a group of Chechens perceived an opportunity for independence and in 1991 declared the new Chechen Republic of Ichkeria to be independent from Russia. Their rationale was that they were no different from the Central Asian, Eastern European, and Baltic states that had also declared their independence. The Russian Federation refused to recognize Chechnya's independence, and in 1994 invaded with 40,000 troops. The Chechens resisted fiercely, inflicting severe casualties on Russian forces, and in 1996, Russia agreed to withdraw its troops after approximately 80,000 Russians and Chechens had died.

Tensions mounted again in 1999 as Russian troops prepared to reenter Chechnya. In September

*(Continued)*

---

[12]Hewitt, Christopher. "Public's Perspectives." In *Terrorism and the Media*, edited by David L. Paletz and Alex P. Schmid. Newbury Park, CA: Sage, 1992, p. 182.

(Continued)

1999, several blocks of apartments were destroyed by terrorist explosions in Dagestan and Moscow; hundreds were killed. The Russian army invaded Chechnya, thus beginning a protracted guerrilla war that also witnessed repeated Chechen terrorist attacks in Russia. Although guerrillas inside Chechnya were mostly suppressed, approximately 100,000 Russians and Chechens died during the second invasion.

Because Chechnya is a Muslim region, Russian authorities have tried to link their conflict with the global war on terrorism. At the same time, some Chechen fighters have become Islamists and sought support from the Muslim world. Russian President Vladimir Putin repeatedly voiced a strong and aggressive tone against Chechen terrorists, stating on one occasion that "Russia doesn't conduct negotiations with terrorists—it destroys them."[a]

During the Russian occupation, Chechen separatists waged an ongoing terrorist campaign on Russian soil. Their attacks have been dramatic and deadly. Examples of the quality of their attacks include the following incidents:

On October 23 through 26, 2002, approximately 50 Chechen terrorists seized approximately 800 hostages during the performance of a musical in a Moscow theater. During the 57-hour crisis, the Chechens wired the theater with explosives and threatened to destroy the entire building with everyone inside. Several of the female terrorists also wired themselves with explosives. Russian commandos eventually pumped an aerosol anesthetic, or "knockout gas" (possibly manufactured with opiates), into the theater, and 129 hostages died—most of them from the effects of the gas, which proved to be more lethal than expected in a confined area. All of the Chechens were killed by the commandos as they swept through the theater during the rescue operation.

On February 6, 2004, a bomb in a Moscow subway car killed 39 people and wounded more than 100.

On August 24, 2004, two Russian airliners crashed, virtually simultaneously. Investigators found the same explosive residue at both crash sites. Chechen suicide bombers were suspected, and a group calling itself the Islambouli Brigades of Al-Qa'ida claimed responsibility.

On August 31, 2004, a woman detonated a bomb near a Moscow subway station, killing herself and nine other people and wounding 100. The Islambouli Brigades of Al-Qa'ida claimed responsibility.

On September 1, 2004, Chechens seized a school in Beslan, taking 1,200 hostages. On September 3, as explosives were detonated and special forces retook the school, more than 330 people were killed, about half of them schoolchildren. Russian authorities displayed the bodies of 26 Chechens.

The number and intensity of terrorist incidents declined in 2005 and 2006, largely because of negotiations and Russian success in eliminating prominent Chechen opposition leaders. In March, the president of a separatist Chechen government was killed by Russian troops, and in July 2006, famed rebel leader Shamil Basayev was killed by an explosion that many attributed to Russian security forces.

The conflict has by no means ended. "Incidents of violence rose from 795 in 2008 to 1,100 in 2009, and suicide bombings quadrupled in 2009, the majority of which occurred in Chechnya."[b] In 2010, 39 people were killed when two metro stations in Moscow were attacked by two female suicide bombers, for which Chechen leader Doku Umarov claimed responsibility. A Chechen suicide assault on the Domodedovo Airport in Moscow in 2011 killed 36 people. The National Consortium for the Study of Terrorism and Responses to Terrorism reported that in 2012, 150 terrorist attacks occurred in Russia from all sources.

## Notes

a. Ingram, Judith. "Rush Hour Blast Hits Moscow Metro." *Washington Post,* February 6, 2004.

b. Bhattacharji, Preeti. "Chechen Terrorism (Russia, Chechnya, Separatist)." *Backgrounder.* Washington, DC: Council on Foreign Relations, 2010.

## Revolutionaries, Nihilists, and Nationalists: Freedom Fighters?

Regardless of their ideology, methodology, or goals, there is unanimity in positive self-perception—terrorists perceive themselves as members of an enlightened, fighting elite. The names adopted by terrorist organizations reflect this self-perception, but as indicated in Table 5.2, organizational names often have nothing to do with the reality of the group's actual composition. Table 5.2 gives examples of how terrorists perceive themselves.

**Table 5.2  Self-Perception or Self-Deception? Dissident Terrorists as Freedom Fighters**

Dissident terrorists adopt organizational names that characterize themselves as righteous defenders of a group or principle. These monikers are always positive representations that project the "higher purpose" of the group. The following categories and examples illustrate the self-perception of armed dissident groups.

| Liberation Fighters | Military Units | Defensive Movements | Retribution Organizations | Inconsequential Alliances |
|---|---|---|---|---|
| Basque Fatherland and Liberty | Alex Boncayo Brigade | Islamic Resistance Movement | Revolutionary Justice Organization | Aum Shinrikyo (Supreme Truth) |
| Liberation Tigers of Tamil Eelam | Irish Republican Army | Revolutionary People's Struggle | International Justice Group | Middle Core Faction |
| Palestine Islamic Jihad | Japanese Red Army | National Council of Resistance | Palestinian Revenge Organization | Al-Qa'ida ("The Base") |
| Revolutionary People's Liberation Party | New People's Army | Jewish Defense League | Black September | Orange Volunteers |

## ❖ Warring Against the State: Antistate Dissident Terrorism

A good deal of "terrorism from below" is antistate in nature. It is directed against existing governments and political institutions, attempting to destabilize the existing order as a precondition to building a new society. Antistate dissidents can have a clear vision of the new society (revolutionary dissidents), a vague vision of the new society (nihilist dissidents), national aspirations (nationalist dissidents), or a profit motive (criminal dissidents). Regardless of which model fits a particular antistate movement, their common goal is to defeat the state and its institutions.

### Intensities of Conflict: Antistate Terrorist Environments

With few exceptions, antistate terrorism is directed against specific governments or interests and occurs either within the borders of a particular country or where those interests are found in other countries. Thus, antistate terrorist environments are defined by the idiosyncrasies of each country, each dissident movement, and each terrorist organization. The histories of every nation give rise to specific antistate environments that are unique to their societies. The following examples from North America and Europe illustrate this point.

In the United States, leftist terrorism predominated during the late 1960s through the late 1970s, at the height of the anti–Vietnam War and people's rights movements. Acts of political violence—such as bank robberies, bombings, and property destruction—took place when some black, white, and Puerto Rican radicals engaged in armed protest. This changed in the 1980s, when the leftist remnants either gave up the fight or were arrested. Around this time, right-wing terrorism began to predominate when some racial supremacists, religious extremists, and antigovernment members of the Patriot movement adopted strategies of violence.[13]

In West Germany from the late 1960s through the mid-1980s, the leftist **Red Army Faction (RAF)** engaged in a large number of bank robberies, bombings, assassinations, and other acts of antistate violence aimed at destabilizing the West German government. The RAF also targeted the North Atlantic Treaty Organization (NATO) presence in West Germany, primarily focusing on U.S. military personnel. After the fall of the communist Eastern bloc in 1989 and the reunification of Germany, RAF-style leftist terrorism waned. Around this time, rightist neo-Nazi violence increased—much of it directed against non-German *Gastarbeiters,* or "guest workers." The perpetrators of this violence were often young skinheads and other neofascist youths. Many of these rightist attacks occurred in the region that formerly comprised East Germany.

In Italy, the leftist Red Brigades group was responsible for thousands of terrorist incidents from the early 1970s through the mid-1980s. Originating in the student-based activism of the late 1960s and early 1970s, Red Brigades members were young urban terrorists whose terrorist campaign can best be described as a nihilist attempt to undermine capitalism and democracy in Italy. By the late 1980s, Italian police had eliminated Red Brigades cells and imprisoned their hard-core members. During this period, Italian neofascists also engaged in terrorist violence, eventually outlasting the leftist campaign, and they remained active into the 1990s.

In Spain, antistate terrorism has generally been nationalistic or leftist. General Francisco Franco, who seized power after leading the fascist revolt against the Republican government during the Spanish Civil War of 1936 to 1939,[14] ruled as a right-wing dictator until his death in 1975. Small, violent leftist groups have appeared in Spain—such as the Anti-Fascist Resistance Group of October First and the Maoist Patriotic and Anti-Fascist Revolutionary Front. Without question, the most prominent antistate dissident group in Spain is the nationalist and vaguely Marxist ETA. ETA was founded in 1959 to promote the independence of the Basque region in northern Spain. The Basques are a culturally and linguistically distinct people who live in northern Spain and southwestern France. Although ETA adopted terrorism as a tactic in response to the Franco government's violent repression of Basque nationalism, "of the more than 600 deaths attributable to ETA between 1968 and 1991, 93 per cent occurred after Franco's death."[15] ETA was rife with factional divisions—at least six ETA factions and subfactions were formed—but their terrorist campaign continued, despite the granting of considerable political rights by the Spanish government and the loss of popular support for ETA among the Basque people. A right-wing terrorist group, Spanish National Action (*Accion Nacional Espanila*), was formed as a reaction to ETA terrorism.

Sometimes antistate dissident movements, because of their history and political environment, take on elements of both antistate and communal conflict. In Israel, for example, the Palestinian nationalist movement is made up of numerous organizations and movements that have mostly operated under the umbrella of the **Palestine Liberation Organization (PLO)**, founded by **Yasir Arafat** and others in 1959. From its inception, the PLO has sought to establish an independent Palestinian state. Because the organization claims the same territory as the state of Israel, the PLO and its affiliates have attacked targets inside Israel and abroad. Until recently, Palestinian armed resistance was characterized by a series of dramatic hit-and-run raids, hijackings, bombings, rocket attacks, and other

---

[13]An excellent discussion of this progression is found in Smith, Brent L. *Terrorism in America: Pipe Bombs and Pipe Dreams.* Albany: State University of New York Press, 1994.

[14]An interesting compilation of British newspaper reports from the Spanish Civil War is published in Haigh, R. H., D. S. Morris, and A. R. Peters, eds. *The Guardian Book of the Spanish Civil War.* Aldershot, UK: Wildwood House, 1987.

[15]Whittaker, *The Terrorism Reader,* p. 126.

acts of violence. Israeli and Jewish civilians were often targeted. On May 15, 1974, for example, 16 Jewish teenagers were killed and 70 wounded when three Palestinian terrorists seized a school and demanded that Israel free 23 Palestinian prisoners; all of the gunmen were killed when Israeli soldiers stormed the school.

Since September 28, 2000, Palestinian resistance has taken on the characteristics of a broad-based uprising—and communal terrorism. On that date, Israeli General Ariel Sharon visited the Temple Mount in Jerusalem. The Temple Mount is sacred to both Muslims and Jews. Muslims believe that the prophet Muhammed ascended to heaven from the site, upon which was constructed the Al-Aqsa Mosque. Jews believe that the patriarch Abraham prepared to sacrifice his son on the Temple Mount in accordance with God's wishes, and that Judaism's First and Second Temples were located at the site. After Sharon's visit, which was perceived by Palestinians to be a deliberate provocation, enraged Palestinians began a second round of massive resistance—the "shaking off," or *intifada*. The new dissident environment included violent demonstrations, street fighting, and suicide bombings. The violence was regularly characterized by bombings, shootings, and other attacks against civilian targets. On March 27, 2002, for example, 29 people were killed and 100 injured when a suicide bomber attacked a hotel in the Israeli city of Netanya. Thus, the Palestinian nationalist movement entered a phase distinguished by the acceptance of communal dissident terrorism as a strategy.

Chapter Perspective 5.2 summarizes the coalitional features of the Palestinian movement. Attention should be given to the PLO and its role as an umbrella organization for numerous ideological factions.

## CHAPTER PERSPECTIVE 5.2: The Palestinian Movement

Some antistate dissident environments are long-standing and have generated many contending factions. A good example of this phenomenon is the Palestinian movement. Palestinian activism against the state of Israel has as its ultimate goal the creation of an independent Palestinian state. The antistate strategies of most of these groups were replaced by a broad-based communal dissident environment (the *intifada*), combined with maintaining Palestinian governing authority in Gaza and the West Bank. The following organizations have been prominent in the Palestinian nationalist movement.[a]

### Palestine Liberation Organization

Formed in 1964, the Palestine Liberation Organization (PLO) is not a religious movement but rather a secular nationalist umbrella organization comprising numerous factions. Its central and largest group is **Al Fatah,** founded by PLO chair Yasir Arafat in October 1959. The PLO is the main governing body for the Palestinian Authority in Gaza and the West Bank. **Force 17** is an elite unit that was originally formed in the 1970s as a personal security unit for Arafat. It has since been implicated in paramilitary and terrorist attacks. The **Al-Aqsa Martyr Brigades** is a "martyrdom" society of fighters drawn from Al Fatah and other factions; it includes suicide bombers. Traditionally a secular nationalistic movement, the PLO has received significant challenges from Hamas for the mantle of champion of the Palestinian people.

### Islamic Resistance Movement (Harakt al-Muqaqama Al-Islamiya, or Hamas, meaning "zeal")

**Hamas** is an Islamic fundamentalist movement founded in 1987, with roots in the Palestinian branch of the Muslim Brotherhood. Hamas is a comprehensive movement rather than simply a terrorist group, providing social services to

*(Continued)*

(Continued)

Palestinians while at the same time committing repeated acts of violence against Israeli interests. Its armed groups operate as semi-autonomous cells and are known as the **Izzedine al-Qassam Brigade** (named for a famous *jihadi* in the 1920s and 1930s). Hamas has always been at the forefront of the communal dissident *intifada*. In February 2006, Hamas assumed control of the Palestinian parliament, and in June 2007, the movement seized military control of Gaza from the PLO after fierce fighting. After several years of negotiations, in 2011, Hamas and Fatah reached an accord in Cairo seeking gradual rapprochement and operational cooperation. However, fundamentalist splinter factions such as the Al-Qa'ida–inspired Jund Ansar Allah (Soldiers of the Companions of God) group formed to challenge Hamas as being too moderate. A second round of reconciliation talks between Hamas and Fatah resulted in an April 2014 accord. During this period, tensions escalated markedly between Israel and Hamas, as Hamas fired hundreds of rockets into Israeli territory, eventually resulting in an Israeli military suppression campaign in July 2014. Fighting ended in August 2014 after thousands of casualties.

## Palestine Islamic Jihad

The **Palestine Islamic Jihad** is not a single organization but a loose affiliation of factions. It is an Islamic fundamentalist revolutionary movement that seeks to promote *jihad*, or holy war, to form a Palestinian state. It is responsible for assassinations and suicide bombings. Like Hamas, it is actively promoting the *intifada.*

## Abu Nidal Organization

Led by Sabri al-Banna, the **Abu Nidal Organization (ANO)** is named for al-Banna's *nom de guerre*. The ANO split from the PLO in 1974 and is an international terrorist organization, having launched attacks in 20 countries at the cost of 900 people killed or wounded. The ANO has several hundred members and a militia in Lebanon. It has operated under other names, including Fatah Revolutionary Council, Arab Revolutionary Council, and Black September. The ANO has operated from bases in Libya, Lebanon, and Sudan.

## Popular Front for the Liberation of Palestine

The **Popular Front for the Liberation of Palestine (PFLP)** was founded in 1967 by George Habash. It is a Marxist organization that advocates a multinational Arab revolution. With about 800 members, the PFLP was most active during the 1970s but has continued to commit acts of terrorism. The PFLP is responsible for dramatic international terrorist attacks. Its hijacking campaign in 1969 and 1970, its collaboration with West European terrorists, and its mentorship of Carlos the Jackal arguably established the model for modern international terrorism. Habash died in January 2008.

## Popular Front for the Liberation of Palestine–General Command

Ahmed Jibril formed the **Popular Front for the Liberation of Palestine–General Command (PFLP-GC)** in 1968 when he split from the PFLP because he considered the PFLP to be too involved in politics and not sufficiently committed to the armed struggle against Israel. The PFLP-GC has several hundred members, is probably directed by Syria, and is responsible for many cross-border attacks against Israel.

## Palestine Liberation Front

The **Palestine Liberation Front (PLF)** split from the PFLP-GC in the mid-1970s and further split into pro-PLO, pro-Syrian, and pro-Libyan factions. The pro-PLO faction was led by **Abu Abbas,** who committed a number of attacks against Israel. It is a small organization, with about 50 members.

## Democratic Front for the Liberation of Palestine

The **Democratic Front for the Liberation of Palestine** split from the PFLP in 1969 and further split into two factions in 1991. It is a Marxist organization that believes in ultimate victory through mass revolution. With about 500 members, it has committed primarily small bombings and assaults against Israel, including border raids.

### Note

a. Most of these data were found in *Country Reports on Terrorism 2009*. Washington, DC: U.S. Department of State, 2010, pp. 121ff.

## Defeat Is Unthinkable: The Terrorists' Faith in Victory

Why do small groups of individuals violently confront seemingly invincible enemies? Why do they engage powerful foes by force of arms when their envisioned goal is often illogical or unattainable? From the perspective of antistate dissidents, their armed struggle is never in vain. They believe not only that their cause is *likely* to end in victory, but that victory is in fact *inevitable*. From the perspective of outside observers of terrorist groups and terrorist campaigns, terrorists are almost certainly fighting a losing battle, with a slim-to-none likelihood of eventual victory; yet the terrorists persist in their war.

Although antistate dissident terrorists avoid direct confrontation out of a pragmatic acceptance of their comparative weakness, they nevertheless believe in the ultimate victory of

Keystone/Hulton Archive/Getty Images

❖ **Photo 5.3**

Yasir Arafat, chair of the Palestine Liberation Organization (PLO). Arafat successfully united disparate Palestinian nationalist factions under the PLO umbrella. A number of these factions regularly engaged in terrorism against the state of Israel. Arafat died in 2004.

their cause. They have a utopian vision that not only justifies their means but also (in their worldview) guarantees the triumph of their idealized ends. Violent confrontation in the present—often horrific in scope—is acceptable because of the promised good at the end of the struggle. Religious antistate dissidents believe that God will assure them final victory. A 1996 pronouncement by an Egyptian terrorist organization, the Islamic Group (al-Gama'at al-Islamiyya), stated,

> They plot and plan and God too plans . . . but the best of planners is God. . . . [The Islamic Group will] pursue its battle . . . until such time as God would grant victory—just as the Prophet Muhammed did with the Quredish[16] until God granted victory over Mecca.[17]

Nonreligious antistate dissidents also hold an enduring faith in final victory. Some have adopted a strategy similar to the urban terrorist (or "urban guerrilla") model developed by Carlos Marighella. According to Marighella's strategy, rebels should organize themselves in small cells in major urban areas. He argued that terrorism, when correctly applied against the government, will create sympathy among the population, which in turn forces the government to become more repressive—thus creating an environment conducive to a mass uprising.[18] Although this model has failed repeatedly (the people tend not to rise up, and repressive states usually crush the opposition), it exemplifies the faith held by

---

[16]Also known as the Quraysh, who were the tribe into which the prophet Muhammed was born. Muhammed split from his tribe to gather together his Muslim followers in 622 during "the migration" (*hijrah*). The Quraysh never forgave him for leaving the tribe and became his most formidable foes. The Muslims were eventually victorious over the Quraysh. See Armstrong, Karen. *Islam: A Short History*. New York: Modern Library, 2000, pp. 13–23.

[17]Hoffman, Bruce. *Inside Terrorism*. New York: Columbia University Press, 1998, p. 169.

[18]See Marighella, Carlos. "Mini-Manual of the Urban Guerrilla." In *Terror and Urban Guerrillas: A Study of Tactics and Documents,* edited by Jay Mallin. Coral Gables, FL: University of Miami Press, 1971, pp. 110–2.

antistate dissidents in their victory scenarios—no matter how far-fetched those scenarios may be. Thus, comparatively small in number, limited in capabilities, isolated from society, and dwarfed by both the vast resources of their enemy and the enormity of their task, secular terrorists necessarily function in an inverted reality where existence is defined by the sought-after, ardently pursued future rather than the oppressive, angst-driven, and incomplete present.[19]

## ❖ Warring Against a People: Communal Terrorism

Dissident terrorism is not always directed against a government or national symbols. It is often leveled against entire population groups—people who are perceived to be ethnonational, racial, religious, or ideological enemies. Because the scope of defined enemies is so broad, it is not unusual for this type of terrorism to be characterized by extreme repression and violence on a massive scale. Often deeply rooted in long cultural memories of conflict, communal terrorism sometimes descends into genocidal behavior because

> while the rival combatants often lack the weapons of destruction available to the major powers, they often disregard any recognized rules of warfare, killing and maiming civilians through indiscriminate car bombings, grenade attacks and mass shootings.[20]

Communal terrorism is essentially "group-against-group" terrorism, whereby subpopulations of society wage internecine (i.e., mutually destructive) violence against one another. As with other types of terrorist violence, it occurs in varying degrees of intensity and in many different contexts. Sometimes it can occur on a massive scale, such as the periodic outbreaks of genocidal violence between Hutus and Tutsis in Rwanda and Burundi, which have killed hundreds of thousands. At other times—and on a lower scale of intensity—a politically dominant ethnic or racial group may seek to terrorize a subordinate ethnic or racial group into submission, as occurred in the American South from 1882 to 1930, when more than 3,000 southern African Americans were lynched (publicly murdered) by white mobs and vigilantes.[21] The scale of violence frequently surprises the world, for these conflicts "often do not command the headlines that rivet world attention on international wars and guerrilla insurgencies, but they frequently prove more vicious and intractable."[22]

There are many sources of communal violence, and it is useful to review a few broad categories and illustrative cases in point. These categories—ethnonationalist, religious, and ideological—are explored in the following discussion.

### Ethnonationalist Communal Terrorism

**Ethnonationalist communal terrorism** involves conflict between populations that have distinct histories, customs, ethnic traits, religious traditions, or other cultural idiosyncrasies. Numerous adjectives have been used to describe this type of dissident terrorism, including "separatist, irredentist, . . . nationalist, tribal, racial, indigenous, or minority."[23] It occurs when one group asserts itself against another

---

[19]Hoffman, *Inside Terrorism,* p. 169.

[20]Podesta, Don. "The Terrible Toll of Human Hatred." *Washington Post National Weekly Edition,* June 8, 1987. Quoted in Schechterman, Bernard, and Martin Slann, eds. *Violence and Terrorism.* 3rd ed. Guilford, CT: Dushkin, 1993, p. 33.

[21]Barkan and Snowden, *Collective Violence,* p. 67.

[22]Podesta, "The Terrible Toll."

[23]Thomas, Trent N. "Global Assessment of Current and Future Trends in Ethnic and Religious Conflict." In *Ethnic Conflict and Regional Instability,* edited by Robert L. Pfaltzgraff Jr. and Richard A. Schultz. Carlisle, PA: Strategic Studies Institute, 1994, pp. 33–41. Quoted in Schechterman, Bernard, and Martin Slann, eds. *Violence and Terrorism.* 5th ed. Guilford, CT: Dushkin, 1999, p. 24.

group—many times to "defend" its cultural identity. This defensive rationale for violent communal behavior is not uncommon and has been used in communal conflicts in Bosnia, the Caucasus, Sri Lanka, Indonesia, and elsewhere. In these conflicts, all sides believe themselves to be vulnerable and use this perception to rationalize engaging in terrorist violence.

Regionally, Africa leads in the number of ethnonationalist communal conflicts, with long-term discord in Sierra Leone, Liberia, Nigeria, Chad, Sudan, the Horn of Africa, Congo, Burundi, Rwanda, South Africa, and elsewhere. Typical of the African conflicts is the case of the fighting that occurred during the apartheid era in South Africa between the nationalist African National Conference (ANC) and the Zulu-based Inkatha Freedom Party.[24] South and Central Asia probably ranks second, with ethnic and nationalist sentiment strongest in Chechnya, Afghanistan, Kashmir, and Sri Lanka. The Middle East has several simmering conflicts, such as the Kurdish and Palestinian–Israeli conflicts. East Asia and Southeast Asia also have several armed movements that represent ethnic and nationalist sentiments, such as the Moro National Liberation Front in the Philippines (which has signed a cease-fire but has some renegade fighters) and the Kachin Independence Army in Myanmar (Burma). Latin America has occasionally experienced ethnonationalist communal violence; the worst in scale in recent decades occurred during Guatemala's anti-Indian racial violence, which caused approximately 200,000 deaths before officially ending in 1996, after 35 years of genocidal communal conflict. Western Europe, aside from periodic discord in the Basque region of Spain, has been relatively free of ethnonationalist violence since World War II, as has North America (with the exception of violence in Chiapas, Mexico, during the 1990s).

The scale of ethnonationalist communal violence can vary considerably from region to region, depending on many different factors—such as unresolved historical animosities, levels of regional development, and recurrent nationalist aspirations. It can be waged across national borders (as in the Congo-Rwanda-Burundi region of East Africa), inside national borders (as in Afghanistan), within ethnically polarized provinces (as in the Nagorno-Karabakh territory of Azerbaijan), at the tribal level (as in Liberia), and even at the subtribal clan level (as in Somalia).

The following cases of ethnonationalist communal conflict exemplify two levels of intensity of such conflicts:[25]

### Corsica: Low-Intensity Communal Conflict

France has ruled Corsica since 1796. Migrants from the French mainland have settled in Corsica since its annexation to France. Beginning in the 1960s, separatists from groups such as the Front for the National Liberation of Corsica (FLNC) committed approximately 5,000 attacks on the interests of French mainlanders in an ongoing campaign for independence. Several hundred bombings, assaults, and incidents of vandalism occurred each year, as separatists targeted French mainlander businesses, homes, and offices. In 1997, the FLNC bombed more than 50 banks, government buildings, and other targets in a single day. A turning point in the conflict occurred in June 2014, when the FLNC announced the beginning of a "demilitarization process" and a unilateral cessation of armed protest.

### Nigeria: High-Intensity Communal Conflict

Since gaining independence from Britain in 1960, Nigeria has experienced recurrent outbreaks of ethnic, tribal, and religious violence. The overwhelmingly Muslim north and west is populated mostly by Fulanis, Hausas, and Yorubas. The largely Christian south comprises mostly Ibos. During the 1967 to 1970 civil war, approximately 1 million people died when Ibo separatists unsuccessfully tried to establish the nation of Biafra in southern Nigeria. About 200 people were killed in Kano in northern Nigeria when ethnic and religious riots broke out after the U.S. bombing of Afghanistan began in

---

[24]The Inkatha Freedom Party's website can be accessed at http//www.ifp.org.za/.

[25]Information mostly derived from Central Intelligence Agency. *The World Fact Book 2013–14*. Washington, DC: Central Intelligence Agency, 2014; and U.S. Department of State. *Country Reports on Terrorism, 2013*. Washington DC: U.S. Department of State, April 2014.

October 2001. A particularly violent Islamist movement known as Boko Haram (loosely translated as "Western Education Is Forbidden") was founded in 2002 in the Muslim region of northeastern Nigeria. The operational intensity and sophistication of Boko Haram steadily increased during the following decade, eventually posing a significant threat to Nigeria's and the region's security. Boko Haram is discussed in greater detail in Chapter 6.

## Religious Communal Terrorism

**Sectarian violence** refers to conflict between religious groups and is sometimes one element of discord in a broader conflict between ethnonational groups. Many of the world's ethnic populations define their cultural identity partly through their religious beliefs, so that violence committed by and against them has both ethnic and religious qualities. This link is common in regions where ethnic groups with dissimilar religious beliefs have long histories of conflict, conquest, and resistance. In Sri Lanka, for example, the civil war between the Hindu Tamils and the Buddhist Sinhalese was exceptionally violent, with massacres and indiscriminate killings a common practice. The war ended with the defeat of the Tamil Tigers in 2009.

Two examples further illustrate this point:

### Nagorno-Karabakh Territory, Azerbaijan

After the Soviet bloc collapsed in 1989, fighting in the Nagorno-Karabakh territory of the Caucasus nation of Azerbaijan pitted majority Orthodox Christian Armenians in the territory against minority Muslim Azeri Turks. This conflict is both ethnic and religious, with the Armenians receiving military support for their national aspirations from the Republic of Armenia, which eventually occupied 20% of Azerbaijan, including Nagorno-Karabakh. The Azeris have received support from the Republic of Azerbaijan.

### Yugoslavia

Some intraethnic internecine conflict occurs because of combined nationalist aspirations and regional religious beliefs. The breakup of Yugoslavia led to internecine fighting, the worst of which occurred in Bosnia in 1992–1995. During fighting between Orthodox Christian Serbs, Muslim Bosnians, and Roman Catholic Croats, *ethnic cleansing*—the forcible removal of rival groups from claimed territory—was practiced by all sides. Significantly, all three religious groups are ethnic Slavs.

In both of the foregoing cases, regional nationalism was suppressed under the communist regimes in the Soviet Union and Yugoslavia. However, neither the Soviets nor national hero and ruler Josip Broz Tito's style of Yugoslav nationalist communism could eliminate centuries of ethnic and religious differences. When these regimes ended, those differences led to brutal communal violence.

### Israel

In Israel, religion is used by both Jewish and Muslim militants to justify communal violence. For example, militant members of the Jewish settler community have regularly engaged in violence against Palestinians, usually retaliatory in nature. The religious nature of many of these attacks has been encouraged by members of radical organizations such as the late Rabbi Meir Kahane's **Kach** ("thus") movement, which has advocated the expulsion of all Arabs from biblical Jewish territories. Settlers generally rationalize their attacks as reprisals for Palestinian attacks and sometimes cite Jewish religious traditions as a basis for their actions. This kind of justification was used after an attack in 1983; when settlers

killed an eleven-year-old Palestinian girl in the city of Nablus on the West Bank, a religious text was used in their defense. The chief rabbi of the Sephardic Jewish community referred to the talmudic text, which justified killing an enemy if one can see from a child's eyes that he or she will grow up to be your enemy.[26]

Thus, intractable religious sentiment exists on both sides of the conflict in Israel and Palestine, with Islamic extremists waging a holy war to expel Jews and Jewish settler extremists seeking to reclaim biblical lands and expel Arabs.

Not all **religious communal terrorism** occurs in an ethnonationalist context. For example, religious campaigns are sometimes directed against perceived blasphemy to "purify" a religious belief. Religious fundamentalists of many religions have been known to chastise, denounce, and attack members of their own faiths for failing to follow the spiritual path of the fundamentalists. The perceived transgressors can be members of the same ethnonational group who are members of the same religion as the fundamentalists. Thus, the Algerian fundamentalist **Armed Islamic Group** waged a brutal religious communal war against its fellow Algerians that took 75,000 lives during the 1990s. Similarly, the Egyptian fundamentalist Islamic Group, a cell-based organization, targeted fellow Muslims and Egyptian government officials, as well as Coptic Christians.[27]

Examples of religious communal conflict have occurred in the following countries and regions:[28]

### Northern Ireland[29]

In Northern Ireland, communal dissident terrorism between Catholic nationalists (Republicans) and Protestant unionists (Loyalists) became a regular occurrence during unrest that began in 1969. The nationalist Provisional IRA[30] was responsible for most acts of antistate political violence directed against British administration in Northern Ireland. During the same period, Protestant Loyalist terrorism tended to meet the criteria for communal terrorism rather than antistate terrorism, as Loyalist paramilitaries targeted pro-IRA Catholics rather than symbols of governmental authority. Targets included civilian leaders, opposition sympathizers, and random victims. From 1969 to 1989, of the 2,774 recorded deaths, 1,905 were civilians; of the civilian deaths, an estimated 440 were Catholic or Protestant terrorists.[31] Between 1969 and 1993, 3,284 people died. During this period, Loyalist paramilitaries killed 871 people, Republican paramilitaries killed 829 people, and British forces killed 203 people.[32] Violence continued from IRA splinter groups at a much-reduced level of intensity. These groups included the Continuity Irish Republican Army (founded 1994) and the Real Irish Republican Army (founded 1997). The Irish National Liberation Army, an older splinter group and previous rival to the Provisional IRA, continued to exist but eventually became known more for organized criminal activity than political activism.

### Sudan

In Sudan, long-term animosity exists between the mostly Arabized[33] Muslim north and mostly black Christian and animist (traditional religions) south. Civil war has been a feature of Sudanese

---

[26]Kelly, Robert J., and Jess Maghan. *Hate Crime: The Global Politics of Polarization.* Carbondale: Southern Illinois University Press, 1998, p. 91.

[27]Copts are Orthodox Christians whose presence in Egypt predates the Arab conquest.

[28]Central Intelligence Agency, *World Fact Book;* Podesta, "The Terrible Toll."

[29]For an excellent analysis of the IRA and "the Troubles" in Northern Ireland, see Bell, J. Boywer. *The IRA 1968–2000: Analysis of a Secret Army.* London: Frank Cass, 2000.

[30]The Provisional IRA was formed in 1969 when radicals broke from the official IRA, which was more political than military.

[31]Clutterbuck, Richard. *Terrorism, Drugs, and Crime in Europe After 1992.* New York: Routledge, 1990, p. 73.

[32]*Irish News,* November 30, 1993. Reporting on a joint study by the Northern Ireland Economic Research Centre in Belfast and the Economic and Social Research Institute in Dublin.

[33]Some northerners are ethnic Arabs, but many are not. Nevertheless, non-Arab Muslims have been heavily influenced by their Arab neighbors and fellow Muslims, and hence have developed an "Arabized" culture.

political life since its independence in 1956, generally between progovernment Muslim groups and antigovernment Christian and animist groups. The war has been fought by conventional troops, guerrilla forces, undisciplined militias, and vigilantes. In addition, the Sudanese government began arming and encouraging Arabized militants in the Darfur region to attack black Muslims. Tens of thousands died in this conflict, which approached genocide in scale.

### Lebanon

In Lebanon, bloody religious communal fighting killed more than 125,000 people during the 16-year Lebanese civil war that began in 1975. Militias were formed along religious affiliations, so that Maronite Christians, Sunni Muslims, Shi'a Muslims, and Druze all contended violently for political power. Palestinian fighters, Syrian troops, and Iranian revolutionaries were also part of this environment, which led to the breakdown of central government authority.

## Ideological Communal Terrorism

**Ideological communal terrorism** in the post–World War II era reflected the global rivalry between the United States and the Soviet Union. The capitalist democratic West competed with the authoritarian communist East for influence in the postcolonial developing world and in countries ravaged by invading armies during the war. A common pattern was for civil wars to break out after European colonial powers or Axis armies[34] were driven out of a country. These civil wars were fought by indigenous armed factions drawn from among the formerly occupied population. In China, Yugoslavia, Malaysia, and elsewhere, communist insurgents vied with traditional monarchists, nationalists, and democrats for power. Civilian casualties were high in all of these conflicts.

Examples of ideological communal conflict have occurred in the following countries and regions:[35]

### Greece

The 5-year-long civil war in Greece from 1944 to 1949 was a complicated and brutal affair that in the end took at least 50,000 to 65,000 lives. It involved fighting among conventional troops, guerrilla groups, gendarmerie (armed police), and armed bands. The Greek Communist Party, which had led a resistance group during World War II, fought against the Greek government in several phases after liberation in 1944. The Greek Communist Party eventually lost, in the only attempted communist takeover in postwar Europe to be defeated by force of arms.

### Angola

In Angola, former anti-Portuguese allies fought a long conflict after independence in 1975. The ruling Movement for the Liberation of Angola (MPLA) is a Marxist-Leninist party whose ideology promotes a multicultural and nationalistic (rather than ethnic or regional) agenda. Its principal adversary is the National Union for the Total Independence of Angola (UNITA), mostly made up of the Ovimbundu tribal group. Because the MPLA leadership identified with the international ideological left, the Soviet Union, Cuba, the United States, and South Africa supported either the MPLA or UNITA. This is a rare example of conflict between a multicultural ideological movement and a regional ethnic movement.

### Indonesia

In Indonesia, the Indonesian Communist Party (PKI) was implicated in an October 1965 abortive coup attempt. While the army rounded up PKI members and sympathizers, many Indonesians took

---

[34]The Axis powers were an alliance of Germany, Japan, Italy, and their allies.

[35]Podesta, "The Terrible Toll."

to the streets to purge the communist presence. During a wave of anticommunist communal violence, much of it done by gangs supported by the government, roughly 500,000 communists, suspected communists, and political opponents to the government were killed.

Ideology was used repeatedly in the 20th century to bind together nations or distinctive groups. It has become, in many conflicts, a means to discipline and motivate members of a movement. When applied to rationalize behavior in communal conflicts, the effect can be devastatingly brutal.

Antistate and communal terrorist environments are very dynamic over time, and never static. Table 5.3 reports the top 10 perpetrator groups with the most attacks worldwide in 2013.

## ❖ Operational Shifts: Dissidents and the New Terrorism

The dissident terrorist paradigm is a good model for understanding the environments, motives, and behaviors of modern terrorism. Categorizing the goals and strategies of dissident terrorists as revolutionary, nihilistic, or nationalistic is a useful method for understanding dissident violence. However, one must remember that terrorism is an evolutionary phenomenon, and terrorist environments are never static. Terrorist methodologies and organizational configurations undergo changes over time. In the modern era, these methodologies and organizational configurations have continued to evolve.

❖ **Photo 5.4**
Replica of an explosive suicide vest. Suicide attacks became increasingly common during insurgencies in the post–September 11 era.

Jeff Fusco/Getty Images

| Table 5.3 | Ten Perpetrator Groups With the Most Attacks Worldwide, 2013 |

| Perpetrator Group Name | Total Attacks | Total Killed | Average Number Killed per Attack |
|---|---|---|---|
| Taliban | 641 | 2,340 | 3.65 |
| Al-Qa'ida in Iraq/Islamic State of Iraq and the Levant | 401 | 1,725 | 4.30 |
| Boko Haram | 213 | 1,589 | 7.46 |
| Maoists (India)/Communist Party of India–Maoist | 203 | 190 | 0.94 |
| Al-Shabaab | 195 | 512 | 2.63 |
| Tehrik-i-Taliban Pakistan (TTP) | 134 | 589 | 4.40 |
| New People's Army (NPA) | 118 | 88 | 0.75 |
| Al-Qa'ida in the Arabian Peninsula (AQAP) | 84 | 177 | 2.11 |
| Revolutionary Armed Forces of Colombia (FARC) | 77 | 45 | 0.58 |
| Bangsamoro Islamic Freedom Movement (BIFM) | 34 | 23 | 0.68 |

*Source:* U.S. Department of State, Office of the Coordinator for Counterterrorism. *Country Reports on Terrorism 2013.* Washington, DC: U.S. Department of State, 2014.

Toward the end of the 20th century, two important developments came to characterize the terrorist environment, moving it into a new phase: a new morality and organizational decentralization

## The New Dissident Terrorist Morality

The morality of dissident terrorism in the latter decades of the 20th century differed from 19th-century anarchist terrorism and other violent movements. The new generation did not share the same moralistic scruples of the previous generation. Terrorism in late 19th- and early 20th-century Russia, for example, was "surgical" in the sense that it targeted specific individuals to assassinate, specific banks to rob, and specific hostages to kidnap. In fact, not only did the **Social Revolutionary Party** in Russia (founded in 1900) engage in an extensive terrorist campaign in the early 20th century, but its tactics actually became somewhat popular because its victims were often government officials who were hated by the Russian people.

In contrast, during the postwar era, the definitions of who an enemy was, what a legitimate target could be, and which weapons to use became much broader. This redefining of what constitutes a legitimate target, as well as the appropriate means to attack that target, led to a new kind of political violence. Late 20th-century dissident terrorism was "new" in the sense that it was "indiscriminate in its effects, killing and maiming members of the general public . . . , arbitrary and unpredictable . . . , refus[ing] to recognize any of the rules or conventions of war . . . [and] not distinguish[ing] between combatants and non-combatants."[36] Operationally, the new terrorist morality can be spontaneous and quite gruesome. For example, in March 2004, four American private contractors were killed in an ambush in the Iraqi city of Fallujah. Their corpses were burned, dragged through the streets, and then displayed from a bridge. In Iraq and Syria in 2014, the Islamic State of Iraq and al-Sharm (ISIS) recorded and promulgated the beheadings of several Western civilian prisoners on social networking media.

When terrorists combine this new morality with the ever-increasing lethality of modern weapons, the potential for high casualty rates and terror on an unprecedented scale is very real. This combination was put into practice in September 2001 in the United States, March 2004 in Spain, and July 2005 in Great Britain and Egypt. It was especially put into practice during the long-term terrorist suicide campaign in Israel during the Palestinians' *intifada*. Should terrorists obtain high-yield weapons— such as chemical, biological, nuclear, or radiological weapons—the new morality would provide an ethical foundation for their use.

Regarding operational shifts and the new dissident morality, Chapter Perspective 5.3 explores a troubling practice found among many revolutionary, nihilist, and nationalist paramilitaries and rebel groups. It is the phenomenon of recruiting and training so-called child soldiers to fight on behalf of dissident movements.

## Terrorist Cells and Lone Wolves: New Models for a New War

### Terrorist Cells

A newly predominant organizational profile—the **terrorist cell**—also emerged as the 20th century drew to a close. Terrorist organizations had traditionally been rather clearly structured, many with hierarchical command and organizational configurations. They commonly had aboveground political organizations and covert "military wings."

During the heyday of group-initiated New Left and Middle Eastern terrorism from the 1960s to the 1980s, it was not unusual for dissident groups to issue formal communiqués. These communiqués

---

[36]Crosbie-Weston, R. "Terrorism and the Rule of Law." In *20th Century,* edited by R. W. Cross. London: Purnell Reference Books, 1979, p. 2715.

## CHAPTER PERSPECTIVE 5.3: Child Soldiers

One disturbing—and common—trend among paramilitaries and other armed groups has been the conscription of children as fighters. **Child soldiers** are a serious humanitarian issue, with "children as young as six . . . being used in combat by government and rebel forces in civil wars throughout the world."[a] Around the world, "[t]housands of children are serving as soldiers in armed conflicts. . . . These boys and girls, some as as young as 8-years-old, serve in government forces and armed opposition groups. They may fight on the front lines, participate in suicide missions, and act as spies, messengers, or lookouts. Girls may be forced into sexual slavery. Many are abducted or recruited by force, while others join out of desperation, believing that armed groups offer their best chance for survival."[b] For example,

- In India, "Maoist 'Naxalite' rebels in Chhattisgarh use children as soldiers. The Maoists induct children as young as six into children's associations and use children as young as 12 in armed squads that receive weapons training and may participate in armed encounters with government security forces."[c]

- In Sierra Leone during the 1990s and early 2000s, the Revolutionary United Front abducted thousands of children and organized those under the age of 15 into Small Boy Units and Small Girl Units.[d]

- In Democratic Republic of Congo, "[c]hildren serve in the government armed forces as well as various rebel forces. At the height of DRC's war, the UN estimated that more than 30,000 boys and girls were fighting with various parties to the conflict."[e]

- In Central African Republic, "hundreds of children, some as young as 12, serve with various rebel groups."[f]

- In Colombia, "[t]housands of children—both boys and girls—serve in Colombia's irregular armed groups. The majority serve in the FARC guerrillas, with smaller numbers in the UC-ELN guerrillas. Children are also recruited into successor groups to paramilitaries."[g]

- In Afghanistan, "[i]nsurgent groups, including the Taliban and other armed groups, use children as fighters, including in suicide attacks. The UN also reports recruitment of children by the Afghan National Police."[h]

- Paramilitaries and rebel movements have assigned child soldiers to heavy combat on the front lines. Some children are drugged prior to entering into combat and have been known to commit atrocities under orders.

### Notes

a. Amnesty International. *Killings by Government.* London: Amnesty International, 1983. Quoted in Iadicola, Peter, and Anson Shupe. *Violence, Inequality, and Human Freedom.* Dix Hills, NY: General Hall, 1998, p. 255.

b. Human Rights Watch. "Child Soldiers." New York: Human Rights Watch, 2014: http://www.hrw.org/node/105699/.

c. Human Rights Watch. "Child Soldiers Worldwide." New York: Human Rights Watch, 2014: http://www.hrw.org/node/105699/.

d. The anarchic war in Sierra Leone is discussed further in Chapter 9.

e. Human Rights Watch. "Child Soldiers Worldwide." New York: Human Rights Watch, 2014: http://www.hrw.org/node/105699/.

f. Ibid.

g. Ibid.

h. Ibid.

would officially claim credit for terrorist incidents committed on behalf of championed causes, and formal press conferences were held on occasion.

The "vertical" organizational models began to be superseded by less structured "horizontal" models during the 1990s. These cell-based movements have indistinct command and organizational configurations.

❖ **Photo 5.5**

Child soldiers in training. Adults drill armed young boys at a stadium in Angola.

Keystone/Hulton Archive/Getty Images)

Modern terrorist networks are often composed of a "hub" that may guide the direction of a movement but that has little direct command and control over operational units. The operational units are typically autonomous or semiautonomous cells that act on their own, often after lying dormant for long periods of time as "sleepers" in a foreign country. The benefit of this type of organizational configuration is that if one cell is eliminated or its members are captured, they can do little damage to other independent cells. This configuration also permits aboveground supporters to have "deniability" over the tactics and targets of the cells.

### The Lone Wolf Model

Many incidents of terrorist violence have been committed by individual extremists who act alone without clearly identifiable associations with terrorist organizations or networks. Such individuals certainly profess an intellectual or ideological identification with extremist causes, but they are lone operators who act on their own initiative or are sent on lone missions by extremist organizations. A good example of how a cell can be as small as a single individual—the **lone wolf model**—is the case of **Richard C. Reid**, a British resident who converted to Islam and who became known as the **"shoe bomber."** Reid was detected by an alert flight attendant and overpowered by passengers on December 22, 2001, when he attempted to ignite plastic explosives in his shoe on American Airlines Flight 63, a Boeing 767 carrying 198 passengers and crew from Paris to Miami.[37] In Reid's case, he was a self-professed follower of Al-Qa'ida and may have been trained by the organization in Afghanistan. He was sentenced to life imprisonment in a super-maximum-security prison after pleading guilty before a federal court in Boston.

## Chapter Summary

This chapter provided readers with an understanding of the nature of dissident terrorism. The purpose of this discussion was to identify and define several categories of dissident behavior, to classify antistate dissident terrorism, to describe types of communal dissident terrorism, and to offer examples of these concepts.

The dissident terrorist paradigm identified several categories of dissident terrorism. Included in this model were revolutionary, nihilist, and nationalist dissident terrorism. These environments were defined and discussed with the underlying recognition that they are ideal categorizations, and it should be remembered that some terrorists will exhibit characteristics of several categories. It should also be understood that new models became more common as the 20th century drew to a close—the cell organizational structures and

"lone wolf" attacks are now integral elements of the modern terrorist environment.

Antistate dissident terrorism was defined as terrorism directed against existing governments and political institutions, attempting to destabilize the existing environment as a precondition to building a new society. Several antistate terrorist environments were presented as cases in point for understanding why violent antistate agitation may arise. The cases included the United States, several European societies, and a look at the nexus of antistate and communal violence in Israel. The seemingly irrational faith in ultimate victory despite overwhelming odds was examined; this faith in the inevitability of success is at the center of antistate dissident campaigns.

Communal terrorism was defined as "group-against-group" terrorism, wherein

[37]Associated Press. "Did Shoe Bombing Suspect Act Alone?" *Christian Science Monitor,* December 27, 2001.

subpopulations of society wage interne-cine violence against one another. Several environments were discussed to illustrate differences in motivations, manifestations of violence, and environments conducive to communal conflict. The categories that were evaluated were ethnonationalist, religious, and ideological communal terrorism. Cases in point were identified that illustrated each concept.

In Chapter 6, readers will explore religious motives for terrorist behavior. The discussion will focus on specific case studies as well as the contexts for armed religious dissident movements. Reasons for religious violence will also be evaluated.

## Key Terms and Concepts

The following topics are discussed in this chapter and can be found in the glossary:

Abbas, Abu

Abu Nidal Organization (ANO)

Al-Aqsa Martyr Brigades

Al Fatah

antistate terrorism

Arafat, Yasir

Armed Islamic Group

child soldiers

communal terrorism

criminal dissident terrorism

Democratic Front for the Liberation of Palestine

dissident terrorism

ethnonationalist communal terrorism

Force 17

Freedom Birds

Hamas

ideological communal terrorism

Izzedine al-Qassam Brigade

Kach

Liberation Tigers of Tamil Eelam (Tamil Tigers)

lone wolf model

nationalist dissident terrorism

nihilism

nihilist dissident terrorism

Palestine Islamic Jihad

Palestine Liberation Front (PLF)

Palestine Liberation Organization (PLO)

Popular Front for the Liberation of Palestine (PFLP)

Popular Front for the Liberation of Palestine–General Command (PFLP-GC)

Provisional Irish Republican Army (Provos)

Red Army Faction (RAF)

Red Brigades

Reid, Richard C.

religious communal terrorism

revolutionary dissident terrorism

sectarian violence

"shoe bomber"

*Sic semper tyrannis*

Social Revolutionary Party

terrorist cells

Tupamaros

Weather Underground Organization

Zapatista National Liberation Front

## Discussion Box: The Tamil Tigers

*This chapter's discussion box is intended to stimulate critical debate about the legitimacy of dissident movements using guerrilla and terrorist tactics.*

The Democratic Socialist Republic of Sri Lanka is an island nation in the Indian Ocean off the southeast coast of India. Its population is about 74% Sinhalese and

*(Continued)*

(Continued)

18% Tamil; the rest of the population is a mixture of other ethnic groups.[a]

In April 1987, more than 100 commuters were killed when terrorists—most likely **Liberation Tigers of Tamil Eelam (Tamil Tigers)**—exploded a bomb in a bus station in the capital city of Colombo. This type of attack was typical in the Tigers' long war of independence against the Sri Lankan government. The organization was founded in 1976 and champions the Tamil people of Sri Lanka against the majority Buddhist Sinhalese.

The goal of the movement was to carve out an independent state from Sri Lanka, geographically in the north and east of the island. To accomplish this, the Tamil Tigers used conventional, guerrilla, and terrorist tactics to attack government, military, and civilian targets. A unit known as the Black Tigers specialized in terrorist attacks, often committing suicide in the process. Sinhalese forces and irregular gangs often used extreme violence to repress the Tamil uprising.

About half the members of the Tiger movement were teenagers. Indoctrination of potential Tigers included spiritual purity, nationalist militancy, a higher morality, and a glorification of death. At the conclusion of training and indoctrination, young Tiger initiates were given a vial of cyanide, which was worn around the neck to be taken if capture were inevitable. Songs, poetry, and rituals glorified the Tamil people and nation. The Tamil Tigers were very shrewd with public relations, making extensive use of the media, video, and the Internet. They also established a foreign service presence in numerous countries and apparently became adept at transnational organized crime, raising revenue for the cause by trading in arms and drugs.

Estimates of membership numbers ranged between 6,000 and 15,000 fighters. They were well organized and disciplined. Women, called **Freedom Birds**, took on important leadership positions over time

as Tamil male leaders died. About one third of the movement were women.

Some Tamil Tiger attacks were spectacular. In May 1991, a young Tamil woman detonated a bomb, killing herself and Indian Prime Minister Rajiv Gandhi. In 1996, Tigers surrounded and annihilated a government base, killing all 1,200 troops. Also in 1996, a Tiger bomb at Colombo's Central Bank killed scores and injured 1,400 others. In 1997, the new Colombo Trade Center was bombed, causing 18 deaths and more than 100 injuries. The Tamil Tigers operated a small naval unit of speedboats (the Sea Tigers) that intercepted Sri Lankan shipping. Fighting centered repeatedly on the Jaffna peninsula in the north, with both sides capturing and losing bases.

By 1997, the war had claimed at least 58,000 military and civilian lives, including 10,000 Tigers. By 2002, the combatants had fought to a stalemate. In early 2002, both sides agreed to Norwegian mediation to negotiate terms for a lasting peace settlement. Several hundred thousand Tamils eventually fled the island, with more than 100,000 living in India and about 200,000 in the West.

Beginning in 2006, the Sri Lankan government began a massive expansion of its armed forces, doubling its size by late 2008. After a protracted and massive government offensive, the Tamil Tigers were overrun in May 2009, thus ending the 26-year conflict.

## Discussion Questions

- Is terrorism a legitimate tactic in a war for national independence? Does the quest for national freedom justify the use of terrorist tactics?

- When a cause is considered just, is it acceptable to use propaganda to depict the enemy as uncompromisingly corrupt, decadent, and ruthless, regardless of the truth of these allegations?

- Is suicidal resistance merely fanatical and irrational, or is it a higher form of commitment to one's struggle for freedom? Is this type of indoctrination and myth building necessary to sustain this level of commitment to a just cause?

- When a cause is just, are arms smuggling and drug trafficking acceptable options for raising funds?

- Were the Tamil Tigers terrorists or freedom fighters?

## Source:

Data mostly derived from Central Intelligence Agency. *The World Fact Book 2013–14.* Washington, DC: U.S. Central Intelligence Agency, 2014.

## On Your Own

The open-access Student Study Site at **http://study.sagepub.com/martin5e** has a variety of useful study aids, including eFlashcards, quizzes, audio resources, and journal articles. The websites, exercises, and recommended readings listed below are easily accessed on this site as well.

## Recommended Websites

The following websites provide links to dissident revolutionary organizations, movements, and information:

Foreign Terrorist Organizations: http://www.state.gov/s/ct/rls/

Intifada.com: http://www.intifada.com/

Irish Northern Aid (Noraid): http://inac.org/

Naval Postgraduate School (Terrorist Group Profiles): http://www.nps.edu/Library/Research/SubjectGuides/SpecialTopics/TerroristProfile/TerroristGroupProfiles.html/

PLO Negotiations Affairs Department (NAD): http://www.nad-plo.org/

## Web Exercise

Using this chapter's recommended websites, conduct an online investigation of dissident terrorism.

1. How would you describe the self-images presented by dissident movements?
2. Based on the information given by the monitoring organizations, are some dissident movements seemingly more threatening than others? Less threatening? Why?
3. Compare the dissident websites to the monitoring agencies' sites. Are any of the dissident groups *unfairly* reported by the monitoring agencies?

For an online search of dissident terrorism, readers should activate the search engine on their Web browser and enter the following keywords:

"Revolutionary Movements"

The names of specific dissident organizations

"Terrorist Organizations (or Groups)"

# Recommended Readings

The following publications provide discussions on dissident activism, protest movements, and violence:

Barkan, Steven E., and Lynne L. Snowden. *Collective Violence*. 2nd ed. Cornwall-on-Hudson, NY: Sloan Publishing, 2007.

Bell, J. Boywer. *The IRA 1968–2000: Analysis of a Secret Army*. London: Frank Cass, 2000.

Cambanis, Thanassis. *A Privilege to Die: Inside Hezbollah's Legions and Their Endless War Against Israel*. New York: Free Press, 2010.

Cromer, Geralde. *Insurgent Terrorism*. Aldershot, UK: Ashgate, 2006.

Dekker, Ted, and Carl Medearis. *Tea With Hezbollah: Sitting at the Enemies' Table*. New York: Doubleday, 2010.

Follian, John. *Jackal: The Complete Story of the Legendary Terrorist, Carlos the Jackal*. New York: Arcade Publishing, 2011.

Horne, Alistair. *A Savage War of Peace: Algeria 1954–1962*. New York: New York Review Books, 2006.

Hughes, James. *Chechnya: From Nationalism to Jihad*. Philadelphia: University of Pennsylvania Press, 2007.

Jaber, Hala. *Hezbollah: Born With a Vengeance*. New York: Columbia University Press, 1997.

Karmon, Eli. *Coalitions Between Terrorist Organizations: Revolutionaries, Nationalists, and Islamists*. Boston: Martinus Nijhoff, 2005.

Mallin, Jay, ed. *Terror and Urban Guerrillas: A Study of Tactics and Documents*. Coral Gables, FL: University of Miami Press, 1971.

Mitchell, Thomas G. *When Peace Fails: Lessons From Belfast for the Middle East*. Jefferson, NC: McFarland, 2010.

Norton, Augustus R. *Hezbollah: A Short History*. Princeton, NJ: Princeton University Press, 2009.

Raab, David. *Terror in Black September: The First Eyewitness Account of the Infamous 1970 Hijacking*. New York: Palgrave Macmillan, 2007.

Rosen, David M. *Armies of the Young: Child Soldiers in War and Terrorism*. New Brunswick, NJ: Rutgers University Press, 2005.

Shay, Shaul. *Islamic Terror Abductions in the Middle East*. Portland, OR: Sussex Academic Press, 2007.

Shirlow, Peter. *The End of Ulster Loyalism?* New York: Manchester University Press, 2012.

Spaaij, Ramon. *Lone-Wolf Terrorism*. The Hague, Netherlands: COT Institute for Safety, Security and Crisis Management, 2007.

Wickham-Crowley, Timothy P. *Guerrillas and Revolution in Latin America: A Comparative Study of Insurgents and Regimes Since 1956*. Princeton, NJ: Princeton University Press, 1993.

# Violence in the Name of the Faith

CHAPTER 6

## Religious Terrorism

Religious extremism is a central attribute of the New Terrorism. It has become a binding ideology for many extremists, in part because it provides an uncomplicated sense of purpose and a clear worldview. But how do individuals come to adopt religious revolution as their primary purpose in life? What kind of personal journey leads them to view the world through the lens of religious intolerance?

The case of **Abu Musab al-Zarqawi** is an important study of how young Muslims turn to *jihad*. During the U.S.-led occupation of Iraq after the invasion of March 2003, al-Zarqawi became a primary symbol of Islamist resistance. His likeness and name became as well known as Osama bin Laden's, and he became synonymous with the type of adversary the United States expected to fight in the war on terrorism. Al-Zarqawi's ideology encompassed a fervent internationalism, believing that all Muslim-populated countries should be governed in accordance with Islamic law, and that *jihad* must be waged to protect the faith.

Born Ahmed Khalayleh in the Jordanian town of Zarqa (from which he adopted his name), al-Zarqawi was a young man who lived a fast and nonreligious life during his early years. He fought, drank alcohol, was heavily tattooed, dropped out of high school, and had a reputation for being incorrigible. However, he joined many other young men by volunteering to serve as a fighter in the anti-Soviet *jihad* in Afghanistan during the 1980s. It was during this service that al-Zarqawi began to become deeply religious by immersing himself in reading the Qur'an

and accepting the worldview that the "Muslim nation" should be defended from nonbelievers. As was the case with many who served in Afghanistan, he returned home in 1992 with a global religious outlook.

In Jordan, al-Zarqawi became a follower of the radical cleric Sheikh Abu Muhammed al-Maqdisi, a Palestinian who advocated the overthrow of all secular governments. Because of his association with al-Maqdisi, al-Zarqawi and other followers were jailed as political prisoners. During several years in prison, al-Zarqawi stood out as a temperamental leader who eventually eclipsed his mentor al-Maqdisi. He became a radical among radicals, arguably more extremist in his ideology than Osama bin Laden. To al-Zarqawi, all who did not share his interpretation of Islam were unbelievers and therefore enemies—even Shi'a Muslims were enemies.

After his release from prison in Jordan, he apparently drifted to Pakistan and then Afghanistan, where he allegedly had poor relations with Al-Qa'ida. Sometime around the time of the U.S.-led invasion of Afghanistan, al-Zarqawi made his way to Iraq and eventually became a major symbol of Sunni Islamist resistance to the occupation. As a result, Osama bin Laden apparently solicited al-Zarqawi to put aside their differences, and they declared al-Zarqawi's movement to be the **Al-Qa'ida Organization for Holy War in Iraq**. This movement became a prototypical predecessor for later Sunni Islamist movements such as the Islamic State of Iraq and the Levant (ISIS).

In July 2005, al-Zarqawi announced on behalf of Al-Qa'ida in Iraq that the organization would wage war against members of the Iraqi armed forces because they were "apostates," as well as against the Badr Brigade (formally known as the Badr Organization), a powerful Shi'a militia.[b] Despite a massive manhunt in Iraq and a $25 million bounty, al-Zarqawi managed to elude American forces until June 2006, when he was killed by an American air strike in a farmhouse near Baqubah.[c]

## Notes

a. The "ISIS" designation is derived from either "Islamic State of Iraq and al-Sham" or "Islamic State of Iraq and Syria."

b. See Reuters. "Zarqawi Says Qaeda Forms Wing to Fight Shi'ites—Web." *New York Times,* July 5, 2005.

c. See Allen, Mike, and James Carney. "Funeral for Evil." *Time,* June 19, 2006. See also Powell, Bill, and Scott MacLeod. "How They Killed Him." *Time,* June 19, 2006.

Terrorism in the name of religion has become the predominant model for political violence in the modern world. This is not to suggest that it is the only model, because nationalism and ideology remain as potent catalysts for extremist behavior. However, religious extremism has become a central issue for the global community.

In the modern era, religious terrorism has increased in its frequency, scale of violence, and global reach. At the same time, a relative decline has occurred in secular—nonreligious—terrorism. The old ideologies of class conflict, anticolonial liberation, and secular nationalism have been challenged by a new and vigorous infusion of sectarian (religious) ideologies. Grassroots extremist support for religious violence has been most widespread among populations living in repressive societies that do not permit demands for reform or other expressions of dissent. In this regard,

it is perhaps not surprising that religion should become a far more popular motivation for terrorism in the post–Cold War era as old ideologies lie discredited by the collapse of the Soviet Union and communist ideology, while the promise of munificent benefits from the liberal-democratic, capitalist state . . . fails to materialize in many countries throughout the world.[1]

❖ **Photo 6.1**

Abu Musab al-Zarqawi. From a video of the Jordanian-born leader of Al-Qa'ida in Iraq. Al-Zarqawi was accused of leading a campaign of kidnappings and beheadings of foreign workers as well as for scores of bombings that killed hundreds of Shi'as and U.S. forces. He was killed in a U.S. air strike in June 2006.

© handout/Reuters/Corbis

What is religious terrorism? What are its fundamental attributes? How is religion-inspired violence rationalized? Religious terrorism is a type of political violence that is motivated by an absolute belief that an otherworldly power has sanctioned—and commanded—the application of terrorist violence for the greater glory of the faith. Acts that are committed in the name of the faith will be forgiven by the otherworldly power and perhaps rewarded in an afterlife. In essence, one's religious faith legitimizes violence so long as such violence is an expression of the will of one's deity.

Table 6.1 presents a model that compares the fundamental characteristics of religious and secular terrorism. The discussion in this chapter will review the following:

- Primary and Secondary Motives: The Idiosyncratic Quality of Religious Terrorism
- Historical Cases in Point: Fighting, Dying, and Killing in the Name of the Faith
- State-Sponsored Religious Terrorism in the Modern Era
- Dissident Religious Terrorism in the Modern Era
- The Future of Religious Terrorism

[1]Hoffman, Bruce. *Inside Terrorism*. New York: Columbia University Press, 1998, p. 92.

| Table 6.1 | Case Comparison: Religious and Secular Terrorism |
|---|---|

Religious and secular terrorism have contrasting activity profiles. Both environments certainly pose threats to targeted systems, but the manifestations of dissent differ in potential scale and scope of impact.

The quality of violence, constituency profile, and relationship to the existing system are summarized in the following table.

| Environment | Activity Profile | | | |
|---|---|---|---|---|
| | Quality of Violence[a] | Scope of Violence | Constituency Profile | Relationship to Existing System |
| **Religious** | Unconstrained scale of terrorist violence | Expansive target definition | Narrow, insular, and isolated | Alienated "true believers" |
| | Result: Unconstrained choice of weapons and tactics | Result: Indiscriminate use of violence | Result: No appeals to a broader audience | Result: Completely reconfigured social order |
| **Secular** | Constrained scale of terrorist violence | Focused target definition | Inclusive, for the championed group | Liberators |
| | Result: Relative constraint in choice of weapons and tactics | Result: Relative discrimination in use of violence | Result: Appeals to actual or potential supporters | Result: Restructured or rebuilt society |

*Source:* Hoffman, Bruce. *Inside Terrorism.* New York: Columbia University Press, 1998, pp. 94–5.

a. Communal terrorism is rarely constrained and is a case in point of convergence in the quality of violence used by religious and secular terrorism.

# ❖ Primary and Secondary Motives: The Idiosyncratic Quality of Religious Terrorism

Religious terrorism is an idiosyncratic type of terrorism; it originates from countless national, cultural, and historical contexts. Unlike secular terrorism, which usually has an inherent (but fringe) rationality, religious terrorism is often an expression of unquestioned faith in a supernatural purpose. It is, therefore, very much contingent on trends within specific religions, the historical experiences of ethnonational groups, and the unique political environments of nations. As a basis for terrorism, religious faith has been applied in different ways, depending on the cultural and political environments of each terrorist movement. In some environments, religion is the primary motive for terrorist behavior. In other contexts, it is a secondary motive that is part of an overarching cultural identity for politically violent movements.

As a primary motive, religion is at the very core of an extremist group's political, social, and revolutionary agenda. Within this context, the religious belief system is the driving force behind the group's behavior. Examples of this profile are found in the Middle East and elsewhere among *jihadi* Islamic fundamentalists, in India among Hindu extremists, and in the United States among violent Christian antiabortionists. In the United States, the Army of God has expressed support for and advocated violent attacks against abortion clinics and providers. The following quotation is an excerpt from a declaration in "The Army of God Manual":[2]

---

[2]Army of God. "The Army of God Manual: Declaration." Army of God: http://armyofgod.com/ (accessed June 17, 2005).

We, the remnant of God-fearing men and women of the United States of Amerika [*sic*], do officially declare war on the entire child-killing industry. After praying, fasting, and making continual supplication to God for your pagan, heathen, infidel souls, we then peacefully, passively presented our bodies in front of your death camps, begging you to stop the mass murder of infants. . . . Yet you mocked God and continued the holocaust. . . . No longer! All of the options have expired. Our Most Dread Sovereign Lord God requires that whosoever sheds man's blood, by man shall his blood be shed . . . we are forced to take arms against you. . . . You shall not be tortured at our hands. Vengeance belongs to God only. However, execution is rarely gentle.

As a secondary motive, religion represents one aspect of an extremist group's overall identity and agenda. For many ethnonationalist and other revolutionary movements, national independence or some other degree of autonomy forms the primary motivation for their violent behavior. Religious affiliation can be important because it is an element of their ethnic or national identity, but their ultimate goal is grounded in their secular identity. Examples of this profile are found in Northern Ireland among Catholic and Protestant terrorists, in southern Sudan among Christians and believers in traditional faiths, and in pre-independence Palestine among Jewish terrorists. In Palestine, the Jewish terrorist group Lohmey Heruth Israel (Fighters for the Freedom of Israel)—commonly known as the **Stern Gang**—issued the following (mostly nationalistic) rationalization for the group's violence against the British occupation of Palestine:

Now this is the law of our war. So long as there is fear in the heart of any Jew in the world, so long as there are embers burning under our feet anywhere in the world, so long as there is a foreign policeman guarding the gates of our homeland, so long as there is a foreign master over our country, so long as we do not rule our own land, so long shall we be in your way. You will look around you and fear day and night.[3]

It should be understood that the concept of primary vis-à-vis secondary motives is not exclusively an attribute of religious extremism but also exists among secular extremist groups. For example, Marxism has been applied in different ways, depending on the political environment of each extremist movement. Ideological groups such as Italy's Red Brigade were motivated *primarily* by Marxist ideals during the 1970s and 1980s, but nationalist movements such as Vietnam's Viet Cong were motivated *secondarily* by ideology during the 1960s and 1970s—the Viet Cong's primary motivation was its national identity.

## Understanding *Jihad* as a Primary Religious Motive: An Observation and Caveat

Keeping the idiosyncratic quality of religious terrorism in mind, it is arguably necessary to make a sensitive observation—and caveat—about the study of religious terrorism in the modern era. The observation is that in the modern era, the incidence of religious terrorism is disproportionately committed by radical Islamists:

Popular Western perception equates radical Islam with terrorism. . . . There is, of course, no Muslim or Arab monopoly in the field of religious fanaticism; it exists and leads to acts of violence in the United States, India, Israel, and many other countries. But the frequency of Muslim- and Arab-inspired terrorism is still striking. . . . A discussion of religion-inspired terrorism cannot possibly confine itself to radical Islam, but it has to take into account the Muslim countries' preeminent position in this field.[4]

---

[3]From the Stern Gang's journal, *Hazit,* quoted in Hurwood, Bernhardt J. *Society and the Assassin: A Background Book on Political Murder.* New York: Parents' Magazine Press, 1970, p. 149.

[4]Laqueur, Walter. *The New Terrorism: Fanaticism and the Arms of Mass Destruction.* New York: Oxford University Press, 1999, p. 129.

The caveat is that there is much misunderstanding in the West about the historical and cultural origins of the growth of radical interpretations of Islam. One such misunderstanding is the common belief that the concept of "holy war" is an underlying principle of the Islamic faith. Another misunderstanding is that Muslims are united in supporting *jihad*. This is simplistic and fundamentally incorrect. Although the term *jihad* is widely presumed in the West to refer exclusively to waging war against nonbelievers, an Islamic *jihad* is *not* the equivalent of a Christian Crusade (the Crusades are discussed later in this chapter). In this regard,

> most Muslims, even most fundamentalists, are not terrorists. Instead, they have overwhelmingly been the victims of violent conflicts. Hundreds of thousands of Muslims were killed in the war between Iran and Iraq, and the civil wars in Afghanistan and Algeria led to similarly horrific numbers of casualties. Noncombatant Muslims have suffered untold losses in the war between Chechnya and Russia, in the turmoil in Indonesia, and throughout much of Africa and the Middle East.[5]

Chapter Perspective 6.1 provides some clarification of the concept of *jihad*.

## CHAPTER PERSPECTIVE 6.1: *Jihad*: Struggling in the Way of God

The concept of *jihad* is a central tenet in Islam. Contrary to misinterpretations common in the West, the term literally means a sacred "struggle" or "effort" rather than an armed conflict or fanatical holy war.[a] Although a *jihad* can certainly be manifested as a holy war, it more correctly refers to the duty of Muslims to personally strive "in the way of God."[b]

This is the primary meaning of the term as used in the Qur'an, which refers to an internal effort to reform bad habits in the Islamic community or within the individual Muslim. The term is also used more specifically to denote a war waged in the service of religion.[c]

Regarding how one should wage *jihad*,

> The *greater jihad* refers to the struggle each person has within himself or herself to do what is right. Because of human pride, selfishness, and sinfulness, people of faith must constantly wrestle with themselves and strive to do what is right and good. The *lesser jihad* involves the outward defense of Islam. Muslims should be prepared to defend Islam, including military defense, when the community of faith is under attack.[d] (italics added)

Thus, waging an Islamic *jihad* is not the same as waging a Christian crusade—it has a broader and more intricate meaning. Nevertheless, it is permissible—and even a duty—to wage war to defend the faith against aggressors. Under this type of *jihad*, warfare is conceptually defensive in nature; in contrast, the Christian Crusades were conceptually offensive in nature. Those who engage in armed *jihad* are known as *mujahideen*, or holy warriors. *Mujahideen* who receive **"martyrdom"** by being killed in the name of the faith will find that

> awaiting them in paradise are rivers of milk and honey, and beautiful young women. Those entering paradise are eventually reunited with their families and as martyrs stand in front of God as innocent as a newborn baby.[e]

The precipitating causes for the modern resurgence of the armed and radical *jihadi* movement are twofold: the revolutionary ideals and ideology of the 1979 Iranian Revolution and the practical application of *jihad* against the Soviet Union's occupation of Afghanistan.

*(Continued)*

---

[5]Griset, Pamala L., and Sue Mahan. *Terrorism in Perspective*. 3rd ed. Thousand Oaks, CA: Sage, 2013, p. 99.

(Continued)

Some radical Muslim clerics and scholars have concluded that the Afghan *jihad* brought God's judgment against the Soviet Union, leading to the collapse of its empire. As a consequence, radical *jihadis* fervently believe that they are fighting in the name of an inexorable force that will end in total victory and guarantee them a place in paradise. From their perspective, their war is a just war.[f]

### Notes

a.  Armstrong, Karen. *Islam: A Short History.* New York: Modern Library, 2000, p. 201.

b.  Burke, Josh, and James Norton. "Q&A: Islamic Fundamentalism: A World-Renowned Scholar Explains Key Points of Islam." *Christian Science Monitor,* October 4, 2001.

c.  Armstrong, *Islam,* p. 201.

d.  Burke and Norton, "Q&A."

e.  Laqueur, Walter. *The New Terrorism: Fanaticism and the Arms of Mass Destruction.* New York: Oxford University Press, 1999, p. 100.

f.  See Goldstein, Evan R. "How Just Is Islam's Just-War Tradition?" *The Chronicle Review,* April 18, 2008.

## A Case of Secondary Religious Motive: *The Protocols of the Learned Elders of Zion*

Extremist religious and secular ideologies have historically scapegoated undesirable groups. Many conspiracy theories have been invented to denigrate these groups and to implicate them in nefarious plans to destroy an existing order. Some of these conspiracy theories possess quasi-religious elements that in effect classify the scapegoated group as being in opposition to a natural and sacred order.

Among right-wing nationalists and racists, there often exists a convergence between scapegoating and mysticism. Just as it is common for rightists to assert their natural and sacred superiority, it is also normal for them to demonize a scapegoated group, essentially declaring that the entire group is inherently evil. One quasi-religious conspiracy theory is the promulgation of a document titled ***The Protocols of the Learned Elders of Zion***.[6]

The *Protocols* originated in czarist Russia and were allegedly the true proceedings of a meeting of a mysterious committee of the Jewish faith, during which a plot to rule the world was hatched—in league with the Freemasons. The *Protocols* are a detailed record of this alleged conspiracy for world domination, but they were, in fact, a forgery written by the secret police (**Okhrana**) of Czar Nicholas II around 1895 and later published by a Russian professor named Sergei Nilus. Many anti-Semitic groups have used this document to justify the repression of European Jews, and it was an ideological foundation for the outbreak of anti-Jewish violence in Europe, including massacres and **pogroms** (violent anti-Jewish campaigns in Eastern Europe).

The National Socialist (Nazi) movement and Adolf Hitler used the *Protocols* extensively. Modern Eurocentric neo-Nazis, Middle Eastern extremists (both secular and religious), and Christian extremists continue to publish and circulate the *Protocols* as anti-Semitic propaganda. In this regard, neo-Nazis and Middle Eastern extremists have found common cause in quasi-religious anti-Semitism. In 1993, a Russian court formally ruled that the *Protocols* are a forgery.[7] Nevertheless, the document continues to be referenced by anti-Semitic and other extremists as a historical document.

---

[6]*The Protocols of the Learned Elders of Zion* has been extensively published on the Internet. It is readily available from websites promoting civil liberties, neo-Nazi propaganda, anti-Semitism, and Islamist extremism.

[7]See Hiltzik, Michael A. "Russian Court Rules 'Protocols' an Anti-Semitic Forgery." *Los Angeles Times,* November 28, 1993.

# ❖ Historical Cases in Point: Fighting, Dying, and Killing in the Name of the Faith

Terrorism carried out in the name of the faith has long been a feature of human affairs. The histories of people, civilizations, nations, and empires are replete with examples of extremist "true believers" who engage in violence to promote their particular belief system. Some religious terrorists are inspired by defensive motives, others seek to ensure the predominance of their faith, and others are motivated by an aggressive amalgam of these tendencies.

Why do some movements and ethnonational groups link their cause to an underlying spiritual principle? Is it accurate to characterize all spiritually rooted violence as terrorist or extremist? What kinds of historical cases illustrate the idiosyncratic qualities of religious violence? To begin, we may observe that faith-based violence exhibits the same qualities as other terrorist environments. Religious terrorism can be communal, genocidal, nihilistic, or revolutionary. It can be committed by lone wolves, clandestine cells, large dissident movements, or governments. And, depending on one's perspective, there is often debate about whether the perpetrators should be classified as terrorists or religious freedom fighters.

The following cases are historical examples of the idiosyncratic qualities of religious violence. This is a selective survey (by no means exhaustive) that will demonstrate how some examples of faith-based violence are clearly examples of terrorism, how others are not so clear, and how each example must be considered within its historical and cultural context.

## Judeo-Christian Antiquity

Within the Judeo-Christian belief system, there are references in the Bible not only to assassinations and conquest but also to the complete annihilation of enemy nations in the name of the faith. One such campaign is described in the Book of Joshua.

The story of Joshua's conquest of Canaan is the story of the culmination of the ancient Hebrews' return to Canaan. To Joshua and his followers, this was the "Promised Land" of the covenant between God and the chosen people. According to the Bible, the Canaanite cities were destroyed and the Canaanites themselves were attacked until "there was no one left who breathed."[8] Assuming that Joshua and his army put to the sword all the inhabitants of the 31 cities mentioned in the Bible, and assuming that each city averaged 10,000 people, his conquest cost 310,000 lives.[9]

Within the context of this account, to the ancient Hebrews the Promised Land had been occupied by enemy trespassers. To fulfill God's covenant, it was rational and necessary from their perspective to drive them from the land, exterminating them when deemed necessary.

Hulton Archive/Getty Images

❖ **Photo 6.2**
The conquest of Bethlehem. A romanticized depiction of victorious Christian Crusaders, who seized Bethlehem in June 1099 during the First Crusade. The Crusaders subsequently killed virtually all of the town's inhabitants.

## Christian Crusades

During the Middle Ages, the Western Christian (i.e., Roman Catholic) Church launched at least nine invasions of the Islamic east, the first one in 1095. These invasions were termed **Crusades** because they were conducted in the name of the Cross. The purpose of the Crusades was to recapture the holy lands from the disunited Muslims, whom they referred to collectively as Saracens.

---

[8]Joshua 11, in *The Holy Bible, New Revised Standard Version*.

[9]Iadicola, Peter, and Anson Shupe. *Violence, Inequality, and Human Freedom*. New York: General Hall, 1998, p. 175. Citing Scott, Ralph A. *A New Look at Biblical Crime*. Chicago: Nelson-Hall, 1979, p. 66.

Christian knights and soldiers answered the call for many reasons. The promises of land, booty, and glory were certainly central secular reasons. Another important reason was the idealistic spiritual promise, made by Pope Urban II, that fighting and dying in the name of the Cross would ensure martyrdom and thereby guarantee a place in heaven. Liberation of the holy lands would bring eternal salvation. Thus, "knights who with pious intent took the Cross would earn a remission from temporal penalties for all his sins; if he died in battle he would earn remission of his sins."[10] This religious ideology was reflected in the war cry of the early Crusades: *Deus vult!* ("God wills it!").[11]

During the First Crusade, Western knights—primarily Frankish soldiers—captured a broad swath of biblical lands, including Jerusalem and Bethlehem. When cities and towns were captured, most of the Muslim and Jewish inhabitants were killed outright, a practice that was common in medieval warfare. When Jerusalem was captured in July 1099, Frankish knights massacred thousands of Muslim, Jewish, and Orthodox Christian residents. An embellished Crusader letter sent to Pope Urban II in Rome boasted that the blood of the Saracens reached the bridles of the Crusaders' horses.

Not all Christian Crusades were fought in Muslim lands. The Western Church also purged its territories of Jews and divergent religious beliefs that were denounced as heresies. The zealousness and violence of these purges became legendary. During the brutal Albigensian Crusade in southern France during the 13th century, the story was told that concerns were raised about loyal and innocent Catholics who were being killed along with targeted members of the enemy Cathar sect. The pope's representative, Arnaud Amaury, allegedly replied, "Kill them all, God will know his own."

The Church-sanctioned invasions and atrocities were deemed to be in accordance with God's wishes and therefore perfectly acceptable. An extreme and unquestioning faith in the cause led to a series of campaigns of terror against the non-Christian (and sometimes the Orthodox Christian) residents of conquered cities and territories. In a typical and tragic irony of the time, the Greek Orthodox city of Constantinople, center of the Byzantine Empire and one of the great cities of the world, was captured and sacked by Western Crusaders in 1204 during the Fourth Crusade. The Crusaders looted the city and created a short-lived Latin Empire, which lasted until 1261.

## The Assassins[12]

The **Order of Assassins** (sometimes referred to as the Brotherhood of Assassins) was founded by Hasan ibn al-Sabbah in 11th-century Persia. Al-Sabbah was a caliph (religious head) of the Ismaili sect of Islam. He espoused a radical version of Ismaili Islam and founded the Order of Assassins to defend this interpretation of the faith. Beginning in 1090, he and his followers seized a string of fortresses in the mountains of northern Persia, the first of which was the strong fortress of Alamut near Qazvin. Because of these origins, al-Sabbah was called "The Old Man of the Mountain."

The word *assassin* was allegedly derived from the drug hashish, which popular opinion has long suggested al-Sabbah's followers ate prior to committing acts of violence in the name of the faith.[13] They referred to themselves as *hashashins* or *hashishis,* reputedly meaning "hashish eaters," although this is widely considered by historians to be an apocryphal attribution. During the early years of the movement, Assassin followers spread out of the mountains to the cities of Persia, modern Iraq, Syria, and the Christian Crusader–occupied areas of Palestine. The Assassins killed

---

[10]Cohn, Norman. *The Pursuit of the Millennium*. New York: Oxford University Press, 1971, p. 61. Quoted in Iadicola and Shupe, *Violence*, p. 177.

[11]The correct Classical Latin translation is *Deus vult*. At the time of the Crusades, a popular corruption of the Classical Latin by many Europeans led to adopting the war cry of *Deus lo volt!*

[12]For a history of the Assassin movement, see Lewis, Bernard. *The Assassins: A Radical Sect in Islam*. New York: Oxford University Press, 1987.

[13]Lewis discounts the assertion that the Assassins drugged themselves. He argues that "in all probability it was the name that gave rise to the story, rather than the reverse." Lewis, *The Assassins*, p. 12.

many people, including fellow Muslims who were Sunnis, and Christians. Suicide missions were common, and some Crusader leaders went so far as to pay tribute to the Assassins so that the Assassins would leave them alone.

The Assassins were very adept at disguise, stealth, and surprise killings, and thus the word *assassination* was coined to describe this tactic. A key component of the Assassins' beliefs was the absolute righteousness of their cause and methodology. To kill or be killed was a good thing because it was done in the name of the faith and ensured a place in paradise after death. This belief in complete justification and ultimate reward is practiced by many modern-day religious terrorists.

Although their political impact was negligible and the Assassin organization was eliminated in 1256, they left a profound psychological mark on their era and, in many ways, on the modern era.

## A Secret Cult of Murder

In India during the 13th through the 19th centuries, the **Thuggee** cult existed among some worshippers of the Hindu goddess Kali, the destroyer. They were called by various names, including Phansigars ("noose operators") and Dacoits ("members of a gang of robbers"). Thuggee comes from *thag*, Hindi for thief, from which the English word *thug* is derived.

Thuggees were a fraternal band of robbers whose behavior they believed glorified Kali. They raised their sons (and often kidnapped children) to become members of the cult, thus passing the tradition to the next generation. Members would strangle sacrificial victims—usually travelers—with a noose called a ***phansi*** in the name of Kali and then rob and ritually mutilate and bury them. Offerings would be made to Kali.

The British eventually destroyed the movement during the 19th century, although the death toll of Thuggee victims was staggering: "This secretive cult is believed to have murdered 20,000 victims a year . . . perhaps dispatching as many as several million victims altogether before it was broken up by British officials."[14] There are few debatable counterpoints about this cult—the Thuggees waged a campaign of religious and criminal terror for centuries.

## Modern Arab Nationalism and the Rise of Islamist Extremism

The Arab world passed through several important political phases during the 20th century. Overlordship by the Ottoman Empire ended in 1918 after World War I. This was followed by European domination, which ended in the years after World War II. New Arab and North African states were initially ruled primarily by monarchs or civilians who were always authoritarian and frequently despotic. A series of military coups and other political upheavals led to the modern era of governance. These phases had a significant influence on activism among Arab nationalists and intellectuals, culminating in the late 1940s when the chief symbol of Western encroachment became the state of Israel. Postwar activism in the Arab Muslim world likewise progressed through several intellectual phases, most of them secular expressions of nationalism and socialism. The secular phases included the following:

- Anticolonial nationalism, during which Arab nationalists resisted the presence of European administrators and armed forces
- Pan-Arab nationalism (Nasserism), led by Egyptian President Gamel Abdel-Nasser, which advocated the creation of a single dynamic United Arab Republic
- Secular leftist radicalism, which was adopted by many activists to promote Marxist or other socialist principles of governance, sometimes in opposition to their own governments

[14]Iadicola and Shupe, *Violence,* p. 181. Citing Haught, James A. *Holy Horrors.* Buffalo, NY: Prometheus, 1990, p. 34.

Many activists and intellectuals became disenchanted with these movements when they failed to deliver political reforms, economic prosperity, and the desired degree of respect from the international community. In particular, several humiliating military defeats at the hands of the Israelis—and the seemingly intractable plight of the Palestinians—diminished the esteem and deference once enjoyed by the secular movements. Arab nationalists—both secular and sectarian—had struggled since the end of World War II to resist what they perceived to be Western domination and exploitation, and some tradition-oriented nationalists began to interpret Western culture and values to be alien to Muslim morality and values.

As a result, new movements promoting Islamist extremism began to overshadow the ideologies of the previous generation. This has placed many Islamists at odds with existing Arab governments, many of which are administered under the principles of the older ideologies.

In the post–Cold War political environment, the adoption of Islam as a vehicle for liberation is a logical progression. When radical secular ideologies and movements achieved minimal progress in resisting the West and Israel, and when secular Arab governments aggressively repressed any expressions of domestic dissent, many activists and intellectuals turned to radical interpretations of Islam. This should not be surprising, because

> the discrediting of leftist ideologies within the Muslim world, like the earlier loss of respect for Nasserite pan-Arabism . . . has . . . meant that political Islam has become the main vehicle there for expression . . . of strongly held dissent. A young man in a Muslim country who wants to make a forceful statement against the existing order has few avenues for doing so except through membership in a radical Islamic group.[15]

There is a sense of collegiality and comradeship among many Islamists, but there are also differences within the ideologies of many leaders, as well as between the Sunni and Shi'a traditions. However, the Islamist movement has transcended most ethnic and cultural differences and is a global phenomenon.

## Cult Case: Mysticism and Rebellion in Uganda[16]

### Phase 1: The Holy Spirit Mobile Force

Uganda in 1987 was a hotbed of rebellion, with several rebel groups opposing the new government of President Yoweri Museveni. One rebel group was the **Holy Spirit Mobile Force**, inspired and led by the mystic Alice Lakwena. Lakwena claimed to be inspired by the Christian Holy Spirit and preached that her movement would defeat Musevani's forces and purge Uganda of witchcraft and superstition. Because her followers championed the Acholi tribe (which she declared to be God's chosen people), the Holy Spirit Mobile Force attracted some 10,000 followers, many of them former soldiers from previous Ugandan government armies. In late 1987, she led thousands of her followers against Museveni's army. To protect themselves from death, Holy Spirit Mobile Force fighters anointed themselves with holy shea nut butter oil, which they believed would turn the enemy's bullets into water. She also told her followers that the stones they threw at the enemy would become hand grenades. When they met Museveni's forces, thousands of Lakwena's followers were slaughtered in the face of automatic weapons and artillery fire. Alice Lakwena fled the country to Kenya, where she lived until her death in January 2007.

### Phase 2: The Lord's Resistance Army

Josef Kony reorganized the Holy Spirit Mobile Force into the **Lord's Resistance Army**. Kony blended together Christianity, Islam, and witchcraft into a bizarre, mystical foundation for his

---

[15]Pillar, Paul R. *Terrorism and U.S. Foreign Policy.* Washington, DC: Brookings Institution Press, 2001, pp. 45–6.

[16]Much of the discussion has been adapted from Human Rights Watch. *The Scars of Death: Children Abducted by the Lord's Resistance Army in Uganda.* New York: Human Rights Watch, 1997.

movement. Kony proclaimed to his followers that he would overthrow the government, purify the Acholi people, and seize power and reign in accordance with the principles of the biblical Ten Commandments.

From its inception, the Lord's Resistance Army was exceptionally brutal and waged near-genocidal terrorist campaigns—largely against the Acholi people whom it claimed to champion. The movement destroyed villages and towns, killed thousands of people, drove hundreds of thousands more from the land, abducted thousands of children, and routinely committed acts of mass rape and banditry. With bases in southern Sudan, the Lord's Resistance Army proved to be extremely difficult for the Ugandan government to defeat in the field.

An estimated 30,000 children became kidnap victims, and 1.6 million Ugandans were displaced into refugee camps. These camps became regular targets of the Lord's Resistance Army, which raided them for supplies, to terrorize the refugees, and to kidnap children. Among the kidnapped children, boys were forced to become soldiers and girls became sex slaves known as bush wives. There has been some hope of ending the conflict. In 2005, a top Lord's Resistance Army commander surrendered, the government claimed a temporary cease-fire, and Sudan began to stabilize its border with Uganda after its own southern civil war ended. Unfortunately, the Lord's Resistance Army continued its pattern of violence and abductions, and from 2008 through 2011 the group conducted destructive raids into the neighboring Democratic Republic of Congo. The resilience of the Lord's Resistance Army was unmistakable, as it repeatedly survived a series of operations designed to neutralize its effectiveness.

As in the case of the Thuggees, the Lord's Resistance Army is unquestionably an example of a cultic movement that waged a campaign of religious terrorism.

# ❖ State-Sponsored Religious Terrorism in the Modern Era

State terrorism is the most organized, and potentially the most far-reaching, application of terrorist violence. Governments possess an array of resources that are unavailable to substate dissident groups, which means that the state is unmatched in its ability to commit acts of violence. Government sponsorship of terrorism is not limited to providing support for ideological or ethnonational movements. It also incorporates state sponsorship of religious revolutionary movements.

## National Case: Iran

Iran became a preeminent state sponsor of religious terrorism after the overthrow of the monarchy of Shah Muhammed Reza Pahlavi in 1979 and the creation of the theocratic Islamic Republic of Iran soon thereafter.

Iran has been implicated in the sponsorship of a number of groups that are known to have engaged in terrorist violence, making it a perennial entry on the U.S. Department of State's list of state sponsors of terrorism.[17] The 125,000-member **Revolutionary Guards Corps** has a unit—the **Qods (Jerusalem) Force**—that promotes Islamic revolution abroad and the "liberation" of Jerusalem from non-Muslims. Members of the Revolutionary Guards have appeared in Lebanon and Sudan, and the United States designated the entire corps a terrorist group in August 2007.[18] Significantly, Iranian officials have repeatedly announced the formation of Iranian "martyrdom" units that are prepared to engage in suicide attacks against American and Israeli targets.[19]

---

[17]For a good policy discussion of Iran's involvement in terrorism, see Sick, Gary. "Iran: Confronting Terrorism." *The Washington Quarterly* (Autumn 2003): 83–98. See also Pollack, Kenneth, and Ray Takeyh. "Taking on Tehran." *Foreign Affairs* (March/April 2005).

[18]Wright, Robin. "Iranian Unit to be Labeled 'Terrorist.'" *Washington Post,* August 15, 2007.

[19]Alfoneh, Ali. "Iran's Suicide Brigades." *Middle Eastern Quarterly* 14, no. 1 (2007).

### Case in Point: Iranian Support for Lebanon's Hezbollah

An important example of Iranian support for politically sympathetic groups is the patronage and assistance given by Iran to Lebanon's **Hezbollah** movement. The Iran–Hezbollah relationship is important because of the central role Hezbollah has played in the region's political environment.

Lebanon's Shi'a, who comprise roughly half of Lebanon's Muslims, have been a historically poorer and less politically influential population among Lebanon's religious groups. The Sunnis, Maronite Christians, and Druze typically wielded more authority. Hezbollah ("Party of God") is a Shi'a movement in Lebanon that arose to champion the country's Shi'a population. The organization emerged during the Lebanese civil war and Israel's 1982 invasion as a strongly symbolic champion for Lebanese independence and justice for the Shi'a population. Hezbollah was responsible for hundreds of incidents of political violence during the 1980s and 1990s. These incidents included kidnappings of Westerners in Beirut, suicide bombings, attacks against Israeli interests in South Lebanon, and attacks against Israel proper. They operated under various names, such as Islamic Jihad and Revolutionary Justice Organization. Hezbollah is a good case study for a number of issues, including the following:

- Proxies for state-sponsored terrorism
- Practitioners of religious dissident terrorism
- Participation in international terrorism
- Application of asymmetrical methods such as high-profile kidnappings and suicide bombings

Although it has proven to be an effective guerrilla and terrorist force, it is also a very diversified social activist organization. For example,

> Hezbollah provides social services to its followers, such as schools and medical services. It has engaged in a variety of business ventures, including supermarkets, bakeries, building, farming, bookshops, and clothing sales to true believers, partly to finance its terrorist activities.[20]

For some time, Hezbollah has been closely linked to Iran. Hezbollah's leaders, while sometimes guarded about their identification with Iran, have overtly stated that they support the ideals of the Iranian Revolution. Their ultimate goal is to create an Islamic republic in Lebanon, and they consider Israel to be an enemy of all Muslims. Hezbollah tends to consider Iran a "big brother" for its movement. As one leader stated, "Our relationship with the Islamic revolution [in Iran] is one of a junior to a senior . . . of a soldier to his commander."[21] Thus, at their root, the ideological bonds between the movement and the Iranian Revolution are strong.

These bonds allowed Iran's support to extend beyond ideological identification toward overt sponsorship. Beginning in the 1980s, Iran deployed members of its Revolutionary Guards Corps into Lebanon's Beka'a Valley—then under Syrian occupation—to organize Hezbollah into an effective fighting force. Iran provided training, funding, and other logistical support. This was done with the acquiescence of Syria, so that Hezbollah is also a pro-Syrian movement.

### Case in Point: Iranian Support for Palestinian Islamists

Iran has also promoted religion-motivated movements that are directly confronting the Israelis in Gaza, the West Bank, and inside Israel's borders. Since the early days of the Iranian Revolution, the Iranian regime has never been guarded about its goal to "liberate" Jerusalem. To achieve this goal, Iran has likewise never been guarded about its overt support for Palestinian organizations that

---

[20]Laqueur, *The New Terrorism*, p. 137.

[21]Kramer, Martin. "The Moral Logic of Hizballah." In *Origins of Terrorism: Psychologies, Ideologies, Theologies, States of Mind*, edited by Walter Reich. Washington, DC: Woodrow Wilson Center, 1998, p. 138. Quoting interview with Tufayli, *Ettela'at* (Tehran), August 20, 1985.

reject dialogue and negotiations with the Israelis. It has, in fact, provided significant assistance to the Palestinian cause by promoting the operations of religious movements. For example, two militant Islamic organizations—Palestine Islamic Jihad (PIJ) and Hamas (Islamic Resistance Movement)—are Palestinian extremist groups that received important support from Iran. Both groups perpetrated many acts of terrorism, including suicide attacks, bombings, shootings, and other violent assaults.

PIJ is not a single organization; rather, it is a loose affiliation of factions. It is an Islamic revolutionary movement that advocates violent *jihad* to form a Palestinian state. Iranian support to PIJ includes military instruction and logistical support. PIJ members have appeared in Hezbollah camps in Lebanon's Beka'a Valley and in Iran, and planning for terrorist attacks has apparently taken place in these locations. Members who received this training were infiltrated back into Gaza and the West Bank to wage *jihad* against Israel.

Hamas's roots lie in the Palestinian branch of the Muslim Brotherhood. It operates as both a social service organization and an armed resistance group that promotes *jihad*. Because of its social service component, Iran's **Fund for the Martyrs** has disbursed millions of dollars to Hamas. Hamas posted a representative to Iran who held a number of meetings with top Iranian officials. Iran has also provided Hamas with the same type of support that it provides PIJ; this includes military instruction, logistical support, training in Hezbollah's Beka'a Valley camps (prior to the Syrian withdrawal), and training in Iran. Hamas operatives returned from these facilities to Gaza and the West Bank.

## Regional Case: Pakistan and India

India and Pakistan are seemingly implacable rivals. Much of this rivalry is grounded in religious animosity between the Hindu and Muslim communities of the subcontinent, and the sponsorship of terrorist proxies has kept the region in a state of nearly constant tension.

Hindus and Muslims in Southwest Asia have engaged in sectarian violence since 1947, when British colonial rule ended. The spiritual and political architect of the movement against British rule was Indian leader Mahatma Gandhi, who led an independence movement based on nonviolence and principles of inclusive community. Unfortunately, Gandhi's deep spiritual convictions could not forestall sectarian confrontation in the new nation. During and after the British withdrawal, communal fighting and terrorism between Hindus and Muslims led to the partition of British India into mostly Muslim East Pakistan and West Pakistan (now Bangladesh) and mostly Hindu India. During the partition, Hindus and Muslims migrated across the new borders by the hundreds of thousands. Since independence, conflict has been ongoing between Pakistan and India over many issues, including Indian support for Bangladesh's war of independence from Pakistan, disputed borders, support for religious nationalist terrorist organizations, the development of nuclear arsenals, and the disputed northern region of Jammu and Kashmir.

Pakistan, through its intelligence agency, the **Directorate for Inter-Services Intelligence (ISI)**, has a long history of supporting insurgent groups fighting against Indian interests. Religious terrorist groups in the Indian state of Punjab and in Jammu and Kashmir have received Pakistani aid in what has become a high-stakes conflict between two nuclear powers that can also field large conventional armies. The Pakistan–India conflict is arguably as volatile as the Arab–Israeli rivalry, but with many times the manpower and firepower. This is especially noteworthy because both countries possess nuclear arsenals.

### Case in Point: The War in Jammu and Kashmir

In the Jammu and Kashmir region, which is occupied by Pakistan, India, and China, a sustained insurgency supported by the ISI led to human rights violations and a campaign of terrorism. The fighting was between Pakistani proxies and Muslim Kashmiris on one side and the Indian army on the other side. About 70% of Jammu and Kashmir's population is Muslim; the rest are Hindus, Sikhs, and Buddhists.

Islamic fighters from a number of groups supported by Pakistan have waged a protracted war against the Indian presence, using terrorism to attack Indian forces and interests. Their goal is independence for Jammu and Kashmir. Pro-Pakistan Muslim fighters have included an international assortment of *mujahideen* from Pakistan, Afghanistan, Kashmir, and Arab countries. Groups involved in the insurgency and terrorist campaign have included the following:

- **Harkat-ul-Ansar**, which kidnapped six Western hostages in 1995
- **Jammu and Kashmir Islamic Front**, another Pakistani proxy supported by the ISI
- **Jammu Kashmir Liberation Front**, a long-standing independence movement
- **Lashkar e Taiba**, a large Pakistani proxy based in Pakistan

### Case in Point: The Golden Temple Massacre (and Aftermath)

Sikhism is a religion that was founded about 500 years ago. One of its fundamental beliefs is that only a single all-powerful God should be worshipped, although its followers accept the existence of lesser gods. With approximately 20 million followers, Sikhism is centered in the Indian state of Punjab. The most sacred temple of the Sikh religion is the **Golden Temple** in the city of Amritsar, Punjab.

Punjab is rife with discord, originating in Sikh nationalism, the policies of the Indian army, Punjabi interests, and Pakistani agitation. With training and support from Pakistan's ISI, Sikh nationalists have agitated since at least the 1970s for the creation of the Sikh state of Khalistan in Punjab. In May 1984, armed Sikh militants—among them leaders of a terrorist campaign—occupied the Golden Temple. After negotiations failed, the Indian government of Indira Gandhi (no relation to Mahatma Gandhi) sanctioned an assault. When Indian troops stormed the temple in early June 1984, they were met by greater firepower than they anticipated. Tanks and artillery were called in, and hundreds were killed or wounded before the temple was retaken.

The assault on the Golden Temple inflamed tensions in Punjab, leading to communal violence and terrorism between Sikhs and Punjabis. Nationalists declared independence for Khalistan in 1987, but 500,000 Indian troops violently occupied the Punjab, causing an estimated 250,000 Sikh deaths between 1984 and 1992. Significantly, Indian Prime Minister Indira Gandhi was assassinated in October 1984 by Sikh bodyguards in revenge for the Golden Temple attack. Included among the many Sikh terrorist groups are Dal Khalsa, Bhinderanwala Tiger Force, Saheed Khalsa Force, the Khalistan Liberation Front, and the Khalistan Commando Force.

Chapter Perspective 6.2 discusses the 2008 assault on Mumbai, India, by highly trained members of Lashkar e Taiba.

## CHAPTER PERSPECTIVE 6.2: Assault on Mumbai

Mumbai (formerly Bombay) is India's largest city, the country's financial hub, and home to the famous and lucrative "Bollywood" Hindi-language film industry. Its reputation is one of prosperous cosmopolitanism, and Western tourists are drawn to reputable hotels, an active nightlife, and rich cultural history. Unfortunately, in recent years, the port city has experienced a series of lethal terrorist attacks. These incidents include the detonation of two car bombs in August 2003 that killed approximately 50 people and seven bombs aboard passenger trains that killed more than 200 in July 2006.

On November 26 through 29, 2008, Mumbai was attacked by 10 determined terrorists who entered the city from the sea aboard dinghies. The attackers spread out to assault high-profile targets throughout Mumbai's urban center, firing at victims randomly and throwing explosives. Tourist sites, hotels, and a Jewish center were specifically selected for their symbolic value and to inflict maximum casualties. The ferocity of the assault is reflected in the following events:

- More than 50 people were killed at the Taj Mahal Palace and Tower hotel. During the initial assault on the night and early morning of November 26 to 27, terrorists seized and killed hostages. A large fire broke out as they fought National Security Guard commandos and police officers when the troops and officers conducted room-to-room searches. Dozens of hostages were rescued during the operation. Firefights continued for days as the terrorists evaded the security sweep, finally ending on the morning of November 29.

- More than 30 people were killed at the Oberoi Hotel, which was attacked at the same time and in a similar manner as the Taj Mahal Palace and Tower. Terrorists at the Oberoi seized and killed hostages on November 26 to 27 and began hide-and-seek gun battles with members of the National Security Guard. The Guard restored order during the afternoon of November 28.

- Eight people were killed at Nariman House, an ultra-orthodox Jewish Lubavitch-Chabad center. On the night of November 26 to 27, terrorists attacked the center and seized hostages, including the center's rabbi and his wife. As gunshots were intermittently heard inside Nariman House, commandos assaulted the building on the morning of November 28 and secured the center by nighttime. Although many hostages were freed, others were killed by the terrorists. Victims included the rabbi and his wife.

- Members of the terrorist unit struck several other targets around the city, including the Chhatrapati Shivaji Terminus (where dozens were killed), the popular Leopold Café (frequented by tourists), and the Cama and GT Hospitals.

Indian security forces were caught off guard by the scope and violence of the assault. By the time order was restored, more than 160 people were killed and hundreds more injured. Nine terrorists and approximately 20 police officers and soldiers were killed. The lone survivor among the terrorists signed a seven-page confession approximately 2 weeks after the attack in which he confirmed that the men were members of Lashkar e Taiba (Army of the Pure), a Pakistan-based Islamist organization. He described his weapons training at several Lashkar camps in Pakistan and his indoctrination on alleged Indian atrocities against Muslims. Training in Karachi, Pakistan, included how to operate fast boats. When he and nine others embarked on a ship in late November, each man was issued an AK-47 assault rifle, hand grenades, and ammunition. They were ordered to maximize casualties on their mission.

The involvement of Lashkar e Taiba resulted in an escalation in tensions between India and Pakistan. Distrust was exacerbated because of Lashkar's long affiliation with Pakistan's Directorate for Inter-Services Intelligence (ISI). This affiliation was instrumental in the group's rise to prominence and viability within the Islamist movement, largely because ISI allowed the group to engage in recruitment, training, logistical support, and networking. In fact, ISI patronage allowed the group to operate rather openly in Pakistan. Lashkar's initial role as a Pakistani proxy against India in Kashmir eventually grew into a sizeable movement with wealthy patrons from Saudi Arabia and other countries. Their sophisticated use of the Internet permitted the group to communicate with fellow Islamists in Asia and the Middle East, thus enhancing its international image and contacts. Significantly, Lashkar operatives fought in Iraq against the American-led occupation.

## ❖ Dissident Religious Terrorism in the Modern Era

Dissident religious terrorism is political violence conducted by groups of religious "true believers" who fervently have faith in the sacred righteousness of their cause. Any behavior carried out in the defense of this sacred cause is considered to be not only justifiable but blessed. Most major religions—in particular,

Christianity, Islam, Judaism, and Hinduism—possess extremist adherents, some of whom have engaged in terrorist violence. Smaller religions and cults have similar adherents. Among the ubiquitous principles found among religious extremists are their convictions that they are defending their faith from attack by nonbelievers, or that their faith is an indisputable and universal guiding principle that must be advanced for the salvation of the faithful. These principles are manifested in various ways and to varying degrees by religious extremists, but they are usually at the core of their belief system.

## Regional Case: Religious Zealotry in the Middle East

From the perspective of religious radicals in the Middle East, violence done in the name of God is perfectly rational behavior because God is on their side. Many of the holy sites in the region are sacred to more than one faith, as in the case of Jerusalem, where a convergence of claims exists among Muslims, Jews, and Christians. When these convergences occur, some extremists believe that the claims of other faiths are inherently blasphemous. Because of this sort of indisputable "truth," some extremists believe that God wishes for nonbelievers to be driven from sacred sites or otherwise barred from legitimizing their claims. As Sheik Ahmed Yassin, the assassinated founder of the Palestinian Islamist group Hamas, explained in a 1998 justification of defensive religious violence,

> First of all . . . these are not suicide operations. [Islam forbids suicide.] We are protecting ourselves. . . . The Jews attack and kill our civilians—we will kill their civilians, too. . . . From the first drop of blood [the bomber] spills on the ground, he goes to Paradise. The Jewish victims immediately go to Hell.[22]

A great deal of violence has been motivated by such sentiments, as illustrated by the following cases in point.

### Case in Point: The Grand Mosque Incident

The framework for Muslim life is based on the Five Pillars of Islam. The Five Pillars are faith, prayer, *zakat* (alms, or charity), fasting during the month of Ramadan, and the *hajj* (pilgrimage) to the holy city of Mecca, Saudi Arabia, for those who are able. In November 1979 during their *hajj,* 300 radicals occupied the Grand Mosque in Mecca. Their objective was to foment a popular Islamic uprising against the ruling Saud royal family. After nearly 2 weeks of fighting, the Grand Mosque was reoccupied by the Saudi army, but not before the Saudis called in French counterterrorist commandos to complete the operation. More than 100 radicals were killed, and scores were later executed by the Saudi government. During the fighting, Iranian radio accused the United States and Israel of plotting the takeover, and a Pakistani mob attacked the U.S. embassy, killing two Americans.

### Case in Point: The Hebron Mosque Massacre

On February 25, 1994, a New York–born physician, **Baruch Goldstein**, fired on worshippers inside the Ibrahim Mosque at the Cave of the Patriarchs holy site in the city of Hebron, Israel. As worshippers performed their morning prayer ritual, Goldstein methodically shot them with an Israel Defense Forces Galil assault rifle. He fired approximately 108 rounds in about 10 minutes before a crowd of worshippers rushed and killed him. According to official government estimates, he killed 29 people and wounded another 125;[23] according to unofficial estimates, approximately 50 people

[22]Frankel, Glenn, Barton Gellman, and Laura Blumenfeld. "Sheik Ahmed Yassin, Founder of Hamas." *Washington Post,* March 22, 2004.

[23]Kelly, Robert J., and Jess Maghan, eds. *Hate Crime: The Global Politics of Polarization.* Carbondale: Southern Illinois University Press, 1998, p. 105.

died.[24] In reprisal for the Hebron massacre, the Palestinian Islamic fundamentalist movement Hamas launched a bombing campaign that included the first wave of human suicide bombers.

### Case in Point: The Rabin Assassination

On November 4, 1995, Israeli Prime Minister Yitzhak Rabin was assassinated by **Yigal Amir**, who considered Rabin to be a traitor and had stalked him for about a year.[25] He shot Rabin in the back with hollow-point bullets in full view of Israeli security officers. Amir was a Jewish extremist who said that he acted fully within the requirements of *Halacha,* or the Jewish code. The following account describes the religious justification Amir used for the assassination:

> Asked where he got his ideas, Yigal Amir told the magistrate that he drew on the Halacha, which is the Jewish legal code. "According to the Halacha, you can kill the enemy," Amir said. "My whole life, I learned Halacha. When you kill in war, it is an act that is allowed." When asked whether he acted alone, Amir replied: "It was God."[26]

The foregoing cases in point confirm that religious terrorism in the Middle East occurs between and within local religious groups. Radical true believers of many faiths not only attack those who are of other religions but also readily attack "fallen" members of their own religion. These attacks against proclaimed apostasies can be quite violent.

## Movement Case: The International *Mujahideen* (Holy Warriors for the Faith)

The *mujahideen* are Islamic fighters who have sworn a vow to take up arms to defend the faith. They tend to be believers in fundamentalist interpretations of Islam who have defined their *jihad,* or personal struggle, to be one of fighting and dying on behalf of the faith.

The modern conceptualization of the *mujahideen* began during the Soviet war in Afghanistan, which dated from the time of the Soviets' invasion of the country in December 1979 to their withdrawal in February 1989. Although several Afghan rebel groups (mostly ethnically based) fought the Soviets, they collectively referred to themselves as *mujahideen.* To them, their war of resistance was a holy *jihad.* Significantly, Muslim volunteers from around the world served alongside the Afghan *mujahideen.* These **"Afghan Arabs"** played an important role in spreading the modern *jihadi* ideology throughout the Muslim world.

Reasons for taking up arms as a *jihadi*[27] vary, depending on one's personal or national context. Some *mujahideen* recruits answer calls for holy war from religious scholars who might declare, for example, that Islam is being repressed by the West. Others respond to clear and identifiable threats to their people or country, such as the Soviet invasion of Afghanistan, the U.S.-led occupation of Iraq, or the Israeli occupation of Gaza and the West Bank. And others may join as *mujahideen* on behalf of the cause of other Muslims, such as the wars fought by Bosnian Muslims or Algerian rebels. Following the 2011 Arab Spring protests, thousands of Islamist fighters volunteered to wage *jihad* against the Assad regime in Syria and the Shi'a-led government in Iraq. Several thousand of these volunteers were Westerners.

Regardless of the precipitating event, *mujahideen* are characterized by their faith in several basic values. The ideology of the modern *mujahideen* requires selfless sacrifice in defense of the faith.

---

[24]See Katz, Samuel M. *The Hunt for the Engineer: How Israeli Agents Tracked the Hamas Master Bomber.* New York: Fromm International, 2001, pp. 97–9.

[25]Ibid., p. 225.

[26]CNN. "Rabin's Alleged Killer Appears in Court." *CNN World News,* November 7, 1995.

[27]A *jihadi* is one who wages *jihad,* regardless of whether it is an armed *jihad. Mujahideen* are *jihadis* who have taken up arms.

Accepting the title of *mujahideen* means that one must live, fight, and die in accordance with religious teachings. They believe in the inevitability of victory because the cause is being waged on behalf of the faith and in the name of God; both the faith and God will prevail. During this defense of the faith, trials and ordeals should be endured without complaint because the pain suffered in this world will be rewarded after death in paradise. If one lives a righteous and holy life—for example, by obeying the moral proscriptions of the Qur'an—one can enjoy these proscribed pleasures in the afterlife. Thus, the essence of modern *mujahideen* ideology is

> a hybrid and simplistic blend of Islamic fundamentalism. This "Islam" seeks to eradicate all forms of Islam other than its own strict literal interpretation of the Koran. It comes packaged with a set of now well-known political grievances . . . and justifies violence as a means of purging nations of corruption, moral degradation, and spiritual torpor.[28]

❖ **Photo 6.3**

Holy war against Communist invaders. Afghan *mujahideen* during their *jihad* against occupying Soviet troops.

David Stewart-Smith/Hulton Archive/Getty Images

As applied by the *mujahideen,* the defensive ideology of *jihad* holds that when one defends the faith against the unfaithful, death is martyrdom, and through death paradise will be achieved. One oath of commitment made by a recruit to the anti-Soviet *jihad* in Afghanistan read,

> I . . . state in the presence of God that I will slaughter infidels my entire life. . . . And with the will of God I will do these killings in the supervision and guidance with Harkat ul-Ansar. . . . May God give me strength in fulfilling this oath.[29]

## Organization Case: Al-Qa'ida's Religious Foundation

The modern era's most prominent Islamic revolutionary organization is Saudi national **Osama bin Laden**'s cell-based Al-Qa'ida (The Base), which seeks to unite Muslims throughout the world in a holy war. Al-Qa'ida is not a traditional hierarchical revolutionary organization; nor does it call for its followers to do much more than engage in terrorist violence in the name of the faith. Al-Qa'ida is best described as a movement or a loose network of like-minded Islamic revolutionaries. Compared to other movements in the postwar era, it is a different kind of network because Al-Qa'ida

- holds no territory,
- does not champion the aspirations of an ethnonational group,
- has no "top-down" organizational structure,
- has virtually nonexistent state sponsorship,
- promulgates political demands that are vague,
- is completely religious in its worldview.

Experts do not know how many people count themselves as Al-Qa'ida operatives, but estimates range from 35,000 to 50,000. Of these, perhaps 5,000 received training in camps in Sudan and Afghanistan.[30] Others are new recruits from around the Muslim world and Europe, and many others are veteran Afghan Arabs who fought in the *jihad* against the Soviets and later against the

[28]Marquand, Robert. "The Tenets of Terror: A Special Report on the Ideology of Jihad and the Rise of Islamic Militancy." *Christian Science Monitor,* October 18, 2001.

[29]Rohde, David, and C. J. Chivers. "Al Qaeda's Grocery Lists and Manuals of Killing." *New York Times,* March 17, 2002.

[30]McFadden, Robert D. "Bin Laden's Journey From Rich Pious Lad to the Mask of Evil." *New York Times,* September 30, 2001.

post–September 11, 2001, American-led coalition forces in Afghanistan. With a presence in an estimated 50 to 60 countries, it is likely that new recruits will continue to join the Al-Qa'ida cause (or Al-Qa'ida–inspired causes) in the aftermath of the September 11, 2001, attacks.

Al-Qa'ida's religious orientation is a reflection of Osama bin Laden's sectarian ideological point of view. Bin Laden's worldview was created by his exposure to Islam-motivated armed resistance. As a boy, he inherited between $20 million and $80 million from his father, with estimates ranging as high as $300 million. When the Soviets invaded Afghanistan in 1979, bin Laden eventually joined with thousands of other non-Afghan Muslims who traveled to Peshawar, Pakistan, to prepare to wage *jihad*. However, his main contribution to the holy war was to solicit financial and matériel contributions from wealthy Arab sources. He apparently excelled at this. The final leg of his journey toward international Islamic terrorism occurred when he and thousands of other Afghan veterans—the Afghan Arabs—returned to their countries to carry on their struggle in the name of Islam. Beginning in 1986, bin Laden organized a training camp that grew in 1988 into the Al-Qa'ida group. While in his home country of Saudi Arabia, bin Laden "became enraged when King Fahd let American forces, with their rock music and Christian and Jewish troops, wage the Persian Gulf war from Saudi soil in 1991."[31]

GOVERNMENT EXHIBIT AQ00107 01-455-A (ID)

U.S. Federal Bureau of Investigation

❖ **Photo 6.4**

Khalid Sheikh Mohammed, a central member of Al-Qa'ida. A handout photograph released in March 2006 by a U.S. district court as it was introduced during the trial of Zacarias Moussaoui. According to the Pentagon, Khalid Sheikh Mohammed confessed to his role as the alleged mastermind of the 9/11 attacks and 29 other terror plots around the world.

After the Gulf War, bin Laden and a reinvigorated Al-Qa'ida moved to its new home in Sudan for 5 years. It was there that the Al-Qa'ida network began to grow into a self-sustaining financial and training base for promulgating *jihad*. Bin Laden and his followers configured the Al-Qa'ida network with one underlying purpose: "launching and leading a holy war against the Western infidels he could now see camped out in his homeland, near the holiest shrines in the Muslim world."[32]

Al-Qa'ida has inspired Islamic fundamentalist revolutionaries and terrorists in a number of countries. It became a significant source of financing and training for thousands of *jihadis*. The network is essentially a nonstate catalyst for transnational religious radicalism and violence.

When Al-Qa'ida moved to Afghanistan, its reputation as a financial and training center attracted many new recruits and led to the creation of a loose network of cells and "sleepers" in dozens of countries. Significantly, aboveground radical Islamic groups with links to Al-Qa'ida took root in some nations and overtly challenged authority through acts of terrorism. Two of these groups—Abu Sayyaf in the Philippines and Laskar Jihad in Indonesia—are discussed in the following sections.

### The Abu Sayyaf Group

The Republic of the Philippines experienced several insurgencies and terrorist campaigns in the postwar era. The country's first serious left-wing rebellion occurred after World War II. The rebellion, as well as the government's response to it, was the only case in Southeast Asia of a major communist insurgency that was defeated without foreign military assistance. Later, a nationalistic Muslim rebellion in the southern islands, led by the Moro National Liberation Front, scored a number of military and political successes.

[31]Ibid.

[32]Reeve, Simon. *The New Jackals: Ramzi Yousef, Osama bin Laden, and the Future of Terrorism*. Boston: Northeastern University Press, 1999, p. 181.

The religious demographics of the Philippines are roughly 92% Christian, 5% Muslim, and 3% Buddhist,[33] with Muslims living primarily on islands in the southern rim of the Philippines. The Philippines has also been home to **Abu Sayyaf**, a Muslim insurgency on the island of Basilan with ideological and other links to Al-Qa'ida. Abdurajak Janjalani, who was killed by Filipino police in 1998, founded Abu Sayyaf. Like a few other Filipino Islamic militants, Janjalani fought in the *jihad* in Afghanistan against the Soviets, where he may have known Osama bin Laden. After the war, he returned to the Philippines to wage *jihad* to create a Muslim state in the southern Philippines. Al-Qa'ida funds were apparently sent to Abu Sayyaf, and radical Muslims from the Middle East arrived to provide military and terrorist training for Filipino Muslims.

In April 2000, Abu Sayyaf kidnapped 20 hostages in a Malaysian resort and received $25 million in ransom for their release. The ransom money was used to buy weapons and boats and to recruit and train new fighters. In May 2001, the group kidnapped 20 more people, including three American hostages. One of the Americans was beheaded, probably in June 2001. After the September 11, 2001, attacks, the Filipino government—with advice from hundreds of American Special Forces troops—launched a vigorous campaign to wipe out Abu Sayyaf. The government campaign was successful, and hundreds of Abu Sayyaf fighters were killed or captured or went home. In June 2002, Filipino Special Forces troops identified the location of the two surviving Americans and one Filipina nurse who was also held hostage. During a firefight, one of the Americans and the Filipina were killed, and the other American was wounded.

Abu Sayyaf has proven to be resilient despite setbacks. The Philippine government blamed the group for an October 2002 bomb near a military base that killed an American serviceman, and in February 2004, the group bombed a ferry in Manila Bay, which killed 132 people.

### Laskar Jihad

Under the leadership of Ja'afar Umar Thalib, the armed Islamic group called **Laskar Jihad (Militia of the Holy War)** waged communal holy war in Indonesia. Thousands of fighters joined Laskar Jihad, which was organized in April 2000 to confront Christians in a holy war on Indonesia's Molucca Islands. The Molucca conflict became a communal confrontation between Christians and Muslims in January 1999. The group was based on the island of Java but arrived in the Moluccas in force to champion indigenous Muslims when the fighting broke out. Terrorism and human rights violations became common on both sides—the conflict cost thousands of lives and forced hundreds of thousands of people from their homes.

Although Thalib denied any linkage between Laskar Jihad and Al-Qa'ida, Western intelligence agencies claimed that the Al-Qa'ida link existed. Thalib had in fact met Osama bin Laden in 1987 in Pakistan during the *jihad* in Afghanistan against the Soviets. However, Thalib argued that bin Laden's interpretation of the Islamic struggle was incorrect and that his war against Islamic governments was wrong. Before disbanding in October 2002, Thalib and Laskar Jihad engaged in terrorism and forged ties with Malaysia's terrorist Mujahideen Group.

## Transnational Case: The Algerian *Jihadis*

### Prelude: Civil War in Algeria

The first multiparty elections in Algeria were scheduled to be held in 1992. When it became apparent that an Islamic movement, the Islamic Salvation Front (Front Islamique de Salut, or FIS), would win the election, the elections were canceled by the government of President Chadli Ben Djedid, a former army colonel. FIS incited violent strikes and demonstrations, and the government responded by declaring a state of emergency, postponing the general elections, and seizing control of FIS offices. An antigovernment campaign of terrorism began, growing into a large-scale insurgency that regularly

---

[33]Central Intelligence Agency. "Philippines." *The World Factbook.* https://www.cia.gov/library/publications/the-world-factbook/geos/rp.html/.

committed acts of terrorism. Typical of these attacks were indiscriminate bombings in August 1992 at the Algiers airport and in front of the Algiers headquarters of the Sûreté Nationale; the latter bomb killed 42 people and injured 250.[34]

By the mid-1990s, several Islamic terrorist movements were waging a campaign of terror in the countryside and in the cities of Algeria. These groups, which included the **Armed Islamic Group** (Groupe Islamique Armé) and the **Armed Islamic Movement** (Mouvement Islamique Armé), used exceptionally violent tactics. Thousands of secular teachers, journalists, doctors, academics, and others were assassinated. Foreigners were also singled out for assassination, including French Christian priests, nuns, and monks. In the countryside, bands of Islamic militants swept through villages and towns, killing, kidnapping, and raping noncombatants of all ages. The government responded with a brutal suppression campaign that included massacres and the use of death squads. The government also armed local civilian paramilitary units, many of which included veterans of the anticolonial war against France. Between 1992 and 1997, approximately 120,000 people were killed.[35] In 1999, an amnesty was offered, and about 5,000 militants surrendered.[36]

### Postscript: Spreading the Jihad

Many of Algeria's Islamic militants were veterans of the *jihad* in Afghanistan. Others had been trained in Al-Qa'ida camps. During the Algerian insurgency, many Algerians and other North Africans apparently moved abroad to set up support networks for the struggle. The purpose was to establish arms and financing pipelines to the insurgent groups. Some of these support cells apparently became independent "sleeper" cells committed to waging holy war against the West in their home countries. These cells were informally organized and shared "common participants, communications . . . and shared training experiences in Bin Laden–run camps."[37] One such cell plotted to detonate a bomb at Los Angeles International Airport around the time of the 2000 millennial celebrations. It was foiled when **Ahmed Ressem**, an Algerian who lived in Montreal, was arrested as he tried to cross the Canadian border into the United States with bomb-making components.[38] During captivity in the United States, Ressem exchanged a great deal of information about Al-Qa'ida operatives for privileges.[39] In one such exchange, he admitted that he had been trained in an Al-Qa'ida camp, and in other exchanges, he gave information about his former associations. Ressem was sentenced to 22 years in prison in July 2005.[40]

The Algerian *jihad* is an example of a nexus of religious terrorism, transnational solidarity among religious fighters, and the spread of revolutionary religious fervor beyond Algeria to cells in the West.

## Internecine Case: Sectarian Civil War in Iraq

Iraq is a multicultural nation that incorporates significant numbers of people who have very strong ethnonational, tribal, and religious identities. The demography of Iraq consists of the following subpopulations:[41]

---

[34]Stone, Martin. *The Establishment of Algeria.* London: Hurst, 1997, pp. 1–3. Quoted in Whittaker, David J., ed. *The Terrorism Reader.* New York: Routledge, 2001, pp. 141–2.

[35]Whitaker, *The Terrorism Reader.*

[36]Daley, Suzanne. "French Leader Visits Algiers to Shore Up Terrorism War." *New York Times,* December 2, 2001.

[37]Ibid.

[38]Pyes, Craig, Josh Meyer, and William C. Rempel. "U.S. Sees New Terrorist Threat From North Africa." *Los Angeles Times,* July 8, 2001.

[39]Meyer, Josh. "Records Show Man in LAX Plot Gave U.S. Key Terrorist Details." *Los Angeles Times,* April 27, 2005.

[40]Tizon, Thomas Alex, and Lynn Marshall. "Would-Be Millennium Bomber Ressam Gets 22-Year Sentence." *Los Angeles Times,* July 28, 2005.

[41]Data derived from U.S. Central Intelligence Agency. *World Fact Book.* https://www.cia.gov/library/publications/the-world-factbook/geos/iz.html/ (accessed July 13, 2014).

Arab: 75%–80%

Shi'a Muslim: 60%–65%

Sunni Muslim: 32%–37%

Kurdish: 15%–20%

Turkoman, Assyrian, or other: 5%

Christian or other: 3%

In recent history, expressions of nationalism or religious independence were harshly repressed. The regime of Saddam Hussein favored Sunni Muslims, repressed expressions of religious independence by Shi'a Muslims, and fought brutal military campaigns against the Kurds. After the collapse of the Hussein regime in March 2003, previously repressed ethnonational and religious groups began to openly display their cultural heritages.

Tensions that had simmered during the Hussein years led to difficulty in fully integrating all groups into accepting a single national identity. For example, many Arabs who had moved into northern Kurdish regions after native Kurds were forced out became pariahs when Kurds returned to reclaim their homes and land. Some violence was directed against the Arab migrants. More ominously, the Sunni minority—which had dominated the country under Hussein—found itself recast as a political minority when the country began to move toward democracy, after an interim government was established in June 2004. Sunnis expressed their dissatisfaction when large numbers refused to participate in elections to form a Transitional National Assembly in January 2005.

Sectarian tensions between Shi'a and Sunni Iraqis became increasingly violent, beginning during a poor security environment in 2004 and 2005 that pitted U.S.-led occupation forces against Iraqi and foreign insurgents. Acts of religion-inspired violence were directed against members of the Shi'a and Sunni communities. For example, scores of Shi'a were killed in March 2004 by suicide bombers in Baghdad and the holy city of Karbala; the Karbala bombing specifically targeted pilgrims celebrating Ashura, the holiest Shi'a holiday.[42] In a series of other incidents, hundreds of bodies were found around Iraq in ditches and fields, along roads, and in rivers.

During one period in April and May 2005, scores of bodies were found floating in the Tigris River. Officials blamed these killings not on the insurgency, per se, but on revenge killings between the two communities. Sunni insurgents assassinated Shi'a leaders, bombed or shot at mosques, attacked Shi'a neighborhoods, disrupted religious festivals, and generally targeted centers of Shi'a authority. For the most part, Shi'a leaders strongly denounced the violence and urged members of their community not to retaliate. However, some Shi'a militias armed themselves as an expression of independence and protection. One such militia was organized by cleric Moqtada al-Sadr, whose father (Muhammed Saiq al-Sadr) was assassinated by the Hussein regime in 1999. The younger al-Sadr stated that Shi'a should "terrorise your enemies as we cannot remain silent at their violations."[43]

Also in Iraq, religious extremists—it is unclear whether they were Sunnis or Shi'a— conducted a series of attacks on "non-Muslim" cultural institutions. These included liquor stores (often owned by Christians) and barber shops that designed Western-style haircuts.[44] It is estimated that perhaps 50% of Iraq's Christian population relocated to neighboring countries (Syria, Jordan, and Lebanon) following the collapse of the Hussein regime in 2003.

---

[42]Rotella, Sebastian, and Patrick J. McDonnell. "Death Toll in Twin Strikes on Iraqi Shiites Rises to 143." *Los Angeles Times,* March 3, 2004.

[43]BBC News. "Who's Who in Iraq: Moqtada Sadr." *BBC News World Edition,* August 27, 2004.

[44]See Morin, Monte. "In Iraq, to Be a Hairstylist Is to Risk Death." *Los Angeles Times,* February 22, 2005.

### Case in Point: The Rise of the Islamic State of Iraq and the Levant[45]

In early 2014 the international community was surprised when a little-known Sunni insurgent movement overran significant swaths of territory in northern Iraq. The international community was further alerted when these insurgents seized major population centers in Iraq—particularly the cities of Mosul and Tikrit (Saddam Hussein's home city)—as the Iraqi army and other security forces were routed. The movement was the **Islamic State of Iraq and the Levant**, also known as the Islamic State of Iraq and al-Sham, or ISIS.

ISIS (also known as ISIL) was formally declared to exist in April 2013 during the Syrian civil war that began in the aftermath of the 2011 Arab Spring protests, and that subsequently escalated to internecine warfare in 2012. The central tenets of ISIS are its refusal to recognize the borders of Syria, Iraq, and other Eastern Mediterranean nations, and its war to achieve the avowed goal of establishing a renewed **caliphate** (Islamic state) transcending these borders. This doctrine brought the movement into political opposition with Al-Qa'ida's central leadership, in particular leader Ayman al-Zawahiri, who disavowed ISIS when the group refused to limit its operations only to Syria. This disavowal did nothing to diminish ISIS's operations on the battlefield. In Iraq, ISIS became the de facto successor to Abu Musab al-Zarqawi's Al-Qa'ida Organization for Holy War in Iraq (AQI), which had waged an intensive Islamist insurgency from about 2005 to 2006 against U.S.-led occupation forces, the Iraqi army, and the Shi'a Badr Brigade.

ISIS adopted brutal tactics from the beginning of its war. The movement regularly executed captured Iraqi soldiers and police officers, imprisoned and tortured Iraqi civilians, kidnapped and executed Western civilians, and imposed draconian *shari'a* law and order in the territory it occupied. ISIS routinely recorded and broadcast beheadings, crucifixions, and massacres via social networking

---

**Table 6.2**   Two Traditions, One Religion

Sunni and Shi'a Muslims represent the two predominant traditions in Islam. Demographically, Sunni Islam represents about 85% to 90% of all Muslims, and Shi'a Islam represents about 10% to 15%. They are distinct practices that originate from, and worship within, a core system of belief.

Unlike Christian denominations, which can diverge quite markedly, Sunni and Shi'a differ less in interpretations of religious faith and more on historical sources of religious authority. The two paths in Islam hearken back to the death of the prophet Muhammed and the question of who among his successors represented true authority within the faith.

The differences between Sunni and Shi'a beliefs are summarized in the following table:

| Sunni Muslims | Shi'a Muslims |
|---|---|
| Historically accept all four caliphs (successors to Muhammed) as being legitimate, including the caliph Ali, Muhammed's son-in-law and cousin. | Historically reject the first three caliphs before Ali as being illegitimate successors to Muhammed. |
| Only the prophet Muhammed and the holy Qur'an are authorities on questions of religion. The Shi'a succession of imams is rejected. | As the first legitimate caliph, Ali was also the first in a historical line of imams, or leaders within Muslim communities. |
| Historically, leaders within the Islamic world have been political leaders and heads of governments rather than religious leaders. | Imams serve as both political and religious leaders. |
| There is no strictly organized clergy. For example, no single religious leader can claim ultimate authority, and nonclergy may lead prayers. | Imams have strict authority, and their pronouncements must be obeyed. Imams are without sin, and appoint their successors. |

---

[45]The Levant refers to the Eastern Mediterranean region, traditionally encompassing Syria, Lebanon, Israel, Jordan, and Cyprus.

media. As knowledge of ISIS's tactics spread, thousands of members of the Iraqi army and security forces literally shed their uniforms and abandoned weapons when relatively small numbers of ISIS fighters advanced.

ISIS successfully inspired international fighters to join the movement in Syria and Iraq, many of whom were volunteers from North Africa, Chechnya, Europe, and the United States. A stated goal by ISIS was to have these volunteers return to their home countries to wage *jihad* domestically.

Because ISIS and other similar Sunni movements are often in conflict with Shi'a Muslims, readers should be familiar with the essential distinctions between the Sunni and Shi'a Islamic traditions. Table 6.2 summarizes these differences.[46]

## National Case: Boko Haram in Nigeria

The **Boko Haram** organization was founded in 2002 in the city of Maiduguri in northeastern Nigeria. Originally little more than a religious complex with a school and mosque, the organization also espoused a political agenda with the goal of establishing an Islamic state. The Islamic school actively recruited adherents for waging *jihad*, and in 2009 Boko Haram launched sporadic attacks against government installations and personnel in Maiduguri. Since 2009, Boko Haram has attacked military and police targets, schools, Christian churches, and gathering places such as bars. It has been responsible for thousands of casualties, kidnappings, and population displacements, with the weekly death toll sometimes above one hundred victims.

The term *Boko Haram* is loosely translated as "Western Education Is Forbidden," a reference in part to the legacy of British colonial missionary work and the presence of a significant Christian population in Nigeria. The group also holds that participation in Western social or political activity is forbidden, including participating in elections and wearing Western dress. In April 2014 Boko Haram kidnapped approximately 200 schoolgirls, vowing to hold them as "wives" for its fighters.

❖ **Photo 6.5**

The aftermath of the March 1995 Sarin nerve gas attack on the Tokyo subway system. The case of the Aum Shinrikyō cult represents the feasibility of deploying such weapons by dedicated extremists.

Noboru Hashimoto/Sygma/Corbis

## Cult Case: Aum Shinrikyō (Supreme Truth)

**Aum Shinrikyō** is a Japan-based cult founded in 1984 by **Shoko Asahara**. Its goal under Asahara's leadership was to seize control of Japan and then the world. The core belief of the cult is that Armageddon—the final battle before the end of the world—is imminent. One component of this doctrine is that the United States will wage World War III against Japan.[47] As one top member of the cult explained, "This evil [of the modern age] will be shed in a 'catastrophic discharge' . . . [and only those who] repent their evil deeds . . . [will survive]."[48]

At its peak membership, Aum Shinrikyō had perhaps 9,000 members in Japan and 40,000 members around the world—thousands of them in Russia.[49] Asahara claimed to be the reincarnation of Jesus Christ and Buddha and urged his followers to arm themselves if they were to survive Armageddon. This apocalyptic creed led to the stockpiling of chemical and biological weapons, including nerve gas,

---

[46]For an analysis of the conflict between Sunni and Shi'a Muslims, see Ghosh, Bobby. "Why They Hate Each Other." *Time,* March 5, 2007.

[47]U.S. Department of State. "Aum Supreme Truth (Aum)." *Patterns of Global Terrorism, 2000.* U.S. Department of State, April 2001.

[48]Marshall, Andrew. "It Gassed the Tokyo Subway, Microwaved Its Enemies and Tortured Its Members. So Why Is the Aum Cult Thriving?" *The Guardian,* July 15, 1999.

[49]U.S. Department of State, "Aum."

anthrax, and Qfever. One report indicated that Aum Shinrikyō members had traveled to Africa to acquire the deadly Ebola virus. Several mysterious biochemical incidents occurred in Japan, including one in June 1994 in the city of Matsumoto, where 7 people died and 264 were injured from a release of gas into an apartment building.[50]

### The Tokyo Subway Nerve Gas Attack

On March 20, 1995, members of Aum Shinrikyō positioned several packages containing Sarin nerve gas on five trains in the Tokyo subway system. The trains were scheduled to travel through Tokyo's Kasumigaseki train station. The containers were simultaneously punctured with umbrellas, thus releasing the gas into the subway system. Twelve people were killed and an estimated 5,000 to 6,000 were injured.[51] Tokyo's emergency medical system was unable to respond adequately to the attack, so that only about 500 victims were evacuated, with the remaining victims making their own way to local hospitals. The police were also surprised by the attack, and

> it took . . . several weeks to narrow their search to the Aum sect, locate its leaders, and seize some of their arsenal, despite the fact that Aum was not a secret organization but one that paraded through the streets of Tokyo—albeit in masks that depicted the face of their guru and leader, Shoko Asahara.[52]

The police seized tons of chemicals stockpiled by the cult. Asahara was arrested and charged with 17 counts of murder and attempted murder, kidnapping, and drug trafficking. A new leader, Fumihiro Joyu, assumed control of Aum Shinrikyō in 2000 and renamed the group Aleph (the first letter in the Hebrew and Arabic alphabets). He has publicly renounced violence, and the cult's membership has enjoyed new growth in membership.

Aum Shinrikyō is an example of the potential terrorist threat from apocalyptic cults and sects that are completely insular and segregated from mainstream society. Some cults are content simply to prepare for the End of Days, but others—like Aum Shinrikyō—are not averse to giving the apocalypse a violent "push."

A Japanese court sentenced cult leader Shoko Asahara to death by hanging on February 27, 2004.

Table 6.3 summarizes the activity profiles of several of the terrorist groups and movements discussed in this chapter.

## ❖  The Future of Religious Terrorism

The new millennium began with a resurgence of religious terrorism. Unlike previous terrorist environments, the new era of terrorism is largely shaped by the international quality of this resurgence—in essence, modern religious terrorism is a global phenomenon affecting every member of the international community. The current ideological profile of this development is one of activism and momentum among radical Islamists. Although extremist members of other faiths will certainly strike periodically, the Islamist tendency continues to attract new cadres of *jihadis* who oppose secular governments and Western influence in the Middle East.[53] Many new adherents originate from Western countries.

Religion is a central feature of the New Terrorism, and the New Terrorism is characterized by asymmetrical tactics, cell-based networks, indiscriminate attacks against "soft" targets, and the threatened use of high-yield weapons technologies. Al-Qa'ida and its Islamist affiliates pioneered this strategy,

---

[50]Marshall, "It Gassed"; Laqueur, *The New Terrorism,* p. 54.

[51]Initial reports cited this figure. Later studies suggest that physical injuries numbered 1,300 and that the rest were psychological injuries. U.S. Department of State, "Aum."

[52]Laqueur, *The New Terrorism,* p. 129.

[53]Juergensmeyer, Mark. "Holy Orders: Religious Opposition to Modern States." *Harvard International Review* (Winter 2004): 34–8.

| Table 6.3 | Religious Terrorism |
|-----------|---------------------|

Although religious terrorist groups and movements share the general profile of religious identity and often are rooted in similar belief systems, they arise out of unique historical, political, and cultural environments that are peculiar to their respective countries. With few exceptions, most religious movements are grounded in these idiosyncratic influences.

| Group | Activity Profile | |
|-------|------------------|---|
| | *Constituency* | *Adversary* |
| Aum Shinrikyō | Fellow believers | The existing world order |
| Lord's Resistance Army | Fellow believers and members of the Acholi tribe | Ugandan government and "nonpurified" Acholis |
| Palestine Islamic Jihad | Palestinian Muslims | Israel |
| Hamas | Palestinian Muslims | Israel |
| Al-Qa'ida | Faithful Muslims, as defined by Al-Qa'ida | Secular governments, nonbelievers, the West |
| Abu Sayyaf | Filipino Muslims | Filipino government, Western influence |
| Laskar Jihad | Moluccan Muslims | Moluccan Christians |
| Jammu-Kashmir groups | Jammu-Kashmir Muslims | India |
| Sikh groups | Punjabi Sikhs | India |
| Algerian/North African cells | Algerian Muslims and Muslims worldwide | Secular Algerian government, the West |
| Boko Haram | West Africa Muslims | Nigerian, West African nonbelievers, the West |
| Islamic State of Iraq and the Levant (al-Sham) | Levant Sunnis | Secular Arab nations, Shi'a, nonbelievers |

and it serves as a model for new similarly motivated individuals and groups. Religious extremists understand that by adopting these characteristics, their agendas and grievances will receive extensive attention, and their adversaries will be sorely challenged to defeat them. It is therefore reasonable to presume that religious terrorists will practice this strategy for the near future.

Having made this observation, it is important to critically assess the following questions: What trends are likely to challenge the global community in the immediate future? Who will enlist as new cadres in extremist religious movements? Who will articulate the principles of their guiding ideologies? The following patterns, trends, and events are offered for critical consideration:

- **Extremist religious propaganda cannot be prevented.** All religious extremists—Christian, Islamic, Jewish, and others—have discovered the utility of the Internet, the global media, and social networking media. They readily communicate with one another through the Internet, and their websites have become forums for propaganda and information.[54] Cable television and other members of

---

[54]For interesting insight about Al-Qa'ida's use of computers, see Cullison, Alan. "Inside Al-Qaeda's Hard Drive." *The Atlantic,* September 2004.

the globalized media frequently broadcast interviews and communiqués. Social networking media are readily accessible dissemination outlets for "live" events as they occur in real time.

- **A new generation of Islamist extremists has been primed.** In a prescient study reported in January 2005, the Central Intelligence Agency's National Intelligence Council concluded that the war in Iraq created a new training and recruitment ground for potential terrorists, replacing Afghanistan in this respect. One official stated, "There is even, under the best scenario . . . the likelihood that some of the jihadists [will go home], and will therefore disperse to various other countries."[55] This assessment accurately predicted the rise of a new generation of *jihadis*—especially after the Arab Spring in 2011, when international fighters enlisted in newly emergent Islamist movements in Syria, Iraq, Libya, and elsewhere.

- **Al-Qa'ida has become more than an organization; it evolved to become a symbol and ideology.** Osama bin Laden, founder and leader of Al-Qa'ida, presented himself in a series of communiqués as an "elder statesman" and intellectual of Islam. He recast himself as a symbolic mentor for the next generation of fighters.[56] After bin Laden's death in 2011 many *jihadis* considered him a martyr.

- **The *jihadi* movement has become a globalized phenomenon.** The dissemination of information and images via the media, the Internet, and social networking media created a global sense of solidarity among Islamists. Potential recruits easily access information, and many new volunteers are young people who live in the West, often in Europe.[57] The influx of Western volunteers who fought with Islamist movements such as ISIS confirmed the international scope and influence of the *jihadi* movement.

- **Christian extremists continue to promote a religious motivation for the war on terrorism.** Postings on some Christian websites and comments from some Christian leaders, usually in the United States, intimate that the Islamic faith is wrong and/or evil, and the war on terrorism is part of a divine plan pitting the "true faith" against Islam.[58]

## Chapter Summary

Religious movements are motivated by a belief that an otherworldly power sanctions and commands their behavior. Some religious terrorists are motivated primarily by faith, whereas other terrorists use religion secondarily. The latter movements are motivated by nationalism or some other ideology as a primary inspiration, but they are united by an underlying religious identity that is incorporated into their belief system. The goals of both primary and secondary religious terrorism are to construct a new society based on their religious or ethnonational identity. The terrorist behavior of both tendencies is active and public.

State-sponsored religious terrorism emanates from governments that pursue international agendas by mentoring and encouraging religious proxies. The case of Iranian support for religious dissident terrorists is an example of a theocracy that is promoting its own revolutionary agenda. The case of Syria is an example of a secular government that supports religious movements out of a sense of common cause against a mutual enemy. Dissident religious terrorism involves attacks by self-proclaimed "true believers" against members of other faiths and perceived apostasies within their own faith. Some dissident groups espouse mystical

---

[55]Priest, Dana. "Report Says Iraq Is New Terrorist Training Ground." *Washington Post,* January 14, 2005.

[56]Meyer, Josh. "Bin Laden, in Tape, May Have Sights on New Role." *Los Angeles Times,* October 31, 2004.

[57]See Cowell, Alan. "British Muslims Are Seen Moving Into Mideast Terrorism." *New York Times,* May 1, 2003; Cowell, Alan. "Zeal for Suicide Bombing Reaches British Midlands." *New York Times,* May 2, 2003; Whitlock, Craig. "Moroccans Gain Prominence in Terror Groups." *Washington Post,* October 14, 2004; Czuczka, Tony. "Germans Suspect Terror Pipeline." *Dallas Morning News,* January 9, 2005; Rotella, Sebastian. "Europe's Boys of Jihad." *Los Angeles Times,* April 2, 2005.

[58]Within popular culture, pundits, bloggers, and others dubbed the war on terrorism as a Tenth Crusade.

or cult-like doctrines that are outside the belief systems of major religions.

In Chapter 7, readers will review extremist ideologies and terrorist behavior. The discussion will focus on specific cases in point as well as the contexts for armed ideological dissident movements. Reasons for ideological violence in liberal democracies will also be evaluated.

## Key Terms and Concepts

The following topics are discussed in this chapter and can be found in the glossary:

Abu Sayyaf

"Afghan Arabs"

Al-Qa'ida Organization for Holy War in Iraq

al-Zarqawi, Abu Musab

Amir, Yigal

Armed Islamic Group

Armed Islamic Movement

Asahara, Shoko

Aum Shinrikyō (Supreme Truth)

bin Laden, Osama

Boko Haram

caliphate

Crusades

Directorate for Inter-Services Intelligence (ISI)

Fund for the Martyrs

Golden Temple

Goldstein, Baruch

greater *jihad*

Harkat-ul-Ansar

Hezbollah

Holy Spirit Mobile Force

Islamic State of Iraq and the Levant (ISIS)

Jammu and Kashmir Islamic Front

Jammu Kashmir Liberation Front

Jewish Defense League

*jihad*

*jihadi*

Kahane, Rabbi Meir

Lashkar e Taiba

Laskar Jihad (Militia of the

Holy War)

lesser *jihad*

Lord's Resistance Army

martyrdom

Okhrana

Order of Assassins

*phansi*

pogroms

*Protocols of the Learned Elders of Zion, The*

Qods (Jerusalem) Force

Ressem, Ahmed

Revolutionary Guards Corps

Stern Gang

Thuggee

## Discussion Box: The One True Faith

*This chapter's Discussion Box is intended to stimulate critical debate about faith-motivated terrorism within major religions.*

Most religious traditions have produced extremist movements whose members believe that their faith and value system is superior to other beliefs. This concept of the "one true faith" has been used by many fundamentalists to justify violent intolerance on behalf of their religions. Religious terrorists are modern manifestations of historical traditions of extremism within the world's major faiths. For example,

- Within *Christianity,* the medieval Crusades were a series of exceptionally violent military campaigns against Muslims, Jews, and heretical Christian sects. Later, during the 16th and 17th centuries, Catholic and Protestant Christians waged relentless wars against each other, which were marked by extreme brutality. In the modern era, Christian terrorists and extremists have participated in communal fighting in numerous countries and, in the United States, have bombed abortion clinics and committed other acts of violence.

- Within *Judaism,* the Old Testament is replete with references to the ancient Hebrews' faith-based mandate to wage war against non-Jewish occupiers of the Promised Land. In the modern era, the late **Rabbi Meir Kahane**'s Kach (Kahane Chai) movement in Israel has likewise advocated the expulsion of all Arabs from Israel. Two members of the **Jewish Defense League** were arrested in the United States in December 2001 on charges of conspiring to bomb Muslim mosques and the offices of a U.S. congressman in Los Angeles.

- Within *Islam,* the relative religious tolerance of the 15th and 16th centuries is counterbalanced against modern intolerance among movements such as Afghanistan's Taliban, Palestine's Hamas, and Lebanon's Hezbollah. Numerous examples exist of political and communal violence waged in the name of Islam. Overt official repression has also been imposed in the name of the Islamic faith, as in Saudi Arabia's policy of relegating women to second-class status.

Modern religious extremism is arguably rooted in faith-based natural law. Natural law is a philosophical "higher law" that is theoretically discoverable through human reason and references to moral traditions and religious texts. In fact, most religious texts have passages that can be selectively interpreted to encourage extremist intolerance. To religious extremists, it is God's law that has been revealed to—and properly interpreted by—the extremist movement.

### Discussion Questions

- Is faith-motivated activism a constructive force for change?
- At what point does the character of faith-motivated activism become extremist and terrorist?
- Does faith-based natural law justify acts of violence?
- Why do religious traditions that supposedly promote peace, justice, and rewards for spiritual devotion have so many followers who piously engage in violence, repression, and intolerance?
- What is the future of faith-based terrorism?

## On Your Own

The open-access Student Study Site at **http://study.sagepub.com/martin5e** has a variety of useful study aids, including eFlashcards, quizzes, audio resources, and journal articles. The websites, exercises, and recommended readings listed below are easily accessed on this site as well.

## Recommended Websites

The following websites provide links to discussions of religious terrorism and extremism:

Army of God: http://www.armyofgod.com/

Christian Exodus: http://christianexodus.org/

Hezbollah (Islamic Resistance): http://www.english.moqawama.org/

Islamic Propagation Organization: http://www.al-islam.org/short/jihad/

Muslim Brotherhood Movement: http://www.ikhwanweb.com/

Radio Islam: http://www.radioislam.org/

# Web Exercise

Using this chapter's recommended websites, conduct an online investigation of religious extremism.

1. What commonalities can you find among the religious websites? What basic values are similar? In what ways do they differ?

2. Are the religious sites effective propaganda? How would you advise the site designers to appeal to different constituencies?

For an online search of historical and cultural issues pertaining to religious extremism, readers should activate the search engine on their Web browser and enter the following keywords:

"Christian Crusades"                                    "Jihad"

# Recommended Readings

The following publications discuss the motives, goals, and characteristics of religious extremism:

Allen, Tim. *Trial Justice: The International Court and the Lord's Resistance Army*. New York: Zed Books, 2006.

Bader, Eleanor J., and Patricia Baird-Windle. *Targets of Hatred: Anti-Abortion Terrorism*. New York: Palgrave, 2001.

Bhutto, Benazir. *Reconciliation: Islam, Democracy, and the West*. New York: Harper, 2008.

Crews, Robert D., and Amin Tarzi, eds. *The Taliban and the Crisis of Afghanistan*. Cambridge, MA: Harvard University Press, 2009.

Fishman, Brian. *Dysfunction and Decline: Lessons Learned From Inside al-Qa'ida in Iraq*. West Point, NY: Harmony Project, The Combating Terrorism Center, 2009.

Gerges, Fawaz A. *Journey of the Jihadist: Inside Muslim Militancy*. Orlando, FL: Harcourt, 2006.

Halevi, Yossi Klein. *Memoirs of a Jewish Extremist: An American Story*. New York: Little, Brown, 1995.

Huband, Mark. *Warriors of the Prophet: The Struggle for Islam*. Boulder, CO: Westview, 1999.

Jamal, Arif. *Shadow War: The Untold Story of Jihad in Kashmir*. Hoboken, NJ: Melville, 2010.

Kelsay, John. *Arguing the Just War in Islam*. Cambridge, MA: Harvard University Press, 2007.

Kepel, Gilles, and Jean-Pierre Milelli, eds. Trans., Pascale Ghazaleh. *Al Qaeda in Its Own Words*. Cambridge, MA: Belknap of Harvard University Press, 2008.

Lifton, Robert Jay. *Destroying the World to Save It: Aum Shinrikyō, Apocalyptic Violence, and the New Global Terrorism*. New York: Holt, 2000.

Miniter, Richard. *Mastermind: The Many Faces of the 9/11 Architect, Khalid Shaikh Mohammed*. New York: Sentinel HC, 2011.

Norton, Augustus Richard. *Hezbollah: A Short History*. Princeton, NJ: Princeton University Press, 2007.

Rashid, Ahmed. *Taliban: Militant Islam, Oil and Fundamentalism in Central Asia*. 2nd ed. New Haven, CT: Yale University Press, 2010.

Reidel, Bruce. *The Search for al Qaeda: Its Leadership, Ideology, and Future*. Washington, DC: Brookings Institution Press, 2010.

Rotberg, Robert I., ed. *Battling Terrorism in the Horn of Africa*. Washington, DC: Brookings Institution Press, 2005.

Schofield, Victoria. *Kashmir in Conflict: India, Pakistan, and the Unending War*. New York: I. B. Tauris, 2010.

Stern, Jessica. *Terror in the Name of God: Why Religious Militants Kill*. New York: Ecco/HarperCollins, 2003.

Tamimi, Azzam. *Hamas: A History From Within*. Northampton, MA: Olive Branch, 2007.

# Violent Ideologies

## CHAPTER 7

# Terrorism From the Left and Right

OPENING VIEWPOINT: RACIST SKINHEADS AS A SUPPORTIVE ENVIRONMENT

**Skinheads** are associations of youths who live a countercultural, and often antisocial, lifestyle. The term *skinhead* is derived from their distinctive appearance, which includes closely cropped hair, suspenders, T-shirts, tattoos, blue jeans, and boots (traditionally manufactured by Dr. Martens). Some skinheads have organized themselves into gangs, but others simply live the lifestyle. Although they have a popular reputation for advocating racial supremacy, the fact is that many have no racial animosity, and some actively confront racist skinheads. An international movement known as **Skinheads Against Racial Prejudice (SHARP)** specifically challenges racist skinhead gangs, although the SHARP designation is often an individual statement rather than participation in an established group.

The skinhead movement began in the United Kingdom in the early 1970s among working-class youths as a countermovement to the hippies. They were known for hard drinking (usually beer) and fighting. Some began to engage in racial harassment of, and assaults on, Asians and blacks. This was the beginning of the racist skinhead movement, which has since adopted supremacist values, Nazi symbols, and Nazi slogans. The movement's lifestyle has become international, with thousands of skinhead youths found in dozens of countries.

Skinhead gangs have been actively courted by extremist organizations in the United Kingdom, Germany, the United States, and elsewhere. They are often viewed as a potential recruitment reservoir that simply requires the discipline of the organized neofascist and neo-Nazi groups and parties. Some of these linkages have been successful, but the movement is by no means directed by organized neofascists.

## The Racist Skinhead Counterculture

An important aspect of the racist skinhead lifestyle is an active counterculture. It is expressed through magazines and music. The magazines—called "**skinzines**" or "**zines**"—generally report on skinhead lifestyle and music. Advertising includes standard ads for clothing, flamboyant grooming tips, and music. Skinheads—both racist and nonracist—promote a strong music style that is rooted in the punk music that began in the mid-1970s. It is a "hard" rock-and-roll style with driving beats and rhythms and a heavy emphasis on guitars, drums, and racially charged lyrics.

The following are typical lyrics from the international racist skinhead music scene:

United Kingdom's Skrewdriver (entitled "White Warriors"):

> Fighting in the city,
> It's a matter of life and death,
> It's as easy as black and white,
> You'll fight till your last breath . . .
> When the battle is over,
> And the victory is won,
> The White man's lands are owned
> By the White people,
> The traitors will be all gone.[a]

Germany's Tonstörung (entitled "Doitsche Musik"):

> Sharpen your knife on the sidewalk,
> let the knife slip into the Jew's body.
> Blood must flow

and we shit on the freedom of this Jew republic . . .

oiling the guillotine with the Jew's fat.[b]

Hungary's Mos-Oi (entitled "Gypsy-Free Zone"):

We will do away with everything bad;
Everything base and evil will disappear;
A blazing gun is the
Only weapon I can win with.
I will kill every Gypsy, adult or child . . .
When the job is done, we can post
[the sign] "Gypsy-free Zone."[c]

## Notes

a. Quoted in Anti-Defamation League. *The Skinhead International: A Worldwide Survey of Neo-Nazi Skinheads*. New York: Anti-Defamation League, 1995, p. 76. © Anti-Defamation League. Reprinted with permission. All rights reserved.

b. From Anti-Defamation League (note a), p. 38. © Anti-Defamation League. Reprinted with permission. All rights reserved.

c. From Anti-Defamation League (note a), p. 46. © Anti-Defamation League. Reprinted with permission. All rights reserved.

n this chapter, readers will acquire a fundamental understanding of the radical left and reactionary right by reviewing the following:

- Reactionaries and Radicals: The Classical Ideological Continuum
- Left-Wing Ideologies and Activism
- Class Struggle and National Liberation: The Terrorist Left
- Right-Wing Activism and Extremism
- Race and Order: The Terrorist Right
- Violent Ideologies in the New Era of Terrorism

## ❖ Reactionaries and Radicals: The Classical Ideological Continuum

There are literally scores of belief systems that have led to acts of terrorist violence. Because there are so many belief systems, it is difficult to classify them with precision. Nevertheless, a **classical ideological continuum** rooted in the politics of the French Revolution has endured to the present time.[1] This is instructive for our discussion of politically motivated violence because the concepts embodied in the continuum continue to be relevant in the modern era.

At the beginning of the French Revolution in 1789, a parliament-like assembly was convened to represent the interests of the French social classes. Although its name changed during the revolution—from Estates-General to National Constituent Assembly to Legislative Assembly—the basic ideological divisions were symbolically demonstrated by where representatives sat during assembly sessions. On the left side of the assembly sat those who favored radical change, some advocating a complete reordering of French society and culture. On the right side of the assembly sat those who favored either the old order or slow and deliberate change. In the center of the assembly sat those who favored either moderate change or simply could not make up their minds to commit to either the left or right. These symbolic designations—**left**, **center**, and **right**—have become part of our modern political culture.

Table 7.1 summarizes the progression of these designations from their origin during the French Revolution.

It is readily apparent from the French Revolution that the quality of the classical continuum depended very much on the political environment of each society. For example, within American

---

[1]The politics of the French Revolution are evaluated in Skocpol, Theda. *States and Social Revolutions: A Comparative Analysis of France, Russia, and China*. Cambridge, UK: Cambridge University Press, 1990, pp. 174–205.

**Table 7.1** The Classical Ideological Continuum: The Case of the French Revolution

After the dissolution of the monarchy, the victorious revolutionaries began a complete restructuring of French society. Perhaps the most important priority was to create a new elective constituent assembly to represent the interests of the people. The configuration of this new assembly changed repeatedly as the revolution progressed from one ideological phase to the next.

| Legislative Body | Political and Ideological Orientation | | |
| --- | --- | --- | --- |
| | Left | Center | Right |
| **National Constituent Assembly 1789–1791** | Patriots (republicans) | Moderates (constitutional monarchists) | Blacks (reactionaries) |
| **Legislative Assembly 1791–1792** | Mountain (republicans) | Plain (near-republicans) | Constitutionalists (constitutional monarchists) |
| **National Convention 1792** | Mountain (radicals) | Marsh (uncommitted bourgeois) | Girondins (bourgeois republicans) |

culture, mainstream values include free enterprise, freedom of speech, and limited government.[2] Depending on where one falls on the classical continuum, the interpretation of these mainstream values can be very different. In the American example:

- Free enterprise might be viewed with suspicion by the far left but might be considered sacrosanct (untouchable) by the far right.

- Freedom of speech would seem to be a noncontroversial issue, but the right and left also disagree about what kinds of speech should be protected or regulated.

- The role of government is a debate that has its origins from the time of the American Revolution. The right and left disagree about the degree to which government should have a role in regulating private life.

Mainstream American values of past generations—such as Manifest Destiny and racial segregation—were rejected by later generations as unacceptable extremist ideologies. Thus, the concepts of left, center, and right shift during changes in political and social culture.

In the modern era, many nationalist or religious terrorists do not fit easily into the classical continuum. For example,

to argue that the Algerian terrorists, the Palestinian groups, or the Tamil Tigers are "left" or "right" means affixing a label that simply does not fit. . . . The Third World groups . . . have subscribed to different ideological tenets at different periods.[3]

---

[2]For a comparative discussion of ideological conflict in revolutionary environments, see Skocpol, *States.* For seminal discussions that formed the ideological foundation for the U.S. Constitution and Bill of Rights, see Hamilton, Alexander, John Jay, and James Madison. *The Federalist: A Commentary on the Constitution of the United States, Being a Collection of Essays Written in Support of the Constitution Agreed upon September 17, 1787.* New York: Modern Library, 2000.

[3]Laqueur, Walter. *The New Terrorism: Fanaticism and the Arms of Mass Destruction.* New York: Oxford University Press, 1999, p. 230.

An interesting case in this regard is the National Union for the Total Independence of Angola (UNITA) guerrilla movement, which fought in Angola during the 1970s and thereafter. UNITA was avowedly leftist when it fought alongside the Marxist Movement for the Liberation of Angola (MPLA) against the Portuguese colonialists. However, the group became strongly anti-Communist and pro-Western when it was supported by the United States and South Africa during its civil war against the MPLA after the Portuguese withdrawal. The war in Angola exemplifies a classic "proxy war" between the United States and the Soviet Union.

Nevertheless, the classical continuum is still very useful for categorizing terrorist behaviors and extremist beliefs. Table 7.2 compares the championed groups, methodologies, and desired outcomes of typical political environments on the continuum.

## An Ideological Analysis: From the Left Fringe to the Right Fringe

It is not difficult to draw a conceptual distinction between right-wing and left-wing ideologies. The term **reactionary** has been affixed to far- and fringe-rightist ideologies, and **radical** has been affixed to far- and fringe-leftist ideologies. These terms are, of course, exercises in semantics. As such, they can be at best imprecise and, at worst, confusing. Rather than enter into an academic debate about the meaning of these terms, it is instructive for readers to understand the following two concepts:

- *Right-wing extremism* is generally a reaction against perceived threats to a group's value system, its presumption of superiority, or its sense of specialness. Rightists often try to preserve their value system and special status by aggressively asserting this claimed status. They frequently desire to return to a time of past glory, which in their belief system has been lost or usurped by an enemy group or culture. In this sense, right-wing extremism is *nostalgic*.

- *Left-wing extremism* is future oriented, seeking to reform or destroy an existing system prior to building a new and just society. To the extent that leftists champion a special group, it is usually one that is perceived to be oppressed unjustly by a corrupt system or government. This group is commonly a class or ethnonational category that, in the leftists' belief system, must receive the justice and equality that has been denied them. In doing so, leftists believe that reform of the system, or revolution, is needed to build a just society. In this sense, left-wing extremism is *idealistic*.

**Fringe-left ideology** is usually an extreme interpretation of Marxist ideology, using theories of class warfare or ethnonational liberation to justify political violence. At the leftist fringe, violence is seen as a perfectly legitimate option because the fringe group considers itself to be at war with an oppressive system, class, or government. The key justification is that the fringe group pictures itself as a righteous champion of the poor and downtrodden.

This type of ideological movement frequently concerns itself only with destroying an existing order in the name of the championed class or national group, not with building the new society in the aftermath of the revolution. For example, Gudrun Ensslin, a leader of the terrorist Red Army Faction in West Germany, stated, "As for the state of the future, the time after victory, that is not our concern. . . . We build the revolution, not the socialist model."[4]

**Far-left ideology** frequently applies Marxist theory to promote class or ethnonational rights. It is best characterized as a radical worldview because political declarations often direct public attention against perceived forces of exploitation or repression. Far-left groups do not necessarily engage in political violence and often fully participate in democratic processes. In Western Europe, for example, communist parties and their affiliated communist labor unions have historically been overt

---

[4]Kellen, Konrad. "Ideology and Rebellion: Terrorism in West Germany." In *Origins of Terrorism: Psychologies, Ideologies, Theologies, States of Mind*, edited by Walter Reich. Washington, DC: Woodrow Wilson Center, 1998, p. 57.

**Table 7.2** The Classical Ideological Continuum: Modern Political Environments

Activism on the left, right, and center can be distinguished by a number of characteristics. A comparison of these attributes is instructive. The representation here compares their championed groups, methodologies, and desired outcomes.

| | Fringe Left | Far Left | Liberalism | Moderate Center | Conservatism | Far Right | Fringe Right |
|---|---|---|---|---|---|---|---|
| Championed groups | Class/nationality | Class/nationality | Demographic groups | General society | General society | Race, ethnicity, nationality, religion | Race, ethnicity, nationality, religion |
| Methodology/process | Liberation movement | Political agitation | Partisan democratic processes | Consensus | Partisan democratic processes | Political agitation | "Order" movement |
| Desired outcome | Radical change | Radical change | Incremental reform | Status quo, slow change | Traditional values | Reactionary change | Reactionary change |

in their agitation for reform through democratic processes.[5] The French Communist Party regularly had its members elected at the national level,[6] as did the Italian Communist Party.[7] In March 1977, the Spanish, Italian, and French communist parties embarked on an independent, yet undefined, course setting them apart from the orthodox, Moscow-inspired path. The new path was called Eurocommunism.[8]

This environment of relatively peaceful coexistence occurs only in societies where dissent is tolerated. In countries with weaker democratic traditions, far-left dissent has erupted in violence and been met by extreme repression. Latin America has many examples of this kind of environment.

**Liberalism** is a concept that has been defined differently depending on the historical or national context in which it has been used. In its original context, European liberalism arose as a philosophical challenge to the absolutism practiced by monarchies. It advocated the rights of the individual vis-à-vis the monarch and the state. Liberty in political expression and equality under the law were the ideals of liberalism, although as practiced, these ideals were not enjoyed by every person in society. For example, the French and American revolutions embodied liberal principles, but the French state fell into civil war and Napoleonic imperialism, and American constitutional rights were not afforded to women or African Americans until well into the 20th century. Thus, 19th-century liberalism was highly contextualized and even conservative by modern standards.

In the modern era, particularly in the American and British contexts, liberalism "expects to use government in a positive and expansive role . . . motivated by the highest sentiments," and "it sees as both necessary and good that the policy agenda and the public interest be defined in terms of the organized interests in society."[9] From this perspective, the various *people's rights* movements—such as the human, civil, women's, and gay rights movements—are usually considered to be liberal in nature.

The **moderate center** is best described as the stable, balancing segment of the political environment. Political expression is conducted within accepted traditional institutions and rarely exhibits sustained group-centered activism or agitation. In a democracy, the moderate center is ideally the largest segment in the political environment, drawing support from both liberal and conservative ranks that need its political backing. Consensus, not adversarial confrontation, is the hallmark of the moderate center.

**Conservatism**, like liberalism, is a concept that evolved over time and within the context of political and social conflict. The French Revolution and subsequent upheavals in Europe caused a backlash that sought to reestablish order, the rule of law, and often monarchy. **Edmund Burke**, who criticized the excesses of the French Revolution, is considered to be the founder of modern conservatism. Conservatives of the 19th century argued that, rather than rejecting the past in favor of an idealized vision of how humans *ought* to live, one should preserve (conserve) the good features of the existing order. Conservatives held that change, especially radical change, ought to be questioned.

In the modern era, traditional "conservatism is committed to a discriminating defense of social order against change and reform."[10] Traditional conservatism questions government intervention in the private sector, especially regulation of the market, and questions international intervention. Having said this, in the United States, a new conservatism (termed **neoconservatism**) eschews the lack of activism among traditional conservatives and advocates strong international intervention. The core trait of neoconservative ideology is the aggressive promotion of democracy among allies and

[5]See Ellis, Harry B. *Ideals and Ideologies: Communism, Socialism, and Capitalism.* New York: World, 1972.

[6]See Cobban, Alfred. *A History of Modern France.* New York: Penguin, 1965.

[7]Pryce, Roy. "Italy, the New Republic." In *20th Century,* edited by R. W. Cross. London: Purnell Reference Books, 1979, pp. 2109ff.

[8]Murphy, Brian. "Achieving a United Europe." In *20th Century,* edited by R. W. Cross. London: Purnell Reference Books, 1979, p. 2344.

[9]Lowi, Theodore J. *The End of Liberalism: Ideology, Policy, and the Crisis of Public Authority.* New York: W. W. Norton, 1969, p. 71.

[10]Rossiter, Clinton. *Conservatism in America.* New York: Knopf, 1955, p. 12. Quoted in Lowi, *The End,* p. 56.

adversaries alike, with the idealistic aim of doing so "in every nation and culture, with the ultimate goal of ending tyranny in our world."[11] To achieve this idealistic end, global intervention is necessary, and preemptive wars sometimes need to be fought.

**Far-right ideology** is characterized by strong adherence to social order and traditional values. There is often a chauvinistic racial or ethnic dimension to the worldview of the far right, as well as an undercurrent of religion or mysticism—the latter is especially prevalent in the United States. As with the case of the far left, far-right groups do not necessarily engage in political violence and have fully participated in democratic processes. Organized political expression is often overt. For example, right-wing political parties in many European countries are a common feature of national politics. Their success has been mixed, and their influence varies in different countries. In Spain, Greece, and Great Britain, these parties have little popular support.[12] However, the far-right parties in Austria, Belgium, France, and Italy have enjoyed significant popular support in the recent past.

Not all far-right political movements are the same, and a comparison of the American and European contexts is instructive. In Europe, some rightist parties are nostalgic neofascist, such as the German People's Union. Others are more populist, such as the National Front in France.[13] They all tend to favor an open market, "articulate a low-tax, anti-welfare-state ideology . . . may support 'law and order' and a vigorous military . . . [and] condemn bureaucracy [and] excessive state control."[14] In the United States, the far right is characterized by activism among local grassroots organizations and has no viable political party. Some American groups have a religious orientation, others are racial, others embody a politically paranoid survivalist lifestyle, and some incorporate all three tendencies.

**Fringe-right ideology** is usually rooted in an uncompromising belief in ethnonational or religious superiority, and terrorist violence is justified as a protection of the purity and superiority of the group. Terrorists on the fringe right picture themselves as champions of an ideal order that has been usurped or attacked by inferior interests or unwanted religious values. Violence is an acceptable option against those who are not members of the group or religion because they are considered to be obstacles to the natural assumption of power by the favored group or belief. Like terrorists on the fringe left, right-wing terrorists often have only a vague notion of the characteristics of the new order after the revolution. They are concerned only with asserting their value system and, if necessary, destroying the existing order. Significantly, rightist terrorists have been more likely than violent leftists to engage in indiscriminate bombings and other attacks that produce higher numbers of victims.

## Ideologies and Ideals

**Ideologies** are *systems of belief;* they are derived from theories that explain human social and political conditions. Lowi describes one element of ideology as "a source of principles and a means of justifying behavior."[15] Some ideologies are very intricate, intellectual, and dynamic, such as Marxism. Other ideologies are rather uncomplicated and straightforward, such as nationalism in East Africa,[16]

---

[11]Quotation from a speech delivered by U.S. President George W. Bush. In McManus, Doyle. "Bush Pulls 'Neocons' Out of the Shadows." *Los Angeles Times,* January 22, 2005.

[12]Weinberg, Leonard. "An Overview of Right-Wing Extremism in the Western World: A Study of Convergence, Linkage, and Identity." In *Nation and Race: The Developing Euro-American Racist Subculture,* edited by Jeffrey Kaplan and Tore Bjørgo. Boston: Northeastern University Press, 1998, pp. 8ff.

[13]Ibid., p. 10.

[14]Ibid., p. 11.

[15]Lowi, *The End of Liberalism,* p. 3.

[16]Communal violence between Hutus and Tutsis in Rwanda and Burundi has claimed hundreds of thousands of lives in the postwar era. The International Committee of the Red Cross estimated in its *Annual Report 1996* that hundreds of thousands were killed or injured in 1996 in Burundi alone.

the Balkans,[17] and elsewhere. And some ideologies are nothing more than paranoid conspiracy theories, such as the one-world government and New World Order conspiracies underlying the Patriot movement in the United States.[18]

Ideologies can constitute political, social, or economic programs. They can also constitute religious, racial, or ethnic systems of belief. The common attribute of all ideologies is that they guide the worldview and manner of living for individuals, groups, and nations. In their most extreme application, ideologies permit no deviation from their perceived truth and are completely intolerant of any criticism.

It is critical to grasp the influence of ideological systems on the modern era. For this reason, several ideologies—**anarchism**, **Marxism**, and **fascism**—are discussed in the following sections.

### Anarchism

Anarchism is a leftist philosophy that was an ideological by-product of the social upheavals of mid-19th-century Europe, a time when civil unrest and class conflict swept the continent, culminating in the revolutions of 1848. Anarchists were among the first antiestablishment radicals who championed what they considered to be the downtrodden peasant and working classes. They abhorred central government control and private property. Frenchman **Pierre-Joseph Proudhon**, who published a number of articles and books on the virtues of anarchism, coined an enduring slogan among anarchists: **"Property is theft!"** In his 1840 publication *What Is Property? An Inquiry Into the Principle of Right and of Government,* Proudhon wrote,

> If I had to answer the following question, "What is slavery?" and if I should respond in one word, "It is murder," my meaning would be understood at once. I should not need a long explanation to show that the power to deprive a man of his thought, his will, and his personality is the power of life and death. So why to this other question, "What is property?" should I not answer in the same way, "It is theft," without fearing to be misunderstood.[19]

❖ **Photo 7.1**

A portrait of Pierre-Joseph Proudhon, the ideological father of anarchism. His slogan, "Property is theft!" became a rallying cry for anarchists during the 19th and 20th centuries.

Hulton Archive/Getty Images

Thus, the radical undercurrent for anarchist thought began with the proposition that *property is theft.* **Mikhail Bakunin** and his philosophical associates **Sergei Nechayev** and **Petr Kropotkin**, all Russians, were the founders of modern anarchism. They supported destruction of the state, radical decentralization of power, atheism, and individualism. They also opposed capitalism and Karl Marx's revolutionary doctrine of building a socialist state. Among these early anarchists, Bakunin's theories had a particularly international influence.

Anarchists never offered a concrete plan for replacing centralized state authority because they were not concerned about building a clearly defined vision of postrevolutionary society. Instead, early anarchists considered the destruction of the state alone to be their contribution to the future. In the ***Revolutionary Catechism***, Nechayev wrote,

The revolutionary . . . must have a single thought, a single goal—implacable destruction. Pursuing this goal coldly and relentlessly, he must be prepared to perish himself and to

---

[17]Since the breakup of Yugoslavia, wars have been fought in Slovenia, Croatia, Bosnia, Macedonia, and the Kosovo region of Serbia.

[18]See Stern, Kenneth S. *A Force Upon the Plain: The American Militia Movement and the Politics of Hate.* New York: Simon & Schuster, 1996.

[19]Kelley, Donald R., and Bonnie G. Smith, eds. *Proudhon: What Is Property?* Cambridge, UK: Cambridge University Press, 1994, p. 13.

cause to perish, with his own hands, all those who would prevent him from achieving his goal.[20]

Bakunin, Nechayev, and Kropotkin believed that revolutionary violence was needed to destroy capitalism and state socialism. Bakunin rejected publication of the anarchists' cause through traditional media such as newspapers or leafleting. Instead, he advocated achieving propaganda victories by violently pursuing the revolution, which became known as *propaganda by the deed*. Terrorism was advocated as a principal means to destroy state authority. Interestingly, they argued that terrorists should organize themselves into small groups, or cells—a tactic that has been adopted by modern terrorists.

Anarchists actively practiced propaganda by the deed, as evidenced by many acts of violence against prominently symbolic targets. In Russia, People's Will (Narodnaya Volya) conducted a terrorist campaign from 1878 to 1881, and other anarchist terrorist cells operated in Western Europe. Around the turn of the 20th century, anarchists assassinated Russian Czar Alexander II (1881), French President Sadi Carnot (1894), Austro-Hungarian Empress Elizabeth (1898), Italian King Umberto I (1900), and American President William McKinley (1901)—the latter by self-professed anarchist Leon Czolgosz.

### Marxism

Radical socialism, like anarchism, is a leftist ideology that began in the turmoil of mid-19th-century Europe and the uprisings of 1848. Socialists championed the emerging industrial working class and argued that the wealth produced by these workers should be more equitably distributed, rather than concentrated in the hands of the wealthy elite.

**Karl Marx** is regarded as the founder of modern socialism. He and his associate **Friedrich Engels**, both Germans, argued that their approach to socialism was grounded in the scientific "discovery" that human progress and social evolution are the result of a series of historical conflicts and revolutions. Each era was based on the working group's unequal relationship to the means of production (e.g., slaves, feudal farmers, industrial workers) vis-à-vis the ruling group's enjoyment of the fruits of the working group's labor. In each era, a ruling *thesis* group maintained the status quo and a laboring *antithesis* group challenged the status quo (through agitation and revolution), resulting in a socioeconomic *synthesis* that created new relationships with the means of production. Thus, human society evolved into the next era. According to Marx, the most advanced era of social evolution would be the synthesis Communist era, which Marx argued would be built after the antithesis industrial working class overthrows the thesis capitalist system. Marx theorized that the working class would establish the **dictatorship of the proletariat** in the Communist society and build a just and egalitarian social order.

Marx and Engels collaborated on the ***Manifesto of the Communist Party***, a short work completed in 1847 and published in 1848. It became one of the most widely read documents of the 20th century. In it, Marx and Engels explained the revolutionary environment of the industrial era and how this era was an immediate precursor to the Communist era. They wrote,

> The Communists disdain to conceal their views and aims. They openly declare that their ends can be attained only by the forcible overthrow of all existing social conditions. Let the ruling classes tremble at a Communist revolution. The proletarians have nothing to lose but their chains. They have a world to win. Working Men of All Countries, Unite!

Marxist socialism was pragmatic and revolutionary. It was action oriented and was adopted by many revolutionary leaders and movements throughout the 20th century. For example, **Vladimir Ilich Lenin** in Russia, **Mao Zedong** in China, **Ho Chi Minh** in Vietnam, and **Fidel Castro** in Cuba all based their revolutionary doctrines on Marx's precepts. Terrorism, both state and dissident, was used during these revolutions and during the consolidation of power after victory.

---

[20]Quoted in Ferracuti, Franco. "Ideology and Repentance: Terrorism in Italy." In *Origins of Terrorism: Psychologies, Ideologies, Theologies, States of Mind,* edited by Walter Reich. Washington, DC: Woodrow Wilson Center, 1998, p. 60.

Keystone/Hulton Archive/Getty Images

❖ **Photo 7.2**

Architects of Communism. Russian revolutionary leader Vladimir Ilich Lenin (left) with Leon Trotsky, head of the Red Army and future ideological rival of Joseph Stalin.

Interestingly, Marx championed the industrial working class and dismissed any attempt to mobilize either the peasantry or the marginalized sectors of society (the **Lumpenproletariat**). To Marx, the peasants' relationship to the means of production (agricultural laborers) meant that they were socially and politically isolated from one another. Because of this, they could never develop lasting revolutionary political organization. This analysis was proven wrong. Despite Marx's emphasis on the revolution of the industrial working class, successful Marxist rebellions during the 20th century occurred not in industrialized nations but in preindustrial and agrarian peasant-based societies in the developing world. This occurred in Russia, China, Cuba, Vietnam, and Nicaragua. Other successful non-Marxist, rural-based rebellions in the 20th century occurred in Mexico and Algeria.

### Fascism

Fascism was a rightist ideological counterpoint to Marxism and anarchism that peaked prior to World War II. Its name is derived from the Latin word *fasces*, which was a bundle of wooden rods bound together with an axe protruding from the center; it was the Roman imperial symbol of strength and power and was carried before processions of Roman officials.

Like Marxism and anarchism, fascism's popular appeal grew out of social turmoil in Europe—this time as a reaction to the 1917 Bolshevik (Communist) Revolution in Russia, the subsequent Bolshevik-inspired political agitation elsewhere in Europe, and the widespread unrest during the Great Depression of the 1930s. It was rooted in a brand of extreme nationalism that championed the alleged superiority of a particular national heritage or ethnoracial group. Fascism was anti-Communist, antimonarchist, antidemocratic, and anti-intellectual (although there were some fascist writers). It demanded extreme obedience to law, order, and the state. Fascism also required cultural conservatism—often looking backward in history to link the ancient past to the modern state. Fascists created their own conceptualizations of traditional values such as military duty, the Christian church, and motherhood. Strong antidemocratic leadership was centralized in the state, usually under the guidance of a single charismatic leader who symbolically embodied the virtues of the state, the people, and the underlying fascist ideology.

Italian dictator **Benito Mussolini** was the first to consolidate power and create a fascist state. Beginning with his March on Rome in 1922, he gradually eliminated all opposition and democratic institutions. He was a mentor for **Adolf Hitler**, who led the fascist National Socialist German Worker's (Nazi) Party to power in Germany in 1933. Both the Italian and German fascist regimes sent troops to fight on the side of right-wing Spanish rebels led by **Francisco Franco** during the Spanish Civil War.[21] These regimes—fascist Italy, Nazi Germany, and Falangist Spain—represented three strains of fascism that reflected their own cultural and national idiosyncrasies:

1. *Italian fascism* was nationalistic and expansionistic. It hearkened back to Italy's ancient past, seeking to symbolize the rise of a new Roman Empire. Mussolini sent his fascist legions on wars of conquest in Abyssinia, North Africa, the Balkans, and Greece.

2. *German fascism* was also nationalistic and expansionistic. Unlike Italian fascism, the Nazis practiced an ideology of racial supremacy. Nazism looked back to the Germanic people's ancient past, seeking to symbolize a time of Teutonic tribal and racial glory.

---

[21]For a good journalistic chronology of the Spanish Civil War, see Haigh, R. H., D. S. Morris, and A. R. Peters. *The Guardian Book of the Spanish Civil War*. Aldershot, UK: Wildwood House, 1987.

3. *Spanish fascism* was also nationalistic but strongly rejected an expansionist ideology. The Franco regime successfully resisted intimidation from Adolf Hitler to enter World War II on the side of Germany and Italy. Spanish rightists looked to Spanish institutions and history to consolidate power domestically. They had a strong ideological influence in Latin America that lasted throughout the latter half of the 20th century.

The power of all three regimes was rooted in a disciplined political party, a charismatic leader, glorification of the military, and an organized elite. Fascist regimes during this period also took root in Hungary (1930s), Bulgaria (1934), and Romania (1938). Only Franco's Falangist (phalanx) regime survived World War II, lasting until his death in 1975.

Although the first fascist movement largely collapsed in 1945, right-wing groups and political parties have continued to promote neofascist ideals. Some terrorist groups in Europe and the United States have been overtly fascist and racist. Also, dictatorships have arisen since World War II that adopted many features of prewar fascism. For example, Latin American regimes arose in Chile, Argentina, Uruguay, and El Salvador—to name a few—that fit the fascist pattern.

Table 7.3 summarizes the ideals and ideologies discussed here.

Hulton Archive/Getty Images

❖ **Photo 7.3**

Architects of fascism. German Führer (leader) Adolf Hitler (front left) stands beside Italian Duce (leader) Benito Mussolini. Behind them are ranking members of the Nazi and fascist regimes.

## ❖ Left-Wing Ideologies and Activism

Leftist agitation is group oriented. Emphasis has traditionally been placed on creating a collective political consciousness—a class or national consciousness—within the championed group. On the far and fringe left, this collective political consciousness is considered a precondition to successful revolution. Hence, indoctrination has been used by radical leftists to fashion a disciplined and motivated **cadre group**, which represents the interests of the class or national group. At the vanguard of the struggle, then, are the political and military cadres—those who have been indoctrinated to engage in political agitation and armed conflict on behalf of the championed group. This concept of a politically disciplined cadre group has been applied by leftist extremists in many contexts, including nonviolent agitation, guerrilla warfare, and terrorist campaigns.

| Table 7.3 | A Comparison of Ideologies |
|---|---|

Social conflict in the 20th century was deeply rooted in the application of ideals and ideologies to practice. The adoption of these social and philosophical systems frequently inspired individuals and motivated movements to engage in armed conflict with perceived enemies. The following table matches proponents, outcomes, and case studies of four ideals and ideologies.

| | *Ideological Orientation* | | | |
|---|---|---|---|---|
| | *Anarchism* | *Marxism* | *Fascism* | *Just War* |
| **Proponents** | Proudhon/Bakunin | Marx/Engels | Mussolini/Hitler | Augustine |
| **Desired social outcome** | Stateless society | Dictatorship of the proletariat | New order | Legitimized conflict |
| **Applications** | Narodnaya Volya | Russian Revolution | World War II–era Italy and Germany | State and dissident violence |

Many leftists, especially Marxists, believe that capitalism inherently causes social and economic inequities that relegate working people and other groups (such as racial minorities)[22] to a subordinate political status. The political agenda on the left frequently reflects this fundamental principle.

The following propositions summarize the quality of activism by modern leftists:

1. *Radical leftists tend to emphasize "economic rights" as a priority.* Because orthodox Marxists and other radical socialists represent ideological and class interests, "rights" are defined within the context of redistributing the wealth and basic services to lower classes and groups. It was, therefore, not uncommon for radicals on the left to conclude that political rights are secondary to economic rights. Examples of economic rights include guaranteed health care, a job, enough income to support a household, and retirement benefits. Unlike coalitional political parties in the United States and elsewhere—which build broad demographic bases of political support—communist and socialist parties are usually affiliated with labor unions, minority or exploited demographic groups, or other political and economic interests.

2. *Democratic socialism emphasizes reform, not revolution.* Democratic socialist political parties—usually called Social Democrat parties—are quite common around the world and are affiliated with one another through the Socialist International. Although socialists seek to redistribute wealth and services to a subordinate group, this is usually done nonviolently. The democratic socialist movement seeks to influence policy democratically, although selective demonstrations or labor strikes are sometimes advocated to pressure the governing authorities. In many democracies—particularly in Europe—Social Democrat parties wield significant political influence and have large delegations in parliaments and other elected assemblies.

3. *Communists traditionally emphasize revolution, not reform.* Orthodox communism offers a vision of doing away with the capitalist system completely and reconfiguring society as a model of complete economic equality—ideally with no dominant or subordinate classes. Orthodox Marxism claims to be a scientific theory, so that class conflict is inevitable and a future communist society is ensured. Some communist movements and communist parties were violently activist, adopting armed insurgency and terrorism as viable options. In the developing world, this insurgent variant of Marxist activism continued well into the 1980s; some insurgencies in countries such as Colombia and Peru continued through the 1990s. Other communist parties, especially those in Western Europe, adapted to specific democratic environments, so that by the mid-1970s, "democratic communism" became fashionable.

4. *Because democratic socialists are traditionally reformers, and communists are traditionally revolutionaries, they tend to distrust each other.* The history of interaction between communist and democratic socialist parties has been contentious. Although democratic socialist parties have acquired sufficient respectability to become a mainstream force in many countries, communist parties have never acquired lasting mainstream support.

5. *Leftist terrorists in Western democracies often considered the working class to be corrupted or co-opted by capitalism.* The Weather Underground in the United States and the Red Army Faction in West Germany claimed to fight on behalf of the oppressed of their countries and the exploited people of the developing world. They held little faith that the working classes in their countries would develop a revolutionary class consciousness sufficient for them to identify with the oppressed of the world.

Chapter Perspective 7.1 summarizes the Marxist-influenced political philosophies of the New Left, which arose in Western countries during the 1960s.

---

[22]For a Marxist analysis of the African American rights movement, see Thomas, Tony, ed. *Black Liberation and Socialism*. New York: Pathfinder, 1974.

## CHAPTER PERSPECTIVE 7.1: Required Reading on the "New Left"

In the postwar West, many leftist terrorists were inspired not by orthodox Marxism but by examples of revolutionaries in the developing world such as Mao Zedong, Ho Chi Minh, Fidel Castro, and Che Guevara. Realizing as a practical matter that building guerrilla units in the countryside was impossible—and that the working class was not sufficiently prepared for revolution—many young radicals became nihilistic dissident revolutionaries. They concluded that revolution was a goal in itself, and "revolution for the hell of it"[a] became a slogan and a practice for many left-wing radicals in the West. For them, there was little vision of what kind of society would be built on the rubble of the old. In fact,

> The central question about the rationality of some terrorist organizations, such as the West German groups of the 1970s or the Weather Underground in the United States, is whether or not they had a sufficient grasp of reality . . . to calculate the likely consequences of the courses of action they chose.[b]

Nevertheless, from the perspective of radical activists and intellectuals, nihilist dissident behavior was rational and logical.

Several books inspired radical leftists in the West. These books provided a rational justification for revolutionary agitation against democratic institutions in relatively prosperous societies. They came to define the New Left of the 1960s and 1970s, which rejected the rigid ideological orthodoxy of the "Old Left" Marxists. They created a new interpretation of revolutionary conditions. On the short list of "required reading" among radical activists were three books:[c]

- Frantz Fanon's *The Wretched of the Earth*
- Herbert Marcuse's *One-Dimensional Man*
- Carlos Marighella's *Mini-Manual of the Urban Guerrilla*

### The Wretched of the Earth

In *The Wretched of the Earth,* Fanon analyzed the role of indigenous people living in countries controlled by imperial governments that exploited local resources and imposed a foreign culture and values. He concluded that revolutionary violence was perfectly justifiable under these conditions. In fact, it was required because, in addition to liberating one's country, one had to liberate oneself as an individual; only "liberating violence" could do this. Young radicals in the West agreed with this analysis, and some concluded that liberating violence in a prosperous society was justified. They also rationalized their violent political behavior by establishing a sense of revolutionary solidarity with "the wretched of the earth."

### One-Dimensional Man

Marcuse was a German philosopher who, along with Jean-Paul Sartre, was prominent among existentialist writers. He argued in *One-Dimensional Man* that capitalist society—no matter how prosperous or democratic—created "manacles" of privilege that kept the public docile and content. He explained that the people's oppression should be measured by how much they had been co-opted by the accoutrements of capitalist comfort. Using this analysis, middle-class college students who considered themselves to be Marxists could justify revolutionary activism, even though they were far removed from the working class. Thus, they were rejecting their "manacles" of privilege and fighting in common cause with other revolutionaries worldwide.

### Mini-Manual of the Urban Guerrilla

As discussed in Chapter 5, Carlos Marighella's book was extremely influential on leftist revolutionary strategy in Latin America, Western Europe, and the United States. It was a blueprint for revolution in urban societies, and Marighella's guidelines for using urban terrorism to create revolutionary conditions were widely followed. However, as noted previously, the assumption

*(Continued)*

(Continued)

that the exploited group would join the revolution at the right time rarely happened in practice.

These works of dissident philosophy shaped the ideological justifications for the tactics of many revolutionary movements. For example, the motivation behind West Germany's Red Army Faction has been described as having three central elements. These elements reflect the revolutionary literature and theory of the time:[d]

- The concept of the "armed struggle" and the model of Third World liberation movements
- The Nazi "connection" and "formal democracy" in the Federal Republic
- The rejection of consumer society[e]

**Notes**

a. The title of a book by the American New Left radical Abbie Hoffman. See Hoffman, Abbie. *Revolution for the Hell of It.* New York: Dell, 1968.

b. Reich, Walter. *Origins of Terrorism: Psychologies, Theologies, States of Mind.* Washington, DC: Woodrow Wilson Center, 1990, p. 9.

c. Fanon, Frantz. *The Wretched of the Earth.* New York: Grove, 1963; Marcuse, Herbert. *One-Dimensional Man.* Boston: Beacon, 1964; Marighella, Carlos. *Mini-Manual of the Urban Guerrilla.* Chapel Hill, NC: Documentary Publications, 1985.

d. Marighella, *Mini-Manual.*

e. Pridham, Geoffrey. "Terrorism and the State in West Germany During the 1970s: A Threat to Stability or a Case of Political Over-Reaction?" In *Terrorism: A Challenge to the State,* edited by Juliet Lodge. Oxford, UK: Martin Robinson, 1981. Quoted in Whittaker, David J., ed. *The Terrorism Reader.* New York: Routledge, 2001, pp. 189–91.

Three subjects of leftist activism are discussed below: class struggle, leftist nationalism, and special-interest extremism.

## For the Exploited: Class Struggle

Marxists have traditionally focused their attention on being a vanguard movement on behalf of the working class. They faithfully believe that this class struggle will end in victory by the working class.

*Class struggle* refers to more than simply competition between people with different job incomes. In fact, orthodox Marxists would argue that one's income alone does not confer class status. According to Karl Marx, one's class is determined by one's relationship to the **means of production**. Because Marx and Engels wrote *Manifesto of the Communist Party* and other documents[23] during the Industrial Age, one's relationship to the means of production referred to whether one was a wage-earning worker (the **proletariat**), a small-time shop owner or wage-owning manager (the **bourgeoisie**), or an owner of an industrial enterprise. The political power of each group, as well as the degree of exploitation suffered by each group, was determined by that group's relationship to the means of production.

According to Marx, the owners are the political and economic ruling class, the bourgeoisie are a co-opted middle class, and the proletariat is a class of exploited labor. After the proletarian revolution, he envisioned the creation of a communist society under the leadership of the working class—a society that he termed the dictatorship of the proletariat. There was no blueprint for the creation of this new society; instead, Marx believed that the state would simply wither away after the revolution.

Figure 7.1 illustrates the class pyramid during the Industrial Age, which Marx considered to be the final age of human society prior to the dictatorship of the proletariat.

---

[23]For a good compilation of the writings of Marx and Engels, see Tucker, Robert C., ed. *The Marx-Engels Reader.* New York: Norton, 1972.

**Figure 7.1**  Marx: The Industrial Age Class Pyramid

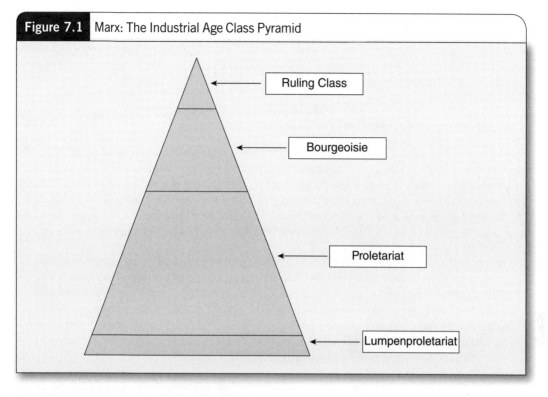

## For the People: Leftist Nationalism

Nationalism is a concept that promotes the aspirations of groups of people who are distinguished by their cultural, religious, ethnic, or racial heritage. It is difficult to apply the categories of the classical ideological continuum (fringe left to fringe right) to nationalist movements because the guiding motivation behind these movements is national identity. In cases where ideological theory becomes secondary to promoting one's national identity, the labels of *right wing* and *left wing* become imprecise.

Nationalist movements have selectively applied Marxism as required by their unique circumstances. These movements were, in fact, an adaptation of orthodox Marxist theory to the reality of 20th-century political conflict. For Karl Marx, guerrilla warfare in the developing world did not enter into his calculation for bringing about the workers' revolution, and nationalism was certainly subordinate to class consciousness. In theory, the workers would simply rise up under the leadership of their party (the Communist Party). In practice, nationalists often adopted a political ideology in their struggle for national independence, and Marxism was frequently their ideology of choice.

During the Cold War rivalry between the United States and the Soviet Union, each superpower displayed a persistent pattern of international behavior. The Soviets tended to side with nationalist insurgencies in the developing world, whereas the United States supported the embattled established governments. These insurgencies took on the characteristics of Marxist revolutions, and the embattled governments became, from the perspective of the United States, bulwarks against the spread of communism. The Soviets and, to a lesser extent, the Chinese armed and financed many of these **wars of national liberation** against U.S.-supported regimes.

Nationalism and Marxism were synthesized repeatedly by 20th-century revolutionaries in the developing world. Three of these conflicts—led by Mao Zedong in China, Ho Chi Minh in Vietnam, and Fidel Castro in Cuba[24]—came to symbolize the new phenomenon of leftist nationalism. Left-wing revolutionaries in the

---

[24]For further information about Mao's ideology, see Schram, Stuart R. *The Political Thought of Mao Tse-tung*. New York: Praeger, 1974. For a discussion of the Vietnamese and American perspectives during the war in Vietnam, see FitzGerald, Frances. *Fire in the Lake: The Vietnamese and the Americans in Vietnam*. New York: Vintage, 1972. For a good analysis of revolution in Cuba, see del Aguila, Juan M. *Cuba: Dilemmas of a Revolution*. Boulder, CO: Westview, 1988.

West drew on these examples and developed theories of solidarity with Marxist nationalists to justify acts of violence in Western democracies. As discussed later in this chapter, many New Left revolutionaries in the West were particularly receptive to the theory that their terrorist campaigns in Western democracies were linked to the nationalistic armed insurgencies in the developing world. From their perspective, all of these struggles were part of a worldwide war against capitalism, imperialism, and exploitation.

## Special-Interest Extremism

Special-interest extremism is also described as "single-issue" terrorism. Unlike the global scope of Marxist ideology or the nation-building goal of nationalism, special-interest extremism involves agitation on behalf of a narrowly drawn political interest. These political interests are often very specific, so that violence is usually carefully focused. For example, animal rights activists have repeatedly vandalized, or "trashed," laboratories.

The key feature of this type of terrorist behavior is that its motives are confined to the single cause, and its goals are limited. As noted by former U.S. Federal Bureau of Investigation (FBI) director Louis Freeh,

> Special interest terrorism differs from traditional right-wing and left-wing terrorism in that extremist special interest groups seek to resolve specific issues, rather than effect more wide-spread political change. Special interest extremists . . . conduct acts of politically motivated violence to force segments of society, including the general public, to change attitudes about issues considered important to their causes. . . . Some special interest extremists—most notably within the animal rights and environmental movements—have turned increasingly toward vandalism and terrorist activity in attempts to further their causes.[25]

Mainstream special-interest movements on the left include left-wing environmentalism, the peace movement, the antinuclear movement, the civil rights moment, feminism, and alternative lifestyle groups. Extremists within each of these movements include radical animal rights groups, neo-anarchist groups, Black Power advocates, and radical feminist groups. One commonality among modern special-interest extremists is that they believe their narrow issue is universally important and is linked to other "rights" movements. Hence, animal rights and neo-anarchist radicals find common cause on the question of exploitation by international business interests.

For many radicals, political dissent and terrorist violence are necessary to "save" a fundamental truth. For those on the fringes of these movements, the only means to save their fundamental truth may be the destruction of an existing social order or economic system. Thus, ecological and animal rights terrorists have engaged in politically motivated vandalism and arson to "save the planet" from human exploitation. This is obviously a nihilist dissident strategy.

## Problems on the Radical Left

The radical left was never a monolithic or united belief system. It was always factionalized and under-went a never-ending process of internecine feuding that ended in ideological and organizational splits. Many of these feuds ended in bloodshed.

A number of theoretical and practical challenges arose on the radical left, several of which have been alluded to. The following four problems are illustrative of these challenges.

The first problem was that Marx and other orthodox socialist revolutionaries assumed that the communist revolution would occur in one or both of the two most industrialized nations of the time—either Great Britain or Germany. Despite this fundamental faith, the first communist revolution occurred in Russia, which was a preindustrial, peasant-based, semifeudal society. This presented Marxists with a problem because history was not unfolding as they thought it would. The solution was one that was repeated again and again on the radical left: Simply redesign the basic ideology to reflect the new reality, and reassess the revolution's strategy and tactics. Thus,

[25]Freeh, Louis J. *Statement for the Record on the Threat of Terrorism to the United States.* U.S. Senate Committees on Appropriations and Armed Services, and Select Committee on Intelligence. May 10, 2001.

- Vladimir Ilich Lenin organized the Communist Party as a vanguard party;

- Joseph Stalin consolidated communism in one country, thus rejecting Trotsky's theory of "permanent revolution" (described later);

- Mao Zedong designed a revolutionary philosophy and strategy that was adopted extensively in the developing world; and

- Nationalists used Marxism to organize, discipline, and motivate their followers in their quest for national independence.

A second problem was the revolutionary party. Once Lenin and others accepted the need to give the revolution a "push," they designed a revolutionary party as the mechanism to do so. The new Communist Party was a vanguard party and a combat party. It was nothing like traditional political parties in democratic societies. However, the communist movement could not determine what kind of revolutionary party should represent the workers. This question was at the heart of infighting in the communist movement and led to repeated splits in the Communist Party, as dissident factions either broke away or were expelled. As expected, each new faction considered itself to be the true heir of Karl Marx's vision.

The first great split occurred between the followers of Stalin and the followers of Leon Trotsky. **Stalinists** worked to consolidate communism in the Soviet Union, known in the movement as **socialism in one country**. They also tried to rally all communist parties worldwide under the leadership and inspiration of the Communist Party of the Soviet Union. **Trotskyites** rejected the idea of building socialism in one country and promoted international agitation as a worldwide revolutionary movement—a theory referred to as the **permanent revolution**. This split in the movement continued into the 21st century, with Trotskyites continuing to refer to the Soviet Union as an excellent example of a **degenerate workers' state**.

A third problem involved the application of theory to practice. The communist pantheon (leadership in the movement) from the Soviet perspective moved from Marx to Lenin to Stalin. When Stalin died in 1953, the most important figure in the international communist movement was China's Mao Zedong. However, the Soviets never considered Mao to be an heir of Stalin, and another split occurred in the ranks of international communism. Soviet communism was centered in Eastern Europe, with allies among insurgent movements and newly formed leftist regimes such as in Cuba, Angola, and Ethiopia. The Chinese became prominent for their contribution to revolutionary and guerrilla theory in the developing world; they considered the Soviets to be "social imperialists."

A fourth problem was the reality that the working class in the liberal democratic West would likely never acquire a sufficiently revolutionary class consciousness. This realization was a blow to orthodox Marxists and radical leftists, who had long considered the working class to be the true standard bearers of revolution and human progress. The radical left adapted their ideological foundation to allow for the inclusion of peasant-based rural revolutionaries as their new championed class. These "Third World revolutionaries" became iconic on the radical left, and many Western leftists chose these revolutionaries as the new championed group. In addition, young members of the New Left during the 1960s largely rejected orthodox Marxism and took on the revolutionary theories of Fanon, Marcuse, and Marighella. Nevertheless, some radical leftists—especially the Trotskyites—maintained the orthodox Marxist fiction that the workers of the world would someday unite.

# ❖ Class Struggle and National Liberation: The Terrorist Left

Leftist terrorism in its modern context originated after the 1848 revolutions in Europe. Anarchism and Marxism provided the philosophical basis for revolutionary violence, and many who adopted these ideologies engaged in acts of terrorism. Throughout the 20th century and into the present, variations of anarchism and Marxism have repeatedly adapted to unique socio-political conditions.

Historically, left-wing terrorism has not been a method of first resort. It usually occurred after other options were tried and abandoned, sometimes as an expression of frustration with the pace of change, and other times after the state repressed leftist dissent. In fact, "traditional left-wing doctrine has favored terrorism only in rare cases . . . not because they were humanitarians but because they feared that terrorism opened the door to all kinds of possibilities that might endanger their own cause."[26]

Once the line had been crossed between peaceful dissent and a strategy of violent agitation, terrorism repeatedly became an accepted option among left-wing extremists. Chapter Perspective 7.2

## CHAPTER PERSPECTIVE 7.2: Vanguard Theory

Fringe-left ideology at the beginning of the 21st century was usually an extreme application of Marxist ideology, and it generally adopted the doctrines of class warfare or national liberation to justify political violence. On the radical left wing, violence has been seen as a perfectly legitimate option because the terrorist group considers itself to be at war against an oppressive class, government, or system. The terrorist group pictures itself as a righteous champion of the poor and downtrodden.

One theoretical pattern that has appeared repeatedly on the radical left is the adoption of a **vanguard strategy** by leftist activists. This strategy is, in essence, a belief that revolutionary conditions will rarely occur *spontaneously* from within the exploited lower classes or group. Instead, revolutionary conditions must be *created* by a committed and disciplined revolutionary movement, which will build a generalized climate of change. When this happens, the exploited class or group will become "politically conscious" and will accept revolution as a preferable alternative to the existing system. Those activists who would create this climate of change are the "vanguard" of the soon-to-be revolutionary exploited classes or group. Not surprisingly, the vanguard group's membership tends to be drawn from among a young, educated elite that became disaffected by what they perceived to be a system of exploitation and privilege.

Vanguard theory was put into practice time after time during the 20th century. Two short cases in point illustrate this pattern:

### Russian Vanguard of the Proletariat

The vanguard strategy was adopted by Russian communists during the creation of the first successful Communist Party and was applied worldwide by other communist parties.[a] Lenin and the Bolsheviks (literally, "majoritarians") who built the party required their followers to consider themselves to be the **vanguard of the proletariat** (*proletariat* was Marx's term for the working class); they were an elite who would bring about the revolution and build the communist society.

### Che Guevara's *Foquismo*

In another application of the vanguard strategy, Latin American revolutionary **Ernesto "Che" Guevara** believed after the Cuban Revolution that a transnational climate of revolutionary change could be created in South America and that all of Latin America could be swept by revolution—all that was needed was a revolutionary "push" by a vanguard of dedicated revolutionaries. Guevara and his followers were annihilated in Bolivia while trying to deliver that push in 1967.[b] Guevara's (and the Cuban) variant on this theory was termed **foquismo**, or "armed struggle" (also known as Foco Theory). It included an emphasis on creating an immediate impact on the general political environment rather than engaging in a long process of "consciousness building" among the lower classes.

### Notes

a. A good history of the Russian Revolution is found in Ulam, Adam B. *The Bolsheviks: The Intellectual and Political History of the Triumph of Communism in Russia.* Cambridge, MA: Harvard University Press, 1998.

b. For insight into Guevara's Bolivian campaign, see James, Daniel, ed. *The Complete Bolivian Diaries of Che Guevara and Other Captured Documents.* Lanham, MD: Cooper Square Press, 2000.

---

[26]Laqueur, *The New Terrorism*, p. 106.

presents a discussion of vanguard theory, an interesting strategic doctrine that was widely adopted by members of the revolutionary left.

## Regional Case: Latin America

Latin America has a long history of political agitation, repression, and rebellion. The postwar era has seen dozens of revolutions, coups, attempted coups, civil wars, military dictatorships, and proxy wars. Although most modern Marxist and other leftist movements engage in relatively nonviolent political agitation,[27] there are many examples of terrorism from the left.

Armed leftist activism in the postwar era has posed serious challenges to many established governments. Armed Marxist guerrillas have operated in the countryside of several nations, and urban terrorists—who resolutely applied Marighella's *Mini-Manual*—have appeared repeatedly in Latin America. Although leftist nationalism did occur in the postwar era, most leftist insurgents were dedicated Marxists. Some similarities can be found in many of these insurgencies, including the following:

- Virtually all left-wing Latin American revolutionaries applied versions of Marxist ideology to their causes.
- The United States was considered to be an imperialist power that propped up repressive right-wing dictatorships; thus, opposing the United States became central to their "anti-imperialist" wars.
- Many revolutionaries were inspired by the Cuban Revolution.
- Rural rebels tended to train and fight using classic guerrilla tactics and tried to create "liberated zones" as bases for military operations.
- Urban rebels practiced terrorist methodologies that included kidnappings, extortion, bombings, shootings, and other examples of politically motivated criminal behavior.
- Strategies were adopted that used "urban guerrilla warfare" to provoke the state and politicize the lower classes.

Cases of armed extremist movements in Colombia, Peru, and Argentina are discussed in the following section. All engaged in terrorist violence to some degree.

### Colombia

Colombia has a long history of communal violence. For example, 200,000 people died during a civil war known as *La Violencia,* which lasted from 1946 to 1966. Modern Colombia experienced a different type of terrorist environment, with dissident violence being committed by left-wing rebels, right-wing paramilitaries (death squads), and drug lords (*narcotraficantes*).[28] A culture of political violence and intimidation became endemic to Colombia during the 1960s to early 2000s, so that likely and unlikely alliances were formed: The weakened government was accused of aiding and abetting the work of the paramilitaries, the paramilitaries and *narcotraficantes* cooperated against the Marxist rebels, and the Marxist rebels moved into drug-producing regions to generate revenue for their causes. In fact, drug-related income became a significant factor in securing the financial independence of the Marxist rebellion. The result was that approximately 3,500 Colombians—the vast majority civilians—died annually in the fighting during this period.

On the left, two intractable Marxist insurgencies had continued for decades.[29] The strategies of both insurgent groups allowed for the use of classic guerrilla tactics and terrorism. Beginning in 2002,

---

[27]For a discussion of modern leftist politics in Latin America, see Castañeda, Jorge G. "Latin America's Left Turn." *Foreign Affairs* (May/June 2006): 28–43. See also Vargas Llosa, Alvaro. "The Return of the Idiot." *Foreign Policy* (June 2007): 54–61.

[28]For an interesting discussion of radical Colombian politics and the drug trade, see Ehrenfeld, Rachel. *Narco-Terrorism.* New York: Basic Books, 1990, pp. 74–112.

[29]A third group is the small terrorist April 19 Movement, also known as M-19.

the Colombian conflict decreased in intensity as the principal insurgent groups suffered military reversals and defections among followers.

***Revolutionary Armed Forces of Colombia.*[30]** The **Revolutionary Armed Forces of Colombia** (Fuerzas Armadas Revolucionarias de Colombia, or **FARC**) was organized in 1964 as a Marxist rebel organization that operated primarily in the Colombian countryside. Its role in the overall revolution was to operate as the armed wing of the originally pro-Soviet Colombian Communist Party. FARC's anti-imperialist political position labeled the United States as an imperial power and the Colombian government as a right-wing oligarchy. The group historically enjoyed widespread support among many peasants and farmers, and FARC successfully created "liberated zones" in central Colombia, including a large "demilitarized" zone that the Colombian government temporarily ceded to FARC. With about 17,000 fighters at its peak,[31] FARC became a formidable fighting force and scored numerous victories using guerrilla tactics against Colombian security forces. FARC's terrorist activities included kidnapping, robberies, assassinations, and other violent tactics. It also conscripted child soldiers into its ranks. In the largest cocaine-producing country in the world, FARC participated in the drug trade to finance its revolution and became independent from outside aid. By 2002, FARC's military and political initiatives declined significantly due to pressure from the Colombian military. In 2008, FARC suffered several serious reversals, including when the group's second-in-command was killed by the Colombian army in a cross-border assault in Ecuador, the fatal heart attack of its commander in chief, and the rescue of 15 hostages from a jungle base—including former presidential candidate Ingrid Betancourt—by Colombian commandos using an intricate ruse. By 2014, FARC's strength had declined to an estimated 7,000 fighters, who rarely directly battled the Colombian military or police.

***National Liberation Army.*[32]** The **National Liberation Army** (Ejercito de Liberación Nacional, or **ELN**) was organized as a pro-Cuban Marxist rebel organization that, like FARC, operated primarily in the countryside of Colombia. Its ideological icons were Fidel Castro and Ernesto "Che" Guevara. Also like FARC, it followed an anti-imperialist line that fought to end what it considered to be U.S.-backed oppression in Colombia. Unlike FARC, its ideology has been more Maoist in outlook. With 3,000 fighters at its peak, the ELN was always smaller than FARC, but it also largely fought the Colombian army to a standstill. The ELN engaged in bombings, extortion, and kidnappings. Targets included foreign businesses and oil pipelines. The ELN also participated in the drug trade to fund its insurgency.

### Peru

The Peruvian government was besieged by a dissident terrorist environment from the 1970s through the 1990s. By the late 1990s, security forces had delivered serious setbacks to the primary terrorist organizations.

***Shining Path.*[33]** **Shining Path (Sendero Luminoso)** is an interesting case because of its uniqueness. It was radically Maoist, but unlike other Latin American revolutionary groups, it did not completely accept orthodox Marxist theory. Nor did Shining Path accept the New Left theories of Fanon, Marcuse, or Marighella. Instead, Shining Path members considered the teachings of their supreme leader, former university professor Abimael Guzmán, to be the highest evolution of Marxist thought, directly

[30]For further information, see "Revolutionary Armed Forces of Colombia (FARC)." *Terrorist Group Profiles.* Dudley Knox Library, Naval War College. Website: http://www.nps.edu/Library/Research/SubjectGuides/SpecialTopics/TerroristProfile/Current/Revolutionary%20Armed%20Forces%20of%20Colombia%20(FARC).html/ (accessed June 10, 2008).

[31]Miller, Christian T. "Colombia, Rebels Set New Talks." *Los Angeles Times,* January 15, 2002.

[32]For further information, see "National Liberation Army (Colombia)." *Terrorist Organization Profiles.* National Consortium for the Study of Terrorism and Responses to Terrorism, University of Maryland. Website: http://www.start.umd.edu/tops/terrorist_organization_profile.asp?id=218/ (accessed July 13, 2014).

[33]For further information, see "Shining Path." *Terrorist Organization Profiles.* National Consortium for the Study of Terrorism and Responses to Terrorism, University of Maryland. Website: http://www.start.umd.edu/tops/terrorist_organization_profile.asp?id=111/ (accessed July 13, 2014).

superseding Marx, Lenin, Stalin, Trotsky, and Mao. Guzmán's philosophy was a hybrid of Marxism, Maoism, and native Indian traditionalism that championed Peru's Quechua-speaking Incans and mixed-race *mestizos*. This racial dimension was melded with a quasi-mystical philosophy that was considered to be the "shining path" to liberation; Guzmán was referred to as the "Fourth Sword of Marxism." In practice, Shining Path's methods paralleled those of the ruthless Khmer Rouge movement in Cambodia, which was responsible for approximately 2 million Cambodian deaths. Shining Path members were racial and xenophobic, rejecting all outside influences—including orthodox Marxist revolutionary theory. They used brutal intimidation to force support from the Quechua-speaking and *mestizo* Peruvians whom they championed. They also set about waging a campaign of widespread terror against Peruvian society in cities, towns, villages, and the countryside. Anyone who did not join them was considered to be their enemy. Shining Path's campaign cost Peru nearly 70,000 lives during two decades of violence. In September 1992, Guzmán was captured, and he was sentenced to life in prison in October 2006.

Because support for Shining Path largely depended on the cult of personality that was built around him, Shining Path gradually withered after Guzmán's capture and the capture of other leaders. In 1993, when Guzmán renounced violence, 5,500 of his followers accepted a government amnesty. Nevertheless, a few hundred diehards remained active and eventually rebuilt the movement to several thousand followers. Shining Path detonated at least two bombs in 2001, and an explosion near the U.S. embassy in March 2002 bore the Shining Path signature.[34] The group carried out bloody attacks during the early 2000s and continued to participate in the cocaine trade. However, the elimination of cadres and central leaders in 2010–2013 seriously degraded Shining Path's operational capabilities.

***Tupac Amaru Revolutionary Movement.*[35]** The **Tupac Amaru Revolutionary Movement** (Movimiento Revolucionario Tupac Amaru, or **MRTA**) was an orthodox Marxist organization that had no connection whatsoever to the Tupamaros of Uruguay. Founded in 1983, MRTA was an anti-imperialist movement that sought to create a Marxist state. It applied Carlos Marighella's strategy to Peru and therefore engaged in urban terrorism. Its membership was never large, and it operated in urban areas rather than the countryside, which was probably impractical because of the presence of Shining Path. Its most dramatic—and, as it happened, its last—major attack was on December 17, 1996, when it seized the Japanese ambassador's residence in Lima and held hundreds of guests hostage. This feat received worldwide attention. The crisis lasted for 4 months as negotiations ebbed and flowed, with many hostages being released. Finally, after an impasse—and after the Peruvian army had tunneled beneath the residence—on April 22, 1997, soldiers stormed the residence. They literally burst from tunnels on the grounds, and after about 40 minutes, all of the MRTA terrorists were killed and 25 hostages injured. Two soldiers were killed. The incident was disastrous for the MRTA, which was unable to restore its operational initiative.

### Argentina

The complicated political environment of postwar Argentina centered on tension among several movements, including the populism of President Juan Perón, the right-wing military establishment, Spanish-inspired fascism, and leftist activism. Peronism was a populist and nationalist ideology that split into leftist and rightist factions. The Argentine left was primarily Marxist, and several small armed dissident groups appeared in the late 1960s and early 1970s. However, one group, the **Montoneros**, was unique. Montoneros members were originally young leftist Peronists but eventually came to advocate several distinctly Argentine sentiments: radical Catholic principles of justice, Peronist populism, and leftist nationalism. They were young radicals who championed justice and unity for "the people" in Argentina.

During the early 1970s, these armed dissident movements gradually disbanded or coalesced around the Marxist People's Revolutionary Army and the Montoneros.

---

[34]Faiola, Anthony, and Lucien Chauvin. "Peruvian Attaché Raises Fears of Rebel Resurgence." *Washington Post,* March 21, 2002.

[35]For further information, see "Tupac Amaru Revolutionary Movement." *Terrorist Organization Profiles.* National Consortium for the Study of Terrorism and Responses to Terrorism, University of Maryland. Website: http://www.start.umd.edu/tops/terrorist_organization_profile.asp?id=121/ (accessed July 13, 2014).

***Ideology of the Armed Argentine Left.*** The Montoneros accepted Ernesto "Che" Guevara's theory that a dedicated and focused revolutionary group could bring about a generalized revolutionary environment. Thus, the theory of *foquismo* infused a Cuban-inspired addition into their unique Argentine ideology. The People's Revolutionary Army was originally a Trotskyite group that eventually adopted the Maoist theory of building a revolutionary base in the countryside. Like the Montoneros, the members applied Che Guevara's theory of *foquismo*.

***Montonero and People's Revolutionary Army Terrorism.*** The Montoneros inspired young leftists with their slogan "Fatherland or Death." Although the nationalism of the Montoneros attracted a numerous and loyal following, the **People's Revolutionary Army** never became as prominent. Both groups engaged in urban terrorism, à la Carlos Marighella. The Montoneros became skillful kidnappers and extorted an estimated $60 million in ransom payments. Shootings, bombings, and assassinations were also pervasive. Their campaign caused widespread disorder and even spawned a retaliatory right-wing death squad, the Argentine Anti-Communist Alliance, whose brutality caused hundreds of intellectuals to flee the country. When Juan Perón died in 1974, the political situation became precarious. In March 1976, the military seized control in Argentina. Under President Jorge Rafael Videla, all political opposition was crushed, including the terrorist campaign. Torture, murder, assassinations, and "disappearances" were used. Thousands of Montoneros and People's Revolutionary Army members were killed.

## Regional Case: Europe

Prior to the tearing down of the Berlin Wall in 1989, very little terrorism of any kind occurred in the communist Eastern bloc. However, democratic Western Europe experienced a wave of leftist terrorism that began during the student and human rights movements in the 1960s. This wave of political violence occurred in numerous Western countries. Although some nationalist terrorism took place—in Northern Ireland and Spain—most terrorist groups were ideologically motivated. The latter style of terrorism exhibited certain similarities across national boundaries, including the following:

- Origins in leftist activism on university campuses
- Origins in youthful members of the middle class
- The application of New Left theories that justified violence committed by middle-class terrorists in prosperous democracies
- Methodologies that included kidnappings, extortion, bombings, shootings, and other examples of politically motivated criminal behavior
- Adoption of strategies similar to those of Latin American terrorists, using "urban guerrilla warfare" to provoke the democratic state and politicize the working class
- Nihilistic dissident activism, with no clear vision for the new postrevolutionary society

Cases of armed movements active in Italy, Germany, and Northern Ireland are discussed in the following section.

### Italy[36]

Postwar Italy was a unique democracy. Although its democratic institutions were rarely if ever threatened by street-level unrest, its parliamentary politics were chaotic. Governments rose and fell regularly, and, with one of the few strong communist parties in the West, the left was quite influential in setting the political agenda. As in most Western democracies, the 1960s were a time of political activism among the young generation. In addition to activism on college campuses, Italy in 1969 experienced significant union unrest in the north. Out of this environment arose a strong radical leftist movement, as well as a significant terrorist campaign from the left.

---

[36]See Clutterbuck, Richard. *Terrorism, Drugs and Crime in Europe After 1992.* New York: Routledge, 1990, pp. 30–45.

***The Red Brigade.***[37] In 1969, Italy's most notable leftist terrorist group was formed. It was a Marxist revolutionary movement that sought to create a revolutionary environment by waging a widespread campaign of urban terrorism. It practiced nihilist dissident terrorism and never developed a clear vision of postrevolutionary Italy. Although the Red Brigade operated in solidarity with the goals of other terrorist groups—as well as liberation movements in the developing world—it never collaborated with other organizations to any significant extent. It apparently did receive weapons from Palestinian sources. The Red Brigade's first base of operations was in Milan, but it gradually spread to Rome, Genoa, Turin, and other cities. Aside from the Irish dissident terrorists, the Red Brigade constituted the most active terrorist group in Europe. During its first 10 years of existence, the Red Brigade committed about 14,000 terrorist attacks.

***Years of Lead.*** The politically violent years of the 1970s and 1980s in Italy have been termed the **Years of Lead**. During that period, the Red Brigade group was exceptionally active. The Red Brigade initially committed symbolic attacks against property. However, beginning in about 1972, it began a campaign of violence that included shootings, bombings, kidnappings, and other violent criminal acts. Kidnap victims included Genoa's Assistant Attorney General Mario Sossi (1974), former Italian prime minister Aldo Moro (1978), and American Brigadier General James Dozier (1981). Of these cases, Sossi was released, Moro was executed, and Dozier was rescued from a "people's prison" run by the Red Brigade. During Moro's kidnapping, five of his bodyguards were slain. He was very prominent in Italian politics at the time and would have likely become president of Italy. By the mid-1990s, the Red Brigade had declared an end to "military" operations.

❖ **Photo 7.4**

Prisoner of the Red Brigade. A photograph of former Italian prime minister Aldo Moro, taken during his captivity by the Red Brigade. Moro was later executed by the terrorists.

Central Press/Hulton Archive/Getty Images

### Germany[38]

The partition of Germany after World War II symbolized the Cold War rivalry between the democratic capitalist West and the totalitarian communist Eastern bloc. The Federal Republic of Germany (West Germany) was pro-Western, and the Soviet troops stationed in the German Democratic Republic (East Germany) ensured that it would be part of the pro-Eastern bloc. No terrorist movement existed in East Germany, but at least three violent leftist groups emerged in West Germany. These groups were avowedly Marxist or anarchist but practiced nihilist dissident terrorism. They were certainly New Left in orientation, having read and put into practice the theories of Fanon, Marcuse, Marighella, and other new revolutionary thinkers.

An interesting feature of the German groups was the level of collaboration with one another and with Palestinian terrorist groups. The German terrorists included the following groups.

***Red Army Faction.***[39] The Marxist **Red Army Faction** (RAF, or Baader-Meinhof Gang) was the most prominent terrorist group in Germany in the postwar era. From its beginning in 1970, the RAF committed many politically motivated bank robberies, kidnappings, murders, bombings, and other crimes. RAF members quickly established links with Palestinian terrorists, and some members received

[37]For further information, see "Red Brigades." *Terrorist Organization Profiles.* National Consortium for the Study of Terrorism and Responses to Terrorism, University of Maryland. Website: http://www.start.umd.edu/tops/terrorist_organization_profile .asp?id=92/ (accessed July 13, 2014).

[38]See Clutterbuck, *Terrorism,* pp. 46–52.

[39]For further information, see "Red Army Faction." *Terrorist Organization Profiles.* National Consortium for the Study of Terrorism and Responses to Terrorism, University of Maryland. Website: http://www.start.umd.edu/tops/terrorist_ organization_profile.asp?id=163/ (accessed July 13, 2014).

❖ **Photo 7.5**

Prisoner of the Red Army Faction. A photograph of West German industrialist Hanns-Martin Schleyer, taken during his captivity by the Red Army Faction (also known as the Baader-Meinhof Gang). The RAF later executed Schleyer.

Keystone/Hulton Archive/Getty Images

weapons training in the Middle East. This was the beginning of a long collaboration between German and Palestinian terrorists, especially the Marxist Popular Front for the Liberation of Palestine. This collaboration was based on a sense of ideological solidarity, the RAF's internationalist worldview, and its conclusion that the capitalist West and Israel were common foes. Joint operations between the RAF and Palestinian terrorists included the June 1976 hijacking of an Air France airliner to Entebbe, Uganda. Two German terrorists participated in the hijacking. The RAF remained active well into the 1990s, officially ceasing "military" operations in 1998.

***June 2nd Movement.*** The **June 2nd Movement** (Bevegung 2. Juni), founded in West Berlin in 1971, was named for the date in 1967 when a German pacifist, Benno Ohnesorg, was killed by the police during a demonstration in West Berlin. Unlike the RAF and Red Cells (discussed next), June 2nd Movement was more anarchistic in its ideology. It was known for bombings of property targets in West Berlin. June 2nd Movement's most famous action was the 1975 kidnapping of Peter Lorenz, a Berlin mayoral candidate. He was released in one day after four June 2nd comrades were released and flown to Yemen. After the group disbanded in the 1980s, many members joined the RAF.

***Red Cells.*** **Red Cells** (Rote Zelles) is a shadowy Marxist organization that was founded in Frankfurt, probably in 1972 or 1973. Members adopted an underground cell-based strategy, believing (correctly) that the RAF's organizational structure made the group easier to penetrate. They disappeared into the middle class by holding jobs, owning homes, and raising families. Their terrorist activity included bombings and other criminal activity. A women's "auxiliary" called **Red Zora** (Rota Zora) was formed and later became independent of Red Cells.

The RAF—and arguably the other German terrorists—considered itself to be in ideological solidarity with the anticolonial sentiment of the people of the developing world, and that adopting terrorism as a strategy was the most viable stratagem of relatively small revolutionary organizations.[40] Some important events in the history of the violent German left are discussed in the following sections.

***Origin of the RAF.*** Like many other leftist organizations, the RAF grew out of the activism of the 1960s. **Gudrun Ensslin** and her boyfriend, **Andreas Baader**, were prominent in student protests at Berlin Free University during the 1960s. Both were imprisoned in 1968 when convicted of attempted arson by firebombing department stores in the city of Frankfurt. After being released a year later during a grant of temporary amnesty, they fled the country illegally, but Baader was imprisoned when he later returned. In May 1970, Ensslin and **Ulrike Meinhof** collaborated with others on a successful jailbreak of Baader. From that point on, the group was popularly referred to as the **Baader-Meinhof Gang** (although Ensslin was more of a leader than Meinhof). They officially referred to themselves as the Red Army Faction.

***Death Night.*** In 1972, approximately 100 members and supporters of the RAF were arrested and imprisoned, including founders Ensslin, Baader, and Meinhof. In prison, Ulrike Meinhof hanged herself on May 9, 1976. On October 18, 1977—known as **Death Night**—Andreas Baader, Gudrun Ensslin, and Jan-Carl Raspe were shot in prison. West German authorities officially concluded that Ensslin hanged herself and that Baader and Raspe shot themselves with guns smuggled into their cells—ostensibly for a jailbreak. A fourth terrorist (Irmgard Möller) stabbed herself four times with a knife but missed her heart. Many Germans have never believed the official version of their deaths, although attorneys for the RAF are known to have smuggled other illegal contraband into what had been touted as the most secure prison in the world.

---

[40]See Whittaker, David J., ed. *The Terrorism Reader.* 4th ed. New York: Routledge, 2012. At 234, *et. seq.*

***The OPEC Raid.*** On December 21, 1975, members of the RAF, June 2nd Movement, and Red Cells collaborated with Palestinian terrorists in a hostage-taking raid on the Vienna headquarters of the Organization of Petroleum Exporting Countries (OPEC). The group was led by Carlos the Jackal, the *nom de guerre* for Ilich Ramírez Sánchez. During the course of the raid, the terrorists and some of the hostages were flown to Algiers, Algeria, and then to Tripoli, Tunisia. The hostages were released (and the terrorists disappeared into the Middle East) when a $5 million ransom was paid for Palestinian causes.

### Northern Ireland

Most terrorism in the British Isles has been related to the sectarian conflict between Catholics and Protestants in Northern Ireland—commonly termed **the Troubles**—the current manifestation of which began in West Belfast and Londonderry in 1969. Catholic Republicans had initially tried to emulate Dr. Martin Luther King Jr.'s leadership of the African American civil rights movement in the American South. When this failed in the summer of 1969, Catholic and Protestant extremists organized themselves into a terrorist underground.

Although the violent Catholic groups are included under the category of "left wing" because of their professed adoption of socialist ideology, their primary goal was reunification with the Irish republic. The following groups became prominent during the sectarian fighting:

***Provisional Irish Republican Army.***[41] The Provos, as the Provisional IRA is often referred to, is a mildly socialist nationalist "military" organization that seeks reunification with the Irish republic. Its leftist rhetoric moderated significantly during the 1980s. The Provisional IRA split in the 1960s from the **Official Irish Republican Army** when the latter group continued to pursue a less militant line than the Provos. The Provos was initially organized to respond to bombings and other attacks on Catholic neighborhoods by Protestant gangs. At first, it was a somewhat disorganized and undisciplined organization, but it eventually became a highly militarized group organized into three- or four-member cells. Although it never fielded more than 1,000 "soldiers" at any one time and usually numbered about 250, it became the most notorious armed Catholic dissident group. Provos members engaged in urban terrorist strikes in Northern Ireland and mainland Britain.

***Irish National Liberation Army.*** The **Irish National Liberation Army (INLA)**, founded in the early 1970s, grew out of the split in the IRA. The group followed the pattern of many radical nationalist organizations at the time and adopted Marxist theory as its guiding ideology. Like the Provos, the INLA fought to reunite Northern Ireland with Ireland. The INLA is unique in that it envisioned the creation of a socialist Irish republic. In fact, the INLA considered itself to be fighting in unity with other terrorist groups that championed oppressed groups around the world. The INLA's heyday was during the 1970s and mid-1980s. It operated in urban areas, primarily in the cities of Londonderry and Belfast. Although it never fielded more than several dozen "soldiers," it was exceptionally violent and ruthless—arguably more so than the Provos. An internal feud significantly debilitated the group during the 1990s, and the INLA became heavily involved in organized criminal activity.

Table 7.4 summarizes the championed constituencies and enemies of left-wing terrorists.

## ❖ Right-Wing Activism and Extremism

Terrorism on the modern right is an outgrowth of fascist, National Socialist (Nazi), Falangist, and other reactionary movements that existed in Europe between the First and Second World Wars. The between-war era was a heyday for mass agitation on the far and fringe right. It was a period in history when rightist nationalism in Europe was very strong—and popular—among large segments of the public. Fascists, Nazis, Falangists, and others were certainly dictatorial, but they adroitly

[41]For further information, see "Irish Republican Army." *Terrorist Organization Profiles.* National Consortium for the Study of Terrorism and Responses to Terrorism, University of Maryland. Website: http://www.start.umd.edu/tops/terrorist_organization_profile.asp?id=55/ (accessed July 13, 2014).

**Table 7.4** Terrorism on the Left

Although left-wing terrorist groups share similar values and often are rooted in Marxist theory, they arise out of unique political environments that are peculiar to their respective countries. In Latin America and Asia, members of these movements have fought on behalf of identifiable domestic constituencies against identifiable domestic adversaries. In Europe, regional nationalist movements similarly champion identifiable constituencies against identifiable adversaries. However, the New Left constituencies and adversaries have tended to be ideological conceptualizations.

The following table summarizes the constituencies and adversaries of several politically violent dissident movements.

**Latin America**

| Group | Constituency | Adversary |
| --- | --- | --- |
| **FARC** | Workers, peasants | The oligarchy |
| **National Liberation Army** | Workers, peasants | Government, imperialists |
| **Shining Path** | Indians, oppressed classes | Government, imperialists |
| **MRTA** | Workers, peasants | Government |
| **Montoneros** | The people | Government, right wing |
| **People's Revolutionary Army** | Workers, peasants | Government, right wing |

**Europe**

| Group | Constituency | Adversary |
| --- | --- | --- |
| **Red Brigade** | Workers, the oppressed | Government, imperialists |
| **Red Army Faction** | Oppressed classes and people | Government, imperialists |
| **June 2nd Movement** | Oppressed classes and people | Government, imperialists |
| **Revolutionary Cells** | Oppressed classes and people | Government, imperialists |
| **Provisional IRA** | Northern Irish Catholics | British, Northern Irish government |
| **Irish National Liberation Army** | Northern Irish Catholics | British, Northern Irish government |

marshaled the nationalistic spirit of millions of Europeans. These were, without question, mass movements that waged a concerted struggle against communism and Western-style democracy.

The interwar history has been nostalgically recaptured in the ideologies and symbolism of reactionaries on the modern right. Modern activists have selectively chosen specific facets of certain right-wing movements for their causes. For example, right-wing ideologies in Latin America have historically promoted fascist and Falangist-style militarism, anticommunism, traditional values, and authoritarian rule. German extremists use neo-Nazi slogans, symbols, and doctrines, as do some racial supremacists in the United States. Italian activists have looked to their between-war past and adopted fascist traditions and values. These and other commonalities (which are discussed later) continue to invigorate the extreme right wing.

## Political Parties and Dissident Movements

Political parties and dissident movements on the right reflect the distinctive features of their national environments.

Right-wing political parties are most viable in countries with strong traditions of parties that embody the values of grassroots political movements. These traditions have led to the formation of class-specific and ideology-specific political parties. Thus, rightist parties in Europe and Latin America are often represented in their elected assemblies, but such parties are negligible in the United States, where the political system is coalitional.[42] In Europe, right-wing political parties tend to be nationalistic; they advocate traditional national values, promote national culture, and demand strict limitations on immigration. The British National Party in the United Kingdom, the National Front (Front National) in France, and the National Alliance (Alleanza Nazionale) in Italy are typical right-wing parties in Europe. These parties represent movements that are aboveground and that are "mainstreamed" in the sense that they participate in democratic processes. They are also fascist in their ideology. For example, Italy's Alleanza Nazionale is considered to be the heir to Mussolini's Fascist Party. In Russia, the neofascist party Russian National Unity was banned in Moscow because of its overtly fascist ideology.

In comparison to the neofascist political parties, the unorganized or partly organized right-wing dissident movements have varied in how overtly they state their political agendas. Some are frank in their ideological linkages to reactionary traditions, whereas others use contemporary language and code words for their beliefs. For example, rightists in the United States and Europe make references to "international bankers" as a code phrase for Jewish interests. Many right-wing dissidents in Europe, Russia, the United States, and elsewhere have borrowed or imitated the symbolism and mythology of Nazi Germany and other war-era fascist traditions. It is not uncommon for dissidents to use the stiff-armed fascist salute at demonstrations or to adopt reconfigured swastikas, Nordic runes, or other Nazi-era emblems. For example, South Africa's **Afrikaner Resistance Movement** (Afrikaner Weerstandsbeweging, or AWB) is overtly racist and has adopted as its organizational symbol a reconfigured swastika called the "Three Sevens."[43] It also overtly uses the rhetoric of racial supremacy and purity.

## Tradition and Order

Nostalgia for a lost utopia is a common theme on the reactionary right. It is frequently expressed as a desire to reclaim the past supremacy of a championed group. Recapturing past traditions, symbols, and values becomes an important priority to justify their self-perception as defenders of a supreme principle. These traditions, symbols, and values are often portrayed as bulwarks of order against the threat of chaos; they are the keys to a people's supremacy. Thus, whereas leftists might describe their postrevolutionary society as a "people's republic" or "socialist state," rightists are likely to defend their behavior by describing their goals as a "new order" or **Lebensraum** (the Nazis' concept of "room to live"). They seek to preserve hallowed traditions and create an idealized order.

A new mythology is frequently created to explain the superior group's fall from glory—a mythology that claims the lost utopia has been stolen (or is threatened) by an enemy group. If the traditional values can somehow be resurrected or preserved, the ascendancy of the group will be assured. Once the "truth" of this new mythology is revealed, many right-wing extremists conclude that their group's rightful status must be recouped from (or protected against) the usurper group. As a result, the usurper group becomes an enemy group, and therefore **scapegoating** is a common trait of the far and fringe right wing. For example, German "guest workers" (*Gastarbeiter*) from Italy, Spain, Greece, Turkey, Morocco, and Portugal were originally invited (dating to the 1950s) to help in postwar recovery.[44] They are now fully integrated into the economy and have a significant presence in

---

[42]The American Democratic and Republican Parties reflect the American political tradition of coalitional political representation. For example, organized labor in the United States has never been represented by a viable political party, although the Socialist Party did have a period of political influence in the early decades of the 20th century.

[43]For a display of *Afrikaner Weerstandsbeweging* symbolism, see http://www.awb.co.za/.

[44]See Harnishmacher, Robert, and Robert J. Kelly. "The Neo-Nazis and Skinheads of Germany: Purveyors of Hate." In *Hate Crime: The Global Politics of Polarization,* edited by Robert J. Kelly and Jess Maghan. Carbondale: Southern Illinois University Press, 1998, p. 44.

| Table 7.5 | Usurpers of the Chosen People? Scapegoats of the Reactionary Right |

Scapegoating is a common theme among right-wing extremists. Reactionaries tend to champion their favored group by creating a mythology of past glory that has been lost to the interests of an unworthy or inferior group. There is also a strong call to defend the championed group against the threat of subjugation or extermination at the hands of the scapegoated group. The following table lists groups that are typically scapegoated in the United States, Germany, and the United Kingdom.

| United States | Germany | United Kingdom |
| --- | --- | --- |
| Homosexuals | *Ausländer* (foreigners) | Asians ("Paki-bashing") |
| Illegal aliens/immigrants | Jews | Blacks |
| Jews | Leftists | Homosexuals |
| Hispanics | Racial minorities | Jews |
| Racial minorities | Turks | Muslims |

many West German cities. This, combined with an influx of 1 million refugees during the 1990s from the Balkans and elsewhere, has created a significant population of non-Germans. These foreigners (**Ausländer**) have been targets of right-wing violence.

Table 7.5 provides a comparison of scapegoated groups in the United States, Germany, and the United Kingdom.

## Right-Wing Nationalism

The reactionary right has, at its core, a concept of group loyalty and unity. The basic issue is whether one's primary loyalty should be to country, race, ethnonational identity, or another attribute. In the history of the right, there has been no unanimity on the selection of to which "group" one should pledge loyalty. For example, in the modern era, nationalism and racism were commonly invoked as ways to rally the championed group to the cause and to scapegoat a perceived enemy group. The Nazis were originally pan-Germanic, militaristic, and virulently anti-Semitic. They did not, however, initially promote a global white supremacist ideology approximating that of modern neo-Nazis until well into their regime. In fact,

> Hitler's original program did not call for racial unity on the basis of a transnational white or Aryan identity. A racially based transnational doctrine with the explicit goal of bringing all Germanic and Nordic nations together in one united Germanic Reich was not developed . . . until 1940–1941.[45]

Thus, although general trends exist on the reactionary right, and although rightist political parties have been formed throughout Europe, some ideological differences exist on the question of group loyalty and nationalism. A brief examination of divergences on this point is instructive. Three cases in point, two European and one from the United States, are discussed in the following paragraphs. One of the cases—Norway—is an interesting example of the characteristics of activism from the reactionary right in Scandinavia.

---

[45]Kaplan, Jeffrey, and Tore Bjørgo, eds. *Nation and Race: The Developing Euro-American Racist Subculture.* Boston: Northeastern University Press, 1998, p. xi.

In Germany, those on the fringe right exhibit affinity with their National Socialist past. Activist associations include political parties, paramilitaries, and a youth subculture.[46] Prior to the 1980s, the right wing in Germany was suppressed in the West by laws prohibiting the display of Nazi-era symbols and in the East by communist proscriptions against fascist activities. During the 1980s, right-wing parties and organizations began to be organized in the West, and a rightist youth movement began to grow. Around the time of the tearing down of the Berlin Wall, East Germany experienced a rapid growth in right-wing sentiment. Its isolation from the West and lack of foreigners and ethnic minorities may have been responsible for the relative lack of tolerance for non-Germans in the East. In the East after the tearing down of the Wall,

> it is the small far-right parties that have taken root and are growing fast. Their message of nationalism, racism, and xenophobia set against a background of high unemployment, reduced wages, and inflation has a wide and growing appeal.[47]

There was, in fact, an outbreak of xenophobic violence in the East after the Wall was torn down.[48] Thus, in Germany, the extreme right wing is characterized by xenophobia, nationalism, and secularism.

In Norway, although activism on the right has historically been nationalistic rather than National Socialistic in nature, there has been some divergence in focus among different groups.[49] The modern Norwegian right

> consists of three layers characterized by rather different lifestyles and ideologies: paramilitaries, Nationalist Socialist skinheads, and ideologists . . . the main ideological dimensions that divide the underground [are]: nationalism versus Germanism, culture versus race, and Right versus Left.[50]

For Norwegians, "the paramilitaries are those who best fit the nationalist label,"[51] and the skinhead youths are those who are closest to Nazi-like ideology. Interestingly, racial supremacist skinheads have adopted some of the ideological theories of the American racist right wing. For example, many accept the Zionist Occupation Government theory of American neo-Nazis.

In the United States, the nationalist right is by no means monolithic. It has been characterized by a number of movements, including pro-American movements, anticommunist movements, religious extremism, racial supremacy, and opposition to the influx of "foreigners" and their culture.

The American variant of rightist extremism is highly suspicious of a strong central government. This is because conspiracy theories are common on the American right, with some members of the militia movement arming themselves to prepare for war against the New World Order and international bankers (i.e., Jewish interests). Some add religion to their favored conspiracy theory and actively engage themselves in looking for signs of the Rapture and the Anti-Christ. Neo-Nazis tend to demonize the federal government as having been co-opted by Jewish interests, known as the Zionist Occupation (or Occupied) Government.

---

[46]See Kühnel, Wolfgang. "Hitler's Grandchildren? The Reemergence of a Right-Wing Social Movement in Germany." In *Nation and Race: The Developing Euro-American Racist Subculture,* edited by Jeffrey Kaplan and Tore Bjørgo. Boston: Northeastern University Press, 1998, pp. 148ff.

[47]Harnishmacher and Kelly, "The Neo-Nazis," p. 38.

[48]Ibid., pp. 154–6.

[49]See Fangen, Katrine. "Living Out Our Ethnic Instincts: Ideological Beliefs Among Right-Wing Activists in Norway." In *Nation and Race: The Developing Euro-American Racist Subculture,* edited by Jeffrey Kaplan and Tore Bjørgo. Boston: Northeastern University Press, 1998, pp. 202ff.

[50]Ibid., p. 202.

[51]Ibid., p. 214.

## Religion and Mysticism

Religion and mysticism are not universal traits of the fringe right. Even though religious convictions obviously motivate overtly religious right-wingers—such as politicized fundamentalist Christians, Muslims, and Jews—the modern neofascist movement (especially in Europe) does not always appeal to a deity or spiritual foundation. However, the Christian church as an institution has been upheld as a symbol of tradition and order. It is not uncommon for neofascists to reference the values of an orthodox religious tradition or to adopt these values as an element in their defense of an overarching value system.

In Europe, the war-era Nazis flirted with mysticism, neopaganism, and the occult by using astrology and reintroducing ancient Nordic ceremonies and rites. This is now rarely part of the European right-wing milieu, with modern European rightists tending to be nonreligious. Their affiliations, symbols, and culture are politically secular, and their racial beliefs are essentially nationalistic in character. When referenced at all, religion and the church are simply another institution to be managed in the new order.

By contrast, American rightists have historically used religious and mystical symbols and myths as foundations for their ideology—the burning cross of the Ku Klux Klan is one example, as are the references to God's will by antiabortion terrorists. Many right-wing American terrorists try to create a supernatural quality for the superiority of their championed cause or group, as evidenced on the American racial supremacist right. The modern supremacist right has adopted a variety of cult-like beliefs, such as Creativity,[52] Christian Identity,[53] and Ásatrú.[54] These beliefs will be explored further in Chapter 12.

Thus, although European rightists promote the secular nature of their political parties and street gangs, their American counterparts are likely to appeal to otherworldly authority.

## ❖ Race and Order: The Terrorist Right

Right-wing terrorism in the postwar era has not been as well organized, focused, or sustained as left-wing terrorism. There has not been an overarching movement or political environment to support the terrorist right; nor has there been an ideology that bound together dissidents in different countries. Exceptions to this general observation are found in countries with unstable political environments that allow for the operation of armed paramilitaries or **death squads** in long-term campaigns of terror. These paramilitaries have been notoriously brutal, and many were closely affiliated with government security agencies, such as during the Argentine "Dirty War."

Other than the paramilitaries, rightist terrorism has been characterized by indiscriminate attacks carried out by small cells and street toughs. This characterization can be summarized as follows:

- **Organization.** Organizationally, right-wing terrorists normally operate clandestinely in small groups or overtly as street militias and gang-like brawlers. On occasion, the violent right has operated as paramilitaries who attack perceived enemies of the state and established traditions and order, but these incidents are regionally specific. Latin America and Northern Ireland provide examples of paramilitary violence.

- **Focus.** The focus of the violent right is generally much broader than that of leftist terrorists. Right-wing terrorists have typically been indiscriminate in their selection of targets. They have defined members of entire ethnonational groups as enemies and hence have categorized whole civilian populations as legitimate targets. For example, right-wing bombers in Europe during the 1980s were more likely to randomly select targets than were their leftist counterparts, with the result being higher casualty counts.

---

[52] An anti-Christian mystical doctrine adopted by World Church of the Creator.

[53] Adapted from an 18th-century doctrine originating in Great Britain called Anglo-Israelism. The belief system reinterprets the biblical creation story and the concept of the Chosen People.

[54] A neopagan belief based on the pantheon of ancient Norse gods.

- **Longevity.** It is rare for right-wing terrorist campaigns to be *sustained*. An important exception to this observation is activism by paramilitaries and street militias during times of national crisis, when governments are weak or besieged. Other than this kind of deeply unstable political environment, right-wing terrorist campaigns have never had the longevity or staying power seen in leftist terrorist campaigns.

The goals and objectives of dissident right-wing terrorism are best described as nihilistic because the majority of right-wing groups do not espouse any specific program of reform, preferring to hide behind vague slogans of strident nationalism, the need for racial purity, and the reassertion of governmental strength.[55]

Nevertheless, as the cases of the paramilitary activity in Latin America and Northern Ireland indicate, in some political environments, the goals and objectives of the violent right can be very clear. In these cases, death squad activity seeks to preserve law and order, protect the state, and eliminate dangerous (defined as leftist) movements. Assassinations, massacres, and the terrorizing of civilian populations are considered to be necessary methods to achieve the desired goal.

Chapter Perspective 7.3 examines key commonalities among adherents of the violent right.

## CHAPTER PERSPECTIVE 7.3: Violent Reactionaries: Characteristics of the Extreme Right

Fringe-right ideology typically promotes an uncompromising belief in ethnonational, ideological, or religious superiority. Terrorist violence is sometimes selected as a justifiable option because an extremist group believes that it is defending the purity of an ethnonational group, rightist ideology, or religion. Right-wing terrorists picture themselves as champions of an ideal order that has been usurped or attacked by inferior ethnonational interests or religious values. They faithfully believe that final victory will result in the natural assumption (or restoration) of power by the favored group or belief. These uncompromising beliefs are typical among right-wing advocates who act on behalf of national groups, regional minorities, religious fundamentalists, or other groups with a distinctive identity. The identity is championed as being more legitimate, more sacred, or otherwise superior to other identities.

Although right-wing terrorists have a much less sophisticated ideological foundation in comparison to leftist terrorists, their behavior and activism do exhibit common themes. Tendencies among right-wing terrorists at the beginning of the 21st century included the following:

- *Theory,* in the broadest sense, has been far less important for the extreme right . . . , but this has traditionally been true for political movements of the right as well as for terrorist movements.

- There has been a considerably larger incidence of *nonpolitical criminality* among the extreme right.

- Much of right-wing terrorism is *single-issue* in character.

- Much terrorism . . . is vigilante or reactive terrorism . . . terrorism not so much aiming at radical change as at *preserving the status quo.*[a]

In a broader context, both violent and nonviolent activism on the extreme right possess basic common characteristics. The following commonalities are typical elements found in right-wing movements and political parties:[b]

- *Nationalism:* Only people belonging to a particular nationality have a right to reside within that group's country. Moreover, all people

*(Continued)*

---

[55]Hoffman, Bruce. *Inside Terrorism*. New York: Columbia University Press, 1998, p. 165.

(Continued)

belonging to that particular group, wherever they reside, should have the right to live within that country's borders.

- *Racism:* The notion that there are natural and permanent differences between groups of people.
- *Xenophobia:* **Xenophobia** is the fear of strangers or foreigners. In its current manifestation, it also posits the superiority of the group to which the fearful belong.
- *Antidemocracy:* An aversion to the democratic rules of the game; a rejection of the principle of equality; opposition to a pluralist conception of society.
- *Strong state:* Support for militarism and for "law and order" against the threat of crime and chaos. However, the American right's adherence to conspiracy theories has made it suspicious of strong central government.

Right-wing political parties and dissident movements do not share the same degree of solidarity as seen on the left. Rather, they have maintained an idiosyncratic quality that has not been consolidated into a global movement. World circumstances and domestic political environments have not given rise on the right to the same kind of international common cause that was seen on the left during the 20th century.

## Notes

a. Laqueur, Walter. *The New Terrorism: Fanaticism and the Arms of Mass Destruction.* New York: Oxford University Press, 1999, p. 125.

b. Adapted and quoted from Weinberg, Leonard. "An Overview of Right-Wing Extremism in the Western World: A Study of Convergence, Linkage, and Identity." In *Nation and Race: The Developing Euro-American Racist Subculture,* edited by Jeffrey Kaplan and Tore Bjørgo. Boston: Northeastern University Press, 1998, pp. 7–8; Mudde, Cas. "Right-Wing Extremism Analyzed." *European Journal of Political Research* 27 (1995): 203–24.

## Regional Case: Europe

Right-wing violence during the postwar era in Europe has been characterized primarily by a combination of attacks by terrorist cells and hate crimes by individuals or small gangs of people—many of them racist skinheads. Organized rightist terrorism in Europe never approximated the scale or intensity of leftist terrorism. Operationally, whereas leftist groups were active throughout Western Europe, organized groups on the right have tended to engage in sudden and singular attacks rather than terrorist campaigns. Organizationally, European rightist terrorists operate in small, clandestine cells or as gang-like skinhead street toughs. Some neofascists and other rightists have tried to organize themselves into militias, but these groups are apparently not prototerrorist cells, and true paramilitaries are rare.

One distinguishing characteristic of the right, vis-à-vis the left, is that left-wing terrorists were much more discriminating in choosing their targets. The violent left typically engaged in "surgical" acts of violence such as political assassinations, kidnappings, or symbolic bombings. The violent right was almost nonselective, preferring to plant bombs in public places (as occurred in Italy and Germany during the early 1980s) or to randomly seek out and attack members of unwanted ethnonational groups.

Cases from four countries are presented in the following sections. They summarize the types of right-wing terrorist environments common to Europe.

### Germany

During the 1970s, most terrorism in Germany came from the radical left. A small number of neo-Nazi groups did exist during the 1970s and 1980s, including the National Democratic Party, but there were relatively few right-wing incidents during those decades. In 1980 and 1981, during a peak of right-wing violence, 36 people were killed by bombs, including a bombing at the famous Munich Oktoberfest beer festival in October 1980.[56] After the tearing down of the Berlin Wall, the incidence of left-wing violence declined, and right-wing violence increased. This was especially true in the former communist East Germany. Among the reasons given for rightist violence emanating from the East were that East Germans were unaccustomed to living among significant numbers of non-Germans and that the former communist state had never accepted responsibility for Nazi atrocities, instead ascribing blame to the "fascists" in the West.

Right-wing violence in Germany has come mostly from street-level confrontations rather than from terrorist cells or organizations. It has been random and spontaneous rather than politically focused or part of an ongoing terrorist campaign. The most common type of right-wing violence can be broadly described as hate crime activity. The number of these incidents spiked in the early part of the 1990s, declined in the mid-1990s, and then rose again. During this period,

> the number of right-wing actions rose dramatically . . . to a high of 2,600 in 1992, before falling to 1,489 in 1994 and 781 in 1996, levels still considerably above the average of the 1980s. . . . There was another upswing of right-wing terrorist activities in 1997–98, particularly in eastern Germany.[57]

The targets of this violence were usually *Ausländer* (foreign workers and immigrants), Jews, and occasionally U.S. interests. Those responsible were mostly young street toughs, some of them racist skinheads. These attacks and other harassment were perpetrated by individuals and small groups of racially motivated Germans, not organized terrorist cells or paramilitaries.

### Italy

Right-wing terrorism in Italy has been sporadic but deadly. It is characterized by neofascist ideology, randomly placed bombs, and higher body counts than those incurred during leftist terrorist incidents. During the peak years of terrorist violence in Italy (1969–1987), the violent right committed only 27 (7.5%) of the attacks that caused death or injury. However,

> in those 27 attacks, the right killed more victims than the left—193 compared to 145. Of the 193, 85 were killed by a single bomb at Bologna railway station, and 52 in four other indiscriminate bomb attacks in public places.[58]

Despite a spike in right-wing terrorism in the early 1980s, few attacks have occurred since the middle part of that decade. Unlike the rightist environment in Germany, Italy has not experienced a surge of street-level violence from the right. An underlying culture of street toughs and skinheads is not widespread in Italy. Instead, the most significant examples of neofascist violence have come from terrorist cells. Two organizations typify right-wing violence in Italy.

***New Order.*** **New Order** (Ordine Nuovo) carried out several attacks in the late 1960s and early 1970s. On December 12, 1969, New Order bombed the famous Piazza Fontana in Milan, causing 16 deaths and 90 injuries. The group bombed a train in July 1970, killing 6 people and injuring 90, and in May 1974, New Order detonated a hand grenade in Brescia during an antifascist demonstration, killing 8 people.

***Armed Revolutionary Nuclei.*** The **Armed Revolutionary Nuclei** split from New Order. Its most notorious act was the bombing of the main train station in Bologna, which killed 85 and injured 180.

---

[56]Campbell, Bruce B. "Death Squads: Definition, Problems, and Historical Context." In *Death Squads in Global Perspective: Murder With Deniability,* edited by Bruce B. Campbell and Arthur D. Brenner. New York: St. Martin's, 2000, pp. 1–2.

[57]Laqueur, *The New Terrorism,* p. 119.

[58]Campbell, "Death Squads," p. 26.

As in Germany, the Italian terrorists on the right seem to be indiscriminate in the selection of their targets. Bombings and other attacks are typically directed against exposed targets with undifferentiated victims.

### Turkey

Modern Turkish nationalism dates to the founding of the Republic of Turkey in 1923 under the leadership of Kemal Atatürk. Atatürk created a secular, Westernized republic out of the ruins of the autocratic Ottoman Empire. He was a nationalist who, among other reforms, liberated women, adopted a Western alphabet, promoted Western dress, and ended the designation of Islam as a state religion. His goal was to create a secular, modernized republic. This ideology formed the foundation of Turkey's democracy.

Reactionary right-wing nationalists have been active since the 1980s. The **National Movement Party** (Milliyetci Hareket Partisi, or **MHP**) is an ultranationalist political movement that was first organized in the 1960s. MHP's ideology centers on unifying all Turkic peoples and creating **Turan**, or the Great Turkish Empire. This new state would unite Turkic peoples who now live in independent states founded after the collapse of the Soviet Union. Ethnic Turks are demographically significant throughout the Caucasus region and Central Asia in Turkmenistan, Kazakhstan, Azerbaijan, Kyrgyzstan, and Uzbekistan. MHP's ideology also strongly supports the war against the Kurdish rebels in southeastern Turkey, using this conflict to rally its followers around Turkish nationalism. MHP has links to a clandestine paramilitary known as the **Grey Wolves**.

***The Grey Wolves.*** The most prominent organization of the violent right wing in Turkey is the Grey Wolves. The Grey Wolves are named for a mythical she-wolf who led ancient Turks to freedom. Its wolf's-head symbol is displayed by MHP members and other nationalists. Grey Wolves have been implicated in many attacks against leftists, Kurds, Muslim activists, and student organizations. They have also been implicated in attacks supporting the Turkish occupation of Cyprus. **Mehmet Ali Agca**, who was convicted of shooting Pope John Paul II, was a former Grey Wolf.

The Grey Wolves have typically targeted leftists, minority nationalists, religious activists, and others opposed to their nationalist agenda. Attacks have included shootings, bombings, and kidnappings.

### Northern Ireland

The armed Catholic dissident groups are nominally "leftist" because of their adoption of variations on socialist ideology. The armed Protestant Loyalist groups—which are arguably paramilitary militias rather than underground terrorist movements—reject reunification with the Irish republic. They operate as a reaction to Catholic Republican nationalism.

***Ulster Volunteer Force.*** The **Ulster Volunteer Force (UVF)** is the main Protestant Loyalist paramilitary and has its roots in the anti-Republican movement of the early 1900s. Its membership since that time has totaled about 40,000. The mission of the modern UVF was to retaliate against and suppress Provo violence against Protestants. Its members have frequently resorted to acts of terrorism against Catholics.

Protestant paramilitaries typically target Catholic activists, suspected IRA sympathizers, and suspected IRA members. They have been implicated in dozens of assassinations and many more acts of violence.

Table 7.6 summarizes the perceived championed constituencies and enemies of right-wing terrorists.

## ❖ Violent Ideologies in the New Era of Terrorism

## The "New Terrorism"

Referring to the classical ideological continuum is useful for developing a critical understanding of modern extremist behavior. However, it is equally important to understand that the growing

## Table 7.6   Terrorism on the Right

Right-wing terrorist groups have arisen as a reaction against perceived domestic ideological and ethnic enemies. Although they share basic characteristics, their values and ideologies are rooted in their domestic political contexts. They do not share an overarching ideology similar to Marxist theory on the left. In essence, right-wing terrorists develop characteristics that arise out of unique political environments and are peculiar to their respective countries. In Latin America, right-wing terrorists have tended to be paramilitaries that engage in terrorist campaigns arising out of destabilized domestic environments. In Europe, violence on the right has come from either street-level toughs or clandestine terrorist cells.

The following table summarizes the constituencies and adversaries of several politically violent movements.

Latin America

| Group | Constituency | Adversary |
| --- | --- | --- |
| Colombian death squads | Rich, government, traffickers | FARC, ELN, sympathizers |
| Argentine Anticommunist Alliance | Right wing, military | Leftists, perceived opponents |
| ORDEN | Government, right wing | Leftists, sympathizers |
| Battalion 3-16 | Government, military | Leftists, sympathizers |

Europe

| Group | Constituency | Adversary |
| --- | --- | --- |
| German neo-Nazis | Native Germans | *Ausländers*, Jews, United States |
| New Order | Italian right wing | Anyone not in support |
| Armed Revolutionary Nuclei | Italian right wing | Anyone not in support |
| Revolutionary Cells | Oppressed classes and people | Government, imperialists |
| Grey Wolves | Native Turks, Turkic people | Non-Turks, Nonsupporters |
| Ulster Volunteer Force | Northern Irish Protestants | Republicans and supporters |
| Loyalist Ulster Volunteer Force | Northern Irish Protestants | Republicans and supporters |

threat of the New Terrorism adds a unique dimension to the emerging terrorist environment of the 21st century. This is because "the new terrorism is different in character, aiming not at clearly defined political demands but at the destruction of society and the elimination of large sections of the population."[59]

The new breed of terrorists "would feel no compunction over killing hundreds of thousands if they had the means to do so."[60] In addition, the emerging terrorist environment is characterized by a "horizontal" organizational arrangement wherein independent cells operate autonomously without reporting to a hierarchical ("vertical") command structure. Many of these new terrorists are motivated by religious or nationalist precepts that may not fit easily into the classical continuum. The attacks in September 2001 in the United States, March 2004 in Spain, and July 2005 in Great Britain and Egypt represent the full genesis of this new environment.

[59]Laqueur, *The New Terrorism,* p. 81.

[60]Ibid., p. 82.

## The Terrorist Left in the New Era

Since its origins in 19th-century Europe, leftist activism has undergone several generational shifts in ideology, methodology, and purpose. Ideologically, New Left and nationalist liberation theories predominated in the postwar era, gradually displacing orthodox Marxism among the new generation of young, middle-class activists. Methodologically, Soviet-style communist parties were superseded by nationalist movements and Eurocommunism, and labor agitation was supplanted by student and ethnic and national activism. In addition, the purpose of leftist activism on the far and fringe left became nihilistic in the West, as activists rationalized their behavior by referencing New Left revolutionary philosophy and solidarity with the developing world.

The driving forces behind political agitation on the left have been and remain class struggle, leftist nationalism, and special-interest activism. By the beginning of the 21st century, although vestiges of the armed left continued in some regions of the world, these were mere pockets of violent revolutionary sentiment. They did not compare in scale to the revolutionary fervor that existed earlier in the 20th century, nor to the wave of urban guerrilla warfare toward the end of the century. And although a few leftist nationalist and orthodox Marxist insurgencies continued to be fought in the countryside of some countries, they likewise did not compare in scale or frequency to similar wars in the postwar era.

### The Defeat of the Urban Guerrillas

The 1960s through the 1980s were the high tide for the theory of urban guerrilla warfare. Ideological revolutionaries applied Carlos Marighella's strategy repeatedly in Latin America, Western Europe, and (to a lesser extent) the United States. Frantz Fanon's and Herbert Marcuse's theories had allowed middle-class revolutionaries to rationalize armed rebellion in the democratic and relatively prosperous West. The intensity of urban guerrilla violence was significant in several countries, including Italy, West Germany, Argentina, and Uruguay. Nevertheless, the urban guerrillas were ultimately defeated and their strategy discredited.

In the near term, this type of urban violence from the left is unlikely to be replicated, absent new crises of faith and new revolutionary theorists. Left-wing revolutionary activism is unlikely to match the scale or scope of the past unless there is a new ideological revolutionary system or movement similar to 20th-century Marxism as a foundation. In the long term, there simply is not a large pool of new revolutionaries, and without a clear vision for the postrevolutionary society, this pool will continue to be small at best.

### Rebels in the Hills

By the late 1980s, the wars of national liberation of the postwar era had been largely fought and either won or lost. The postwar rivalry between the Soviet Union and the United States ended with the tearing down of the Berlin Wall in 1989 and the subsequent collapse of Soviet communism. The symbol of developing world revolutionaries rising up against colonial and imperial exploitation waned as developing world countries gained independence and consolidated power.

Although Marxist insurgencies continued through the 1990s in a few countries—such as Colombia and the Philippines—they no longer had strong benefactors in the communist world. Significantly, the record of human rights violations in communist societies became well known, so that the idealism and leadership from educated elites became much weaker than it had been during the postwar anticolonial period.

It is therefore likely that although a few leftist insurgencies will linger, the worldwide political environment will not provide strong support for the same scale of left-wing nationalist fervor as in its heyday.

### New Seeds for a Resurgent Left?

Leftist activism has certainly not disappeared. Protests against a globalized economy have rallied activists ranging in ideology from liberal trade unionists to radical anarchists. New symbols—exemplified by demonstrations against meetings of the World Trade Organization—have attracted the attention of a new far-left movement. The "Battle of Seattle" in November 1999 (protesting globalization); violent clashes in Rostock, Germany, in June 2007 (protesting a G-8 conference there); and demonstrations in Rome and Paris in April 2014 (protesting government economic austerity measures) are typical of an ongoing pattern of activism. Leftist protesters continue to rally around perceived inequalities created by exploitation from global corporate and national interests.

The more committed activists have labeled themselves anarchists but have yet to create a generalized activist environment similar to those that occurred after the Bolshevik Revolution or during the 1960s and 1970s. Absent a poignant and overt issue to arouse passions—such as the war in Vietnam or the people's rights movements during the 1960s—it is unlikely that mass far-left activism will become widespread in the near future. Nevertheless, the seeds of resurgent leftist terrorism could be sown among those who rally against issues such as globalization.

Internationally, the problems of unemployment, poverty, and perceived exploitation have traditionally given rise to leftist sentiment. Thus,

> in the West, the dismantling of the welfare state, especially in Europe, is having a divisive effect on societies with high rates of unemployment. Elsewhere, economic reform and higher rates of economic growth are producing marked disparities in income and a mounting perception of inequality . . . the divide between "haves" and "have nots" is making issues of class and economic opportunity central to political change.[61]

Should these factors stimulate renewed social discontent, with renewed analysis from a reinvigorated leftist intelligentsia, it is possible that a "new" New Left may yet arise.

## The Terrorist Right in the New Era

Terrorism from the right has generally increased since its spike in activity during the early 1980s. It has also developed several terrorist environments, including terrorist cells, paramilitary death squads, and gang-like hate movements. These environments differ from region to region and within distinct political environments. The incidence of rightist violence has ebbed and flowed, so that there have not been sustained right-wing terrorist campaigns—with the exception of political environments conducive to paramilitary activity.

Rightist terrorism is likely to continue to be characterized by xenophobic violence in Europe, paramilitary violence in Latin America, and militia-religious-supremacist violence in North America. The current right-wing terrorist environments in North America and Europe will not dramatically change, absent a significant shift in their respective political environments. However, right-wing activism will continue to occur, particularly in the following manner:

- **Scapegoating.** Political and social forces that produced right-wing activism immediately before and after the tearing down of the Berlin Wall are likely to continue to stimulate a rightist reaction. Immigration and discomfort with influences from nonnative cultures have historically caused rightist reactions, especially during periods of domestic uncertainty. During these periods, terrorists are likely to blame ethnonationalist, religious, or political scapegoats for domestic problems. Should domestic problems such as unemployment or inflation become severe, right-wing scapegoating and ethnonational chauvinism are also likely to increase in severity.

- **Rejection of Unpopular Agendas.** The fringe right wing has historically reacted to unpopular agendas, considering them to be threatening to traditional values and group supremacy. Even during times of relative prosperity and stability, some domestic policies and programs will

---

[61]Lesser, Ian. "Countering the New Terrorism: Implications for Strategy." In *Countering the New Terrorism,* edited by Ian Lesser, Bruce Hoffman, John Arquilla, David Ronfeldt, Michele Zanini, and Brian Michael Jenkins. Santa Monica, CA: RAND, 1999, p. 103.

stimulate terrorism from the right wing. In North America, tax policy, abortion rights, alternative lifestyles, and subsidy programs for demographic groups have traditionally aroused reactions from the right. In Europe, foreign worker laws, immigration, and European Union issues ("Europeanization") are likely to arouse reaction from the right.

### A New Future for the Right?

The prospects for an international revolutionary movement on the right—akin to the left-wing environment in the postwar era—are very unlikely. This is because right-wing political environments are uniquely peculiar to specific domestic environments. For example, it is unlikely that American religious extremists will find common cause with European neofascists. Nor will organizations such as the Ku Klux Klan appear in Latin America. At the same time, paramilitary activity similar to the Latin American case is unlikely to take root except in the most unstable of regions, such as the Balkans. Thus, aside from regional trends such as xenophobia in Europe or reactionary sentiment in Latin America, deep-seated international linkage or solidarity is unlikely on the right wing.

In Europe, violence by right-wing terrorists is likely to continue to be xenophobic, selecting as scapegoated enemies foreign workers, Jews, socialists, and immigrants. Neofascist and nationalist political parties and organizations will remain active. Among young right-wing adherents, the strongest and most enduring movement will continue to be the amorphous and nihilistic youth subculture. The music, lifestyle, and lack of organizational focus will provide a supportive environment for a generalized continuation of right-wing sentiment. The type of violence that this is likely to translate into will be street-level hate crimes and other assaults. It is also likely that terrorist cells will occasionally strike.

In the United States, the most likely future scenario is the continuation of sporadic violence from militia members, racial supremacists, and single-issue terrorists. A racist youth culture exists, but it is unlikely to become a significant grassroots youth movement for two reasons: First, the population of right-wing youths has never been as large as its European counterpart; second, right-wing agitation in the United States has historically come from older activists. Members of militias, racial supremacist groups, and religious terrorists can be expected to occasionally target government symbols, ethnic and religious minority groups, and single-issue victims.

In Latin America, unstable political environments will continue to produce paramilitary activity. Should a strong revival of leftist activism emerge, there may very well be a resurgence of rightist reaction from regimes, the armed forces, and paramilitary death squads. However, strong left-wing provocation is unlikely to resurface on the same scale as during the postwar era, except in isolated cases.

## Chapter Summary

The imprecise—and confusing—term *radical* has been used to describe leftist extremism, and the term *reactionary* has been affixed to rightist extremism. Because of the imprecision of these terms, the following concepts are what should be kept in mind:

- Leftist extremism is future oriented, seeking to reform or destroy an existing system prior to building a new and just society. In this sense, the extreme left is *idealistic*.

- When leftists champion a particular group, the group is one that is perceived to be oppressed unjustly by a corrupt system or government.

- Right-wing extremists try to protect their value system and affirm their special status, frequently expressing a desire to return to a time of past glory. In this sense, the extreme right is *nostalgic*.

- Rightist ideologies tend to be a reaction against perceived threats to a group's value system and presumption of superiority.

Reactionaries on the right and radicals on the left have characteristics peculiar to each ideological extreme. A comparison of these distinguishing qualities is instructive because, unlike the fringe left, the fringe right never developed an orthodox system similar to Marxism as an ideological "anchor." Basic distinguishing characteristics include the following:

- There was no singular event such as the Revolution of 1848 to inspire the rise of a right-wing version of Karl Marx.

- No seminal core document, such as the *Manifesto of the Communist Party,* was written to inspire generations of rightists. Hitler's *Mein Kampf* is the closest comparison, but it was a German fascist document and was never universally adopted on the right as were Marx's theories on the left.

- No leadership pantheon exists on the right that is similar to the Marx–Lenin–Stalin/Trotsky–Mao pantheon.

- There was never a long-term intellectual evolution of right-wing theory that allowed for its adaptation to history-making events such as the mostly leftist anticolonial and nationalist wars of the post–World War II era.

The postwar left produced many revolutionary icons who were revered by dissidents and rebels on the left—such as Latin America's Che Guevara, Congo's Patrice Lumumba, Vietnam's Ho Chi Minh, and Cuba's Fidel Castro. The postwar left also produced intellectuals and writers who introduced fairly sophisticated systems of analysis that were operationalized by leftist radicals—such as Herbert Marcuse, Frantz Fanon, and Carlos Marighella (discussed in Chapter Perspective 7.1). There was no postwar rightist equivalent of these revolutionary icons or intellectuals and writers. In fact, terrorists on the right eschew strong intellectualism, rejecting it in favor of simplistic analyses and conclusions.

In essence, right-wing ideology is less systematic and focused than that of the left. It tends to be less intellectual in its analysis of environmental conditions, relying instead on racial or other stereotyping of perceived enemies to mobilize followers. Thus,

whereas the left-wing terrorists of the 1970s emerged from the clubs and cafeterias of the universities, those of the right have more in common with bars and street corners. While those on the left spent inordinate time in ideological discussions . . . those on the right have not the slightest interest in doctrine, do not include even pseudo-intellectuals, and would have had no time for them were they to encounter them.[62]

This chapter provided readers with insight into the characteristics of left-wing and right-wing terrorism. On the left, Marxism was identified as the principal ideology underlying left-wing terrorist behavior, even though the political environments where Marxism became strongest were not those originally envisioned by Karl Marx. On the right, although the historical roots of right-wing violence lie in the rightist movements of Europe in the period between the world wars, modern terrorists have developed their own idiosyncratic qualities.

The right wing is much less ideologically centered than the left and is arguably anti-intellectual. Similarly, right-wing terrorism has not been as concerted or sustained as left-wing terrorism in the recent past, other than extensive violence by paramilitaries in politically fractured societies.

On the left, the quality of activism can be summarized in five propositions: The radical left emphasizes "economic rights"; democratic socialism emphasizes reform, not revolution; communists emphasize revolution, not reform; democratic socialists and communists tend to distrust each other; and leftist terrorists in the West considered the working class to be corrupted or co-opted by capitalism. On the right, although there is no strong ideology comparable to orthodox Marxism, the quality of activism can be summarized in several common themes: nationalism, racism, xenophobia, antidemocracy, and a strong state.

In Chapter 8, readers will investigate international terrorism and the concept of terrorist spillovers. The discussion will focus on defining international terrorism, the reasons for international terrorism, and the perceptions of international terrorism. Consideration will also be given to the question of whether international terrorist networks exist and to examples of cooperation between terrorist movements.

---

[62]Laqueur, *The New Terrorism,* p. 122.

## Key Terms and Concepts

The following topics are discussed in this chapter and can be found in the glossary:

Afrikaner Resistance Movement

Agca, Mehmet Ali

anarchism

Armed Revolutionary Nuclei

Ásatrú

*Ausländer*

Avengers of the Martyrs

Baader, Andreas

Baader-Meinhof Gang

Bakunin, Mikhail

bourgeoisie

Burke, Edmund

cadre group

Castro, Fidel

classical ideological continuum

conservatism

Death Night

death squads

degenerate workers' state

dictatorship of the proletariat

Engels, Friedrich

Ensslin, Gudrun

far-left ideology

far-right ideology

*fasces*

fascism

*foquismo*

Franco, Francisco

fringe-left ideology

fringe-right ideology

Grey Wolves

Guevara, Ernesto "Che"

Hitler, Adolf

Ho Chi Minh

ideologies

Irish National Liberation Army (INLA)

June 2nd Movement

Kropotkin, Petr

*Lebensraum*

left, center, right

Lenin, Vladimir Ilich

liberalism

Lumpenproletariat

*Manifesto of the Communist Party*

Mao Zedong

Marx, Karl

Marxism

means of production

Meinhof, Ulrike

moderate center

Montoneros

Mussolini, Benito

National Liberation Army (ELN)

National Movement Party (MHP)

Nechayev, Sergei

neoconservatism

New Order

Official Irish Republican Army

*One-Dimensional Man*

People's Revolutionary Army

permanent revolution

proletariat

"Property is theft!"

Proudhon, Pierre-Joseph

radical

reactionary

Red Army Faction

Red Cells

Red Zora

Revolutionary Armed Forces of Colombia (FARC)

*Revolutionary Catechism*

scapegoating

Shining Path (Sendero Luminoso)

skinheads

Skinheads Against Racial Prejudice (SHARP)

"skinzines" (or "zines")

socialism in one country

Stalinists

Trotskyites

Troubles, the

Tupac Amaru Revolutionary Movement (Movimiento Revolucionario Tupac Amaru, or MRTA)

Turan

Ulster Volunteer Force (UVF)

vanguard of the proletariat

vanguard strategy

Viet Minh

wars of national liberation

*Wretched of the Earth, The*

xenophobia

Years of Lead

# Discussion Box 7.1: Young Nationalist Idealists

*This chapter's first Discussion Box is intended to stimulate critical debate about the appeal of leftist ideologies to educated leaders of anticolonial insurgencies in the developing world.*

Until 1989, the Cold War rivalry between the communist East and the democratic West dominated the international relations and domestic politics of many nations. Nationalist movements often adopted leftist and Marxist ideology, and the Soviets supported a number of these movements.

The outcomes of these movements and the fates of their leaders are now the subject of history books. The early years of these leaders are intriguing stories and good case studies for our analysis of leftist dissent. The background and questions about three nationalist leaders are presented here.

## Patrice Lumumba—Fallen National Hero or Communist Sympathizer?

Patrice Lumumba was a Congolese nationalist who became a martyred national hero. The first prime minister of Congo, he was executed by a rebel faction when he fled a military coup in 1961 that was instigated by Mobutu Sese Seko. Mobutu became dictator of Congo (which he renamed Zaire) for three decades.

Lumumba was born in colonial Belgian Congo in 1925 and was strongly influenced by French existentialism (particularly Jean-Paul Sartre) and Marxism. He was a writer and activist who advocated Congolese independence from Belgium. A leftist but not a communist, he was president of the National Congolese Movement and became a pan-Africanist. During the anticolonial period in Africa, pan-Africanists advocated the unity of all African religions and people.

When the Belgians withdrew under pressure in 1960, Lumumba became prime minister. The new country was torn apart by a secessionist war in Katanga province (where Lumumba was killed), civil war, United Nations intervention, and rogue units of European mercenaries. Lumumba, who tried desperately to create a stabilized economy and government, asked for aid from the Soviet Union. He was thereafter branded a communist by the West. Lumumba, who was declared a national hero in 1966, also became a nationalist hero in the pan-Africanist movement.

## Fidel Castro—The Revolutionary in America's Backyard

Fidel Castro seized power in Cuba in 1959 after leading a revolution that successfully waged an urban terrorist and rural guerrilla campaign against the United States–supported government of Fulgencio Batista. Castro later openly declared himself to be a communist and became an important ally of the Soviet Union.

When young, Castro's observations of Cuban poverty and American condescension toward Cubans shaped his nationalistic beliefs. Castro was a student of Cuban nationalism and history, and when he enrolled at the University of Havana law school, he participated in violent political activism. At this point, he was certainly a leftist but most likely not a communist. In Havana, he met radical exiles from other Caribbean countries and participated in an abortive attempt to overthrow the dictator of the Dominican Republic. Castro was very active in international Latin American conferences and movements that opposed U.S. hegemony over the region.

In 1951, Castro was still a believer in democratic reform and ran for political office in the Cuban legislature. Unfortunately, Batista led a coup before the election could be held, and this was the end of Castro's belief in democratic change; thereafter, he was an advocate of armed rebellion.

*(Continued)*

(Continued)

### Ho Chi Minh—Master of Guerrilla Warfare

Ho Chi Minh was a committed communist nationalist who fought a long war against Japanese, French, and American adversaries. He successfully applied terrorist and guerrilla tactics, and his forces eventually achieved victory after a conventional invasion of South Vietnam in 1975.

Ho was born in French Indochina in 1890. As a young man, he traveled the world while working on a French steamliner. It was during this period that he became acquainted with the writings of Karl Marx and the ideals of the French and American revolutions. Ho eventually took residence in Paris, and after World War I, he became a founding member of the French Communist Party. After visiting the Soviet Union in 1923, he traveled through China and met other Vietnamese nationalists.

Ho cofounded the Indochinese Communist Party in Hong Kong in 1930. Eventually returning to Vietnam in 1941, he organized the Vietnam Independence Brotherhood League (Viet Nam Doc Lap Dong Minh Hoi)—known as the **Viet Minh**—which began fighting first against the Japanese conquerors of French Indochina and then against the French colonial forces. Its goal was to "overthrow the Japanese and French and their [Vietnamese] jackals."[a] Ho's forces regularly used assassinations and other acts of terrorism as part of their overall military and political strategy.

### Discussion Questions

- What are common themes in these case studies of revolutionary nationalists?

- In what ways do these examples differ?

- Were these leaders freedom fighters? Were they terrorists?

- Compare and contrast the points in their lives at which these individuals became radicals.

- Were Fidel Castro and Ho Chi Minh justified in taking up arms against their respective enemies?

a. Sheehan, Neil. *A Bright Shining Lie: John Paul Vann and America in Vietnam*. New York: Random House, 1988, p. 159.

## Discussion Box 7.2: Order From Chaos

*This chapter's second Discussion Box is intended to stimulate critical debate about the role of the military in preserving tradition and order in some societies when civilian governments are unable to do so.*

In some political environments, the military has come to symbolize tradition and order. When civilian governments have been unable to preserve a traditional or orderly society, the military has stepped in to "save" the nation. Latin America from the 1960s through the 1980s was often beset by conflict between the right and left. The military was often a violent institutional bulwark on behalf of the right.

The Chilean and Argentine dictatorships of the 1970s and 1980s are discussed here.

## Chile

Salvador Allende, a democratic socialist, was elected president of Chile in 1970, the first democratically elected socialist in Latin America. His policies of nationalizing (seizing control of) industries and banking angered many owners and the traditional upper class. His attempt to control the economy by keeping consumer product prices low and raising the minimum wage created rampant inflation, seriously damaging the economy. Demonstrations broke out in the capital of Santiago, as did labor strikes around the country. During his 3 years in power, Allende also brought in advisers from communist countries, Cubans, Spanish communists, and thousands of leftists from other countries.

The military, led by General Augusto Pinochet, seized control in a bloody *coup d'état* on September 11, 1973. Allende was killed during the coup. General Pinochet was a neofascist, and his rule was brutal. To suppress the left, the government arrested, tortured, and killed suspected subversives. A government-sponsored death squad—the **Avengers of the Martyrs**—operated under the direction of the security forces. More than 3,000 people "disappeared" or were killed during the regime. When Pinochet stepped down in March 1990, the economy had been stabilized, and the left had been crushed.

## Argentina

The unstable political environment in Argentina during the early 1970s was exacerbated by the significant activities of the leftist Montonero and ERP urban terrorist movements. With the inability of the Peronist government to curb mass unrest and the Montonero insurgency, the right wing responded violently. The Argentine Anticommunist Alliance paramilitary was encouraged by government agents.

In March 1976, the Argentine military seized power. General Jorge Videla eventually rose to leadership of the new government. A campaign of state-sponsored terror was waged during the military regime, known as the Dirty War. Tens of thousands of people were tortured, made to "disappear," or killed. Detention camps were constructed in which much of this activity was carried out. During this period, the Montoneros and ERP were eliminated, the left was crushed, and all political opposition was silenced.

## Discussion Questions

- Should the mission of the armed forces include stepping in to save the nation, even at the expense of democratic liberties?

- Was the Argentine military *coup d'état* necessary, considering the violent political environment?

- Was the Chilean military *coup d'état* justifiable, considering the damage Allende's policies had caused the economy and the influx of communist aid and left-wing activists?

- What are the reasons for the strong undercurrent of fascism in many Latin American armed forces?

- To what degree did the United States benefit from the coups in Chile and Argentina? To what degree was the United States harmed by these coups?

# On Your Own

The open-access Student Study Site at **http://study.sagepub.com/martin5e** has a variety of useful study aids, including eFlashcards, quizzes, audio resources, and journal articles. The websites, exercises, and recommended readings listed below are easily accessed on this site as well.

## Recommended Websites

The following websites provide information about leftist and rightist organizations, movements, and goals:

Afrikaner Resistance Movement (South Africa): http://www.awb.co.za/

Earth Liberation Front: http://www.earthliberationfront.com/

Front National (France): http://www.frontnational.com/

National Liberation Army (Colombia): http://www.eln-voces.com/

Sinn Féin (UK): http://sinnfein.ie/

Socialist International: http://www.socialistinternational.org/

## Web Exercise

Using this chapter's recommended websites, conduct an online investigation of left-wing dissident movements.

1. How would you describe the self-images presented by left-wing dissident movements?

2. Review the goals and objectives of these organizations. Do they seem reasonable to you? Do they justify violent behavior?

3. If you were a violent leftist dissident, how would you design your own website?

Using this chapter's recommended websites, conduct an online investigation of right-wing dissident movements.

1. How would you describe the self-images presented by rightist dissident movements?

2. Review the goals and objectives of these organizations. Do they seem reasonable to you? Do they justify violent behavior?

3. If you were a violent right-wing dissident, how would you design your own website?

For an online search of violent left-wing dissident movements, readers should activate the search engine on their Web browser and enter the following keywords:

"Marxist Revolution"

"National Liberation"

The names of specific dissident organizations

For an online search of violent right-wing dissident movements, readers should activate the search engine on their Web browser and enter the following keywords:

"Aryan Revolution"

"Neo-Nazism"

The names of specific dissident organizations

# Recommended Readings

The following publications give insight into leftist ideologies, movements, and personalities:

Djilas, Milovan. *The New Class: An Analysis of the Communist System*. New York: Praeger, 1957.

Djilas, Milovan. *The Unperfect Society: Beyond the New Class*. New York: Harcourt, Brace & World, 1969.

Fanon, Frantz. *The Wretched of the Earth*. New York: Grove, 1963.

Kropotkin, Peter. *The Black Flag: Peter Kropotkin on Anarchism*. St. Petersburg, FL: Red and Black Publishers, 2010.

Marcuse, Herbert. *One-Dimensional Man*. Boston: Beacon, 1964.

Marighella, Carlos. *Mini-Manual of the Urban Guerrilla*. Chapel Hill, NC: Documentary Publications, 1985.

Marshall, Peter. *Demanding the Impossible: A History of Anarchism*. Oakland, CA: PM Press, 2010.

Schiller, Margit. *Remembering the Armed Struggle: Life in Baader Meinhof*. Darlington, NSW, Australia: Zidane Press, 2009.

Tucker, Robert C., ed. *The Marx-Engels Reader*. New York: Norton, 1972.

The following publications give insight into rightist ideologies, movements, and personalities:

Anti-Defamation League. *The Skinhead International: A Worldwide Survey of Neo-Nazi Skinheads*. New York: Anti-Defamation League, 1995.

Bar-On, Tamir. *Where Have All the Fascists Gone?* Aldershot, UK: Ashgate, 2007.

Kaplan, Jeffrey, and Tore Bjørgo, eds. *Nation and Race: The Developing Euro-American Racist Subculture*. Boston: Northeastern University Press, 1998.

Kelly, Robert J., and Jess Maghan, eds. *Hate Crime: The Global Politics of Polarization*. Carbondale: Southern Illinois University Press, 1998.

Lee, Martin A. *The Beast Reawakens: Fascism's Resurgence From Hitler's Spymasters to Today's Neo-Nazi Groups and Right-Wing Extremists*. New York: Routledge, 1999.

Lipstadt, Deborah E. *Denying the Holocaust: The Growing Assault on Truth and Memory*. New York: Plume, 1994.

## CHAPTER 8

# Terrorist Spillovers

## International Terrorism

The New Terrorism has become a principal attribute of the modern era and poses a significant challenge to the affairs of the global community. "In this new era, advanced communications technologies such as the Internet and cable news outlets confer an unprecedented ability for terrorists to influence the international community quickly, cheaply, and with little risk to the extremists themselves."[a] Terrorists understand the value of disseminating their message to a global audience, and they carefully adapt their tactics to manipulate modern information technologies for their benefit. The New Terrorism represents a manifestation of the sophistication of modern extremists who have acquired advanced proficiency in coordinating their tactics with globalized information technologies. Independent stateless terrorist groups operate "within the context of modern integrated economies and regional trade areas."[b]

Political and economic integration has created a new field of operations for international terrorists—in effect, globalization accommodates the operational choices of committed extremists. Global trade and political integration permit extremists to provoke the attention of targeted audiences far from their home territories. In many respects, because of globalized information and integration, terrorists are able to operate on a virtual battlefield and cross virtual borders to strike their enemies. Globalized political and economic arrangements offer terrorists the capability to affect the global community much faster and more intensely than could previous generations of terrorists. Technologies are quite capable of broadcasting visual images and political interpretations of attacks to hundreds of millions of people instantaneously.

The globalization of political violence is a manifestation of new information technologies, mass audiences, and the features of the New Terrorism. "These potentialities, if skillfully coordinated, provide unprecedented opportunities for small groups of violent extremists to broadly influence targeted audiences."[c]

### Notes

a. Martin, Gus. "Globalization and International Terrorism." In *The Blackwell Companion to Globalization*, edited by George Ritzer. Malden, MA: Blackwell, 2006.
b. Ibid.
c. Ibid.

This chapter investigates the dimensions of international terrorism. International terrorism is terrorism that "spills over" onto the world's stage, usually to focus world attention on an otherwise domestic conflict. Targets are selected because of their value as symbols of international interests and the impact that attacks against these targets will have on a global audience. Terrorism in the international arena has been a common feature of political violence since the late 1960s, when political extremists began to appreciate the value of allowing their revolutionary struggles to be fought in a global arena. By doing so, relatively low-cost incidents reaped significant propaganda benefits that were impossible when radicals limited their revolutions to specific regions or national boundaries. Because of their adoption of terrorism on an international scale, revolutionary movements have been very successful in moving terrorism—and their underlying grievances—to the forefront of the international agenda. It is not an exaggeration to conclude that "international terrorism represents one of the defining elements of politics on the world's stage today."[1]

International terrorism affords one of the best examples of **asymmetrical warfare**, a term that refers to unconventional, unexpected, and nearly unpredictable acts of political violence. Although it is an old practice, asymmetrical warfare has become a core feature of the New Terrorism. In the modern era of asymmetrical warfare, terrorists can theoretically acquire and wield new high-yield arsenals, strike at unanticipated targets, cause mass casualties, and apply unique and idiosyncratic tactics. The dilemma for victims and for counterterrorism policy makers is that by using these tactics, the terrorists can win the initiative and redefine the international security environment. In this way, the traditional protections and deterrent policies used by societies and the global community can be surmounted by dedicated terrorists.

When violent dissidents limit their activism to *domestic* victims and domestic environments, they often do not receive a great deal of world attention. This is because the world community usually considers domestic political violence to be a localized issue unless it affects in some way the national interests of other countries. As a matter of domestic policy, some governments will not hesitate to suppress the media's access to information or to mete out swift and brutal reprisals against dissenters. The cumulative impact of repressive government policies toward dissent is that domestic attacks against domestic symbols can become very risky and costly for dissidents, with uncertain prospects for world attention or sympathy.

In the modern era of immediate media attention, small and relatively weak movements have concluded that worldwide exposure can be achieved by committing acts of political violence against international symbols. These groups have discovered that politically motivated hijackings, bombings, assassinations, kidnappings, extortion, and other criminal acts can be quite effective when conducted under an international spotlight. Thus, the international realm guarantees some degree of attention and affords greater opportunities for manipulating the world's political, popular, and media sentiments.

In practical terms, these points are illustrated by the case of the Palestinian cause. It is, in fact, the beginning point for understanding

U.S. Air Force

❖ **Photo 8.1**

The rubble of Khobar Towers. An indication of the destruction in the aftermath of a 1996 terrorist attack against the American military facility in Dharan, Saudi Arabia.

---

[1]Kegley, Charles W., Jr. "The Characteristics, Causes, and Controls of International Terrorism: An Introduction." In *International Terrorism: Characteristics, Causes, Controls,* edited by Charles W. Kegley Jr. New York: St. Martin's, 1990, p. 3.

modern international terrorism because Palestinian nationalists engaged in tactics that were widely emulated by others in the global arena.

Palestinian nationalists were the first revolutionaries to shape the framework for modern international terrorism. From the perspective of Palestinian activists, the global community ignored the plight of the Palestinian people while their struggle was being fought domestically on Israeli soil. Using high-profile international violence such as airline hijackings, shootings, and the taking of hostages, they effectively applied "propaganda by the deed" to force the international community to recognize the plight of the Palestinian people. For many Palestinian nationalists, any means were justifiable— including international terrorism—because their cause was just. From their perspective, the methods that many in the global community condemned as "terrorism" were the legitimate tactics of freedom fighters. As Leila Khaled, who participated in two airline hijackings, wrote,

> Our struggle will be long and arduous because the enemy is powerful, well organised and well-sustained from abroad. . . . We shall win because we represent the wave of the future . . . because mankind is on our side, and above all because we are determined to achieve victory.[2]

Other nationalist causes emulated the Palestinian model. Radical Kurdish, Armenian, and South Moluccan groups also took their domestic causes into the international arena. These groups committed kidnappings, assassinations, hijackings, and bombings in third countries far from their homelands. In addition, ideological radicals in Europe established common cause with the Palestinians, sometimes carrying out high-profile and dramatic joint operations with them. This created an international terrorist environment during the late 1960s through the 1980s that was dominated by left-wing and ethnonationalist movements.

Chapter Perspective 8.1 summarizes the changing environments of international terrorism, focusing on the predominant dissident profiles during the latter part of the 20th century.

## CHAPTER PERSPECTIVE 8.1: The Changing Environment of International Terrorism

International terrorism is in many ways a reflection of global politics, so that the international terrorist environment is dominated at different times by different terrorist typologies. Thus, one may conclude that the profile of international terrorism has progressed through several phases in the postwar era, which can be roughly summarized as follows:[a]

- From the 1960s through the early 1980s, *left-wing* terrorists figured prominently in international incidents. For example, Western European groups frequently attacked international symbols "in solidarity" with defined oppressed groups. Only a few leftist groups remain, and most of them (such as Colombia's FARC) do not often practice international terrorism.

- From the beginning of the modern era of international terrorism in the late 1960s, *Palestinian nationalists* were perhaps the leading practitioners of international terrorism. Participating in their struggle were Western European and Middle Eastern extremists who struck targets in solidarity with the Palestinian cause. By the late 1990s, with the creation of the governing authority on the West Bank and Gaza, Palestinian-initiated terrorism focused primarily on targets inside Israel and the occupied territories. Their radical Western comrades ceased their violent support by the late 1980s, but many Middle Eastern extremists continued to cite the Palestinian cause as a reason for their violent activism.

---

[2]Khaled, Leila. *My People Shall Live: The Autobiography of a Revolutionary.* London: Hodder & Stoughton, 1973, p. 209. Quoted in Hoffman, Bruce. *Inside Terrorism.* New York: Columbia University Press, 1998, p. 169.

- Throughout the postwar era, *ethnonational* terrorism occupied an important presence in the international arena. Its incidence has ebbed and flowed in scale and frequency, but ethnonationalist violence has never completely disappeared. By the late 1990s, these groups operated primarily inside their home countries but continued to occasionally attack international symbols to bring attention to their domestic agendas.

- By the end of the 20th century, the most prominent practitioners of international terrorism were *religious* extremists. Although Islamic movements such as Al-Qa'ida–generated groups were the most prolific international religious terrorists, extremists from every major religion have operated on the international stage.

- During the early decades of the 21st century, *religious* international terrorism firmly eclipsed international practitioners espousing other extremist causes. In the modern era, extremist religious ideologies have inspired followers via the Internet and other technologies.

**Note**

a. Adapted from Pillar, Paul R. *Terrorism and U.S. Foreign Policy.* Washington, DC: Brookings Institution, 2001, pp. 44–5.

International terrorism has two important qualities: First, it is a methodology that is specifically selected by violent extremists, and second, it is an identifiable brand of terrorism. International terrorism is, in other words, a tactical and strategic instrument of political violence as well as a category of terrorism. In the discussion that follows, the special features of what gives some terrorist incidents an international quality will be explored—primarily within the following dimensions:

- **Defining International Terrorism.** International terrorism must be defined by identifying the core attributes that make some terrorist acts "international" in character. All incidents of international terrorism exhibit one or more of these core attributes.

- **Globalized Revolution: Reasons for International Terrorism.** A critical examination of international terrorism will naturally raise the question of why extremist violence takes place so frequently—and so publicly—on the world's stage. Several advantages and disadvantages of global terrorism can be identified that enter into the extremists' cost-benefit calculus. Included in this analysis are *perceptions of international terrorism.* One important focus of an inquiry into the attributes of international terrorism is the question of perception—more precisely, how various international actors perceive the legitimacy of using international terrorism as a method of political dissent. For example, Western democracies abhor and denounce international terrorism, whereas many regimes and leaders elsewhere in the world have been either weak in their denunciations or have on occasion expressed their approval of international extremist violence.

- **Globalized Solidarity: International Terrorist Networks.** Since the days of the Cold War rivalry between the democratic West and the communist East, scholars and policy makers have frequently posed the question of whether cooperation exists between international terrorist groups—and whether international terrorist networks exist.

- **The International Dimension of the New Terrorism.** Stateless revolutionary networks such as Al-Qa'ida, motivated revolutionaries such as the Afghan Arabs, and the new generation of Al-Qa'ida–inspired movements have created an international terrorist environment that reflects the characteristics of the New Terrorism and the globalization of the world community.

# ❖ Defining International Terrorism

International terrorism and domestic terrorism differ in both quality and effect. *Domestic terrorism* occurs when several factors are present:

- Terrorist incidents are confined to a domestic venue.
- Targets represent domestic symbols.
- Political and psychological "terrorist" effects are primarily domestic.

Previous discussions presented a number of cases that explored dissident movements and incidents that were limited in scope to the borders of one country or region and where domestic targets symbolizing domestic interests were attacked. Many of these cases also evaluated incidents of state terrorism as domestic policy that were confined to the borders of the nation.

*International terrorism* occurs when the target is an international symbol and when the political-psychological effects go beyond a purely domestic agenda. It will be recalled that state terrorism as foreign policy is often characterized by state sponsorship of dissident movements. In addition, many dissident terrorist groups and extremist movements have regularly acted "in solidarity" with international interests such as class struggle or national liberation. It is not uncommon for domestic groups and movements to travel abroad to attack targets symbolizing their domestic conflict or some broader global issue. And especially in the post–World War II world, terrorist groups have selected targets that only tangentially symbolize the sources of their perceived oppression. Thus, linkages often exist between seemingly domestic-oriented dissident terrorist groups and international terrorism. Table 8.1 illustrates this point by reviewing the activity profiles of several dissident terrorist groups that were implicated in acts of international terrorism.

| **Table 8.1** | **Dissident Terrorism on the World's Stage** |
| --- | --- |

During the latter quarter of the 20th century, dissident terrorist groups attacked symbols of international interests many times. Some groups traveled abroad to strike at targets, whereas others attacked domestic symbols of international interests.

The following table summarizes a variety of international incidents conducted by dissident terrorist groups.

| | Activity Profile | | | |
| --- | --- | --- | --- | --- |
| *Dissident Group* | Home Country | *Incident* | *Target* | *International Effect* |
| ***Abu Sayyaf*** | Philippines | April 2000 kidnapping | 20 Asian and European tourists in Malaysia | Increased profile; $20 million ransom |
| ***Provos*** | Northern Ireland | December 1983 bombing | Harrods department store in London | National security crisis in United Kingdom |
| ***Shining Path*** | Peru | March 2002 bombing | Near U.S. embassy | Renewed profile; domestic spillover |
| ***Red Brigades*** | Italy | December 1981 kidnapping | U.S. Brigadier General James Dozier | Increased profile; NATO security crisis |
| ***Black September*** | Palestinian diaspora | Summer 1972 kidnapping | Israeli athletes at summer Olympics | Increased profile; international crisis |

Two contexts provide a model for defining international terrorism. The first context is the centrality of the **spillover effect**, which occurs when violent domestic conflicts are played out internationally, so that revolutionary struggles "spill over" national borders into the global arena. The second context is the interplay between international terrorism and terrorist environments such as state, dissident, religious, and ideological terrorism. Much of the violence conducted within the framework of these environments can be classified as international terrorism. Both of these contexts—the spillover effect and the environmental interplay, as well as unambiguous international implications—are discussed next.

## Expanding the Struggle: The Spillover Effect

Terrorist violence frequently occurs beyond the borders of the countries that are the targets of such violence. Those who engage in political violence on an international scale do so with the expectation that it will have a positive effect on their cause at home—thus reasoning that international exposure will bring about compensation for perceived domestic injustices. Using this logic, terrorists will either go abroad to strike at targets or remain at home to strike internationally symbolic targets. The following characteristics distinguish international terrorism as a specific type of terrorism:

- Domestic attacks against victims with an international profile
- Operations in a foreign country

### Domestic Attacks Against Victims With an International Profile

Most experts would agree that international terrorism by definition does not require terrorists to leave their home countries; they can strike domestically, depending on the symbol represented by the target. As a result, terrorist spillovers do not always occur in foreign countries. They are frequently domestic targets that signify international interests. In this way, domestic extremist movements can commit acts of international terrorism by selectively attacking internationally symbolic targets that are present in their home countries.

Examples of domestic targets with symbolic international links include diplomats, businesspeople, military personnel, and tourists. An important and disturbing result of these attacks has been a repeated trend in which terrorists recognize no qualitative difference between their victim group and the enemy interest that it represents. Thus, innocent business travelers, civilians, academics, and military personnel are considered to be legitimate targets and fair game for terrorist violence because they symbolize an enemy interest.

The long Lebanese Civil War in the 1970s and 1980s is a good example of domestic attacks against victims with an international profile. During the war, militant Islamic groups targeted symbols of international interests with great drama. The Shi'a group Hezbollah was responsible for most of these incidents, but claims for responsibility were usually made under different names, such as **Islamic Jihad**, **Organization of the Oppressed**, and the **Revolutionary Justice Organization**. Examples of terrorist attacks included the bombing of the U.S. embassy in Beirut and attacks against French and American peacekeeping troops in Beirut. In addition, the kidnapping of foreign nationals by Islamic extremists came to be a prominent characteristic of the civil war. Kidnapping victims were often non-Lebanese nationals (many of them American and French), such as journalists, academics, an envoy of the Archbishop of Canterbury, a station chief of the U.S. Central Intelligence Agency, and others. Some hostages were kept in captivity for years, and others were executed.

Other examples of domestic attacks against victims symbolizing international interests include the following:

- In Rwanda on January 18, 1997, Hutu militants shot and killed three Spanish workers from the international aid society Doctors of the World.[3] One American aid worker was seriously wounded, requiring his leg to be amputated.

---

[3]The Doctors of the World UK website may be accessed at http://www.doctorsoftheworld.org.uk/.

- In Colombia on February 7, 1997, Revolutionary Armed Forces of Colombia (FARC) guerrillas kidnapped two German and two Austrian tourists from a park and demanded $15 million in ransom for their release. On March 4, Colombian soldiers spotted them and attacked. During the firefight, FARC rebels killed two of the hostages, and the army killed four rebels.

### Operations in a Foreign Country

The history of terrorism is replete with examples of extremists who deliberately travel abroad to strike at an enemy. Their targets often include nationals that the terrorists symbolically associate with the policies of their perceived enemy. Some are representatives of these policies, such as diplomats or political officials, whereas others are only minimally linked to national policy, such as business travelers, tourists, or other civilians. For example, the Algerian Armed Islamic Group launched a terrorist campaign in metropolitan France from July to October 1995. Eight people were killed and 180 injured during bombings of trains, schools, cafés, and markets. In another example, the Irish Republican Army (IRA) in June 1996 fired three mortar rounds into a British army barracks at Osnabreuck, Germany. In both cases, terrorists selected marginally linked targets that were far removed from the center of their conflict.

In the modern era of the New Terrorism, terrorist plots have taken on a decidedly transnational dimension, with cells linked to one another across several countries. Extremist groups have deliberately positioned terrorist operatives and autonomous cells in foreign countries. Their purpose is to attack enemy interests with a presence in those countries. For example, during the 1990s, Latin American and U.S. security officials identified an apparent threat in South America, which indicated that Middle Eastern cells became active in the 1990s along the triangular border region where Brazil, Argentina, and Paraguay meet. These concerns arose in part from two incidents in July 1994. In the first incident, the Lebanese Shi'a movement Hezbollah was suspected of committing a deadly suicide bombing at the Argentine–Israelite Mutual Association in Buenos Aires, Argentina, where 85 people were killed and more than 200 were injured. Although the media reported that a group calling itself **Ansar Allah** claimed credit, Hezbollah (using the name Islamic Jihad) had previously claimed responsibility for the 1992 bombing of the Israeli embassy in Buenos Aires. In the second incident, an apparent suicide bomb exploded aboard a Panamanian airliner, killing 21 people, 12 of whom were Jewish.

The extent of transnational operations in foreign countries is illustrated by the following examples of investigations that occurred in the aftermath of the attacks against the United States on September 11, 2001:

❖ **Photo 8.2**
Death in Kenya. A Kenyan man is lifted out of the rubble of the U.S. embassy in Nairobi, Kenya. On August 7, 1998, the U.S. embassy in Nairobi was bombed by an Al-Qa'ida cell, which coordinated the assault with an attack conducted by another cell against the U.S. embassy in Dar es Salaam, Tanzania.

U.S. Department of State

- According to the U.S. Department of Justice, a terrorist cell based in Hamburg, Germany, included three of the September 11 hijackers and three others who were implicated in the attacks.[4] The cell had apparently been positioned in Hamburg since 1999.

- In November 2001, a Spanish judge indicted several alleged members of an Al-Qa'ida cell that had apparently begun to organize in Spain in 1994. The indictment was based on wiretaps of conversations between the Spanish cell, the Hamburg cell, and others who may have been linked to the September 11 attacks.[5]

- On March 3, 2002, Macedonian security officers killed seven members of an apparent terrorist cell that was allegedly planning to bomb the American, British, and German embassies in the capital city of Skopje. It was a multinational cell, with most members coming from Pakistan or

---

[4]Associated Press. "Ashcroft Says Terrorist Cell Based in Germany Included Hijackers." *New York Times,* October 23, 2001.

[5]Dillon, Sam. "Indictment by Spanish Judge Portrays a Secret Terror Cell." *New York Times,* November 20, 2001.

the Middle East. In February 2002, Macedonian police had arrested two Jordanians and two Bosnians and had seized computer disks that contained information about embassies and Macedonian government offices.[6]

## Unambiguous International Implications

Regardless of whether political violence is directed against domestic targets that are international symbols or take place in third countries, the fundamental characteristic of international terrorism is that international consequences are clearly apparent. For example, the February 1993 terrorist attack on the World Trade Center in New York City had clear international consequences, as did the terrorist attacks of September 11, 2001. In those incidents, foreign terrorist cells and the Al-Qa'ida network had used transnational resources to position terrorist operatives in the United States, their targets were prominent symbols of international trade and power, and their victims were citizens from many countries.

### Case in Point: Attacks on Embassies

International law recognizes the embassies as legal representations of nations in foreign countries. Diplomats have special status as representatives of their governments, and because of this special status, embassies and diplomats are afforded recognized legal protections. It is therefore not uncommon that embassies and diplomats have been targets of terrorist attacks. The following plots against American diplomatic missions are typical:

- India (January 21, 2002): Armed militants on motorcycles fire on the U.S. consulate in Kolkata, killing five Indian security personnel.
- Pakistan (June 14, 2002): A bomb explodes outside the American consulate in Karachi, killing 12.
- Uzbekistan (July 30, 2004): A suicide bomber detonates explosives at the U.S. embassy in Tashkent, killing two Uzbek security guards.
- Saudi Arabia (December 6, 2004): Militants storm the U.S. consulate compound in the Red Sea city of Jeddah, killing five non-American consular staff. Four of the five attackers die in the attack and a fifth is wounded and arrested.
- Pakistan (March 2, 2006): A car bomb outside the U.S. consulate in Karachi kills four people, including an American foreign service officer.
- Syria (September 12, 2006): Four Syrians try to blow up the U.S. embassy in Damascus, but the plot fails after Syrian guards kill three of the assailants in a shootout. The fourth man later dies of his wounds. A Syrian guard and bystander are also killed.
- Yemen (December 4, 2006): Yemeni security forces shoot and wound, as well as arrest, a gunman after he opens fire on the U.S. embassy in Sanaa.
- Greece (January 12, 2007): Attackers fire a rocket at the U.S. embassy in Athens. Authorities say anonymous callers claim that the attack was staged by Greek leftists.[7]
- Afghanistan (July 7, 2008): A large car bomb in Kabul kills more than 41 people at the gates of the Indian embassy.
- Libya (September 11, 2012): An attack on the U.S. consulate in Benghazi leaves four people dead, including the U.S. ambassador to Libya.
- Lebanon (November 19, 2013): The Iranian embassy in Beirut is bombed, killing and injuring more than 70 people.

---

[6]Finn, Peter. "Macedonian Police Kill 7 in Suspected Terror Cell." *Washington Post,* March 3, 2002.

[7]Reuters. "Chronology: Previous Attacks on American Embassies." *New York Times,* January 12, 2007.

### Case in Point: Hijackings as International Spillovers

A good example of unambiguous international implications is the selection of international passenger carriers—that is, ships and aircraft—as targets by terrorists. They are relatively "soft" targets that easily garner international media attention when attacked. The passengers on these carriers are considered to be legitimate symbolic targets, so that terrorizing or killing them is justifiable in the minds of the terrorists.

Beginning in the late 1960s, terrorists began attacking international ports of call used by travelers. International passenger carriers—primarily airliners—became favorite targets of terrorists. In the beginning, hijackings were often the acts of extremists, criminals, or otherwise desperate people trying to escape their home countries to find asylum in a friendly country. This profile changed, however, when the Popular Front for the Liberation of Palestine (PFLP) staged a series of aircraft hijackings as a way to publicize the cause of the Palestinians before the world community. The first successful high-profile PFLP hijacking was Leila Khaled's attack in August 1969. The PFLP struck again in September 1970, when it tried to hijack five airliners, succeeding in four of the attempts. These incidents certainly directed the world's attention to the Palestinian cause, but they also precipitated the Jordanian army's Black September assault against the Palestinians. Nevertheless, passenger carriers became frequent targets of international terrorists.

## Terrorist Environments and International Terrorism

Several cases presented in previous chapters were international in character, but they were evaluated within other contexts. It is therefore useful to briefly summarize terrorist environments within the context of international terrorism.

### International State Terrorism

Many governments have used terrorism as an instrument of foreign policy. These policies have been characterized by state sponsorship of terrorist movements and direct state involvement in terrorist incidents or campaigns. Although international state terrorism in the modern era has mostly involved the use of proxy groups by radical regional powers, it has also been used by global powers. For example, during the Cold War, the superpowers engaged in behavior that can be labeled as international terrorism. The United States carried out the Phoenix Program in cooperation with its South Vietnamese allies. It was a 3-year program that was militarily successful, but there were also many civilian deaths attributable to the campaign. The Soviet Union regularly supported dissident "national liberation" movements that used terrorism, giving rise to a theory in the West that the Soviets and their allies were the primary sources of international terrorism. This theory of a monolithic (single-source) conspiracy is discussed later in this chapter.

### International Dissident Terrorism

Many examples exist of dissident terrorists selecting domestic targets that have a symbolic international connection. Some of these attacks are carried out as a way to express solidarity with foreign movements or demographic groups; other attacks have been directed against perceived foreign enemies. For example, during the late 1970s and early 1980s, the Cuban American terrorist group **Omega 7** was responsible for "more than fifty bombings and assassination attempts in the United States against Cuban diplomats and businesses involved with Cuba."[8] Omega 7 is a good case in point of a domestic dissident terrorist group that engaged in international terrorism. Its targets during the 1970s included the following:

---

[8]Barkan, Steven E., and Lynne L. Snowden. *Collective Violence*. Boston: Allyn & Bacon, 2001, p. 75.

- the Venezuelan consulate in New York City in 1975
- the Cuban delegation to the United Nations in 1976
- a Soviet ship docked at the New Jersey coast in 1976
- several travel agencies in New Jersey in 1977 and 1978
- New York City's Lincoln Center in 1978
- both the Cuban Mission to the United Nations and a Soviet airlines ticket office in New York in 1979[9]

### International Religious Terrorism

Religious terrorism epitomizes the international terrorist environment of the 1990s and the present. Much of the religion-motivated international violence is a result of growth in radical Islamist ideologies. This resurgence has grown out of the rejection of traditional secular ideologies such as Marxism, as well as disillusionment with pan-Arab nationalist sentiment. The examples of the Iranian Revolution and the international *mujahideen* in Afghanistan inspired a number of movements in predominantly Muslim countries, and the presence of international volunteers in Iraq formed a crucible for creating new fighters. The result has been that a new revolutionary consciousness is promoting a sense of common cause among revolutionary brethren throughout the world. Operationally, pan-Islamic networks such as Al-Qa'ida have significantly influenced the growth of transnational radical Islamist terrorist cells.

### International Left-Wing Terrorism

Many armed left-wing movements resorted to international terrorism, and in fact, these movements significantly shaped the international environment from the 1960s through the 1980s. It was not uncommon for leftist groups to attack Western "imperialist" targets in the groups' home country or in countries far afield from the root causes of the groups' revolutionary movement. For example, Latin American leftists initiated a cycle of kidnappings of American and other nations' businesspeople and diplomats during the 1960s and 1970s. The kidnappers sometimes profited handsomely from ransoms that were paid for the hostages' release. These targets were interpreted by leftist groups to be symbols of repression; they were considered to represent the economic and political supports that were propping up enemy domestic governments.

### International Right-Wing Terrorism

The incidence of international terrorism by right-wing movements has been rather low. Unlike left-wing terrorism, there has not been a consistent cycle of rightist terrorism on an international scale. Right-wing terrorist movements have been idiosyncratic in the sense that they are strongly rooted in the political and cultural environments of their home countries. There has not been a transnational rightist movement since the fascist movement of the 1930s and 1940s, so that modern right-wing extremists do not have a common ideological source that has motivated them to form a global movement. Hence, they have rarely engaged in international terrorist violence as a way to express solidarity with one another; nor have they established important international terrorist networks. In essence, dissident right-wing terrorism has not been a significant factor in the international arena.

### International Criminal Terrorism

Terrorists who are members of traditional criminal enterprises (such as the Italian Mafia or Chinese Triads) tend to be reactive and anonymous in their political agitation. Members of criminal enterprises have occasionally engaged in international terrorism, but these incidents are exceptions to the general pattern of refraining from global exposure. They rarely seek out high-profile attention

---

[9]Ibid., pp. 75–6.

for their illicit "business" activities, unless threatened by governments that aggressively try to suppress their criminal endeavors; when this occurs, criminal dissident terrorism tends to be domestic rather than international. Terrorism from traditional criminal enterprises has not been a significant factor in the international arena.

Table 8.2 summarizes the interplay between international terrorism and terrorist environments.

| Table 8.2 | International Terrorism and Terrorist Environments |
|---|---|

Although cases of international terrorism exist for most terrorist environments, right-wing and traditional criminal terrorists tend to refrain from violence in the international arena.

The following table identifies incidents of international terrorism within the framework of several terrorist environments.

| Environment | Activity Profile | | | |
| | Incident | Perpetrator | Target | International Effect |
|---|---|---|---|---|
| **State** | Car bomb in Washington, DC | Chile Security Service, DINA (Chilean secret service) | Orlando Letelier | Minimal effect; domestic spillover |
| **Dissident** | Bomb in London | Irish Republican Army | Canary Wharf business district | Significant effect; ended IRA's cease-fire |
| **Left-wing** | Hostages taken in Lima, Peru | Peru's Tupac Amaru Revolutionary Movement | Japanese ambassador's residence | Minimal effect; domestic spillover |
| **Right-wing** | Arson attacks in former East Germany | Neo-Nazis and supporters | Foreign "guest workers" | Minimal effect; domestic spillover |
| **Religious** | Attacks of September 11, 2001 | Al-Qa'ida cells | World Trade Center, Pentagon | Significant effect; international crisis and war |
| **Criminal** | Kidnapping, murder | Mexican *narcotraficantes* | U.S. DEA Special Agent Enrique Camarena | Significant effect; enhanced war on drugs |

# ❖ Globalized Revolution: Reasons for International Terrorism

Extremist groups and movements resort to international terrorism for a number of reasons. Some movements act in cooperation with other groups, waging an international campaign against a perceived global enemy. For example, France's Direct Action, Germany's Red Army Faction, and Italy's Red Brigades frequently attacked symbolic targets as expressions of solidarity with international causes. Other groups are motivated by idiosyncrasies that are unique to the group or movement. For example, the **Armenian Secret Army for the Liberation of Armenia (ASALA)**, the **Justice Commandos of the Armenian Genocide**, and the **Armenian Revolutionary Army** waged a campaign of international terrorism against Turkish interests in Europe and the United States during the

1970s and 1980s. To support their demands for autonomy for the Armenian region of Turkey, these groups bombed Turkish interests, killed and wounded Turkish diplomats, and bombed airports. One such bomb, at Orly airport near Paris, killed about 10 people and wounded 70.

The following discussion summarizes several underlying reasons for the selection of international terrorism as a strategy by extremists:

- Ideological Reasons: Modern "isms" and International Revolutionary Solidarity
- Practical Reasons: Perceived Efficiency
- Tactical Reasons: Adaptations of Revolutionary Theory to International Operations
- Historical Reasons: Perceptions of International Terrorism

## Ideological Reasons: Modern "isms" and International Revolutionary Solidarity

Conflict in the postwar era was largely a by-product of resistance in many countries against former colonial powers. These indigenous "wars of national liberation" were global in the sense that insurgents established a common cause among themselves against what they perceived to be domination by repressive and exploitative imperial powers and their local allies. Marxism and generalized leftist sentiment provided a common bond among radicals in the developing world and among Western dissidents.

Reasons for this resistance included, of course, the overt presence of foreign troops, administrators, and business interests in the newly emerging countries. From a broader global perspective, other reasons included the policies and ideologies of the Western powers. These policies and ideologies were given negative labels that insurgents affixed to the Western presence in the developing world. If one were to apply Marxist interpretations of class struggle and national liberation, these indigenous wars could easily be interpreted as representing an internationalized struggle against global exploitation by the West. The conceptual labels commonly used by violent extremists—both secular and religious—include the following:

### "Imperialism"

Postwar dissidents fought against what they considered to be the vestiges of European colonial empires. Western powers had traditionally deemed empire building (**imperialism**) to be a legitimate manifestation of national prestige and power, an ideology that existed for centuries and was not finally ended until the latter decades of the 20th century. For example, the European "scramble for Africa" during the late 19th century was considered to be completely justifiable. During the wars of national liberation, foreign interests and civilians were attacked because they were labeled as representatives of imperial powers.

### "Neocolonialism"

**Neocolonialism** refers to exploitation by Western interests, usually symbolized by **multinational corporations**. Even when Western armies or administrators were not present and when indigenous governments existed, insurgents argued that economic exploitation still relegated the developing world to a subordinate status. From their perspective, the wealth of the developing world was being drained by Western economic interests. Domestic governments thus became targets because they were labeled as dupes of Western interests. Multinational corporations and other symbols of neocolonialism became targets around the world, so that facilities and employees were attacked internationally.

### "Zionism"

**Zionism** historically refers to an intellectual movement that sought to establish the proper means, conditions, and timing to resettle Jews in Palestine. Zionism was officially sanctioned by the Balfour Declaration of November 2, 1917; this was a statement by the British government that favored the establishment of a Jewish nation in Palestine as long as the rights of non-Jewish residents were guaranteed. The concept has become a lightning rod for resistance against Israel and its supporters. One significant difference in the international character of anti-Zionist terrorism—vis-à-vis resistance against imperialism and neocolonialism—is that international terrorists have attacked Jewish civilian targets around the world as symbols of Zionism. This adds a religious and ethnonational dimension to anti-Zionist terrorism that does not necessarily exist in the other concepts just discussed.

Symbols of the foregoing concepts have been attacked repeatedly by dissident terrorists. They have also been the objects of state-sponsored terrorism by enemy governments. An unfortunate consequence of this type of labeling is that diplomats have been victimized as imperialists, bankers have been attacked as neocolonialists, and Jewish civilians have been singled out as Zionists. In effect, these labels confer an enemy status on individuals who otherwise have little or nothing to do with the extremists' grievances.

## Practical Reasons: Perceived Efficiency

One basic (and admittedly simplified) reason for the high incidence of international terrorism is that it is perceived by many extremists to be "a highly efficient (if repugnant) instrument for achieving the aims of terrorist movements."[10] Within the context of this assessment, the extremists' calculation to engage in international terrorism certainly incorporates the *perception* of efficiency. The desired effect is to link a violent international incident to a domestic agenda for maximum effect.

Using this rationale of perceived efficiency as a core motivation, practical reasons for international terrorism include several factors:

### The Potential for Maximum Publicity

Terrorists practice "propaganda by the deed" and understand that international deeds will reap maximum media exposure. The media have never been reluctant to move dramatic terrorist attacks to the top of their reporting agenda; international terrorism is always depicted as "important" news. In November 1979, the American embassy was attacked in Tehran, Iran, and 53 Americans were held hostage until January 1981, a total of 444 days. During that time, Iran was at the center of media attention, and the revolutionaries manipulated the press to publicize their revolutionary agenda. They also embarrassed the most powerful nation in the world.

### The Potential for Inflicting Maximum Psychological Anxiety

Terrorism against enemy interests on a global scale theoretically creates security problems everywhere that the target commands a political or economic presence. When travelers, airliners, and diplomats are attacked internationally, an enemy will give attention to the grievances of the movement that is the source of the violence.

### Pragmatism

Demanding concessions from adversaries who become the focus of worldwide attention has been successful occasionally. Terrorists and extremists have sometimes secured ransoms for hostages, prisoner releases, and other concessions.

Thus, international terrorism is a functional operational decision that offers—from the perspective of the terrorists—greater efficiency in promoting the goals of the cause.

## Tactical Reasons: Adaptations of Revolutionary Theory to International Operations

Mao Zedong, Carlos Marighella, and Frantz Fanon provided influential analyses of the practicality of revolutionary violence, and international extremists apply modern adaptations of their ideas on a global scale.

---

[10]Kegley, "Characteristics," p. 21.

### *Mao: Fish Swimming in the Sea of the People*

With the inexorable trend toward globalization, many national, information, and communication barriers have been dramatically altered. Members of dissident movements are now able to reside in multiple countries while remaining in regular contact with one another via the Internet and other communications technologies. Adapting Mao Zedong's maxim to the modern post–Cold War international environment, terrorists can become "fish swimming in the sea of the global community." It is much more difficult to root out a movement that uses cells pre-positioned in several countries, as became apparent during the post–September 11, 2001, war against terrorism.

### *Marighella: Enraging the Beast*

Relatively weak groups continue to attempt to provoke governments into reacting in ways that would be detrimental to the governments' interests. By doing so, new supporters will arise to join the cause. Adapting Carlos Marighella's theory of provoking a powerful adversary into overreacting—and thus creating a heightened revolutionary consciousness among the people—international terrorists can now provoke a nation on a global scale. These provocations provide effective propaganda if the offending nation can be depicted as an international bully. This is not difficult to do because modern information technology allows for dramatic images and messages to be disseminated worldwide. During the 2001–2002 coalition campaign against the Taliban in Afghanistan and the 2003 invasion of Iraq, images of wounded and killed civilians were regularly and graphically broadcast throughout the Muslim world. Similarly, the Islamic State of Iraq and the Levant (ISIS) skillfully used social networking media to promulgate its fighters in battle and gruesome executions.

### *Fanon: Liberating Violence*

It is apparent that terrorists continue to believe that they represent a superior calling and morality. Modern religious extremists in particular believe that killing or dying in defense of the faith will ensure them a place in paradise. On an international scale, this superior calling, morality, and promised reward are a kind of "liberation." Adapting Frantz Fanon's analysis that oppressed people psychologically need to engage in revolutionary resistance against their oppressor, terrorists can use the international arena as a means to "liberate" themselves and thereby obtain vengeful justice against an adversary.

## Historical Reasons: Perceptions of International Terrorism

Governments in developing countries do not always share the West's interpretations when political violence is used in the international arena. Western democracies regularly abhor and denounce international terrorism, whereas many regimes and leaders elsewhere in the world either have been weak in their denunciations or have on occasion expressed their approval of international extremist violence.

Three factors illustrate why terrorism is *unacceptable* from the perspective of Western governments:

- First, Western governments have adopted an ideology of democratic justice as a norm. A *norm* is an accepted standard for the way societies ought to behave. Within the context of these norms, terrorism is perceived to be inherently *malum in se* criminal behavior.

- Second, the West is often a target of terrorism. This is a practical consideration.

- Third, the West recognizes accepted methods of warfare. These include rules that define which modes of conflict constitute a legal manner to wage war and that only just wars should be fought. If possible, so-called collateral damage (unnecessary casualties and destruction) is to be avoided.

In the developing world, wars waged to gain independence or to suppress political rivals were commonly fought by using "irregular" tactics. Combatants often used guerrilla or terrorist tactics against colonial opponents or against indigenous adversaries during civil wars. In fact, many of the leaders who rose to prominence after the formation of the new nations were former insurgents who were previously referred to by their adversaries as terrorists. From their perspective, terrorism and other violent methods were necessary weapons for waging "poor man's warfare" against enemies who were sometimes many times stronger than themselves.

Three factors demonstrate why terrorism is often *acceptable* from the perspective of governments in the developing world:

1. Many anticolonial extremists became national leaders. They were freedom fighters and heroes in the eyes of their people. A large number of revolutionaries became national leaders in Asia, Africa, and the Middle East.

2. Terrorism was used as a matter of practical choice during insurgencies. It provided armed propaganda, sowed disorder, and demoralized their adversaries. At some point in many postwar conflicts, the cost of war simply became unacceptable to the colonial powers.

3. Many developing-world insurgents crafted an effective fusion of ideology and warfare. Terrorism was a justifiable and legitimate method of warfare as long as the cause was just and the fighters were cadres who understood why they were fighting.

The massacre of 11 Israeli athletes by Black September terrorists at the 1972 Munich Olympics exemplifies how divergent the foregoing perspectives can be. In the aftermath of the tragedy, Western and developing-world members of the United Nations engaged in sometimes acrimonious debate about the use of political violence in the international arena. The debate centered on whether "terrorist acts" should be defined by referencing the perspectives of the victims or the assailants. There were important differences between the positions of the developing-world nations and those of the Western members, especially NATO countries[11]: "[Western countries contended that] murder, kidnapping, arson and other felonious acts constitute criminal behavior, but many non-Western nations have proved reluctant to condemn as terrorist acts what they consider to be struggles for national liberation."[12]

Keystone/Hulton Archive/Getty Images

❖ **Photo 8.3**
The 1972 Munich Olympics. A hooded Black September terrorist peers over a balcony during the tragic crisis that ended with the deaths of all of the Israeli hostages.

Some Arab, African, and Asian nations considered the underlying motives for the Munich attack to be the determining criteria for whether the assault was a terrorist incident. Because of the status of some ethnonational groups, one developing-world delegate observed, "The term 'terrorist' could hardly be held to apply to persons who were denied the most elementary human rights, dignity, freedom and independence, and whose countries objected to foreign occupation."[13]

## ❖ Globalized Solidarity: International Terrorist Networks

Historically, many revolutionary movements have proclaimed their solidarity with other movements. In some cases, these movements engaged in coordinated attacks or other behaviors that intimated the

---

[11]At that time, NATO was made up of the Western democracies, excluding France.

[12]North Atlantic Assembly Papers, Sub-Committee on Terrorism. *Terrorism.* Brussels: International Secretariat, January 1989, p. 34. Quoted in Hoffman, *Inside Terrorism,* p. 32.

[13]Sofaer, Abraham D. "Terrorism and the Law." *Foreign Affairs* 64 (Summer 1986): 904. Quoted in Hoffman, *Inside Terrorism.*

existence of terrorist networks. The concept of an international terrorist network naturally presumes one or more of the following environments:

- Terrorist groups talk to one another.
- Terrorist groups support one another.
- Governments sponsor terrorists.
- The international terrorist environment is basically conspiratorial.

Using these characteristics as criteria for determining whether there is such a thing as an "international terrorist network," one can conclude that networks have existed and continue to exist. A number of dissident terrorist movements—such as European leftists and Palestinian nationalists—have cooperated with one another. They frequently establish common cause and act in solidarity to promote a generalized global struggle against "imperialism," "Zionism," or other perceived forces of oppression. In addition, governments (such as those of Syria and Iran) have sponsored terrorist movements as instruments of foreign policy. There are many cases of terrorist incidents or movements that owe their operational viability to linkages with government sponsors.

Chapter Perspective 8.2 discusses a noteworthy example of cooperation between Japanese Red Army terrorists and the Popular Front for the Liberation of Palestine.

## CHAPTER PERSPECTIVE 8.2: A Remarkable Example of International Terrorism: The Japanese Red Army and the Lod (Lydda) Airport Massacre

The **Japanese Red Army** (JRA) was a nearly fanatical international terrorist organization founded in about 1970. It participated in a series of terrorist incidents, including assassinations, kidnappings, and airline hijackings. The JRA on one occasion tried to occupy the U.S. embassy in Kuala Lumpur, Malaysia. On another occasion, the group bombed a United Service Organizations club in Naples, Italy. Members have been arrested in a number of countries, including one who was caught with explosives on the New Jersey Turnpike. Others who were not arrested were thought to have joined Latin American revolutionaries in Colombia and Peru.

The JRA committed a number of terrorist acts in cooperation with other terrorist groups. On May 30, 1972, three members of the organization fired assault rifles into a group of religious pilgrims and other travelers at Israel's Lod (Lydda) Airport. The death toll was high—26 people were killed and about 80 were wounded. Most of the injured were travelers from Puerto Rico on a religious pilgrimage.

During the firefight that ensued, two of the terrorists were killed by security guards, and one was captured. The Japanese terrorists had been retained by the Popular Front for the Liberation of Palestine (PFLP) for the attack, and the PFLP had sent the three operatives on their mission on behalf of the Palestinian cause.

The attack is a remarkable example of international terrorism in its purest form: Leftist Japanese terrorists killed Christian pilgrims from Puerto Rico arriving on a U.S. airline at an Israeli airport on behalf of the nationalist Popular Front for the Liberation of Palestine.

As a postscript, the one survivor of the Lod attack—Kozo Okamoto—was tried and sentenced to life imprisonment in Israel but was later released in a 1985 prisoner exchange with other Palestinian prisoners. He lived in Lebanon's Beka'a Valley until 1997 but was arrested by the Lebanese with four other members of the JRA. After serving three years in prison, all five members were freed in 2000.

## Cold War Terrorist-Networking Theory

During the Cold War rivalry between the Western allies and the Eastern bloc, many experts in the West concluded that the communist East was responsible for sponsoring an international terrorist network.[14] The premise was that the Soviet Union and its allies were at least an indirect—and often a direct—source of most international terrorism. Under this scenario, state-sponsored terrorism was a significant threat to world security and was arguably a manifestation of an unconventional World War III. It represented a global network of state-sponsored revolutionaries whose goal was to destabilize the democratic West and its allies in the developing world (referred to at that time as the **Third World**).

The Western democracies were able to cite evidence to support their claim that global terrorism related back to a Soviet source. One source of evidence was the fact that the Soviets never denied that they supported revolutionary groups. However, they labeled them freedom fighters waging wars of national liberation rather than as terrorists. Another source of evidence was the truism that the West was the most frequent target of international terrorism; Soviet interests were rarely attacked. Perhaps the most credible evidence was that a number of regimes were clearly implicated in supporting terrorist movements or incidents. Many of these regimes were pro-Soviet in orientation, or at least recipients of Soviet military aid. Thus, when Soviet- or Chinese-manufactured weapons were found in terrorist arms caches, it was clear that these regimes were conduits for Soviet support for radical movements.

Despite these indications, one significant problem with the Soviet sponsorship scenario was that most of the evidence was circumstantial and inconclusive. For instance, many of the world's terrorist movements and extremist governments were either non-Marxist in orientation or only secondarily Marxist. They were comfortable with accepting assistance from any willing donor, regardless of the donor's ideological orientation. Although some nationalist movements, such as the Palestine Liberation Organization, certainly had Marxist factions that received training and support from the Soviets, and although some governments, such as those of Cuba and Syria, received Soviet military and economic aid, it is questionable how much actual *control* the Soviets had over their proxies. And, very significantly, many dissident movements and state sponsors of terrorism—such as the Provisional Irish Republican Army and revolutionary Iran—were completely independent of Soviet operational or ideological control.

Thus, the belief that terrorism was part of a global conflict between democracy and communism (and hence an unconventional World War III) was too simplistic. It did not take into account the multiplicity of ideologies, motivations, movements, or environments that represented international terrorism. Having said this, there was without question a great deal of state sponsorship of terrorism that emanated at least indirectly from the communist East. Ideological indoctrination (e.g., at Patrice Lumumba Peoples' Friendship University), material support, and terrorist training facilities did provide revolutionary focus for extremists from around the world. Therefore, although there was not a communist-directed terrorist network, and the Soviets were not a "puppet master" for a global terrorist conspiracy, they did actively inflame terrorist behavior.[15]

## International Terrorist Environments

Several terrorist environments are theoretically possible at different times and in different regional contexts. These are not, of course, exclusive descriptions of every aspect of international terrorism. They are, however, useful models for framing a generalized interpretation of international terrorism. The following discussion summarizes four environments that range in structure and cohesion from

[14]See Sterling, Claire. *The Terror Network: The Secret War of International Terrorism*. New York: Holt, Rinehart & Winston, 1981. See also Cline, Ray S., and Yonah Alexander. *Terrorism: The Soviet Connection*. New York: Crane Russak, 1984.

[15]For an argument that the Soviet sponsorship theory was simply a new Red Scare, see Herman, Edward S. *The Real Terror Network: Terrorism in Fact and Propaganda*. Boston: South End, 1982.

tightly knit single-sourced threats to loosely linked multiple-source threats.[16] The four environments are the following:

- Monolithic terrorist environment
- Strong multipolar terrorist environment
- Weak multipolar terrorist environment
- Cell-based terrorist environment

### Monolithic Terrorist Environment

The emphasis in the **monolithic terrorist environment** model is on state-centered behavior. The old model of a global Soviet-sponsored terrorist threat described a terrorist environment wherein terrorism was a monolithic (singular) threat emanating from a single source. This presupposed that Soviet assistance and Marxist ideology were binding motivations for international terrorism. As a matter of counterterrorism policy, if this had been correct, combating the threat would have been uncomplicated because in theory, the source (i.e., the Soviets) might be induced or co-opted to reduce or end their sponsorship.

### Strong Multipolar Terrorist Environment

In the **strong multipolar terrorist environment**, the emphasis is also on state-centered behavior. This model presumes that state sponsorship guides terrorist behavior but that several governments support their favored groups. It also presumes that there are few truly autonomous international terrorist movements; they all have a link to a state sponsor. Unlike the theory of a monolithic Soviet-sponsored threat, this scenario suggests that regional powers use terrorism to support their own agendas and that many proxies exist. To counter this type of environment, the several sources theoretically would each have to be co-opted independently of the others.

### Weak Multipolar Terrorist Environment

The model of the **weak multipolar terrorist environment** shifts the emphasis away from the state toward the terrorist movements. Unlike the strong multipolar model, the weak multipolar model presupposes that state sponsorship exists but that the terrorist groups are more autonomous. Under this scenario, several governments support their favored groups, but many of these groups are relatively independent international terrorist movements. The terrorist groups would be content with *any* state sponsor so long as they received enough assistance to continue their revolutionary struggle. Countering this environment is more difficult than countering the monolithic or strong multipolar models because the dissident movements are more flexible and adaptable. Cutting off one source of assistance would theoretically have little effect other than to cause a temporary disruption in operations.

### Cell-Based Terrorist Environment

In the model of the **cell-based terrorist environment**, the emphasis is centered on the terrorist movement. This model presumes that state sponsorship may exist to some extent but that the revolutionary movement is independent of governmental constraints. It is a kind of "free-floating" revolution that maintains its autonomy through its own resources. In this kind of environment, the movement is based on the viability of small cells that are loosely affiliated with one another. Thus, the movement will prevail even when some of its cells are destroyed or otherwise compromised. Because of the fluid character of its organizational structure, this environment is the most difficult to counter.

Table 8.3 summarizes the activity profiles for the foregoing international terrorist environments.

---

[16]See Sederberg, Peter C. *Terrorist Myths: Illusion, Rhetoric, and Reality.* Englewood Cliffs, NJ: Prentice Hall, 1989, pp. 117ff.

| Table 8.3 | Understanding International Terrorist Environments |
|-----------|----------------------------------------------------|

International terrorism occurs within the context of international social and political environments. These environments are not static and can vary from time to time and region to region.

The following table suggests a model for understanding the features of several international terrorist environments.

| Environment | Activity Profile | | | |
|-------------|-------------------------|------------------|----------------|------------------------|
| | *Foremost Participant* | *State Control* | *Group Autonomy* | *Difficulty in Countering* |
| **Monolithic** | Single state sponsor | Strong and direct | Minimal | Clear options; easiest to counter |
| **Strong multipolar** | Several state sponsors | Strong and direct | Minimal | Clear options |
| **Weak multipolar** | Dissident groups; several state sponsors | Weak and insecure | Strong | Problematic and unpredictable |
| **Cell-based** | Dissident groups | Weak | Strong | Problematic and unpredictable; most difficult to counter |

## ❖ The International Dimension of the New Terrorism

### Movement Case: The Afghan Arabs at War

The series of wars in Afghanistan, which began with the 1979 Soviet invasion, produced a large cadre of hardened Islamic fighters. The invasion and occupation by Soviet forces led to a sustained guerrilla insurgency that eventually forced the Soviet army to withdraw after losing 15,000 of its men. The war was considered by the insurgents to be a *jihad*, and they declared themselves to be *mujahideen* in a holy war against nonbelievers.

Muslims from around the world volunteered to fight alongside or otherwise support the Afghani *mujahideen*. This created a pan-Islamic consciousness that led to the creation of the Al-Qa'ida network and domestic *jihadi* movements as far afield as the Philippines, Malaysia, Central Asia, and Algeria. The Muslim volunteers—**Afghan Arabs**—became a legendary fighting force among Muslim activists. It is not known exactly how many Afghan Arabs fought in Afghanistan during the anti-Soviet *jihad*. However, reasonable estimates have been calculated:

> [A former] senior CIA official . . . claims the number is close to 17,000, while the highly respected British publication *Jane's Intelligence Review* suggests a figure of more than 14,000 (including some 5,000 Saudis, 3,000 Yemenis, 2,000 Egyptians, 2,800 Algerians, 400 Tunisians, 370 Iraqis, 200 Libyans, and scores of Jordanians).[17]

---

[17]Reeve, Simon. *The New Jackals: Ramzi Yousef, Osama bin Laden, and the Future of Terrorism*. Boston: Northeastern University Press, 1999, p. 3.

After the Soviet phase of the war, many of the Afghan Arabs carried on their *jihad* in other countries, becoming **international *mujahideen***, who were first introduced in Chapter 6. For example, many Algerian Afghan Arabs returned home to fight on the side of Muslim rebels in the brutal Algerian insurgency during the 1990s. Others fought in Bosnia and gained a reputation for their fervor, fighting skills, and brutality. Many Afghan Arabs traveled to Muslim communities in Asia and Africa, assisting indigenous Muslim groups in their causes. They provided technical assistance and other resources to these groups. For example, Filipino and Indonesian *jihadis* had frequent interaction with the Al-Qa'ida network and Afghan Arabs. Afghan Arabs also fought in Chechnya, and some Chechens subsequently fought on behalf of the Taliban in Afghanistan and elsewhere.

The Afghan Arabs symbolize a phenomenon that carried on well into the second decade of the 21st century. They represent the "first generation" of international Islamist fighters who inspired younger *mujahideen* recruits to join the cause, a process that continued on in the post–2011 Arab Spring conflicts.

### Case in Point: Mujahideen *in Bosnia*

The first wars that were fought after the breakup of Yugoslavia were between the Serbs, Croatians, and Bosnian Muslims. When Bosnia declared independence, it precipitated a brutal civil war that at times had all three national groups fighting one another simultaneously. The war between the Bosnians and Serbs was particularly violent and involved genocidal "ethnic cleansing" that was initiated by the Serbs and imitated later by other national groups.

From the beginning, the Bosnian Muslims were severely pressed by their adversaries and were nearly defeated as town after town fell to the Serbs. Overt international arms shipments were prohibited, although some Islamic countries did provide covert support. Into this mix came Muslim volunteers who fought as *mujahideen* on behalf of the Bosnians. Most were Middle Eastern Afghan Arabs. An estimated 500 to 1,000 *mujahideen* fought alongside the Bosnians, coming from nearly a dozen countries. Many came from Afghanistan, Algeria, Egypt, Tunisia, and Yemen. Although the international *mujahideen* were motivated by religious zeal, the Bosnians are traditionally secular Muslims, so that they were motivated by nationalist fervor.[18] This was a cause for some friction, but a handful of Bosnians also took an oath to become *mujahideen*.

After the war, *mujahideen* maintained a presence in Bosnia, as did Al-Qa'ida. Some were active in hatching plots to attack U.S. and Western interests, including one conspiracy to attack Eagle Base, the main facility for 3,000 American peacekeeping troops who were stationed in the country.[19] Evidence suggests that Bosnia and neighboring regions developed a fairly well-entrenched *mujahideen* and Al-Qa'ida presence. The following are examples of this presence:

- After the Bosnian war, at least 200 *mujahideen* remained in Bosnia, some working for relief agencies or other social services.
- In 1998, Talaat Fouad Qassem, a member of Egypt's Islamic Group, was seized in Croatia and flown to Egypt. He had been traveling to Bosnia from Denmark.[20]
- In October 2001, 10 suspected *mujahideen* terrorists were arrested in Bosnia; at least five of them were Algerians.[21]
- In January 2002, five Algerians and a Yemeni were seized by U.S. forces in Bosnia and flown to the U.S. detention camp at Guantánamo Bay, Cuba.[22]

[18]Bruce, James. "Arab Veterans of the Afghan War." *Jane's Intelligence Review,* April 1, 1995, pp. 175ff.

[19]Purvis, Andrew. "The Suspects: A Bosnian Subplot." *Time,* November 12, 2001.

[20]Chandrasekaran, Rajiv, and Peter Finn. "U.S. Behind Secret Transfer of Terror Suspects." *Washington Post,* March 11, 2002.

[21]Ibid.

[22]Ibid.

# Organization Case: Al-Qa'ida and International Terrorism

Al-Qa'ida is a loose network of Islamic revolutionaries that has shown remarkable resilience despite setbacks such as the 2011 death of Osama bin Laden. It is unique compared with other movements because it

- holds no territory,
- does not champion the aspirations of an ethnonational group,
- has no "top-down" organizational structure,
- has virtually nonexistent state sponsorship, and
- promulgates political demands that are vague at best.

Al-Qa'ida is a transnational movement with members and supporters throughout the Muslim world. It is, at its very core, an international revolutionary movement that uses terrorism as a matter of routine. Al-Qa'ida has two overarching goals: to link together Muslim extremist groups throughout the world into a loose pan-Islamic revolutionary network and to expel non-Muslim (especially Western) influences from Islamic regions and countries. Osama bin Laden established training camps in Sudan and Afghanistan, where an estimated 5,000 men received direct training. Other Al-Qa'ida operatives are drawn from a pool of new recruits from Muslim and European countries and the Afghan Arab veterans who fought in Afghanistan. For example, many young North African Islamists were recruited to fight in Iraq and Syria, or eventually carried out terrorist attacks in their home countries.[23] Furthermore, the rise of Al-Qa'ida–inspired movements in Africa and the Arabian Peninsula has inducted a fresh generation of followers who continue to broaden the international scope of the Al-Qa'ida model.

### International Cells

Operatives who were trained or inspired by Al-Qa'ida established cells in dozens of countries and regions. For instance, cells and larger groups became resident in the following predominantly Muslim countries and regions: Afghanistan, Algeria, Bosnia, Chechnya, Indonesia, Iraq, Kosovo, Lebanon, Malaysia, Pakistan, the southern Philippines, Somalia, Sudan, the West Bank, and Yemen. Other cells were covertly positioned in the following Western and non-Muslim countries: Britain, France, Germany, Israel, Spain, the United States, and the border region of Argentina, Brazil, and Paraguay.

Members communicate with one another using modern technologies such as faxes, the Internet, cell phones, and e-mail. Most Al-Qa'ida cells are small and self-sustaining and apparently receive funding when activated for specific missions. For example, the bombings of the American embassies in Kenya and Tanzania may have cost $100,000.[24] Not all cells are **sleeper cells**, defined as groups of terrorists who take up long-term residence in countries prior to attacks. For example, most of the September 11, 2001, hijackers entered the United States for the express purpose of committing terrorist acts; they were never pre-positioned as sleepers to be activated at a later date.

Al-Qa'ida has been rather prolific in its direct and indirect involvement in international terrorism. Its operatives or sympathizers have been implicated in numerous terrorist incidents, including the following plots:

- 1994: A Filipino airliner was bombed.
- 1994–1995: Filipino security thwarted an ambitious plot that included bombing airliners and assassinations of U.S. President Bill Clinton and Pope John Paul II during state visits.

---

[23]Whitlock, Craig. "Terrorist Networks Lure Young Moroccans to War in Far-Off Iraq." *Washington Post,* February 20, 2007; Whitlock, Craig. "From Iraq to Algeria, Al-Qaeda's Long Reach." *Washington Post,* May 30, 2007.

[24]McNeil, Donald G. "What Will Rise if bin Laden Falls?" *New York Times,* December 2, 2001.

- 1995: An assassination attempt was made against Egyptian President Hosni Mubarak during a state visit to Ethiopia.

- 1995: A car bomb was detonated in Saudi Arabia at a Saudi National Guard facility.

- 2002: An attempted bombing of a Paris-to-Miami airline flight was thwarted; the plan was to ignite explosives hidden inside a shoe.

- 2003: More than 40 people were killed and about 100 were wounded in Casablanca, Morocco, when synchronized bombs—including suicide devices—were detonated.

- 2003: Dozens of people were killed in Riyadh, Saudi Arabia, when bombs exploded at two compounds housing mainly Western workers.

- 2004: In Madrid, Spain, 191 people were killed and hundreds were wounded when 10 synchronized bombs were detonated aboard several commuter trains.

- 2005: Four bombs exploded in London, three simultaneously aboard London Underground trains and one aboard a bus. The attacks, carried out by suicide bombers, killed more than 50 people and injured more than 700. A second, virtually identical, attack was attempted mere days later, but four bombs failed to detonate, and a fifth bomb was abandoned in a London park.

- 2005: Bombs were detonated in an area frequented by tourists in Bali, Indonesia.

- 2008: The Marriott hotel in Islamabad, Pakistan, was bombed by a truck bomb, killing more than 50 people and injuring hundreds.

- 2009: Seven Central Intelligence Agency operatives were killed at Camp Chapman, Afghanistan, in a suicide bombing by a Jordanian man whom the CIA believed would work for them to infiltrate Al-Qa'ida.

- 2013: Approximately 800 people at a gas facility in Algeria were taken hostage. During the ensuing crisis, nearly 40 foreign hostages were killed.

The group was also implicated in the following attacks against American interests:

- 1993: Bombing of the World Trade Center in New York City
- 1998: Bombings of two American embassies in East Africa
- 2000: Attack on the destroyer **USS Cole** in Aden, Yemen (discussed further in Chapter 10)
- 2001: Attacks on the World Trade Center in New York City and the Pentagon in Arlington, Virginia

The following cases of international Al-Qa'ida terrorist activity illustrate the scope, skill, and operational design of the network.

### The Hijacking of Air France Flight 8969

In December 1994, **Air France Flight 8969** was hijacked in Algeria by an Algerian Islamic extremist movement, the Armed Islamic Group (GIA). The GIA apparently has ties to Al-Qa'ida, and many members of its movement are Afghan Arab war veterans. After hijackers killed three passengers, the plane was permitted to depart the Algerian airfield and made a refueling stop in Marseilles. Intending to fly to Paris, the hijackers demanded three times the amount of fuel needed to make the journey. The reason for this order was that they planned to blow up the aircraft over Paris—or possibly crash it into the Eiffel Tower—thus killing themselves and all

❖ **Photo 8.4**
Air France Flight 8969 after the rescue of hostages by French GIGN *gendarme* commandos.

George Gobet/AFP/Getty Images

of the passengers as well as raining flaming debris over the city. French GIGN *gendarme* police commandos disguised as caterers stormed the plane in Marseilles, thus bringing the incident to an end. The assault was broadcast live on French television.

### The Singapore Plot

During December 2001 and January 2002, security officers in Singapore, Malaysia, and the Philippines arrested more than three dozen terrorist suspects. Thirteen were arrested in Singapore, 22 in Malaysia, and 4 in the Philippines. The sweep apparently foiled a significant plot by Al-Qa'ida to attack Western diplomatic missions and personnel in Singapore. The arrests were made after Northern Alliance forces in Afghanistan captured a Singaporean of Pakistani descent who was fighting for the Taliban. The prisoner gave details about "plans to bomb U.S. warships, airplanes, military personnel and major U.S. companies in Singapore [as well as] American, Israeli, British and Australian companies and government offices there."[25]

Members of the Singaporean cell had been trained by Al-Qa'ida in Afghanistan, and Al-Qa'ida operatives had traveled to Singapore to advise some of the suspects about bomb construction and other operational matters. During their preparations for the strike, the cell had sought to purchase 21 tons of ammonium nitrate—by comparison, Timothy McVeigh's ANFO (ammonium nitrate and fuel oil) truck bomb had used only 2 tons of ammonium nitrate, enough to virtually demolish the Alfred P. Murrah Federal Building in Oklahoma City during his attack in 1995. The Singaporean cell organized itself as the Islamic Group (Jemaah Islamiah). The Malaysian cell called itself the Kumpulan Militan Malaysia. In an interesting twist, the Malaysian group apparently had indirect ties to the October 2000 bombing of the *USS Cole* in Yemen; the September 11, 2001, attacks in the United States; and perhaps to Zacarias Moussaoui, the French Moroccan implicated as affiliated with the September 11 terrorists.[26]

### Northwest Airlines Flight 253 in Detroit

On December 25, 2009, Nigerian national Umar Farouk Abdulmutallab ignited explosive chemicals aboard Northwest Airlines Flight 253 with approximately 290 people aboard as it approached Detroit, Michigan, in the United States. According to a federal criminal complaint and FBI affidavit, Abdulmutallab attempted to detonate an improvised explosive containing PETN (pentaerythritol tetranitrate), which had been attached to his leg. He used a syringe to detonate the PETN, but fortunately the device merely caught fire and did not fully detonate. Passengers reported that immediately prior to the incident, Abdulmutallab had been in the restroom for approximately 20 minutes. He pulled a blanket over himself, and passengers heard cracking sounds comparable to firecrackers, sensed an odor, and observed Abdulmutallab's pants leg and the airplane wall on fire. Abdulmutallab was subdued by passengers and members of the crew, who also extinguished the fire. He was calm throughout the incident, and replied "explosive device" when asked by a flight attendant what he had in his pocket.

Abdulmutallab had recently associated with religious militants in Yemen and had visited there from August to December 2009. He said to officials that he had been trained in Yemen to make explosives; he also claimed that Yemenis had given him the chemicals used on Flight 253. His name had been listed in a U.S. terrorism database during November 2009 after his father reported to the U.S. embassy in Nigeria that his son had been radicalized and was associating with religious extremists. However, Abdulmutallab was not placed on an airlines watch list for flights entering the United States because American authorities concluded they had insufficient information to do so. In fact, Abdulmutallab possessed a 2-year tourist visa, which he received from the U.S. embassy in London in June 2008, and he had traveled to the United States on at least two occasions. In October 2011, Abdulmutallab pleaded guilty to eight counts of terrorism-related criminal charges.

---

[25]From Paddock, Richard C., and Bob Drogin. "A Terror Network Unraveled in Singapore." *Los Angeles Times,* January 20, 2002. Quoted with permission.

[26]Ibid.

Chapter Perspective 8.3 explores the bona fide threat from terrorist organizations that have been inspired by the Al-Qa'ida model.

## CHAPTER PERSPECTIVE 8.3: Beyond Al-Qa'ida

It is well known that the idea of Al-Qa'ida was born in the crucible of the anti-Soviet *jihad* in Afghanistan. International fighters were brought together under the banner of *jihadi* solidarity, and those who passed through the Al-Qa'ida network became imbued with a global and extreme belief system.

Because Al-Qa'ida's belief system is grounded in fundamentalist religious faith, the organization evolved into an ideology and an exemplar for other radical Islamists.[a] In a sense, Al-Qa'ida "franchised" its methods, organizational model, and international-ist ideology.[b] As the original leadership and Afghan Arabs were killed, captured, or otherwise neutralized, new personnel stepped to the fore, many of whom had minimal contacts with the original Al-Qa'ida network. New Islamist terrorist movements inspired by Al-Qa'ida's ideology and reputation were formed, and new extremists thus became affiliated with Al-Qa'ida by virtue of their replication of the Al-Qa'ida model.

Although Al-Qa'ida remains actively engaged in its war against Western influence and perceived Muslim apostasies, its role has in part become that of an instigator and mentor. For example, the Islamists who joined the anticoalition resistance in Iraq became an Al-Qa'ida–affiliated presence. Jordanian-born Abu Musab al-Zarqawi was an important symbol of Islamist resistance in Iraq, and Osama bin Laden communicated with him. Al-Zarqawi and his followers eventually claimed credit for terrorist attacks under the banner of a hitherto unknown group called Al-Qa'ida Organization for Holy War in Iraq. This example is not unique, as evidenced by Al-Qa'ida movements in Yemen, North Africa, Syria, and Nigeria.

In effect, a robust pattern of terrorist behavior arose, involving claims of responsibility for terrorist attacks around the world by Al-Qa'ida–inspired or loosely affiliated groups.[c]

One scenario offered by experts during the height of the U.S.-led wars in Iraq and Afghanistan was that the unanticipated resistance resulted in a new generation of extremists with a similar inter-nationalist mission as the original Afghan Arabs.[d] It is plausible that this occurred, as the global *jihad* evolved beyond the Al-Qa'ida network into a formi-dable web of similar organizations and networks.

### Notes

a. Rotella, Sebastian, and Richard C. Paddock. "Experts See Major Shift in Al Qaeda's Strategy." *Los Angeles Times*, November 19, 2003.

b. Farah, Douglas, and Peter Finn. "Terrorism, Inc." *Washington Post*, November 21, 2003.

c. Meyer, Josh. "Al Qaeda 'Co-Opts' New Affiliates." *Los Angeles Times*, September 16, 2007.

d. Priest, Dana. "Report Says Iraq Is New Terrorist Training Ground." *Washington Post*, January 14, 2005.

## Wartime Case: Terrorist Violence in Iraq

The U.S.-led invasion of Iraq, designated Operation Iraqi Freedom, commenced with an early morn-ing "decapitation" air strike intending to kill Iraqi leaders on March 20, 2003. Ground forces crossed into Iraq from Kuwait on the same day. During the drive toward Baghdad (March 21 to April 5), coali-tion forces encountered some stiff resistance from regular and irregular Iraqi forces, but such opposi-tion was overcome or bypassed. American armored units swept through Baghdad on April 5, British troops overcame resistance in Basra on April 7, and Baghdad fell on April 9. On May 1, the coalition declared that major combat operations had ended.

Unfortunately for the coalition, the security environment and quality of life in Iraq became pro-gressively poorer in the immediate aftermath of the fall of Saddam Hussein's government. Crime became widespread, and basic services such as electricity and water became sporadic. Most ominously, an insurgency took root and increased in intensity.

A classic guerrilla insurgency spread during the first year of the occupation. The insurgents—a collection of pro-Saddam Iraqis, Iraqi nationalists, *jihadis,* and foreign fighters—organized themselves into resistance cells and armed themselves from looted arsenals and smuggled weapons. Iraqi guerrillas received monetary and military assistance from supporters and operated openly in cities such as Fallujah and other locations where coalition forces were weak. Significant numbers of volunteers from Muslim countries and Europe enlisted to fight alongside the Iraqis; many of these volunteers were Islamists motivated by *jihad* in much the same manner as foreign volunteers during the anti-Soviet *jihad* in Afghanistan.

The insurgents engaged in classic guerrilla attacks (some of them professionally and intricately planned) against occupation troops and Iraqi security forces. Roadside bombs, ambushes, harassing mortar fire, and firefights occurred in many areas. Insurgents also used terrorism and assassinations against foreign contract workers and those whom they defined as "collaborators" with the occupation. The latter designation meant that terrorist violence was directed against police officers, Iraqi soldiers, moderate leaders, election workers, and many others.

In addition to the politically motivated insurgency against occupiers and perceived collaborators, a decidedly communal quality of violence also spread. For example, bombs were indiscriminately detonated in Shi'a neighborhoods, mosques were attacked, leaders were assassinated, and dozens of bodies were found in rivers, mass graves, and other locations. These incidents were the results of communal terrorism and tit-for-tat revenge killings.

The insurgency in Iraq had international implications from the outset because the intensity of the resistance was widely admired throughout the Arab world. The insurgency also became a focal point for debate about the prosecution of the war against terrorism. For example, some leaders and supporters of the occupation reasoned that terrorists were being "flushed out" and that it would be better to fight them in Iraq than elsewhere. Other leaders and opponents of the occupation reasoned that Iraq had never posed a direct threat of Al-Qa'ida–style terrorism, that resources were needlessly expended in an unnecessary war, and that a significant number of new extremists became inspired by the Iraqi insurgency.

## ❖  Postscript: The "Stateless Revolutionaries"

Some terrorist movements operate exclusively on an international scale and have little or no domestic presence in a home country. There are different reasons for this strategy: Some groups espouse a global ideological agenda that requires them to fight on behalf of a vague concept of "the oppressed" of the world. Other groups operate within an environment that mandates as a matter of practicality that they operate internationally. They strike from operational havens across state borders and often move around from country to country.

These movements are essentially "stateless" in the sense that they have no particular home country that they seek to liberate, there is no homeland to use as a base, or their group has been uprooted from the land for which they are fighting. Among these stateless extremist movements are secular ideological revolutionaries, sectarian radicals fighting on behalf of a faith, and representatives of stateless ethnonational groups. Examples of **stateless revolutionaries** include the following familiar cases:

### The Japanese Red Army

The Japanese Red Army (JRA) represents an example of a *secular* stateless revolutionary movement. Although the JRA claimed that one of its core goals was to overthrow the Japanese monarchy and end Japanese capitalism, its activity profile suggests that it had a more global outlook. JRA members considered themselves to be international revolutionaries fighting on behalf of the oppressed of the world against international capitalism, imperialism, and Zionism. Operationally, they acted in coordination with other terrorist groups and extremist movements to promote their global revolutionary agenda.

## Al-Qa'ida

The Al-Qa'ida network is an example of a *sectarian* stateless revolutionary movement. Pan-Islamist ideologies began to transcend limitations imposed by national boundaries in the 1980s and 1990s. This new revolutionary consciousness was a direct result of the Iranian Revolution and the *jihad* against the Soviet Union in Afghanistan. The Al-Qa'ida network epitomizes the modern profile of a transnational revolutionary consciousness among Islamist radicals, and serves as an inspirational template for newly emerging movements.

Tom Stoddart/Hulton Archive/Getty Images

❖ **Photo 8.5**

The remains of Pan Am Flight 103 after being bombed in the skies over Lockerbie, Scotland. The attack led to economic sanctions against Libya and the trial of two members of the Libyan security service.

## Palestinian Nationalism

The Palestinian cause prior to the establishment of the governing authority in Gaza and on the West Bank exemplified a stateless ethnonational revolutionary movement. Until their strategy for revolution shifted to an internal *intifada* inside the old borders of Palestine, Palestinian nationalists were forced to operate from bases in third countries. These countries included Jordan, Lebanon, Tunisia, Syria, and Iraq. Acts of terrorism usually occurred in the international arena, originating from the safe havens provided by these sympathetic governments. The movement was essentially stateless until the Palestinian Authority was established, which allowed relatively steady internal operations to be conducted against Israel.

Table 8.4 summarizes the activity profiles of secular, sectarian, and ethnonational "stateless revolutions."

| Table 8.4 | The Stateless Revolutions |
| --- | --- |

Some movements operate almost exclusively in the international arena. The reasons why include ideologies of transnational revolution, global spiritual visions, or simple practicality brought on by their political environment.

The following table describes the activity profiles of three such radical movements.

| Political Orientation | Activity Profile | | | | |
| --- | --- | --- | --- | --- | --- |
| | Group | Constituency | Adversary | Benefactor | Goal |
| **Secular** | Japanese Red Army | Oppressed of the world | Capitalism, imperialism, Zionism | Unclear; probably PFLP, maybe Libya | International revolution |
| **Sectarian** | Al-Qa'ida | Muslims of the world | Foes of Islam | Self-supporting; maybe radical states | International Islamic revolution |
| **Ethnonationalist** | Palestinian nationalists | Palestinians | Israel | Government sponsors | Palestinian nation |

## Chapter Summary

This chapter provided readers with a critical assessment of international terrorism. International terrorism was defined from the point of view of the motives of the perpetrators and the symbolism of their selected targets; terrorists who choose to operate on an international scale select targets that symbolize an international interest. Within the framework of the reasons identified for international terrorism—ideological, practical, tactical, and historical—readers were asked to apply adaptations of revolutionary theory to international operations. Recalling previous discussions about Mao's doctrine for waging guerrilla warfare as "fish swimming in the sea of the people," Fanon's "liberating violence," and Marighella's strategy for destabilizing established governments, it is no surprise that modern terrorists would carry variations of these themes onto the international stage.

International terrorist networks have been a facet of international terrorism since the 1960s. The models presented in this chapter are useful for understanding the networking features of terrorist environments. The cases of Al-Qa'ida and the international *mujahideen* illustrate the nature of modern terrorist networks.

In Chapter 10, readers will be introduced to the tactics and targets of terrorists. The discussion will center on terrorist objectives, methods, and targets. The discussion will also ask whether, and to what extent, terrorism is effective.

## Key Terms and Concepts

The following topics are discussed in this chapter and can be found in the glossary:

Afghan Arabs

Air France Flight 8969

Ansar Allah

Armenian Revolutionary Army

Armenian Secret Army for the Liberation of Armenia (ASALA)

asymmetrical warfare

cell-based terrorist environment

imperialism

international *mujahideen*

Islamic Jihad

Japanese Red Army

Justice Commandos of the Armenian Genocide

monolithic terrorist environment

multinational corporations

neocolonialism

Omega 7

Organization of the Oppressed

Revolutionary Justice Organization

sleeper cells

spillover effect

stateless revolutionaries

strong multipolar terrorist environment

Third World

*USS Cole*

weak multipolar terrorist environment

Zionism

## Discussion Box: Understanding Terrorist "Spillovers"

### Middle Eastern and North African Spillovers in Europe

*This chapter's Discussion Box is intended to stimulate critical debate about whether* spillover incidents are a legitimate expression of grievances.

Terrorist spillovers have occurred regularly since the 1960s. The most common sources of spillovers since that time have been from the Middle East and North Africa, and the most frequent venue for these spillovers has been Western Europe. For example, during the 1980s, hundreds of Middle Eastern and North African terrorist incidents occurred in more than a dozen countries, causing hundreds of deaths and hundreds of people wounded. Outside of the Middle East and North Africa, Europe is the favored theater of operations.

There are several types of Middle Eastern and North African spillovers in Europe: Some result from the foreign policies of governments, others are PLO-affiliated groups, and others are attacks by Islamist revolutionaries.

The motives behind these incidents have included:

- The silencing or intimidating of exiles
- Attempts to influence European policies
- Retaliation against a person or state
- "Solidarity" attacks by indigenous European groups

  Europe has been an attractive target for many reasons, including:
- The presence of large Middle Eastern and North African communities

- Many "soft" targets
- Immediate publicity
- Open borders and good transportation
- Proximity to the Middle East and North Africa

These attacks have been widespread geographically, and many have been indiscriminate.

## Discussion Questions

- Is the international arena a legitimate option for the expression of grievances?

- Is Europe an appropriate venue for conflicts originating in the Middle East or North Africa?

- Are some grievances more legitimate, or more acceptable, for spillovers?

- What is the likely future of spillover attacks in Europe?

- Since Europe has historically been perceived to be an easy battlefield with soft targets, should the European Union "harden" itself?

## On Your Own

The open-access Student Study Site at **http://study.sagepub.com/martin5e** has a variety of useful study aids, including eFlashcards, quizzes, audio resources, and journal articles. The websites, exercises, and recommended readings listed below are easily accessed on this site as well.

## Recommended Websites

The following websites provide links to organizations that report research on or discuss international terrorism and conflict:

Air University Library: http://www.au.af.mil/au/aul/lane.htm/

Homeland Security.com: http://www.homelandsecurity.com/

International Policy Institute for Counter-Terrorism: http://www.ict.org.il/

Naval Postgraduate School Center on Terrorism & Irregular Warfare: http://www.nps.edu/Academics/Centers/CTIW/index.html

South Asia Terrorism Portal: http://www.satp.org/

# Web Exercise

Using this chapter's recommended websites, conduct an online investigation of international terrorism.

1. From your review of these websites, how significant do you think the threat is from international terrorist groups?
2. Which groups do you think pose a serious threat of international terrorism?

Which groups do you think present less serious threats?

3. Critique the websites of the international monitoring organizations. Are some more helpful than others?

For an online search of international terrorism, readers should activate the search engine on their Web browser and enter the following keywords:

"Global Terrorism"

"International Terrorism" (or "International Terrorists")

# Recommended Readings

The following publications provide discussions about the nature of international terrorism and cases in point about international terrorists:

Follain, John. *Jackal: The Complete Story of the Legendary Terrorist, Carlos the Jackal*. New York: Arcade Publishing, 2011.

Gartenstein-Ross, Daveed, and Laura Grossman. *Homegrown Terrorists in the U.S. and U.K.* Washington, DC: FDD Press, 2009.

Gerges, Fawaz A. *The Far Enemy: Why Jihad Went Global*. Cambridge, UK: Cambridge University Press, 2009.

Gunaratna, Rohan. *Inside Al Qaeda: Global Network of Terror*. New York: Columbia University Press, 2002.

Herman, Edward S. *The Real Terror Network: Terrorism in Fact and Propaganda*. Boston: South End Press, 1982.

Kegley, Charles W., Jr., ed. *The New Global Terrorism: Characteristics, Causes, Controls*. New York: Prentice Hall, 2002.

Lutz, James M., and Brenda J. Lutz, eds. *Global Terrorism*. New York: Routledge, 2008.

Perkins, Samuel, ed. *Homegrown Terror and American Jihadists: Assessing the Threat*. Hauppauge, NY: Nova Publishers, 2011.

Pillar, Paul R. *Terrorism and U.S. Foreign Policy*. Washington, DC: Brookings Institution, 2001.

Reeve, Simon. *The New Jackals: Ramzi Yousef, Osama bin Laden, and the Future of Terrorism*. Boston: Northeastern University Press, 1999.

Sageman, Marc. *Leaderless Jihad: Terror Networks in the Twenty-First Century*. Philadelphia: University of Pennsylvania Press, 2008.

Siniver, Asaf, ed. *International Terrorism Post-9/11: Comparative Dynamics and Responses*. London: Routledge, 2010.

## CHAPTER 9

# Emerging Terrorist Environments

## Gender-Selective Political Violence and Criminal Dissident Terrorism

**OPENING VIEWPOINT: THE JANJAWEED CAMPAIGN AGAINST "ENEMY" WOMEN IN DARFUR, SUDAN**

Darfur is a region in western Sudan with a population that is almost entirely Muslim. Although inhabitants are classified as either African or Arab, these distinctions are largely cultural. In practical terms, those classified as Arabs are mostly culturally "Arabized" Africans, and the government of Sudan is dominated by Arabized Sudanese.

In early 2003, two Darfur rebel movements, the Sudanese Liberation Army (SLA) and the Justice and Equality Movement (JEM), attacked government troops stationed in Darfur. Because the government had few soldiers in the region, and because it did not trust those who were there, it organized an alliance of Arab militias known as the **Janjaweed.** The term *Janjaweed* is roughly translated as "men on horses" because the Arabized population are herdsmen and often travel on camels with horses tied behind them. African residents in Darfur tend to be farmers.

From its inception, the war was brutal. With government arms and air support, the Janjaweed embarked on a policy of de facto ethnic cleansing and methodically burned African villages, killed many inhabitants, and drove others off the land.[a] About 2 million Africans were forced from the land, many taking refuge in neighboring Chad. Although both the Janjaweed and their adversaries are Muslims, Janjaweed fighters burned mosques. More than 50,000 people died.

As has occurred in many communal conflicts elsewhere, African women and girls were systematically sexually assaulted by Janjaweed fighters. One purpose of the assaults was to debase the culture of African Muslims by "defiling" their women. Another, more genocidal, purpose was to impregnate the women and thereby create "light" babies, which under local tradition would take on the ethnicity of their fathers.[b]

Governments and human rights agencies declared the Janjaweed campaign of systematic rape to be a conscious policy of using sexual assault as a weapon of war.[c]

### Notes

a. For a discussion of genocide in Darfur, see DeWine, Mike, and John McCain. "It's Happening Again." *Washington Post*, June 23, 2004.

b. Wax, Emily. "'We Want to Make a Light Baby.'" *Washington Post*, June 30, 2004.

c. See Amnesty International. *Darfur: Rape as a Weapon of War: Sexual Violence and Its Consequences.* London: Amnesty International, July 19, 2004.

This chapter is "cutting-edge" in the sense that it discusses the global community's growing recognition of two emerging terrorist environments: gender-selective political violence and criminal dissident terrorism. Until recently, neither environment received consistent recognition as discernible terrorist environments. However, it may be argued that both environments have identifiable characteristics that pose serious challenges to domestic populations, governments, and the international community. In the case of gender-selective terrorist violence, such behavior was historically subsumed under other events, such as war and rebellion. In the case of criminal dissident terrorism, powerful criminal enterprises rarely engaged in the same quality of violence as began during the late 20th century.

The following attributes characterize the basic qualities of political violence against genders and dissident terrorists who are affiliated with criminal enterprises:

*Gender-selective political violence* refers to systematic violence directed against men and women that specifically targets them because of their gender. It can occur in a variety of environments, usually as the result of political conflict (including genocide), an enemy male population's perceived status as potential fighters, or perceived deviations from a female population's "proper place" within traditional cultures and belief systems. For example, gender-selective violence against women can be cultural in nature, reflecting violent reactions by mainstream groups (familial or social) against women who violate norms for women's conformity in society (usually as a lower status). Or violence can occur when dissident movements (such as ethnonationalist militias) specifically target the women of an enemy group as a method to terrorize them or destroy the group's cultural identity. Governments may also violently repress identifiably unacceptable behaviors among women.

**Criminal dissident terrorism** is motivated by sheer profit. This profit can be invested differently, depending on the goals of the criminal enterprise. **Traditional criminal enterprises** (such as Mexican drug cartels and the Italian Mafia) accumulate profits from criminal activity for personal pleasure and aggrandizement; they use violence so that the government will leave them

❖ **Photo 9.1**

War in Colombia. A Colombian policeman takes a break after an attack in Granada, Colombia.

© Reuters/Corbis

| Table 9.1 | Characteristics of Gender-Focused and Criminal Dissident Terrorism |
|---|---|

The actions of gender-motivated and criminal dissident terrorists can be contrasted in several ways, as can the actions of traditional criminal enterprises and criminal-political enterprises. When the decision has been made by these extremists to engage in terrorism, their activity profiles become very distinguishable.

The following table illustrates differences between these environments in their motives, goals, targets, personnel, and degrees of political agitation.

| Environment | Activity Profile | | | | |
|---|---|---|---|---|---|
| | *Motives* | *Goals* | *Targets* | *Personnel* | *Political Agitation* |
| **Gender-focused terrorism** | Cultural or political | Repression or cultural destruction | Enemy men and women or nonconformist women | Soldiers or militias or civilians | Active and public |
| **Traditional criminal enterprises** | Financial | Passive government | Active governments | Criminals | Reactive and anonymous |
| **Criminal-political enterprises** | Political | Revolutionary victory | Agents and symbols of oppression | Dissident activists | Active and public |

alone. In contrast, **criminal-political enterprises**, such as Sri Lanka's Tamil Tigers and Colombia's Revolutionary Armed Forces of Colombia (FARC), accumulate profits from criminal activity to sustain their movement; they use violence to advance their political agendas.

Table 9.1 presents a model that compares the fundamental characteristics of gender-selective terrorism and criminal dissident terrorism. The discussion in this chapter will review the following:

- Culture and Conflict: Gender-Selected Victims of Terrorist Violence
- Protecting the Enterprise: Criminal Dissident Terrorism
- A Global Problem: Regional Cases of Criminal Dissident Terrorism

# ❖ Culture and Conflict: Gender-Selected Victims of Terrorist Violence

Gender-selective political violence is the discriminate use of force purposely directed against males or females of a particular group. It is often the product of communal discord, and it can become genocidal in scope. Thus, the degree of violence can range from violence committed by marauding guerrillas or armies to systematic abuse and killings as a matter of policy.

Historically, males and females have been specially selected for violent treatment because of their gender. Men and boys have been massacred en masse, women and girls have been the victims of mass rape, and both genders have suffered under the threat of gender-associated violence during times of war and hostile occupation. These behaviors were traditionally considered to be the unfortunate consequences of war. Recently, however, the United Nations and human rights agencies such as Amnesty International and Human Rights Watch have construed systematic gender-selective violence as more than an unfortunate outcome. As discussed in the following sections, such violence has been redesignated as fundamentally genocidal and terrorist. In essence, gender-selective violence is a specific subset of horrific treatment that should be identified and considered. Common rationales for subjecting men and boys to gender-selective political violence include the following:

- Eliminate potential enemy fighters or soldiers
- Massacre existing fighters or soldiers who have been captured
- Destroy a patriarchal culture

Common rationales for subjecting women and girls to gender-selective political violence include the following:

- Broad cultural repression of women and girls to force them to submit to their traditional roles
- Take enemy females as "spoils" of war
- Symbolically destroy the "cultural chastity" of an enemy group through mass rape

## Gender-Selective Terrorism Against Men

During the 20th century, males were selectively targeted during periods of conflict and unrest. They were typically selected as a way to eliminate potential fighters or during violent communal campaigns against enemy groups. Historical examples of gender-selective political violence against males include the following incidents:

- During the 1915 to 1917 Armenian Genocide, the Ottoman Empire exterminated most of the male Armenian population.
- During the 1941 to 1945 German war against the Soviet Union (Operation Barbarossa), an estimated 2.8 million Soviet prisoners of war died.
- During the 1988 Anfal Campaign, the Iraqi army killed thousands of military-age Kurdish males.

- During the 1994 Rwandan Genocide, Hutu militias killed many thousands of Tutsi and moderate Hutu males.

### Case in Point: Ethnic Cleansing and Males in Bosnia-Herzegovina

The civil wars in the former Yugoslavia during the 1990s periodically descended into a three-way conflict between Croats, Bosnians, and Serbs. During the 1992 to 1995 war in Bosnia-Herzegovina, about 200,000 Bosnian Muslims died, and more than 2 million were forced from their homes as a result of fighting and ethnic cleansing sweeps. Although ethnic cleansing in Bosnia-Herzegovina began during the initial phase of Serb aggression, and Serbs were responsible for most "cleansing" campaigns, all three sides practiced it to some degree. Paramilitaries were particularly responsible for some of the most infamous incidents of the war. These paramilitaries included the Serb White Eagles, the Bosnian Muslim Patriotic League, and the Croat Defense Forces.

During the early phases of the conflict, regular Yugoslav (in effect, Serb) troops and Bosnian Serb militias rounded up Croat and Bosnian Muslim men for deportation to detention camps. For the first time since World War II, images were broadcast of gaunt men who had been detained in detention camps. Within these camps, murder and torture were common. Many other cases exist of killings of males by Bosnian Serb forces during ethnic cleansing sweeps against Bosnian Muslim municipalities.

❖ **Photo 9.2**

Forensic experts uncover the remains of victims of the 1995 Srebrenica massacre. The bodies had been transferred from an original burial site in an attempt to hide evidence from war crimes investigators.

© Reuters/Corbis

One case of gender-selective political violence against males in Bosnia-Herzegovina occurred in July 1995, when more than 7,000 Bosnian Muslim men and boys were rounded up and killed by Bosnian Serb security forces. The massacre occurred in the aftermath of the collapse of Muslim defenses inside the besieged United Nations (UN)–protected "safe area" of Srebrenica, Bosnia-Herzegovina. The battle took place during a prolonged genocidal drive by Bosnian Serbs to create an "ethnically pure" Serb state within Bosnia, and the subsequent massacre was the worst mass killing in Europe since the end of World War II.

The selective killings of Bosnian males and many of the atrocities in the camps were prosecuted by the **International Criminal Tribunal for the Former Yugoslavia (ICTY)** as genocide and crimes against humanity.[1]

## Background to Terrorism Against Women: Cultural Repression and Violence

Although extremism is often a precursor to terrorism, not all extremism leads to terrorist violence. The same is true when evaluating the precursors to political violence against women.

For readers to critically assess the nature of terrorist violence directed against women, it is important to understand that, in many societies, rigorous cultural restrictions exist that relegate women and girls to second-class status. These cultural restrictions may regulate the behavior and dress of females, their independence from men, their access to basic services, the quality of their education, and their employment opportunities. Within some ethnonational and religious cultures, traditional customs coercively (on occasion violently) impose significant restrictions on the ability of women and girls to be coequal members of society with men and boys. Many of these restrictions are quite repressive and can be forcefully imposed in the extreme. Gender-related restrictions may be officially enforced by law, and they may also be unofficially enforced in compliance with tribal, clan, or family customs.

Two modern cases in point—Saudi Arabia and Taliban Afghanistan—will facilitate readers' critical assessment of gender-specific cultural restrictions. In the case of Saudi Arabia, gender segregation and

---

[1]See *Prosecutor of the Tribunal v. Radovan Karadzic*, Ratko Mladic, IT-95-5-I, July 24, 1995; see also *Prosecutor of the Tribunal v. Radovan Karadzic*, amended indictment, May 31, 2000.

male-centered authority are imposed by law and custom. In the case of Taliban Afghanistan, gender segregation and male-centered authority were imposed with revolutionary fervor. In both cases, fundamentalist interpretations of religion form the underlying justification for gender-specific laws and customs.

### Case in Point: The Status of Women in Saudi Arabia

Since the founding of the Kingdom of Saudi Arabia by the al-Saud dynasty in 1932, Saudi society and government have been predicated on the strict implementation of the Wahhabi[2] interpretation of Islam and Islamic law. In accordance with this theocratic ideology, gender segregation is officially enforced throughout Saudi society. Women live restrictive lives and cannot drive motorized vehicles, attend the cinema, or observe sport events. These restrictions are rigorously enforced under law. Also in Saudi Arabia:[3]

- Women cannot vote.
- A woman must obtain permission to travel abroad in writing from a significant male, such as her father or husband. Authorities may require that the significant male travel with her.
- By custom, women should not walk in public unless accompanied by a male relative. Should they do so, it is presumed that such women are immoral. The same is true if women are found alone with an unrelated man.[4]
- By custom and law, women must comply with mandated codes of dress.[5]

Religious doctrines are enforced by a religious police force known as the Authority for the Promotion of Virtue and Prevention of Vice, or the **Mutaween**. In 2002, the *Mutaween* were the focus of a public outcry (including government censure) when 15 girls died in a fire because they tried to escape the blaze without proper head coverings. Officers from the *Mutaween* had forced them to remain inside the burning building.

### Case in Point: Cultural Repression Under the Taliban in Afghanistan[6]

Afghanistan has undergone several regime changes in recent history, almost all of them through force of arms. The Soviet intervention in Afghanistan (1978 to 1992) fomented an insurgency that became a *jihad* against the occupation. After the Soviets withdrew, internecine fighting among the *mujahideen* became stalemated between several warlord-led factions. One faction of strict Islamists, the Taliban, gained superiority over the other factions, and it controlled about 90% of the country from 1998 until the U.S.-led invasion in late 2001. The Taliban applied its own interpretation of Islamic law, which in regard to women mandated the following practices:

- Women were required to wear the *burka,* which completely covered their bodies from head to toe.
- Women were forbidden to work outside the home, except to provide health care to other women.

---

[2]Faithful Wahhabis ban photographs, video, singing, musical instruments, and celebrating the birthday of the prophet Muhammed.

[3]For a discussion of women's rights in the Middle East, see Esfandiari, Haleh. "The Woman Question." *Wilson Quarterly* (Spring 2004): 56–63; see also Inglehart, Ronald, and Pippa Norris. "The True Clash of Civilizations." *Foreign Policy* (March/April 2003): 63–70.

[4]In December 2007, King Abdullah of Saudi Arabia pardoned a rape victim who had been sentenced to 200 lashes. She had been punished because the seven rapists had assaulted her as she was sitting with her boyfriend; it is illegal in Saudi Arabia for an unmarried woman to be alone with a male who is not a relative. Zoepf, Katherine. "Pardon Reported for Saudi Rape Victim." *New York Times,* December 18, 2007.

[5]For further information from a human rights perspective, see Amnesty International. "Saudi Arabia: Gross Human Rights Abuses Against Women." September 27, 2000; see also Amnesty International. "Saudi Arabia: Time Is Long Overdue to Address Women's Rights." September 27, 2000.

[6]For a good historical and cultural discussion of the Taliban, see Rashid, Ahmed. *Taliban: Militant Islam, Oil, and Fundamentalism in Central Asia.* 2nd ed. New Haven, CT: Yale University Press, 2010.

- Women were not permitted to be educated.
- Houses with women living inside were required to have windows facing the street covered with black paint so that the women would not be seen.
- Photographs and images of women could not be pictured or framed. For example, images of women in photo frames or on television were forbidden.
- Women's shoes could not make noise.
- Women could not appear at tourist areas or picnics.

### Other Cases: Violent Cultural Repression of Women

In the modern era, there exists an array of cultural sanctions—many of them unofficially enforced—directed against women who violate established cultural norms. Historically, these sanctions have varied in degree of severity and include ostracism from the group, public shaming, physical assaults, corporal punishment, maiming, and execution. Such punishments are rationalized as necessary to preserve indispensable values that guard the culture from undesirable change and an erosion of fundamental beliefs. For example, so-called **honor killings** occur with some frequency around the world, and they involve murders of women and girls who are perceived to have dishonored their family, clan, or tribe by their behavior. Members of the victim's family, clan, or tribe mete out such killings.[7]

Violent enforcement of traditional customs occurs in many cultures, so that honor killings and other violence against women and girls remain acceptable practices in some societies. For example, culturally accepted violence against women and girls occurs under the following circumstances:

- In China and India, female infanticide continues to be practiced in some areas. The rationale is that boys are more desirable than girls.
- In some tradition-bound areas of the Muslim world, girls who have been sexually assaulted may be forced to marry their assailant to preserve the honor of her family.[8]
- In some traditional southern African societies, new widows are expected to submit to "cleansing" sexual relations with a relative of her deceased husband as a way to exorcise her husband's spirit and thus save her and her village from mental and physical disease.[9]
- In some countries, mainly in traditional Middle Eastern and African societies, girls are subjected to ritualized genital mutilation (usually clitorectomies) prior to reaching puberty.[10] Amnesty International reports that approximately 135 million women have undergone the procedure, at a rate of perhaps 6,000 per day. The procedure is commonly referred to as **female genital mutilation (FGM)**, female genital cutting, or female circumcision.[11] In some nations the rate of FGM is extremely high—in Egypt, an estimated 90% of women have undergone FGM.

## An Emerging Recognition: Terrorism Against Women

### State Terrorism Against Women

State terrorism is characterized by official government support for policies of violence, repression, and intimidation. Although soldiers or other government security personnel may participate in terrorist violence, surrogates of the state may also be supplied, supported, or otherwise encouraged

---

[7]See, e.g., Fleishman, Jeffrey. "'Honor Killings' Show Culture Clash in Berlin." *Los Angeles Times,* March 20, 2005.

[8]See, e.g., Zaman, Amberin. "Where Girls Marry Rapists for Honor." *Los Angeles Times,* May 24, 2005.

[9]LaFraniere, Sharon. "AIDS Now Compels Africa to Challenge Widows' 'Cleansing.' " *New York Times,* May 11, 2005.

[10]See, e.g., Hecht, David. "African Women Standing Up to Ancient Custom." *Christian Science Monitor,* June 3, 1998.

[11]See Amnesty International. "Fight Against Female Genital Mutilation Wins UN Backing." http://www.amnesty.org/en/for-media/press-releases/fight-against-female-genital-mutilation-wins-un-backing-2012-11-26/ (accessed July 13, 2014).

to engage in terrorism. In effect, governments either directly engage in terrorism or unleash violent proxies to do so.

Most state-mandated terrorism against women is conducted by the armed forces of the state or state-supported proxies such as paramilitaries. Underlying reasons given for such violence include cowing an enemy into submission or the genocidal destruction of a culture. Such violence often accompanies a warlike political environment. Historically, state-mandated violence against women usually has arisen in two circumstances:

- At campaigns of conquest during wartime
- When there exists an overriding threat to the authority of the state from an indigenous ethnonational or religious group—in essence, when a potential uprising or other resistance is sensed

As with any case of state terrorism, the potential magnitude of state-mandated violence against women can be quite extreme. The following discussion explores two examples of large-scale terrorist violence against women (and men) by regular soldiers during wartime.

***War of Conquest in East Asia: The "Rape of Nanking."***[12] The practice of committing sexual violence against enemy females as a mode of warfare is very ancient. Such violence can occur on a massive scale over a period of time. Throughout the history of warfare, up to the present day, many armies have used rape to brutalize defeated enemies. For example, during World War II in China, the Japanese army seized the Chinese capital city of Nanking (modern-day Nanjing) after heavy fighting in October to December 1937. What followed was an intensive campaign of brutalization by the Japanese occupiers, which became known as the **Rape of Nanking**.

Throughout a 6-week campaign, between 200,000 and 300,000 Chinese were killed, many thousands of whom were bayoneted, beheaded, or tortured. Captured Chinese soldiers and military-aged males were used for bayonet practice (see Photo 3.4 in Chapter 3) or were beheaded with Samurai swords in accordance with the code of Bushido. An estimated 20,000 to 80,000 Chinese women and girls were raped by Japanese soldiers, and thousands of women and girls either were forced into sexual slavery as **"comfort women"** or were made to perform in perverse sex shows and pose for pornographic photographs as entertainment for Japanese troops. A large number of Chinese women and girls were killed by the Japanese. In the postwar era, Japanese political leaders have repeatedly denied that the Rape of Nanking occurred, or the existence of "comfort women," during the war.[13]

***Suppressing Independence in South Asia: The Bangladesh Liberation War.***[14] The war for Bangladesh's independence was fought from March to December 1971. It began as an attempt by Pakistan to suppress an independence movement in what was then a territory known as East Pakistan. The war is an example of a national policy of political suppression that included widespread violence against an indigenous female population.

In 1971, approximately 25 years after the partition of the Indian subcontinent into the nations and territories of India, West Pakistan, and East Pakistan (now Bangladesh), extensive fighting broke out in East Pakistan when the Pakistani army was sent in to quell an independence movement. The invasion and suppression campaign were conducted with strong elements of religious and ethnonationalist vehemence. Although about 85% of the residents of East Pakistan were Muslims, they were more secular than the West Pakistanis, and most residents were ethnically related to the Bengalis of India. During the 9-month war, Pakistani forces systematically raped or killed hundreds of thousands of Bengali women and girls and executed males of military age. Perhaps 3 million Bengalis died, and the fighting did not end until the Indian army intervened on behalf of Bangladesh.

---

[12]For a groundbreaking discussion of the Rape of Nanking, see Chang, Iris. *The Rape of Nanking: The Forgotten Holocaust of World War II*. New York: Basic Books, 1997.

[13]See Wallace, Bruce. "Japan's Abe Sticks to Comments on 'Comfort Women.'" *Los Angeles Times*, March 18, 2007.

[14]For an eyewitness account of the war in Bangladesh, see Imam, Jahanara. *Of Blood and Fire: The Untold Story of Bangladesh's War of Independence*. New Delhi, India: Sterling, 1989.

### Dissident Terrorism Against Women

Most dissident terrorism against women is conducted by bands of insurgents or paramilitaries. Underlying reasons given for such violence include ethnic cleansing campaigns to remove an enemy group from a desired region or attacking enemy women as symbols of a cultural identity. Such violence often occurs when central government authority is weak or when an insurgency is especially active. For example, in April 2014 Boko Haram insurgents in northeastern Nigeria kidnapped nearly 300 mostly Christian schoolgirls, avowedly as war booty to be held as slaves and wives. The Nigerian military apparently received 4 hours' warning prior to the incursion, but was unable to mobilize troops to prevent the kidnappings.

Dissident violence against women often occurs under circumstances that cause such gender-selective violence to be obscured by other circumstances. Many terrorist environments are communal in nature, so that entire ethnonational, ideological, or religious groups become participants (and victims) in bloodshed against rival groups. Within these environments, reports of communal violence against women are sometimes overshadowed by reporting on other aspects of the conflict.

The following discussion explores two examples of dissident terrorist violence against women by irregular militias during periods of communal warfare.

***Ethnic Cleansing and Violence Against Women in Bosnia-Herzegovina.*** Ethnic cleansing sweeps in Bosnia-Herzegovina could be quite violent, and many civilians were killed. During the communal campaign against enemy civilians, paramilitaries and regular forces in Bosnia-Herzegovina specifically targeted the female population, and an estimated 20,000 women and girls were systematically raped during the war, most of them Bosnian Muslims. Investigations identified a particularly notorious practice among Serb paramilitaries of abducting women and imprisoning them in militia bases and "rape camps" and "rape hotels," where they were repeatedly assaulted over long periods of time. Because of the magnitude and official planning of these assaults, in 2001, the International Criminal Tribunal for the Former Yugoslavia formally held that systematic rape is genocide and can be prosecuted as a war crime. This decision was the first formal and official legal pronouncement on this issue by an international body.[15]

❖ **Photo 9.3**

A mother and child lie dead after a "cleansing" sweep by paramilitaries in Bosnia.

U.S. Department of State

***Anarchy in Sierra Leone.***[16] The West African nation of Sierra Leone was founded as a British Crown Colony for freed slaves in 1808. A republic was established after independence in 1961, but the country descended into a brutal civil war in 1991. In 1991, the **Revolutionary United Front (RUF)**, led by Foday Sankoh, rebelled against the government. A rival rebel force, the **Armed Forces Revolutionary Council (AFRC)**, is typical of several other rebel movements that were organized, thus creating an increasingly anarchic environment.[17] Widespread human rights abuses of civilians occurred as government forces either resisted or allied themselves with rebel factions during several phases of the war. These phases were anarchic and included the following events:

---

[15]*Prosecutor v. Dragoljub Kunarac, Radomir Kovac, and Zoran Vukovic,* International Prosecution for Persons Responsible for Serious Violations of International Humanitarian Law Committed in the Territory of the Former Yugoslavia Since 1991. Case No. IT-96–23-T & IT-96–23/1-T, February 22, 2001.

[16]For a good summary of the conflict in Sierra Leone and eyewitness accounts, see Human Rights Watch. *Sierra Leone: Getting Away With Murder, Mutilation, Rape.* New York: Human Rights Watch, July 1999.

[17]Other rebel movements included the National Patriotic Front for Liberia, United Liberation Movement of Liberia for Democracy, and the West Side Boys.

- A military coup in May 1997
- Intervention by a West African multinational armed force known as the ECOWAS[18] Cease Fire Observer Group (ECOMOG)
- Reinstatement of civilian government
- A peace agreement
- Collapse of the peace agreement
- Intervention by troops under the direction of the United Nations Mission in Sierra Leone (UNAMISIL)
- Shifting alliances between government and rebel forces

The war caused at least 50,000 deaths and displaced more than 2 million people (out of a population of about 5.5 million).[19] In the countryside, rebels systematically abused civilians in horrific ways, including a notorious policy of chopping off hands, arms, and legs. Thousands of children were kidnapped, as were thousands of women and girls. Females who were abducted were systematically gang-raped or forced into sexual bondage, and many were tortured and killed, especially those who resisted assaults.[20] Rebel fighters regularly took in young women as sexual consorts, known as "bush wives." These atrocities were largely contained in the countryside until January 1999, when RUF forces attacked the capital of Freetown in a major offensive. ECOMOG troops were initially overrun and forced onto the defensive, but they eventually regained RUF-occupied sections of the city after 3 weeks of heavy fighting. During the RUF offensive, rebels systematically maimed, killed, and raped thousands of civilians as "punishment" for their support of the government. As they withdrew, RUF troops kidnapped a large number of young women and girls, thus repeating the pattern of group rape, sexual bondage, torture, and murder.

## Responding to Gender-Selective Political Violence

The international community did not collectively respond to gender-selective political violence until the close of the 20th century. At that time, prosecutions in international courts resulted in guilty verdicts for gender-motivated war crimes, crimes against humanity, and genocide.

In September 1998, the United Nations **International Criminal Tribunal for Rwanda (ICTR)** convicted a Hutu former mayor on nine counts of war crimes, crimes against humanity, and genocide.[21] Embedded in the ICTR decision were explicit references to sexual violence and rape as acts of genocide.

In February 2001, the ICTY convicted three Bosnian Serb men of war crimes and crimes against humanity.[22] In this case—designated the "Foca" decision after the location of the crimes—the court explicitly held that these crimes included the rape of Bosnian Muslim women and girls, as well as holding several victims in sexual slavery. Prior to these verdicts, most nations had classified wartime rape and other incidents of political violence against women as an unfortunate consequence of war.

During ongoing indictments and prosecutions, the Srebrenica massacre of men and boys and other incidents of violence against males were prosecuted by the ICTY in the Hague as acts of genocide and crimes against humanity.[23]

---

[18]Economic Community of West African States.

[19]For an interesting study of the human rights dimension of the war, see Smith, Alison L., Catherine Gambette, and Thomas Longley. *Conflict Mapping in Sierra Leone: Violations of International Humanitarian Law from 1991 to 2002.* New York: No Peace Without Justice, March 2004.

[20]See Amnesty International. *Sierra Leone: Rape and Other Forms of Sexual Violence Against Girls and Women.* London: Amnesty International, June 29, 2000.

[21]See *Prosecutor v. Jean-Paul Akayesu,* International Criminal Tribunal for Rwanda. ICTR-96–4-T, September 2, 1998.

[22]*Prosecutor v. Dragoljub Kunarac, Radomir Kovac, and Zoran Vukovic,* International Prosecution for Persons Responsible for Serious Violations of International Humanitarian Law Committed in the Territory of the Former Yugoslavia Since 1991. Case No. IT-96–23-T & IT-96–23/1-T, February 22, 2001.

[23]See, e.g., *Prosecutor of the Tribunal v. Radovan Karadzic,* Ratko Mladic. IT-95–18, November 16, 1995.

Private international agencies have also begun to actively investigate, document, and report gender selective political violence, particularly violence against women and girls. These agencies include international human rights organizations such as Amnesty International and Human Rights Watch, which have been instrumental in investigating and reporting campaigns of systematic terrorism against women in many conflicts. Other organizations such as Médecins Sans Frontières (Doctors Without Borders) and Doctors of the World have documented systematic violence against women in the war zones where they carry out humanitarian missions. These organizations also document and report many testimonials by individual female victims of politically motivated rape, torture, and murder. The work of humanitarian agencies can be hazardous. For example, two members of Médecins Sans Frontières were arrested by the Sudanese government in May 2005, in retaliation for the organization's publication of a document in late March 2005 titled *The Crushing Burden of Rape: Sexual Violence in Darfur [Sudan]*. They were charged with publishing false information but were released in late June 2005.

In a remarkable example of widespread international opposition to gender-focused terrorism, the global human rights community focused attention on a 2012 Taliban assassination attempt in Pakistan. Malala Yousafzai was a teenage girl who from a young age engaged in activism on behalf of the education of girls in Afghanistan. She was fairly public in her activities, including writing a blog on behalf of the rights of girls in Pakistan. In October 2012 a gunman attempted to assassinate Malala, shooting her in the face with a .45 caliber firearm. She survived the attack, and the global human rights community presented her case as an example of the plight of women in extreme political environments.

## ❖ Protecting the Enterprise: Criminal Dissident Terrorism

The modern era has witnessed the growth of a huge system of **transnational organized crime**. Organized crime exhibited minimal transnational characteristics in the past, but it in no way resembled the billion-dollar enterprises of modern arms and drug traffickers. Transnational organized crime has become an intricate web of illegal enterprise that incorporates both large and small criminal organizations that operate across national borders. Organizationally, some illegal enterprises are unsophisticated and gang-like in their operations, whereas others are highly sophisticated and organized as illicit businesses. The latter organizations have joined together from time to time to create international **criminal cartels** that try to regulate "product lines" such as refined cocaine.

Within this transnational web, criminal organizations have engaged in documented cases of terrorist violence, the characteristics of which can be summarized with at least two models:

1. Profit-motivated traditional criminal enterprises
2. Politically motivated criminal-political enterprises

Perhaps the most fundamental distinguishing characteristic between the two models (aside from motive) is that traditional criminal enterprises are illicit businesses whose participants normally desire a minimal amount of public attention for their activities. In contrast, criminal-political enterprises are dissident movements that frequently desire a high public profile for their activities. As previously indicated in Table 9.1, when the decision is made to engage in extremist violence, the activity profiles of traditional criminal enterprises and criminal-political enterprises are distinguishable in their motives, goals, targets, personnel, and degrees of political agitation.

### The Criminal and Political Terrorism Nexus

Before proceeding to discuss the threat of terrorism from traditional criminal and criminal-political enterprises, there is another dimension to the modern international environment that poses an inherent danger to security: cooperation and coordination between these groups.

Terrorist groups and criminal enterprises are by their nature secretive, antisocial, and underground. Transnational criminal enterprises are adept at smuggling drugs and weapons to the highest bidder through covert international networks. This black market exists purely for profit and is highly lucrative. Hence, it is acknowledged that transnational criminal enterprises can—and have—covertly provided terrorist groups with arms and other goods.

It is likely that terrorists have solicited criminal groups for "special-order" goods, such as certain types of weapons or chemicals, as have ideologically motivated authoritarian governments. For example, in March 2005, Ukrainian prosecutors reported that members of Ukrainian transnational organized crime smuggled 18 Soviet-era cruise missiles to China and Iran in 2000 and 2001, respectively.[24] The officials further reported that at least 12 of the missiles were capable of carrying a 200-kiloton nuclear warhead. Should a transnational criminal enterprise acquire nuclear, biological, or chemical weapons, it is conceivable that such weapons could be sold on the black market to the highest bidder—all without personal qualms about their use, so long as the price is right. This kind of convergence poses a serious security threat to the global community.

Chapter Perspective 9.1 discusses the case of the Beka'a Valley in Lebanon, which became a prominent example of the nexus between crime and political extremism.

## CHAPTER PERSPECTIVE 9.1: Lebanon's Beka'a Valley

The Beka'a Valley is located in the east-central region of Lebanon. Beginning in the 1970s, it became a nexus of state-sponsored terrorism, religious revolution, drug production, and counterfeiting.

Syria asserted itself as the predominant political and military force in Lebanon when it deployed thousands of troops to the Beka'a Valley in 1976. Syria's objective was to influence the behavior of its proxies among Lebanese and Palestinian dissident movements. Adding to the revolutionary environment in the Beka'a was Syria's permission for the presence of members of Iran's Revolutionary Guards; their mission was to sponsor and train Hezbollah and various Palestinian groups who were provided safe haven in the Beka'a. Groups that were based in the valley and protected by the Syrian military presence included Hamas, Palestine Islamic Jihad, Abu Nidal, Popular Front for the Liberation of Palestine–General Command, the Kurdistan Workers' Party, and the Japanese Red Army.

The Beka'a Valley is also a historic center of drug production—primarily hashish and opium. Although its percentage of global drug production has been relatively small, profits from the trade were enough to support the activities of dissident groups in the valley. For example, evidence strongly implicated Hezbollah in the production and sale of drugs to support themselves and to offset reductions in support from Iran.[a] Markets for Lebanese drugs included North Africa, the United States, Israel, and Europe. In an aggressive antidrug campaign, the Lebanese government greatly reduced drug production to negligible levels during the mid-1990s. There is, however, evidence that recurrent attempts were made to reinvigorate drug-related agriculture.

Sophisticated counterfeiting operations were also conducted in the Beka'a Valley. The industry produced a large quantity of high-grade international U.S. dollars. The decision by the United States to redesign its paper currency during the 1990s was due in part to the excellent quality of dollars produced by the Beka'a Valley's counterfeiting industry.

With the withdrawal of Syrian troops from Lebanon in April 2005 after 29 years of military intervention, the Beka'a Valley returned to Lebanese government control.

**Note**

a. Cilluffo, Frank. "The Challenge We Face as the Battle Lines Blur." Statement before the U.S. House Committee on the Judiciary, Subcommittee on Crime. December 13, 2000.

## Traditional Criminal Enterprises

The overriding imperative for traditional criminal enterprises is to profit from their criminal endeavors and protect their illegal enterprise. Because they are motivated by sheer profit, crime-motivated

---

[24]Holley, David. "China, Iran Missile Sales Confirmed." *Los Angeles Times,* March 19, 2005.

enterprises are political only to the extent that they wish to create a safe environment for their illicit business. In essence, traditional criminal enterprises do not seek to destroy the system; rather, they wish to subvert or otherwise manipulate it for their benefit. They are not necessarily interested in active political participation, other than to subvert or co-opt government officials. They desire a stable environment for their enterprise, so that governments that are either too weak to interfere with the enterprise or that lack the motivation to do so are unlikely to be targeted by traditional criminal enterprises. Conversely, some criminal organizations have violently resisted government law enforcement campaigns that interfere with their enterprises. This is by no means a universal reaction, but it is nevertheless one that has occurred repeatedly.

Examples of traditional criminal enterprises include the Chinese Triads, Japanese Yakuza, American La Cosa Nostra, Colombian drug cartels, Russian Mafia, Italian organized crime, and Southeast Asian drug lords. Most of these enterprises have been politically passive and have engaged in political violence reactively rather than actively. In essence, the likelihood of antistate violence by these organizations depends on the social and political environments of their national bases of operation.

## Criminal-Political Enterprises

Dissident movements have become increasingly involved in transnational organized crime, having concluded out of pragmatic necessity that there is a benefit to be gained from trading arms or drugs on the illicit market. Some movements—primarily from Latin America and Asia—have even occupied drug-producing regions as a matter of strategic choice. The reasons for this strategy are uncomplicated: Participation in the drug or arms trades is quite lucrative. A dissident movement can guarantee its financial independence from state sponsorship if it can establish its own niche in an illicit enterprise.

In the modern era, the formerly clear delineation between organized crime, political extremism, and illegal trafficking has become blurred. An overlap between crime and extremist politics has occurred, so that some politically motivated movements and individuals actively participate in the international smuggling of arms and drugs. Alliances are forged between exclusively profit-motivated traditional criminal enterprises and politically violent movements.

The following survey of regional cases illustrates the linkages between terrorism, transnational criminal activity, traditional criminal enterprises, and criminal-political enterprises.

## Case in Point: The Logic of Narco-terrorism

The drug trade has become particularly prominent in the financing of some extremist movements, and many terrorists and extremist movements have become adept drug traffickers. This is a result of the enormous profits derived from the global underground drug market, to which American drug users contribute $64 billion each year.[25] Having made these observations, the reality is that there is no grand revolutionary conspiracy to control the drug trade; rather, there is a very fluid and intricate web that links profit-motivated traditional criminal enterprises to ideologically motivated criminal-political enterprises.

The term **narco-terrorism** was first used in 1983 by Peruvian President Belaunde Terry when Peruvian drug traffickers waged war against antidrug security forces. The concept describes "the use of drug trafficking to advance the objectives of certain governments and terrorist organizations."[26] Although its original meaning referred to a theorized semimonolithic Marxist (hence, Soviet) control of the trade,[27] narco-terrorism continues to be an important concept in the post–Cold War world.[28]

---

[25]U.S. Drug Enforcement Administration. "Drugs and Terrorism: A New Perspective." *Drug Intelligence Brief.* Washington, DC: U.S. Department of Justice, September 2002. Data derived from estimates by the Office of National Drug Control Policy.

[26]Ehrenfeld, Rachel. *Narco-Terrorism.* New York: Basic Books, 1990, p. xiii.

[27]For an interesting discussion about drug-related criminal terrorism, see ibid.

[28]Use of the term has been debated, and some controversy regarding its use still exists. See Laqueur, Walter. *The New Terrorism: Fanaticism and the Arms of Mass Destruction.* New York: Oxford University Press, 1999, p. 211.

Officially, the U.S. Drug Enforcement Administration (DEA) defines a narco-terrorist group as "an organized group that is complicit in the activities of drug trafficking in order to further, or fund, premeditated, politically motivated violence perpetrated against noncombatant targets with the intention to influence (that is, influence a government or group of people)."[29] The DEA also differentiates between narco-terrorism and **drug-related violence**, pointing out that the latter is "financially motivated violence perpetrated against those who interfere with or cross the path of a drug trafficking organization."[30] Drug-related violence occurs visibly and every day in major urban areas around the world, whereas narco-terrorism is less visible and not as pervasive.

Among criminal-political enterprises, the logic of narco-terrorism is uncomplicated: Because of the frequent difficulty in obtaining direct state sponsorship, some indigenous terrorist and revolutionary groups have turned to drug trafficking and arms trading to raise money for their movements. Among traditional criminal enterprises, drug traffickers have been especially prone to engage in criminal dissident terrorism because their product must be grown, refined, packaged, and transported from production regions within the borders of sovereign nations. Thus, among transnational criminals, drug traffickers in particular must necessarily establish a political environment that is conducive to their illegal enterprise.

An example of a long campaign of narco-terrorism illustrates its logic. The campaign occurred in Colombia during the 1980s and early 1990s. Drug cartel *narcotraficantes* (drug traffickers), based in the city of Medellin and led by Pablo Escobar, were notorious during the 1980s and early 1990s for their violence against police officers, prosecutors, journalists, and judges who attempted to interfere with cocaine production and trafficking. The Medellin cartel's rival *narcotraficantes* in the city of Cali were also known to react violently when challenged by Colombian officials, though they were more sophisticated in their manipulation of the government through bribery and corruption. Both cartels were eventually dismantled by Colombian law enforcement agencies with the assistance of the United States, but new lower-profile drug gangs rose to prominence in Colombia, as did criminal-political adversaries in Colombia's internecine fighting. For example, in May 2005, more than 13 tons of cocaine were found in underground chambers in Nariño state in Colombia.[31] The cache was apparently owned by leftist rebels and paramilitary fighters, and it was valued at more than $350 million. The Latin American connection is explored further as a regional case study in the next section.

Chapter Perspective 9.2 discusses the case of the Tri-Border Area in South America, a lawless region posing a plausible threat to the security of the Western Hemisphere from organized crime and political extremism.

## CHAPTER PERSPECTIVE 9.2: The Tri-Border Area of South America

The Tri-Border Area, also known as the Triple Frontier, is a region in central South America straddling the borders of Brazil, Paraguay, and Argentina. It is a remote area in which government authority is weak, and it has become home to an illicit economy specializing in drug trafficking, money laundering, and the transfer of financial resources to the Middle East, including to extremist groups. Much of the smuggling network is coordinated by Lebanon's Hezbollah, an operation that is possible because the Tri-Border Area is home to a diaspora of approximately 25,000 Arab residents whose ancestral homes are largely from the Levant of Lebanon.

The region is known for its thriving illegal smuggling and financial criminal activities. Smugglers regularly cross international borders, and Hezbollah is quite adept at raising money and laundering it to extremist causes. Narcotics trafficking alone generates billions of dollars in profit, and other contraband goods (including cash) add to the lucrative illicit economy.

*(Continued)*

---

[29]U.S. Drug Enforcement Administration, "Drugs."

[30]Ibid.

[31]Times Wire Reports. "Authorities Seize More Than 13 Tons of Cocaine." *Los Angeles Times,* May 14, 2005.

(Continued)

Ready access to three countries friendly to the United States poses a plausible security risk to the region because extremists could pose as travelers and enter the United States through neighboring countries. Motivated extremists could also travel to Mexico and easily cross the border into the United States. Other countries are also vulnerable to attack, as evidenced by Hezbollah's 1992 bombing of the Israeli embassy in Buenos Aires and the July 1994 bombing of the Argentine Israelite Mutual Association in Buenos Ares.

The Tri-Border Area's nexus of weak government control, an organized and vibrant criminal economy, and political extremism pose a significant security challenge to the region.

Table 9.2 summarizes the activity profiles of several traditional criminal and criminal-political enterprises.

## Table 9.2  Criminal Dissident Terrorism

*Criminal dissident terrorism*, as defined here, refers to traditional criminal enterprises and criminal-political enterprises. They are differentiated primarily by motive, with traditional criminal enterprises motivated by profit and criminal-political enterprises motivated by a dissident cause.

The following table summarizes the activity profiles of several traditional criminal and criminal-political enterprises.

| Group and Type | Activity Profile | | |
| --- | --- | --- | --- |
| | *Criminal Enterprise* | *Motive* | *Quality of Violence* |
| **Taliban (Afghanistan: criminal-political)** | Opium and heroin production | Consolidate the movement; promote *jihad* | Domestic terrorism; *jihad* against opponents |
| **Tamil Tigers (Sri Lanka: criminal-political)** | Arms and drug trafficking | National independence | Terrorism, insurgency |
| **Myanmar groups (traditional criminal)** | Opium and heroin production | Profit; regional autonomy | Insurgency |
| **Abu Sayyaf (Philippines: criminal-political)** | Kidnapping, extortion, drug trafficking | *Jihad* against the Filipino government | Terrorism, insurgency |
| **Italian organized crime (traditional criminal)** | Broad variety of activities | Profit | Terrorism, extortion, intimidation |
| **Russian Mafia (traditional criminal)** | Broad variety of activities | Profit | Terrorism, extortion, intimidation |
| **Irish dissidents (criminal-political)** | Drug trade | Republicanism or loyalism | Terrorism |
| **Kosovo Liberation Army/ National Liberation Army (criminal-political)** | Arms and drug trafficking | Albanian nationalism | Terrorism, insurgency |

| | | | |
|---|---|---|---|
| *Colombian cartels (traditional criminal)* | Drug trade | Profit | Narco-terrorism |
| *FARC (Colombia: criminal-political)* | Drug trade | Revolution | Terrorism, insurgency |
| *AUC (Colombia: criminal-political)* | Drug trade | Counterinsurgency | Terrorism, counterinsurgency |
| *Shining Path (Peru: criminal-political)* | Drug trade | Revolution | Terrorism |
| *Mexican narcotraficantes (traditional criminal)* | Drug trade | Profit | Narco-terrorism |

# ❖ A Global Problem: Regional Cases of Criminal Dissident Terrorism

## Regional Case: Latin America

Criminal terrorism in Latin America is directly linked to the lucrative drug trade, which primarily involves cocaine and marijuana but also includes relatively small quantities of heroin. Traditional criminal enterprises thrive on the drug trade, as do criminal-political enterprises. Latin American drug traffickers are known as *narcotraficantes,* and many traditional criminal enterprises are **drug cartels**. A cartel is "an international syndicate, combine or trust generally formed to regulate prices and output in some field of business."[32] Under this definition, Mexico's and Colombia's traditional criminal enterprises have been classic drug cartels.

### Narcotraficantes in Mexico

Criminal gangs in Mexico have historically been involved in banditry and traditional organized criminal activity such as extortion and prostitution. With the rise of the cocaine trade in the 1970s and 1980s, Colombian drug cartels (discussed later) hired Mexican gangs to transship cocaine overland to the United States. They were subordinate to the cartels and were initially paid in cash. As Mexican gangs became proficient smugglers, they began to demand marijuana and cocaine as payment, which they then sold to their own customers. The gangs eventually became independent and coequal partners with the Colombians, growing into criminal cartels.[33] They also became adept at using narco-terrorism to defend their enterprises.

Several large and lucrative criminal enterprises were organized. By 1999, the most important of these were the Carillo Fuentes organization in Ciudad Juárez, the Caro-Quintero organization in Sonora, and the Arellano-Félix organization in Mexicali and Tijuana. Newer organizations eventually arose, including Los Zetas, Cartel Pacifico Sur, the Gulf Cartel, and La Familia Michoacana. They have prospered as drug traffickers, and the Mexican trade in marijuana and cocaine became a multibillion-dollar industry.

***Case in Point: The Arellano-Félix Group.*** The Arellano-Félix group (also known as the Tijuana Cartel) is an excellent case study of the rise, fall, and rebirth of a transnational criminal enterprise in

---

[32]*The American College Dictionary.* New York: Harper & Brothers, 1947.

[33]Constantine, Thomas A. "DEA Congressional Testimony." Statement before the U.S. Senate Drug Caucus. February 24, 1999.

Mexico because the group was considered for some time to be the most profitable and violent of the Mexican organizations. The cartel operated on the border with and inside the territory of the United States, and its territory centered on the corridor from Mexico to San Diego and Los Angeles. Principally run by brothers Benjamin and Ramón, the **Arellano-Félix cartel** corrupted some government officials, tried to intimidate those whom it could not corrupt, and killed others.[34] Victims of the group included Mexican police chiefs, prosecutors, police officers, journalists, critics, and children. The targeting of civilians was intentional; in one incident in 1998, the group killed three families from a rival enterprise. As one former American drug agent noted about the Arellano-Félix tactics, "If you are late paying the Arellanos, you won't get a nicely worded letter saying your 30 days were up. . . . But you might get a finger of your child in the mail."[35]

The Arellano-Félix cartel was severely damaged when its leaders were eliminated. On February 10, 2002, Ramón Arellano-Félix was killed in a shootout. On March 9 of the same year, his brother Benjamin was imprisoned in Mexico's high-security La Palma prison. The near collapse of the cartel was, however, by no means the end of Mexican narco-terrorism or the drug trade. In fact, there were indications that the cartel merged with the so-called Gulf Cartel of Osiel Cardenes in 2004 or 2005 as a way to consolidate the operations of both cartels and to jointly resist other groups who might otherwise seize the Arellano-Félix market.[36] There were also deadly confrontations between factions of the Arellano-Félix cartel in Tijuana, indicating the resilience of the factions' claims over lucrative trade.

***The Mexican Drug War.*** Unlike their Colombian colleagues, and except for the apparent Arellano-Félix/Gulf Cartel alliance, the Mexican criminal enterprises tend to not cooperate with one another. Feuding is common, and the demise of one cartel leads to exceptional drug-related violence over its former turf. For example, during 2004, scores of bodies were found in Ciudad Juarez and dozens of others in Tijuana, Mexicali, and Tecate.[37] In the Sinaloa state alone in 2004, about 300 bodies were discovered. At the same time, narco-terrorist activities of the groups continued to include attacks against government officials, journalists, and other critics. Also, Mexican President Felipe Calderon launched a crackdown on drug traffickers in December 2006. The toll from drug-related violence has been high. By 2013, approximately 60,000 Mexicans had been killed by the cartels, with more than 13,000 deaths between January and September 2011.

The following incidents are typical examples of Mexican narco-terrorism and violence:

- Since 2000, more than 30 news reporters have disappeared or been killed by *narcotraficantes*.

- In June 2004, an editor for a Tijuana newsweekly was murdered, allegedly by rogue Zeta special antinarcotics troops who worked for the Gulf Cartel.

- In September 2004, several *narcotraficantes* and a state police commander were killed by gunmen in Culiacan. The assailants were allegedly rogue members of an elite antidrug unit of the Mexican military known as **Los Zetas**. Rogue Zetas were implicated in several assassinations conducted on behalf of the Gulf Cartel.

- In December 2004, the brother of a top *narcotraficante* was shot to death in La Palma prison, reputedly Mexico's most secure prison, apparently with the collaboration of corrupt prison officials. He was the third top *narcotraficante* to be killed in La Palma prison, apparently with staff complicity. In October 2004, another trafficker was shot to death in the cafeteria, and in May 2004, another was strangled in a shower. La Palma prison was raided by 750 Mexican troops and police in January 2005.

- In January 2005, two state police officers were assassinated.

---

[34]See Kraul, Chris. "The Collapse of Mexico's 'Invincible' Drug Cartel." *Los Angeles Times,* March 16, 2002.

[35]Ibid.

[36]Kraul, Chris. "Mexican Official Says Tijuana, Gulf Cartels Have United." *Los Angeles Times,* January 14, 2005.

[37]Kraul, Chris. "Drug Cartels Battle Over Mexican Turf." *Los Angeles Times,* September 14, 2004.

- In May 2005, the police chief of Rosarito and the director of Mexicali's Municipal Jail were assassinated.

- In September 2005, the state of Michoacan's chief of security police was assassinated during a birthday dinner by men firing AK-47 assault rifles.

- Eighty-nine soldiers were killed between December 2006 and May 2007 during the first phase of a crackdown against drug traffickers.

- In December 2007, the entire Rosarito police force was disarmed following the attempted assassination of the town's police chief after concerns were raised that the police had been infiltrated by drug traffickers.

- In May 2008, the chief of Mexico's federal police was assassinated in Mexico City.

- In May 2008, a mass grave with 33 bodies was found in Ciudad Juarez, the victims of drug violence.

- From July 5 to July 8, 2008, authorities found the bodies of 11 men at two sites, executed by *narcotraficantes* in Tijuana. This was despite the presence of 3,000 soldiers in the city.

- In August 2010, the bodies of 72 migrants from South and Central America were found on a ranch in Tamaulipas state. They were probably kidnapped by the Los Zetas cartel and murdered for refusing to traffic drugs.

- In April 2011, mass graves with 177 bodies were found in the same area where 72 bodies were found in 2010.

- In May 2012, authorities found nearly 50 decapitated bodies along a highway in Nuevo Leon state.

- In February 2014, Joaquin "El Chapo" Guzman, the head of one of the wealthiest drug cartels, was captured.

### Colombia's Drug Cartels and Gangs

*Narcotraficantes* in Colombia have historically been highly organized, resilient, and terrorist, and Colombia's first large traditional criminal enterprises were classic drug cartels.

The Cali and Medellin cartels dominated the worldwide cocaine trade during the 1980s through the mid-1990s. Named for their home cities, they waged a campaign of criminal dissident terrorism against anyone opposed to them, frequently targeting government officials. During the 1980s alone, cartel terrorists killed

- 3,000 soldiers and police officers,
- more than 1,000 public officials,
- 170 judicial employees,
- 50 lower judges,
- dozens of journalists,
- 12 Supreme Court judges,
- three presidential candidates,
- one attorney general, and
- one newspaper publisher.[38]

The cartels were also very adept at co-opting government officials through bribery, extortion, and intimidation. However, partly because of the cartels' high profile, the Colombian government was eventually able to dismantle the big cartels with the assistance of the United States. One interesting

---

[38]Ehrenfeld, *Narco-Terrorism*, pp. 86–7.

twist to the offensive against the cartels was a paramilitary terrorist campaign that was waged against the Medellin cartel and its leader, Pablo Escobar. The paramilitary, calling itself **People Persecuted by Pablo Escobar**, or **"Pepes,"** assassinated at least 50 cartel members and targeted Escobar's family for assassination.[39] Pepes was apparently a death squad made up of former Medellin operatives and backers with a history of supporting paramilitaries; they claimed that they acted out of a sense of patriotism and a code of vengeance.[40] Escobar was eventually killed in 1993 during a shootout with Colombian troops and police.

A new *narcotraficante* model replaced the old drug cartels—smaller drug gangs in Colombia and new Mexican cartels. After the demise of the Cali and Medellin cartels, the Colombian drug trade was reconfigured around these smaller criminal enterprises. The new enterprises have kept a lower profile than during the heyday of the cartels and have not engaged in narco-terrorism on the same scale as their predecessors. As a result, drugs have continued to flow into the global drug market, and these gangs continue to send tons of cocaine, marijuana, and other drugs to the United States and Europe.

❖ **Photo 9.4**

Colombian Special Forces surrounded by coca plants near a cocaine processing lab in the heart of the Colombian jungle.

Tom Stoddart/Hulton Archive/Getty Images

### FARC's Drug Connection

The Revolutionary Armed Forces of Colombia (FARC) and the National Liberation Army (ELN) in Colombia have partly financed their revolutions with drug money. Both groups have used terrorist and guerrilla tactics in their war, and they have become self-sufficient largely through the drug trade.

Since the early period of its insurgency, FARC has permitted cocaine traffickers to operate without interference so long as the *narcotraficantes* paid a "tax" to the movement.[41] This was a pragmatic arrangement. FARC's pragmatism progressed during the 1990s when the rebels cut out the middlemen and began to deal directly with marijuana and coca farmers, trafficking their produce to the Colombian drug cartels. They also protected the trade in their "liberated zones," promising to liberate and protect peasants from exploitation by the drug lords.

FARC established a kind of law, order, and predictability in its liberated zones that became popular among local peasants and small-time drug traders. Because of this new enterprise, "the changes in FARC . . . have been significant. As the revenue from the drug trade . . . expanded, so [did] the power and influence of FARC."[42] For example, some FARC units promote or manage coca cultivation, cocaine laboratories, trafficking, and bartering drugs-for-weapons arrangements with transnational organized crime groups. Other FARC units have been very active in the drug-producing southwestern province of Nariño, where ambushes of government troops are common.[43]

Estimates of FARC's revenues from the cocaine trade were in the hundreds of millions of dollars.[44] There is evidence that the rebel group has forged close ties to the Russian Mafia, supplanting the Colombian drug cartels as clients after the large cartels were dismantled and reformed as smaller drug gangs. Airlifted deliveries of arms were made by the Russian Mafia to FARC in exchange for cocaine, which was then flown back to Russia for distribution to the Russian drug market.[45] There is also evidence of a FARC link to the Tijuana Cartel in Mexico.

---

[39]Ambrus, Steven. "Vigilantes Target Drug Chief: Effective Paramilitary Squad Raises Ethical Dilemma for Colombian Government." *Christian Science Monitor,* March 5, 1993.

[40]Cilluffo, Frank. "The Challenge We Face as the Battle Lines Blur." Statement before the U.S. House Committee on the Judiciary, Subcommittee on Crime. December 13, 2000.

[41]Ibid.

[42]Ibid.

[43]Van Dongen, Rachel. "Rebels Kill 14 Troops in Raid on Colombian Military Facility." *Los Angeles Times,* February 2, 2005.

[44]Walters, John. Press briefing by the director of the Office of National Drug Control Policy. February 12, 2002.

[45]Cilluffo, "The Challenge."

### Colombia's AUC

Colombian landowners and government officials organized regional right-wing paramilitaries to oppose the FARC and ELN insurgency. The United Self-Defense Forces of Colombia, or AUC, was long the most prominent alliance of these paramilitaries. Human rights agencies implicated the AUC in a number of incidents involving death squad attacks, civilian massacres, and political terrorism.[46]

Although the AUC was able to field 11,000 fighters, the paramilitary alliance eventually split into at least five factions in 2002. In June 2003, a classified report on the AUC indicated that the paramilitary had become a primary participant in the drug trade. The report stated that "it is impossible to differentiate between the self-defense groups and narco-trafficking organizations."[47] Like FARC, a large proportion of AUC's funding came from drug trafficking, the report estimating that about 80% of the group's revenues came from drugs. Continuing negotiations on demobilization were somewhat successful—for example, top AUC leaders were arrested by Colombian authorities in 2005—but participation in the drug trade continued. In May 2008, Colombia extradited 14 ranking paramilitary leaders to the United States to stand trial on drug-trafficking charges.[48]

### Shining Path in Peru

Peru's Shining Path (Sendero Luminoso) regularly engaged in acts of terrorism during its insurgency under the tutelage of Abimael Guzmán, the self-professed Fourth Sword of Marxism. Shining Path's ideology had racial and mystical elements to it, championing the Quechua-speaking Indians and mixed-race *mestizos*. The insurgency gradually withered after Guzmán's capture in 1992, although diehards remained active into the new millennium.

In the mid-1980s, Shining Path aggressively—and violently—vied for a share in Peru's drug trade. During the 1980s, Peru's Upper Huallaga Valley region was the world's richest producer of coca leaf. It was also a top exporter of cocaine paste, which is used to manufacture refined cocaine. Colombian *narcotraficantes* would purchase the coca leaf and cocaine paste for transshipment to Colombia to be refined into cocaine. Shining Path operatives moved into the valley in about 1983, claiming that they were liberating and protecting peasant farmers from exploitation by the Colombian drug cartels and the Peruvian government.[49] In the meantime,

> it is believed that Sendero garnered a minimum of $10 million a year (some estimates range as high as $100 million) between 1987 and 1992 from "taxes" on a large portion of the valley's 80,000 coca growers and from levies of up to $15,000 a flight on the mostly Colombian traffickers as they landed on the scores of clandestine runways in the valley to pick up their cargoes of cocaine paste.[50]

At its height, Shining Path seized control of towns in the Upper Huallaga Valley, expelled government administrators and police, and created its own moralistic model of law and order—which included killing homosexuals and ending prostitution. Before Guzmán's capture, Shining Path had become a self-sufficient terrorist movement, with most of its self-sufficiency derived from the drug trade. When a fungus ravaged the Upper Huallaga's coca leaf crop in the mid-1990s, the movement received a final blow because its primary financial resource was removed.[51]

---

[46]For further information, see Human Rights Watch at http://hrw.org/.

[47]Wilson, Scott. "Colombian Fighters' Drug Trade Is Detailed." *Washington Post,* June 26, 2003.

[48]Romero, Simon. "Colombia Extradites 14 Paramilitary Leaders." *New York Times,* May 14, 2008.

[49]Ehrenfeld, *Narco-Terrorism,* p. 125.

[50]Scott Palmer, David. "The Revolutionary Terrorism of Peru's Shining Path." In *Terrorism in Context,* edited by Martha Crenshaw. State College: Pennsylvania State University Press, 1995. Quoted in Whittaker, David J., ed. *The Terrorism Reader.* New York: Routledge, 2001, p. 160.

[51]Laqueur, *The New Terrorism,* p. 187.

## Regional Case: Asia

Asian drug production is centered on two regions: Southwest Asia and Southeast Asia. The drug-producing regions of Southwest Asia are referred to as the **Golden Crescent**, and the drug-producing regions of Southeast Asia are referred to as the **Golden Triangle**. Dissident terrorists and extremists in both regions have profited from the drug trade. The Golden Triangle—known for its cultivation of opium poppies and the manufacturing of refined opium and heroin—consists of the countries of Myanmar (Burma), Laos, and Thailand. The Golden Crescent—known for its cultivation of opium poppies and the manufacturing of heroin—consists of the countries of Iran, Afghanistan, and Pakistan. Because of the fall of the Soviet Union, the drug production industry in the Golden Crescent has found a lucrative transshipment industry in Central Asia, where organized crime and Islamic extremists have profited from transshipping heroin into the Russian and European drug markets.

### Afghanistan

Afghanistan has historically been an important producer of opium and heroin and eventually became the world's chief supplier of illegal opiates. It has also historically been a major supplier of hashish. In the modern era, warlords, revolutionaries, and holy warriors have all profited enormously from the trade.

During Taliban rule (September 1996 to January 2002), Afghanistan's traditional cultivation of opium flourished to record levels. Although the Taliban government cracked down on drug production in 2000, the movement allegedly earned approximately 80% of its income from the opium poppy and heroin trade. It also produced more than 70% of the world's supply of opium after production fell off in Southeast Asia's Golden Triangle (discussed later). There have been reports that while in Afghanistan, Osama bin Laden approached opium manufacturers in Afghanistan and Pakistan. The Taliban's radical interpretation of Islam allowed the cultivation of opium poppies but strictly forbade and severely punished the use of opium or heroin. Citing religious grounds, the Taliban forbade the cultivation of opium poppies in 2000, resulting in the near eradication of Afghanistan's drug trade.

Afghan warlords moved into opium-producing regions after the U.S.-led invasion, and the country again became a premier producer of opium. In a single year (2003 to 2004), cultivation of opium poppies grew from approximately 150,000 acres to about 510,000 acres.[52] In comparison, the Taliban's peak cultivation had been 160,000 acres in 2000.[53] By 2005, Afghanistan was producing record crops of poppies despite Afghanistan President Hamid Karzai's official policy of opposing opium production.[54] In addition, experts estimated that nearly 90% of the world's heroin was produced from Afghan poppies. In the aftermath of the coalition invasion, warlords continued to store large quantities of opium, which could theoretically continue supplying heroin laboratories for years. In essence, opium cultivation steadily increased from the time of the U.S.-led invasion, often significantly each year. For example, in 2013 opium production reached record levels.

❖ **Photo 9.5**

Drugs that fund the cause. An Afghan fighter sits in a field of ripe opium poppies.

Peter Jouvenal/Hulton Archive/Getty Images

### Sri Lanka

Until their defeat in 2009, the Liberation Tigers of Tamil Eelam sustained their movement in part by establishing themselves as middlemen in the illicit arms and drug trades. Evidence suggested that the Tamil Tigers received drugs and arms "on consignment" from traditional criminal enterprises in Myanmar and

---

[52]Efron, Sonni. "An Afghan Quandary for the U.S." *Los Angeles Times,* January 2, 2005.

[53]Miller, T. Christian. "Post-Invasion Chaos Blamed for Drug Surge." *Los Angeles Times,* October 4, 2004.

[54]Watson, Paul. "Karzai Takes Oath, Vows to Tackle Drug Trafficking." *Los Angeles Times,* December 7, 2004.

India.[55] The Tamil Tigers sold the consigned drugs, paid for the weapons, and repeated the cycle as a method to build their arsenals. This was very similar to the arrangement used by Albanian criminals and dissidents in their management of the Balkan Route.

### Myanmar (Burma)

Until the mid-1990s, Khun Sa, the commander of the Shan United Army, controlled much of the heroin production coming out of the Golden Triangle. Based in Myanmar, Khun Sa claimed to champion the ethnic Shan people, but in reality he was a traditional warlord, and his army was a renegade force. The Shan United Army waged an occasional insurgency against the government as a way to establish regional autonomy from central control, thus ensuring its profits from the heroin trade.

At its height, the Golden Triangle produced 75% of the world's heroin, largely within the operational area of the Shan United Army. When Khun Sa retired in 1996,[56] a vacuum was created in the trade, so that the drug flow declined significantly from Myanmar's old heroin-producing regions. Taliban-controlled Afghanistan more than made up for this shortfall on the world market. After the Taliban's late-2000 crackdown on opium cultivation, the Golden Triangle saw a resurgence in production, regaining its prominence as a top producer of opium. Groups such as the United Wa State Army, an old splinter group of the Burmese Communist Party, moved into the Shan United Army's old operational areas in northern Myanmar.

### The Philippines

Abu Sayyaf, the southern Filipino Islamic terrorist organization discussed in Chapter 6, was known to engage in criminal enterprise. Although its activities never approximated the scale of other movements, Abu Sayyaf resorted to kidnapping, extortion, and drug trafficking as tactics in its cause of waging a *jihad*. Reports indicated that it moved into southern Filipino marijuana fields to reap the benefits of the marijuana trade, raising revenues for its war against the Filipino government.[57]

## Regional Case: Europe

Europe has a highly active criminal underground. The most historically established criminal enterprises are found in Italy. Recently established enterprises are found in the former communist Eastern bloc, mainly in Russia. The incidence of terrorism by criminal enterprises occurs to greater or lesser degrees from country to country, with the most serious incidence found in Italy and Russia.

### Italian Organized Crime

The word *mafia* is commonly used to describe organized criminal activity anywhere in the world. However, it originally referred to traditional organized crime societies in southern Italy and Sicily. The derivation of the word is unknown, although there is some speculation that it is Arabic in origin. Regardless, the original mafia groups were secret associations of Sicilian resistance fighters who opposed the occupation of Sicily by the Spanish and French. A tradition grew out of these origins that demanded the following:

- Secrecy under a code of silence (*omerta*)
- Opposition to, and noncooperation with, security and law enforcement officials and agencies
- A code of honor
- Absolute obedience and loyalty toward the respected heads of mafia groups

---

[55]Cilluffo, "The Challenge."

[56]Khun Sa died at the age of 73 in November 2007.

[57]Ibid.

This concept was adopted throughout southern Italy, so that in Naples, a Neapolitan secret society was created called the **Camorra**, and in Calabria, the **N'drangheta** was organized. These secret societies have long been criminal enterprises and are best characterized as profit-making traditional organized crime groups. The **Sicilian Mafia**, Camorra, and N'drangheta became entrenched at all levels of southern Italian society, including business and government. One report by Italy's leading trade organization has argued that one business in five has been penetrated by organized crime.[58] Immigrants from these cultures brought these traditions with them to the United States, where **La Cosa Nostra** ("our thing" or "this thing of ours") was organized as "families" in urban areas. La Cosa Nostra has been traditionally associated with the Sicilian Mafia.

The Sicilian Mafia, Camorra, and N'drangheta have used corruption, violence, and extortion to keep opponents not only from interfering with their criminal enterprises, but also from being too public in their criticism. Assassinations, bombings, and other terrorist acts have been committed against politicians, journalists, and law enforcement officials. Examples of this violence include the following:

- In 1971, the Sicilian Mafia assassinated the chief prosecutor in Palermo, Sicily.
- In 1983, the Camorra assassinated a Neapolitan journalist who had written articles criticizing organized crime.
- In July 1992, the Sicilian Mafia assassinated an anti-Mafia judge in dramatic fashion when a bomb exploded outside the judge's mother's home in Sicily, killing him and five bodyguards.
- In 1992, the Sicilian Mafia assassinated the top anti-Mafia prosecutor.
- In 1993, bombs in Florence, Milan, and Rome killed 10 people and wounded 32. One of the bombs damaged the famous Uffizi Gallery in Florence.
- In July 2000, a Calabrian provincial official was assassinated, apparently by the N'drangheta.

The style of these attacks is typical of violence by Italian organized crime. It is usually "surgical," in the sense that specific officials are singled out for intimidation or assassination. However, it has taken a toll in lives. From 1971 to 1991, about 40 judges, law enforcement officers, politicians, and others were assassinated. The death toll has been higher among feuding organized crime groups and civilians. In Sicily alone, an average of 100 people are killed each year by Sicilian Mafia violence.[59] In Calabria, the N'drangheta shifted to drug and weapons trafficking, and its profits run into the billions of dollars annually.[60]

### The Russian Mafia

In the aftermath of the dissolution of the Soviet Union, the **Russian Mafia** has grown into a massive network of criminal enterprise—it is, in fact, the largest organized crime environment in the world. The Russian Ministry of Interior has estimated that as of 1996, the Russian Mafia had 5,000 to 8,000 groups and perhaps 100,000 members.[61] By comparison, the United States has 24 traditional La Cosa Nostra families, with an estimated 2,000 members.[62] The Russian Mafia is not a single organization; rather, it is a loosely organized network of gangs with between 50 and

---

[58]BBC News. "Mafia 'Gripping Italian Economy.'" November 14, 2000. This report was challenged by Italian officials.

[59]De Gennaro, Giovanni. "The Threat of International Organized Crime and Global Terrorism." Statement before the U.S. House Committee on International Relations. October 1, 1997.

[60]Wilkinson, Tracy, and Maria De Cristofaro. "Killings Cast Light on an Italian Mob." *Los Angeles Times,* August 24, 2007.

[61]Ibid.; remarks of the Honorable Louis Freeh, director of the Federal Bureau of Investigation.

[62]Ibid.

1,000 members.[63] Some of these gangs are quite large. For example, the **Solntsevskaya Gang**, named after a Moscow suburb, has an estimated 5,000 members.[64] A staggering 40% of private businesses, 60% of state-owned companies, and 80% of banks were estimated to be under Russian Mafia control in 1998.[65] Within the Russian criminal underworld, Georgians and Chechens became disproportionately prominent.

It is important to understand the quality of violence perpetrated by the Russian Mafia and the nature of its criminal enterprises. The scale and types of violence perpetrated by the Russian Mafia are often terrorist in nature. Gangs have regularly killed private businesspeople, journalists, politicians, and others. An estimated 600 murders per year are contract killings, and 95 bankers were assassinated from 1993 to 1998.[66] The enterprises of the Russian Mafia include arms smuggling, drug smuggling, extortion, murder, racketeering, and other illicit activities. Significantly, there have been indications that the Russian Mafia has transferred weapons to violent organizations and terrorists in the developing world. These transfers apparently have been done with the collaboration of former Soviet KGB (secret service) officers. Because of the KGB connection, many fear that if the Russian Mafia obtains weapons of mass destruction, these weapons will be sold to terrorists on the black market.

### Irish Dissidents

Allegations have been made that dissident movements in Northern Ireland have been involved in the illicit sale of drugs. Both Catholic and Protestant militant groups apparently traded in drugs to generate revenue for their causes. British and Northern Irish law enforcement agencies implicated extremists in the trade, despite protestations from these groups that they were opposed to drug sales and use. Nevertheless,

> [w]hile publicly crusading against the drug trade in Ireland, there is compelling evidence that the Irish Republican Army (IRA) and its radical offshoot, the Real IRA, are involved in an unholy alliance with the Middle Eastern narcotics industry. . . . The IRA is not the only guilty party in the conflict. Protestant paramilitaries are also heavily involved in using the profits from drug sales to finance their organizations.[67]

The Royal Ulster Constabulary assigned increasing numbers of personnel to narcotics duty and seized significant amounts of marijuana and ecstasy.

### The "Balkan Route"

The fervor of ethnic Albanian nationalism grew dramatically during the collapse of communism in Albania and Yugoslavia, when ethnic Albanians in the southern Yugoslav regions of Kosovo and Macedonia sought independence from Yugoslavia. Macedonia successfully separated from Yugoslavia and was subsequently pressed by an Albanian rebel force called the National Liberation Army (NLA). Kosovo did not separate from Yugoslavia, but Serb forces were forced by North Atlantic Treaty Organization (NATO) forces to withdraw from the region after prolonged fighting with an Albanian nationalist group called the **Kosovo Liberation Army (KLA)**. Both the NLA and KLA used terrorism in their wars for independence.

Albanian separatists such as the KLA and Macedonia's NLA received arms and financing from drug trafficking via the so-called **Balkan Route**. Arsenals stockpiled prior to the fighting in Kosovo and Macedonia were purchased largely with proceeds from the heroin trade.

---

[63]BBC News. November 21, 1998.

[64]BBC News. "So Who Are the Russian Mafia?" April 1, 1998.

[65]BBC News. November 21, 1998.

[66]Cilluffo, "The Challenge."

[67]Ibid.

The Balkan Route is a drug trafficking crossroads between the European drug-consuming market and the heroin-producing countries of Afghanistan and Pakistan. Approximately 80% of Europe's heroin has historically passed through the former Yugoslavia. Prior to the disintegration of Yugoslavia, Western Europe's heroin was shipped from Turkey through Serbia, Croatia, and Slovenia.[68] Afterward, the Balkan Route shifted through Bulgaria, Hungary, Slovakia, and the Czech Republic. With the rise of Albanian nationalism, the route again flowed through the former Yugoslavia. European law enforcement experts universally agree that Albanian organized criminal enterprises became the primary traffickers of heroin in Europe during the 1990s. Estimates suggest that Albanian criminal enterprises controlled 70% of the heroin trade in Germany and Switzerland.[69]

Albanian nationalists and foreign drug traffickers engaged in heroin and weapons exchanges. For example, criminal enterprises in Georgia and Chechnya are known to have supplied weapons and heroin to Albanian traffickers, who sold the heroin in Europe to pay for the arms and then repeated the cycle.[70] This was done in league with traditional criminal enterprises in the West, such as the Italian criminal organizations. This nexus between Albanian nationalism and Albanian organized crime is further illustrated by the example of links between illicit Albanian groups and Macedonia's Albanian nationalist Party for Democratic Prosperity (PDP). Top PDP leaders were arrested and prosecuted for crimes that indicated their direct involvement in the smuggling into Macedonia of arms trafficked illegally from Serbia, Albania, Western Europe, and Bulgaria.[71]

# Chapter Summary

This chapter discussed two emerging terrorist environments: gender-selective political violence and criminal dissident terrorism. Each has distinguishable motivations, characteristics, and goals in the application of terrorist violence.

Gender-selective political violence occurs for a number of reasons. It often occurs during communal conflicts, which obscures the gender-focused nature of many incidents. Men and boys become targets of gender-selective terrorism either because an enemy wishes to eliminate potential fighters or because of a genocidal agenda. Terrorist violence against women has occurred on a massive scale and has been carried out by states during wartime and dissidents during rebellions and communal conflicts. It was not until the late 20th century that the international community began to recognize gender-selective violence as a specific kind of crime against humanity or genocidal violence.

Criminal terrorism is generally motivated by profit. Traditional criminal enterprises have no overarching reason for acquiring profit by illicit means, other than to enjoy the perquisites of accumulated wealth. Newer criminal-political enterprises have an overarching political motivation that guides their behavior. The latter model uses profits derived from illicit enterprises to finance their cause. The goals of traditional criminal enterprises are simply to generate profit and to be left alone in this endeavor. Their terrorist behavior tends to be reactive. The goals of criminal-political enterprises are revolutionary victory and the reconstruction of society. Their terrorist behavior tends to be active and public. A key concept to understand about criminal terrorism is that there is significant convergence between traditional and criminal-political enterprises. This is an intricate and fluid web of transnational cooperation.

In Chapter 10, readers will explore the tactics and targets of terrorists. The discussion centers on terrorist objectives, methods, and targets. The discussion will also ask whether, and to what extent, terrorism is effective.

[68]Chazan, Yigal. "Albanian Mafias Find New Drug Routes Around Yugoslavia." *Christian Science Monitor,* October 20, 1994.

[69]Milivojevic, Marko. "The 'Balkan Medellin.'" *Jane's Intelligence Review,* February 1, 1995, p. 68.

[70]James, Barry. "In Balkans, Arms for Drugs." *International Herald Tribune—Paris,* June 6, 1994.

[71]Milivojevic, "The 'Balkan Medellin.'"

# Key Terms and Concepts

The following topics are discussed in this chapter and can be found in the glossary:

Arellano-Félix cartel

Armed Forces Revolutionary Council (AFRC)

Balkan Route

Camorra

"comfort women"

criminal cartels

criminal dissident terrorism

criminal-political enterprises

drug cartels

drug-related violence

female genital mutilation (FGM)

gender communal terrorism

Golden Crescent

Golden Triangle

honor killings

International Criminal Tribunal for the Former Yugoslavia (ICTY)

International Criminal Tribunal for Rwanda (ICTR)

Janjaweed

Kosovo Liberation Army (KLA)

La Cosa Nostra

*Mutaween*

narco-terrorism

*narcotraficantes*

N'drangheta

People Persecuted by Pablo Escobar ("Pepes")

Rape of Nanking

Revolutionary United Front (RUF)

Russian Mafia

Sicilian Mafia

Solntsevskaya Gang

traditional criminal enterprises

transnational organized crime

Zetas, Los

# Discussion Box: Political Violence Against Women: Gender Communal Terrorism?

*This chapter's Discussion Box explores the hypothesis that mass violence against women is a type of communal terrorism. Communal terrorism, like other terrorist environments, is not static and continues to evolve. As war crimes are redefined to incorporate crimes such as rape conducted by combatants, it is appropriate to consider the inclusion of politically motivated gender-based violence.*

Violence against women has been an integral feature of wartime atrocities for centuries. In many conflicts, regular armies, irregular fighters, and politically motivated gangs have routinely selected the women of enemies to be kidnapped, raped, or killed. This type of violence has often been committed as a matter of policy and has been both systematic and methodical. As expressed by some violators, one motive behind systematic rape is to impregnate the women of an enemy group—thus "achieving forced pregnancy and thus poisoning the womb of the enemy."

The question is whether these gender-focused atrocities can be defined as **gender communal terrorism**.

The following are examples of government-initiated violence against women.

- During World War II, Japan provided "comfort women" to its armed forces.

These were women from Korea, China, and other conquered territories who were forced into sexual slavery. In December 1937, thousands of Chinese women were raped, humiliated, and killed during the "Rape of Nanking."

- The Taliban regime in Afghanistan repressed women with edicts that forbade them from working, receiving an education, showing any portion of their body, and even wearing certain kinds of shoes. Reports indicate that some Taliban and tribal commanders kidnapped girls and women to serve as sexual concubines and servants for their fighters.[a]

The following are examples of communal gender violence against women.[b]

- During the 1992 to 1995 war in Bosnia, an estimated 20,000 to 50,000 women were raped as part of ethnic cleansing campaigns. "Rape camps" and "rape hotels" were set up by Serb militia forces, where Muslim women were methodically raped, tortured, or killed.

- Hutu troops and militiamen in Rwanda systematically raped Tutsi women during the 1994 genocide.

- During the mid-1990s, the Armed Islamic Group in Algeria kidnapped and raped hundreds of women and young girls.

- During the 1998 rioting and looting of ethnic Chinese neighborhoods in Jakarta, Indonesia, hundreds of ethnic Chinese women were allegedly raped by organized gangs.

During investigations and prosecutions of war crimes committed in the Balkans, the United Nations International Criminal Tribunal for the Former Yugoslavia—for the first time in the history of war crimes tribunals—officially recognized rape as a war crime.

## Discussion Questions

- Why was systematic violence against women historically defined as something other than terrorism? Does it make sense to define such violence as terrorism in the modern era?

- At what point does violence against women become an act of terrorism? What are the parameters of terrorism against women?

- What are the causes of systematic violence against women? Is it likely to occur more often in some sociopolitical environments than others?

- How should governments and international organizations respond to gender-selective terrorism against women?

- What are the long-term implications of the emerging recognition of the existence of terrorism against women?

*Source:* Crossette, Barbara. "An Old Scourge of War Becomes Its Latest Crime." *New York Times.* June 14, 1998. Used by permission.

## Note

a. In Afghanistan, the Revolutionary Association of the Women of Afghanistan was founded in 1977 to combat abuses against women. It actively opposed the Taliban government and has continued to fight for basic civil liberties. Its website can be accessed at http://www.rawa.org/.

## On Your Own

The open-access Student Study Site at **http://study.sagepub.com/martin5e** has a variety of useful study aids, including eFlashcards, quizzes, audio resources, and journal articles. The websites, exercises, and recommended readings listed below are easily accessed on this site as well.

## Recommended Websites

The following websites provide links to discussions of gender-selective and criminal terrorism and extremism:

Drug Enforcement Administration (DEA): http://www.usdoj.gov/dea/

Gendercide Watch: http://www.gendercide.org/

International Criminal Tribunal for the Former Yugoslavia: http://www.un.org/icty/

International Criminal Tribunal for Rwanda: http://www.ictr.org/

Office of National Drug Control Policy (ONDCP): http://www.whitehouse.gov/ONDCP/

## Web Exercise

Using this chapter's recommended websites, conduct an online investigation of gender-selective terrorist violence.

1. What recommendations are made by medical human rights agencies to address the problem of gender-selective political violence?

2. Do the medical human rights agencies have enough resources to treat female victims of political violence?

3. Why is gender-selective political violence largely communal in nature?

Using this chapter's recommended websites, conduct an online investigation of criminal terrorism as it pertains to narco-terrorism.

4. How adequately do the DEA and ONDCP websites address the threat from narco-terrorism?

5. Does the DEA discussion of narco-terrorism present a thorough analysis of the problem?

6. Based on the discussion in this chapter, how would you advise these agencies to inform the public online about criminal terrorism?

For an online search of issues pertaining to gender-selective and criminal terrorism, readers should activate the search engine on their Web browser and enter the following keywords:

"Gendercide"

"Narco-terrorism"

# Recommended Readings

The following publications discuss the motives, goals, and characteristics of gender-selective and criminal extremism:

Ehrenfeld, Rachel. *Narco-Terrorism*. New York: Basic Books, 1990.

Farr, Kathryn. *Sex Trafficking: The Global Market in Women and Children*. New York: Worth, 2004.

Grabosky, Peter, and Michael Stohl. *Crime and Terrorism*. Thousand Oaks, CA: Sage, 2010.

Grayson, George W. *Narco-violence and a Failed State?*. Piscataway, NJ: Transaction Publishers, 2010.

Holmes, Jennifer S. *Guns, Drugs, and Development*. Austin: University of Texas Press, 2009.

Jones, Adam, ed. *Gendercide and Genocide*. Nashville, TN: Vanderbilt University Press, 2004.

Kenney, Michael. *From Pablo to Osama: Trafficking and Terrorist Networks, Government Bureaucracies, and Competitive Adaptation*. University Park: Pennsylvania State University Press, 2007.

Prunier, Girard. *Darfur: The Ambiguous Genocide*. Ithaca, NY: Cornell University Press, 2005.

Reichel, Philip, ed. *Handbook of Transnational Crime and Justice*. Thousand Oaks, CA: Sage, 2005.

Tarazona-Sevillano, Gabriela. *Sendero Luminoso and the Threat of Narcoterrorism*. Westport, CT: Praeger, 1990.

Voeten, Teun. *How de Body? One Man's Terrifying Journey Through an African War*. New York: Thomas Dunne, 2002.

# PART III

# The Terrorist Trade and Counterterrorism

Asymmetrical warfare. The remains of a vehicular bomb inside the heavily fortified Green Zone of Baghdad. A suicide bomber attacked the U.S.-occupied area during the post-2003 insurgency phase of the war in Iraq.

U.S. Department of Defense

# Tools of the Trade

CHAPTER 10

## *Tactics and Targets of Terrorists*

### OPENING VIEWPOINT: THE ENGINEER[a]

**Yehiya Ayyash**, a master bomb maker better known as **"the Engineer,"** was a model activist within Hamas's cell-based organizational structure. Unlike PLO-style groups, Hamas required its operatives to organize themselves into small, semi-autonomous units. Ayyash was an Al-Qassam cell (and later a "brigade") commander, but he had very few outside contacts and built his bombs in an almost solitary setting. He taught others to make bombs and how **suicide bombers** should position themselves for maximum effect.

The Engineer's first bomb was a Volkswagen car bomb that was used in April 1993. When Hamas began its suicide bombing campaign after the February 1994 Hebron massacre, Ayyash was the principal bomb maker. His bombs were sophisticated and custom made for each mission. They were particularly powerful compared to others previously designed by Hamas.

Ayyash was killed in January 1996. The cell phone he was using to carry on a conversation with his father had been booby-trapped by Israeli security agents and was remotely detonated. The assassination occurred as follows:

Fifty grams of RDX [plastic] explosives molded into the battery compartment of a telephone had been designed to kill only the man cradling the phone to his ear. The force of the concentrated blast caused most of the right side of Ayyash's face to implode. . . . The booby-trapped cellular phone had been . . . so target specific, that the left side of Ayyash's face had remained whole. The right hand which held the telephone was neither burnt nor damaged.[b]

The Engineer had been directly and indirectly responsible for killing approximately 150 people and injuring about 500 others.

#### Notes

a. Primarily from Katz, Samuel M. *The Hunt for the Engineer: How Israeli Agents Tracked the Hamas Master Bomber.* New York: Fromm International, 2001.

b. Ibid., pp. 260–1.

n this chapter, readers will investigate terrorist objectives, methods, and targets. The discussion focuses on the rationale behind the calculation of terrorists' ends and means—*what* terrorists are trying to do and *how* they try to do it. Weaponry is, of course, an integral factor in the evaluation of ends and means, so attention will also be given to the terrorists' arsenal.

*Terrorism*—however defined—is usually officially condemned, even by movements and governments that most of the global community would consider to be terrorists (they, of course, consider themselves to be freedom fighters, or the champions of freedom fighters). This is because much of the discussion about the objectives and methods of politically violent movements is a *moralistic debate,* centering on whether one can legitimately select certain methods as an expression of dissent. When terrorists adopt methods that will inevitably cause the deaths of defined enemies—including innocent civilians—a process of "moral disengagement" occurs that allows them to justify their actions.[1] Thus,

> the conversion of socialized people into dedicated combatants is not achieved by altering their personality structures, aggressive drives, or moral standards. Rather, it is accomplished by cognitively restructuring the moral value of killing.[2]

Previous chapters stressed the importance of *perspective* in the debate about the morality of extremists' tactics and targets, including the important role of codes of self-sacrifice that essentially "cleanse" those who follow the code, regardless of the scale of the violence committed in support of the cause. The following concepts are particularly pertinent for understanding terrorist behavior:

- "It became necessary to destroy the town to save it."[3]
- "Extremism in defense of liberty is no vice."[4]
- "One person's terrorist is another person's freedom fighter."
- "One man willing to throw away his life is enough to terrorize a thousand."[5]

Ironically, many people sympathize with the goals and objectives of violent extremist movements but oppose the means they use to accomplish those ends. The problem for some sympathizers is the seeming senselessness of certain types of violence. To most onlookers, many methods appear to be senseless and random; however, from the perspective of terrorists, these methods are neither. Two commonalities must be remembered about terrorist violence from the perspective of terrorists:

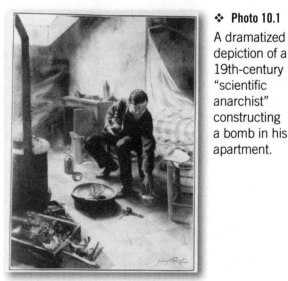

❖ **Photo 10.1**

A dramatized depiction of a 19th-century "scientific anarchist" constructing a bomb in his apartment.

Hulton Archive/Getty Images

---

[1]For a discussion of moral disengagement in the use of political violence, see Bandura, Albert. "Mechanisms of Moral Disengagement." In *Origins of Terrorism: Psychologies, Ideologies, Theologies, States of Mind,* edited by Walter Reich. Washington, DC: Woodrow Wilson Center, 1998, pp. 161ff.

[2]Ibid., p. 164.

[3]This quotation was more widely reported after the war as "we had to destroy the village to save it." The accuracy and source of the statement have been debated by journalists, scholars, and policy makers. See Oberdorfer, Don. *Tet!* Garden City, NY: Doubleday, 1971, pp. 184–5, 332. See also Sheehan, Neil. *A Bright Shining Lie: John Paul Vann and America in Vietnam.* New York: Random House, 1988, p. 719.

[4]A statement made by Republican Senator Barry Goldwater of Arizona during his bid for the presidency in 1964 against President Lyndon Johnson.

[5]A statement made by Chinese military philosopher Wu Ch'i.

- **Terrorist violence is rarely senseless.** It is usually well thought out and not an exercise in irrationality. Within the context of their circumstances, extremists conclude that terrorist methods make perfect sense. Regardless of the ultimate scale of violence applied or the number of civilian casualties, these are considered to be logical and sensible consequences of waging a just war.

- **Terrorist violence is rarely random.** Targets are specifically selected and represent the outcome of careful deliberation. An element of randomness occurs when "targets of opportunity" are attacked without a period of careful pre-planning.

Extremist movements justify the selection of terrorist methods in different ways. Among extremists, acceptance is almost universal that terrorist violence is a kind of "poor man's warfare" the weak use against stronger opponents. According to this rationale, terrorism is a weapon used by the downtrodden poor against brutally intransigent regimes. There is also a rationale that politically violent groups have no recourse other than to engage in terrorism because their opponents are unreceptive (perhaps violently so) to peaceful or democratic methods of dissent. As a matter of practicality, extremists adopt terrorist methods for several reasons:

- Terror tactics are relatively easy to use and therefore commend themselves to an organization without sophisticated weapons or popular support.

- Terrorism produces disproportionate publicity, which is highly prized by separatist movements or political factions that may feel they have no other way of seizing the world's attention.

- Spectacular atrocities illustrate a government's inability to rule. If a government is perceived to be weakened, exasperated security forces may be provoked to overreaction.[6]

Based on such justifications and practical considerations, terrorists have selected methods and targets from a menu of options derived from their interpretation of their environment. Many terrorists in the past were known to discriminate in selecting methods and targets. Conversely, practitioners of the New Terrorism are apt to wield any available weapon against broadly defined enemy interests.

Table 10.1 reports the incidence of terrorism against specific types of targets worldwide in 2013. The discussion in this chapter will review the following:

- The Purpose: Terrorist Objectives
- The Means: Terrorist Methods
- The Focus: Terrorist Targets
- The Outcome: Is Terrorism Effective?

## ❖ The Purpose: Terrorist Objectives

Objectives and goals are theoretical concepts that help explain the actions taken by extremist groups and movements during the course of their struggle; they are descriptions of processes that move toward final outcomes. An *objective* is an incremental step in the overall process that leads to an ultimate goal. A *goal* is the final result of the process, the terminal point of a series of objectives. Thus, a desired objective in a revolutionary campaign could be the overthrow of an enemy government or social order; the goal could be the establishment of a new society. During a revolutionary campaign, many objectives would have to be achieved to reach the final goal. For example, an objective for Marxists would be the revolutionary overthrow of a capitalist government. Their goal would be the construction of a new, classless society.

---

[6]See Keegan, John, and Richard Holmes. *Soldiers: A History of Men in Battle*. New York: Elisabeth Sifton Books, 1986, pp. 252–3.

| Table 10.1 | Targets of Terrorist Attacks Worldwide, 2013 |
| --- | --- |

| Target Type | Number of Targets |
| --- | --- |
| Private citizens and property | 3,035 |
| Police | 2,388 |
| Government (general) | 1,376 |
| Business | 862 |
| Military | 621 |
| Religious figures and institutions | 383 |
| Educational institutions | 354 |
| Terrorists and nonstate militia | 270 |
| Transportation | 253 |
| Utilities | 244 |
| Journalists and media | 167 |
| Violent political party | 137 |
| Government (diplomatic) | 102 |
| Telecommunication | 68 |
| NGO | 51 |
| Other | 41 |
| Airports and airlines | 29 |
| Tourists | 16 |
| Maritime | 11 |
| Food or water supply | 7 |
| Total | 10,415 |

*Source:* Office of the Coordinator for Terrorism. *Country Reports on Terrorism 2013*. Washington, DC: U.S. Department of State, 2014.

## Typical Objectives

Similarities in objectives can be identified among politically violent groups and movements. These objectives tend to fall somewhere within the range of minimal and optimal desirability: "For most terrorists, the *minimal* objective is increased public recognition that they are a political actor to contend with. The *optimal* objective is movement toward achieving their communal, revolutionary, or other political objective."[7]

The following discussion identifies a few commonalities in objectives. The selected list is by no means common to all violent extremists at all phases of their campaigns, and this is not an exhaustive

---

[7]Weimann, Gabriel, and Conrad Winn. *The Theater of Terror: Mass Media and International Terrorism*. New York: Longman, 1994, p. 173 (italics added).

analysis of every objective.[8] However, it is instructive to review a few central objectives.[9] These common objectives are the following:

- Changing the existing order
- Psychological disruption
- Social disruption
- Publicizing the cause
- Creating a revolutionary environment

### Changing the Existing Order

At some level, all terrorists seek to change an existing order, even if it is simply a short-term objective to disrupt the normal routines of society by inflicting maximum casualties. When evaluating what it means to change an existing order, one must take into consideration the different profiles of terrorist movements, their motives, and the idiosyncrasies of individual terrorists. Several examples follow:

- *Ethnonationalist* terrorists seek to win recognition of their human rights, or a degree of national autonomy, from the present order.
- *Nihilists* wish to destroy systems and institutions without regard for what will replace the existing order.
- *Religious* terrorists act on behalf of a supernatural mandate to bring about a divinely inspired new order.
- *"Lone wolves"* have a vague and sometimes delusional assumption that their actions will further a greater cause against a corrupt or evil social order.

### Psychological Disruption

An obvious objective is to inflict maximum psychological damage by applying dramatic violence against symbolic targets. "From the terrorists' perspective, the major force of terrorism comes not from its physical impact but from its psychological impact."[10] When terrorist violence is applied discerningly, the weak can influence the powerful, and the powerful can intimidate the weak. Cultural symbols, political institutions, and public leaders are examples of iconic (nearly sacred) targets that can affect large populations when attacked.

Although it is seemingly simplistic to state that terrorists strike these targets to spread terror, this is not an inaccurate characterization of the trauma that follows from a particularly dramatic terrorist incident. For example, many New Yorkers exhibited strong manifestations of stress and anxiety long after the September 11, 2001, attacks.[11]

### Social Disruption

Social disruption is an objective of propaganda by the deed. The ability of terrorists and extremists to disrupt the normal routines of society demonstrates both the weakness of the government and the strength of the movement; it provides terrorists with potentially very effective propaganda.

---

[8]For a good discussion of the objectives of states vis-à-vis dissidents, see Sederberg, Peter C. *Terrorist Myths: Illusion, Rhetoric, and Reality.* Englewood Cliffs, NJ: Prentice Hall, 1989, pp. 92ff.

[9]Another inventory of objectives is presented by Pillar, Paul R. *Terrorism and U.S. Foreign Policy.* Washington, DC: Brookings Institution, 2001, pp. 130–1.

[10]Heymann, Philip B. *Terrorism and America: A Commonsense Strategy for a Democratic Society.* Cambridge, MA: MIT Press, 1998, p. 9.

[11]Kershaw, Sarah. "Even 6 Months Later, 'Get Over It' Just Isn't an Option." *New York Times,* March 11, 2002.

When governments fail to protect the normal routines of society, discontent may spread throughout society, thus making the population susceptible to manipulation by a self-styled vanguard movement. For example, social disruption could be accomplished—and government weakness could be demonstrated—by bombing attacks on public transportation systems. These kinds of attacks have occurred many times in Israel, including a Jerusalem attack in February 1996 when Hamas bombed a bus, killing 22 Israelis. Similarly, a **suicide bombing** on December 25, 2003, at a bus station killed four Israelis; it was carried out by a 17-year-old member of the Popular Front for the Liberation of Palestine (PFLP). In another scenario, a targeted group could be attacked specifically to deter it from traveling through a region or territory; this group could be an ethnonational group or simply an economic group, such as the customers of a tourism industry. Tourists, for example, have been targeted repeatedly in Egypt:

- November 1997 incident in the ancient ruins of Luxor by Islamists, in which more than 60 people (mostly tourists) were killed
- July 2005 bombing incident in the resort city of Sharm el Sheikh on the Sinai Peninsula, which killed approximately 90 people
- A 2014 ultimatum attributed to the Islamist group Ansar Beit al-Maqdis that warned tourists to leave Egypt immediately

### Publicizing the Cause

Terrorists practice propaganda by the deed as a way to achieve exposure for their cause. When successfully manipulated, specific populations, governments, or other interests will focus on the extremists and their grievances. In the modern era, this means that a great deal of terrorist violence is **media-oriented terrorism**. Live broadcasting of violent incidents and their aftermath is *de rigueur* for media networks that wish to remain competitive in the global audience market. Television can bring terrorism, warfare, or other violence into hundreds of millions of households within seconds. Thus, with proper planning, terrorists can succeed not only in publicizing their cause but also in causing significant psychological disruption. In this way, the cause receives maximum exposure, and the target audience becomes victimized. All that is required is to attack a symbol that moves the targeted audience.

### Creating a Revolutionary Environment

Dissident extremists understand that they cannot hope to win in their struggle against the state without raising the revolutionary consciousness of the people. Theoretically, this objective can be achieved through the cumulative effect of the objectives just discussed. For many terrorists, propaganda by the deed is considered to be the most direct method for creating a broad-based revolutionary environment, so that "the destruction of one troop transport truck is more effective propaganda for the local population than a thousand speeches."[12] Revolutionary theorists predicted that terrorism would force the state to overreact, the people would understand the true repressive nature of the state, and a mass rebellion would occur—led by the revolutionary vanguard movement.

## Playing to the Audience: Objectives, Victims, and Constituencies

Terrorists adapt their methods and selection of targets to the characteristics of their championed group and the idiosyncrasies of their environment. Targets are selected for specific symbolic reasons, with the objectives of victimizing specific groups or interests and sending symbolic messages to the terrorists' constituency. In a sense, the targeted groups or interests serve as conduits to communicate the extremist movement's message. Thus,

---

[12]Debray, Regis. *Revolution in the Revolution?* Westport, CT: Greenwood, 1967. Quoted in Hewitt, Christopher. "Public's Perspectives." In *Terrorism and the Media,* edited by David L. Paletz and Alex P. Schmid. Newbury Park, CA: Sage, 1992, p. 189.

the act of victimizing captures the attention of particular audiences and allows the terrorist to communicate more specific messages tailored to each one. . . . The use of threat and violence against victims—the kidnappings, the bombings, the assassinations, the killings—serves to transmit specific demands to certain targets and different messages to other targets.[13]

If skillfully applied, propaganda by the deed can be manipulated to affect specific audiences. These audiences can include the following segments of society:[14]

- **Politically Apathetic People.** The objective of terrorist violence directed toward this group is to force an end to their indifference and, ideally, to motivate them to petition the government for fundamental changes.
- **The Government and Its Allied Elites.** Terrorists seek to seriously intimidate or distract a nation's ruling bodies to force them to deal favorably with the underlying grievances of the dissident movement.
- **Potential Supporters.** An important objective of propaganda by the deed is to create a revolutionary consciousness in a large segment of society. This is more easily done within the pool of those who are sympathetic to the extremists' objectives but who do not yet approve of their methods.
- **Confirmed Supporters.** Terrorists seek to assure their members and confirmed supporters that the movement continues to be strong and active. They communicate this through acts of symbolic violence.

Depending on whom they claim to champion, extremist movements adapt their tactics to their environment as a way to communicate with (and attract) their defined constituency. Consider, for example, the perspective from two familiar environments (ethnonationalism and ideology):

*Ethnonationalist terrorists* have tended to be focused and surgical, with the important exception of extreme examples of communal violence. Their objectives are to win improved conditions or autonomy for their championed group. Even when the scale of violence has escalated to the point of near civil war, the enemy group has usually been clearly (if broadly) defined, and the targeted symbols have been interpreted as representations of the enemy group. Attacks against rival ethnonational groups certainly cause civilian casualties, but these civilians have been defined as legitimate targets because of their ethnonational affiliation. Thus, aside from extreme communal terrorist environments,

> these terrorist movements . . . see themselves as a revolutionary vanguard—if not in classic Marxist-Leninist terms, at least as a spearhead, similarly using violence to "educate" fellow members of their national or ethnic group about the inequities imposed upon them by the ruling government and the need for communal resistance and rebellion.[15]

*Left-wing ideological terrorists* historically tended to be focused and relatively surgical in their objectives and methods. Their overriding objective has been to use propaganda by the deed to create a revolutionary consciousness in their championed group and thereby to attract the championed group to the cause. Leftists traditionally have been careful about attacking clearly symbolic targets such as buildings, offices, interests, and officials. Based on their interpretation of the existing social and political environment, "the overriding tactical—and indeed ethical—imperative for left-wing terrorists has been the deliberate tailoring of their violent acts to appeal to their perceived 'constituencies.'"[16]

---

[13]Crelinsten, Ronald D. "Victims' Perspectives." In *Terrorism and the Media,* edited by David L. Paletz and Alex P. Schmid. Newbury Park, CA: Sage, 1992, p. 212.

[14]See Heymann, *Terrorism,* pp. 10–1.

[15]Ibid., p. 161.

[16]Hoffman, Bruce. *Inside Terrorism.* New York: Columbia University Press, 1998, p. 158.

*Right-wing ideological terrorists* have been much less likely to be either focused or surgical in their political objectives. This is perhaps because their objectives are often quite vague, and their constituencies are not clearly defined. Right-wing ideology is very idiosyncratic to specific national political environments, and rarely is there a global philosophy that seeks to bind together the violent right. Within the context of terrorist objectives, right-wing terrorist violence has been described as nothing more than

> an egocentric pleasure derived from brawling and bombing, preening or parading in 1940s-era Nazi regalia . . . given that the majority of right-wing groups do not espouse any specific programme of reform, preferring to hide behind vague slogans of strident nationalism, the need for racial purity and the re-assertion of governmental strength.[17]

Thus, with a few exceptions, appeals to specific constituencies are commonly made by terrorists and extremists. These appeals are peculiar to the environment and idiosyncrasies of the movement, although leftists and ethnonationalists have sometimes championed the same groups out of a sense of revolutionary solidarity. Table 10.2 illustrates the relationship between several extremist groups and movements and their constituencies, objectives, methods, and targeted interests.

## Table 10.2   Constituencies and Enemies: Selecting Tactics and Targets

Terrorists select their methods within the context of their social and political environments. They appeal to specific constituencies and justify their choice of methods by championing the political cause of their constituencies. Their targeted interests (that is, enemy interests) can be defined narrowly or broadly, so that civilian populations can be included as legitimized targets.

The following table summarizes the constituencies, objectives, methods, and targeted interests of several terrorist groups and movements.

| Group or Movement | Activity Profile | | | |
| --- | --- | --- | --- | --- |
| | Constituency | Objectives | Methods | Targeted Interest |
| **Al-Aqsa Martyr Brigades** | Palestinians | Palestinian state | Suicide bombings; small-arms attacks | Israeli civilians; Israeli military |
| **Iraqi and Syrian Islamist insurgents** | Sunni Muslims | Collapse of Syrian and Iraqi regimes; establishment of Islamist state | Terrorist attacks; guerrilla warfare | Regime institutions; non-Sunnis |
| **Al-Qa'ida and affiliates** | Devout Muslims | Worldwide Islamic revolution | Well-planned bombings; indigenous insurrections | The West; secular Islamic governments |
| **Provos** | Irish Catholics | Union with the Irish Republic | Small-arms attacks; bombings | British; Ulster Protestants |
| **Bosnian Serb militias** | Bosnian Serbs | Serb state | Ethnic cleansing; communal terrorism | Bosnian Muslims; Bosnian Croats |
| **Tamil Tigers** | Sri Lankan Tamils | Tamil state | Terrorist attacks; guerrilla warfare | Sri Lankan government; Sinhalese |

[17]Ibid., p. 161.

# The New Terrorism and New Objectives

The New Terrorism is different from previous models because it is characterized by vaguely articulated political objectives, indiscriminate attacks, attempts to achieve maximum psychological and social disruption, and the potential use of weapons of mass destruction. It also includes an emphasis on building horizontally organized, semi-autonomous cell-based networks.

## Weapons of Mass Destruction and the Objectives of the New Terrorism

Terrorist violence is, at its core, symbolic in nature. With notable exceptions, methods and targets have tended to be focused and relatively surgical, and they have been modified to accommodate the terrorists' definitions of who should be labeled as a championed group or as an enemy. However, the redefined morality of the New Terrorism opens the door for methods to include high-yield weapons and for targets to include large populations. Symbolic targets and enemy populations can now be hit much harder than in the past; all that is required is the will to do so.

Why would terrorists deliberately use high-yield weapons? What objectives would they seek? Depending on the group, many reasons have been suggested, including the following general objectives:[18]

- **Attracting Attention.** No one can ignore movements that carry out truly devastating attacks. This is the ultimate manifestation of armed propaganda and propaganda by the deed.

- **Pleasing God.** Divinely inspired terrorists seek to carry out what they believe to be a mandate from God. For example, Christian terrorists believing in the inevitability of the apocalypse might wish to hasten its arrival by using a weapon of mass destruction.

- **Damaging Economies.** This could be accomplished by the contamination of food or other consumer products. A few poisoning events or other acts of consumer-focused sabotage could damage an economic sector.

- **Influencing Enemies.** Terrorists may be moved to wield exotic weapons as a way to influence a large population. After using these weapons, their demands and grievances would receive serious scrutiny.

In the era of the New Terrorism, terrorists may strike with the central objective of killing as many people as possible. For example, in late 2006 and early 2007, a series of vehicular bombs used by Islamist extremists in Iraq were constructed using chorine-filled tanks. However, violent extremists are not necessarily interested in overthrowing governments or changing policies as their primary objectives. Rather, their intent is simply to deliver a high body count and thereby terrorize and disrupt large audiences. For example, the 1993 and 2001 attacks on the World Trade Center in New York City by radical Islamists, Aum Shinrikyō's 1995 **Sarin nerve gas** attack in Tokyo, and the 1995 bombing in Oklahoma City by American terrorists were all intended to kill as many civilians as possible and to demonstrate the vulnerability of society. There was little if any consideration given to changing government policies.

The following examples are cases of attempted and actual acquisitions of **chemical agents** by extremists. They demonstrate how the underlying characteristic of groups willing to use these weapons is that their objectives (often very vague) permit indiscriminate targeting. These groups also exhibit a minimal intention to pursue concrete political objectives.

***The Covenant, the Sword, and the Arm of the Lord.*** **The Covenant, the Sword, and the Arm of the Lord (CSA)** was an apocalyptic religious and racial supremacist survivalist community in the Ozark Mountains of Arkansas. The group was effectively disbanded in 1985 after prosecutions by federal authorities for, among other charges, possessing a large quantity of poisonous **potassium cyanide**.

---

[18]See Stern, Jessica. *The Ultimate Terrorists.* Cambridge, MA: Harvard University Press, 1999, pp. 70ff.

CSA had intended to use the toxin to poison water supplies in U.S. cities.[19] Its objective was to fulfill its apocalyptic vision of hastening the end of time and the coming of a new racial and religious age. CSA is an important example of the threat from committed fringe communities (a number of which exist in the United States) and how such communities can easily acquire chemical agents if motivated to do so.

***Ramzi Yousef.*** Yousef masterminded the first World Trade Center attack in February 1993. Some authorities claimed that he had incorporated toxic **sodium cyanide** into the bomb, intending to create a toxic chemical cloud.[20] This is unlikely,[21] but Yousef apparently did attempt to procure chemical agents prior to the attack but was unable to do so. Yousef's case confirms that some activists in the new international terrorist environment have no compunction about using chemical agents (if available) to inflict as high a death toll as possible. This kind of objective is purely terroristic in character.

***Aum Shinrikyō.*** The Aum Supreme Truth cult released Sarin nerve gas into the Tokyo subway system in March 1995, killing 12 and injuring thousands. The Aum example is significant because it provides several important lessons: First, the attack was easily planned; second, the attack was easily carried out; third, the chemical agent was easily manufactured; fourth, the potential death toll from this kind of attack is massive; and fifth, the emergency medical systems of major cities may be unable to respond effectively to this kind of attack.

## ❖ The Means: Terrorist Methods

The terrorist environment today is shaped by advances in technology, information, and transnational interconnectivity. This truly globalized environment has given rise to new possibilities in terrorist methodology.[22] Two factors in particular are believed by experts to contribute significantly to the distinctiveness of methodologies in the era of the New Terrorism. The first is "the diffusion of information technology and advanced communications":

> The concern about chemical, biological, radiological, or nuclear . . . terrorism is based partly on the increased ease of finding pertinent information on [the] Internet. The principal impact of the new electronic technologies, however, has not been to move the terrorists toward more exotic methods of attack, but rather . . . to improve the efficiency of all of their activities. . . . Computers and satellite phones have become standard equipment in terrorist groups.[23]

A second distinction of the New Terrorism's methods is the "increased movement, and ease of movement, across international boundaries":

> The terrorists' greater ability to operate over long distances has manifested itself [in] . . . the building by several terrorist groups of globe-circling infrastructures [and] . . . the rise of ad hoc terrorists—small cabals of extremists who do not belong to any larger, established, previously known group.[24]

---

[19]See Stern, Jessica Eve. "The Covenant, the Sword, and the Arm of the Lord (1985)." In *Toxic Terror: Assessing Terrorist Use of Chemical and Biological Weapons,* edited by Jonathan B. Tucker. Cambridge, MA: MIT Press, 2000, pp. 139–57.

[20]See Judge Kevin T. Duffy. Sentencing Statement. *United States of America v. Mohammad A. Salameh, et al.,* S593CR.180 (KTD), May 24, 1994, p. 36. Quoted in Parachini, John V. "The World Trade Center Bombers (1993)." In *Toxic Terror: Assessing Terrorist Use of Chemical and Biological Weapons,* edited by Jonathan B. Tucker. Cambridge: MIT Press, 2000, pp. 185–6.

[21]See Parachini, "The World Trade Center," pp. 186–7.

[22]For a discussion of terrorism in the age of globalization, see Martin, Gus. "Globalization and International Terrorism." In *The Blackwell Companion to Globalization*, edited by George Ritzer. Malden, MA: Blackwell, 2006.

[23]Pillar, *Terrorism,* p. 47.

[24]Ibid., pp. 48–9.

The following discussion reviews common methods used by terrorists to achieve their objectives, including their selection of weapons.

## Concept: Asymmetrical Warfare

The concept of **asymmetrical warfare** has been adapted to the characteristics of contemporary political violence.[25] Modern asymmetrical warfare refers to the use of unconventional, unexpected, and nearly unpredictable methods of political violence. Terrorists intentionally strike at unanticipated targets and apply unique and idiosyncratic tactics. This way, they can seize the initiative and redefine the international security environment and overcome the traditional protections and deterrent policies that societies and the international community use.

### The Appeal of Asymmetrical Conflict

Asymmetrical warfare as a method of confrontation arose "from the perception that the United States, and the West (including Israel) more generally, have developed an unassailable capacity for conventional warfare."[26] Because of this reality, state-level rivals must resort to unconventional and subversive methods to confront U.S. and Western interests—they could never otherwise confront them using conventional means. At the same time, dissidents must adopt unorthodox methods that can deliver maximum propaganda and symbolic blows against the seemingly overwhelming power of enemy states or societies. Hence, the New Terrorism is characterized by a new doctrine that allows for the use of weapons of mass destruction, indiscriminate attacks, maximum casualties, technology-based terrorism, and other exotic and extreme methods.

This methodology is particularly appealing to antistate movements. Dissident terrorists are quantitatively and qualitatively weaker than conventional security forces. In today's intensive security environment, they simply cannot prevail or last indefinitely in an urban-based guerrilla campaign—readers may recall the fates of the Montoneros and Tupamaros (cited later in this chapter as cases of unviable movements). Modern terrorists who understand this are more willing than before to deploy unconventional weapons and use highly destructive tactics. Through the adoption of asymmetrical methods, "the weaker forces are seeking total war, encompassing all segments of society."[27] They are trying to break the enemy's will to resist through whatever means are at their disposal.

### Netwar: A New Organizational Theory

The New Terrorism incorporates maximum flexibility into its organizational and communications design. Semi-autonomous cells either are pre-positioned around the globe as sleepers (such as the March 11, 2004, Madrid terrorists) or they travel to locations where an attack is to occur (such as the September 11 hijackers in the United States). They communicate using new cyber and digital technologies. An important concept in the new terrorist environment is the **netwar** theory, which refers to

an emerging mode of conflict and crime . . . in which the protagonists use network forms of organization and related doctrines, strategies, and technologies attuned to the information age. These protagonists are likely to consist of dispersed small groups who communicate, coordinate, and conduct their campaigns in an internetted manner, without a precise central command.[28]

---

[25]The term was used in a study conducted by the National Defense Panel titled "Transforming Defense: National Security in the 21st Century." The 1997 report warned that "unanticipated asymmetries" in the international security environment would likely result in an attack on the American homeland. Leiby, Richard. "Rueful Prophets of the Unimaginable: High-Level Studies Warned of Threat." *Washington Post,* September 22, 2001.

[26]Lesser, Ian O. "Countering the New Terrorism: Implications for Strategy." In *Countering the New Terrorism,* edited by Ian O. Lesser, Bruce Hoffman, John Arquilla, David Ronfeldt, and Michele Zanini. Santa Monica, CA: RAND, 1999, p. 94.

[27]Haselkorn, Avigdor. "Martyrdom: The Most Powerful Weapon." *Los Angeles Times,* December 3, 2000.

[28]Arquilla, David Ronfeldt, and Michele Zanini. "Networks, Netwar, and Information-Age Terrorism." In *Countering the New Terrorism,* edited by Ian O. Lesser, Bruce Hoffman, John Arquilla, David Ronfeldt, and Michele Zanini. Santa Monica, CA: RAND, 1999, p. 47.

The new "internetted" movements have made a strategic decision to establish virtual linkages via the Internet and other technologies. They represent modern adaptations of the following organizational models:[29]

- **Chain Networks.** People, goods, or information move along a line of separated contacts, and end-to-end communication must travel through the intermediate nodes.

- **Star, Hub, or Wheel Networks.** A set of actors is tied to a central node or actor and must go through that node to communicate and coordinate.

- **All-Channel Networks.** There is a collaborative network of small militant groups, and every group is connected to every other group.

### Case in Point: The "Martyr Nation" as an Asymmetrical Strategy

The application of asymmetrical warfare is evident in the conflict between the Palestinians and Israelis during 2001 to 2002. The doctrine of engagement used by Palestinian nationalists called for incessant confrontation with the Israelis, using guerrilla, terrorist, and suicidal martyrdom tactics to strike unexpectedly at soft civilian targets. As one Palestinian leader said, "Our ability to die is greater than the Israelis' ability to go on killing us." Nationalists contended that "Israel is confronting a martyr 'nation,' not just individual fanatics or militant groups."[30] Thus, the Maoist concept of *people's war* arguably has had an asymmetrical application in the martyrdom tactics used by Palestinian extremists, because it suggests that an entire people is willing to sacrifice a great deal to achieve its goals.

This concept of a **martyr nation** as a doctrine for engagement is an example of modern asymmetrical warfare, and it has been applied outside of Israel and the occupied territories. The Palestinians' notion that their ability to die is greater than their enemy's ability to go on killing them was not lost on Iraqi insurgents, who regularly employed suicidal martyrdom tactics after 2003 against U.S.-led occupation troops and perceived Iraqi collaborators.

## An Introduction to Common Methods of Terrorists

Methods adopted by modern terrorists reflect the idiosyncrasies of their political environments, so that no single factor explains the adoption of specific tactics by different groups. For example, some methods can become routine among a number of groups but are then rarely employed by other groups. Nevertheless, some commonalities do exist, and "the bomb and the gun" remain as staples in the terrorist arsenal. A number of tactics and weapons are recurrently encountered:

- *Bombings* are a very common terrorist method because they allow the extremist movement to inflict maximum physical and psychological damage with minimum casualties. *Suicide bombings* are particularly effective in the maximization of casualties and psychological consequences.

- *Sidearms* (pistols and rifles) are likewise commonly employed to ambush, assassinate, or otherwise inflict casualties on an enemy.

- *Kidnappings* are conducted for different reasons; they are done sometimes to extort ransoms and at other times for purely propaganda purposes. In the latter scenario, the hostages are sometimes executed.

- *Hijackings* of airliners, seagoing vessels, trains, and other modes of transportation are generally conducted for maximum propaganda effect. This is because they generally have an international profile and are conducted in conjunction with seizing hostages.

---

[29]See ibid., p. 49.

[30]Haselkorn, "Martyrdom."

Methods have occasionally become "signatures" of terrorist movements. These are methods that become closely affiliated with the operational activities of specific extremist groups. An example of a **signature method** is a technique used by the Irish Republican Army, Irish Protestant loyalists, and Italy's Red Brigades known as **"kneecapping."** The technique involved shooting a victim in the back of the knee joint, thus shooting off the kneecap. Other signature methods have included kidnappings (Abu Sayyaf in the Philippines and Brazilian leftists), hijackings (Popular Front for the Liberation of Palestine), and suicide bombings (Iraqi insurgents and Liberation Tigers of Tamil Eelam).

The weapons employed by terrorists are integral features of their overall methodologies. Firearms and explosives have historically been the weapons of choice for terrorists. This has not changed appreciably in the modern era, although available firepower has greatly increased, and the selection of targets has arguably become more indiscriminate. Weapons typically include small arms, commercial- and military-grade explosives, rocket-propelled grenades, vehicular (car and truck) bombs, and sometimes suicide bombs. Sophisticated weapons have occasionally been used, such as **precision-guided munitions** (shoulder-fired anti-aircraft rockets) and high-technology triggering devices for bombs. Very few examples exist of the use of weapons of mass destruction, such as chemical, biological, radiological, or nuclear devices. Although the *threat* from terrorists' acquisition of weapons of mass destruction increased during the 1990s, the overarching profile of terrorists and extremists is that they typically wield conventional firearms and explosives.

❖ **Photo 10.2**

Anthrax-laced letters sent to Capitol Hill offices. Several letters were mailed during the immediate aftermath of the September 11 homeland attack.

U.S. Federal Bureau of Investigation

## Weapons Old and New

In the modern era, weaponry can be classified along a sliding scale of technological sophistication and threat potential. This scale includes a high, medium, and low range, summarized as follows:[31]

- **High Range.** The New Terrorism is defined in part by the threatened acquisition of chemical agents, **biological agents**, or **nuclear weapons**. This threat includes the development of **radiological agents** that spread highly toxic radioactive materials by detonating conventional explosives. The first case of widespread use of a biological agent by terrorists occurred when **anthrax** was deliberately sent through the mail in the United States in the aftermath of the September 11, 2001, attacks.

- **Medium Range.** Terrorists currently have extensive access to military-style weaponry. These include automatic weapons, rocket launchers, and military-grade explosives of many varieties. Sympathetic state sponsorship and the international arms black market permit the procurement of a virtually unlimited array of conventional small arms and munitions. These arms have been the weapons of choice for terrorists in innumerable examples.

- **Low Range.** Often forgotten in the discussions about the threat from medium- and high-range weaponry are the powerful homemade weapons that can be manufactured from commercial-grade components. For example, ammonium nitrate and fuel oil (ANFO) bombs can be easily manufactured from readily available materials. Iraqi insurgents became quite adept at deploying **improvised explosive devices (IEDs)**, commonly referred to as **"roadside bombs,"** against U.S.-led occupation troops.

Contrary to popular assumptions, terrorists and extremists have historically been selective about their choice of weapons and reserved about their use. They have not, as a rule, been particularly

---

[31]See Hoffman, Bruce. "Terrorism Trends and Prospects." In *Countering the New Terrorism,* edited by Ian O. Lesser, Bruce Hoffman, John Arquilla, David Ronfeldt, and Michele Zanini. Santa Monica, CA: RAND, 1999, pp. 28ff.

adventurous about the quality of violence that they employ. Although modern terrorists have used improvements in the technology of firearms and explosives, they are similar to their violent predecessors in the basic kinds of weaponry that they elect to use:

> Previously, most terrorists had shown an aversion to the esoteric and exotic weapons of mass destruction. . . . Radical in their politics, the majority of terrorists were equally conservative in their methods of operation. Indeed, from the time of the late nineteenth-century Russian revolutionaries and the [Irish] Fenian dynamiters . . . terrorists have continued to rely almost exclusively on the same two weapons: the gun and the bomb.[32]

### Firearms

Small arms and other handheld weapons have been, and continue to be, the most common types of weapons employed by terrorists. These are light and heavy infantry weapons and include pistols, rifles, submachine guns, assault rifles, machine guns, **rocket-propelled grenades**, mortars, and precision-guided munitions. Typical firearms found in the hands of terrorists include the following:

- **Submachine Guns.** Originally developed for military use, **submachine guns** are now mostly used by police and paramilitary services. Although new models have been designed, such as the famous Israeli Uzi and the American Ingram, World War II–era models are still on the market and have been used by terrorists.

- **Assault Rifles.** Usually capable of both automatic (repeating) and semiautomatic (single-shot) fire, **assault rifles** are military-grade weapons that are used extensively by terrorists and other irregular forces. The **AK-47**, invented by **Mikhail Kalashnikov** for the Soviet army, is the most successful assault rifle in terms of production numbers and its widespread adoption by standing armies, guerrillas, and terrorists. The American-made **M-16** has likewise been produced in large numbers and has been adopted by a range of conventional and irregular forces.

- **Rocket-Propelled Grenades (RPGs).** Light, self-propelled munitions are common features of modern infantry units. The **RPG-7** has been used extensively by dissident forces throughout the world, particularly in Latin America, the Middle East, and Asia. The weapon was manufactured in large quantities by the Soviets, Chinese, and other communist nations. It is an uncomplicated and powerful weapon that is useful against armor and fixed emplacements such as bunkers or buildings.

- **Precision-Guided Munitions (PGMs).** Less commonly found among terrorists, but extremely effective when used, are weapons that can be guided to their targets by using infrared or other tracking technologies. The American-made **Stinger** is a shoulder-fired surface-to-air missile that uses an infrared targeting system. It was delivered to the Afghan *mujahideen* during their anti-Soviet *jihad* and was used very effectively against Soviet helicopters and other aircraft. The Soviet-made **SA-7**, also known as the **Grail**, is also an infrared-targeted surface-to-air missile. Both the Stinger and the Grail pose a significant threat to commercial airliners and other aircraft.

### Common Explosives

Terrorists regularly use explosives to attack symbolic targets. Along with firearms, explosives are staples of the terrorist arsenal. The vast majority of terrorists' bombs are self-constructed, improvised weapons rather than premanufactured, military-grade bombs. The one significant exception to this rule is the heavy use of military-grade **mines** by the world's combatants. These are buried in the soil or rigged to be detonated as booby traps. Antipersonnel mines are designed to kill people, and antitank mines are designed to destroy vehicles. Many millions of mines have been manufactured and are available on the international market.

---

[32]Hoffman, *Inside Terrorism*, p. 121.

Some improvised bombs are constructed from commercially available explosives such as **dyna-mite** and **TNT**, whereas others are manufactured from military-grade compounds. Examples of compounds found in terrorist bombs include the following:

- **Plastic Explosives. Plastic explosives** are putty-like explosive compounds that can be easily molded. The central component of most plastic explosives is a compound known as **RDX**. Nations that manufacture plastic explosives often use chemical markers to "tag" each batch that is made. The tagged explosives can be traced back to their source if used by terrorists. Richard C. Reid, the "shoe bomber" aboard American Airlines Flight 63, attempted to detonate a bomb crafted from plastic explosives molded into his shoe in December 2001.

- **Semtex. Semtex** is a very potent plastic explosive of Czech origin. During the Cold War, Semtex appeared on the international market, and a large quantity was obtained by Libya. It is popular among terrorists. For example, the Irish Republican Army (IRA) has used Semtex-based bombs in Northern Ireland and England.

- **Composite-4 (C-4). Composite-4 (C-4)** is a high-grade and powerful plastic explosive. It is more expensive and more difficult to obtain than Semtex. The availability of C-4 for use by terrorists became apparent when a renegade CIA agent was convicted of shipping 21 tons of the compound to Libya during the 1970s. About 600 pounds of C-4 was used in the October 2000 attack against the American destroyer *USS Cole* in Yemen, and it was evidently used to bomb the American facility at Khobar Towers in Dhahran, Saudi Arabia, in June 1996.

- **ANFO Explosives. Ammonium nitrate and fuel oil (ANFO) explosives** are manufactured from common ammonium nitrate fertilizer that has been soaked in fuel oil. Using ammonium nitrate as a base for the bomb, additional compounds and explosives can be added to intensify the explosion. These devices require hundreds of pounds of ammonium nitrate, so they are generally constructed as car or truck bombs. ANFO explosives were used by the IRA in London in 1996; American extremist Timothy McVeigh used a 2-ton device in Oklahoma City in 1995. Sri Lanka's Tamil Tigers also used ANFO-based devices during their decades-long insurgency.

### Triggers

Regardless of the type of explosive that is used, some bomb makers construct sophisticated triggering devices and are able to shape explosive charges to control the direction of the blast. Examples of triggering devices include the following:

- **Timed Switches.** Time bombs are constructed from acid-activated or electronically activated triggers. They are rigged to detonate after the passage of a period of time.

- **Fuses.** A very old and low-technology method to detonate bombs is to light a fuse that detonates the explosives. It can be timed by varying the length of the fuse. Shoe bomber Richard Reid was overpowered after a flight attendant smelled burning matches as he tried to light a fuse in his shoe.

- **Pressure Triggers.** Using **pressure triggers**, weapons such as mines are detonated when physical pressure is applied to a trigger. Car bombers in Iraq apparently attached broom handles or other poles to the front of their vehicles as plungers and then rammed their target with the plunger. A variation on physical pressure triggers are trip-wire booby traps. More sophisticated pressure triggers react to atmospheric (barometric) pressure, such as changes in pressure when an airliner ascends or descends.

- **Electronic Triggers.** Remotely controlled bombs are commonly employed by terrorists. **Electronic triggers** are activated by a remote electronic or radio signal.

- **High-Technology Triggers.** Some sophisticated devices may use triggers that are activated by motion, heat, or sunlight. The technologies for such devices are readily available. For example, household lighting and other devices commonly utilize motion- and solar-activated sensors.

### Types of Bombs

© Joseph Faddoul/epa/Corbis

❖ **Photo 10.3**
Car bomb in Beirut. Flames rise from the wreckage of a burnt-out car after a bomb was exploded in it.

- **Gasoline Bombs.** The most easily manufactured (and common) explosive weapon used by dissidents is nothing more than a gasoline-filled bottle with a flaming rag for its trigger. It is thrown at targets after the rag is stuffed into the mouth of the bottle and ignited. Tar, Styrofoam, or other ingredients can be added to create a gelling effect for the bomb, which causes the combustible ingredient to stick to surfaces. These weapons are commonly called **"Molotov cocktails,"** named for Vyacheslav Molotov, the Soviet Union's foreign minister during World War II. During the war, Red Army soldiers and partisans (guerrillas) hurled **gasoline bombs** at German tanks.

- **Pipe Bombs.** These devices are easily constructed from common pipes, which are filled with explosives (usually gunpowder) and then capped on both ends. Nuts, bolts, screws, nails, and other shrapnel are usually taped or otherwise attached to pipe bombs. Many hundreds of pipe bombs have been used by terrorists. In the United States, pipe bombs were used in several bombings of abortion clinics and at the 1996 Summer Olympics in Atlanta. Modified pipe bombs have also been used by Palestinian suicide bombers during the *intifada*.

- **Vehicular Bombs.** Ground vehicles that have been wired with explosives are a frequent weapon in the terrorist arsenal. **Vehicular bombs** can include car bombs and truck bombs; they are mobile, are "covert" in the sense that they are not readily identifiable, are able to transport large amounts of explosives, and are rather easily constructed. They have been used on scores of occasions throughout the world. Examples of groups that regularly used vehicular bombs include Shining Path (Sendero Luminoso) in Peru, the IRA, the Tamil Tigers in Sri Lanka, Palestinian groups, the Basque Fatherland and Liberty (ETA) in Spain, Iraqi insurgents, and Lebanese groups. Some of these attacks have been quite devastating:

  o February 1993: Four hundred people were killed and 1,000 wounded in 13 simultaneous vehicular bombings in Bombay, India. The attacks were carried out to avenge an attack on a Muslim shrine by Hindus.

  o April 1995: One hundred sixty-eight people were killed, including 19 children, when Timothy McVeigh used a truck bomb to destroy the Alfred P. Murrah Federal Building in Oklahoma City.

  o June 1996: A truck bomb killed 19 people in an attack on the U.S. Air Force barracks in Dhahran, Saudi Arabia. Anti-Saudi Islamic revolutionaries were responsible.

  o August 1998: Twenty-nine people were killed and more than 220 were injured when a car bomb exploded in the town of Omagh, Northern Ireland. The Real Irish Republican Army claimed credit for the attack in an attempt to derail peace negotiations.

  o 2000–2001: The Basque terrorist group ETA ended its cease-fire and began a bombing campaign in Spain. A number of these bombs were car bombs.

  o February 2005: Rafiq Hariri, former prime minister of Lebanon, was assassinated by a car bomb; 20 other people were killed. Syrian agents were suspected.

  o June 2005: Dhari Ali al-Fayadh, a member of Iraq's newly constituted parliament, was assassinated by a suicide car bomb in Baghdad.

- **Improvised Rockets.** Examples exist of the deployment of self-designed rockets by terrorist groups. These are basic designs that are fired without precision at intended targets, but some designs have been significantly upgraded in sophistication. The most famous and frequently used improvised rocket is the **Qassam**, deployed by Hamas and Palestine Islamic Jihad against Israel.

Fired from Gaza, Qassams are imprecisely aimed and directed against Israeli territory. They are responsible for killing or wounding hundreds of Israelis. The term *Qassam* is used generically to refer to several types of rockets, which also include multiple-tube Katyushas and Grads (Soviet-designed) and Iranian Fajr-5 rockets. Israel responded by deploying its **Iron Dome** missile defense network, widely credited with successfully intercepting many Palestinian improvised rockets.[33]

- **Barometric Bombs.** These bombs use triggers that are activated by changes in atmospheric pressure. An altitude meter can be rigged to become a triggering device when a specific change in pressure is detected. Thus, an airliner can be blown up in midair as the cabin pressure changes. These are sophisticated devices.

### Case in Point: Weapons of Mass Destruction

Within the context of threats from high-range weapons, it is important to distinguish basic differences between four types of weapons: biological agents, chemical agents, radiological agents, and nuclear weapons.

*Biological Agents.* These weapons are "living organisms . . . or infective material derived from them, which are intended to cause disease or death in man, animals, and plants, and which depend on their ability to multiply in the person, animal, or plant attacked."[34] Viruses, fungi, and bacteria are all labeled as "biological" weapons, but once biological components are obtained, the problem of "weaponizing" them can be difficult.[35] Toxins such as botulism (discussed in this section) are easier to obtain or manufacture than other potential weapons-grade biological components. The threat from such attacks comes mostly from possible poisoning of food or water rather than causing a catastrophic epidemic. Poisoning attacks would have limited but potentially severe casualties.

Experts generally agree that the most likely biological agents (whether bacteria or not) to be used by terrorists would be the following:

- **Anthrax.** Anthrax is a disease that afflicts livestock and humans. It can exist as spores or be suspended in aerosols. Humans contract anthrax either through cuts in the skin (cutaneous anthrax), through the respiratory system (inhalation anthrax), or by eating contaminated meat. Obtaining lethal quantities of anthrax is difficult but not impossible. Anthrax-infected letters were sent through the mail in the eastern United States immediately after the September 11, 2001, attacks. Those who died from anthrax exposure suffered from inhalation anthrax. The anthrax case is discussed further in Chapter 14.

- **Smallpox.** Eradicated in nature, **smallpox** is a virus that is very difficult to obtain because samples exist solely in laboratories, apparently only in the United States and Russia. Its symptoms appear after about 12 days of incubation and include flu-like symptoms and a skin condition that eventually leads to pus-filled lesions. It is a highly contagious disease and can be deadly if it progresses to a hemorrhagic (bleeding) stage known as the "black pox."

- **Botulinum Toxin (Botulism).** Also known as **botulism, botulinum toxin** is a rather common form of food poisoning. It is a bacterium rather than a virus or fungus and can be deadly if inhaled or ingested even in small quantities.

- **Bubonic Plague.** A bacterium that led to the disease known as the Black Death in medieval Europe, **bubonic plague** is spread by bacteria-infected fleas that infect hosts when bitten. The disease is highly infectious and often fatal.

---

[33]See Witte, Griff, and Ruth Eglash. "Iron Dome, Israel's Missile Defense System, Changes Calculus of Fight With Hamas." *Washington Post,* July 14, 2014.

[34]Stern, "The Covenant," citing UN General Assembly (UNGA). *Report of the Secretary-General on Chemical and Bacteriological (Biological) Weapons and the Effects of Their Possible Use.* UNGA. A/7575, 1969, p. 6.

[35]See Mintz, John. "Technical Hurdles Separate Terrorists From Biowarfare." *Washington Post,* December 30, 2004.

***Chemical Agents.*** These weapons are "chemical substances, whether gaseous, liquid, or solid, which are used for hostile purposes to cause disease or death in humans, animals, or plants, and which depend on direct toxicity for their primary effect."[36] Some chemical agents, such as pesticides, are commercially available. Other chemical agents can be manufactured by extremists using available instruction guides. Because of many plausible threat scenarios,[37] experts believe that chemical weapons in the possession of terrorists pose a more likely possibility than do biological, radiological, or nuclear weapons.[38]

Examples of possible weaponized chemical agents in the arsenals of terrorists could include the following:

- **Phosgene gas** causes the lungs to fill with water, choking the victim.
- **Chlorine gas** destroys the cells that line the respiratory tract.
- **Mustard gas** is actually a mist rather than a gas. It is a blistering agent that blisters the skin, eyes, and nose, and can severely damage the lungs if inhaled.
- **Nerve gases,** such as Sarin, Tabun, and VX, block (or "short-circuit") nerve messages in the body. A single drop of a nerve agent, whether inhaled or absorbed through the skin, can shut down the body's neurotransmitters.

***Radiological Agents.*** These weapons are materials that emit radiation that can harm living organisms. To become threatening to life or health, these radioactive substances must be "ingested, inhaled, or absorbed through the skin" in sufficient quantities.[39] Non–weapons-grade radiological agents could theoretically be used to construct a toxic **"dirty bomb"** that would use conventional explosives to release a cloud of radioactive contaminants. Radioactive elements that could be used in a dirty bomb include plutonium, uranium, cobalt 60, strontium, and cesium 137.[40] Conceptually, radiological weapons are not unlike chemical or biological weapons in the sense that the effectiveness of each is based on contaminating or infecting living organisms. Absent large quantities of radioactive materials, this type of weapon would likely cause minimal casualties outside of the blast radius of the bomb, but its psychological effect could be quite disruptive. Radiological materials are available, making the threat from a radiological weapon a plausible scenario—much more than nuclear weapons.

***Nuclear Weapons.*** Nuclear weapons are high-explosive military weapons using weapons-grade plutonium and uranium. Explosions from nuclear bombs devastate the area within their blast zone, irradiate an area outside the blast zone, and are capable of sending dangerous radioactive debris into the atmosphere that descends to the Earth as toxic **fallout**. Nuclear devices are sophisticated weapons that are difficult to manufacture, even for highly motivated governments. Modern nuclear arsenals include large strategic weapons powerful enough to lay waste to large areas and smaller, relatively compact tactical nuclear weapons that were originally developed to support ground troops. Although it is conceivable that terrorists could construct a nuclear device, this would be a very difficult technical and logistical endeavor.[41] Therefore, most threat scenarios envision the acquisition of tactical nuclear

---

[36]Stern, "The Covenant," pp. 21–2.

[37]The threat scenarios are very plausible. In early 2007, Iraqi insurgents detonated several chlorine bombs, killing a number of people and injuring hundreds. See Cave, Damien, and Ahmad Fadam. "Iraq Insurgents Employ Chlorine in Bomb Attacks." *New York Times,* February 22, 2007. See also Brulliard, Karin. "Chlorine Bombs Kill 10, Injure at Least 350 in Iraq." *Washington Post,* March 17, 2007. See also Therolf, Garrett, and Alexandra Zavis. "Bomb Releases Chlorine in Iraq's Diyala Province." *Los Angeles Times,* June 3, 2007.

[38]See Warrick, Joby. "An Easier, but Less Deadly, Recipe for Terror." *Washington Post,* December 31, 2004.

[39]Stern, "The Covenant," p. 26.

[40]For a discussion of the nuclear threat, see Laqueur, Walter. *The New Terrorism: Fanaticism and the Arms of Mass Destruction.* New York: Oxford University Press, 1999, pp. 70ff.

[41]See Linzer, Dafna. "Nuclear Capabilities May Elude Terrorists, Experts Say." *Washington Post,* December 29, 2004.

weapons such as artillery shells by terrorists. The Soviets apparently developed several so-called suitcase bombs—nuclear weapons that are quite compact.

### Case in Point: The Suicide Bombers[42]

"Human bombs" have become an accepted method of political violence in a number of conflicts. Although some examples of suicidal behavior by ideological extremists can be found, most incidents have been committed by ethnonational and religious terrorists. When considering the tactical and symbolic value of suicide attacks, it is instructive to recall the words of the Chinese military philosopher Wu Ch'i: "One man willing to throw away his life is enough to terrorize a thousand," although the gender-related suggestion is inapplicable in the modern era.[43] Women also sacrifice themselves as suicide bombers, having participated in more than 230 suicide attacks between 1985 and 2008, and many more since that time.[44] The attraction for deploying suicide squads is simply stated: Human bombs

- possess an intelligence and flexibility that other weapons do not have;
- inflict significant psychological damage on an enemy;
- are relatively "cheap" weapons, so long as the reservoir of volunteers is maintained; and
- exact a high human toll from an enemy while at the same time incurring acceptable losses.

In some conflicts, suicide bombings have rarely occurred. For example, the IRA, ETA, and European leftists and rightists did not use suicidal violence. In other conflicts, suicide attacks became a common method of waging war against the defined enemy. The Tamil Tigers in Sri Lanka, Hezbollah (Islamic Jihad) in Lebanon, several Palestinian groups in Israel, Al-Qa'ida internationally, and Islamist insurgencies are all examples of movements that have used this tactic regularly. In other conflicts, suicide operations became the signature methods of Chechen rebels and Syrian/Iraqi insurgents. The following cases in point illustrate this behavior:

***Nationalism-Motivated Suicide Among the Tamil Tigers.*** The civil war between the Sri Lankan government and Tamil separatists involved the extensive use of terrorist methods by the Tamil Tigers. Throughout the 1990s, the movement committed a series of assassinations, detonated a number of car and truck bombs, and regularly engaged in suicide bombing incidents. Tens of thousands of people died during this period. Some suicide attacks were significant events during the course of the war, including the following incidents:

- In May 1991, former Indian prime minister Rajiv Gandhi was assassinated in India by a Tamil woman who detonated a bomb as she stood next to Gandhi. She was probably affiliated with Sri Lanka's Tamil Tigers movement. In 1998, 26 people were sentenced to death by an Indian court for complicity in the assassination.
- In May 1993, Sri Lankan Prime Minister Ramasinghe Premadasa was assassinated by a suicide bomber.
- In December 1999, Sri Lankan President Chandrika Kumaratunga was injured and narrowly escaped death when a suicide bomber attempted to assassinate her at an election rally.

***Religion-Motivated Suicide and the Lebanon Model.*** Lebanon descended into anarchy for approximately 15 years during the 1970s and 1980s. The fighting was mostly religious, among contending paramilitaries drawn from the Shi'a, Sunni, Druze, and Christian communities. The Palestine

---

[42]For an excellent discussion of suicide attacks in the modern era, see Pape, Robert Anthony. *Dying to Win: The Strategic Logic of Suicide Terrorism.* New York: Random House, 2005.

[43]Sun Tzu. *The Art of War.* New York: Oxford University Press, 1963, p. 168.

[44]Bloom, Mia. *Bombshell: Women and Terrorism.* Philadelphia: University of Pennsylvania Press, 2011.

Liberation Organization (PLO) also had a strong presence. During the war, these factions carved out de facto fiefdoms that were secured by the paramilitaries. Terrorism and atrocities regularly occurred, and methods included suicide bombings.

The group that pioneered suicide bombing as an effective method of terrorist violence in the Middle East was Lebanon's Hezbollah.[45] Hezbollah is a Lebanese Shi'a movement that has historically received significant state support from Iran and Syria. The group conducted a series of suicide bombings in 1983 through 1985 against Israeli, American, and French interests. Credit for the bombings was usually taken by a group calling itself **Islamic Jihad**, a radical splinter group from Hezbollah. The October 1983 suicide attacks against the French and American peacekeeping troops in Beirut were particularly effective—the attackers killed 58 French paratroopers and 241 American Marines, forcing the withdrawal of the peacekeepers. This tactic continued through the 1990s during Hezbollah's campaign against the Israeli occupation of Lebanon's southern border region. These attacks were directed against Israeli troops and Israel's proxy, the mostly Christian South Lebanon Army.

An important aspect of the Lebanese example is that each suicide bomber was later glorified as a martyr. This concept of *martyrdom* is an important motivation behind the recruitment of young suicide bombers. In Israel, Hamas, Palestine Islamic Jihad, and Al-Aqsa Martyr Brigades all cited the Lebanon model as the inspiration for their renewed *intifada* against the Israelis.

***Intifada-Motivated Suicide in Israel.*** Israel has experienced a large number of suicide attacks. The Islamic Resistance Movement (Hamas)[46] was founded in December 1987 when the first Palestinian *intifada* broke out. Hamas's "military wing" is the Izzedine al-Qassam Brigade, which first appeared in January 1992.

Hamas made a concerted effort from 1994 to 1996 to establish itself as the preeminent Palestinian liberation organization. At that time, the PLO was deeply committed to the peace process, and Hamas was equally committed to sabotaging it. The movement conducted a significant number of bombings, shootings, and acts of sabotage. It was during this period that Hamas set the precedent—and honed the methodology—for Palestinian suicide bombings.

In 1995 and 1996, Hamas's bombing campaign became more deadly as its bombs became increasingly sophisticated. This was the handiwork of an electrical engineer named Yehiya Ayyash, the master bomb maker better known as "the Engineer."

Hamas was the first Palestinian group to initiate a suicide bombing campaign. It launched the operation in retaliation for the February 1994 Hebron massacre when Baruch Goldstein killed and wounded scores of Muslim worshippers at the Ibrahim Mosque on the holy site of the Cave of the Patriarchs. After Goldstein's attack, Hamas recruited human-bomb candidates into its Izzedine al-Qassam Brigade cells, with the specific mission to attack Israeli civilian targets—primarily at commuter transportation sites. The suicide bombers used shrapnel-laden vehicular bombs, satchel charges (bagged bombs), and garment-strapped bombs. These attacks inflicted significant damage on Israel in terms of the number of Israeli casualties. For example, four Hamas bombers killed 59 people in 1996.[47]

Beginning in 2001, suicide bombers from sectarian Hamas and the secular PLO-affiliated Al-Aqsa Martyr Brigades carried out dozens of attacks against civilian targets, killing scores of people during a deadly bombing campaign. The targets were selected to disrupt everyday life in Israel, often buses and other public sites. This was not the first suicide bombing campaign in Israel, but it was by far the most sustained and lethal one. During 2001 to 2006, approximately 125 suicide bombings occurred, many carried out by young women. The following time line summarizes the number of suicide attacks against Israel immediately before and after the bombing mission.[48]

---

[45]For a good discussion of Hezbollah's rationale in deploying suicide bombers, see Kramer, Martin. "The Moral Logic of Hezbollah." In *Origins of Terrorism: Psychologies, Ideologies, Theologies, States of Mind,* edited by Walter Reich. Washington, DC: Woodrow Wilson Center, 1998, pp. 131ff.

[46]HAMAS means "zeal" and is an acronym for *Harakt al-Muqaqama al-Islamiya*.

[47]The 1996 attacks by Hamas led to the election of a hawkish Israeli administration.

[48]From Ripley, Amanda. "Why Suicide Bombing Is Now All the Rage." *Time,* April 15, 2002.

- 1993: 13 attacks
- 1994: 7 attacks
- 1995: 8 attacks
- 1996: 4 attacks
- 1997: 4 attacks
- 1998: 2 attacks
- 1999: 0 attacks

- 2000: 4 attacks
- 2001: 36 attacks
- 2002: 60 attacks[49]
- 2003: 26 attacks[50]
- 2004: 14 attacks[51]
- 2005: 7 attacks[52]
- 2006: 4 attacks[53]

***Al-Qa'ida and Martyrdom in the New Era of Terrorism.*** Operatives of the Al-Qa'ida network, affiliated movements, and other similar Islamist extremist groups have demonstrated a propensity for suicidal violence. Members of the network have committed a series of highly destructive suicide bombing attacks against American interests. They have also been known to carry out attacks against rival factions. Examples of these methods include the following incidents:

- August 1998: Suicide bombers struck the American embassies in Nairobi, Kenya, and Dar es Salaam, Tanzania, killing more than 200 people and wounding 5,000.
- October 2000: The American destroyer *USS Cole* was severely damaged by two suicide bombers while berthed in the port of Aden, Yemen. The bombers detonated a boat bomb next to the *Cole,* killing themselves and 17 crew members and wounding 39 other Navy personnel. In September 2004, a judge in Yemen sentenced two people to death for the attack and imprisoned four others.[54]
- September 2001: Ahmad Shah Massoud was assassinated by two Arab suicide bombers posing as a film crew for an interview. Massoud was a highly regarded Afghan commander who fought very well during the anti-Soviet *jihad.* He was also the most effective commander fighting against the Taliban movement. The bombers were Afghan Arabs who used a booby-trapped camera.
- April 2002: A natural gas truck exploded on Djerba Island in Tunisia at the oldest synagogue in North Africa. Seventeen people, 12 of them German tourists, were killed.[55]
- November 2003: Two car bombs were detonated at two synagogues in Istanbul, Turkey.
- May and June 2005: About 130 suicide attacks occurred in Iraq.[56]
- July 2005: Three suicide bombs were detonated at the Egyptian resort town of Sharm el Sheik, killing more than 60 people.
- February 2008: Two mentally disabled women in Iraq, who were strapped with explosives, killed nearly 100 people and wounded about 200 at two pet markets when they were blown up by remote control.

---

[49]Federman, Josef. "Israel to Target More Hamas Leaders." *Washington Post,* March 23, 2004. Other data, derived from the Israel Ministry of Foreign Affairs, list about 40 attacks. Website: http://www.mfa.gov.il (accessed July 3, 2008).

[50]Ibid. Other data, derived from the Israel Ministry of Foreign Affairs, list about 20 attacks.

[51]Ibid.

[52]Ibid.

[53]Ibid.

[54]See MacFarquhar, Neil. "Two Sentenced to Death in Yemen for Bombing U.S.S. *Cole*." *New York Times,* September 29, 2004.

[55]MacFarquhar, Neil. "Qaeda Says Bin Laden Is Well, and It Was Behind Tunis Blast." *New York Times,* June 23, 2002.

[56]For a discussion of suicide bombers in Iraq, see Ghosh, Aparisim. "Inside the Mind of an Iraqi Suicide Bomber." *Time,* July 4, 2005.

- March 2008: A female suicide bomber in Iraq assassinated a prominent Sunni sheik, who had denounced Al-Qa'ida, in his home.
- January 2012: A suicide bomber killed and injured dozens of people in Burgas, Bulgaria. The bombing occurred near a tour bus transporting Israeli tourists.
- October 2013: A member of Syria's Al-Nusra Front detonated a truck bomb near Hama, killing approximately 30 people.
- January 2014: A Boko Haram suicide bomber killed and wounded scores in a crowded market area in Maiduguri, Nigeria.

Interestingly, Al-Qa'ida apparently designed an internal consensus about how to conduct terrorist operations. Members of the network committed to writing what are best described as operational protocols, discovered during searches of Al-Qa'ida hideouts in the aftermath of the September 11 attacks. Manuals—including a six-volume, 1,000-page CD-ROM version—were found in locations as diverse as Chechnya, the United States, Afghanistan, and Manchester, England. Chapter Perspective 10.1 presents sample guidelines designed for Al-Qa'ida operatives.

## CHAPTER PERSPECTIVE 10.1: The Al-Qa'ida "Terrorist Manual"[a]

In May 2000, a document written in Arabic was found during the search of a home of an alleged Al-Qa'ida member in Manchester, England. The document was a manual, approximately 180 pages in length, titled "Military Studies in the Jihad Against the Tyrants." It is essentially an operations manual, or blueprint, for engaging in cell-based terrorist activities in foreign countries. Excerpts from the manual include the following passages:

### Goals and Objectives

The confrontation that we are calling for with the apostate regimes does not know Socratic debates . . . Platonic ideals . . . nor Aristotelian diplomacy. . . . But it knows the dialogue of bullets, the ideals of assassination, bombing and destruction, and the diplomacy of the cannon and machine gun.

**Missions Required:** The main mission for which the Military Organization is responsible is: the overthrow of the godless regimes and the replacement with an Islamic regime. Other missions consist of the following:

1. Gathering information about the enemy, the land, the installations, and the neighbors.

2. Kidnapping enemy personnel, documents, secrets and arms.

3. Assassinating enemy personnel as well as foreign tourists.

4. Freeing the brothers who are captured by the enemy.

5. Spreading rumors and writing statements that instigate people against the enemy.

6. Blasting and destroying the places of amusement, immorality, and sin; not a vital target.

7. Blasting and destroying the embassies and attacking vital economic centers.

8. Blasting and destroying bridges leading into and out of the cities.

### The following security precautions should be taken:

1. Keeping the passport in a safe place so it would not be ceized [sic] by the security apparatus, and the brother it belongs to would have to negotiate its return (I'll give you your passport if you give me information).

*(Continued)*

(Continued)

2. All documents of the undercover brother, such as identity cards and passport, should be falsified.

3. When the undercover brother is traveling with a certain identity card or passport, he should know all pertinent [information] such as the name, profession, and place of residence.

4. The brother who has special work status . . . should have more than one identity card and passport.

5. The photograph of the brother in these documents should be without a beard. . . .

**Measures that should be taken by the undercover member:**

1. Not reveal his true name to the Organization's members who are working with him . . .

2. Have a general appearance that does not indicate Islamic orientation (beard, toothpick, book, long shirt, small Koran).

3. Be careful not to mention the brothers' common expressions or show their behaviors . . .

4. Avoid visiting famous Islamic places . . .

5. Not park in no-parking zones and not take photographs where it is forbidden. . . .

**Operations**

Cell or cluster methods should be adopted by the Organization. It should be composed of many cells whose members do not know one another. . . .

Facsimile and wireless: . . . Duration of transmission should not exceed five minutes in order to prevent the enemy from pinpointing the device location. . . .

**Important note:** Married brothers should observe the following: Not talking with their wives about Jihad work.

**Note**

a. U.S. Department of Justice website: http://www.justice.gov/ag/manualpart1_1.pdf (accessed November 13, 2002).

Table 10.3 summarizes the scale of violence experienced during the suicide bombing campaign waged by Palestinians during a 9-month period of the *intifada*.[57] The targets were almost exclusively civilians, and the death toll was "acceptable" from the perspective of the terrorists—200 people were killed during this time line, at a cost of 13 "human bombs."

## ❖ The Focus: Terrorist Targets

Brazilian revolutionary Carlos Marighella advocated the adoption of terrorism and **armed propaganda** as justifiable tactics in waging urban guerrilla warfare. He wrote that armed propaganda is a symbolic process in which targets should be chosen after a period of careful deliberation about the effect an attack will have on a larger audience. In his *Mini-Manual of the Urban Guerrilla*, Marighella recommended specific targets to be attacked for maximum propaganda effect. He suggested that careful selection would psychologically damage an enemy and attract supporters to the cause. Marighella wrote,

Bank assaults, ambushes, desertions and diverting of arms, the rescue of prisoners, executions, kidnappings, sabotage, terrorism, and the war of nerves, are all cases in

[57]See Ratnesar, Romesh. "Season of Revenge: The Inside Story of How Israel Imprisoned Arafat—and Why the Rage Keeps Burning." *Time,* April 8, 2002; and ibid.

## Table 10.3  The *Intifada* Suicide Bombers

The Palestinian *intifada* increased in scale and ferocity during 2001 and 2002. Fighting in Gaza and the West Bank became pitched battles between Palestinian guerrillas and the Israeli military. Street fighting broke out in Bethlehem, Nablus, Ramallah, and other ancient cities. At the same time, a deadly and unpredictable new weapon was applied extensively by the Palestinians—the human bomb.

Initially used by radical Islamic movements such as Hamas and Palestine Islamic Jihad, suicide bombing became a regular weapon of secular Palestine Liberation Organization fighters. The Al-Aqsa Martyr Brigades was a secular "martyrdom" society linked to the mainstream Fatah organization of the PLO.

The following table is a 9-month snapshot of the activity profiles of human bombing incidents.

| "Martyr" Profile | Activity Profile | | |
| --- | --- | --- | --- |
| | Date | Target | Fatalities |
| 22-year-old man, Jordanian | June 1, 2001 | Tel Aviv discothèque | 20 killed |
| 23-year-old man, Hamas activist | August 9, 2001 | Jerusalem pizzeria | 15 killed, including 7 children |
| 48-year-old man, first known Arab Israeli bomber | September 9, 2001 | Train depot | 3 killed |
| 21-year-old man, engaged to be married | December 2, 2001 | Haifa passenger bus | 15 killed |
| 28-year-old woman, first female suicide bomber | January 27, 2002 | Jerusalem shopping district | 1 elderly man killed |
| 21-year-old woman, English student | February 27, 2002 | Israeli roadblock | 3 hurt |
| 19-year-old man | March 2, 2002 | Bar Mitzvah celebration | 9 killed |
| 20-year-old man | March 9, 2002 | Café near Prime Minister Ariel Sharon's residence | 11 killed |
| 20-year-old man | March 20, 2002 | Commuter bus | 7 killed |
| 23-year-old man, wanted fugitive | March 27, 2002 | Passover celebration Seder | 21 killed |
| 18-year-old woman, engaged to be married | March 29, 2002 | Jerusalem supermarket | 2 killed |
| 23-year-old man | March 30, 2002 | Tel Aviv restaurant | 32 hurt |
| 22-year-old man | March 31, 2002 | Haifa restaurant | 15 killed |

*Source:* Primarily from Ripley, Amanda. "Why Suicide Bombing Is Now All the Rage." *Time.* April 15, 2002. Used with permission.

point. . . . Airplanes diverted in flight by revolutionary action, moving ships and trains assaulted and seized by guerrillas, can also be solely for propaganda effect.[58]

Terrorists select their targets because of the expectation that any moral ambiguities of the deed will be outweighed by the target's propaganda value. Terrorists must calculate that they can

---

[58]Marighella, Carlos. "Mini-Manual of the Urban Guerrilla." In *Terrorism and Urban Guerrillas: A Study of Tactics and Documents,* edited by Jay Mallin. Coral Gables, FL: University of Miami Press, 1971, pp. 103–4.

manipulate the incident into a positive propaganda context. The following sampling of typical targets indicates that terrorists and extremists must rely on a process of redefining who constitutes an enemy group, thereby turning them into a legitimate target. Terrorists

- take innocent civilians hostage—if the civilian is a symbolic person, they have not hesitated to execute them;
- attack and murder third-country military personnel who have no direct connection to their cause;
- indiscriminately attack civilians as part of terrorist and reprisal campaigns against enemy interests; and
- regularly target symbolic buildings such as embassies.[59]

In many terrorist campaigns, the objective has been to disrupt society to the point where the routines of life cannot be managed and the government cannot maintain order. To accomplish this goal, some terrorist movements have incrementally adapted their methods to new targets. This point is exemplified by Algeria's Armed Islamic Group and Armed Islamic Movement, which escalated their terrorist campaign by gradually shifting their emphases to new targets, managing to move through several phases during their insurgency:[60]

- Beginning in 1992, the first targets were security forces, who were ambushed in the countryside and in towns. Civilians were also targeted to keep them from revealing where the rebels were based.
- Next, assassinations were carried out. Suspected collaborators (broadly defined), government officials, party officials, and professionals were killed.
- Beginning in 1993, the terrorists redefined who their enemies were and began killing family members of government officials.
- Terrorists also began to target foreign workers and tourists in 1993.
- Women became specific targets for assassination. These victims included professionals and female family members of government officials.
- Indiscriminate bomb attacks began in 1994, escalating into a campaign of suicide bombings in Algiers in June 1995.

Figure 10.1 is a representation of tactics used in terrorist attacks worldwide in 2013.

## The Symbolism of Targets

In light of our previous discussions about terrorist groups, environments, and incidents, one conclusion should now be readily apparent: Terrorists select their targets because of their symbolic and propaganda value. High-profile, sentimental, or otherwise significant targets are chosen with the expectation that the terrorists' constituency will be moved and that the victims' audience will in some way suffer.

On occasion, terrorists attempt to demonstrate the weakness of an enemy and terrorize those who place their trust in that enemy. For example, in October 2004, during a ceremony in Baghdad to celebrate the opening of a U.S.-funded sewage facility, two suicide car bombs killed 42 people and wounded many more. At least 35 of the dead were children, many of whom were caught in the first blast as they gathered around U.S. soldiers for candy. The other children were killed when they rushed to the scene and a second car bomb was detonated.[61]

---

[59]See Hoffman, *Inside Terrorism,* pp. 34–5.

[60]See Stone, Martin. *The Establishment of Algeria.* London: Hurst, 1997. In *The Terrorism Reader,* edited by David J. Whittaker. New York: Routledge, 2001, pp. 146–7.

[61]See Sanders, Edmund. "35 Children Die in Baghdad Bombings." *Washington Post,* October 1, 2004. See also Sanders, Edmund, and Raheem Salman. "Children's Curiosity Proved All Too Deadly This Time." *Washington Post,* October 1, 2004.

**Figure 10.1** Tactics Used in Terrorist Attacks Worldwide, 2013

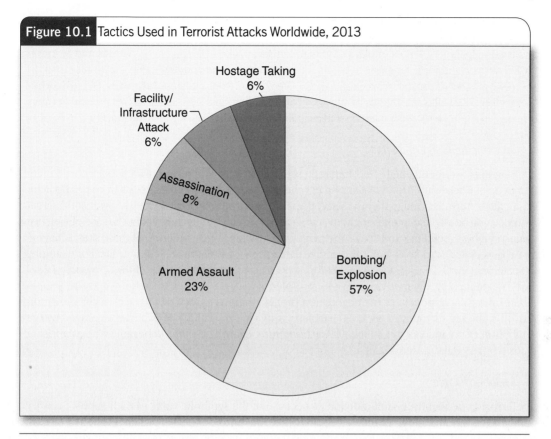

*Source:* Office of the Coordinator for Counterterrorism. *Country Reports on Terrorism 2013.* Washington, DC: U.S. Department of State, 2014.

The following targets are often selected because terrorists conclude that they offer a high return in propaganda value.

### Embassies and Diplomatic Personnel

The symbolism of embassy attacks and operations against diplomats can be quite profound. Embassies represent the sovereignty and national interests of nations. Diplomatic personnel are universally recognized as official representatives of their home countries, and attacks on embassy buildings or embassy personnel are conceptually the same as direct attacks on the nations they represent. Assaults on embassies also guarantee a large audience. For example, the 1996 to 1997 attack and hostage seizures by Peru's Tupac Amaru Revolutionary Movement (MRTA) on the Japanese ambassador's residence in Lima, Peru, garnered worldwide attention. The incident ended with the deaths of the MRTA members and dealt a severe blow to the movement, but it demonstrated how a relatively small dissident movement can otherwise score significant propaganda successes. In another example, Iraqi insurgents began a campaign of attacks on Muslim diplomats in July 2005 to force their governments to sever ties with the newly installed Iraqi government.[62]

### International Symbols

Many nations deploy military representatives to other countries. They also encourage international investment by private corporations, which consequently set up offices and other facilities. These interests are understandable targets for terrorists because they can be manipulated symbolically to depict

---

[62]See Mosher, Andy. "Gunmen Mount Attacks on Diplomats in Iraq." *Washington Post,* July 5, 2005.

exploitation, imperialism, or other representations of repression. Thus, terrorists and extremists redefine military facilities, corporate offices, military personnel, and company employees as enemy interests and legitimate targets. For example, Colombian leftists attacked U.S. business interests and Mormon missionaries—and took American citizens hostage—during the country's 1994 election season. In another example, during the winter of 1991, the Greek terrorist group **Revolutionary Organization November 17** carried out a series of attacks against international businesses in Greece. Their targets symbolized the interests of the international coalition opposing Iraq during the Gulf War.[63]

### Symbolic Buildings and Sites

Buildings and sentimental sites often represent the prestige and power of a nation or the identity of a people. These sites can evoke strong psychological and emotional reactions from people who revere them. Terrorists and extremists select these cultural symbols because they know that the target audience will be affected. Interestingly, the target audience can be affected without the use of violence against symbolic buildings and sites—the perception (by the target audience) of these sites as having been "desecrated" can involve nothing more than a show of strength at a cultural site. For example, in September 2000, Israeli leader Ariel Sharon, who was at that time the chair of the opposition Likud Party, made a politically motivated visit to Jerusalem's Al-Aqsa Mosque (also known as the Temple Mount). A strong opponent of the negotiation process that led to the Oslo (Peace) Accords, Sharon arrived at the site surrounded by 1,000 Israeli security officers. Palestinians became enraged by the symbolism of the incursion, and the Al-Aqsa *intifada* began. The *intifada* became a mass uprising marked by reprisals and terrorism.

### Symbolic People

Terrorists frequently assault individuals because of the symbolic value of their status. Security personnel, political leaders, journalists, business executives, and others are often selected as targets. Kidnappings and physical violence are common methods used by terrorists against human symbols. In kidnapping and hostage situations, videotapes and photographs are sometimes released for propaganda purposes. For example, in September 1977, the leftist Red Army Faction/Baader-Meinhof Gang kidnapped German industrialist Hanns-Martin Schleyer. He was murdered by the group in October 1977. Beginning in 2014, the Islamic State of Iraq and the Levant regularly broadcast images of its fighters and executions using video and social media technologies.

### Passenger Carriers

From the perspective of terrorists, passenger carriers are logical targets. If the carrier is big, such as an airliner, it provides a large number of potential victims or hostages who are confined inside a mobile prison. International passenger carriers readily lend themselves to immediate international media and political attention. For example, the nationalist Popular Front for the Liberation of Palestine repeatedly used airline hijackings to achieve maximum propaganda exposure for their movement. In Israel, Hamas regularly attacked buses, often assigning suicide bombers to the task. In a typical attack, Hamas suicide operatives attacked two buses virtually simultaneously in the city of Beersheba, killing at least 15 people and wounding dozens. Chapter Perspective 10.2 applies the foregoing discussion to symbolic attacks against American interests.

## Case in Point: The Threat From Cyberterrorism

Information and computer technologies can be used offensively as a mode of warfare, commonly termed **cyberwar**. The adoption of cyberwar techniques by extremists has already occurred, and it is

---

[63]November 17, a Marxist terrorist movement, had a long history of attacks against NATO and American interests. The group was finally suppressed in 2002 after a series of arrests by Greek security officers.

## CHAPTER PERSPECTIVE 10.2: The Symbolism of Targets

### Terrorist Attacks Against the United States

Many targets are selected because they symbolize the interests of a perceived enemy. This selection process requires that these interests be redefined by extremists as representations of the forces against whom they are waging war. This redefinition process, if properly communicated to the terrorists' target audience and constituency, can be used effectively as propaganda on behalf of the cause.

The following attacks were launched against American interests.

### Embassies

- June 1987: A car bombing and mortar attack were launched against the U.S. embassy in Rome, most likely by the Japanese Red Army.
- February 1996: A rocket attack was launched on the American embassy compound in Greece.

### International Symbols

- April 1988: A USO club in Naples, Italy, was bombed, most likely by the Japanese Red Army. Five people were killed.
- November 1995: Seven people were killed when anti-Saudi dissidents bombed an American military training facility in Riyadh, Saudi Arabia.

### Symbolic Buildings and Sites

- January 1993: Two were killed and three injured when a Pakistani terrorist fired at employees outside the Central Intelligence Agency (CIA) headquarters in Langley, Virginia.
- February 1993: The World Trade Center in New York City was bombed, killing 6 and injuring more than 1,000.
- September 2001: Attacks in the United States against the World Trade Center and the Pentagon killed approximately 3,000 people.

### Symbolic People

- May 2001: The Filipino Islamic revolutionary movement Abu Sayyaf took three American citizens hostage. One of them was beheaded by members of the group in June 2001.
- January 2002: An American journalist working for the *Wall Street Journal* was kidnapped in Pakistan by Islamic extremists. His murder was later videotaped by the group.

### Passenger Carrier Attacks

- August 1982: A bomb exploded aboard Pan Am Flight 830 over Hawaii. The Palestinian group 15 May committed the attack. The plane was able to land.
- April 1986: A bomb exploded aboard TWA Flight 840. Four were killed and nine injured, including a mother and her infant daughter who fell to their deaths when they were sucked out of the plane. Flight 840 landed safely.

quite conceivable that new technologies could be used by terrorists to destroy information and communications systems. Three examples from 1998 illustrate the potential damage that can be wrought by motivated activists:

- Members of the Liberation Tigers of Tamil Ealam (also known as the Tamil Tigers) inundated Sri Lankan embassies with 800 daily e-mails during a 2-week period. The e-mail messages read, "We are the Internet Black Tigers and we're doing this to disrupt your communications." This attack was the first known cyberattack by a terrorist organization against an enemy country's computer grid.

- Animal liberation activists dropped an "e-mail bomb" on the server of Sweden's Smittskyddinstitutet. Its entire database crashed when 2,000 e-mail messages were sent on a single day, followed on a second day by 3,000 messages. The institute was targeted because of its use of monkeys in medical experiments.
- A 3-week e-mail campaign targeted approximately 100 Israeli Internet sites, resulting in the destruction of data. The campaign was launched by Lebanese Americans living in Texas.

## ❖ The Outcome: Is Terrorism Effective?

Does terrorism work? When we consider the effectiveness of terrorism, the basic question to be answered is: Do the methods used by terrorists against their selected targets promote their goals and objectives? Terrorism is arguably effective—however defined—in some manner to someone.[64] The key (for terrorists) is to establish a link between terrorist methods used in incidents and desirable outcomes. Of course, success and effectiveness can be very subjective considerations. In this regard, there is a tendency for terrorists to use unconventional factors as measures for their effectiveness. For example, terrorists have been known to declare victory using the following criteria:

- Acquiring global media and political attention
- Having an impact on a target audience or championed constituency
- Forcing concessions from an enemy interest
- Disrupting the normal routines of a society
- Provoking the state to overreact

The following discussion reviews these criteria. This is not an exhaustive evaluation of measures of effectiveness, but it demonstrates commonalities found among modern terrorist acts.

### Media and Political Attention

At times, the focusing of world attention on the terrorists' cause is itself a measure of success. One central fact in the age of instantaneous media attention is that

> for the terrorist, success . . . is most often measured in terms of the amount of publicity and attention received. Newsprint and airtime are thus the coin of the realm in the terrorists' mind-set: the only tangible or empirical means they have by which to gauge their success and assess their progress. In this respect, little distinction or discrimination is made between good or bad publicity.[65]

Many terrorist groups engage in violence that is, at least in part, media oriented. As one Red Army Faction/Baader-Meinhof Gang member[66] reflected after his "retirement" from the terrorist trade, "We always immediately looked at how the newspapers, especially in Berlin, reacted to our actions, and

---

[64]For a discussion of several myths about terrorism, including the notion that it is highly effective, see Shermer, Michael. "The Five Myths About Terrorism—Including That It Works (Why Terror Doesn't Work)." In *Scientific American* 309, no. 2 (July 17, 2013). See also Heymann, Philip B. *Terrorism and America: A Commonsense Strategy for a Democratic Society.* Cambridge, MA: MIT Press, 1998, pp. 12ff. Another good discussion of effectiveness is found in Laqueur, Walter. "The Futility of Terrorism." In *International Terrorism: Characteristics, Causes, Controls,* edited by Charles W. Kegley Jr. New York: St. Martin's, 1990, pp. 69ff. And also Sederberg, Peter C. *Terrorist Myths: Illusion, Rhetoric, and Reality.* Englewood Cliffs, NJ: Prentice Hall, 1989, pp. 96ff.

[65]Hoffman, *Inside Terrorism,* p. 176.

[66]The Red Army Faction/Baader-Meinhof Gang is discussed in detail in Chapter 7.

how they explained them, and thereupon we defined our strategy."[67] The June 1985 hijacking of TWA Flight 847, with its odyssey through several countries and the hijackers' manipulation of the world's media, is a classic example of a media-oriented terrorist incident. The epic case of Flight 847 and the role of the media will be explored further in Chapter 11.

## Having an Impact on an Audience

Terrorists use propaganda by the deed to affect audiences, hoping to rouse them to action or incite a society-level response. Victim audiences, neutral audiences, and championed groups can all be affected by a terrorist event. When an incident occurs, extremists and their supporters assess reactions from these audiences. From the terrorists' perspective, the effectiveness of an attack requires successful manipulation of various audiences' reactions. If, for example, a victim audience is successfully manipulated, members of the audience

> change [their] travel habits or [their] vacation destinations out of fear of becoming victims. The rationale for this fear is small . . . but the fear of victimization is real, especially among heavy media consumers. . . . A process of identification takes place not only with former victims and likely future victims but with all those in the audience who share some "victim characteristics."[68]

### CHAPTER PERSPECTIVE 10.3: Tactical Horror: Digital, Video, and Audio Terrorism

With the advent of the Internet, cable news networks, and social media, terrorists now possess unprecedented access to global audiences. Communications technologies quickly and cheaply bring symbolic images and extremist messages to the attention of policy makers and civilians around the world. Terrorists have adapted their tactics to these new technologies, and many utilize them to broadcast their messages and operations.

During the early millennium, hostage-takers discovered that the plight of their victims would garner intensive global attention so long as their images were promulgated to noteworthy cable news networks.

The typical pattern was for an international figure—often a foreign worker—to be seized by extremists, followed by a communiqué claiming credit for the abduction. A video or series of videos would be delivered to a news outlet, with images of the victim pleading for his or her life while seated before a flag and surrounded by hooded and armed terrorists. The outcome was sometimes satisfactory, with the hostage being granted freedom; at other times, the video incidents ended horrifically.

The first noted incident was the kidnapping and videotaped murder of American journalist Daniel Pearl in Pakistan in January 2002. Since then, Islamist insurgents in Iraq and Syria, terrorists in Saudi Arabia, and violent *jihadis* elsewhere have either issued Internet, cable news, and social media communiqués, or videotaped their hostages, or executed them, or committed all of these actions. After the Daniel Pearl murder, a gruesome cycle of beheadings occurred, as illustrated by the following incidents from Iraq:

*(Continued)*

---

[67]Weimann, Gabriel, and Conrad Winn. *The Theater of Terror: Mass Media and International Terrorism.* New York: Longman, 1994, p. 59.

[68]Schmid, Alex P. "Terrorism and the Media: Freedom of Information vs. Freedom From Intimidation." In *Terrorism: Roots, Impact, Responses,* edited by Lawrence Howard. New York: Praeger, 1992, pp. 101–2.

(Continued)

- Victims represent the international community, and have included citizens from Bulgaria, Pakistan, South Korea, Nepal, Norway, the United States, Great Britain, Turkey, and Iraq.

- Al-Qa'ida in Iraq and other Islamist or other sectarian movements appeared to be responsible for most of the kidnappings and murders.

- A number of hostages were beheaded, sometimes on video recordings that were posted on the Internet.

In the aftermath of the initial cycle of broadcasts, subsequent cycles of media-oriented terror have included social media images of killings and other incidents, such as mass executions of prisoners in 2014 by the Islamic State of Iraq and the Levant (ISIS).

Chapter Perspective 10.3 explores a tactic adopted by insurgent groups and hostage takers of recording their victims and promulgating their images in the mass media, on social networking media, and on the Internet. This tactic will be further discussed in Chapter 11.

An unusual example of an *unsuccessful* campaign to generate this measure of effectiveness is found in the motives of South Africa's **People Against Gangsterism and Drugs** (PAGAD). Founded in 1996, PAGAD waged a campaign of violence to protest the values of what it considered to be an immoral South African society. Originally a vigilante anticrime group, PAGAD evolved into a dissident terrorist group. It espoused an antigovernment and anti-Western ideology, supposedly on behalf of South Africa's Muslim population, but its attacks focused largely on moral targets. PAGAD selected these targets—primarily in Cape Town—as a way to promote moralistic Islamic values and to cleanse society. Targets included fast-food restaurants, gay bars, tourist sites, and other symbols of Western decadence and immorality. Unfortunately for PAGAD, South Africa's population was minimally affected, and there was not a societal reaction to PAGAD's attacks (other than revulsion). Interestingly, PAGAD promoted its cause in part by maintaining a website.[69]

## Forcing Concessions From an Enemy Interest

Enemy interests—broadly defined—will sometimes concede to the demands of a politically violent movement. Concessions vary in magnitude. They can be made as short-term and immediate concessions or as long-term and fundamental concessions whereby an entire society essentially concedes to a movement. At the level of immediate concessions, accommodations could include ransoms paid by companies for the release of employees who are being held hostage. At the societal level, laws might be changed or autonomy granted to a national group. One repeated method used by terrorists to force concessions is **kidnapping/hostage taking**. This is because

> hostage takers may influence the government's decision by promising rewards for compliance. . . . The release of hostages unharmed when ransom is paid underwrites a promise in the future. Sequential release of selected hostages makes promises credible. Maintaining secrecy about a government's concessions is an additional reward for compliance.[70]

For example, in 1969, two radical Brazilian organizations—National Liberation Action and MR-8—collaborated in the kidnapping of the American ambassador to Brazil, Charles Burke. They demanded and received radio airtime in exchange for his release. The groups were permitted to broadcast their indictment of Brazil's authoritarian government to a broad audience.

---

[69]For more information, see PAGAD website: http://www.pagad.co.za/.

[70]Crenshaw, Martha. "The Logic of Terrorism: Terrorist Behavior as a Product of Strategic Choice." In *Origins of Terrorism: Psychologies, Ideologies, Theologies, States of Mind*, edited by Walter Reich. Washington, DC: Woodrow Wilson Center, 1998, p. 22.

## Disruption of Normal Routines

An obvious measure of effectiveness is whether the normal routines of society can be affected or halted by a terrorist incident or campaign. Some targets—such as the commercial transportation industry—can be selectively attacked to the point where their operations will be disrupted. When this happens, the daily habits of individuals and routines of society will change. In this way, large numbers of people in the broader society in essence respond to the tactics of a relatively weak movement. For example, the American airline industry lost $2.2 billion during the first quarter of 2002 as a direct result of changes in Americans' travel behavior following the September 11, 2001, attacks.[71]

## Provoking the State to Overreact

One outcome that terrorists allude to as a measure of effectiveness is the state's imposition of violent security countermeasures in response to a terrorist environment. This notion of "enraging the beast" is common across the spectrum of terrorist environments. Terrorists, of course, anticipate that the state will become violently repressive, the people will suffer, and the masses will rise up in rebellion after experiencing the true nature of the enemy. This theory has had only mixed success, as evidenced in the following cases in point that are now familiar to readers.

### Viable Movements

Some movements proved to be viable after provoking the state, as demonstrated by the examples of the Irish Republican Army and the Palestine Liberation Organization.

Northern Ireland's Irish Republican Army fought in an environment wherein Irish Catholics were subjected to violence perpetrated by Protestant paramilitaries, British security forces, and the Royal Irish Constabulary. The IRA had a significant amount of popular support. Because of this support—and because its opponents could not end the violence—the aboveground Sinn Féin party was welcomed as an equal partner by the British during several rounds of peace talks in the late 1990s, also known as the decommissioning process.

The Palestine Liberation Organization survived countless crises that might have defeated other movements. It maintained a consistent level of international and domestic violence directed against Israel for decades. Despite significant applications of force by the Israelis—including assassinations, surgical reprisals, reprisal campaigns, and conventional warfare—the PLO continued to garner worldwide attention and regional support from sympathetic governments.

### Unviable Movements

Some movements proved to be unviable after provoking the state, as demonstrated by the examples of the Montoneros and Tupamaros.

Argentina's Montoneros were effective according to several measures: They successfully received media and political attention, affected target audiences, received concessions from enemy interests, and disrupted societal routines. Unfortunately for the Montoneros, they were wiped out during the Argentine military's violently repressive Dirty War after having provoked the state into using authoritarian methods.

Uruguay's Tupamaros were likewise successful in achieving the first four measures of effectiveness and, like the Montoneros, provoked the state into adopting violent security measures. Unfortunately for the Tupamaros, the group was annihilated during a somewhat popular suppression campaign waged by the Uruguayan military.

Table 10.4 summarizes measures of effectiveness, the cited cases, and outcomes.

---

[71]*Time,* April 11, 2002.

**Table 10.4** Measures of Effectiveness

When extremist movements adopt terrorism as a methodology, they measure the effectiveness of their violent behavior by linking the incident to identifiable outcomes. These measures of effectiveness are unconventional in the sense that they are frequently media oriented and audience oriented.

The following table summarizes measures of effectiveness by illustrating the linkage between terrorist incidents and outcomes.

| Measure of Effectiveness | Activity Profile | |
|---|---|---|
| | Incident | Outcome |
| *Media and political attention* | Hijacking of TWA Flight 847 | Global media and political attention |
| *Impact on an audience* | PAGAD's moralist terrorist campaign | Failed campaign to bring about a societal response |
| *Concessions from an enemy interest* | Kidnapping of U.S. ambassador to Brazil | Broadcast of terrorists' political manifesto |
| *Disruption of societal routines* | Suicidal hijackings of four airliners on September 11, 2001 | Fewer Americans traveled via airlines; industry suffered revenue losses |
| *Provoke the state* | Viable: provocations by IRA and PLO | Government methods failed to eradicate opposition |
| | Unviable: provocations by Montoneros and Tupamaros | Violent military governments crushed the opposition |

## Effective Terrorism: The King David Hotel Bombing

The 1946 King David Hotel Bombing by the Jewish terrorist group the **Irgun** (acronym for "National Military Organization in the Land of Israel") was a successful terrorist operation because the attack produced all five of the measures of effectiveness and desired outcomes presented earlier.

**❖ Photo 10.4**

The rubble of the King David Hotel in Jerusalem. The hotel, which housed British administrative offices for their Palestine mandate, was bombed by the Jewish terrorist group Irgun.

Fox Photos/Hulton Archive/Getty Images

After the dissolution of the Ottoman Empire following World War I, the British Empire occupied and governed Palestine. During the 1930s, communal violence between Palestinian Arabs and Jews led to an unsuccessful rebellion by Arabs. In 1937, a Jewish organization calling itself the Irgun began engaging in revenge attacks against Palestinian Arabs. When the Irgun's leaders, **Vladimir Jabotinsky** and **David Raziel**, were killed in 1940 and 1941, a young **Menachem Begin** and other leaders reinvigorated the Irgun's violent resistance in 1944. Irgun's membership was small, so its strategy was to engage in urban terrorist attacks against British institutions, such as immigration department, land registry, and taxation offices, as well as British security forces.

The King David Hotel in Jerusalem housed the headquarters of the British military and the government secretariat. On July 22, 1946, the Irgun bombed the hotel, killing 91 persons and wounding 45 others.[72] Its victims included civilians, Jews, Palestinian Arabs, and British.

---

[72]Menachem Begin said later that the Irgun placed at least three telephone calls warning of the attack—to the hotel, the French consulate, and the *Jerusalem Post* newspaper.

The bombing achieved worldwide attention and began a debate in Great Britain about the failure of the British administration to bring peace to Palestine. The British responded with an increase in the authoritarian policies that it had already imposed prior to the bombing. These policies included mass arrests of Jews, military roadblocks, random personal and dwelling searches, and curfews. These measures were unpopular in Britain and the United States and led to a gradual shift in political opinion against the British occupation.

When the British executed three Irgun members, the Irgun retaliated in July 1947 by beating and hanging two British sergeants, photographing their hanged corpses, and then releasing the pictures to the media. The effect was the final straw for British public opinion, which turned irrevocably against Britain's administration of Palestine.

On May 15, 1948, the British mandate in Palestine ended. The Irgun, a small, determined, urban terrorist group, had successfully implemented Carlos Marighella's strategy of pushing the state to the point of unacceptable authoritarian measures that ultimately resulted in the state's inability to sustain its rule.

As a postscript, Menachem Begin served as prime minister in Israel from 1977 to 1983.

## Chapter Summary

This chapter analyzed terrorist objectives, methods, and targets. It also discussed the effectiveness of terrorism.

Typical objectives included the terrorists' desire to change the existing order, to promote the psychological and social disruption of a society, to publicize their cause through propaganda by the deed, and to create a generalized revolutionary environment. To accomplish their objectives, terrorists traditionally have directed their attention to the manipulation of specific audiences. In the era of the New Terrorism, objectives have become characterized by vagueness, and methods have included indiscriminate attacks and the possibility of the use of weapons of mass destruction.

Modern terrorist methods reflect the changing global political environment and are characterized by asymmetrical warfare and new, cell-based organizational models. However, most terrorists rely on age-old methods that can be accomplished by using such conventional weapons as firearms and explosives. Modern technologies such as rocket-propelled grenades, precision-guided munitions, and barometric bombs are updated variations on the same theme. Nevertheless, threats from biological, chemical, radiological, and nuclear weapons are unprecedented in the possible arsenals of terrorists.

Terrorist targets are selected because of their symbolic value and the impact they will have on affected audiences. Typical targets include embassies, international symbols, symbolic buildings and sites, symbolic people, and passenger carriers. These targets are chosen because they represent the interests of a defined enemy.

The effectiveness of terrorist attacks is measured by unconventional criteria. From the terrorists' perspective, these criteria include gaining media and political attention, affecting targeted audiences, gaining concessions from an enemy interest, disrupting normal routines, and provoking the state to overreact.

In Chapter 11, readers will assess the role of the media. The discussion will illustrate how the media can be used to manipulate information, what it means to consider the media to be a "weapon," the language of reporting terrorism, and issues involved in regulating the media.

## Key Terms and Concepts

The following topics are discussed in this chapter and can be found in the glossary:

| | | |
|---|---|---|
| AK-47 | fuel oil (ANFO) explosives | armed propaganda |
| Ammonium nitrate and | anthrax | assault rifles |

asymmetrical warfare

Ayyash, Yehiya ("the Engineer")

Begin, Menachem

biological agents

botulinum toxin (botulism)

bubonic plague

chemical agents

chlorine gas

Composite-4 (C-4)

Covenant, the Sword, and the Arm of the Lord, The (CSA)

"dirty bomb"

dynamite

electronic triggers

fallout

gasoline bombs

improvised explosive devices (IEDs)

Irgun

Iron Dome

Islamic Jihad

Jabotinsky, Vladimir

Kalashnikov, Mikhail

kidnapping/hostage taking

King David Hotel bombing

"kneecapping"

M-16

martyr nation

media-oriented terrorism

mines

"Molotov cocktails"

mustard gas

nerve gases

netwar

nuclear weapons

People Against Gangsterism and Drugs

phosgene gas

plastic explosives

potassium cyanide

precision-guided munitions

pressure triggers

Qassam rocket

radiological agents

Raziel, David

RDX

Revolutionary Organization November 17

"roadside bombs"

rocket-propelled grenades

RPG-7

SA-7 (or Grail)

Sarin nerve gas

Semtex

signature method

smallpox

sodium cyanide

Stinger

submachine guns

suicide bombing

TNT

vehicular bombs

# Discussion Box: Attacks Against the U.S. Marine and French Paratrooper Headquarters in Beirut

*This chapter's Discussion Box is intended to stimulate critical debate about how determined terrorist attacks can affect the policies of nations.*

In September 1982, 5,000 elite French paratroopers, Italian Bersaglieri, and American Marines were sent into Beirut, Lebanon, as members of the peace-keeping Multinational Force (MNF). The purpose of the MNF was to restore order to the city in the midst of a civil war and an Israeli invasion that had been launched to drive the

Palestine Liberation Organization from Lebanon.

Members of radical Lebanese Islamic militia movements, specifically the Sunni Amal and Shi'ite Hezbollah groups, viewed the MNF as an invasion force. From their perspective, the West supported the Lebanese Christian Phalangists and the Israelis. They at first waged low-intensity resistance against the Western presence. A gradual escalation then occurred, with Amal and Hezbollah fighters becoming more aggressive in their opposition. In response to casualties incurred by U.S. Marines and French paratroopers, the United States began shelling Syrian-controlled positions from naval vessels.

On October 23, 1983, two suicide bombers driving vehicular bombs simultaneously struck the U.S. Marines' and French paratroopers' headquarters in Beirut; 241 Marines and 58 paratroopers were killed. The terrorist group Islamic Jihad—probably the Lebanese Shi'ite movement Hezbollah—claimed credit for the attacks. The bombings were hailed by Amal and Hezbollah leadership (who were careful to deny any responsibility for the attacks) as legitimate resistance by patriots against occupying armies.

After the attacks, the United States began using air power and naval artillery to shell hostile positions. However, public opinion had turned against the increasingly complicated "peace-keeping" mission, and MNF troops were withdrawn in early 1984.

### Discussion Questions

- Were the Lebanese militia fighters terrorists or freedom fighters?

- Is terrorism "poor man's warfare" and therefore a legitimate option for waging war?

- Were the suicide bombings acceptable methods for opposing the deployment of the MNF?

- Was the presence of Western soldiers indeed an understandable precipitating cause of Amal's and Hezbollah's resistance?

- Were the targets—the French and American headquarters—logical targets for relatively weak opposition forces?

## On Your Own

The open-access Student Study Site at **http://study.sagepub.com/martin5e** has a variety of useful study aids, including eFlashcards, quizzes, audio resources, and journal articles. The websites, exercises, and recommended readings listed below are easily accessed on this site as well.

U.S. Department of State

❖ **Photo 10.5**
Peacekeeping in Beirut. Two U.S. Marines survey the rubble of the Marine Corps barracks, which had been destroyed by a Lebanese suicide bomber. More than 200 of their comrades died in the attack.

## Recommended Websites

The following websites provide links to discussions and data about terrorist objectives, methods, and targets:

Al-Qa'ida "Training Manual": http://www.justice.gov/ag/manualpart1_1.pdf

*The Anarchist's Cookbook:* Search engine, enter: Anarchist's Cookbook

Center for Defense Information: http://www.cdi.org/

Jaffe Center for Strategic Studies (Tel Aviv): http://www.inss.org.il/

Patterns of Global Terrorism (State Department): http://www.state.gov/s/ct/rls/

*The Terrorist's Handbook:* Search engine, enter: Terrorist's Handbook

# Web Exercise

Using this chapter's recommended websites, conduct an online investigation of terrorist objectives, methods, and targets.

1. What common patterns of behavior and methods can you identify across regions and movements?

2. Conduct a search for other websites that offer advice for organizing terrorist cells and carrying out terrorist attacks. Do you think that the online terrorist manuals and weapons advice are a danger to global society?

3. Compare the websites for the monitoring organizations. How would you describe the quality of their information? Are they providing a useful service?

For an online search of terrorist tactics and targets, readers should activate the search engine on their Web browser and enter the following keywords:

"Terrorist Manuals"

"Terrorist Weapons"

# Recommended Readings

The following publications provide discussions on terrorist objectives and methods:

Bergen, Peter L. Holy War, Inc.: *Inside the Secret World of Osama bin Laden*. New York: Simon & Schuster, 2001.

Berko, Anat. *The Path to Paradise: The Inner World of Suicide Bombers*. Westport, CT: Praeger Security International, 2009.

Cragin, Kim, et al. *Sharing the Dragon's Teeth: Terrorist Groups and the Exchange of New Technologies*. Santa Monica, CA: RAND Corporation, 2007.

Dolnik, Adam. *Understanding Terrorist Innovation: Technology, Tactics, and Global Trends*. London: Routledge, 2007.

Frantz, Douglas, and Catherine Collis. *The Nuclear Jihadist: The True Story of the Man Who Sold the World's Most Dangerous Secrets—And How We Could Have Stopped Him*. New York: Twelve Books, 2007.

Glucklich, Ariel. *Dying for Heaven: Holy Pleasure and Suicide Bombers*. New York: HarperOne, 2009.

Hafez, Mohammed M. *Suicide Bombers in Iraq: The Strategy and Ideology of Martyrdom*. Washington, DC: United States Institute of Peace Press, 2007.

Janczewski, Lech J., and Andrew M. Colarik, eds. *Cyber Warfare and Cyber Terrorism*. Hershey, PA: Information Science Reference, 2008.

Katz, Samuel M. *The Hunt for the Engineer: How Israeli Agents Tracked the Hamas Master Bomber*. New York: Fromm International, 2001.

Levi, Michael. *On Nuclear Terrorism*. Cambridge, MA: Harvard University Press, 2009.

Mueller, Robert. *Atomic Obsession: Nuclear Alarmism From Hiroshima to Al Qaeda*. New York: Routledge, 2009.

Oliver, Anne Marie, and Paul F. Steinberg. *The Road to Martyrs' Square: A Journey Into the World of the Suicide Bomber*. New York: Oxford University Press, 2005.

Pape, Robert Anthony. *Dying to Win: The Strategic Logic of Suicide Terrorism*. New York: Random House, 2005.

Powell, William. *The Anarchist Cookbook*. New York: Lyle Stuart, 1971; assigned to Barricade Books, 1989.

Ranstorp, Magnus, and Magnus Normark, eds. *Unconventional Weapons and International Terrorism: Challenges and a New Approach*. New York: Routledge, 2009.

Stern, Jessica. *The Ultimate Terrorists*. Cambridge, MA: Harvard University Press, 1999.

Thornton, Rod. *Asymmetric Warfare: Threat and Response in the Twenty-first Century*. Cambridge, UK: Polity Press, 2007.

Tucker, Jonathan B., ed. *Toxic Terror: Assessing Terrorist Use of Chemical and Biological Weapons*. Cambridge: MIT Press, 2000.

Zubay, Geoffrey, et al., eds. *Agents of Bioterrorism: Pathogens and Their Weaponization*. New York: Columbia University Press, 2005.

## CHAPTER 11

# The Information Battleground

## Terrorist Violence and the Role of the Media

Lebanon's Hezbollah has long engaged in media-oriented political violence. In the aftermath of its attacks, Hezbollah leaders and supporters—sometimes including the influential Lebanese Sunni Amal militia—engaged in public relations campaigns. Press releases were issued and interviews granted. Statements were made to the world press claiming, for example, that attacks against French and U.S. interests were in reprisal for their support of the Lebanese Christian **Phalangist** militia and the Israelis. This public linkage between terrorist attacks and a seemingly noble cause served to spin the violence favorably and thereby justify it.

Hezbollah intentionally packaged its strikes as representing heroic resistance against inveterate evil and exploitation. It produced audio, photographic, and video images of its resistance for distribution to the press. For example, some of Hezbollah's attacks against the Israelis in South Lebanon were videotaped and sent to the media—with images of dead Israeli soldiers and stalwart Hezbollah attackers.

Young Hezbollah suicide bombers recorded videotaped messages prior to their attacks. These messages explained in very patriotic terms why they intended to attack Israeli interests as human bombs. These tapes were widely distributed, and the suicidal fighters were cast as martyrs in a righteous cause. Photographs and other likenesses of many Hezbollah "martyrs" have been prominently displayed in Hezbollah-controlled areas.

Hezbollah continues to maintain an extensive media and public relations operation and has periodically posted a website. When active, the website contains a great deal of pro-Hezbollah information, including political statements, reports from the "front," audio links, video links, photographs, and e-mail links.

This chapter explores the role of the media in a terrorist environment. There is frequent interplay between media reporting and the use of violence by extremist movements. If terrorism is a strategy characterized by symbolic attacks on symbolic targets, it is also a strategy characterized by the intentional manipulation of the news media. Since the inception of the modern era of terrorism, "terrorist attacks are often carefully choreographed to attract the attention of the electronic media and the international press."[1] In the modern era, the truism that **information is power** is very clearly understood by the media and governments; it is also understood by terrorists, their audiences, and their adversaries.

The ability of modern news agencies to use satellite and digital technologies to broadcast events as they happen "live"—and graphically—to a global audience has not been lost on violent extremists. Terrorists understand that instantaneous media exposure for their grievances simply requires a dramatic incident to attract the world's press. Terrorists seeking publicity are likely to garner a large audience if they dramatically carry out targeted hijackings, bombings, hostage takings, assassinations, or other acts of violence. The press also has its own incentives to report major terrorist incidents. From the media's point of view—and aside from its fundamental responsibility to objectively report the news—drama guarantees increased attention from potential viewers.

## ❖ Two Perspectives: The Media and Governments

A brief introduction to two perspectives is useful for understanding the role of the media; both will be developed further in this chapter. The first is from the media's perspective, and the second is from the perspective of governments.

❖ **Photo 11.1**
An Iraqi police officer surveys the damaged car in which two foreign journalists were killed at the police station in the town of Latifiya. Polish war correspondent Waldemar Milewicz and a Polish Algerian colleague were killed when their car was raked by machine-gun fire in an ambush south of Baghdad.

© Reuters/Corbis

### The Perspective of the Media

For journalists, the time-honored professional ideal is to report the news objectively, without placing too much "spin" on the information. The concept of **media spin** refers to the inclusion of subjective (opinionated) interpretations when reporting the facts. Interpretation is, of course, very desirable at some point during a terrorist incident, but there is an urge within the media to immediately create a mood or a dramatized atmosphere when reporting the news. This is typical of many news outlets and reflects the modern trend toward tabloid talk radio, reality shows, and family-oriented television news—even in major urban outlets. The fact is that a **news triage** (selection process) does occur, so that some news items are given a higher priority than others. Editors must decide what information to report and how it should be reported. As a consequence, dramatic news such as terrorist incidents often reflects the personal, political, and cultural biases of editors and reporters and contains a great deal of emotional human-interest content.

Because the news triage is a significant factor in the processing of information by audiences, it can be a critical element in the audience's analysis of a particular terrorist environment. For example, editors generally focus on and report terrorist violence without critical analysis of the terrorists' cause or the symbolic message conveyed by their behavior. This can leave the recipient audience with an incomplete understanding of the terrorist environment, and it gives rise to misperceptions and misinterpretations of the terrorists, the grievances of their championed group, and government responses.

[1]Jenkins, Brian. Quoted in Hoffman, Bruce. *Inside Terrorism*. New York: Columbia University Press, 1998, p. 132.

## The Perspective of Governments

Policy makers are challenged to develop coherent and consistent policies to respond to acts of terrorism. They are also challenged to develop popular policies that are accepted by the public. When democratic governments try to create a national consensus, they seek to control the media's spins on the terrorist incident. Unfortunately for policy makers, the media can be—and usually are—a source of concern. This is because the press is adept at creating political environments that can sway public opinion. In societies that pride themselves on protecting freedom of the press,

> terrorism . . . can cause enormous problems for democratic governments because of its impact on the psychology of great masses of citizens. . . . Terrorist bombings, assassinations, and hostage-taking have, in nations with a free press, the ability to hold the attention of vast populations.[2]

For this reason, some level of contention or animosity is frequently present in the relationship between government officials and members of the media when terrorism moves to the forefront of public discourse. In the United States, this tension occurs at all levels of government interaction with the media, from the president's spokespersons to cabinet-level federal representatives to local law enforcement officials. At each level, there is often an instinctive (and noticeable) attempt by officials either to keep the media at arm's length or to manipulate the conditions for media access to information. One example of animosity between government and the media occurred in May 2005, when the U.S. newsmagazine *Newsweek* published a report that American interrogators and guards at the detention facility in Guantánamo Bay, Cuba, had desecrated the Qur'an, the Muslim holy book. As a result of the report—which alleged that guards had flushed the Qur'an down a toilet—anti-American protests in the Muslim world were widespread and violent. After strong government denials and after initially (and strongly) defending its position, *Newsweek* retracted its story and apologized for publishing the report without proper confirmation.[3]

The discussion in this chapter will review the following:

- Understanding the Role of the Media
- A New Battleground: The War for the Information High Ground
- The Public's Right to Know: Regulating the Media

## ❖ Understanding the Role of the Media

In societies that champion freedom of the press, a tension exists between the media's professional duty to objectively report the news and the terrorists' desire to use the media to promote their cause. This is a tension between the necessity to keep the public informed and deliberate attempts to manipulate the world's media to disseminate propaganda. **Propaganda** is defined as "any systematic, widespread, deliberate indoctrination or plan for such indoctrination."[4] It is used by organizations, movements, and governments to spread their interpretations of the truth or to invent a new truth. Propaganda can incorporate elements of truth, half-truths, and lies. Underlying all extremist propaganda is a particular political agenda.

The media sometimes tread a fine line between providing news and disseminating the terrorists' message. This happens when they report the details of terrorist incidents, broadcast interviews

---

[2]Heymann, Philip B. *Terrorism and America: A Commonsense Strategy for a Democratic Society.* Cambridge, MA: MIT Press, 1998, p. 9.

[3]Other allegations of desecration of the Qur'an also arose. See Serrano, Richard A., and John Daniszewski. "Dozens Have Alleged Koran's Mishandling." *Los Angeles Times*, May 22, 2005. See also Schmitt, Richard B. "Newsweek Backtracks on Koran Report." *Los Angeles Times*, May 16, 2005.

[4]*Webster's New Twentieth Century Dictionary of the English Language, Unabridged.* 2nd ed. New York: Publishers Guild, 1966.

with terrorists and their extremist supporters, or investigate the merits of the terrorists' grievances. In *theory*, the media will be mindful of this fine line and will carefully weigh what news to report and how to do so. In *practice,* some media outlets are blatantly sympathetic to one side of a conflict and completely unsympathetic to the other side. In authoritarian states, this occurs as a matter of routine because the government heavily regulates the media. In democracies, the free press enjoys the liberty to apply whatever spin is deemed desirable in its reporting practices. Some media purposely use provocative language and photographs to attract an audience.

The following discussion will review several factors one should consider when evaluating the role of the media:

- Publicizing the cause
- Spreading the word: Mass communications and the terrorists' message
- No more printing presses: Mass communications and the "new media"
- Truth and consequences: Reporting terrorism

## Publicizing the Cause

Terrorists frequently try to **publicize their cause**, hoping to reach as broad an audience as possible. They do this by adapting their tactics so that their methods are accredited in a public environment. **Media-oriented terrorism** refers to terrorism that is purposely carried out to attract attention from the media and, consequently, the general public.[5] Methods and targets are selected because they are likely to be given high priority by news outlets. The purpose of media-oriented terrorism is to deliver the terrorists' message. "Thus, terrorism . . . may be seen as a violent act that is conceived specifically to attract attention and then, through the publicity it generates, to communicate a message."[6]

Terrorists and extremist movements that seek broad exposure have been known to directly and indirectly cultivate relationships with reporters and to establish aboveground organizations that promote media relations. For example, the mainstream Irish Republican political party Sinn Féin has long had a sophisticated information operation, which has historically included close relationships with the print and broadcast media.[7] Some terrorists and rebel movements have also cast themselves as the "military wing" of political movements. For example, both Sinn Féin and the Colombian Communist Party engaged in aboveground political public relations while the Irish Republican Army and Revolutionary Armed Forces of Colombia (FARC) waged armed rebellion.

For terrorists concerned about delivering their message, the main questions are, How can the dissident group communicate its grievances to the world (or a regional) community? Which institutions are most likely to publish the underlying reasons for the group's revolutionary violence? Governments and other targeted interests are highly unlikely to "get the word out" about the merits of the cause—if anything, they will denounce the incident and the cause. Governments and targeted interests are also quite likely to try to control the flow of information and to craft their comments in a manner that will sway an audience against the extremist movement. The best solution to this problem is for terrorists to access and use the technologies of **mass communications**. They can do this in a number of ways, including appropriation of technologies for their own use to personally send their message to the public (perhaps through aboveground sympathizers) and skillful "packaging" of their message, hoping to send it through international media outlets.

---

[5]See Weimann, Gabriel, and Conrad Winn. *The Theater of Terror: Mass Media and International Terrorism.* New York: Longman, 1994.

[6]Hoffman, *Inside Terrorism,* p. 131.

[7]See Laqueur, Walter. *The New Terrorism: Fanaticism and the Arms of Mass Destruction.* New York: Oxford University Press, 1999, p. 44.

By cleverly manipulating these technologies and the world's press, terrorists can create a mood among target audiences that can lead to public pressure for the government or other adversary to "do something"—perhaps even grant concessions to the movement. For example, when the media focus on terrorist victimization (which they usually do), "it is clear that media coverage of victimization can aid in the generation of messages from terrorists to their various target audiences."[8] At the same time, media attention can affect the behavior of target governments: "By stimulating and exacerbating public reaction to victim suffering and family tragedy, it is clear that media coverage can also increase pressure on targets of demands."[9]

Thus, when a message is filtered into the intended audience, and this message has been manipulated in an advantageous manner, the terrorists have successfully publicized their cause.

## Spreading the Word: Mass Communications and the Terrorists' Message

Mass communications is the technological ability to convey information to a large number of people. It includes technologies that allow considerable amounts of information to be communicated through printed material, audio broadcasts, video broadcasts, and expanding technologies such as the Internet and social networking media. Modern revolutionaries consider mass communications an invaluable tool for achieving the goals of their cause. In fact, the theories of "armed propaganda" are partly technology driven. For example, in his influential discussion of armed propaganda, Brazilian revolutionary Carlos Marighella wrote,

> The urban guerrilla must never fail to install a clandestine press and must be able to . . . produce small clandestine newspapers, pamphlets, flyers, and stamps for propaganda and agitation against the dictatorship. . . . The urban guerrilla engaged in clandestine printing facilitates enormously the incorporation of large numbers of people into the revolutionary struggle. . . . Tape recordings, the occupation of radio stations, and the use of loudspeakers, drawings on the walls . . . are other forms of propaganda.[10]

For terrorists, efficiency, timeliness, and coherence are critical components to mass communication. *Efficiency* is necessary so that one's message will be delivered in an orderly (as opposed to garbled or chaotic) manner and received in an intelligible and easily understood form. *Timeliness* is also necessary, because the message must be received while it is still fresh and relevant. It makes little sense to send a message before an issue has had an opportunity to ripen; it likewise makes little sense to send a message after an issue has become moot. *Coherence* refers to delivering a message that is easily understood by a target audience. Chapter Perspective 11.1 demonstrates the importance of delivering a coherent message to the target audience.

Thus, if one's message is delivered efficiently and in a timely manner, it will have a stronger impact on the target audience. In fact, if the terrorists can successfully create identification between the audience and some sympathetic symbol of a terrorist incident, the audience could become a factor in resolving the incident. For example, when American hostages were taken during the 1980s in Lebanon and during the hijacking of **TWA Flight 847** (discussed in this chapter), an interesting dynamic occurred:

---

[8]Paletz, David L., and Alex P. Schmid, eds. *Terrorism and the Media*. Newbury Park, CA: Sage, 1992, p. 214.

[9]Ibid., p. 215.

[10]Marighella, Carlos. "Mini-Manual of the Urban Guerrilla." In *Terror and Urban Guerrillas: A Study of Tactics and Documents,* edited by Jay Mallin. Coral Gables, FL: University of Miami Press, 1971, p. 104.

## CHAPTER PERSPECTIVE 11.1: Delivering the Message

Extremist movements will often use coded language to convey their message. This language is often peculiar to the particular group or ideological movement, and is not easily interpreted by nonmembers. From the point of view of laypersons and people not attuned to this language, the group's message is sometimes incoherent. The following example demonstrates how an extremist group's propaganda can become lost in its own rhetoric.[a]

### Against Social-Democracy and Liquidationism— For Steadfast Revolutionary Work!

Reformism does not mean improving the conditions of the masses; on the contrary, the vital role that reformism has played in the capitalist offensive shows that reformism means collaborating with the bourgeoisie in suppressing the mass struggle and implementing the capitalist program. . . .

The work of the Marxist-Leninist Party has been a beacon against the opportunism of the liquidationist and social-democratic trends. The Marxist-Leninist Party has persevered in steadfast revolutionary struggle, while the opportunists, as fair-weather "revolutionaries," are reveling in despondency and renegacy, are denouncing the revolutionary traditions from the mass upsurge that reached its height in the 1960s and early 1970s, and are cowering behind the liberals, labor bureaucrats and any bourgeois who is willing to throw them a crumb.[b]

Communiqué on the Second Congress of the
Marxist-Leninist Party, USA
Fall 1983

### Notes

a. See Sargent, Lyman Tower, ed. *Extremism in America: A Reader.* New York: New York University Press, 1995, pp. 85ff.
b. Communiqué on the Second Congress of the MLP, USA; ibid., pp. 88–9.

Powerful pressure groups [were] created, demanding the safe return of the victims of kidnappings at almost any price. . . . The release of [the Lebanon] hostages was a major reason why the U.S. president sent arms to Iran. In the case of the hijacked TWA Flight 847 (June 14–30, 1985) the media exposure of the hostages generated enough pressure for the American president to make concessions.[11]

Since the advent of printing presses using industrial-age technologies in the 19th century, terrorists and extremist movements have used virtually every available mass communications technology. The following technologies are commonly used by modern political extremists:

- Print media
- Radio
- Television
- The Internet and social networking media

### Print Media

Printed news and propaganda have been used extensively since the 19th century, when the printing press was improved through the use of steam power and then electric power.

---

[11]Schmid, Alex P. "Terrorism and the Media: Freedom of Information vs. Freedom From Intimidation." In *Terrorism: Roots, Impact, Responses,* edited by Lawrence Howard. New York: Praeger, 1992, p. 102.

These technologies permitted the mass production of multiple-page documents. Privately owned newspapers became common, as did the dissemination of politically critical publications and propaganda. Collectively, these outlets constituted the **print media**.

Dissident movements relied on the printed word throughout the 20th century to disseminate their message. Sympathetic publishers and clandestine printing presses were instrumental in promulgating propaganda on behalf of dissident causes. Governments readily understood the power of the press to sway public sentiment, and there were many cases of crackdowns on aboveground newspapers. There were also many examples of the deployment of security forces to locate and shut down clandestine presses. In an interesting example of how political blackmail can be used to promulgate an extremist message, the *New York Times* and *Washington Post* published the political manifesto of Ted Kaczynski, the so-called Unabomber, on September 19, 1995. Earlier in 1995, Kaczynski stated that he would cease his bombing campaign if major newspapers published his manifesto. If they did not do so, he promised to continue his campaign. On the recommendation of the U.S. Department of Justice (which hoped Kaczynski's writing style would be recognized), the *Times* and *Post* published his document, titled "Industrial Society and Its Future."

### Radio

Radio broadcasts were used by many dissident movements prior to the advent of television. Many 20th-century movements continued to issue radio broadcasts in societies where large numbers of people were unable to receive uncensored television broadcasts and where shortwave radio was widely used. In 1969, the Brazilian groups National Liberation Action and MR-8 kidnapped the American ambassador to Brazil; as a consequence of the terms for his release, they successfully demanded that their manifesto be broadcast over the radio. Historically, clandestine radio broadcasts have been instrumental in publicizing the cause to selected audiences, including potential supporters—shortwave radio was particularly effective in reaching a broad audience. As has been the case with dissident printing presses, governments have used security forces to root out clandestine radio stations.

John Downing/Hulton Archive/Getty Images

❖ **Photo 11.2**

The nature of the job. A British war correspondent travels with southern Sudanese rebels. The rebels, who practice Christianity or traditional religions, have fought a long and brutal war against the northern Islamic government.

### Television

The first widespread television broadcasts during the 1950s included news broadcasts. Prior to that time, the only moving visual images of political issues were broadcast in movie houses as newsreel footage. Newsreels were often little more than short propaganda films that presented the government's and mainstream society's points of view; they were useless to extremists unless their movements were depicted as the favored side in the broadcast. With the advent of mass broadcasts during the 1960s, news of the day was received relatively quickly in people's homes. For example, the Vietnam War became the modern era's first "television war," and for the first time, unflattering and even horrific images were regularly seen in American households—this was especially so because the evening news was broadcast in the early evening at dinnertime.

Television has since become the medium of choice for terrorists, especially in the era of cable and digital feeds. It provides immediate visibility and increases the size of the audience. Television also allows for the broadcast of dramatic images, many of which are relatively uncensored in sympathetic markets.

Television news breaks very quickly—often within minutes of an incident—and is broadcast worldwide. Satellite feeds can be linked from almost anywhere in the world. Television has thus become quite useful for promulgating the terrorists' message both visually and with dramatic, on-the-scene audio. All that is required is for the terrorists to manipulate the media into broadcasting a sympathetic spin for their grievances. The terrorists use television as the main instrument for gaining sympathy and supportive action for their plight by presenting themselves as risking their lives for the welfare of a victimized constituency whose legitimate grievances are ignored.[12]

If successful, terrorists can bring images of their war into the homes of hundreds of millions of people worldwide nearly instantaneously—possibly with sentimental content that can potentially sway large audiences to their side.

### The Internet and Social Networking Media

Computer and social communication technologies are now used extensively by many terrorist groups and extremist movements. It is not uncommon for websites to be visually attractive, user friendly, and interactive. Music, photographs, videos, and written propaganda are easily posted on Web pages or disseminated via social networking media.

Tweeting, texting, and other social networking media platforms are used to record incidents (often graphically) and tout claimed successes. The fundamental attraction of social networking media is that it affords the capability to send messages and images "live" as they occur. This is an advantage for media outlets or individuals who wish to be the first to break a story. Activists quickly adapted to this capability, first most notably during the Arab Spring in 2011 when protesters tweeted and texted videos and other information during antigovernment demonstrations. Extremists also took advantage of social networking media by recording and disseminating real-time images of fighting, executions, beheadings, and casualties.

Many Internet postings portray the sense of a peaceful and rich culture of a downtrodden group. Graphic, gory, or otherwise moving images are skillfully posted, sometimes as photo essays that "loop" for continuous replay. Bloggers have posted links to hundreds of websites where viewers may obtain *jihadi* videos.[13] E-mail addresses, mailing addresses, membership applications, and other means to contact the movement are also common, so that a "virtual world" of like-minded extremists thrives on the Internet.[14] An example of the anonymity and scope of the Internet was the activities of a purported member of the Iraqi resistance who called himself Abu Maysara al-Iraqi. Al-Iraqi regularly posted alleged updates and communiqués about the Iraqi resistance on sympathetic Islamic websites. It proved to be very difficult to verify his authenticity or even whether he (or they) was based in Iraq because he was accomplished in the skillful substitution of new online accounts.[15]

As a counterpoint to such online postings, organizations independently monitor extremist websites for their origin and content. For example, the Search for International Terrorist Entities Intelligence Group, also known as the SITE Intelligence Group, maintains a website dedicated to identifying Web postings by several extremist organizations and terrorist groups.[16]

# No More Printing Presses: Mass Communications and the "New Media"

The traditional and new resources just discussed are not the only media outlets. In the United States, there is a growing market in, and consumer demand for, the so-called **New Media**. New Media use

---

[12]Bandura, Albert. "Mechanisms of Moral Disengagement." In *Origins of Terrorism: Psychologies, Ideologies, Theologies, States of Mind,* edited by Walter Reich. Washington, DC: Woodrow Wilson Center, 1998, p. 172.

[13]Moss, Michael. "An Internet Jihad Aims at U.S. Viewers." *New York Times,* October 15, 2007. See also Sheridan, Mary Beth. "Terrorism Probe Points to Reach of Web Networks." *Washington Post,* January 24, 2008.

[14]See Mohamed, Geisal G. "The Globe of Villages: Digital Media and the Rise of Homegrown Terrorism." *Dissent* (Winter 2007): 61–4. See also Gray, John. "A Violent Episode in the Virtual World." *New Statesman,* July 18, 2005.

[15]Cha, Ariana Eunjung. "From a Virtual Shadow, Messages of Terror." *Washington Post,* October 2, 2004.

[16]The Site Intelligence Group's Web page is found at http://www.siteintelgroup.org/.

existing technologies and alternative broadcasting formats to analyze and disseminate information. These formats include talk-show models, tabloid (sensational) styles, celebrity status for hosts, and blatant entertainment spins. Strong and opinionated political or social commentary makes up a significant portion of New Media content. These qualities represent a distinctive media style:

> New media are mass communication forms with primarily nonpolitical origins that have acquired political roles. These roles need not be largely political in nature; in some instances they are only tangentially so. What distinguishes these communication forms . . . is the degree to which they offer political discussion opportunities that attract public officials, candidates, citizens, and even members of the mainstream press corps.[17]

Common types of New Media include "political talk radio . . . television talk . . . electronic town meetings . . . television news magazines . . . MTV . . . and print and television tabloids."[18] These media are innovative in their formats and sensational in their delivery. They do not hesitate to make admittedly provocative and completely biased statements. An important quality of the New Media is that they are very innovative and frequently experiment with untried formats and issues. Some extremist groups have appeared in the New Media, but terrorists have not been particularly active in attempting to manipulate this resource.

## Truth and Consequences: Reporting Terrorism

The print and broadcast media have shown a propensity for giving priority to terrorist incidents in their news reports. This is understandable, given the influence terrorism can have on policy making and domestic or international political environments. However, the media have not been consistent about which incidents they report or how these incidents are reported. The news triage frequently gives extensive coverage to some acts of political violence but provides little if any information about other incidents.[19] For example, during the post–September 11, 2001, invasions of Afghanistan and Iraq, American cable news outlets focused on the military campaign and laced their broadcasts with on-the-scene reporting from embedded journalists who were advancing with the troops. In contrast, Qatar's **Al Jazeera** cable news outlet regularly broadcast images of injured civilians or destruction from the fighting and laced its broadcasts with on-the-scene reporting from journalists on the street and inside hospitals. Hezbollah's television station, Al-Manar TV, likewise provided a popular non-Western perspective on events in Lebanon, Israel, Palestine, and the Middle East.[20]

Thus, media reports attach inconsistent labels to the perpetrators of political violence, and there can be a disproportionate amount of media interest in the sheer violent nature of terrorism, without an exploration of the underlying causes of this violence. Because of these disparities in reporting, organizations such as the Middle East Media Research Institute (MEMRI) have been established to bridge the gap between Western and Middle Eastern media outlets.[21]

Chapter Perspective 11.2 discusses Al Jazeera, the independent satellite news network based in the Persian Gulf nation of Qatar.

### Market Competition

The news media are owned and controlled by large corporations that are mostly motivated by market shares and profits. This affects the style, content, and reporting practices of the modern media.

---

[17]Davis, Richard, and Diana Owen. *New Media and American Politics*. New York: Oxford University Press, 1998, p. 7.

[18]Ibid., pp. 9–15.

[19]For a discussion of selective reporting, see Rainey, James. "Unseen Pictures, Untold Stories." *Los Angeles Times,* May 21, 2005.

[20]See Rafei, Raed. "Hezbollah Wages On-Air War Against U.S." *Los Angeles Times,* July 13, 2008.

[21]MEMRI's Web page is found at http://memri.org.

## CHAPTER PERSPECTIVE 11.2: Al Jazeera

Al Jazeera, literally translated as "the island" in Arabic, is an independent satellite news network based in Qatar. Launched in 1996, it immediately found its market niche as a result of the closure of the BBC's Arabic language feed. The network eventually found its independent presence in Qatar after the Saudi Arabian government attempted to censor a documentary about executions under Islamic law. It has since established respected credentials within the news industry, although governments and political leaders periodically criticize some reports and stories.

Al Jazeera's broadcasting reputation stems from its independent reporting and interviews on controversial subjects. For example, the network filed news reports from Israel, broadcast interviews and statements from insurgents, and provided news analyses from different perspectives on political issues. It was the only network to report live from Iraq during the initial phase of the 2003 war, and its news feeds were broadcast by Western networks. Significantly, Al Jazeera's "on the ground" reporting of civilian casualties led to accusations of bias from Western political leaders. Nevertheless, the network received critical acclaim for objectivity from the journalistic community. The periodic criticism of Al Jazeera has largely come from governments and political leaders who are opposed to the network's depictions of their favored policies.

Al Jazeera English was launched in 2006 and was successful in employing respected journalists for its broadcasts. In the same style, Al Jazeera America began broadcasting in 2013. Al Jazeera also branched into other nonpolitical areas of journalism such as sports reporting. The international team and worldwide reporting of Al Jazeera eventually moved the network into what is widely regarded as the upper tier of satellite news networks.

The fact is that objective reporting is often outweighed by other factors, such as trying to acquire a larger share of the viewing market vis-à-vis competitors. The "scoop" and the "news exclusive" are prized objectives. Thus, coverage can be quite selective, often allowing public opinion and government pronouncements to set the agenda for how the news will be spun. In this type of political and market environment, the media will often forgo criticism of counterterrorist policies. Coverage can also be quite subjective, with the biases of executives, editors, and commentators reported to the public as if they were the most salient features of a particular issue.

The following discussion illustrates the conflict between theoretical objectivity in news reporting and actual inconsistency when these reports are released. It summarizes the dilemma of *which* incidents are reported and *how* they are reported.

### Deciding Which Incidents to Report

The process for deciding which events to report (the news triage) is often driven by evaluating what kind of news is likely to attract a viewing audience. If it is decided that dramatic incidents will bring in sizable shares of viewers, the popular media will not hesitate to give such incidents a high priority for the day's editions or broadcasts.

The media can be highly selective about which terrorist incidents to report. The ultimate decision tends to weigh in favor of news that affects the media's readers or viewing public. In a striking example of this phenomenon, 12 people fell victim to terrorist attacks in Israel in 1985, two British soldiers were killed in Northern Ireland the same year, and the number of Americans killed by terrorists in 1982 was seven. There was great publicity in all these cases, whereas the tens of thousands killed in Iran and Iraq, in the Ugandan civil war, and in Cambodia (where hundreds of thousands were killed) were given far less attention, because Western media either had no access or were not interested.[22]

---

[22]Laqueur, *The New Terrorism*.

The personal stories of participants in a terrorist environment are particularly appealing to the media. Strong emotions such as outrage, grief, and hatred play well to many audiences. Certain kinds of terrorist incidents are particularly susceptible to the media's use of "human-interest" spins because readers and viewers more readily identify with the victims of these incidents. For example, "hostage takings, like kidnappings, are human dramas of universal fascination."[23] Personal identification will always attract the public. The key task for the popular media is to find personal stories that resonate well with their readers or viewers. When this happens, the personal stories that do not resonate are likely to be left out of the mass media news.

### *Deciding How to Report Incidents*

The process of deciding how to report terrorist incidents is, from the readers' or viewers' perspective, seemingly a subjective exercise. Media reports have never been consistent in their descriptions of the perpetrators of terrorist incidents; nor have they been consistent in characterizing examples of extremist violence as terrorism, per se. **Labeling** by reporters vacillates in connotation from the pejorative term *terrorist* to somewhat positive terms such as *commando*. These decisions in semantics sometimes reflect social norms. For example, "democratic societies value compromise and moderation so that the term extremist tends to be opprobrious."[24] This point is further demonstrated by the following sequence of reporting that occurred in 1973:

> One *New York Times* leading article . . . [described] it as "bloody" and "mindless" and [used] the words "terrorists" and "terrorism" interchangeably with "guerrillas" and "extremists." . . . The *Christian Science Monitor* reports of the Rome Pan Am attack . . . avoided "terrorist" and "terrorism" in favour of "guerrillas" and "extremists"; an Associated Press story in the next day's *Los Angeles Times* also stuck with "guerrillas," while the two *Washington Post* articles on the same incident opted for the terms "commandos" and "guerrillas."[25]

These labels reflect a tendency to use euphemistic (indirect or vague) language to describe what might otherwise be appalling behavior.[26] Euphemisms are also used by governments, policy makers, and others to apply words outside of their normal meaning to mask or soften the language of violence. This practice is deliberately media oriented so that the press and general public will more easily accept an incident or policy. Recent examples of **euphemistic language** used by government officials and soldiers at war include the following:

- "collateral damage"—dead civilians
- "deniability"—ability to plead ignorance
- "extraordinary rendition"—kidnapping a person in one country and forcibly sending the person to another country
- "KIA"—killed soldiers
- "neutralize" or "suppress"—destroy or otherwise eliminate
- "preventive reaction strike"—air raid
- "robust"—aggressively violent
- "terminate with extreme prejudice"—assassinate
- "waste"—kill

---

[23]Sick, Gary. "Taking Vows: The Domestication of Policy-Making in Hostage Incidents." In *Origins of Terrorism: Psychologies, Ideologies, Theologies, States of Mind,* edited by Walter Reich. Washington, DC: Woodrow Wilson Center, 1998, p. 241.

[24]Weimann and Winn, *The Theater of Terror,* p. 176.

[25]Hoffman, *Inside Terrorism,* pp. 36–7.

[26]See Bandura, "Mechanisms," p. 169.

- "wet work"—assassinations
- "WIA"—wounded soldiers

### A Word About Terrorist-Initiated Labeling

Terrorist groups also engage in labeling and adopt euphemistic language. They primarily do this in two circumstances: first, when they label enemy interests as potential targets, and second, when they engage in self-labeling. This language is promulgated in communiqués to supporters and journalists.

***Labeling Enemies and Targets.*** Terrorists use symbolism to dehumanize potential targets. This is a universal trait of violent extremists regardless of their ideology. For example, leftists might recast Western business travelers as imperialists. Or Armenian nationalists could symbolically hold Turkish diplomats to account for the Armenian genocide of the early 20th century. Or anti-Semitic and religious terrorists might label a Jewish community center as a Zionist interest. In the era of the New Terrorism, Al-Qa'ida and its sympathizers denounce Western culture and values as being contrary to Islam and the values of the faithful; they also denounce secular Arab governments as apostasies. This labeling process creates important qualifiers for acts of extreme violence, allowing terrorists to justify their behavior even though their victims are often noncombatants.

***Self-Labeling.*** Choosing organizational or movement titles is an important task for terrorists. Those who engage in political violence consider themselves to be an elite—a vanguard—that is waging war against an implacable foe. They consciously use labels and euphemisms to project their self-image. Members of the cause become self-described martyrs, soldiers, or freedom fighters. Hence, organizational and movement

| Table 11.1 | Public Relations: The Organizational Titles of Violent Extremists |

Terrorists seek to project an image that casts them in the role of liberators and soldiers. They are often conscious of their public image and can become quite media savvy.
The following table illustrates how organizational titles reflect terrorists' self-designations as military organizations, the purpose of their movements, and their championed groups.

| Organizational Title | Self-Designation | Purpose | Championed Group |
|---|---|---|---|
| **Popular Front for the Liberation of Palestine** | A united front; a forward position in a war | Liberation of a people | Palestine and Palestinians |
| **Islamic State in Iraq and the Levant** | A prototypical nation | Liberation movement; creating a caliphate | Faithful Muslims in the region |
| **Irish Republican Army** | An army; members are soldiers | Republican unification | Northern Irish Catholics |
| **New People's Army (Philippines)** | An army; members are soldiers | The continuation of a people's liberation movement | The Filipino people |
| **Party of God (Hezbollah)** | Movement representing God's will | Carry out God's will on Earth | Faithful Muslims in the region |
| **Liberation Tigers of Tamil Eelam (Sri Lanka)** | Warriors possessing the fierceness of tigers | Liberation | Tamils |
| **Quebec Liberation Front** | A united front; a forward position in a war | Liberation of a people | Quebec and people of Quebec |

titles always project an image of freedom, sacrifice, or heroism; negative or cowardly images are never conveyed. This pattern is universal among groups on the extremist fringe and is likely to continue. Table 11.1 surveys a few examples of self-labeling and euphemistic language.

## ❖ A New Battleground: The War for the Information High Ground

Mass communications technologies can become weapons of war in modern conventional and asymmetrical conflicts. Because the mass media deliver vast amounts of information to large audiences, this informational battleground has become a front line in modern conflicts. Propaganda has, of course, been used by adversaries since the dawn of organized conflict. However, new technologies provide new opportunities and dangerous pitfalls for combatants. The following discussion surveys the manipulation of the media in terrorist environments.

Adversaries in a terrorist environment frequently try to shape the character of the environment by manipulating the media. For terrorists, the media serve several useful purposes: First, the media may permit the dissemination of information about their cause; second, the media may facilitate the delivery of messages to their supporters and adversaries; and third, the media may serve as a "front" in their war to shape official governmental policies or influence the hearts and minds of their audience. For governments, the media can be a powerful tool for the suppression of terrorist propaganda and for the manipulation of the opinions of large segments of society. This is why every regime will intensively deliver selective information to the media or, as in the case of authoritarian regimes, officially suppress the reporting of some stories.

## Practical Considerations: Using the Media

Terrorists and their supporters use time-honored techniques to attract media attention. In the tradition of mainstream media-savvy organizations (and aside from acts of dramatic violence), terrorists have invited the media to press conferences, issued press releases, granted interviews, released audio and video productions, and produced attractive photographic essays. Two outlets that have greatly expanded the reach and solidarity of extremists are Internet chat rooms and websites that post messages.

Extremists have come to understand that there are many ways in which they can adapt their methods and styles of violence to attract the media.[27] These adaptations can include

- the degree of violence applied,
- the use of symbolism, and
- the performance of very spectacular or special deeds.[28]

These techniques have created environments wherein the media have been eager to receive the terrorists' message. There is a tendency for the media to sensationalize information, so that broadcasts of terrorist audio and video recordings, news conferences, or written statements often take on an entertainment quality.

### Terrorists' Manipulation of the News "Scoop"

News outlets compete in trying to preempt the newsworthiness of their competitors' stories, known colloquially as **media scooping**—that is, being the first to report breaking news. Even when

---

[27]Gerrits, Robin P. J. M. "Terrorists' Perspectives: Memoirs." In *Terrorism and the Media,* edited by David L. Paletz and Alex P. Schmid. Newbury Park, CA: Sage, 1992, pp. 45–9.

[28]Ibid., p. 46.

there is no breaking news, news outlets will often spin human-interest or background stories to give the audience an impression of urgency and drama. To accomplish this task, journalists will frequently probe the feelings of participants in terrorist environments, including the terrorists themselves and their supporters. "This is a situation that, however unwittingly, is tailor-made for terrorist manipulation and contrivance."[29] Terrorists and other radicals have in fact successfully manipulated this propensity for scooping and sensationalizing news on a number of occasions. Several examples follow:

- Ilich Ramírez Sánchez (Carlos the Jackal) did not make his escape during the December 1975 Organization of Petroleum Exporting Countries (OPEC) hostage crisis until the television cameras arrived. After their arrival, he dramatically and publicly made his getaway from Vienna to Algeria with 35 hostages in tow.[30]

- During the November 1979 to January 1981 seizure of the American embassy in Iran, there were several incidents of Iranian crowds playing to the cameras. Crowds would come alive when the cameras were on them, so that some sections of the crowd would act temporarily militant while other sections of the crowd were rather quiescent.[31]

- In May 1986, ABC News broadcast a short interview with Abu Abbas, the leader of the Palestine Liberation Front (PLF). The PLF was notorious at the time because a PLF terrorist unit had carried out the October 1985 hijacking of the *Achille Lauro* cruise ship, in which American passengers were terrorized and one was murdered. During the interview, Abbas threatened to carry out acts of terrorism in the United States and referred to President Ronald Reagan as "enemy number one." The case of the *Achille Lauro* will be explored further in Chapter 13.

One former member of the leftist West German June 2nd Movement terrorist group made the following argument for the manipulation of the media by West German terrorists:

The RAF [Red Army Faction] has said, this revolution will not be built up by political work, but through headlines, through its appearance in the press, which reports again and again that guerrilleros are fighting here in Germany.[32]

### Points of Criticism

Because of these and other examples of overt (often successful) manipulation of the media by terrorists, critics have identified a number of problems in the reporting of the news. These include the following:

- First, critics argue that journalists sometimes cross the line between reporting the news and disseminating terrorist propaganda. The theoretical problem is that propaganda can be spread even when the media objectively report the motives of terrorists. When motives are broadcast, events can be intellectually rationalized.

- Second, critics argue that the media's behavior sometimes shifts from objectivity to sensational opinion during particularly intense incidents. Journalists' urge to create a mood or to adopt roles other than as news reporters—such as de facto negotiators—can complicate terrorist environments.

- Third, critics argue that the ability of the mass media to reach large audiences, when combined with the foregoing factors, can lead to realignments within the political environment. The concern

---

[29]Hoffman, *Inside Terrorism,* p. 142.

[30]Ibid.

[31]Ibid.

[32]Schmid, "Terrorism," p. 98. Quoting Schmid, Alex P., and Janney De Graaf. *Insurgent Terrorism and the Western News Media.* Leiden, the Netherlands: Center for the Study of Social Conflicts, 1980, p. 48.

is that strongly symbolic attacks by terrorists—in combination with skillful publicity operations by aboveground supporters—may be interpreted by audiences as the acts of rightfully desperate people. This could affect the dynamics of the terrorists' behavior and the government's policy-making options.

A possible outcome of these problems is that some types of reporting can interfere with official efforts to resolve crises. In the case of the United States, for example,

> the media contribute to the process of transforming an international issue into a domestic political crisis for the president. There is perhaps no other type of situation that subjects the president to such intense scrutiny, and the president is aware that his image as a decisive and effective leader is constantly at risk.[33]

Thus, in the aftermath of the September 11 attacks, political and media critics hotly debated whether the media should continue to broadcast feeds from Al Jazeera news service. Al Jazeera is one of the rare independent news services in the Middle East, and it has broadcast extensive footage of injured Afghani and Iraqi civilians, whom the U.S. classified as the unfortunate "collateral damage" of war. Al Jazeera also aired film clips of Al-Qa'ida leaders Osama bin Laden and Ayman al-Zawahiri that were delivered to the station by Al-Qa'ida. The fear in the United States was that uninterpreted broadcasts of these images could spread enemy propaganda or send messages to sleeper cells. For this reason, American news services were asked to limit Al Jazeera coverage.

Applying these concerns to our model of participants in a terrorist environment, it is conceivable that interviews with terrorists, media scooping, and other reporting practices may

- send messages to *terrorists,* possibly encouraging or suggesting targets for further acts of political violence;
- encourage *supporters,* thus improving morale and strengthening the terrorists' base of support for ongoing operations;
- cause *victims* to react, possibly demoralizing them or forcing shifts in public opinion and perceptions;
- engage the target in a global (rather than domestic) forum—this can hurt the target politically and can possibly lead to international pressure to moderate behavior toward the terrorists' championed group;
- elicit sympathy—or at least understanding—from *onlookers;* and
- convince political and journalistic analysts to affix favorable labels to the group or movement.

This may affect the world's perception of the terrorists, possibly transforming them into heroic guerrillas or freedom fighters.

### Counterpointing the Criticism

As a counterpoint to the foregoing criticisms, and in defense of journalistic reporting of terrorist incidents, some proponents of the free press argue that full exposure of terrorism and the terrorists' grievances should be encouraged. In this way, the public can become completely informed about the nature of terrorism in general and about the motives of specific terrorists. Thus, "defenders of media coverage feel that it enhances public understanding of terrorism and reinforces public hostility toward terrorists."[34]

---

[33]Sick, "Taking Vows," p. 242.

[34]Barkan, Steven E., and Lynne L. Snowden. *Collective Violence.* Boston: Allyn & Bacon, 2000, p. 84.

## Information Is Power: The Media as a Weapon

The notion that information is power is a concept that politicians, governments, dictators, and extremists have accepted for some time. Controlling informational spins and the mechanisms of distribution are critical components for success, regardless of whether one wishes to sell a product, promote a political agenda, or impose an ideology. As pointed out in previous discussions, information outlets have been purposely sought out to spread the extremists' message, so that the manipulation of information has become a primary strategy in the modern era.

For terrorists and other extremists, information can be wielded as a weapon of war, so **"media as a weapon"** is an important concept. Because symbolism is at the center of most terrorist incidents, the media are explicitly identified by terrorists as potential supplements to their arsenal. When terrorists successfully—and violently—manipulate important symbols, relatively weak movements can influence governments and entire societies. Even when a terrorist unit fails to complete its mission,

❖ **Photo 11.3**

TWA Flight 847. A terrorist waves a gun to cut short a press interview with TWA pilot John Testrake during the hijacked airliner's odyssey around the Mediterranean. The terrorists skillfully manipulated the international press during this operation.

U.S. Department of State

intensive media exposure can lead to a propaganda victory. For example, during the 1972 Munich Olympics attack by Black September terrorists, "an estimated 900 million persons in at least a hundred different countries saw the crisis unfold on their television screens."[35] As one Palestine Liberation Organization (PLO) leader later observed, "World opinion was forced to take note of the Palestinian drama, and the Palestinian people imposed their presence on an international gathering that had sought to exclude them."[36]

### *Case in Point: Hezbollah and the Hijacking of TWA Flight 847*

Lebanon's Hezbollah (first discussed in Chapter 6) has demonstrated its skill at conducting extraordinary strikes, some of which ultimately affected the foreign policies of France, Israel, and the United States. It regularly markets itself to the media by disseminating grievances as press releases, filming and photographing moving images of its struggle, compiling "human-interest" backgrounds of Hezbollah fighters and Shi'a victims, and packaging its attacks as valiant assaults against Western and Israeli invaders and their proxies. This has been done overtly and publicly, and incidents are manipulated to generate maximum publicity and media exposure. For example, the January 1987 kidnapping in Beirut of Terry Waite, the Archbishop of Canterbury's envoy, was broadcast globally. He was released in November 1991.

On June 14, 1985, three Lebanese Shi'a terrorists hijacked TWA Flight 847 as it flew from Athens to Rome. It was diverted to Beirut, Lebanon, and then to Algiers, Algeria. The airliner was flown back to Beirut, made a second flight to Algiers, and then flew back to Beirut. During the odyssey, the terrorists released women, children, and non-Americans, until 39 American men remained on board the aircraft. At the final stop in Beirut, the American hostages were offloaded and dispersed throughout the city.

As the hijacking unfolded, the media devoted an extraordinary amount of airtime to the incident. The television networks ABC, CBS, and NBC broadcast almost 500 news reports, or 28.8 per day, and devoted two thirds of their evening news programs to the crisis.[37] "During the 16 days of the hijacking, CBS devoted 68% of its nightly news broadcasts to the event, while the corresponding figures at ABC and NBC were 62% and 63% respectively."[38]

---

[35]Hoffman, *Inside Terrorism*, p. 74. Citing Taylor, Peter. *States of Terror: Democracy and Political Violence.* London: Penguin, 1993, p. 8.

[36]Ibid., p. 73. Quoting Iyad, Abu, with Eric Rouleau (Trans. Linda Butler Koseoglu). *My Home, My Land: A Narrative of the Palestinian Struggle.* New York: Time Books, 1981, pp. 111–2.

[37]Hoffman, *Inside Terrorism*, p. 132.

[38]Weimann and Winn, *The Theater of Terror,* p. 1.

The hijackers masterfully manipulated the world's media. They granted carefully orchestrated interviews, held press conferences, and selected the information they permitted the news outlets to broadcast. It was reported later that the terrorists had offered to arrange tours of the airliner for the networks for a $1,000 fee and an interview with the hostages for $12,500.[39] After the hostages were dispersed in Beirut, **Nabih Berri**, the leader of Lebanon's Syrian-backed Shi'a **Amal** movement (an ally and occasional rival of the Shi'a Hezbollah movement), was interviewed by news networks as part of the negotiations to trade the hostages for concessions. In the end, the terrorists' media-oriented tactics were quite effective. They successfully broadcast their grievances and demands to the world community and achieved their objectives. "[The] media exposure of the hostages generated enough pressure for the American president to make concessions."[40] In effect,

> the most pernicious effect of the crisis was its validation of terrorism as a tactic. The Reagan administration, driven by intense domestic pressure generated by the hostages' plight, in turn compelled Israel to accede to the hijackers' demands and release 756 Shi'a.[41]

The hostages were released on June 30, 1985.

As a postscript—which was sometimes forgotten during the episode—a U.S. Navy diver had been severely beaten, shot, and thrown down to the Beirut airport's tarmac by the terrorists. The murder occurred during the second stopover in Beirut. The leader of the terrorist unit, Imad Mughniyah, and three others were later indicted by U.S. prosecutors for the killing. One hijacker, Mohammed Ali Hamadi, was convicted in Germany of the Navy diver's murder and sentenced to life in prison.

### The Contagion Effect

The **contagion effect** refers to the theoretical influence of media exposure on the future behavior of other like-minded extremists.[42] This concept can also be applied "to a rather wide range of violent behavior [other than terrorism], including racial disturbances."[43] In theory, when terrorists successfully garner wide exposure or a measure of sympathy from the media and their audience, other terrorists may be motivated to replicate the tactics of the first successful incident. This may be especially true if concessions have been forced from the targeted interest. Assuming that contagion theory has merit (the debate on this point continues), the question becomes the extent to which the contagion effect influences behavior. Examples of the contagion effect arguably include cycles of

- diplomatic and commercial kidnappings for ransom and concessions in Latin America during the 1960s and 1970s;
- hijackings on behalf of Middle East–related causes (usually Palestinian) from the late 1960s to the 1980s;
- similarities in the tactics of left-wing Western European ideological terrorists during their heyday from the late 1960s to the 1980s;
- the taking of Western hostages in Lebanon during the 1980s;
- the taking of hostages and the committing of beheadings and massacres in the Middle East during the 2000s; and
- the skillful use of social networking media during the 2010s to broadcast images for recruiting purposes and to disrupt enemy populations.

---

[39]Barkan and Snowden, *Collective Violence*.

[40]Howard, Lawrence, ed. *Terrorism: Roots, Impact, Responses*. New York: Praeger, 1992, p. 102.

[41]Weimann and Winn, *The Theater of Terror*, p. 133.

[42]For a discussion of the contagion effect and additional discussions, see ibid., pp. 157–60 and 211ff.

[43]Ibid, p. 158. See also Spilerman, C. S. "The Causes of Racial Disturbances." *American Psychological Review* 35 (1970): 627–49; and Berkowitz, L., and J. Macaulay. "The Contagion of Criminal Violence." *Psychometry* 34 (1971): 238–60.

Assessments of the contagion effect produced some consensus that the media do have an effect on terrorist cycles. For example, empirical studies have indicated a correlation between media coverage and time lags between terrorist incidents.[44] These studies have not definitively *proven* that contagion is a behavioral fact, but they do suggest that the theory may have some validity.

The era of the New Terrorism arguably presents an unprecedented dynamic for contagion theory, because transnational cell-based movements are a new model for—and may suggest new assessments of—the theory. Transnational organizations such as Al-Qa'ida engage in a learning process from the lessons of attacks by their operatives around the world. The advent of communications technologies such as faxes, cellular telephones, e-mail, text messaging, and the Internet—especially in combination with focused manipulation of the media—means that the terrorists' international learning curve can be quick and efficient. Hence, in theory, the contagion effect may be enhanced within New Terrorist movements on a global scale.

## Problems on the New Battleground: The Risk of Backlash

As the examples of TWA Flight 847 and other incidents demonstrate, terrorists purposefully try to force concessions or environmental shifts through the media. In a terrorist environment,

> the media, then, do more than inform us when reporting on terrorism. They give tiny numbers of violent men access to millions of homes and allow the terrorist newsmakers to horrify us by sudden unprovoked killings of innocents.[45]

Unfortunately for terrorists, this widespread exposure does not always work to their advantage. Governments are also experts at spinning the nature of terrorist violence to the media. When the violence is truly horrific, and when the victims, targets, or onlooker audiences recoil in popular disgust, the terrorists can significantly diminish their influence over their adversary. They can, in effect, actually strengthen the adversary's resolve. Hence,

> a vital factor in gaining access to the media, lethality, can sow the seeds of a terrorist group's own destruction. Terrorist groups can experience an irremediable backlash, even among supporters, as a result of doing injury to innocents.[46]

Public opinion among victims, targets, and onlooker audiences is critical to the success of media-oriented terrorism. However, one should bear in mind that terrorists often play to their supporter audiences, so that success is always a relative term in the battle for the media.

❖ **Photo 11.4**
Disseminating information. A Rewards for Justice program poster disseminated by the U.S. Department of State's Diplomatic Security Service. It depicts the aftermath of the 1993 bombing of the World Trade Center in New York City.

U.S. Department of State

# ❖   The Public's Right to Know: Regulating the Media

Freedom of the press is an ideal standard—and arguably an ideology—in many democracies. The phrase embodies a conceptual construct that suggests that the press should enjoy the liberty to

---

[44]See ibid., pp. 219ff.

[45]Schmid, "Terrorism," p. 101.

[46]Weimann and Winn, *The Theater of Terror,* p. 144.

independently report information to the public, even when this information might be unpopular. News editors and journalists, when criticized for their reports, frequently cite the people's right to know as a justification for publishing unpleasant information. The counterpoint to absolute freedom of the press is regulation of the press. This issue arises when the media publish unpleasant facts (often in lurid prose and images) about subjects that the public or the government would rather not consider. Regulation is also a genuine option when matters of national security are at stake. When these and other concerns arise, regimes and societies are challenged to address the following policy questions:

- Should the media be regulated?
- If regulation is desirable, how much regulation is acceptable?

The following discussion addresses these questions within the contexts of the **free press** and the **state-regulated press**.

## The Free Press

The international media operate under many rules that emanate from their cultural environments. Some media operate with few if any codes of professional self-regulation, whereas others have adopted rather strict self-standards.[47] For example, the Netherlands Broadcasting Corporation has traditionally had no formal code of operations, whereas the British Broadcasting Corporation operates under a detailed set of rules.[48] Consensus exists that ethical standards should be observed when reporting terrorist incidents. These include the following:

- [Do not] serve as a spokesman/accomplice of the terrorists . . .
- [Do not] portray terror as attractive, romantic, or heroic; [instead, employ an] honest portrayal of motives of terrorists . . .
- Hold back news where there is clear and immediate danger to life and limb . . .
- Avoid . . . unchallenged terrorist propaganda . . .
- Never try to solve a situation.[49]

### Gatekeeping

In societies that champion freedom of the press, one model professional environment is that of **journalistic self-regulation**. Journalistic self-regulation is sometimes referred to as **media gatekeeping**. If conducted under established standards of professional conduct, self-regulation obviates the need for official regulation and censorship. In theory, moral arguments brought to bear on the press from political leaders and the public will pressure them to adhere to model standards of fairness, accuracy, and objectivity.

This is, of course, an *ideal* free press environment; in reality, critics argue that journalistic self-regulation is a fluid and inconsistent process. The media report terrorist incidents using certain labels and often create a mood by spinning their reports. Some media—acting in the tabloid tradition—sensationalize acts of political violence, so that very little self-regulation occurs. Chapter Perspective 11.3 illustrates this criticism by contrasting different standards of gatekeeping by the American media at several points in time when reporting news about several U.S. presidents.

---

[47]See Paletz, David L., and Laura L. Tawney. "Broadcasting Organizations' Perspectives." In *Terrorism and the Media,* edited by David L. Paletz and Alex P. Schmid. Newbury Park, CA: Sage, 1992, pp. 105ff.

[48]Ibid., pp. 107 and 109.

[49]See ibid., p. 126.

# CHAPTER PERSPECTIVE 11.3: Self-Regulation and the American Media

Gatekeeping is a process of self-regulation by the press, using professional standards of restraint and industry guidelines about fair and objective journalism. The American media have traditionally practiced self-regulation with relatively little hindrance from government regulators, except in time of war (particularly during World War II).

Reporters working in the White House press pool, or otherwise reporting on the U.S. presidency, have developed gatekeeping standards that until recently ensured that the personal lives of presidents would not become front-page news. This "hands-off" approach to reporting details of presidential personal qualities has not been consistent. For example:

The reporting of *Franklin Delano Roosevelt*'s (FDR) administration was highly self-censored. FDR was the United States' only president with a limiting disability. His legs were paralyzed, and he used a wheelchair from the age of 39. President Roosevelt wore thick braces on his legs to prop him up when he delivered speeches. And yet, no photographs were published of him in his wheelchair by the media, most likely because American culture at the time was biased against people with disabilities. During his last years in office, he has been described as a dying man. Nevertheless, his declining health was never reported extensively to the public. The press also never reported persistent rumors about FDR's alleged long-term extramarital affair.

Likewise, the reporting of *John F. Kennedy*'s (JFK) administration was self-censored. JFK symbolized the youth and idealism of a new generation. However, he suffered from poor health during much of his adult life. For example, he had Addison's disease, severe allergies, and spinal problems, and he contracted malaria during the Second World War in the South Pacific. The media were captivated by JFK, portraying him as a man of great vigor and youth. As was the case with FDR, the press never reported rumors of alleged extramarital affairs.

In contrast, the reporting of *Bill Clinton*'s personal life was lurid and long term. Extramarital rumors were reported, interviews were broadcast of his accusers, and the Monica Lewinsky episode was front-page news around the world. For Bill Clinton, the media's self-regulatory gatekeeping practices were virtually nonexistent—particularly in comparison with the reporting of the personal lives of previous presidents such as Roosevelt and Kennedy.

## Regulation of the Free Press

Many governments occasionally regulate or otherwise influence their press community while at the same time advocating freedom of reporting. Governments selectively release information, or release no information at all, during terrorist incidents. The rationale is that the investigation of these incidents requires limitations to be placed on which information is made available to the public. This occurs as a matter of routine during wartime or other national crises.

A number of democracies have state-run and semiprivate radio and television stations. For example, Great Britain, France, Germany, and other European democracies all have government-affiliated networks. These networks are expected to promote accepted standards of professional conduct and to practice self-regulation for the sake of good taste and national security. In some democracies, the law permits the government to suppress the reporting of news. Some examples are the following:

- In Great Britain, the televised media were prohibited from broadcasting the statements of Irish terrorists or their supporters. No broadcasts were permitted of the Marxist Irish National Liberation Army. Even aboveground and somewhat mainstream broadcasts were banned, so that television broadcasts of interviews with Sinn Féin leader Gerry Adams were proscribed.

- Also in Great Britain, the **Official Secrets Act** permitted the prosecution of individuals for the reporting of information that was deemed to endanger the security of the British government.

- The Canadian Official Secrets Act proscribes any communication of information that may be prejudicial to the safety or interests of Canada.

## The State-Regulated Press

State-regulated media exist in environments in which the state routinely intervenes in the reporting of information by the press. This can occur in societies that otherwise have a measure of democratic freedoms. For example, Turkey has frequently suppressed its media and has one of the worst records among democracies. Hundreds of journalists were prosecuted in the past, receiving harsh sentences for writing offensive articles. In another example, the state-regulated presses of most countries in the Middle East led many people in those countries to believe that the September 11, 2001, attacks either were not the work of Al-Qa'ida or were the work of "Zionists." Some Middle Eastern media disseminated far-fetched rumors. For example, mainstream commentators reported and supported a popular conspiracy theory that anonymous telephone calls warned thousands of Jewish workers in the World Trade Center to leave the buildings before the attack—and therefore no Jews were casualties.

Different scales of intervention can emanate from the state, ranging from permitting independent (but regulated) newspapers to creating government-controlled propaganda enterprises. Some examples follow:

- Under authoritarianism,[50] the press can be privately owned and may be granted some latitude in reporting the news. However, information is sometimes officially censored, and the publication of unfavorable articles can be punished. Singapore (a democracy) has a history of suppressing articles that make "libelous" accusations against the government.

- Under totalitarianism,[51] the government operates on a more restrictive scale of intervention. In totalitarian systems, the state controls all information reported in the media, and the press is relegated to a state-controlled enterprise. For example, the People's Republic of China permits no independently published criticism from the media. During the bloody June 1989 suppression of the Tiananmen Square protests in Beijing, the Western press interviewed a number of Chinese civilians, eliciting some criticism of the government's actions. The interviewees were reportedly arrested.

In **authoritarian** and **totalitarian regimes**, terrorists have no chance to rely on the media to sensationalize their deeds. In these societies, the media serve to promote the government's interests and often to disseminate government propaganda. There are no gripping stories that might sway an audience. The general public is never privy to sympathetic human-interest stories or to an extremist manifesto's call to arms. When terrorist incidents occur, they are either underreported by the government or manipulated to the absolute advantage of the regime. As a result,

> one of the reasons for the virtual absence of terrorism in totalitarian states and other effective dictatorships, besides the efficacy of the police forces, is the suppression of publicity. Unless the terrorists succeed in killing the dictator, which would be impossible to ignore, their deeds will pass unheralded.[52]

U.S. Department of State

❖ **Photo 11.5**
Daniel Pearl. An American journalist in Pakistan, Pearl was kidnapped and later murdered by Pakistani Islamic terrorists, but not before they disseminated photographs and videotapes to the international media.

---

[50]Defined in Chapter 4 as "a system of government in which authority and power emanate from the state and are not delegated from the people to elected leaders. Law, order, and state authority are emphasized. Authoritarian regimes can have elected leaders, but they have authoritarian power and often rule for indefinite periods of time. Constitutions do not have enough authority to prohibit abuses by the state."

[51]Defined in Chapter 4 as "a system of total governmental regulation. All national authority originates from the government, which enforces its own vision of an ordered society."

[52]Laqueur, *The New Terrorism*, p. 44.

In very restrictive societies, the media are used as outlets for propaganda on behalf of the existing regime. For example, former Iraqi dictator Saddam Hussein created an extensive **cult of personality** not unlike those of dictators Joseph Stalin in the Soviet Union and Kim Il Sung (and son Kim Jong Il and grandson Kim Jong Un) in North Korea. Cults of personality are used by dictatorial regimes to promote the leader or ruling party as the source of absolute wisdom, truth, and benevolence. Likenesses of the leader are widely distributed, usually in a variety of symbolic poses. Saddam Hussein, for example, was regularly depicted as a visionary, a warrior, the good father, a common citizen, a devout Muslim, and the medieval leader Saladin. Hussein, Stalin, and Kim promoted themselves, their regimes, and their policies by completely controlling the dissemination of information.

## Chapter Summary

This chapter investigated the role of the media in terrorist environments. Particular attention was given to efforts by terrorists to publicize the cause, the manipulation of mass communications by terrorists, and the potential impact of the New Media. Issues regarding the reporting of terrorism by the media include questions about which incidents to report and how to report those incidents. The concepts of "information is power" and "media-oriented terrorism" were defined and explored as critical considerations for understanding the role of the media.

Evaluation of the new battleground for information requires that readers first explore this issue from the perspectives of participants in terrorist environments. Practical considerations for terrorists' treatment of the media include their manipulation of the media's desire to "scoop" their competitors. The contagion effect and the example of the hijacking of TWA Flight 847 demonstrate how media exposure can become a weapon in the terrorists' arsenal.

Regulation of the media is a challenge for every government. For authoritarian and totalitarian regimes, this challenge is easily resolved by simply prohibiting certain kinds of reporting practices. It is a more complex issue in most democratic systems, although most have adapted by adopting laws and practices that restrict media access to operational information.

In Chapter 12, readers will review terrorism in the United States. The discussion will investigate domestic sources of terrorism from the right and left, as well as cases of nationalist and international terrorism. Consideration will be given to terrorist environments and the reasons for terrorism in the United States.

## Key Terms and Concepts

The following topics are discussed in this chapter and can be found in the glossary:

| | | |
|---|---|---|
| Al Jazeera | journalistic self-regulation | news triage |
| Amal | labeling | Official Secrets Act |
| authoritarian regimes | mass communications | Phalangist |
| Berri, Nabih | "media as a weapon" | print media |
| contagion effect | media gatekeeping | propaganda |
| cult of personality | media-oriented terrorism | publicize their cause |
| euphemistic language | media scooping | state-regulated press |
| free press | media spin | totalitarian regimes |
| information is power | New Media | TWA Flight 847 |

## Discussion Box: Freedom of Reporting and Security Issues

During times of crisis, governments restrict media access to information about matters that affect security policy. The logic is quite understandable: Governments believe that the war effort (or counterterrorism policy) requires limitations to be imposed to prevent information from helping the enemy and to prevent the enemy from spreading its propaganda. For example, the British Official Secrets Act was designed to manage the flow of information both *from* adversaries and *to* adversaries.

The challenge for democracies is to strike a balance between governmental control over information—for the sake of national security—and unbridled propaganda. The following examples illustrate how the United States and Great Britain managed the flow of information during international crises:

- During the *Vietnam War*, journalists had a great deal of latitude to visit troops in the field and observe operations. Vietnam was the first "television war," so violent and disturbing images were broadcast into American homes on a daily basis. These reports were one reason why American public opinion turned against the war effort.

- During the 1982 *Falklands War*, news about operations was highly controlled and censored by the British government. Press briefings were strictly controlled by the government, under the rationale that useful information could otherwise be received by the Argentines and jeopardize the war effort.

- During the 1990–1991 *Persian Gulf War*, news was likewise highly controlled.

Unlike during the Vietnam War, the media received their information during official military press briefings. They were not permitted to travel into the field except under highly restrictive conditions.

- During the Afghan phase of the *war on terrorism* in late 2001, news was highly restricted. Official press briefings were the norm, and requests were made for cooperation in not broadcasting enemy propaganda.

- During the 2003 conventional phase of the *invasion of Iraq*, reporters were "embedded" with military units and reported events as they unfolded. Official press briefings were the norm.

### Discussion Questions

- Should the United States adopt information-control regulations similar to Britain's Official Secrets Act?

- What are the policy implications of permitting journalists to have the same degree of access to information as occurred during the Vietnam War?

- What are the policy implications of permitting journalists to have the same degree of access to information as occurred during the Gulf War?

- Under what circumstances should the state increase restrictions on the media? How would you justify these restrictions?

- Do you think that the media in democracies are more prone to manipulation by terrorists? Is this a myth?

## On Your Own

The open-access Student Study Site at **http://study.sagepub.com/martin5e** has a variety of useful study aids, including eFlashcards, quizzes, audio resources, and journal articles. The websites, exercises, and recommended readings listed below are easily accessed on this site as well.

## Recommended Websites

The following websites are links to the online addresses of major resources that regularly report news about terrorism:

Al Arabiya News Channel (Dubai): http://www.alarabiya.net/english.html/

Al Jazeera (Qatar): http://america.aljazeera.com/

Al-Manar TV (Lebanon): http://www.almanar.com.lb/english/main.php/

BBC (UK): http://www.bbc.co.uk/

CNN (USA): http://www.cnn.com/

*Dawn* (Pakistan): http://www.dawn.com/

Middle East Media Research Institute: http://memri.org/

*New York Times*: http://www.nytimes.com/

SITE Intelligence Group (USA): http://siteintelgroup.com/

## Web Exercise

Using this chapter's recommended websites, conduct an online investigation of the reporting of terrorism by the media.

1. Compare and contrast the reporting of political violence by the referenced media services. What patterns of reporting can you identify?

2. To what extent are the media services biased in their reporting? How so?

3. To what extent are the media services objective in their reporting? How so?

For an online search of reporting of terrorism by the media, readers should activate the search engine on their Web browser and enter the following keywords:

"Media and Terrorism"

"Propaganda and Terrorism"

## Recommended Readings

The following publications provide discussions for evaluating the role of the media in the reporting of terrorism, national conflict, and political dissent:

Davies, Nick. *Flat Earth News: An Award-Winning Reporter Exposes Falsehood, Distortion, and Propaganda in the Global Media*. London: Vintage Books, 2009.

Davis, Richard, and Diana Owen. *New Media and American Politics*. New York: Oxford University Press, 1998.

Edwards, David, and David Cromwell. *Newspeak in the 21st Century*. London: Pluto Press, 2009.

Gitlin, Todd. *The Whole World Is Watching: Mass Media in the Making and Unmaking of the New Left*. Los Angeles: University of California Press, 1980.

Herbst, Philip. *Talking Terrorism: A Dictionary of the Loaded Language of Political Violence*. Westport, CT: Greenwood, 2003.

Kavoori, Anandam P., and Todd Fraley, eds. *Media, Terrorism, and Theory: A Reader*. Lanham, MD: Rowman & Littlefield, 2006.

Knightley, Phillip. *The First Casualty: The War Correspondent as Hero and Myth Maker From the Crimea to Iraq*. Baltimore: Johns Hopkins University Press, 2004.

Nacos, Brigitte L. *Mass-Mediated Terrorism: The Central Role of the Media in Terrorism and Counterterrorism.* New York: Rowman & Littlefield, 2007.

Paletz, David L., and Alex P. Schmid, eds. *Terrorism and the Media.* Newbury Park, CA: Sage, 1992.

Pludowski, Tomasz. *How the World's News Media Reacted to 9/11: Essays From Around the Globe.* Spokane, WA: Marquette Books, 2007.

Seib, Philip, ed. *New Media and the New Middle East.* New York: Palgrave McMillan, 2007.

Tuman, Joseph S. *Communicating Terror: The Rhetorical Dimensions of Terrorism.* 2nd ed. London: Sage, 2010.

Weimann, Gabriel, and Conrad Winn. *The Theater of Terror: Mass Media and International Terrorism.* New York: Longman, 1994.

# The American Case

## CHAPTER 12

## Terrorism in the United States

### OPENING VIEWPOINT: LYNCHING—VIGILANTE COMMUNAL TERRORISM IN THE UNITED STATES

Lynchings were public communal killings. On most occasions, they were racially motivated hangings or burnings of African American males. Lynch mobs would typically abduct the victim, drag him to the place of execution, physically abuse him (often gruesomely), and then publicly kill him. Lynchings exhibited the following profile:

- White mobs
- Killings of African Americans (usually men) and others
- Physical abuse, including torture, mutilation, and the taking of "souvenirs" from the corpses (bones, toes, etc.)
- Symbolic protection of the white community
- Symbolic "warnings" to the African American community

Photography was commonly used to record lynchings, and it was not uncommon for members of lynch mobs to pose proudly next to the corpses. This is significant, because the use of the camera to memorialize lynchings testified to their openness and to the self-righteousness that animated the participants. Not only did photographers capture the execution itself, but they also recorded the carnival-like atmosphere and the expectant mood of the crowd.[a]

The term *lynching* comes from Charles Lynch, a colonial-era Virginia farmer who, during the American Revolution, acted as a judge who hanged outlaws and Tories (pro-British colonials). From 1882 to 1968, nearly 5,000 African Americans are known to have been lynched. Some had been accused of crimes, but most were simply innocent sacrificial victims.

### Note

a. Litwack, Leon F. "Hellhounds." In *Without Sanctuary: Lynching Photography in America*, edited by James Allen, Hilton Als, Congressman John Lewis, and Leon Litwack. Santa Fe, NM: Twin Palms, 2000, pp. 10–11.

P revious chapters focused on defining terrorism, its causes, motives behind political violence, the terrorist trade, and terrorist typologies. Many examples of post–World War II terrorist movements and environments were presented to illustrate theoretical concepts and trends. The discussion in this and subsequent chapters will investigate terrorist threats in the United States, the concept of American homeland security, the homeland security bureaucracy, and emerging issues and trends likely to affect the United States' response to terrorist threats in the near future.

The quality of post–World War II extremism in the United States reflects the characteristics of the classical ideological continuum. Readers may recall that the classical ideological continuum, discussed earlier, incorporates political tendencies that range from the fringe left to the fringe right, but that many examples of nationalist and religious terrorism do not fit squarely within the continuum categories. However, the United States is an idiosyncratic subject, and most terrorism in the post–World War II era did originate from the left- and right-wing spectrums of the continuum.

Unlike many terrorist environments elsewhere in the world, where the designations of *left* and *right* are not always applicable, most political violence in the United States falls within these designations. Even nationalist and religious sources of domestic political violence have tended to reflect the attributes of leftist or rightist movements. It is only when we look at the international sources of political violence that the left and right designations begin to lose their precision in the United States.

Hulton Archive/Getty Images

❖ **Photo 12.1**
Communal terrorism in America. The lynchings of Tommy Shipp and Abe Smith in Marion, Indiana, on August 7, 1930. The crowd is in a festive mood, including the young couple holding hands in the foreground.

Table 12.1 applies the classical ideological continuum to the American context.

The discussion in this chapter will review the following:

- An Introduction to the American Case
- Background to Terrorism: Left-Wing Activism and Ideological Extremism in America
- Left-Wing Terrorism in the United States
- Background to Terrorism: Right-Wing Activism and Ideological Extremism in America
- Right-Wing Terrorism in the United States
- International Terrorism in the United States

# ❖ An Introduction to the American Case

To facilitate readers' appreciation of the unique qualities of the American case, it is instructive to briefly survey the American left, the American right, and international terrorism in the United States. All of these themes will be explored in later sections.

The *American left* traditionally refers to political trends and movements that emphasize group rights. Several trends characterize the American left: labor activism, "people's rights" movements, single-issue movements, and antitraditionalist cultural experimentation. Examples include the following:

- **Labor Activism.** Historically, labor activism and organizing promoted ideals that are frequently found on the left. The labor movement of the late 19th and early 20th centuries was highly confrontational, with violence emanating from management, the unions, and the state. Socialist labor activists such as Samuel Gompers were quite active in organizing workers. However, the mainstream American labor movement was distinctive, in comparison with European labor movements, in that the dominant labor unions generally rejected Marxist or other socialistic economic ideologies.[1]

---

[1]For a good history of the American labor movement, see Brooks, Thomas R. *Toil and Trouble: A History of American Labor.* New York: Dell, 1971.

## Table 12.1  The Classical Ideological Continuum: The Case of the United States

The United States is a good case in point for the application of the classical ideological continuum. Its political environment has produced organizations that represent the ideologies included in the continuum. The representation here compares organizations that have economic, group rights, faith, and legal agendas.

| | *Fringe Left* | *Far Left* | *Liberalism* | *Moderate Center* | *Conservatism* | *Far Right* | *Fringe Right* |
|---|---|---|---|---|---|---|---|
| **Economic/class agenda** | | | | | | | |
| | May 19 Communist Organization | Communist Party, USA | American Federation of State, County and Municipal Employees | American Federation of Labor and Congress of Industrial Organizations | Teamsters Union | Lyndon Larouche groups | Posse Comitatus |
| **Activist/group rights agenda** | | | | | | | |
| | | Black Panther Party | National Association for the Advancement of Colored People | National Bar Association | Heritage Foundation | National Association for the Advancement of White People | Aryan Republican Army |
| **Religious/faith agenda** | | | | | | | |
| | Liberation theology | Catholic Worker movement | American Friends Service Committee | National Conference of Christians and Jews | Southern Baptist Convention | Moral Majority | Army of God |
| **Legal/constitutional agenda** | | | | | | | |
| | Individual lawyers | National Lawyers Guild | American Civil Liberties Union | American Bar Association | Thomas More Law Center | American Center for Law and Justice | Freemen |

- **"People's Rights."** There have been a number of people's rights movements on the American left. In the modern era, activism on the left has generally promoted the interests of groups that have historically experienced discrimination or a lack of opportunity. Examples of people's rights movements include the civil rights, Black Power, New Left, gay rights, and immigration reform movements.

- **Single Issue.** Single-issue movements such as the environmentalist and peace movements have also been common on the left.

- **Questioning Traditions.** One facet of the left has been a tendency toward antitraditionalist cultural trends. Manifestations of this trend have included experimentation with alternative lifestyles and the promotion of countercultural issues such as drug legalization.[2]

On the far and fringe left, one finds elements of Marxist ideology and left-wing nationalist principles. Terrorist violence from the left has usually been ideological or ethnonationalist in nature. It has typically been carried out by covert underground organizations or cells that link themselves (at least ideologically) to leftist "rights" movements. Although there have been human casualties as a direct result of leftist terrorism, most violence has been directed at nonhuman symbols such as unoccupied businesses, banks, or government buildings. Law enforcement officers were also occasionally targeted, usually by ethnonationalist terrorists. The heyday of leftist terrorism in the United States was from the late 1960s to the mid-1980s.

The *American right* traditionally encompasses political trends and movements that emphasize conventional and nostalgic principles. On the mainstream right, traditional values are emphasized. Examples include family values, educational content, and social order ("law and order") politics. It is also common on the American right (unlike the European and Latin American right) to find an infusion of fundamentalist or evangelical religious principles.

On the far and fringe right, one finds that racial, mystical, and conspiracy theories abound; one also finds a great deal of antigovernment sentiment, with some fringe extremists opting to separate themselves from mainstream society. Terrorist violence has usually been racial, religious, or antigovernment in nature. With few exceptions, terrorism from the right has been conducted by self-isolated groups, cells, or individual lone wolves. Unlike most leftist attacks, many of the right's targets have intentionally included people and occupied symbolic buildings. Most ethnocentric hate crimes—regardless of whether one considers them to be acts of terrorism or aggravated crimes[3]—come from the far and fringe right wing. This type of ethnocentric violence has a long history in the United States:

> Since the middle of the nineteenth century, the United States has witnessed several episodic waves of xenophobia. At various times, Catholics, Mormons, Freemasons, Jews, blacks, and Communists have been targets of groups . . . seeking to defend "American" ideals and values.[4]

Right-wing terrorism has occurred within different political and social contexts, from **Ku Klux Klan (KKK)** violence during the civil rights movement of the 1950s and 1960s, to neo-Nazi violence in the 1980s, to antigovernment and **single-issue terrorism** in the 1990s.

*International terrorism in the United States* has included anti-Castro movements, Jewish groups opposing the former Soviet Union's emigration policy, Irish Provos (Provisional Irish Republican Army, IRA), and sporadic spillovers from conflicts around the world. Since the collapse of the Soviet Union, most international terrorism in the United States has come from spillovers originating in Middle Eastern conflicts. Attacks such as the September 11, 2001, homeland assaults indicate that practitioners of the New Terrorism have specifically targeted the United States as an enemy interest. Operatives

---

[2]Some of the lifestyle issues, such as drug legalization, have been endorsed by libertarian conservatives.

[3]See a discussion of the definitional debate about hate crimes in the Chapter 2 Opening Viewpoint.

[4]Kelly, Robert J. "The Ku Klux Klan: Recurring Hate in America." In *Hate Crime: The Global Politics of Polarization,* edited by Robert J. Kelly and Jess Maghan. Carbondale: Southern Illinois University Press, 1998, p. 54.

carrying out Middle East–related attacks inside the United States have been foreign nationals who attack symbolic targets, specifically intending to kill people. These attacks have usually been carried out by pre-positioned cells. The members of these cells were drawn from groups such as Hamas and Islamic Jihad, which have had operatives and supporters living in the United States. Collaborative efforts by these and other groups illustrate the internationalization of the New Terrorism, its loose organizational structure, and its potential effectiveness inside the United States.

Table 12.2 shows groups responsible for terrorist incidents in the United States, from 2001 to 2011.

| Table 12.2 | Groups Responsible for Most Terrorist Attacks in the United States, 2001–2011[a] | | |
|---|---|---|---|
| Rank | Organization | Number of Attacks | Number of Fatalities |
| 1 | Earth Liberation Front (ELF) | 50 | 0 |
| 2 | Animal Liberation Front (ALF) | 34 | 0 |
| 3 | Al-Qa'ida | 4 | 2,996 |
| 4 | Coalition to Save the Preserves (CSP) | 2 | 0 |
| 4 | Revolutionary Cells-Animal Liberation Brigade | 2 | 0 |
| 5 | Al-Qa'ida in the Arabian Peninsula (AQAP) | 1 | 0 |
| 5 | Ku Klux Klan | 1 | 0 |
| 5 | Minutemen American Defense | 1 | 2 |
| 5 | Tehrik-i-Taliban Pakistan (TTP) | 1 | 0 |
| 5 | The Justice Department | 1 | 0 |

*Note:* These are all groups attributed responsibility for attacks in the GTD between 2001 and 2011. If responsibility for an attack was attributed to more than one group, then both are listed. The total number of attacks with attributed groups is 90. Seven of those attacks list a second perpetrator, resulting in 97 attributions of responsibility.

[a]United States Department of Justice, Federal Bureau of Investigation.

*Source:* Plumer, Brad. "Eight Facts About Terrorism in the United States." *Washington Post,* April 16, 2013.

Table 12.3 summarizes and contrasts the basic characteristics of contemporary left-wing, right-wing, and international political violence in the United States.[5] This is not an exhaustive profile, but it is instructive for purposes of comparison.

## Weighing the Origins of Terrorism in the United States

An investigation of the origins of activism on the American left and right provides insight into the social trends and political environments that eventually produced homegrown terrorist violence. Understanding this background is instructive for evaluating why some members of

---

[5]See Smith, Brent L. *Terrorism in America: Pipe Bombs and Pipe Dreams.* Albany: State University of New York Press, 1994, pp. 35ff.

| Table 12.3 | Attributes of Terrorism in the United States |
|---|---|

In the United States, terrorism has typically been conducted by groups and individuals espousing leftist or rightist ideologies or those who engage in international "spillover" conflicts. These interests are motivated by diverse ideologies, operate from different milieus, possess distinctive organizational profiles, and target a variety of interests.

The following table summarizes these profiles.

| Environment | Activity Profile | | | |
|---|---|---|---|---|
| | Ideological Profile | Bases of Operation | Organizational Profile | Typical Targets |
| **Left-wing** | Marxist; left-wing nationalist | Urban areas; suburbs | Clandestine groups; movement-based | Symbolic structures; avoidance of human targets |
| **Right-wing** | Racial supremacist; antigovernment; religious | Rural areas; small towns | Self-isolated groups; cells; lone wolves | Symbolic structures; human targets |
| **"Old" international terrorism** | Ethnonationalist | Urban areas | Clandestine groups | Symbols of enemy interest |
| **"New" international terrorism** | Religious | Urban areas | Cells | Symbolic structures; human targets |

social movements adopted terrorism as a means toward an end. Although only a small core of activists engaged in terrorism, their decisions to do so originated in uniquely American political environments.

Two sections in this chapter explore the origins of several social and political movements on the left and right. It is not an exhaustive investigation, but the predominant activist trends are identified. Readers should appreciate that most members of these movements did not rationalize, support, or otherwise advocate political violence. Nevertheless, some factions developed extremist tendencies and began to aggressively challenge the nation's basic political and cultural institutions. Factions within a few of these movements concluded that terrorist violence was necessary and then acted on this decision. The origins of these factions frame the social and ideological background to terrorist violence in the postwar United States.

## ❖ Background to Terrorism: Left-Wing Activism and Ideological Extremism in America

The modern American left is characterized by several movements that grew out of the political fervor of the 1960s. They were fairly interconnected, so that understanding their origins provides instructive insight into the basic issues of the left. One should bear in mind that none of these movements was fundamentally violent in nature, and they were not terrorist movements. However, extremist trends within them led to factions that sometimes espoused violent confrontation, and a few engaged in terrorist violence.

## Origins of the Modern Civil Rights Movement[6]

The modern civil rights movement initially centered on the struggle to win equality for African Americans in the South. This was not the only regional emphasis of the movement, but its momentum came out of the battle to end racial segregation and legalized inequality in the South. During the early 1950s, the movement—at first led by the National Association for the Advancement of Colored People—forced an end to segregation on trains and interstate buses by successfully appealing several federal lawsuits to the U.S. Supreme Court. Despite these victories, Southern state laws still allowed segregation on *intra*state transportation.

In December 1955 in Birmingham, Alabama, Rosa Parks was arrested for refusing to give up her seat to a white man and move to the back of the bus, which is where African Americans were required to sit. The Reverend Martin Luther King Jr. led a bus boycott in Birmingham that lasted 13 months. A Supreme Court decision, combined with lost revenues, forced the bus company to capitulate. This was the beginning of the application of civil disobedience using a strategy known as **collective nonviolence**. King and his followers adopted this strategy from the Indian leader Mahatma Gandhi's successful movement to end British colonial rule in India. The theory was that massive resistance, coupled with moral suasion and peaceful behavior, would lead to fundamental change.

A great many other civil rights protests occurred during the 1950s and 1960s, with official and unofficial violence being directed against the movement. There were numerous anti–civil rights bombings, shootings, and beatings in the South during this period. Under the leadership of King and others, the strategy of collective nonviolence—and targeted lawsuits by civil rights attorneys (including future Supreme Court justice Thurgood Marshall)—finally held sway in the South. However, not every member of the civil rights movement accepted collective nonviolence as a fundamental principle, and the strategy was not particularly effective outside of the Southern context.

## The Rise of Black Power

As a direct result of the violence directed against the nonviolent civil rights movement, an emerging ideology of African American empowerment took root among many activists. It began in June 1966, when civil rights activist James Meredith planned to walk through Mississippi to demonstrate that African Americans could safely go to polling places to register to vote. He was ambushed, shot, and wounded early in his walk. The incident caused Martin Luther King Jr. and other national civil rights activists to travel to Mississippi to finish Meredith's symbolic march. One of the leaders was Stokely Carmichael, chair of the Student Nonviolent Coordinating Committee (SNCC).

Carmichael renounced collective nonviolence. He also disagreed with the civil rights movement's strategy of working within mainstream political parties (primarily the Democratic Party). As the SNCC became more radicalized, the group expelled its white members, many of whom went on to become activists in the New Left movement. At a rally in Mississippi, Carmichael roused the crowd to repeatedly shout "Black power!" and adopted the clenched fist as a symbol of defiance. The slogan caught on, as did the clenched-fist symbol, and the **Black Power** movement began.

The Black Power movement occurred at a time when the violence in the South was paralleled by urban activism, unrest, and rioting in the impoverished African American ghettos of the North, Midwest, and West. In the Northeast, prior to Carmichael's Black Power rally, former Nation of Islam advocate Malcolm X had eloquently challenged African Americans to empower themselves economically and culturally. To do so, Malcolm X argued that economic self-sufficiency was essential for African American communities and that it was necessary for African Americans to culturally unite internationally with the emerging independence movements in Africa, as well as with the descendants of African

---

[6]For good histories of the civil rights movement, see Branch, Taylor. *Parting the Waters: America in the King Years, 1954–63.* New York: Simon & Schuster, 1988. See also Hampton, Henry, and Steve Fayer. *Voices of Freedom: An Oral History of the Civil Rights Movement From the 1950s Through the 1980s.* New York: Bantam, 1990.

slaves in the Americas. His autobiography has become an influential document within the greater body of African American literature.[7]

The ideology of Black Power advocated political independence, economic self-sufficiency, and a cultural reawakening. It was expressed in Afrocentric political agendas; experiments in economic development of African American communities; and cultural chauvinism that was expressed in music, art, and dress (the Black Pride movement). Some members of the movement were radicalized by the violence in the South and began to advocate black nationalism. This led to the formation of overtly nationalist and militant organizations such as the **Black Panther Party for Self-Defense**.

## Growth of the New Left

The so-called old left was characterized by orthodox Marxist ideologies and political parties, dating from the time of the Russian Revolution. Other tendencies of the old left included anarchism and traditional socialist ideologies. After revelations about Stalinist brutality, the Soviet Union's suppression of the Hungarian Revolution in 1956, and frustration with the failure of socialist organizing in the United States, the old left movement became discredited among young activists. New issues galvanized a new movement among educated young activists, primarily on the nation's university campuses.

The **New Left** arose in the mid-1960s when a new generation of activists rallied around the antiwar movement, the civil rights movement, women's rights, and other political and social causes. New student organizations such as **Students for a Democratic Society (SDS)** advocated a philosophy of **direct action** to confront mainstream establishment values (SDS is discussed later in the chapter). In the fall of 1964, participants in the Free Speech Movement at the University of California, Berkeley, seized an administration building on the campus. This was a wakeup call for adopting direct action as a central tactic of the fledgling New Left.

New Left movements still reflected the ideals of the new generation of activism even when they revisited orthodox Marxism. For example, one faction of SDS—the **Revolutionary Youth Movement II (RYM II)**—tailored the orthodox ideologies of the old left to the political environment of the 1960s. RYM II argued that the youth movement should be organized

> not as a cultural phenomenon but as members of the working class who had experienced "proletarianization" in schools and the army. In these institutions, the young found themselves in the same boat as the oppressed black community, slaves to the lords of war and industry.[8]

RYM II and the New Left in general adapted their ideological motivations to the political and social context of the 1960s. Many young leftists turned to the ideas of a new generation of radical thinkers, such as Herbert Marcuse, Frantz Fanon, and Carlos Marighella. They also championed contemporary revolutionaries and movements, such as the Cuban, Palestinian, and Vietnamese revolutionaries. At its core, "the [American] New Left was a mass movement that led, and fed upon, growing public opposition to U.S. involvement in Vietnam."[9] The collective term applied by the New Left to the mainstream American political and cultural establishment was the **military-industrial complex**. This term had been used by President Dwight D. Eisenhower to warn against the possible threat to democratic values from corporate and military interests.

---

[7]See Malcolm X. *The Autobiography of Malcolm X*. New York: Grove, 1964. See also Breitman, George, ed. *Malcolm X Speaks*. New York: Grove, 1965.

[8]Jacobs, Ron. *The Way the Wind Blew: A History of the Weather Underground*. New York: Verso, 1997, p. 21. Citing Mellen, Jim. "More on Youth Movement." *New Left Notes*, May 13, 1969.

[9]Gurr, Ted Robert. "Terrorism in Democracies: Its Social and Political Bases." In *Origins of Terrorism: Psychologies, Ideologies, Theologies, and States of Mind*, edited by Walter Reich. Washington, DC: Woodrow Wilson Center, 1998, p. 89.

Just as the Black Power movement incorporated a cultural agenda, so too did the New Left. Many young Americans experimented with alternative lifestyles, drugs, and avant-garde music. They also challenged the values of mainstream American society, questioning its fundamental ideological and cultural assumptions. This component of the New Left was commonly called the **counterculture**. There was also a genuinely idealistic belief that activist youths could bring justice to the world. This period was marked by many experiments in youth-centered culture.

## ❖ Left-Wing Terrorism in the United States

As New Left and Black Power movements and organizations became radicalized, many individuals and groups began to advocate active resistance against **the Establishment**—defined as mainstream American political and social institutions. This resistance included explicit calls for civil disobedience and confrontation with the authorities. Many within these movements referred to themselves as revolutionaries, and some advocated the overthrow of the military-industrial complex. Prototypical revolutionary organizations began to form in the late 1960s, and a few of these groups produced cadres or factions that became terrorist organizations. All of this occurred in a generalized environment of activism and direct action. For example, social tensions were quite volatile during the first half of 1970, as indicated by the following incidents that occurred before the summer college break:

- On May 4 at Kent State University in Ohio, four students were killed and nine wounded by the Ohio National Guard after several days of violent antiwar demonstrations against the U.S. incursion into Cambodia.
- Just after midnight on May 15 at Jackson State University in South Carolina (a historically African American university), one student and one passerby were killed when police fired into a crowd of African American protestors. At least a dozen students were hospitalized.
- Approximately 30 Reserve Officer Training Corps (ROTC) buildings were burned or bombed.
- More than 500 colleges closed early because of student protests.

There were also a large number of politically motivated bombings, shootings, and assaults during this period. The Senate Committee on Government Operations reported the following statistics:[10]

- In 1969, there were 298 explosive and 243 incendiary bombings.
- From January to July 1970, there were 301 explosive and 210 incendiary bombing incidents.
- From January 1968 to June 1970, there were 216 ambushes against law enforcement personnel and headquarters.
- Also from January 1968 to June 1970, there were 359 total assaults against the police, causing 23 deaths and 326 injuries.

Chapter Perspective 12.1 presents two examples of radicalized organizations—one from the New Left (Students for a Democratic Society) and the other from the Black Power movement (the Black Panthers). The story of both groups illustrates the evolutionary process of left-wing revolutionary cadres and factions that eventually advocated political violence.

---

[10]Data are derived from *Riots, Civil and Criminal Disorders—Hearings Before the Permanent Subcommittee on Investigations of the Committee on Government Operations, United States Senate,* Part 25. Washington, DC: Government Printing Office, 1970. Cited in Prosser, George. "Terror in the United States: 'An Introduction to Elementary Tactics' and 'Some Questions on Tactics.'" In *Terror and Urban Guerrillas: A Study of Tactics and Documents,* edited by Jay Mallin. Coral Gables, FL: University of Miami Press, 1971, p. 52.

## CHAPTER PERSPECTIVE 12.1: Seeds of Terrorism: Radicals on the American Left

Two militant case studies are discussed here—the Black Panthers and the radicalized Students for a Democratic Society. Within each movement were groups or cadres who advocated violent revolution.

### Case: The Black Panthers

The Black Panther Party for Self-Defense was organized in 1966 in Oakland, California. The name was selected from an African American organization founded in Alabama called the Lowndes County Freedom Organization. The Lowndes County group had used the symbol of a black panther on voter ballots, ostensibly so that illiterate voters would know who their candidates were.

The Oakland Black Panthers initially imitated a tactic that had been used by the Los Angeles–based Community Alert Patrol, which had been formed after the Watts riot in August 1965.[a] The Community Alert Patrol would dispatch observers to scenes of suspected harassment by the Los Angeles Police Department and observe police stops. In Oakland, the Black Panthers took this tactic one step further and arrived on the scene openly carrying law books and shotguns or rifles (legal at the time in California).[b] The symbolism of young African Americans projecting a paramilitary image in poor urban ghettos attracted members to the Black Panthers around the country. More than 40 chapters were formed, with a total of more than 2,000 members. By 1968, the group made worldwide headlines and came to symbolize the Black Power movement. Public demonstrations by the Black Panthers maximized the use of paramilitary symbolism, with members marching and chanting slogans in precision and wearing black berets and black leather jackets.

Ideologically, the Black Panthers were inspired by Malcolm X,[c] Frantz Fanon, and Mao Zedong. They were advocates of black nationalism and encouraged economic self-sufficiency and armed self-defense in the black community. Black Panther self-help initiatives included free breakfasts for poor schoolchildren in urban areas. The police (at that time all male and mostly white in most cities) were especially singled out and labeled as a kind of "occupation" force in African American communities.

The group's militancy attracted the attention of federal and local law enforcement agencies, who considered the organization to be a threat to national security. The revolutionary and antipolice rhetoric of Black Panther leaders and the militant articles in its newspaper *The Black Panther* increased their concern. Federal Bureau of Investigation (FBI) Director J. Edgar Hoover stated that the Black Panthers were the most significant threat to domestic security in the United States. A series of arrests and shootouts at Black Panther offices occurred. The leadership of the organization was decimated by arrests, police raids, and a successful "**disinformation**" campaign that sowed distrust among central figures. Internal feuds between leaders Huey Newton and Eldridge Cleaver also disrupted the group. Although the Black Panthers continued to be active into the late 1970s—after significantly moderating its militancy by the mid-1970s—its heyday as a paramilitary symbol of black nationalism was during the late 1960s and early 1970s. As it declined under relentless internal and external pressures, some of its more radical members joined the revolutionary underground.

### Case: Students for a Democratic Society

In June 1962, a group of liberal and mildly leftist students—known as Students for a Democratic Society, or SDS, many from the University of Michigan—met to draft a document that became known as the **Port Huron Statement**. In this document, SDS harshly criticized the values of mainstream American society and called for the establishment of a "new left" movement in the United States. The Port

*(Continued)*

(Continued)

Huron Statement was a critique and a call for action directed to middle-class students. At this time, SDS was liberal and leftist but hardly revolutionary. SDS espoused "direct action," which originally referred to peaceful and nonviolent confrontation.

By 1965, SDS had moved to the radical left, and when the bombing of North Vietnam began, its national membership soared. By 1966, its focal point was the war in Vietnam and support for the Black Power movement (SDS's membership was mostly comprised of white students). In 1967, SDS (in a classic Marcuse-like interpretation) cast activist American youth as a "new working class" oppressed by the military-industrial complex. By 1968, SDS's leadership was revolutionary. An SDS-led takeover of Columbia University occurred during the 1968 spring term, when students seized five buildings for 5 days. When the police were called in, a riot ensued; more than 700 people were arrested, and nearly 150 were injured. A student strike—again led by SDS—closed Columbia. SDS also led dozens of other campus disturbances in 1968.

In June 1968, SDS factionalized because of ideological tensions within the group. Some members formed a prototypical Revolutionary Youth Movement, others aligned themselves with developing-world revolutionary heroes, and others (sometimes called Crazies) espoused violent revolution. At its next meeting in June 1969 in Chicago, SDS split along doctrinal and tactical lines into the Maoist **Progressive Labor Party** (also known as the Worker-Student Alliance), Revolutionary Youth Movement II, and the violent revolutionary **Weathermen** group.

## Notes

a. The toll for the Watts disturbance was high; 34 people were killed, more than 1,000 injured, and nearly 4,000 arrested. Approximately 200 businesses were destroyed and about 700 were damaged. For a study of the Watts riot, see Conot, Robert. *Rivers of Blood, Years of Darkness*. New York: Bantam, 1967.

b. The armed patrols ended when California passed a law prohibiting the open display of firearms.

c. For more information about Malcolm X, see X, Malcolm. *The Autobiography of Malcolm X*. New York: Grove, 1964.

❖ **Photo 12.2**

A young woman screams as she kneels over the body of a student during an antiwar demonstration at Kent State University, Ohio, on May 4, 1970. Four students were slain when Ohio National Guard troops fired into a crowd of some 600 antiwar demonstrators.

John Filo/Premium Archive/Getty Images

The following discussion evaluates four trends and one case in point on the violent left:

- Generational Rebellion: New Left Terrorism
- Civil Strife: Ethnonationalist Terrorism on the Left
- The Revolution Continues: Leftist "Hard Cores"
- Case in Point: The United Freedom Front
- Single-Issue Violence on the Left

## Generational Rebellion: New Left Terrorism

The New Left was deeply affected by the war in Vietnam, the civil rights movement, and the turmoil in inner-city African American communities. A number of terrorist groups and cells grew out of this environment. Although the most prominent example was the Weathermen group, other groups such as the Symbionese Liberation Army also engaged in terrorist violence. The United Freedom Front, discussed later in the chapter as a special case, proved to be the most enduring of all New Left terrorist groups of the era.

### The Weathermen/Weather Underground Organization

The Weathermen group—known as the Weathermen—gelled at the June 1969 Students for a Democratic Society national convention in Chicago, when SDS splintered into several factions. The Weathermen derived their name from a popular song of the time written by artist Bob Dylan, which included the lyrics, "You don't need a weatherman to know which way the wind blows." The Weathermen were mostly young, white, educated members of the middle class. They represented in stark fashion the dynamic ideological tendencies of the era, as well as the cultural separation from the older generation. Although they and others were sometimes referred to collectively as the "Crazies," they operated within a supportive cultural and political environment. The following description of this environment is typical:

> Only a handful of the New Left were alienated enough to embrace revolutionary strategies, but many of them agreed with the objectives, if not the tactics, of the militant Weather People, and some provided support for them. . . . Testimony to the effectiveness of that support network is the fact that no Weather People were arrested during the early 1970s or after the voluntary cessation of their bombing campaign in 1975.[11]

From the beginning, the Weathermen were violent and confrontational. In October 1969, they distributed leaflets in Chicago announcing what became known as their **"Days of Rage"** action. They justified their action by declaring,

> We move with the people of the world to seize power from those who now rule. We . . . expect their pig lackeys to come down on us. We've got to be ready for that. This is a war we can't resist. We've got to actively fight. We're going to bring the war home to the mother country of imperialism. AMERIKA: THE FINAL FRONT.[12]

The Days of Rage lasted for 4 days and consisted of acts of vandalism and running street fights with the Chicago police. In December 1969, the Weathermen held a "war council" in Michigan. Its leadership, calling itself the **Weather Bureau**, advocated bombings, armed resistance, and assassinations. One leader, **Bernardine Dohrn**, praised the murders committed in California by the Charles Manson cult, referring to the bloodshed as revolutionary acts and calling the cult's victims "pigs." In March 1970, an explosion occurred in a Greenwich Village townhouse in New York City that was being used as a bomb factory. Three Weathermen were killed, several others escaped through the New York subway system, and hundreds of members went underground to wage war.

By the mid-1970s, the Weathermen—renamed the **Weather Underground Organization**—had committed at least 40 bombings, including the following targets:

- The Pentagon
- The U.S. Capitol (possibly—see United Freedom Front later in chapter)
- Police stations
- National Guard facilities
- ROTC buildings
- The Harvard war research center in Cambridge, Massachusetts
- The Gulf Oil corporate headquarters in Pittsburgh, Pennsylvania

---

[11]Gurr, "Terrorism," p. 89.

[12]Sprinzak, Ehud. "The Psychopolitical Formation of Extreme Left Terrorism in a Democracy: The Case of the Weathermen." In *Origins of Terrorism: Psychologies, Ideologies, Theologies, States of Mind,* edited by Walter Reich. Washington, DC: Woodrow Wilson Center, 1998, p. 65. Quoting Thomas, Tom. "The Second Battle of Chicago." In *Weatherman,* edited by Harold Jacobs. Berkeley, CA: Ramparts, 1970, p. 197.

Aside from these actions, the Weather Underground also freed counterculture guru Timothy Leary from prison,[13] published a manifesto called ***Prairie Fire***, and distributed an underground periodical called ***Osawatomie***. Members established an aboveground support network of **Weather Collectives** organized by a group called the **Prairie Fire Organizing Committee**. Their underground network of safe houses and rural safe collectives—which served to hide themselves and New Left fugitives from the law—was never effectively infiltrated by law enforcement agencies. By the mid-1970s, members of the Weather Underground began to give up their armed struggle and returned to aboveground activism—a process that they called "inversion." Those who remained underground (mostly the East Coast wing) committed acts of political violence into the 1980s, and others joined other terrorist organizations.

### ❖ Photo 12.3

The Symbionese Liberation Army (SLA) in action. A bank camera captures Patricia Hearst exiting a bank after an SLA robbery. Hearst, who joined the group after being kidnapped by them, likely suffered from Stockholm syndrome.

Consolidated News Pictures/Hulton Archive/ Getty Images

### The Symbionese Liberation Army

The Symbionese Liberation Army (SLA) was a violent terrorist cell that gained notoriety for several high-profile incidents in the mid-1970s. The core members were led by **Donald DeFreeze**, who took the *nom de guerre* Cinque (named for the leader of a 19th-century rebellion aboard the slave ship *Amistad*). Members trained in the Berkeley hills of California near San Francisco, rented safe houses, and obtained weapons. In November 1973, the Oakland school superintendent was assassinated when he was shot eight times; five of the bullets were cyanide tipped. In a communiqué, the SLA took credit for the attack, using a rhetorical phrase that became its slogan: "Death to the fascist insect that preys upon the people!"

In February 1974, newspaper heiress Patricia Hearst was kidnapped by the cell. She was kept bound and blindfolded in a closet for more than 50 days while under constant physical and psychological pressure, including physical abuse and intensive political indoctrination. She broke down under the pressure, and a tape recording was released in which she stated that she had joined the SLA. In April 1974, Hearst participated in a bank robbery in San Francisco. This was a classic case of Stockholm syndrome.

In May 1974, five of the SLA's core members, including DeFreeze, were killed in a shootout in a house in the Watts neighborhood of Los Angeles.

Patricia Hearst was a fugitive for approximately 1 year. She was hidden—probably by the Weather Underground—and traveled across the country with compatriots. By 1975, the SLA had a rebirth with new recruits and was responsible for several bank robberies and bombings in California. Members referred to themselves as the **New World Liberation Front**. Hearst was captured in September 1975 in San Francisco, along with another underground fugitive.

Most of the other members either were captured or disappeared into the underground. One member of the renewed SLA, Kathy Soliah, was arrested in July 1999 in a Minneapolis suburb. She had changed her name to Sara Jane Olson and become a typical community-oriented "soccer mom." Soliah was convicted in California on 20-year-old charges of plotting to blow up two Los Angeles Police Department patrol cars.[14] In February 2003, four former members of the SLA (including Soliah) pleaded guilty to participating in an April 1975 bank robbery in Carmichael, California, in which a mother of four was shot to death.[15] A fifth former SLA member who participated in the Carmichael

---

[13]A former professor, Leary was best known for his recreational and spiritual experimentation with the hallucinogenic drug LSD, which he advocated as a "consciousness-raising" drug.

[14]Soliah was paroled from prison in March 2008 after serving about 6 years of her sentence. She was rearrested about a week after being paroled after authorities determined that she had been mistakenly released 1 year early. See Weinstein, Henry, and Andrew Blankstein. "Sara Jane Olson Rearrested." *Los Angeles Times,* March 23, 2008.

[15]See Landsberg, Mitchell. "Only Hard Sell Revived 'Slam Dunk' SLA Case." *Los Angeles Times,* February 14, 2003.

incident (James Kilgore) was arrested near Cape Town, South Africa, in November 2002. Kilgore also pleaded guilty to charges.

## Civil Strife: Ethnonationalist Terrorism on the Left

Ethnonational violence—which is distinguishable from racial supremacist violence—has been rare in the United States. This is primarily because activist environments have not historically supported nationalist terrorism. Exceptions to this general observation grew out of the political environment of the 1960s, when nationalist political violence originated in African American and Puerto Rican activist movements. There have been few nationalist movements outside of these examples. One isolated example of nationalist violence did occur on the island of St. Croix in the territory of the U.S. Virgin Islands. In 1972, eight people—seven whites and one African American employee—were shot execution style at the Fountain Valley Golf Club by Virgin Islands nationalists seeking independence from the United States. This incident (known as the **Fountain Valley Massacre**) was isolated and idiosyncratic; it did not develop into an underground revolutionary movement, as did the Puerto Rican and mainland African American movements.

The following discussion evaluates ethnonational political violence committed by adherents of the Black Liberation and Puerto Rico independence movements. In both examples, the underlying ideological justifications for the violence were Marxist inspired.

### The Black Liberation Movement

Racial tensions in the United States were extremely high during the 1960s. African Americans in the South directly confronted Southern racism through collective nonviolence and the burgeoning Black Power ideology. In the urban areas of the North and West, cities became centers of confrontation between African Americans, the police, and state National Guards. Many Black Power advocates in the North and West became militant as the summers became seasons of urban confrontation. During what became known in the 1960s as the **"long hot summer,"** many cities were social and political powder kegs, and hundreds of riots occurred during the summers from 1964 to 1969. When President Lyndon Johnson and the U.S. Senate organized inquiries into the causes of these disorders, their findings were disturbing. Table 12.4 describes the quality of these findings, which indicate the severity of tensions in urban areas during the mid-1960s.

Within this environment grew cadres of African American revolutionaries dedicated to using political violence to overthrow what they perceived to be a racist and oppressive system. The most prominent example of African American nationalist terrorism is the **Black Liberation Army (BLA)**.

### The Black Liberation Army

The BLA was an underground movement whose membership included former members of the Black Panthers and Vietnam veterans. BLA members were nationalists who were inspired in part by the 1966 film *Battle of Algiers*,[16] a semidocumentary of an urban terrorist uprising in the city of Algiers against the French during their colonial war in Algeria. In the film, Algerian rebels organized themselves into many autonomous cells to wage urban guerrilla warfare against the French. The actual Battle of Algiers is considered by many to be a prototypical example of cell-based irregular and asymmetrical warfare.

There were at least two cells (or groups of cells) of the BLA—the East Coast and West Coast groups. Although the BLA was likely active in late 1970 and early 1971, both cells became known later, and in similar fashion, to law enforcement agencies and the media:

---

[16]The film was directed by Italian filmmaker Gillo Pontecorvo, who died in October 2006. See Times Staff and Wire Services. "Gillo Pontecorvo, Movie Director Best Known for 'The Battle of Algiers,' Dies at 86." *Los Angeles Times,* October 14, 2006.

## Table 12.4  Racial Conflict in America: The "Long Hot Summers" of the 1960s

The urban disturbances in the United States during the 1960s caused a major period of communal discord. The disturbances were widespread and violent and were a culmination of many factors. One factor was the deeply rooted racial polarization in American society. The presidential-appointed National Advisory Commission on Civil Disorders (known as the **Kerner Commission**) reported in 1968 that

> segregation and poverty have created in the racial ghetto a destructive environment totally unknown to most white Americans. What white Americans have never fully understood—but what the Negro can never forget—is that white society is deeply implicated in the ghetto. White institutions created it, white institutions maintain it, and white society condones it.[a]

The following table reports data from a Senate Permanent Subcommittee on Investigations inquiry into urban rioting after the serious disturbances in the summer of 1967.[b] The table summarizes the environment during 3 years of civil disturbances.[c]

| Incident Report | Activity Profile | | |
|---|---|---|---|
| | 1965 | 1966 | 1967 |
| **Number of urban disturbances** | 5 | 21 | 75 |
| **Casualties** | | | |
| **Killed** | 36 | 11 | 83 |
| **Injured** | 1,206 | 520 | 1,897 |
| **Legal sanctions** | | | |
| **Arrests** | 10,245 | 2,298 | 16,389 |
| **Convictions** | 2,074 | 1,203 | 2,157 |
| **Costs of damage (in millions of dollars)** | $40.1 | $10.2 | $664.5 |

a. *Report of the National Advisory Commission on Civil Disorders.* New York: Bantam Books, 1968, p. 2.

b. In 1967, the Senate passed a resolution ordering the Senate Permanent Subcommittee on Investigations to study what had caused the 1967 rioting and to recommend solutions.

c. Senate Permanent Subcommittee on Investigations. Data reported in *Ebony Pictorial History of Black America,* vol. 3. Chicago: Johnson, 1971, p. 69.

- **East Coast Cell.** In May 1971, two New York City police officers were ambushed and killed by .45-caliber fire. A package delivered to the *New York Times* containing, among other items, a communiqué and a .45 bullet, claimed credit for the shootings on behalf of the BLA. This was the beginning of a number of known and suspected BLA attacks in the New York City region.

- **West Coast Cell.** In August 1971, similar attacks were made against police officers in San Francisco. In one ambush, the police were attacked by .45-caliber machinegun fire; two BLA "soldiers" were captured after a shootout in this incident.

The BLA is suspected to have committed a number of attacks in New York and California prior to and after these incidents. Members are thought to have been responsible for numerous bombings, ambushes of police officers,[17] and bank robberies to "liberate" money to support their cause. Their areas of operation were California and New York City, although some BLA members apparently received training in the South.

The symbolic leader of the BLA was JoAnne Chesimard, a former Black Panther who later changed her name to **Assata Shakur**. She was described by admirers as the "heart and soul" of the BLA. In May 1973, a gunfight broke out when she and two other BLA members were stopped on the New Jersey Turnpike by a New Jersey state trooper. The trooper was killed, as was one of the occupants of the automobile. Shakur was captured, tried, and eventually convicted in 1977. She was sentenced to life imprisonment but was freed in 1979 by members of the May 19 Communist Organization (discussed later in the chapter) and spirited to Cuba. She remains there under the protection of the Cuban government.

Most members of the BLA were eventually captured or killed. Those who were captured were sentenced to long prison terms.[18] Unlike the Weather Underground's network, the BLA network was successfully penetrated and infiltrated by the FBI, using informants. Those who escaped the FBI net re-formed to join other radical organizations. Interestingly, the only known white member of the BLA, Marilyn Buck, was a former member of the radicalized SDS who had disappeared into the revolutionary underground.

### Puerto Rican Independencistas

Puerto Rico is a commonwealth of the United States, meaning that it is self-governed by a legislature and an executive (a governor) and has a nonvoting delegate to Congress. The island is exempt from the Internal Revenue Code, and its residents are ineligible to vote in presidential elections. Opinion about the island's political status is divided among a majority who wish for it to remain a commonwealth, a large number who favor statehood, and a minority who desire national independence. Those who desire independence are nationalists called *independencistas*. Most *independencistas* use democratic institutions to promote the cause of independence; they are activists but are not prone to violence. Many are intellectuals and professionals who are working to build pro-independence sentiment. For example, the Puerto Rico Independence Party is a fairly mainstream leftist political movement in Puerto Rico.

Some *independencistas* are revolutionaries, and a small number have resorted to violence. Puerto Rican nationalist violence on the mainland United States has a history dating to the postwar era. Two incidents from the 1950s illustrate this history:

- In November 1950, nationalists attacked Blair House, the president's official state guest house, in Washington, DC, in an attempt to assassinate President Harry Truman. Two people were killed—one terrorist and one Secret Service agent.

- In March 1954, five members of the U.S. House of Representatives were wounded when four nationalists opened fire from the visitors' gallery overlooking the House floor. All of the attackers were captured, tried, and convicted.

President Jimmy Carter granted executive clemency to the perpetrators of these incidents, freeing them from prison.

Modern violent nationalists pattern themselves after Cuban nationalism and view the United States as an imperial and colonial power. Cuba has, in fact, provided support for violent *independencista* groups, especially during the 1980s.

There have been several Puerto Rican *independencista* terrorist organizations. These organizations include the **Macheteros** ("Machete-Wielders"), the **Organization of Volunteers for the**

---

[17]Possibly 26 police officers died in BLA ambushes. Gurr, Ted Robert. "Political Terrorism: Historical Antecedents and Contemporary Trends." In *Violence in America: Protest, Rebellion, Reform,* vol. 2, edited by Ted Gurr. Newbury Park, CA: Sage, 1989.

[18]In January 2007, eight former radicals, seven of them former members of the Black Liberation Army, were arrested for the 1971 slaying of a San Francisco police officer. See Glionna, John M., and Steve Chawkins. "8 Ex-Radicals Arrested in '71 Police Slaying." *Los Angeles Times,* January 24, 2007.

**Puerto Rican Revolution**, and the **Armed Forces of Popular Resistance**. Although most violent *independencistas* carried out their operations in Puerto Rico, one group—the **Armed Forces for National Liberation (Fuerzas Armadas de Liberación Nacional, or FALN)**—was based on the mainland and was highly active from the 1970s through the mid-1980s. The Macheteros were also responsible for attacks on the mainland.

### The FALN

The FALN[19] was a very active terrorist organization that concentrated its activities on the U.S. mainland, primarily in Chicago and New York City. One important fact stands out about the FALN: It was the most prolific terrorist organization in U.S. history. The group became active in 1974, and from 1975 to 1983, approximately 130 bombings were linked to the FALN or the Macheteros, with the vast majority being the responsibility of the FALN. Most attacks by the FALN were symbolically directed against buildings, although some of its attacks were deadly. For example, in January 1975, the FALN detonated a bomb at the trendy restaurant Fraunces Tavern in New York, killing 4 people and wounding more than 50. In another incident in 1983, three New York City police officers were maimed while trying to defuse explosives at the New York police headquarters. The group was also responsible for armored car and bank robberies.

Aside from the FALN's attacks, the political and legal issues surrounding the group were high profile and significant. Two cases in point are instructive:

- In 1977, leader William Morales was captured by the police after being injured in an explosion at a FALN bomb factory in New York City. In 1979, Morales was freed from a hospital in New York by the May 19 Communist Organization, the same group that freed BLA leader Assata Shakur. He escaped to Mexico, where he remained hidden until 1983. In 1983, Morales was captured by Mexican authorities at an international telephone; he was also convicted *in absentia* of sedition by a federal district court in Chicago for participation in 25 bombings. In 1988, Mexico refused to extradite Morales to the United States, and he was allowed to move to Cuba, where he remains under the protection of Cuban authorities.

- In 1980, more than a dozen FALN members were convicted of terrorist-related crimes. Sentences were imposed for seditious conspiracy, possession of unregistered firearms, interstate transportation of a stolen vehicle, interference with interstate commerce by violence, and interstate transportation of firearms with intent to commit a crime. None of these charges were linked to homicides. FALN members' sentences ranged from 15 to 90 years, and they considered themselves to be prisoners of war.

In August 1999, President Bill Clinton proposed executive clemency for 16 imprisoned FALN members. President Clinton offered to commute their sentences if the prisoners agreed to meet three conditions: first, sign agreements to renounce violence; second, admit that they had committed criminal acts; and third, agree not to reestablish their associations with one another after release. In September 1999, clemency was accepted by 14 members, and 2 refused the offer. Under the terms of the clemency agreement, 11 were released, and 1 accepted a grant of parole in 2004. This process was opposed by the FBI, the U.S. Bureau of Prisons, two U.S. attorneys, local law enforcement agencies, and the families of victims of FALN attacks. It was supported by human rights officials (who argued that the sentences were too harsh), mainstream Puerto Rican politicians, and members of the Puerto Rican nationalist movement. It was also popular among large constituencies on the island and mainland.

## The Revolution Continues: Leftist "Hard Cores"[20]

The left-wing revolutionary underground re-formed after the decline of groups such as the Weather Underground and the BLA. These new groups were made up of die-hard former members of the

---

[19]See Smith, *Terrorism in America: Pipe Bombs and Pipe Dreams,* for sources and further discussion of the FALN.

[20]See ibid. for sources and further discussion of left-wing "hard cores."

Weather Underground and BLA, as well as former activists from other organizations such as the radicalized SDS and the Black Panthers. Two cases in point illustrate the character of the reconstituted revolutionary left in the 1980s.

### May 19 Communist Organization

The **May 19 Communist Organization (M19CO)** derives its name from the birthdays of Malcolm X and Vietnamese leader Ho Chi Minh. The symbolism of this designation is obvious—it combines domestic and international examples of resistance against self-defined U.S. racism and imperialism. The group was composed of remnants of the Republic of New Afrika (described later in the chapter), the BLA, the Weather Underground, and the Black Panthers. These cadres included the founders of the Republic of New Afrika and the most violent members of the Weather Underground. Many of its members were people who had disappeared into the revolutionary underground for years.

M19CO was fairly active, engaging in bank and armored car robberies, bombings, and other politically motivated actions. Its more spectacular actions included the following incidents:

- Responsibility for freeing BLA leader Assata Shakur from a New Jersey prison in 1979. M19CO hid Shakur for months before spiriting her to Cuba.
- Responsibility for freeing FALN leader William Morales from a New York City hospital in 1979. The group hid Morales and arranged his flight to Mexico.
- Participation in the October 1981 robbery of a Brinks armored car in suburban Nyack, New York. During the robbery, one security guard was killed. After an automobile chase and shoot-out at a roadblock, four M19CO members were captured. Two police officers had died at the roadblock shootout. One person captured was Kathy Boudin, daughter of prominent attorney Leonard Boudin.[21] She had been one of the survivors of the explosion at the Weatherman group's Greenwich Village townhouse in 1970.[22] Also captured was Donald Weems, a former BLA member and later member of the New Afrikan Freedom Fighters.

M19CO adopted several different names when claiming responsibility for its attacks. These aliases included Red Guerrilla Resistance, Revolutionary Fighting Group, and Armed Resistance Unit. After the Nyack incident, M19CO remained active and engaged in several bombings. The group was finally broken when its remaining members were arrested in May 1985.

### The New Afrikan Freedom Fighters

The **New Afrikan Freedom Fighters** were an unstructured black liberation movement, considered by authorities to be a self-defined "military wing" of a nationalist organization called the Republic of New Afrika. The objective of the Republic of New Afrika was to form a separate African American nation (called the Republic of New Afrika) from portions of several Southern states in which the population was majority African American. Many of the Republic of New Afrika's activities were aboveground, and many of its members were educated intellectuals. Some members opted to engage in political violence under the name of the New Afrikan Freedom Fighters. The group included former members of the BLA and the Black Panthers. They operated in collaboration with other members of the revolutionary underground. The group was eventually broken up in 1985 after members were arrested for conspiring to free from prison Donald Weems, the group's Nyack armored car robbery comrade; bomb the courthouse; and commit other acts of political violence. Interestingly, most members had been educated professionals.

---

[21]Boudin was denied parole at her first parole hearing in 2001. See Associated Press. "Kathy Boudin, 60s Radical, Denied Parole." *New York Times*, August 22, 2001.

[22]Boudin was paroled in August 2003 after serving 22 years in prison.

## Case in Point: The United Freedom Front[23]

One case is unique in comparison with other New Left, nationalist, or hard-core groups. Formed in 1975, the **United Freedom Front (UFF)** was underground and active for approximately 10 years. It was a New Left terrorist organization that grew out of a program by former SDS members to educate prison inmates about the "political" nature of their incarceration. This effort was similar to other radical programs that defined incarcerated African Americans as political prisoners. Activists across the country went into the prisons to develop the revolutionary consciousness of what they perceived to be an oppressed group—much as orthodox Marxist revolutionaries had long used vanguard strategies to politicize the working class and peasantry.

In 1975, the UFF detonated a bomb at the Boston State House under the name of the **Sam Melville–Jonathan Jackson Unit**, named for two politicized inmates. The group was never very large but was very active, peaking in activity during the early 1980s. The UFF is suspected of committing at least 25 bombings and robberies in New York and New England. The attacks were primarily intended to exhibit anticorporate or antimilitary symbolism. A group calling itself the Armed Resistance Unit detonated a bomb on the Senate side of the U.S. Capitol building on November 6, 1983, to protest the U.S. invasion of Grenada. It is possible that the Armed Resistance Unit was the UFF operating under a different name.

UFF members exhibited a great deal of discipline in their activities—for example, taking copious notes at regular meetings that they called "sets." Members went underground in the American suburbs, immersing themselves in the middle class and adopting covers as nondescript residents. The UFF was broken when its members were arrested in late 1984 and early 1985. Few leftist groups had survived by remaining both underground and active for as long as did the UFF.

## Single-Issue Violence on the Left

The left has produced violent single-issue groups and individuals who focus on one particular issue to the exclusion of others. To them, their championed issue is the central point—arguably the political crux—for solving many of the world's problems. For example, Ted Kaczynski, also known as the Unabomber, protested the danger of technology by sending and placing bombs that killed 3 people and injured 22 others during a 17-year campaign.

### Eco-Terrorism

Typical of leftist single-issue extremism is the fringe environmental movement. Groups such as the **Animal Liberation Front (ALF)** and the **Earth Liberation Front (ELF)** have committed hundreds of acts of violence, such as arson, break-ins, and vandalism. Activists refer to their methods euphemistically as "eco-drama," "eco-tage," "monkey-wrenching," and "animal liberation."[24] The U.S. Federal Bureau of Investigation defines **eco-terrorism** as

> The use or threatened use of violence of a criminal nature against innocent victims or property by an environmentally oriented, subnational group for environmental-political reasons, or aimed at an audience beyond the target, often of a symbolic nature.[25]

Most incidents have been directed against property and other economic targets. Their activity profiles are summarized as follows:

- The ALF favors direct action to protest animal abuse, with the objective of saving as many animals as possible. There is no hierarchy within the movement, and it has operated in small groups.

---

[23]See Smith, *Terrorism,* for sources and further discussion of the United Freedom Front.

[24]See National Consortium for the Study of Terrorism and Responses to Terrorism. *Countering Eco-Terrorism in the United States: The Case of "Operation Backfire."* Final Report to the Science and Technology Directorate, U.S. Department of Homeland Security. College Park, MD, September 2012. At 7.

[25]Ibid. at 10–11.

- The ELF was founded in England by activists who split from the environmentalist group Earthfirst! because of its decision to abandon criminal activities. It is potentially more radical than the ALF.

The ALF and ELF have been known to coordinate their activities. Several joint claims have been made about property damage and other acts of vandalism, and it is likely that the two groups have shared the same personnel. However, both groups are comprised of self-described autonomous collectives of activists, much like the cellular structure of other extremist movements.

For the most part, both the ALF and ELF have been nonviolent toward humans, but they have committed many incidents of property destruction. Property targets include buildings, monuments, and other infrastructure. ALF and ELF targets also include laboratories, facilities where animals are kept, and sport utility vehicles (SUVs). Some of these incidents are vandalism sprees. For example, in one spree near Sacramento, California, in late 2004 and early 2005, several acts of arson were attempted and trucks and SUVs were vandalized and spray-painted with the initials *ELF*. In another operation in 2003, a group of activists apparently affiliated with the ELF went on a firebombing and vandalism spree in the San Gabriel Valley east of Los Angeles. About 125 SUVs and other vehicles parked at homes and auto dealerships were burned or damaged. The initials *ELF* were also spray-painted. In the latter operation, a doctoral student attending the California Institute of Technology was found guilty of conspiracy and arson.

Other ALF/ELF actions have included the following:

- Destruction of a forest station in Oregon
- Poisoning Mars candy bars
- Destruction of a University of California, Davis, livestock research laboratory
- Tree "spiking," which involves pounding metal stakes into trees in logging areas; the purpose is to destroy or damage logging equipment
- The "liberation" of minks in Wisconsin
- Arson at the Vail, Colorado, ski resort

The FBI estimates that the ELF alone has engaged in approximately 1,200 criminal acts and caused about $100 million in property damage since 1996. In 2001, an ELF firebomb destroyed the University of Washington's Center for Urban Horticulture, which was rebuilt at a cost of $7 million. In one particularly destructive arson incident in August 2003, the group caused $50 million in damages to a condominium complex under construction in San Diego, California. The ELF has also targeted suburban property developments, as occurred in 2008 when four luxury homes were burned in a suburb north of Seattle, Washington. In September 2009, members of the ELF toppled two radio towers near Seattle.

# ❖ Background to Terrorism: Right-Wing Activism and Ideological Extremism in America

The modern American right is characterized by several trends that developed from cultural and grassroots sources. Unlike the left, whose characteristics reflected the activism of the 1960s, the right is characterized more by self-defined *value systems*. These value systems have been perceived by many on the right to be under attack and hence in need of protection—often by resorting to activist defense. This tendency is rooted in newly emergent trends such as antigovernment and evangelical religious activism, as well as in historical cultural trends such as racial supremacy. Some political controversies, such as illegal immigration, have rallied extremists who promote their own agendas by claiming that such issues justify their extreme beliefs.[26] One interesting ideological juxtaposition has been collabora tion among racial supremacists and other members of the extreme right with Islamist radicals, primar- ily because of anti-Zionist and anti-Semitic common cause.[27]

The following discussion surveys the modern (postwar) characteristics of these trends. They pro- vide a background to contemporary terrorism on the right.

## Religious Politics and the "Christian Right"

The movement commonly termed the **Christian Right** is a mostly Protestant fundamentalist move- ment that links strict Christian values to political agendas. The Christian Right is certainly not unique in making this connection; the civil rights movement was also led by members of the religious community. In both examples, activists sought the "moral high ground" on issues, thus framing the political debate as one of moral urgency rather than political expediency. The modern origins of the Christian Right lie in the conservative political environment of the 1980s. During the 1980s, President Ronald Reagan and other conservative leaders actively embraced many principles of the movement's political agenda.

The Christian Right is not an inherently violent movement, and some activists have practiced variations of collective nonviolence and direct action by blockading and protesting at the offices of abortion providers. The movement has sometimes been highly active and has successfully mobilized voters and other activists at both the national and local levels. There has also been some success in lobbying politicians for support, particularly among conservative members of Congress who repre- sent conservative religious constituencies. Rallying issues include the promotion of traditional family values, denunciations of homosexuality, and opposition to abortion. The ultimate goal of the Christian Right is to make Christian religious values (primarily evangelical Christian values) an integral part of the nation's social and political framework.

Far- and fringe-right members of the Christian Right have adopted a highly aggressive and con- frontational style of activism. For example, a number of blockades and protests at abortion clinics involved harassment and threats directed against employees and patients. Some clinics received death threats, and violence was occasionally directed against facilities—including bombings and shootings. One significant aspect of the more reactionary tendency within the movement is the promotion of a specifically evangelical *Christian* agenda, thus rejecting agendas that are secular, non-Christian, or nonfundamentalist Christian.

## Rise of the Antigovernment Patriots

The Patriot movement came to prominence during the early 1990s. The movement considers itself to represent the true heirs of the ideals of the framers of the U.S. Constitution. Members hearken back to what they have defined as the "true" American ideals of individualism, an armed citizenry, and minimum interference from government. For many Patriots, government in general is not to be trusted, the federal government in particular is to be distrusted, and the United Nations is a danger- ous and evil institution. To them, American government no longer reflects the will of the people; it has become dangerously intrusive and violently oppressive. The Patriot movement is not ideologi- cally monolithic, and numerous tendencies have developed, such as the Common Law Courts and Constitutionalists.

Conspiracy theories abound within the Patriot movement. Some of them have long and murky origins, having been developed over decades. Other theories appear and disappear during

---

[26]See Ressner, Jeffrey. "Rousing the Zealots: Neo-Nazis, White Supremacists and Militamen Are Revivified by the Furor Over Illegal Immigration." *Time,* June 5, 2006.

[27]See Michael, George. "Strange Bedfellows." *Chronicle of Higher Education,* April 21, 2006.

periods of political or social crisis. Nevertheless, three phases of modern conspiracy beliefs may be identified:

- Cold War–era conspiracy theories
- New World Order conspiracies
- Post-9/11 conspiracy beliefs, also referred to as the **"Truther" movement**

Two events from the 1990s served to invigorate paranoid political activism on the Patriot right, giving rise to new conspiracy theories. These events were the tragedies at **Ruby Ridge**, Idaho, and **Waco**, Texas.

- **Ruby Ridge.** In August 1992 at Ruby Ridge, Idaho, racial supremacist Randy Weaver and his family, with compatriot Kevin Harris, were besieged by federal agents for Weaver's failure to reply to an illegal weapons charge. Two members of the Weaver family were killed during the standoff, as was a U.S. marshal. Weaver's teenage son, Sammy, and Marshal William Degan were killed during a shootout that occurred when Sammy, Randy, and Harris were confronted as they walked along a path. Weaver's wife, Vicky, was later fatally shot by an FBI sniper as she held her baby in the doorway of the Weaver home. The sniper had previously fired shots at Randy Weaver and Harris. Members of the Patriot movement and other right-wing extremists cite this incident as evidence of a broad government conspiracy to deprive freedom-loving "true" Americans of their right to bear arms and other liberties. Randy Weaver's story has inspired Patriots and other members of the extreme right.
- **Waco.** In early 1993 at Waco, Texas, federal agents besieged the Branch Davidian cult's compound after a failed attempt in February to serve a search warrant for illegal firearms had ended in the deaths of four federal agents and several cult members. On April 19, 1993, during an assault led by the FBI, about 80 Branch Davidians—including more than 20 children—died in a blaze that leveled the compound. As with Ruby Ridge, Patriots and other rightists consider this tragedy to be evidence of government power run amok.

Rightist conspiracy theories range from the fanciful to the paranoid. For example, Patriots cite evidence that non-American interests are threatening to take over—or have already taken over—key governmental centers of authority. This is part of an international plot to create a one-world government called the **New World Order**. According to one version of this conspiracy theory:

- New World Order troops may already have been pre-positioned inside the United States—as evidenced by sightings of **black helicopters**.
- The black helicopters are possibly United Nations troops conducting reconnaissance in preparation for their seizure of power.
- The tragedies at Ruby Ridge and Waco were trial runs for imposing the New World Order on the United States.
- Background information databases, especially gun registrations, will be used to round up and oppress loyal patriotic Americans.

As discussed in Chapter Perspective 12.2, the New World Order and black helicopters conspiracy is not the only one created by "true believers" on the extreme right. Many new creative conspiracy theories were framed in the post-9/11 era. Chapter Perspective 12.2 summarizes conspiracy theories emanating from the right.

## CHAPTER PERSPECTIVE 12.2: Conspiracy Theories on the American Right

The modern far and fringe right have produced a number of conspiracy theories and rumors. Although they may seem fantastic to nonmembers of the Patriot (and other) movements, many adherents of these theories live their lives as if the theories were an absolute reality. Three phases of modern conspiracy beliefs may be identified.

### Phase 1: Communist Invaders During the Cold War

- Rumors "confirmed" that Soviet cavalry units were preparing to invade Alaska across the Bering Strait from Siberia.

- Thousands of Chinese soldiers (perhaps an entire division) had massed in tunnels across the southwestern border of the United States in Mexico.

- Thousands of Viet Cong and Mongolian troops had also massed in Mexico across the borders of Texas and California.

### Phase 2: The New World Order Replaces the Communist Menace

- Hostile un-American interests (which may already be in power) include the United Nations, international Jewish bankers, the Illuminati, the Council on Foreign Relations, and the Trilateral Commission.

- Assuming it is Jewish interests who are in power, the U.S. government has secretly become the Zionist Occupation Government (ZOG).

- The government has constructed concentration camps that will be used to intern Patriots and other loyal Americans after their weapons have all been seized (possibly by African American street gangs).

- Invasion coordinates for the New World Order have been secretly stuck to the backs of road signs.

- Sinister symbolism and codes have been found in the Universal Product Code (the bar lines on consumer goods), cleaning products, cereal boxes, and dollar bills (such as the pyramid with the eyeball).

- Sinister technologies exist that will be used when ZOG or the New World Order makes its move. These include devices that can alter the weather and scanners that can read the plastic strips in American paper currency.

- FEMA (Federal Emergency Management Agency) has built concentration camps for the day when patriotic Americans will be interned.

With these and other conspiracy theories as an ideological foundation, many within the Patriot movement organized themselves into citizens' **militias**. Scores of militias were organized during the 1990s, and at their peak, it is estimated that 50,000 Americans were members of more than 800 militias, drawn from 5 to 6 million adherents of the Patriot movement.[a] Some members joined to train as weekend "soldiers," whereas other militias organized themselves as paramilitary survivalists. **Survivalism** originated during the Cold War, when many people believed that a nuclear exchange between the superpowers was inevitable. They moved into the countryside, stocked up on food and weapons, and prepared for the nuclear holocaust. Many militias adapted this expectation to the New World Order conspiracy theory. Militia members who became survivalists went "**off the grid**" by refusing to have credit cards, driver's licenses, Social Security numbers, or government records. The purpose of going off the grid was to disappear from the prying eyes of the government and the New World Order. Several principles are common to most militias:

- The people are sovereign. When necessary, they can resist the encroachment of government into their lives. They can also reject unjust government authority.

- Only an armed citizenry can counterbalance the authority of an oppressive government.

- The U.S. government has become oppressive, so the time is right to organize citizens' militias.

- It is necessary for citizens' militias to train and otherwise prepare for the day when an oppressive government or the New World Order moves in to take away the sovereignty of the people.

The potential for political violence from some members of the armed, conspiracy-bound Patriot movement has been cited by experts and law enforcement officials as a genuine threat.

## Phase 3a: 9/11 "Truther" Conspiracy Theories

A number of conspiracy theories emerged in the aftermath of the September 11, 2001, terrorist attacks, part of the so-called "Truther" movement. These include the following theories:

- The U.S. government allowed the attacks to happen.
- Explosives destroyed the Twin Towers in a controlled detonation, as evidenced by the vertical fall of the towers and debris that was pushed through the windows.
- A missile hit the Pentagon, as evidenced by the small size of two holes in the building.
- World Trade Center Building 7 was brought down by controlled explosions.

## Phase 3b: Post-9/11 Conspiracy Theories

Other conspiracy theories gained traction in the years following the September 11 attacks. These include the following theories:

- President Barack Obama was not born in the United States, is a socialist, and is secretly a Muslim. These are central tenets of what became known as "birther" conspiracy theories.
- The New World Order is spraying toxic chemicals in the atmosphere. These may be seen in the contrails of aircraft.
- The Federal Reserve System will be used to create a one-world banking system.

## Note

a. Hoffman, Bruce. *Inside Terrorism.* New York: Columbia University Press, 1998, p. 107. These numbers declined during the late 1990s and then rebounded after the September 11, 2001, attacks on the U.S. homeland. For a discussion of the militia movement in retrospect, see Southern Poverty Law Center. *Intelligence Report.* Summer 2001.

## Racial Supremacy: An Old Problem With New Beginnings

The history of racial supremacy in the United States began during the period of African chattel slavery and continued with the policy to remove Native Americans from ancestral lands. The racial dimensions of these practices became norms (accepted features) of the early American nation. As the nation grew, what had originated before the Civil War as a cultural *presumption* of racial supremacy became entrenched as cultural and political *policy* after the war. For example, African Americans were legally relegated to second-class citizenship, which meant that racial exclusion and social discrimination were practiced with impunity. Most Native Americans were simply removed from society and resettled on reservations.

After the Civil War and prior to World War II, the United States became a highly segregated country. Housing patterns, educational instruction, cultural institutions (such as sports), and national institutions (such as the armed forces) were racially segregated as a matter of policy. The effort to win equality for African Americans was slow, arduous, and often dangerous. As often as not, racial equality was politically unpopular among large blocs of white Americans. Organized supremacist organizations such as the Ku Klux Klan and White Citizens Councils enforced the racial code of separation and white dominance. After World War II, the tide turned against overt and unquestioned racial supremacy. The civil rights movement won significant legal victories before the Supreme Court and found many allies among prominent white political and social leaders. However, supremacist beliefs continued to win adherents in the postwar era.

Modern organized racial supremacist groups include the modern KKK, neo-Nazi movements, racist skinhead youth gangs, and some adherents of the neo-Confederate movement. New non-Klan groups came into their own during the 1980s, when **Aryan Nations**, **White Aryan Resistance**, and the **National Alliance** (explored further in Chapter Perspective 12.3) actively disseminated information about supremacist ideology. Members of the new supremacist groups created their own mythologies and conspiracy theories. For example, the novel *The Turner Diaries*[28] is considered by many neo-Nazis to be a blueprint for the Aryan revolution in America. The book inspired the terrorist group The Order (discussed later in the chapter) in its terrorist campaign. Also on the racist right, the **Fourteen Words** have become a rallying slogan. Originally coined by David Lane, a convicted member of the terrorist group The Order, the Fourteen Words are as follows: "We must secure the existence of our people and a future for White children." The Fourteen Words have been incorporated into the Aryan Nations' "declaration of independence" for the white race, and the slogan is often represented by simply writing or tattooing *14*.

There were terrorist incidents and abortive terrorist plots during the 1980s rebirth, and since then, violent racial supremacists have committed a number of hate crimes. For example, a typical racially motivated assault occurred in November 1988, when a group of racist skinheads in Portland, Oregon, beat to death an Ethiopian immigrant. They had been influenced by White Aryan Resistance.

When assessing the status of organizations such as Aryan Nations and the National Alliance, a central consideration is that they were founded and led by charismatic leaders. These leaders were the guiding personalities behind many supremacist organizations—so much so that the identities of these organizations were bound to the pronouncements and vigor of their leaders. The deaths of these founding personalities led to disarray within these groups, resulting in precipitous declines in membership. Nevertheless, former members retained the central beliefs of the organizations.

## Racial Mysticism

In Europe, neofascist movements and political parties are decidedly secular. They reference religion and the organized Christian church only to support their political agendas; they do not adopt Christian or cult-like mystical doctrines as spiritual bases to justify their legitimacy. In the United States, members of far- and fringe-right movements frequently justify their claims of racial supremacy and cultural purity by referencing underlying spiritual values—essentially claiming that they have a racial mandate from God. Racial supremacists in particular have developed mystical foundations for their belief systems, many of which are cult-like. Two of these cultish doctrines follow.

### The Creativity Movement

The **World Church of the Creator (WCOTC)**, founded by **Ben Klassen** in 1973, practiced a cult-like faith called **Creativity**. WCOTC was later led by **Matthew Hale** until his imprisonment. Creativity is premised on a rejection of the white race's reliance on Christianity, which Klassen believed was created by the Jews as a conspiracy to enslave whites. According to adherents of the Creativity movement, the white race itself should be worshipped. WCOTC declined markedly when Hale was convicted in April 2004 of soliciting a member of WCOTC to assassinate a federal judge in Illinois. Hale was sentenced in April 2005 to 40 years in prison.[29]

---

[28]Many in the racial supremacist movement consider *The Turner Diaries* to be a blueprint for the Aryan revolution. A copy was found with Timothy McVeigh when he was arrested after the Oklahoma City bombing in 1995. See MacDonald, Andrew [William Pierce]. *The Turner Diaries*. New York: Barricade, 1980. "Andrew MacDonald" is a *nom de plume* for William Pierce, leader of the National Alliance.

[29]See Huffstutter, P. J. "40 Years for Plot to Murder Judge." *Los Angeles Times,* April 8, 2005.

## *Ásatrú*

*Ásatrú* is a neopagan movement that worships the pantheon of ancient Norse (Scandinavian) religions. In its most basic form—which is not racial in conviction—Ásatrú adherents worship the Norse pantheon of Odin, Thor, Freyr, Loki, and others. A minority of Ásatrú believers have adopted an activist and racist belief system, linking variants of Nazi ideology and racial supremacy to the Nordic pantheon. Variations on the Ásatrú theme include Odinism, which venerates the Norse god Odin (Wotan) as the chief god of all gods.

## Race and the Bible: The Christian Identity Creation Myth

**Christian Identity** is the Americanized strain of an 18th-century quasireligious doctrine called Anglo-Israelism that was developed by Richard Brothers. Believers hold that whites are descended from Adam and are the true Chosen People of God, that Jews are biologically descended from Satan, and that nonwhites are soulless beasts (also called the **"Mud People"**). Christian Identity adherents have developed two cultish creation stories that are loosely based on the Old Testament. The theories are called **One-Seedline Christian Identity** and **Two-Seedline Christian Identity**.

*One-Seedline Christian Identity* accepts that all humans regardless of race are descended from Adam; however, only Aryans (defined as northern Europeans) are the true elect of God. They are the Chosen People whom God has favored and who are destined to rule over the rest of humanity. In the modern era, those who call themselves the Jews are actually descended from a minor Black Sea ethnic group and therefore have no claim to Israel.

*Two-Seedline Christian Identity* rejects the notion that all humans are descended from Adam. Instead, its focus is on the progeny of Eve. Two-Seedline adherents believe that Eve bore Abel as Adam's son but bore Cain as the son of the Serpent (that is, the devil). Outside of the Garden of Eden lived nonwhite, soulless beasts who are a separate species from humans. They are the modern nonwhite races of the world and are often referred to by Identity believers as Mud People. When Cain slew Abel, he was cast out of the Garden to live among the soulless beasts. Those who became the descendants of Cain are the modern Jews. They are thus biologically descended from the devil and are a demonic people worthy of extermination. There is an international conspiracy by the Jewish devil-race to rule the world. The modern state of Israel and the Zionist Occupation Government in the United States are part of this conspiracy.

# ❖ Right-Wing Terrorism in the United States

Right-wing terrorism in the United States is usually motivated by racial supremacism and antigovernment sentiment. Unlike the violent left, terrorist campaigns by underground rightist organizations and networks have been rare. Massive bombings such as the Oklahoma City attack have also been rather uncommon. It is more typical for the right to be characterized by small-scale, cell-based conspiracies within the Patriot and neo-Nazi movements. In comparison with the left, the violent right has been less organized and less consistent.

The activity profile of the violent right reflects a long history of vigilante behavior, so that most acts of rightist terrorism have been communal incidents, ambushes, and low-yield bombings. Historically, the KKK and its supporters used vigilante communal violence as the preferred model for its terrorism. Vigilante **lynch mobs** came to symbolize the racial nature of right-wing terrorism in the United States during the late 19th century and continuing well into the 20th century. Lynchings were discussed in this chapter's Opening Viewpoint. These incidents were directed primarily against African American men, although a few lynching victims were African American women, white immigrants, Jews, or criminals.

Chapter Perspective 12.3 summarizes several examples of racial supremacist activity on the right in the modern era. These examples illustrate how potentially violent members of the right wing can find organizations to provide direction and structure for their underlying animosity toward target groups.

## CHAPTER PERSPECTIVE 12.3: Seeds of Terrorism: Reactionaries on the American Right

Three reactionary case studies are discussed here—White Aryan Resistance (WAR), Aryan Nations, and the National Alliance. Each case has directly or indirectly influenced activists on the racial supremacist right.

### White Aryan Resistance

White Aryan Resistance—WAR—is an overtly racist organization founded and led by Tom Metzger. Based in California, WAR publishes neo-Nazi propaganda, manages an active website, and has tried to recruit and organize racist skinheads. Implicit in its message is the notion that skinheads should be mobilized as Aryan shock troops in the coming Racial Holy War. WAR has used popular culture and music to appeal to potential skinhead recruits, and its website is largely marketed to racist youth. In October 1990, WAR lost a $12.8 million verdict after the Southern Poverty Law Center litigated a case on behalf of the family of an Ethiopian immigrant who was beaten to death by WAR-inspired racist skinheads.

### Aryan Nations

The "Reverend" **Richard Butler** established the Aryan Nations organization as a political counterpart to his Christian Identity sect, called the Church of Jesus Christ Christian. Aryan Nations established its spiritual and political headquarters in a compound at Hayden Lakes, Idaho. Residents of the compound were overtly neo-Nazi. They adopted a rank hierarchy, established an armed security force, trained as survivalists, worshipped as Identity believers, and took to wearing uniforms. A number of people who passed through the Aryan Nations group eventually engaged in political and racial violence, a pattern that included violence by the Order and **Buford O'Neal Furrow**. This pattern led to its financial ruin. In a celebrated lawsuit brought by the Southern Poverty Law Center, Aryan Nations lost its title to the Hayden Lakes property in September 2000 when a $6.3 million verdict was decided. During the trial, the Southern Poverty Law Center successfully linked Aryan Nations security guards to the terrorizing of a family who had driven to the compound's entrance.

### National Alliance

The National Alliance is historically linked to the now-defunct American Nazi Party, which had been founded and led by George Lincoln Rockwell prior to his assassination. **William Pierce**, the founder and leader of the National Alliance, was long considered by experts and members of the neo-Nazi movement to be the most prominent propagandist of the movement. Prior to his death in July 2002, Pierce authored *The Turner Diaries* (under the *nom de plume* **Andrew MacDonald**), published a magazine called the *National Vanguard*, made regular radio broadcasts, and managed an active website. The National Alliance's original headquarters is a compound in rural Hillsboro, West Virginia, where Pierce's followers try to carry on his tradition. Although some violent neo-Nazis or other reactionaries may have been inspired by the National Alliance's message (recall that *The Turner Diaries* was found in the possession of Timothy McVeigh), no acts of terrorism or hate crimes were directly linked to the original group.

### Postscript: Aryan Nations and National Alliance in Disarray

Two of the most active and influential neo-Nazi organizations were thrown into disarray when their founders and longtime leaders died in the early years of the new millennium. National Alliance's William Pierce died in July 2002, and Aryan Nations' Richard Butler died in September 2004. With the deaths of these leaders, both organizations engaged in bitter infighting over who would assume leadership and whose ideology most reflected the principles of the founding leaders. Infighting led to splits within the organizations, and factions formed claiming to be the heirs of the original groups. Membership declined significantly because of the leadership crisis and internal quarreling, eventually marginalizing both organizations by the end of the first decade of the 2000s.

The following discussion explores the terrorist right by investigating the following subjects:

- Homegrown Racism: The Legacy of the Ku Klux Klan
- Racial Mysticism: Neo-Nazi Terrorism
- Patriot Threats
- Case in Point: Moralist Terrorism

## Homegrown Racism: The Legacy of the Ku Klux Klan

The Ku Klux Klan is a racist movement that has no counterpart among international right-wing movements—it is a purely American phenomenon. Its name comes from the Greek word **kuclos**, or "circle." The KKK is best described as an enduring movement that developed the following ideology:

- Racial supremacy
- Protestant Christian supremacy
- American cultural nationalism (also known as **nativism**)
- Violent assertion of Klan racial doctrine
- Ritualistic symbolism, greetings, and fraternal behavior

Klan terminology in many ways is an exercise in racist secret fraternal bonding. Table 12.5 samples the exotic language of the KKK.

KKK terrorism has been characterized by different styles of violence in several historical periods. Not every Klansman has been a terrorist, nor has every Klan faction practiced terrorism. However, the threat of violence and racial confrontation has always been a part of the Klan movement. In order to understand the nature of Klan violence, it is instructive to survey the historical progression of the movement. There have been several manifestations of the KKK, which most experts divide into five eras.

| Table 12.5 | The Fraternal Klan |
| --- | --- |

From its inception in 1866, the Ku Klux Klan has used fraternity-like greetings, symbolism, and rituals. These behaviors promote secrecy and racial bonding within the organization. Examples of Klan language include the following greeting: Ayak? (Are you a Klansman?) and Akia! (A Klansman I am!). The language used for regional offices is also unique, as indicated in the following examples:

- Invisible Empire National
- Realm       State
- Klavern     Local

The following table summarizes the activity profiles of official Klan organizational designations.

| Klan Official | Duties | Scope of Authority | Symbolic Identification |
| --- | --- | --- | --- |
| **Imperial Wizard** | National leader | Invisible Empire | Blue stripes or robe |
| **Grand Dragon** | State leader | Realm | Green stripes or robe |
| **Exalted Cyclops** | County leader | Klaverns within county | Orange stripes or robe |
| **Nighthawk** | Local security and administration | Klavern | Black robe |
| **Klonsel** | General counsel | Invisible Empire | White robe |
| **Citizen** | Member | Klan faction | White robe |

### First-Era Klan

The KKK was founded in 1866 in the immediate aftermath of the Civil War. Some sources date its origin to Christmas Eve 1865, whereas others cite the year 1866. According to most sources, the KKK was first convened in Pulaski, Tennessee, by a group of Southerners who initially formed the group as a fraternal association. They originally simply wore outlandish outfits and played practical jokes but soon became a full civic organization. Their first Imperial Wizard, or national leader, was former Confederate general and slave trader Nathan Bedford Forrest. Military-style rankings were established, and by 1868, the KKK was a secretive and politically violent underground. Its targets included African Americans, Northerners, and Southern collaborators. Northern victims were those who traveled south to help improve the conditions of the former slaves, as well as profiteering "carpetbaggers." Southern victims were collaborators derisively referred to as "Scalawags." The KKK was suppressed by the Union Army and the anti-Klan "Ku Klux laws" passed by Congress. Nathan Bedford Forrest ordered the KKK to be officially disbanded, and its robes and regalia were ceremoniously burned. It has been estimated that the Klan had about 400,000 members during its first incarnation.

### Second-Era Klan

After the Reconstruction era (following the departure of the Union Army from the South and the end of martial law), the KKK re-formed into new secret societies and fraternal groups. It wielded a great deal of political influence and successfully helped restore racial supremacy and segregation in the South. African Americans lost most political and social rights during this period, beginning a condition of racial subjugation that did not end until the civil rights movement in the mid-20th century. The targets of Klan violence during this period were African Americans, immigrants, Catholics, and Jews.

### Third-Era Klan

During the early part of the 20th century and continuing into the 1920s, the KKK became a broad-based national movement. In 1915, members gathered at Stone Mountain, Georgia, and formed a movement known as the Invisible Empire. The Klan was glorified in the novel *The Clansman* and in the 1915 film *Birth of a Nation,* which was shown in the White House during the administration of President Woodrow Wilson. During this period, the Invisible Empire had between 3 and 4 million members. In 1925 in Washington, DC, 45,000 Klansmen and Klanswomen paraded down Pennsylvania Avenue. Also during this period, Klan and Klan-inspired violence was widespread. Thousands of people—mostly African Americans—were victimized by the KKK. Many acts of terrorism were ritualistic communal lynchings.

### Fourth-Era Klan

After a decline because of revelations about Third-Era violence and corruption, the Klan was reinvigorated in 1946—once again at Stone Mountain, Georgia. At this gathering, the Invisible Empire disbanded, and new independent Klans were organized at local and regional levels. There was no longer a single national Klan; rather, there were autonomous Klan factions. During the civil rights movement, some Klan factions became extremely violent. The White Knights of Mississippi and the United Klans of America (mostly in Alabama) committed numerous acts of terrorism to try to halt progress toward racial equality in the American South. This era ended after several successful federal prosecutions on criminal civil rights charges, although the Klan itself endured.

### Fifth-Era Klan

Violence during the Fifth Era has been committed by lone wolves rather than as organized Klan actions. The modern era of the Ku Klux Klan is characterized by two trends:

- **The Moderate Klan.** Some Klansmen and Klanswomen have tried to moderate their image by adopting more mainstream symbolism and rhetoric. Rather than advocating violence or para-military activity, they have projected an image of law-abiding activists working on behalf of white civil rights and good moral values. Those who promote this trend have eschewed the prominent display of Klan regalia and symbols. For example, former neo-Nazi and Klansman David Duke has repeatedly used mainstream political and media institutions to promote his cause of white civil rights. He is the founder of the National Association for the Advancement of White People and the European-American Unity and Rights Organization (EURO).

- **The Purist Klan.** A traditional and "pure" Klan has emerged that hearkens back to the original traditions and ideology of the KKK. This group has held a number of aggressive and vitriolic rallies—many in public at county government buildings. Its rhetoric is unapologetically racist and confrontational. Some factions of the purist trend prohibit the display of Nazi swastikas or other non-Klan racist symbols at KKK gatherings.

KKK membership has ebbed and flowed in the Fifth Era, in part because of changes in the nation's cultural and political environment, but also because of competition from other racial suprem-acist movements such as the racist skinhead and neo-Nazi groups. There was also fresh competition beginning in the late 1990s from the neo-Confederate movement.

## Racial Mysticism: Neo-Nazi Terrorism

In the modern era, most non-Klan terrorism on the right wing has come from members of the neo-Nazi movement. Recall that the American version of Nazism has incorporated mystical beliefs into its underlying ideology of racial supremacy. This mysticism includes Christian Identity, Creativity, and rac-ist strains of Ásatrú. Neo-Nazi terrorism is predicated on varying mixes of religious fanaticism, political violence, and racial supremacy. Their worldview is predicated on the superiority of the Aryan race, the inferiority of non-Aryans, and the need to confront an evil global Jewish conspiracy. Another common theme is the belief that a **racial holy war**—called **"RaHoWa"**—is inevitable.

Most violence emanating from these beliefs has been expressed as "lone wolf" terrorism and hate crimes. Historically, most lone wolf attacks in the United States have been racially motivated killing sprees committed by individual neo-Nazis or other racial supremacists. A typical example of neo-Nazi lone wolf violence is the case of **Richard Baumhammers**.[30] Baumhammers was a racist immigra-tion attorney influenced by neo-Nazi ideology who murdered five people and wounded one more on April 28, 2000, near Pittsburgh, Pennsylvania. He methodically shot his victims during a 20-mile trek. The victims were a Jewish woman, two Indian men, two Asian men, and an African American man. The sequence of Baumhammers's assault occurred as follows:

- Baumhammers went to his Jewish neighbor's house and fatally shot her. He then set a fire inside her home.

- He next shot two Indian men at an Indian grocery store. One man was killed, and the other was paralyzed by a .357 slug that hit his upper spine.

- Baumhammers shot at a synagogue, painted two swastikas on the building, and wrote the word *Jew* on one of the front doors.

- He then drove to a second synagogue, where he fired shots at it.

- Baumhammers shot two young Asian men at a Chinese restaurant, killing them both.

- Finally, Baumhammers went to a karate school, pointed his revolver at a white man inside the school, and then shot to death an African American man who was a student at the school.

[30]Simonich, Milan. "Victims Left in Wake of Rampage." *Pittsburgh Post-Gazette,* April 29, 2000.

Richard Baumhammers was convicted in May 2001 and received the death penalty.

In addition to the lone wolf profile, several groups have embarked on violent sprees. For example, a group calling itself the **Aryan Republican Army (ARA)** operated in the Midwest from 1994 to 1996.[31] Inspired by the example of the Irish Republican Army, the ARA robbed 22 banks in seven states before the members were captured. Their purpose had been to finance racial supremacist causes and to hasten the overthrow of the Zionist Occupation Government. Some members also considered themselves to be Christian Identity fundamentalists called Phineas Priests, who are discussed later in the chapter. The following case in point further illustrates the nature of neo-Nazi violence.

### Case in Point: The Order

**The Order** was a covert, underground, and violent group that was inspired by a fictional secret organization depicted in the novel *The Turner Diaries*. In the book, the Order is a heroic inner circle and vanguard for the Aryan revolution in the United States. **Robert Jay Mathews**, a racial supremacist activist, was the founder of the actual Order in 1983.

The Order's methods for fighting the war against the Zionist Occupation Government were counterfeiting, bank robberies, armored car robberies, and occasional murders.[32] Its area of operation was primarily in the Pacific Northwest. Its first action in 1983 was a small heist in Spokane, Washington, that netted the group slightly more than $300. Mathews later robbed the Seattle City bank of $25,000. In April 1984, the group bombed a synagogue in Boise, Idaho. In March 1984, members of the Order seized $500,000 from a parked armored car in Seattle; the group detonated a bomb at a theater as a diversion. In May 1984, a peripheral member, Walter West, was executed because he was indiscreet about the group's secrecy. In June 1984, Alan Berg, a Jewish talk-radio host, was murdered in Denver; he had regularly lambasted the neo-Nazi movement. Also in June, a Brinks armored car was robbed near Ukiah, California, with disciplined precision, and the Order made off with $3.6 million. The end of the Order came when the FBI traced a pistol that Mathews had left at the scene of the Brinks robbery. He was eventually tracked to Whidbey Island in Washington in December 1984, and he died when his ammunition exploded and caused a fire during an FBI-led siege. More than 20 members of the Order were prosecuted and imprisoned in December 1985.

Some members of the potentially violent racial supremacist right consider Mathews to be a martyr and interpret the Order's terrorist spree as a "premature" endeavor. Two subsequent incidents with links to the Order are instructive:

- In March 1998, federal agents arrested members of the self-styled New Order in East St. Louis, Illinois. They had modeled themselves after the Order and were charged with planning to bomb the Anti-Defamation League's New York headquarters; the headquarters of the Southern Poverty Law Center in Birmingham, Alabama; and the Simon Wiesenthal Center in Los Angeles.

- In August 1999, Buford O'Neal Furrow went on a shooting spree in the Los Angeles area, including an attack at a Jewish community center in which five people were wounded. He had been an Aryan Nations member and security officer and had married the widow of Robert Jay Mathews in a Christian Identity ceremony.

# Patriot Threats

Although the Patriot movement attracted a significant number of adherents during the 1990s, and although militias at one point recruited tens of thousands of members, no underground similar to that of the radical left was formed. Few terrorist movements or groups emanated from the Patriot

---

[31]For a discussion of the Aryan Republican Army, see Hamm, Mark. *In Bad Company: America's Terrorist Underground.* Boston: Northeastern University Press, 2002.

[32]The chronology of the Order's terrorist spree is adapted from Anti-Defamation League. *Danger: Extremism. The Major Vehicles and Voices on America's Far-Right Fringe.* New York: Anti-Defamation League, 1996, pp. 270–1.

movement—largely because many members were "weekend warriors" who did little more than train and because law enforcement agencies successfully thwarted a number of true plots. Thus, despite many implicit and explicit *threats* of armed violence from Patriots, terrorist conspiracies were rarely carried to completion.

In 1992, former KKK member Louis Beam began to publicly advocate **leaderless resistance** against the U.S. government. Leaderless resistance is a cell-based strategy requiring the formation of **phantom cells** to wage war against the government and enemy interests. Dedicated Patriots and neo-Nazis believe that leaderless resistance and the creation of phantom cells will prevent infiltration from federal agencies. The chief threat of violence came from the armed militias, which peaked in membership immediately prior to and after the Oklahoma City bombing. After the Oklahoma City bombing, federal authorities broke up at least 25 Patriot terrorist conspiracies. Examples of threatened and actual violence from the Patriot movement include the following incidents from the mid-1990s:[33]

- October 1992: A gathering was held at the Estes Park, Colorado, resort to respond to the Ruby Ridge incident. The meeting attracted an assortment of rightists, supremacists, Christians, and Christian Identity members. They called for a united front against the government. The militia movement quickly grew, as did the theory of leaderless resistance.

- August 1994: Members of the Minnesota Patriots Council were arrested for manufacturing ricin, a potentially fatal toxin.

- April 1995: A large truck bomb destroyed the Alfred P. Murrah Federal Building in Oklahoma City, Oklahoma, killing 168 people.

- November 1995: Members of the Oklahoma Constitutional Militia were arrested for conspiring to bomb several targets, including gay bars and abortion clinics.

- July 1996: Members of the Viper Team militia in Arizona were arrested for plotting to bomb government buildings. They had diagrams and videos of possible targets and had trained using ammonium nitrate and fuel oil (ANFO) explosives.

- October 1996: Members of the Mountaineer Militia in West Virginia were arrested for conspiring to bomb the FBI Criminal Justice Information Services building in Clarksburg, West Virginia.

The number of armed militias declined during the period between the April 1995 Oklahoma City bombing and the American homeland attacks of September 11, 2001.[34] By 2000, the number of Patriot organizations was only one fourth of the 1996 peak,[35] and this general decline continued after September 11, 2001.[36] This occurred for several reasons:[37] First, the 1995 Oklahoma City bombing caused many less committed members to drift away. Second, the dire predictions of apocalyptic chaos for the new millennium that were embedded in their conspiracy theories did not materialize, especially the predicted advent of the New World Order. Third, the September 11, 2001, attacks shifted attention from domestic issues to international threats. Experts noted, however, that the most militant and committed Patriot adherents remained within the movement and that these dedicated members constitute a core of potentially violent true believers. This became evident after the 2008 presidential elections, when the number of Patriot organizations and identified armed militia groups increased markedly. Growth continued steadily through 2012 before some groups consolidated their memberships or disbanded, thus reducing the number of organized Patriot groups and armed militias after 2012. The following trend occurred:[38]

---

[33]Time line adapted from Southern Poverty Law Center, Intelligence Project. *Intelligence Report,* Winter 2000.

[34]Southern Poverty Law Center, Intelligence Project. *Intelligence Report,* Summer 2001.

[35]Ibid.

[36]See "Patriot Free Fall." Southern Poverty Law Center. *Intelligence Report,* Summer 2002.

[37]See Barry, Ellen. "It's the Wilderness Years for Militias." *Los Angeles Times,* April 13, 2005.

[38]Southern Poverty Law Center. *Intelligence Report.* 153, Spring 2014.

- 1996: 858 Patriot organizations; 370 armed militias
- 2001: 158 Patriot organizations; 73 armed militias
- 2006: 147 Patriot organizations; 52 armed militias
- 2008: 149 Patriot organizations; 42 armed militias
- 2009: 512 Patriot organizations; 127 armed militias
- 2010: 824 Patriot organizations; 330 armed militias
- 2012: 1,360 Patriot organizations; 321 armed militias
- 2013: 1,096 Patriot organizations; 240 armed militias

### The Oklahoma City Bombing

On April 19, 1995, **Timothy McVeigh** drove a rented Ryder truck to the Alfred P. Murrah Federal Building in Oklahoma City. He deliberately chose April 19 as a symbolic date for the attack—it was the 220th anniversary of the battles of Lexington and Concord and the second anniversary of the law enforcement disaster in Waco, Texas.

McVeigh was a hard-core devotee of the Patriot movement and a believer in New World Order conspiracy theories. He was almost certainly a racial supremacist, having tried to solicit advice from the neo-Nazi National Alliance and the racial separatist Elohim City group about going underground after the bombing. McVeigh had also visited the Branch Davidian site at Waco, Texas,[39] where about 75 members of the Branch Davidian cult died in a fire that was ignited during a paramilitary raid by federal law enforcement officers.

McVeigh had converted the Ryder truck into a powerful mobile **ammonium nitrate and fuel oil (ANFO)**–based bomb. He used "more than 5,000 pounds of ammonium nitrate fertilizer mixed with about 1,200 pounds of liquid nitromethane, [and] 350 pounds of Tovex."[40] When he detonated the truck bomb at 9:02 a.m., it destroyed most of the federal building and killed 168 people, including 19 children. More than 500 others were injured.

McVeigh's attack was in large part a symbolic act of war against the federal government. He had given careful consideration to achieving a high casualty rate, just as "American bombing raids were designed to take lives, not just destroy buildings."[41]

The deaths of the 19 children were justified in his mind as the unfortunate **"collateral damage"** against innocent victims common to modern warfare.[42] Timothy McVeigh was tried and convicted, and he was executed in a federal facility in Terre Haute, Indiana, on June 11, 2001. His execution was the first federal execution since 1963.

❖ **Photo 12.4**

Oklahoma City. The rubble of the Murrah federal building in the aftermath of a bomb attack by a right-wing member of the Patriot movement. This was the worst terrorist incident on American soil prior to the September 11 homeland attacks. It remains the worst incident of domestic terrorism carried out by Americans.

U.S. Federal Emergency Management Agency

## Case in Point: Moralist Terrorism

Moralist terrorism refers to acts of political violence that are motivated by a moralistic worldview. Most moralist terrorism in the United States is motivated by an underlying religious doctrine, and this

---

[39]For a discussion of Timothy McVeigh's immersion in the fringe right—from the perspective of McVeigh himself—see Michel, Lou, and Dan Herbeck. *American Terrorist: Timothy McVeigh and the Oklahoma City Bombing.* New York: HarperCollins, 2001.

[40]Ibid., p. 164.

[41]Ibid., p. 224.

[42]Ibid., p. 234.

is usually a fringe interpretation of Christianity. Abortion clinics and gay bars have been targets of moralist violence.

Examples of moralist terrorism and threats against abortion providers include the following incidents:

- June and December 1984: An abortion clinic was bombed twice in Pensacola, Florida.
- March 1993: A physician was shot and killed outside an abortion clinic in Pensacola.
- July 1994: A physician and his bodyguard were killed outside an abortion clinic in Pensacola.
- October 1997: A physician was wounded by shrapnel in Rochester, New York.
- October 1998: A physician was killed in Amherst, New York.
- 1998–2002: Hundreds of letters with notes claiming to be infected with anthrax bacteria were sent to abortion clinics in at least 16 states. An anti-abortion activist was convicted of sending more than 500 letters.
- Post–September 11, 2001: During an actual anthrax attack in the period following the September 11 attacks, scores of letters were sent to abortion clinics in a number of states, claiming to be infected with anthrax.
- May 2009: A physician was shot and killed inside his church in Wichita, Kansas, during religious services by an anti-abortion activist.
- 2011–2014: Several cases of arson and at least one bombing occurred at abortion clinics nationwide. Most cases were unsolved.

Examples of violent moralist movements include the **Army of God** and the **Phineas Priesthood**. They are both shadowy movements that apparently have little or no organizational structure, operate as lone wolves or cells, and answer to the "higher power" of their interpretations of God's will. They seem to be belief systems in which like-minded activists engage in similar behavior. The Phineas Priesthood is apparently a "calling" (divine revelation) for Christian Identity fundamentalists, and the Army of God membership is perhaps derived from fringe evangelical Christian fundamentalists. These profiles are speculative, and it is possible that they are simply manifestations of terrorist contagion (copycatting). There has also been speculation that both movements are linked. Nevertheless, it is instructive to review their activity profiles.

### Army of God

The Army of God is a cell-based and lone wolf movement that opposes abortion and homosexuality. Its ideology is apparently a fringe interpretation of fundamentalist Protestantism, although it has also exhibited racial supremacist tendencies. The methodology of the Army of God has included the use of violence and intimidation—primarily in attacks against abortion providers and gay and lesbian targets. The Army of God posted a website with biblical references and grisly pictures of abortions, and the manifesto disseminated by the group included instructions for manufacturing bombs. The website also pays homage to those whom the movement considers to be political prisoners and martyrs in its cause.

The Army of God first appeared in 1982 when an Illinois abortion provider and his wife were kidnapped by members of the group. It has since claimed responsibility for a number of attacks, primarily against abortion providers. For example,

- February 1984: A clinic in Norfolk, Virginia, where abortions were performed was firebombed.
- February 1984: A clinic in Prince George's County, Maryland, where abortions were performed was firebombed.
- July 1994: Paul Hill, an anti-abortion activist, shot and killed a physician and his bodyguard, a retired Air Force lieutenant colonel, in Pensacola, Florida. Hill was executed by lethal injection in September 2003. He was the first person to be executed for anti-abortion violence.

- January 1997: A clinic in Atlanta, Georgia, where abortions were performed was bombed.
- February 1997: A nightclub in Atlanta was bombed. Its patrons were largely gays and lesbians.
- January 1998: An abortion clinic in Birmingham, Alabama, was bombed, killing a police officer and severely wounding a nurse.

One apparent affiliate of the Army of God—**Eric Robert Rudolph**—became a fugitive after he was named as a suspect in the Birmingham bombing and the Atlanta bombings. Rudolph was also wanted for questioning because of possible involvement in the July 1996 bombing at Centennial Olympic Park in Atlanta during the Summer Olympic Games and was linked to a militia group in North Carolina. He was captured in May 2003 in the mountains of North Carolina. In April 2005, Rudolph pleaded guilty to the Birmingham and Atlanta bombings, as well as the Centennial Olympic Park attack.

### Phineas Priesthood

Phineas Priests were first described in the 1990 book *Vigilantes of Christendom: The History of the Phineas Priesthood*.[43] The book is a fundamentalist interpretation of Christian Identity. In the book, the alleged history of the Phineas Priesthood is traced from biblical times to the modern era. The name is taken from the Bible at chapter 25, verse 6 of the Book of Numbers, which tells the story of a Hebrew man named Phineas who killed an Israelite man and his Midianite wife in the temple. According to the Book of Numbers, this act stayed the plague from the people of Israel.

Phineas Priests believe that they are called by God to purify their race and Christianity. They are opposed to abortion, homosexuality, interracial mixing, and whites who "degrade" white racial supremacy. Members also believe that acts of violence—called **Phineas Actions**—will hasten the ascendancy of the Aryan race. The Phineas Priesthood is a calling for men only, so no women can become Phineas Priests. The calling also requires an absolute and fundamentalist commitment to Christian Identity mysticism. Some acts of political violence have been inspired by this doctrine. These incidents include the following:

- In 1991, **Walter Eliyah Thody** was arrested in Oklahoma after a shootout and chase. Thody claimed to be a Phineas Priest and stated that fellow believers would also commit acts of violence against Jews and others.
- In 1993, Timothy McVeigh apparently "made offhand references to the Phineas Priesthood" to his sister.[44]
- From 1994 to 1996, the Aryan Republican Army robbed 22 banks throughout the Midwest. Members of the ARA had been influenced by *Vigilantes of Christendom* and the concept of the Phineas Priesthood.[45]
- In October 1996, three Phineas Priests were charged with bank robberies and bombings in Washington State. They had left political diatribes in notes at the scenes of two of their robberies. The notes included their symbol, **"25:6,"** which denotes chapter 25, verse 6 of the Book of Numbers.

Because the Phineas Priesthood has been a lone wolf and cell-based phenomenon, it is impossible to estimate its size or even whether it has ever been much more than an example of the contagion effect. Nevertheless, the fact is that a few true believers have considered themselves to be members of the Phineas Priesthood, and the concept of Phineas Actions was taken up by some adherents of the moralist and racial supremacist right.

---

[43]Hoskins, Richard Kelly. *Vigilantes of Christendom: The History of the Phineas Priesthood*. St. Louis, MO: Virginia, 1995.

[44]Hamm, *In Bad Company,* p. 147.

[45]Ibid.

# ❖ International Terrorism in the United States

International terrorism has been relatively rare in the United States, and the number of international terrorist incidents is much lower than in other countries, such as the United Kingdom and France.

## The Spillover Effect in the United States

During most of the postwar era (prior to the 1990s), international incidents in the United States were spillovers from conflicts in other Western countries and were directed against foreign interests with a domestic presence in the United States. Most of these spillovers ended after a single incident or a few attacks, such as in the following examples:

- In September 1976, a bomb in Washington, DC, killed former Chilean foreign minister Orlando Letelier and his American assistant Ronni Moffitt. He had been assassinated on orders from DINA, the right-wing Chilean government's secret police.
- In August 1978, Croatian terrorists took hostages in the West German consulate in Chicago. In September of the same year, they killed a New York City police officer when they detonated a bomb. The terrorists hijacked a TWA jet, forcing it to fly over London and Paris.

Some terrorist spillovers were ongoing campaigns. As was the case with the short-term incidents, these campaigns were directed primarily against non-American interests. Examples include the following.

### Omega 7

During the late 1970s and early 1980s, anti-Castro Cuban terrorists actively targeted Cuban interests in the United States. Members of **Omega 7** were Cuban-born exiles who fled Cuba for the United States after the 1959 victory of Fidel Castro's forces during the Cuban Revolution. Omega 7 is thought to have been responsible for at least 50 attacks against Cuban businesspersons and diplomats, including attempted assassinations and bombings. Their targets included the Venezuelan consulate in New York City, a Soviet ship in New Jersey, travel agencies in New Jersey, Lincoln Center in New York City, and the Cuban mission to the United Nations. The group's founder, **Eduardo Arocena**, was arrested in July 1983 and sentenced to life imprisonment for murdering a Cuban diplomat.

### Provisional Irish Republican Army

The Provos did not wage a terrorist campaign in the United States. Rather, members of the IRA in the United States and their American supporters were implicated in the purchase and transshipment of armaments to Northern Ireland. The Provo presence was a support operation for terrorist cells in Northern Ireland. For example, in 1984, weapons were seized aboard a vessel off the coast of Ireland. The weapons had been transported to Irish waters aboard a vessel (the *Valhalla*) whose point of origin was the United States. In another incident in 1986, supporters of the Provos were arrested in a plot to fly weapons into Belfast, including a shoulder-fired Redeye anti-aircraft missile.

### Jewish Defense League

The **Jewish Defense League (JDL)** is an example of American extremists who targeted international interests in the United States. The organization was founded in 1968 in New York City by **Rabbi Meir Kahane** as a militant, youth-based Jewish movement. It favored active—and sometimes violent—defense of the Jewish community and a militant variant of Zionism that advocates the expulsion of Arabs from Israel. Kahane was assassinated in November 1990 in New York City by **El-Sayyid Nosair**, a radical Egyptian Islamic revolutionary.

### The JDL Legacy

The JDL's offshoots in Israel are the right-wing Kach ("Only Thus") and Kahane Chai ("Kahane Lives") movements. Both receive support from American and European supporters, and both share common objectives. During the early 1980s in the United States, the JDL and a shadowy group called the **United Jewish Underground** were responsible for several acts of terrorism. These attacks were directed primarily against Soviet targets, such as the offices of the Soviet national airline Aeroflot, and were conducted to protest that government's treatment of Soviet Jews. Their bombings were sometimes lethal, and a number of deaths were attributed to JDL attacks. The movement ended its attacks in the mid-1980s and shifted its political emphasis to militant Zionist activism in Israel, although it is still in existence in the United States. For example, in December 2001, two JDL members (including the group's leader) were indicted in Southern California for plotting to attack the offices of a Lebanese American congressman and two Islamic centers.

## The New Terrorism in the United States

The terrorist environment changed during the 1990s, when American interests began to be directly attacked domestically by international terrorists. A new threat emerged from religious radicals who considered the United States a primary target in their global *jihad*.

### Jihad in America

The American people and government became acutely aware of the destructive potential of international terrorism from a pattern that emerged during the 1990s and culminated on September 11, 2001. The following incidents were precursors to the modern post-9/11 security environment:

- February 1993: In the first terrorist attack on the World Trade Center, a large vehicular bomb exploded in a basement parking garage; it was a failed attempt to topple one tower into the other. Six people were killed, and more than 1,000 were injured. The mastermind behind the attack was the dedicated international terrorist Ramzi Yousef. His motives were to support the Palestinian people, to punish the United States for its support of Israel, and to promote an Islamic *jihad*. Several men, all *jihadis,* were convicted of the attack.

- October 1995: Ten men were convicted in a New York federal court of plotting further terrorist attacks. They allegedly conspired to attack New York City landmarks, such as tunnels, the United Nations headquarters, and the George Washington Bridge.

These incidents heralded the emergence of a threat to homeland security that had not existed since World War II. The practitioners of the New Terrorism apparently concluded that assaults on the American homeland are desirable and feasible. The key preparatory factors for making these attacks feasible were the following:

- They were carried out by operatives who entered the country for the sole purpose of carrying out the attacks.

- The terrorists had received support from cells or individuals inside the United States. Members of the support group facilitated the ability of the terrorists to perform their tasks with dedication and efficiency.

The support apparatus profile in the United States for this was not entirely unknown prior to September 11, 2001, because militants have been known to be in the United States since the late 1980s and 1990s. For example, aboveground organizations were established to funnel funds to the Middle East on behalf of Hamas, Hezbollah, and other movements. These organizations—and other social associations—were deliberately established in many major American cities. The fact is that since at least the late 1980s, anti-American *jihadi* sentiment existed within the United States among some fundamentalist communities. And, significantly, *jihad* has been overtly advocated by a number of fundamentalist leaders who took up residence in the United States.[46]

The modern threat to homeland security from homegrown *jihadis* is discussed further in Chapter 14.

### September 11, 2001

One of the worst incidents of modern international terrorism occurred in the United States on the morning of September 11, 2001. It was carried out by 19 Al-Qa'ida terrorists who were on a suicidal "martyrdom mission." They committed the attack to strike at symbols of American (and Western) interests in response to what they perceived to be a continuing process of domination and exploitation of Muslim countries. They were religious terrorists fighting in the name of a holy cause against perceived evil emanating from the West. Their sentiments were born in the religious, political, and ethnonational ferment that has characterized the politics of the Middle East for much of the modern era.

Nearly 3,000 people were killed in the attack. The sequence of events occurred as follows:

- **7:59 a.m.** American Airlines Flight 11, carrying 92 people, leaves Boston's Logan International Airport for Los Angeles.
- **8:14 a.m.** United Airlines Flight 175, carrying 65 people, leaves Boston for Los Angeles.
- **8:20 a.m.** American Airlines Flight 77, carrying 64 people, takes off from Washington's Dulles International Airport for Los Angeles.
- **8:42 a.m.** United Airlines Flight 93, carrying 44 people, leaves Newark, New Jersey, International Airport for San Francisco.
- **8:46 a.m.** American Flight 11 crashes into the north tower of the World Trade Center.
- **9:03 a.m.** United Flight 175 crashes into the south tower of the World Trade Center.
- **9:37 a.m.** American Flight 77 crashes into the Pentagon. Trading on Wall Street is called off.
- **9:59 a.m.** Two World Trade Center—the south tower—collapses.
- **10:03 a.m.** United Flight 93 crashes 80 miles southeast of Pittsburgh, Pennsylvania.
- **10:28 a.m.** One World Trade Center—the north tower—collapses.[47]

Many saw the attacks of September 11, 2001, as a turning point in the history of political violence. The attacks themselves created a new reference point for Americans: **9/11**. In their aftermath, journalists, scholars, and national leaders repeatedly described the emergence of a new international terrorist environment. It was argued that within this new environment, terrorists were now quite capable of using—and very willing to use—weapons of mass destruction to inflict unprecedented casualties and destruction on enemy targets. These attacks seemed to confirm warnings from experts during the 1990s that a new asymmetrical terrorism would characterize the terrorist environment in the new millennium.

The United States had previously been the target of international terrorism at home and abroad, but the American homeland had never suffered a terrorist strike on this scale. The most analogous historical event was the Japanese attack on the naval base at Pearl Harbor, Hawaii, on December 7, 1941. The last time so many people had died from an act of war committed on American soil was during the Civil War in the mid-19th century.

---

[46]For a documentary discussion of this subject, see *Terrorists Among Us: Jihad in America*. Prod. SAE Productions, Videocassette. SAE Productions, 2001.

[47]National Commission on Terrorist Attacks Upon the United States. *The 9/11 Commission Report*. New York: Norton, 2004, pp. 32–3, 305, 311.

After the Al-Qa'ida assault and the subsequent anthrax crisis (see the next discussion), routine American culture shifted away from complete openness to a period of high security. The adaptation of the American people and political establishment to this new environment was a new experience for the nation. The symbolism of the attack, combined with its sheer scale, drove the United States to war and dramatically changed the American security environment. Counterterrorism in the United States shifted from a predominantly law enforcement mode to a security mode. Security measures included unprecedented airport and seaport security, border searches, visa scrutiny, and immigration procedures. Hundreds of people were administratively detained and questioned during a sweep of persons fitting the terrorist profile of the 19 attackers. These detentions set off a debate about the constitutionality of these methods and the fear by many that civil liberties were in jeopardy. In October 2001, the USA PATRIOT Act was passed. The new law granted significant authority to federal law enforcement agencies to engage in surveillance and other investigative work. On November 25, 2002, 17 federal agencies (later increased to 22 agencies) were consolidated to form a new Department of Homeland Security.

The symbolism of a damaging attack on homeland targets was momentous because it showed that the American superpower was vulnerable to attack by small groups of determined revolutionaries. The Twin Towers had dominated the New York skyline since the completion of Two World Trade Center in 1972. They were a symbol of global trade and prosperity and the pride of the largest city in the United States. The Pentagon, of course, is a unique building that symbolizes American military power, and its location across the river from the nation's capital showed the vulnerability of the seat of government to attack.

On May 30, 2002, a 30-foot-long steel beam was ceremoniously removed from the **"Ground Zero"** site in New York City. It was the final piece of debris to be removed from the September 11 homeland attacks.

### The Anthrax Crisis

After the September 11 attacks, the activity profile of international terrorism in the United States shifted to cell-based religious terrorist spillovers originating in the Middle East. The threat from the New Terrorism in the United States included the very real possibility of a terrorist campaign using high-yield weapons to maximize civilian casualties.

The potential scale of violence was demonstrated by an anthrax attack immediately after the September 11 attacks when, for the first time in its history, the threat of chemical, biological, and radiological terrorism became a reality in the United States. During October through December 2001, more than 20 people were infected by anthrax-laced letters; five victims died. The attack made use of the U.S. postal system when letters addressed to news organizations and two members of the U.S. Senate were mailed from Princeton, New Jersey. Some of the letters contained references to radical Islam, causing a presumption by authorities and the public that the anthrax incident was part of an ongoing assault against the American homeland.

The crisis led to an extensive manhunt by the FBI, which conducted more than 10,000 interviews on six continents, including intensive investigations of more than 400 people. One person under careful investigation was Dr. Bruce Ivins, a microbiologist and U.S. Army biodefense scientist. Ivins worked for decades on the army's anthrax vaccination program at the army biodefense laboratory in Maryland. The FBI's investigation involved detailed scrutiny of his behavioral habits, e-mail, his trash, and computer downloads. The FBI's observation included attaching a global positioning satellite device to his automobile. Ivins committed suicide in July 2008 after he learned that federal authorities were possibly moving forward with a criminal indictment against him. In February 2010, the FBI released an extensive report that closed

❖ **Photo 12.5**
Anti–Vietnam War riot. An antiwar demonstrator at the University of California, Berkeley, throws a tear gas canister at police during a student strike to protest the killing of four students at Kent State University in May 1970.

© Bettmann/Corbis

its investigation of Ivins. However, debate continued about whether Ivins was responsible for the mailings. In January 2011, the National Academy of Sciences questioned the veracity of the FBI's evidence. In March 2011, a panel of psychiatrists developed a psychological profile of Ivins and concluded that the case against him was persuasive. Nevertheless, prominent scientists and investigative journalists continued to raise serious questions about the FBI's testing procedures and the accuracy of the FBI investigation.

## Chapter Summary

This chapter investigated political violence in the United States. Both domestic and international terrorism were discussed. The sources of domestic terrorism were identified as extremist tendencies that grew out of movements and cultural histories, and the sources of international terrorism were identified as terrorist spillover activity.

On the left, modern terrorism originated in the social and political fervor of the 1960s and 1970s. Some members of activist movements became radicalized by their experiences within the context of their environment. A few became dedicated revolutionaries and chose to engage in terrorist violence. Members of New Left and nationalist terrorist groups waged terrorist campaigns until the mid-1980s. Single-issue and nascent anarchist tendencies have replaced the now-defunct Marxist and nationalist movements on the left.

On the right, the long history of racial violence continued into the 21st century. The Ku Klux Klan is a uniquely American racist movement that has progressed through five eras, with terrorist violence occurring in each era. Modern Klansmen and Klanswomen, neo-Nazis, and moralists have also engaged

in terrorist violence. Threats of potential political violence come from antigovernment movements and emerging "heritage" movements. The activity profile of the modern era is primarily a lone wolf and cell-based profile. It has become rare for racial supremacist and moralist terrorists to act as members of established organizations.

International terrorism in the postwar era began as spillover activity directed against non-American targets with established interests in the United States. Most of this activity was of short duration, although several movements waged terrorist campaigns. Fringe Cuban, Irish, and Jewish organizations waged violent campaigns against their perceived enemies but did not target American interests. This profile changed dramatically during the 1990s, when revolutionary Islamic groups began to target American interests inside the United States.

In Chapter 13, readers explore counterterrorist policy options. Theoretical options and responses will be augmented by examples of successful and failed measures. The discussion will investigate legalistic, repressive, and conciliatory responses to terrorism.

## Key Terms and Concepts

The following topics are discussed in this chapter and can be found in the glossary:

Animal Liberation Front (ALF)

Armed Forces for National Liberation (Fuerzas Armadas de Liberación Nacional, or FALN)

Armed Forces of Popular Resistance

Army of God

Arocena, Eduardo

Aryan Nations

Aryan Republican Army (ARA)

Baumhammers, Richard

black helicopters

Black Liberation Army (BLA)

Black Panther Party for Self-Defense

Black Power

Butler, Richard

Christian Identity

Christian Right

"collateral damage"

collective nonviolence

counterculture

Creativity

"Days of Rage"

DeFreeze, Donald

direct action

"disinformation"

Dohrn, Bernardine

Earth Liberation Front (ELF)

eco-terrorism

Establishment, the

Fountain Valley Massacre

Fourteen Words

Furrow, Buford O'Neal

"Ground Zero"

Hale, Matthew

Jewish Defense League (JDL)

Kerner Commission

Klassen, Ben

Ku Klux Klan (KKK)

*kuclos*

leaderless resistance

"long hot summer"

lynch mobs

MacDonald, Andrew

Macheteros

Mathews, Robert Jay

May 19 Communist Organization (M19CO)

McVeigh, Timothy

military-industrial complex

militias

"Mud People"

National Alliance

nativism

New Afrikan Freedom Fighters

New Left

New World Liberation Front

New World Order

9/11

Nosair, El-Sayyid

"off the grid"

Omega 7

One-Seedline Christian Identity

Order, the

Organization of Volunteers for the Puerto Rican Revolution

*Osawatomie*

phantom cells

Phineas Actions

Phineas Priesthood

Pierce, William

Port Huron Statement

*Prairie Fire*

Prairie Fire Organizing Committee

Progressive Labor Party

racial holy war ("RaHoWa")

Revolutionary Youth Movement II (RYM II)

Ruby Ridge

Rudolph, Eric Robert

Sam Melville–Jonathan Jackson Unit

Shakur, Assata

single-issue terrorism

Students for a Democratic Society (SDS)

survivalism

Thody, Walter Eliyah

"Truther" movement

*Turner Diaries, The*

25:6

Two-Seedline Christian Identity

United Freedom Front (UFF)

United Jewish Underground

Waco

Weather Bureau

Weather Collectives

Weather Underground Organization

Weathermen

White Aryan Resistance

World Church of the Creator (WCOTC)

# Discussion Box: Domestic Terrorism in the American Context

*This chapter's Discussion Box is intended to stimulate critical debate about the idiosyncratic nature of domestic terrorism in the United States.*

The subject of domestic terrorism in the United States is arguably a study in idiosyncratic political violence. Indigenous terrorist groups reflected the

American political and social environments during historical periods when extremists chose to engage in political violence.

In the modern era, left-wing and right-wing political violence grew from very different circumstances. Leftist violence evolved from a uniquely American social environment that produced the civil rights, Black Power, and New Left movements. Rightist violence grew out of a combination of historical racial and nativist animosity, combined with modern applications of religious and antigovernment ideologies.

In the early years of the new millennium, threats continued to emanate from right-wing antigovernment and racial supremacist extremists. Potential violence from leftist extremists remained low in comparison with the right. When the September 11, 2001, attacks created a new security environment, the question of terrorism originating from domestic sources remained uncertain; this was especially true after the anthrax attacks on the U.S. East Coast.

## Discussion Questions

- Assume that a nascent anarchist movement continues in its opposition to globalism. How should the modern leftist movement be described? What is the potential for violence originating from modern extremists on the left?

- Keeping in mind the many conspiracy and mystical beliefs of the American right, what is the potential for violence from adherents of these theories to the modern American environment?

- As a matter of policy, how closely should hate and antigovernment groups be monitored? What restrictions should be imposed on their activities? Why?

- Is the American activity profile truly an *idiosyncratic* profile, or can it be compared with other nations' environments? If so, how? If not, why not?

- What is the likelihood that the new millennium will witness a resurgence of a rightist movement on the scale of the 1990s Patriot movement? What trends indicate that it *will* occur? What trends indicate that it *will not* occur?

# On Your Own

The open-access Student Study Site at **http://study.sagepub.com/martin5e** has a variety of useful study aids, including eFlashcards, quizzes, audio resources, and journal articles.

The websites, exercises, and recommended readings listed below are easily accessed on this site as well.

# Recommended Websites

The following websites provide information about extremist movements and ideologies in the United States:

Animal Liberation Front: http://www
.animalliberationfront.com/

Council of Conservative Citizens: http://
cofcc.org/

Hate Directory: http://www.hatedirectory
.com/

Prairie Fire Organizing Committee. http://
www.prairiefire.org/

Revolutionary Communist Party, USA: http://
www.rwor.org/

White Revolution: http://www
.whiterevolution.com/

## Web Exercise

Using this chapter's recommended websites, conduct an online investigation of terrorism in the
United States.

1. How would you describe the typologies
   of groups that predominate in the United
   States?

2. Conduct a Web search of American
   monitoring organizations, read their mission statements, and assess their services.

Which organizations do you think provide
the most useful data? Why?

3. If you were an American dissident
   extremist (leftist or rightist), how would
   you design your own website?

For an online search of terrorism in the United States, readers should activate the search engine on
their Web browser and enter the following keywords:

"Domestic Terrorism"                                    "Homeland Security"

## Recommended Readings

The following publications discuss the nature of terrorism in the United States and the root causes of
political violence in American society:

Dunbar, David, and Brad Reagan, eds. *Debunking 9/11
Myths: Why Conspiracy Theories Can't Stand Up to the
Facts*. New York: Hearst Books, 2006.

Emerson, Steven. *American Jihad: The Terrorists Living
Among Us*. New York: Free Press, 2002.

Emerson, Steven. *Jihad Incorporated: A Guide to Militant
Islam in the U.S*. Amherst, NY: Prometheus, 2006.

George, John, and Laird Wilcox. *American Extremists:
Militias, Supremacists, Klansmen, Communists, and
Others*. Amherst, NY: Prometheus, 1996.

German, Mike. *Thinking Like a Terrorist: Insights of a
Former FBI Undercover Agent*. Washington, DC:
Potomac Books, 2007.

Graebmer, William. *Patty's Got a Gun: Patricia Hearst in
1970s America*. Chicago: University of Chicago Press,
2008.

Kurst-Swanger, Karl. *Worship and Sin: An Exploration of
Religion-Related Crime in the United States*. New York:
Peter Lang, 2008.

MacDonald, Andrew [William Pierce]. *The Turner Diaries*.
New York: Barricade, 1978.

McCann, Joseph T. *Terrorism on American Soil: A Concise
History of Plots and Perpetrators From the Famous to
the Forgotten*. Boulder, CO: Sentient Publications,
2006.

McCarthy, Timothy Patrick, and John McMillian. *The
Radical Reader: A Documentary History of the
American Radical Tradition*. New York: New Press,
2003.

Michel, Lou, and Dan Herbeck. *American Terrorist:
Timothy McVeigh and the Oklahoma City Bombing*.
New York: Regan Books, 2001.

Ogbar, Jeffrey O. G. *Black Power: Radical Politics and
African American Identity*. Baltimore, MD: Johns
Hopkins University Press, 2004.

Ridgeway, James. *Blood in the Face: The Ku Klux Klan,
Aryan Nations, Nazi Skinheads, and the Rise of a New
White Culture*. 2nd ed. New York: Thunder's Mouth,
1995.

Ronczkowski, Michael. *Terrorism and Organized
Hate Crime: Intelligence Gathering, Analysis, and
Investigations*. 2nd ed. Boca Raton, FL: CRC Press, 2006.

Sargent, Lyman Tower, ed. *Extremism in America: A Reader*. New York: New York University Press, 1995.

Smith, Brent L. *Terrorism in America: Pipe Bombs and Pipe Dreams*. Albany: State University of New York Press, 1994.

Stern, Kenneth S. *A Force Upon the Plain: The American Militia Movement and the Politics of Hate*. New York: Simon & Schuster, 1997.

Wilkerson, Cathy. *Flying Close to the Sun: My Life and Times as a Weatherman*. New York: Seven Stories Press, 2007.

Zakin, Susan. *Coyotes and Town Dogs: Earth First! and the Environmental Movement*. Tucson: University of Arizona Press, 2002.

Zeskind, Leonard. *Blood and Politics: The History of the White Nationalist Movement From the Margins to the Mainstream*. New York: Farrar, Straus and Giroux, 2009.

# PART IV

# Securing the Homeland

The war on terrorism. U.S. Army soldiers patrol in Mosul, Iraq, during the U.S.-led occupation.

U.S. Army

# Counterterrorism

CHAPTER 13

## *The Options*

Al-Qa'ida founder Osama bin Laden was killed during a raid by United States naval special forces on May 2, 2011, in Abbottabad, Pakistan. The successful attack by a unit popularly known as SEAL Team Six ended an intensive manhunt for the most wanted terrorist leader in the world.

The successful hunt for Osama bin Laden originated from fragments of information gleaned during interrogations of prisoners over several years beginning in 2002. Believing that bin Laden retained couriers to communicate with other operatives, interrogators focused their attention on questioning high-value targets about the existence and identities of these couriers. This focus was adopted with an assumption that bin Laden and other Al-Qa'ida leaders would rarely communicate using cell phone technology as a precaution against being intercepted by Western intelligence agencies.

Early interrogations produced reports that a personal courier did indeed exist, a man whose given code name was Abu Ahmed al-Kuwaiti. In about 2007, intelligence officers learned al-Kuwaiti's real name, located him, and eventually followed him to a recently built compound in Abbottabad, Pakistan. U.S. intelligence operatives observed the compound locally from a safe house and concluded that it concealed an important individual. Based on other surveillance and circumstantial intelligence information, officials surmised that Osama bin Laden resided at the compound with his couriers and their families.

Options for assaulting the compound included a surgical strike by special forces, deploying strategic bombers to obliterate the compound, or a joint operation with Pakistani security forces. The latter two options were rejected because of the possibility of killing innocent civilians and distrust of Pakistani security agencies. Approximately two dozen SEAL commandos practiced intensely for the assault, and were temporarily detailed to the CIA for the mission. A nighttime helicopter-borne attack was commenced on May 2, 2011. The courier al-Kuwaiti and several others were killed during the assault, and women and children found in the compound were bound and escorted into the open to be found later by Pakistani security forces. Osama bin Laden was located on an upper floor of the main building and shot dead by SEALs. Four others were killed in addition to bin Laden, whose body was taken away by the assault team. He was subsequently buried at sea.

Al-Qa'ida threatened retribution for the attack and named Ayman al-Zawahiri as bin Laden's successor in June 2011.

T his chapter reviews policy options for responding to acts of political violence. The question of how to respond is traditionally regarded as a choice between so-called hard-line and soft-line responses. Hard-line responses include using military and paramilitary measures to punish or destroy the terrorists. No compromise is desired, and no negotiations are accepted. Soft-line responses are a more complicated approach. They incorporate diplomacy, compromise, and social reforms as possible options. Regardless of which category a particular policy option falls under, the key consideration for policy makers is the *practicality* of the counterterrorist option. In other words, will the option work? Will the terrorists' behavior change? Can the terrorist environment be co-opted or suppressed?

Before addressing these bottom-line questions, it is important to consider what is meant by *responding* to terrorism and engaging in *counterterrorism* or *antiterrorism*.

*Responding to terrorism* is defined here as any action taken by a targeted interest in reply to a terrorist incident or terrorist environment. These actions range in scale from very passive to highly active responses. For example, options can be as passive as simply doing nothing, thus calculating that the terrorists will be satisfied by inaction. More intensive responses include covert campaigns to disrupt or otherwise destabilize hostile movements. Very intensive responses include symbolic military strikes against groups and their sponsors, as well as campaigns to completely incapacitate the terrorists.

**Counterterrorism** refers to proactive policies that specifically seek to eliminate terrorist environments and groups. Regardless of which policy is selected, the ultimate goal of counterterrorism is clear: to save lives by proactively preventing or decreasing the number of terrorist attacks. As a corollary, **antiterrorism** refers to target hardening, enhanced security, and other defensive measures seeking to deter or prevent terrorist attacks.

Much of our discussion will focus on categories of responses. Most experts agree that counterterrorist options can be organized into several policy classifications. Examples of these classifications include the following:

❖ **Photo 13.1**

U.S. Army troops search a building for insurgents in the Iraqi city of Fallujah during heavy fighting.

U.S. Army

- Diplomacy, financial controls, military force, intelligence, and covert action[1]
- Legal, repressive, and conciliatory responses to terrorism[2]
- Targeted and untargeted prevention[3]

These are theoretical groupings of policy options that many experts have identified as possible responses to terrorist incidents. However, they should not be considered exact templates for every terrorist contingency, for there are no exact theories of responses or counterterrorism. The fact of the matter is that terrorist environments are in many ways idiosyncratic, as are many terrorist groups. The implications of this for counterterrorist policy are that some methods will be successful in only a few cases, whereas others will be adaptable to many cases. Significantly, some policy options often seem to make perfect theoretical sense when they are developed, but subsequently they make little practical sense. Nevertheless, the categories of available options are fairly clearly drawn; it is the *adaptation* of these options to specific scenarios that can become less certain.

---

[1]Pillar, Paul R. *Terrorism and U.S. Foreign Policy.* Washington, DC: Brookings Institution Press, 2001, pp. 73ff.

[2]Sederberg, Peter C. *Terrorist Myths: Illusion, Rhetoric, and Reality.* Englewood Cliffs, NJ: Prentice Hall, 1989, pp. 136ff.

[3]Heymann, Philip B. *Terrorism and America: A Commonsense Strategy for a Democratic Society.* Cambridge, MA: MIT Press, 1998, pp. 80ff.

## ❖ Responding to Terror: The Scope of Options

Regardless of which label is attached to an option or which categories are developed, there is consensus among policy makers that they have available to them several basic counterterrorist options and suboptions. For the purposes of our discussion, options and suboptions will be classified as follows:

### Use of Force

This is a hard-line policy classification that allows policy makers to use the force of arms against terrorists and their supporters. The objectives of deploying military and paramilitary assets can range from symbolic punitive attacks to the systematic destruction of terrorist personnel and infrastructure. The following are examples of military and **paramilitary repressive options**:

- **Suppression campaigns** are military strikes against targets affiliated with terrorists. The purpose of these strikes is to destroy or severely disrupt terrorist personnel and infrastructure. Suppression campaigns can include **punitive strikes** and **preemptive strikes**, which are attacks that punish terrorist targets. The former occur in *response to* terrorist attacks, and the latter occur in *anticipation of* terrorist attacks. Both can be symbolic strikes that cause limited damage or that are launched to destroy specific facilities or personnel.

- **Covert operations** (coercive) are secretive operations that include assassinations, sabotage, kidnapping (known as extraordinary renditions, discussed in Chapter 14), and other quasi-legal methods. The purpose is to wage low-level and secretive war against terrorist movements. **Special operations forces** are the principal assets used to carry out **coercive covert operations**. These are specially trained units that specialize in irregular missions against terrorist targets.

### Operations Other Than War

#### Repressive Options

**Repressive responses** include nonmilitary operations selected from a range of options that are flexible and can be adapted to specific terrorist environments. The following are examples of **nonmilitary repressive options**:

- Covert operations (nonviolent) are secretive operations that include a number of possible counterterrorist measures, such as infiltration, disinformation, and **cyberwar**. Nonviolent covert programs require creative and imaginative methods that are adapted to each terrorist environment.

- **Intelligence** refers to the collection of data. Its purpose is to create an informational database about terrorist movements and to predict their behavior. This process is not unlike that of criminal justice investigators who work to resolve criminal cases.

- **Enhanced security** refers to the hardening of targets to deter or prevent terrorist attacks. Security barriers, checkpoints, and surveillance are typical security measures. These are critical components of antiterrorism.

- **Economic sanctions** are used to punish or disrupt state sponsors of terrorism. Sanctions can either selectively target specific economic sectors or generally restrict trade. The purpose is to pressure state sponsors to modify or end their support for terrorism.

The successful use of nonmilitary and nonparamilitary assets to suppress terrorism requires the effective deployment of technological and organizational resources. The primary objective of using nonmilitary resources is to disrupt and deter terrorist organizations and their support apparatuses. Nonmilitary options thus require the development of creative security measures and the use of new technologies.

### Conciliatory Options

**Conciliatory responses** is a soft-line classification that allows policy makers to develop a range of options that do not involve the use of force or other repressive methods. The objectives of non-repressive responses depend on the characteristics of the terrorist environment. Examples of these responses include the following:

- **Diplomacy** refers to different degrees of capitulation to the terrorists, which is engaging with the terrorists to negotiate an acceptable resolution to a conflict. Diplomatic solutions can be incident specific, or they can involve sweeping conditions that may completely resolve the conflict.

- **Social reform** is an attempt to address the grievances of the terrorists and their championed group. The purpose is to resolve the underlying problems that caused the terrorist environment to develop.

- **Concessions** can be incident specific, in which immediate demands are met; or generalized, in which broad demands are accommodated.

## Legalistic Options

Nations developed legal protocols to employ in dealing with terrorism. Some of these protocols were implemented to promote international cooperation, and others were adopted as matters of domestic policy. The overall objective of **legalistic responses** is to promote the rule of law and regular legal proceedings. The following are examples of these responses:

- **Law enforcement** refers to the use of law enforcement agencies and criminal investigative techniques in the prosecution of suspected terrorists. This adds an element of *rule of law* to counterterrorism.

- Counterterrorist laws attempt to criminalize terrorist behavior. This can be done, for example, by declaring certain behaviors to be criminal terrorism or by enhancing current laws such as those that punish murder.

- **International law** relies on cooperation among states. Those who are parties to international agreements attempt to combat terrorists by permitting them no refuge or sanctuary for their behavior. In some cases, terrorists may be brought before international tribunals.

Table 13.1 summarizes activity profiles for these counterterrorist policy categories. The discussion in this chapter will review the following responses to terrorism:

- Warlike Operations: Counterterrorism and the Use of Force
- Operations Other Than War: Repressive Options
- Operations Other Than War: Conciliatory Options
- Applying the Rule of Law: Legalistic Options

## ❖ Warlike Operations: Counterterrorism and the Use of Force

The use of force is a hard-line policy approach used by states and their proxies to violently suppress terrorist environments. The goals of this approach are case specific, so that the decision to use violent suppression is based on policy calculations peculiar to each terrorist environment. When states decide to use force against terrorists and their supporters, coercion and violence are considered to be justifiable and desirable policy options. The underlying rationale for many decisions to use force is to

| Table 13.1 | Counterterrorist Options: General Policy Classifications |
|---|---|

Experts have developed categories for counterterrorist options. These policy classifications have been given a variety of labels, but they refer to similar concepts. Each of the categories has been divided into subcategories. The following table illustrates the activity profiles of general counterterrorist policy classifications.

| Counterterrorist Policy Classification | Activity Profile | | |
|---|---|---|---|
| | *Rationale* | *Practical Objectives* | *Typical Resources Used* |
| **Use of force** | Symbolic strength | Punish or destroy the terrorists | Military assets<br><br>Paramilitary assets<br><br>Covert operatives |
| **Operations other than war: repressive options** | Deterrence<br><br>Prediction<br><br>Destabilization | Disruption of the terrorists<br><br>Intelligence<br><br>Coercion of supporters | Technologies<br><br>Intelligence operatives<br><br>Covert operatives |
| **Operations other than war: conciliatory options** | Resolve underlying problems | End immediate crises<br><br>Forestall future crises | Social resources<br><br>Economic assets<br><br>Negotiators |
| **Legalistic options** | Rule of law | International cooperation<br><br>Prosecution, conviction, and incarceration of terrorists | International organizations<br><br>Law enforcement agencies<br><br>Domestic legal establishments |

demonstrate the state's ability to disrupt the operational capabilities of terrorists and, if necessary, to eliminate them. The process of *eliminating* terrorists refers to incapacitating them by disrupting, isolating, capturing, and killing as many cadres as possible.

This policy option requires the deployment of military or paramilitary assets to punish, destabilize, or destroy terrorists and their supporters. *Military assets* are defined as the recognized and official armed forces of a nation. *Paramilitary assets* are defined as irregular armed units or individuals who are supported or organized by regimes. Paramilitaries include irregular civilian "home guard" units armed by the government and stationed in their home villages and towns. A paramilitary asset can also be an individual trained in the use of explosives, small arms, assassination techniques, and other applications of violence.

States have waged military and paramilitary counterterrorist operations domestically and internationally. A comparison of these operational venues may be summarized as follows:

- *Domestic operations* involve the coercive use of military, police, and other security forces against domestic threats. States justify this type of deployment as being necessary to restore order. Unfortunately, historical examples show that a great deal of civilian "collateral damage" occurs in these environments. A number of governments have readily used domestic force when threatened by dissident insurgents, terrorist campaigns, or other antigovernment political movements. In extreme circumstances, some governments have adopted official policies of indiscriminate repression and state-sponsored terrorism.

- *International operations* involve the overt or covert deployment of security assets abroad. These deployments can include ground, air, or naval forces in large or very small operational configurations. The scale of the deployment is, of course, dependent on the goals of state policies and the type of counterterrorist action to be carried out. In some cases, units will be deployed to an allied country that is willing to serve as a base of operations. If a host country is unavailable, or if it imposes restrictive conditions on the deployment, nations with sufficient military resources (such as the United States) will use naval units as seaborne bases for launching military strikes. Or air assets can be flown over long distances from home bases or friendly third countries to attack designated targets.

The following discussion explores several use-of-force options that are commonly adopted by nations.

## Maximum Use of Force: Suppression Campaigns

Counterterrorist campaigns can be undertaken by military and paramilitary forces. These are long-term policies of conducting operations against terrorist cadres, their bases, and their support apparatuses. Suppression campaigns are uniquely adapted to the conditions of each terrorist environment and are usually of indeterminate duration. They are launched within the policy contexts of war or quasi-war and are often waged with the goal of utterly defeating the terrorist movement.

For example, in 2002 and 2003, Israel began a concerted effort to disrupt Hamas and destroy its capability to indefinitely sustain its trademark suicide bombing campaign. Israeli policy included assassinations (discussed later in the chapter under coercive covert operations); military incursions; and a series of raids that resulted in arrests and gunfights with Hamas operatives, as well as many deaths. A sustained military incursion in the West Bank, designed to suppress Hamas activity and called Operation Defensive Shield, began in April 2002. In one typical raid, eight Palestinians were killed in an operation in Gaza that resulted in the arrest of Mohammed Taha, one of the founding leaders of Hamas.[4] In another raid in Gaza, 11 Palestinians were killed and 140 wounded when Israeli tanks and troops attacked a refugee camp after a Hamas suicide bomber killed 15 people on a bus in Haifa.[5] By 2004, the Israeli government credited these operations and other measures with weakening Hamas's infrastructure and reducing the incidence of Hamas bombings.

### Military Suppression Campaigns

Nations sometimes resort to the use of conventional units and special operations forces to wage war against terrorist movements. The goal is to destroy their ability to use terrorism to attack the nation's interests. Military campaigns require the deployment of troops to bases in friendly countries or (in the case of nations with significant seaborne capability)[6] offshore aboard naval vessels. Israel's Operation Peace for Galilee (1982 Lebanon) and the United States' Operation Enduring Freedom (2001 Afghanistan) illustrate the nature of military suppression campaigns.

***Case in Point: Operation Peace for Galilee (and Aftermath).*** In June 1982, the Israeli army invaded Lebanon for the second time to root out Palestine Liberation Organization (PLO) bases of operation.[7] The operation was called **Operation Peace for Galilee** and was launched in reply to ongoing PLO attacks from its Lebanese bases. During the invasion, the Israelis fought and won a war with Syria that lasted 6 days and drove northward through Lebanon to West Beirut by mid-June. The

---

[4]Reuters. "Israelis Arrest a Hamas Leader in Raid That Kills 8 Palestinians." *New York Times*, March 3, 2003.

[5]Reuters. "Israel Kills 11 Palestinians in Raid After Suicide Bombing." *New York Times*, March 6, 2003.

[6]Only the United States, Great Britain, Russia, and France have the capability to deploy large numbers of seaborne troops.

[7]The first invasion occurred in 1978 with the same goal of driving out PLO fighters. A third Israeli invasion took place in 1996 and was directed against Hezbollah.

city was surrounded, and a 3-month siege of trapped PLO and Syrian troops began. The United States brokered an agreement that allowed the PLO and Syrians to withdraw from Beirut in August. The outcome of this phase of the invasion was the successful neutralization of PLO forces south of Beirut. Many Lebanese opposed to the PLO presence had welcomed the Israelis, but this goodwill ended in mid-September. When Israeli troops entered West Beirut, Christian Phalangist militiamen massacred hundreds of Palestinian civilians for 3 days in the Sabra and Shatila refugee camps. The Israeli army did not intervene, its army remained in Lebanon, and Lebanese resistance against the Israeli presence began to grow. The Israelis eventually withdrew from most of Lebanon in 1985, establishing an occupation zone in southern Lebanon that was maintained until their withdrawal in July 2000. During the incursion and occupation, Hezbollah became a prominent symbol of anti-Israeli resistance. Hezbollah's prominence and reputation in this regard were greatly enhanced in July 2006, when the movement fought the Israeli army to a standstill during a large-scale incursion into Lebanon, which had the stated purpose of breaking Hezbollah.

***Case in Point: Operation Enduring Freedom.*** The United States declared itself at war against global terrorism after the attacks of September 11, 2001. It was joined by a number of allies who agreed to commit their armed forces and domestic security services to the new war. Dubbed **Operation Enduring Freedom**, the operation began with the October 2001 invasion of Afghanistan and was defined from the beginning as a long-term suppression campaign. It was also made clear from the outset that the war on terrorism would require extended deployments of U.S. and allied troops around the world, as well as an intensive use of special operations forces, commandos, Marines, and other elite units. The immediate objectives were to destroy Al Qa'ida's safe havens in Taliban-controlled Afghanistan, collect intelligence, disrupt the terrorist network around the world, and capture or kill as many cadres as possible. The long-term goal of the campaign—which policy makers stated would take years to achieve—was to degrade or destroy the operational capabilities of international terrorists. Interestingly, Operation Enduring Freedom was allegedly first called **Operation Infinite Justice** but was renamed after a negative reaction in the Muslim world (the Muslim stance being that only God can provide infinite justice).

### Paramilitary Suppression Campaigns

In some suppression campaigns, military and paramilitary units actively coordinate their operations. A typical policy used in this type of counterterrorist environment has been the government's arming and support of paramilitaries in areas where the military does not have a strong presence. The following examples illustrate the nature of paramilitary suppression campaigns.

***Case in Point: Paramilitary Suppression in Algeria.*** Algeria was beset by intensive terrorist violence from *jihadis* belonging to several radical Islamic groups. The Algerian government was unsuccessful in suppressing the rebels and was accused of committing human rights violations. Many thousands of civilians were killed, mostly at the hands of the *jihadis*. During the suppression campaign, the government organized and armed paramilitary home guard units.[8] These units, which were used as local self-defense forces, effectively staved off attacks from the rebels, thus reducing their operational effectiveness in the countryside. In part because of the paramilitary policy, as well as government-initiated programs and brutal suppression, the rebellion eventually ended in a negotiated amnesty settlement in 1999.

***Case in Point: Paramilitary Suppression in Colombia.*** Paramilitaries such as the United Self-Defense Forces of Colombia (AUC) fought against the Marxist Revolutionary Armed Forces of Colombia (FARC) and National Liberation Army (ELN) rebels using guerrilla tactics and death-squad terrorism. Paramilitaries such as the AUC received overt and covert support from the government and wealthy

---

[8]Whittaker, David J., ed. *The Terrorism Reader*. New York: Routledge, 2001, pp. 144–5.

Colombians. A typical example of the AUC's operational role and the Colombian army's cooperation occurred in May 2002, when AUC and FARC units fought a pitched battle in the town of Bellavista.
Approximately 400 AUC fighters passed through several Colombian army checkpoints on their way to the
town to recapture it from FARC. During intense fighting, a FARC homemade mortar crashed through the
roof of a church, killing 119 civilians (including 46 children) and wounding more than 100. The Colombian
army permitted the AUC to occupy the village and did not arrive until 5 days after the fighting ended.[9]

### Punitive and Preemptive Strikes

Short-duration military and paramilitary operations are usually conducted for a specific purpose
under specific rules of engagement. These actions are designed to send a clear symbolic message to
terrorists. The following two types of short-duration operations have been used:

- *Punitive strikes* are attacks that are launched as reprisals against terrorists for incidents that have
  already taken place. Successful punitive strikes require the attacker to symbolically and politically link the attacks to the terrorist incident.

- *Preemptive strikes* are attacks that are undertaken to hurt terrorists prior to a terrorist incident.
  Preemptive operations are launched as a precautionary measure to degrade the terrorists' ability to
  launch future attacks. Symbolic and political linkage between the attacks and a real threat is often
  difficult.

Punitive strikes are used more commonly than preemptive strikes. These attacks can be justified to some extent, as long as links can be established between the attacks and a terrorist incident.
Linkage must also be made between the specific targets of the reprisal and the alleged perpetrators
of the incident. This latter consideration sometimes goes awry. For example, when the United States
launched cruise missiles against targets in Sudan and Afghanistan in August 1998 (in retaliation for
the bombings of the U.S. embassies in Tanzania and Kenya), the legitimacy of one of the targets was
called into question. A Sudanese pharmaceutical factory was destroyed by the missiles. The United
States claimed that it was an Al Qa'ida operation that produced chemicals that could be used in chemical weapons. Many observers questioned this assertion, thus reducing the veracity of the Americans'
claim that the target was linked to the terrorist attacks.

Preemptive strikes are used less frequently than punitive strikes, partly because *preemption* by
definition means that the attack is a unilateral action conducted in response to a *perceived* threat. Such
attacks are therefore not as easily justified as punitive operations, which is an important consideration
for regimes concerned about world opinion. Unless a threat can be clearly defined, it is unlikely that
preemptive actions will receive widespread support from friends or neutral parties.

Nevertheless, some nations have adopted preemptive operations as a regular counterterrorist
method. Israel has for some time preemptively attacked neighboring countries that harbor anti-Israeli
terrorists and dissidents. For example, Israeli air, ground, and naval raids into Lebanon frequently
targeted PLO and Hezbollah bases. In another context, the United States justified the 2003 invasion
of Iraq as a preemptive war, arguing that Saddam Hussein's regime kept relations with Al Qa'ida and
other terrorists, that the regime possessed weapons of mass destruction, and that these weapons
could have been delivered to terrorists.

Chapter Perspective 13.1 presents an example of a large punitive operation launched by the
United States against Libya in 1986.

## War in the Shadows, Part 1: Coercive Covert Operations

Coercive covert operations seek to destabilize, degrade, and destroy terrorist groups. Targets
include individual terrorists, terrorist networks, and support apparatuses. Although covert assets

---

[9]Miller, Christian T. "A War-Torn Village Finds No Sanctuary." *Los Angeles Times*, May 19, 2002.

## CHAPTER PERSPECTIVE 13.1: Operation El Dorado Canyon

On April 14, 1986, the United States bombed targets in Libya using Air Force bombers based in Great Britain and Navy carrier–borne aircraft based in the Mediterranean. The attacks occurred at the height of tensions between the United States and Libya, which were precipitated by a radically activist Libyan government and its partnership with the Soviet Union.

### Background

During the 1980s, Libya established strong ties with the Communist Eastern bloc (Soviet-dominated Eastern Europe). It also declared itself to be a champion of people "oppressed" by the West and Israel. Libyan leader Muammar el-Qaddafi permitted the Libyan government to build camps to train terrorists from around the world, to stockpile weapons far in excess of Libya's needs, to acquire large amounts of plastic explosives (including powerful Czech-made Semtex), and to directly engage in state-sponsored international terrorism.

In March 1986, the U.S. Mediterranean fleet sailed into a disputed exclusionary zone off the coast of Libya. Qaddafi responded to the American show of force by declaring that a "line of death" had been drawn in the disputed waters—which the U.S. Sixth Fleet then purposefully crossed. Two terrorist bombings blamed on Libya subsequently occurred in Europe. The first bomb killed four Americans aboard a TWA airliner in Greece, and the second bomb killed one U.S. service officer at La Belle Discothèque in West Berlin. The American punitive raids—dubbed **Operation El Dorado Canyon**—were ostensibly in retaliation for these bombings, but they probably would have occurred in any event.

### Aftermath

More than 100 Libyans were killed in Benghazi and Tripoli, including Qaddafi's young adopted daughter. American policy makers considered the attacks to be successful because Libya thereafter temporarily scaled back its international adventurism, and Qaddafi reduced his inflammatory rhetoric. Libya then entered a second, shorter period of international activism and then pulled back—this time for an extended period of time.

It should be noted that the strike force based in Britain was forced to detour around France and the Iberian Peninsula (Spain and Portugal) and enter the Mediterranean through the Straits of Gibraltar, which separate Europe and Africa. This was necessary because the French and Spanish governments refused to permit the bombers to fly over their airspace.

The American air strike was unpopular in Europe. After the attack, demonstrations occurred in several countries, and many Europeans expressed outrage over the bombings. In Beirut, one American and two British hostages were murdered in retaliation for the attack on Libya.

have been developed by nations to wage "shadow wars" using special operatives, conventional forces have also been used to surreptitiously resolve terrorist crises. The following case illustrates the latter type of operation.

### Case in Point: The Achille Lauro Operation

The Italian cruise ship ***Achille Lauro*** was hijacked in October 1985 by four Palestinian terrorists belonging to the Palestine Liberation Front faction of the PLO. During the hijacking, an elderly wheelchair-bound American was executed and thrown into the Mediterranean Sea. Other Americans were terrorized aboard the ship—for example, being forced to hold a live hand grenade after the pin had been removed. The cruise ship eventually stopped in Egyptian waters, where the hostages were released and the terrorists were taken to Port Said. When the United States demanded that the terrorists be extradited, Egyptian President Hosni Mubarak claimed that they had already left the country.

In fact, the terrorists were still in Egypt and had been secretly placed aboard an aircraft to fly them out of the country and to safety. Also aboard the aircraft was the Palestine Liberation Front's leader,

Abu Abbas. U.S. and Israeli intelligence knew where the aircraft was and when it was in flight. Two U.S. warplanes intercepted the Egyptian aircraft and forced it to fly to Sicily. The final resolution of the *Achille Lauro* crisis is described later in the chapter in the section discussing legalistic responses.

Other types of coercive covert operations are more lethal, as indicated in the following examination of adopting assassination as a policy option.

### Case in Point: Assassinations

*Counterterrorist assassination* is easily defined: It involves the intentional killing of terrorist leaders, cadres, and supporters. The underlying rationale for using assassinations as a counterterrorist option is uncomplicated: Because terrorism is itself a human action, the terrorism will end or diminish if the terrorists and their supporters are eliminated. The argument is that because this option is a terminal solution, those targeted for assassination will be permanently removed as threats. It is debatable whether this is an accurate assumption because there is little evidence to support the conclusion that assassinations have ever had an appreciable deterrent effect on determined terrorists; new recruits continue to enlist in movements worldwide. This is because terrorists who operate within supportive environments and who enjoy the approval of a championed group are likely to be viewed as heroes by supporters. A terrorist's death at the hands of a sworn enemy is likely to elevate the terrorist to martyr status. Symbolic martyrdom is actively manipulated by terrorist movements to rally their followers and recruit new fighters.

Needless to say, assassination is highly controversial as a matter of policy. It is always covertly implemented—one does not broadcast when an assassination will take place. Government deniability is usually incorporated into these operations, but not always. Although most nations will readily disavow involvement in assassinations, others admit responsibility when such an admission is deemed useful. A comparison of the American and Israeli approaches is instructive.

After the Vietnam War, the United States officially declared that it would no longer use assassination as a tool of statecraft. In December 1981, President Ronald Reagan's **Executive Order 12333** expressly prohibited employees of the United States from assassinating adversaries. This prohibition, which followed President Gerald Ford's prohibition outlined in Executive Order 11905, also forbade U.S. personnel from using anyone hired as an agent to commit assassinations. This prohibition was applied during the political and terrorist environment that existed prior to the September 11, 2001, homeland attacks. After the attacks, a counterterrorist assassination policy was adopted and carried out.[10] For example, in November 2002 an Al Qa'ida leader was assassinated by an antitank missile fired at his vehicle from a remotely controlled Predator drone aircraft in a remote area in Yemen; and in October 2011 American-born cleric Anwar al-Awlaki was killed by a drone strike.[11] Such deliberate attacks greatly increased as the war on terrorism escalated. For example, in Pakistan from 2004 to mid-2011, nearly 2,000 Taliban, Al-Qa'ida, and affiliates of other movements were killed by U.S. drone airstrikes.[12] Drone strikes are discussed further in the next section.

***The Israeli Approach.*** In comparison, Israel has used assassinations repeatedly in its war on terrorism, primarily targeting Palestinian nationalists. This policy has been in place for many years, and it has often been administered by the **Mossad**, Israel's intelligence and covert operations agency. For example, on July 11, 1970, the Israelis attempted to assassinate two prominent members of the Popular Front for the Liberation of Palestine (PFLP). Israeli covert operatives identified a safe house used by the PFLP in an apartment in Beirut. They rented an apartment across the street from the safe house and rigged six Katyusha rockets on a timer to fire into the PFLP apartment. Their

---

[10]See Risen, James, and David Johnston. "Bush Has Widened Authority of C.I.A. to Kill Terrorists." *New York Times*, December 15, 2002.

[11]See ibid.

[12]Roggio, Bill, and Alexander Mayer. "Charting the Data for U.S. Airstrikes in Pakistan, 2004–2011." *The Long War Journal*: http://www.longwarjournal.org/pakistan-strikes.php (accessed June 22, 2011).

targets were PFLP cofounder Wadi Haddad and young Leila Khaled. Four rockets fired as planned, but Haddad and Khaled survived the attack.

In another example, a covert Israeli unit known as **Wrath of God** (Mivtza Za'am Ha'el) was responsible for tracking and assassinating Black September terrorists after the 1972 Munich Olympics massacre. At least 20 Palestinians were assassinated in Europe and the Middle East. The Wrath of God program went awry in 1973 when Israeli agents shot to death a North African waiter in Norway while his wife looked on; they had mistaken him for a Black September operative.

In October 1995, Israeli agents were the likely assassins of a leader of Palestine Islamic Jihad in Malta. During the Palestinian *intifada,* Israeli personnel targeted for assassination many terrorists, insurgents, and activist leaders. A famous case was the January 1996 assassination of Yehiya Ayyash, also known as the Engineer.[13] An infamous case was the highly publicized September 1997 assassination attempt on a top Hamas leader in Amman, Jordan. When the attempt failed rather publicly, the Israeli government was embarrassed, Mossad was disgraced, and Israeli–Jordanian relations became severely strained. Nevertheless, the assassination campaign against *intifada* leaders and operatives continued. In one particularly bloody incident in July 2002, an Israeli rocket attack assassinated top Hamas leader Sheik Salah Shehadeh. The attack also killed Shehadeh's wife and three children, as well as hitting an apartment building. A total of 14 civilians were killed in the attack.

Israel's war against Hamas took a decidedly deadly turn in early 2004. In March 2004, Hamas founder and chief leader Sheikh Ahmed Yassin was assassinated by missiles fired from Israeli aircraft; this occurred about 8 days after Hamas and the Al-Aqsa Martyr Brigades took joint credit for two suicide bombing attacks that killed 10 Israelis. In April 2004, another senior Hamas official, Abdel Aziz al-Rantisi, was assassinated by missiles within hours after a Hamas suicide bomb attack. The Israeli assassination campaign against Hamas continued as a matter of acknowledged policy, so when an Israeli sniper assassinated a local Hamas commander in Gaza in July 2005, Prime Minister Ariel Sharon stated that the military would continue to act "unrestrainedly to halt Hamas rocket and mortar fire."[14]

In February 2008, a car bomb exploded in Damascus, Syria, killing senior Hezbollah commander Imad Mughniyah. Although Israel was widely accused of perpetrating the attack, Israel neither confirmed nor denied its responsibility for the assassination.[15] In January 2010, Hamas operative Mahmoud al-Mabhou was assassinated in a hotel room in the Persian Gulf nation of Dubai. Mossad agents were accused of carrying out the operation, and 26 alleged suspects were identified and placed on INTERPOL's most-wanted list. Nevertheless, the case went unsolved.

### Case in Point: The Use of Armed Drone Aircraft

Armed, remotely controlled drone aircraft became fixtures in the United States' arsenal during the post-9/11 era. Operated by military and Central Intelligence Agency personnel from remote locations, armed drones proved to be a deadly counterpart to other options involving targeted killings of terrorists. The deployment and use of drones was relatively modest in years immediately following the September 11, 2001, attacks but increased markedly in 2008. From 2008, armed drone aircraft were deployed extensively in Pakistan and Afghanistan. Hundreds of drone airstrikes occurred and thousands of people were killed, including many terrorists. Within 3 years, the United States had launched lethal drone attacks in six countries: Afghanistan, Iraq, Libya, Pakistan, Somalia, and Yemen. In 2011, the United States began a campaign targeting the leadership of the al Shabaab Islamist militia in Somalia. The purpose of the attacks was to disrupt reportedly growing ties between al Shabaab and Al-Qa'ida, which intelligence reports indicated had been established to enhance al Shabaab's capability to launch international attacks. Al Shabaab had previously formed links to Somali American Islamists, who travelled to Somalia for military training provided by the militia. Al-Qa'ida in the

---

[13]The assassination of the Engineer is discussed in detail in Chapter 10.

[14]King, Laura. "Israel Kills Another Hamas Member, Targets Two More." *Los Angeles Times*, July 18, 2005.

[15]See Shadid, Anthony, and Alia Ibrahim. "Top Hezbollah Commander Killed in Syria." *Washington Post*, February 13, 2008. See also Haidar, Ziad, and Jeffrey Fleishman. "Long-Sought Militant Killed in Syria." *Los Angeles Times*, February 14, 2008.

Arabian Peninsula was also targeted, and resulted in the deaths of a number of operatives, including American-born cleric Anwar al-Awlaki.

In Pakistan, the United States deployed drones extensively. The number of known airstrikes in Pakistan and known Taliban or Al-Qa'ida deaths, mostly by drone aircraft, escalated annually as follows:[16]

- 2004: 1 attack; unknown leader or operative casualties
- 2005: 1 attack; unknown leader or operative casualties
- 2006: 3 attacks; 122 leaders or operatives killed
- 2007: 5 attacks; 73 leaders or operatives killed
- 2008: 35 attacks; 286 leaders or operatives killed
- 2009: 53 attacks; 463 leaders or operatives killed
- 2010: 117 attacks; 801 leaders or operatives killed

From 2009 to 2014, approximately 2,400 people were killed, and U.S. officials reported that most were militants.[17] Unfortunately, civilian casualties also occurred—at least 273 during this period[18]—resulting in vigorous denunciations from the governments of Afghanistan and Pakistan. Such casualties resulted from the proximity of targeted individuals to civilian homes and neighborhoods, as well as their practice of living with their families and others in compounds and other structures. Nevertheless, drone attacks became a commonly used lethal option during operations against terrorist havens and individuals. Targeted assassinations of members of Al-Qa'ida and other organizations occurred with regularity, resulting in the deaths of dozens of upper- and middle-echelon commanders.

## Surgical Use of Force: Special Operations Forces

*Special operations forces* are defined here as highly trained military and police units that specialize in unconventional operations. These units are usually not organized in the same manner as conventional forces because their missions require them to operate quickly and covertly in very hostile environments. Operations are frequently conducted by small teams of operatives, although fairly large units can be deployed if required by circumstances. Depending on their mission, special operations forces are trained for long-range reconnaissance, surveillance, surgical punitive raids, hostage rescues, abductions, and liaisons with allied counterterrorist forces. Their training and organizational configurations are ideally suited to counterterrorist operations.

Special operations forces today have become fully integrated into the operational commands of national armed forces worldwide. Their value in counterterrorist operations has been proven many times in the postwar era. Most nations have included specially trained units in their domestic security and national defense commands. Many of these operatives belong to the armed forces, but not all special operations forces are military units—many are elite police forces trained to conduct paramilitary operations. Examples of these units are summarized later in the chapter.

### Special Operations Forces: Military Units

In the modern era, special operations forces have become fully integrated into the operational commands of national armed forces worldwide. Their value in counterterrorist operations has been

---

[16]Roggio and Mayer, "Charting the Data for U.S. Airstrikes in Pakistan, 2004–2011."

[17]Serle, Jack. "More than 2,400 Dead as Obama's Drone Campaign Marks Five Years." The Bureau of Investigative Journalism, January 23, 2014.

[18]Ibid.

❖ **Photo 13.2**

Special Air Service assault. When gunmen from Iran's Arab minority shot 2 of their 19 hostages held at the Iranian embassy in London, tear gas was fired into the building, and the Special Air Service stormed the rooms where the hostages were held.

Keystone/Hulton Archive/Getty Images

proven many times in the postwar era. The following cases in point illustrate the mission and configuration of special operations forces commands.

***United Kingdom.*** The **Special Air Service (SAS)** is a secretive organization in the British army that has been used repeatedly in counterterrorist operations. Organized at a regimental level but operating in very small teams, the SAS is similar to the French 1st Marine Parachute Infantry Regiment and the American Delta Force. The SAS has been deployed repeatedly to assignments in Northern Ireland and abroad, as well as to resolve domestic terrorist crises, such as rescuing hostages in May 1980 inside the Iranian embassy in London. The **Special Boat Service (SBS)** is a special unit under the command of the Royal Navy. It specializes in operations against seaborne targets and along coastlines and harbors. The SBS is similar to the French Navy's Special Assault Units and the American SEALs. The **Royal Marine Commandos** are rapid-reaction troops that deploy in larger numbers than the SAS and SBS. They are organized around units called commandos, which are roughly equivalent to a conventional battalion. Royal Marines were deployed to Afghanistan in the hunt for Al-Qa'ida cadres and Taliban troops.

❖ **Photo 13.3**

French commandos at Orly Airport outside Paris. The group had just secured the release of hostages held by terrorists in January 1975.

Keystone/Hulton Archive/Getty Images

***France.*** The **1st Marine Parachute Infantry Regiment** (1RPIMa) is similar to the British SAS and American Delta Force. Within the 1RPIMa, small **RAPAS** (intelligence and special operations) squads are trained to operate in desert, urban, and tropical environments. Along with the special police unit GIGN (discussed later in the chapter), they form the core of French counterterrorist special operations forces. 1RPIMa has been deployed to crises around the world, particularly in Africa. Five **French Navy Special Assault Units** have been trained for operations against seaborne targets, coastlines, and harbors. Their mission is similar to that of the British SBS and American SEALs. When large elite combat forces must be deployed, the French use their all-volunteer **11th Parachute Division (Paras)** and the commando or parachute units of the famous French **Foreign Legion**.[19]

***Israel.*** The **Sayaret** are reconnaissance units that were organized early in the history of the Israel Defense Forces (IDF). Several Sayaret exist within the IDF, the most noted of which is **Sayaret Matkal**, a highly secretive formation that is attached to the IDF general headquarters. Operating in small units, it has skillfully (and often ruthlessly) engaged in counterterrorist operations. For example, in April 1973, a Sayaret Matkal unit killed several top PLO leaders in Beirut in reprisal for the Munich Olympics massacre. The **Parachute Sayaret** has been deployed in small and large units, often using high mobility to penetrate deep into hostile territory. They participated in the Entebbe operation in Uganda and were used extensively in Lebanon against Hezbollah. The IDF has also deployed undercover agents against suspected terrorist cells. **Duvdevan** is a deep-cover unit that conducts covert special operations in urban areas against suspected militants. Members are noted for dressing as Arabs during these operations, and among other specialized operations they are known for rendering (kidnapping) specific individuals. When large elite combat forces must be deployed, the **Golani Brigade** and its Sayaret are frequently used. The Golani Brigade has been used extensively against Hezbollah in South Lebanon and against Hamas in Gaza.

---

[19]For a history of the Foreign Legion, see Geraghty, Tony. *March or Die: A New History of the French Foreign Legion*. New York: Facts on File, 1986.

***United States.*** U.S. Special Operations Forces are organized under the U.S. **Special Operations Command**. The **Delta Force (1st Special Forces Operational Detachment—Delta)** is a secretive unit that operates in small teams and operates covertly outside of the United States. This unit is similar to the British SAS and the French 1st Marine Parachute Infantry Regiment. Its missions probably include abductions, reconnaissance, and punitive operations. **Green Berets (Special Forces Groups)** usually operate in units called A Teams. These teams comprise specialists whose skills include languages, intelligence, medicine, and demolitions. The traditional mission of the A Team is force multiplication; that is, members are inserted into regions to provide military training to local personnel, thus multiplying their operational strength. They also participate in reconnaissance and punitive raids. U.S. Navy **Sea, Air, Land Forces (SEALs)** are similar to the British SBS and the French Navy's Special Assault Units. Their primary mission is to conduct seaborne, riverine, and harbor operations, though they have also been used extensively on land. When large elite combat units must be deployed, the United States relies on the army's 75th Ranger Regiment and units from the U.S. Marine Corps. The Marines have formed their own elite units, which include force reconnaissance and long-range reconnaissance units (referred to as Recon). These units are organized into teams, platoons, companies, and battalions.

### Special Operations Forces: Police Units

Many nations have special units within their police forces that participate in counterterrorist operations. In several examples, these units have been used in semimilitary roles.

***France.*** The **GIGN (Groupe d'Intervention Gendarmerie Nationale)** is recruited from the French *gendarmerie,* the military police. GIGN is a counterterrorist unit with international operational duties. In an operation that foiled what was arguably a precursor to the September 11 attacks, the GIGN rescued 173 hostages from Air France Flight 8969 in December 1994. Four Algerian terrorists had landed the aircraft in Marseilles, intending to fly to Paris to crash or blow up the plane over the city. GIGN assaulted the plane in a successful and classic operation.

***Germany.*** GSG-9 (Grenzschutzgruppe 9) was organized after the disastrous failed attempt to rescue Israeli hostages taken by Black September at the 1972 Munich Olympics. It is a paramilitary unit that has been used domestically and internationally as a counterterrorist and hostage rescue unit. GSG-9 first won international attention in 1977 when the group freed hostages held by Palestinian terrorists in Mogadishu, Somalia. The Mogadishu rescue was heralded as a flawless operation.

***Israel.*** The **Police Border Guards** are an elite force that is frequently deployed as a counterterrorist force. Known as the **Green Police**, it operates in two subgroups. **YAMAS** is a covert group that has been used extensively during the Palestinian *intifada*. It has been used to neutralize terrorist cells in conjunction with covert IDF operatives. **YAMAM** was specifically created to engage in counterterrorist and hostage rescue operations.

***Spain.*** In 1979, the Spanish National Police organized a counterterrorist and hostage rescue force called **GEO (Grupo Especial de Operaciones)**. Its training has allowed it to be used in both law enforcement and counterterrorist operations. Most of the latter—and a significant proportion of its operations—have been directed against the Basque Fatherland and Liberty (ETA) terrorist movement.

***United States.*** At the national level, the United States has organized several units that have counterterrorist capabilities, all paramilitary groups that operate under the administrative supervision of federal agencies and perform traditional law enforcement work. These units are prepared to perform missions similar to Germany's GSG-9, Spain's GEO, and France's GIGN. Perhaps the best known is the FBI's **Hostage Rescue Team (HRT)**. Not as well known, but very important, is the Department of Energy's **Emergency Search Team**. Paramilitary capabilities have also been incorporated into the Treasury Department's Bureau of Alcohol, Tobacco, Firearms, and Explosives and the Secret

Service. At the local level, American police forces also deploy units that have counterterrorist capabilities. These units are known by many names, but the most commonly known designation is Special Weapons and Tactics (SWAT).

Both military and police special units have been deployed to resolve hostage crises.

Table 13.2 summarizes the activity profile of counterterrorist options that sanction the use of force.

| Table 13.2 | Counterterrorist Options: The Use of Force |
| --- | --- |

The purpose of violent responses is to attack and degrade the operational capabilities of terrorists. This can be done by directly confronting terrorists or destabilizing their organizations.

The following table summarizes basic elements of the use of force.

| Counterterrorist Option | Activity Profile | | |
| --- | --- | --- | --- |
| | Rationale | Practical Objectives | Typical Resources Used |
| **Suppression campaigns** | Symbolic strength  Punitive measures  Preemption | Destruction of the terrorists  Disruption of the terrorists | Military assets  Paramilitary assets |
| **Coercive covert operations** | Symbolic strength  Destabilization  Preemption | Disruption of the terrorists  Deterrent effect on potential terrorists | Military assets  Paramilitary assets |
| **Special operations forces** | Coercive covert operations  Destabilization  Preemption | Disruption of the terrorists  Deterrent effect on potential terrorists | Military and police assets |

## CHAPTER PERSPECTIVE 13.2: Hostage Rescues

When hostage rescue operations succeed, they seem to be almost miraculous victories against terrorism. There have been a number of hostage rescue operations in which well-trained elite units have dramatically resolved terrorist crises. However, there have also been cases when elite units have failed because of poor planning or overly complicated scenarios. The fact is that when they fail, the consequences have been disastrous.

The following cases illustrate the inherently risky nature of hostage rescue operations.

### Successful Operations

**The Betancourt Rescue ("Operation Jaque")**. In July 2008, Colombian special forces rescued 15 hostages held by FARC rebels. Prominent among the hostages, which included three Americans, was former presidential candidate Ingrid Betancourt. Betancourt, who held dual French-Colombian citizenship, had been taken hostage in 2002 while campaigning in rebel-held territory in Colombia's interior region. The three Americans, who were contractors, were captured in 2003 when their antinarcotics surveillance plane went down. The operation, which was accomplished with exceptional stealth and deception, resulted in no casualties. Colombian military intelligence had previously identified the location of the hostages, infiltrated a FARC unit that controlled a group of hostages, and designed an intricate rescue plan. The leader of the FARC unit (*nom de guerre* "Cesar") had been told that the hostages were to be flown to a meeting with another FARC leader aboard a helicopter operated by a human rights organization. The helicopter arrived, the crew assisted in binding over the prisoners, and the aircraft departed. In fact, the story was a ruse. After the hostages and FARC guards entered the helicopter, the guards were overcome and the group was flown to freedom.

**Entebbe.** In June 1977, an Air France Airbus was hijacked in Athens while en route from Tel Aviv to Paris. Seven terrorists—two West Germans and five PFLP members—forced the plane to fly to Entebbe in Uganda. There were 248 passengers, but 142 were released. The remaining 106 passengers were Israelis and Jews, who were kept as hostages. Israeli troops, doctors, and nurses flew 2,620 miles to Entebbe, attacked the airport, killed at least seven of the terrorists and 20 Ugandan soldiers, and rescued the hostages. Three hostages and one Israeli commando died. One British-Israeli woman who had become ill was moved to a Ugandan hospital, where she was murdered by Ugandan personnel after the rescue.

**Mogadishu.** In October 1977, a Lufthansa Boeing 737 was hijacked in midair while en route from Mallorca, Spain, to Frankfurt. The hijackers took the aircraft on an odyssey to Rome, the Persian Gulf, the Arabian Peninsula, and East Africa. The four Palestinian terrorists demanded a ransom[a] and the release of imprisoned Palestinian and West German terrorists. The plane eventually landed in Mogadishu, Somalia. Throughout its odyssey, the aircraft had been shadowed by a plane bearing elite West German GSG-9 police commandos. In Mogadishu, the unit landed, attacked the hijacked aircraft, killed three of the terrorists, and rescued the hostages. None of the hostages or rescuers was killed, and only one person was injured. As a postscript, several imprisoned West German terrorists committed suicide when they learned of the rescue.

## Unsuccessful Operations

**Operation Eagle Claw.** During the consolidation of the Iranian Revolution in November 1979, Iranian radicals seized the American embassy in Tehran. Some hostages were soon released, but more than 50 were held in captivity. In April 1980, the United States launched a rescue attempt that was led by the Delta Force but that included units from all branches of the military. The plan was to establish a base in the Iranian desert, fly commando teams into Tehran, assault the embassy compound, ferry the hostages to a soccer field, have helicopters land to pick them up, shuttle them to an airfield secured by Army Rangers, and then fly everyone to safety. Gunships and other aircraft would provide air cover during the operation. The operation did not progress beyond its first phase. As helicopters approached the desert site—dubbed *Desert One*—they flew into a massive dust storm. Because they were under orders not to exceed 200 feet, they tried to fly through the storm; two helicopters were forced out of the operation, as was a third helicopter that later malfunctioned. On the ground, a helicopter drove into one of the airplanes, and both exploded. Eight soldiers were killed, and the mission was ordered to be cancelled.

**The Munich Olympics.** In September 1972, members of the Black September terrorist organization captured nine Israeli athletes and killed two others at the Olympic Village during the Munich Olympics. They demanded the release of Palestinian and Red Army Faction prisoners, as well as one Japanese Red Army member. West German officials permitted the terrorists to transport their hostages to an airport, using the ruse that they would be flown out of the country. In reality, the plan called for five Bavarian police snipers to shoot the terrorists when they were in the open. At the airport, five terrorists, one police officer, and all of the hostages were killed in a firefight with the Bavarian police. Three terrorists were captured and imprisoned in West Germany, but they were later released and flown to Libya. Israel's Wrath of God program later hunted down and assassinated two of the terrorists.

*(Continued)*

(Continued)

**Force 777.** In 1977, Egypt organized **Force 777** as a small, elite counterterrorist special operations unit. Soon after its creation, Force 777 was twice used to assault aircraft hijacked to other countries by Palestinian terrorists. In the first incident, the PFLP landed a hijacked Cyprus Airways airliner in Nicosia, Cyprus. The Egyptian government dispatched Force 777 but neglected to inform Cypriot authorities. When the Egyptians landed and rushed the hijacked airliner, Cypriot police and other security personnel opened fire, thinking that the commandos were reinforcements for the terrorists. During an 80-minute firefight, more than 15 Egyptians and Cypriots were killed. In the second incident, Abu Nidal Organization terrorists landed Egyptair Flight 648 in Malta in retaliation for the Egyptian government's failure to protect the *Achille Lauro* terrorists.[b] The Egyptian government again dispatched Force 777, this time in larger numbers and after notifying Maltese officials. Unfortunately, the assault plan called for explosive charges to blow a hole in the aircraft's roof so that Force 777 commandos could jump into the cabin. The charges were much too strong, and the explosion immediately killed approximately 20 passengers. During the ensuing 6-hour firefight, a total of 57 passengers were killed. Reports alleged that Egyptian snipers shot at passengers as they fled the aircraft.

**Notes**

a. The ransom demand was directed to the son of industrialist Hanns-Martin Schleyer, who was in the hands of West Germany's Red Army Faction.

b. During the *Achille Lauro* crisis, Flight 648 was the same aircraft that had transported the PLF terrorists when it was diverted by U.S. warplanes to Sicily.

## ❖ Operations Other Than War: Repressive Options

Nonmilitary and nonparamilitary repressive responses can be effective in the suppression of terrorist crises and terrorist environments. The purpose of these responses is to disrupt and deter terrorist behavior. They are unlikely to bring a long-term end to terrorism, but they can reduce the scale of violence by destabilizing terrorist groups and forcing them to be "on the run."

### War in the Shadows, Part 2: Nonviolent Covert Operations

**Nonviolent covert operations** encompass a number of options, and they are often quite creative. They are inherently secretive, and their value lies in manipulating terrorist behavior and surreptitiously taking terrorist groups by surprise. For example, covert operations can create internal distrust, fear, infighting, and other types of discord. The outcome might also be a reduction in operational focus, momentum, and effectiveness. Typical covert operations include the following options.

#### Infiltration

The successful infiltration of operatives into extremist groups can result in the disruption of terrorist operations. Ideally, infiltration will increase the quality of intelligence predictions as well as the possible betrayal of cadres to counterterrorist forces. However, in the era of the New Terrorism, infiltration of terrorist organizations is more difficult because of their cell-based organizational profiles. There is no hierarchy to penetrate, cells are close-knit, they are usually autonomous, and they have few links beyond their immediate operational group.

#### Disinformation

The manipulation of information can be a powerful counterterrorist tool. Disinformation uses information to disrupt terrorist organizations. It is used to selectively create and deliver data that are calculated to create disorder within the terrorist group or its support apparatus. For example, disinformation can be designed to create dissension and distrust or to otherwise manipulate the group's behavior. It can also be used to spread damaging propaganda about terrorist organizations and cadres.

### The Electronic Battlefield: Cyberwar

In the digital age, information is recorded and transferred in forms that can be intercepted, altered, and destroyed. Bank accounts, personal records, and other data are no longer stored on paper but instead in digital databases. Terrorist movements that maintain or send electronic financial and personal information run the risk of having that information intercepted and compromised. Thus, new technologies have become imaginative counterterrorist weapons. They have also become a new mode of warfare, with a hidden and potentially potent array of cyber weaponry and defense systems.

In June 2011, President Barack Obama signed executive orders approving guidelines for military applications of computer-initiated actions against adversaries. The guidelines governed a range of options, including espionage and aggressive cyberattacks. The overall objective of the executive orders was to embed cyber technology into American warfighting capabilities—in essence, to link cyberwarfare to traditional modes of warfare. Examples of using weaponized cyber technologies include uploading destructive computer viruses; hacking secure sites; and carrying out massive attacks to neutralize communications systems, defense networks, and power grids. A natural corollary to the wielding of weaponized cyber technology is the necessity for creating new cyber defenses to protect friendly computers, networks, and grids against attacks from terrorists or hostile nations.

*Modern Surveillance Technologies.* Electronic surveillance has moved far beyond the days when law enforcement officers literally tapped the telephone wires of criminal suspects. In the modern era, digital technologies, fiber optics, and satellite communications have moved state security agencies into the realm of technology-based surveillance. Surveillance can be conducted quite remotely, literally from facilities on other continents.

Some technologies are visible and taken for granted by residents of major cities. For example, remote cameras have become common features on London streets and Los Angeles intersections. Other technologies are neither visible nor well known. For example, **biometric technology** allows digital photographs of faces to be matched against those of wanted suspects; such technology is especially useful for antiterrorist screens at ports of entry, such as airports and border crossings. Interestingly, biometrics was used at American football's 2001 Super Bowl championship, when cameras scanned the faces of fans as they entered the stadium and matched their digital images against those of criminal fugitives and terrorists. The game became derisively known as the "Snooperbowl."

Surveillance technologies are central components of counterterrorist systems. It is technologically feasible to access private electronic transactions, including telephone records and conversations, computer transactions and communications (such as e-mail), social networking media, and credit card records. Digital fingerprinting and facial imaging permit security agencies to access records virtually instantaneously. The FBI has used biometric technologies to collect and analyze unique human traits. These technologies permit the storage of data such as iris scans, facial recognition, fingerprints, hand geometry, speech verification, and vascular recognition.

Because such technologies are inherently intrusive, they have been questioned by political leaders and civil libertarian organizations. The application of these and other technologies in efforts such as the U.S. National Security Agency's PRISM and XKeyscore data-mining operations (discussed further in Chapter 14) have been criticized by civil libertarians as overly broad and intrusive. Nevertheless, surveillance technologies are considered to be invaluable counterterrorist instruments.

*Case in Point: Echelon.* The National Security Agency manages a satellite surveillance network called **Echelon**. The NSA's network is apparently managed in cooperation with its counterparts in Australia, Canada, Great Britain, and New Zealand. Its purpose is to monitor voice and data communications. Echelon is a kind of global "wiretap" that filters communications using antennae, satellites, and other technologies. Internet transfers, telephone conversations, and data transmissions are among the types of communications that can reportedly be intercepted. It is not publicly known how much communications traffic can be intercepted or how it is done, but the network is apparently very capable. How the traffic is tapped is unknown, but it is likely done with technologies that can pinpoint keywords and interesting websites. It can also be done the old-fashioned way: In 1982, an American listening device was reportedly found on a deep-sea communications cable; it was never discovered whether this was an Echelon-style operation.

Chapter Perspective 13.3 explores the utility of monitoring private social networking media by homeland security and emergency response authorities.

## CHAPTER PERSPECTIVE 13.3: The Utility of Monitoring Social Networking Media

Modern social networking media technologies allow users to upload and post information electronically on provider websites. Popular providers include Twitter, Facebook, and dating enterprises, and users typically employ provider websites as social networking resources. Users upload information about themselves that may be accessed by other users and the public. Information typically includes photographs, videos, statements of interest, and personal information.

Social networking media have proven to be very useful systems for disseminating information when natural or intentional disasters occur. Real-time information about the effect of hurricanes, tornadoes, and other natural events has assisted the media and emergency responders in assessing the magnitude and geographic location of critical incidents. Similarly, social media have alerted the public to unfolding terrorist events, such as what occurred in the aftermath of the 2013 Boston Marathon bombing.

Unfortunately, criminals also utilize social media technologies. For example, confidence artists and sexual predators of children have been known to target unknowing potential victims.

Social media provide intelligence and law enforcement officials with resources to monitor individuals and investigate crimes. Law enforcement agencies have found social media information to be a useful forensic tool for pursuing active investigations, and for framing "sting" operations to take criminals into custody. For example, undercover law enforcement officers posing as children online have successfully captured adult predators. Similarly, intelligence analysts are able to examine the use of Web-based social media by extremist individuals and organizations. This can be useful for projecting the intentions of violent extremists. For example, increased "chatter" could suggest an increased likelihood of actual activity by extremists, especially when combined with increased activity on social networking media websites.

### Discussion Questions

1. How should the examination of social media be regulated?

2. Within which scenarios should homeland security authorities be given broad authority to examine social networking media?

3. What kinds of civil liberties issues arise when social networking media are monitored by homeland security authorities?

## Knowing the Enemy: Intelligence

Intelligence agencies involve themselves with the collection and analysis of information. The underlying purpose of intelligence is to construct an accurate activity profile of terrorists. Data are collected from overt and covert sources and evaluated by expert intelligence analysts. This process—intelligence collection and analysis—is at the heart of counterterrorist intelligence. The outcome of high-quality intelligence collection and analysis can range from the construction of profiles of terrorist organizations to tracking the movements of terrorists. An optimal outcome of counterterrorist intelligence is the ability to *anticipate* the behavior of terrorists and thereby to predict terrorist incidents. However, exact prediction is relatively rare, and most intelligence on terrorist threats is generalized rather than specific. For example, intelligence agencies have had success in uncovering threats in specific cities by specific groups but less success in predicting the exact time and place of possible attacks.

### SIGINT—Signal Intelligence

Intelligence collection and analysis in the modern era require the use of sophisticated technological resources. These technological resources are used primarily for the interception of electronic signals—known as SIGINT. **Signal intelligence** is used for a variety of purposes, such as interceptions of financial data, monitoring communications such as cell phone conversations, and reading e-mail messages. The use of satellite imagery is also commonly used by intelligence agencies, and sophisticated computers specialize in code breaking. However, the practicality of these technologies as counterterrorist options is limited in the era of the New Terrorism. Because of the cellular organizational structure of terrorist groups and their insular interactions (i.e., based on personal relationships), technology cannot be an exclusive counterterrorist resource. Human intelligence is also a critical component.

### HUMINT—Human Intelligence

The collection of **human intelligence**, also referred to as HUMINT, is often a cooperative venture with friendly intelligence agencies and law enforcement officials. This sharing of information is a critical component of counterterrorist intelligence gathering. Circumstances may also require the covert manipulation of individuals affiliated with terrorist organizations or their support groups, with the objective of convincing them to become intelligence agents. The manipulation process can include making appeals to potential spies' sense of justice or patriotism, paying them with money and other valuables, or offering them something that they would otherwise be unable to obtain (such as asylum for their family in a Western country). One significant problem with finding resources for human intelligence is that most terrorist cells are made up of individuals who know one another very well. Newcomers are not openly welcomed, and those who may be potential members are usually expected to commit an act of terrorism or other crime to prove their commitment to the cause. In other words, intelligence agencies must be willing to use terrorists to catch terrorists. This has been a very difficult task, and groups such as Al-Qa'ida have proven very difficult to penetrate with human assets.[20]

### Intelligence Agencies

In many democracies, intelligence collection is traditionally divided between agencies that are separately responsible for domestic and international intelligence collection. This separation is often mandated by law. For example, the following agencies roughly parallel one another's missions:

- In the United States, the **Federal Bureau of Investigation (FBI)** performs domestic intelligence collection, and the **Central Intelligence Agency (CIA)** operates internationally. The United States' extensive **intelligence community** is discussed in detail in Chapter 14.

- In Great Britain, **MI-5** is responsible for domestic intelligence, and **MI-6** is responsible for international collection.

- In Germany, the **Bureau for the Protection of the Constitution** shares a mission similar to MI-5 and the FBI, and the **Military Intelligence Service** roughly parallels MI-6 and the CIA.

---

[20]Whitlock, Craig. "After a Decade at War With the West, Al-Qaeda Still Impervious to Spies." *Washington Post*, March 20, 2008.

## Hardening the Target: Enhanced Security

Target "hardening" is an antiterrorist measure that makes potential targets more difficult to attack. This is a key component of antiterrorism, which attempts to deter or prevent terrorist attacks. Enhanced security is also intended to deter would-be terrorists from selecting hardened facilities as targets. These measures are not long-term solutions for ending terrorist environments, but they serve to provide short-term protection for specific sites. Target hardening includes increased airport security, the visible deployment of security personnel, and the erection of crash barriers at entrances to parking garages beneath important buildings. In the United States, the digital screening of fingerprints and other physical features is one technological enhancement at ports of entry.[21]

Typical examples of target hardening include the following:

- Vehicular traffic was permanently blocked on Pennsylvania Avenue in front of the White House because of the threat from high-yield vehicular bombs in the aftermath of the 1993 World Trade Center and 1995 Oklahoma City bombings. The area became a pedestrian mall.
- During the 1990s, Great Britain began to make widespread use of closed-circuit surveillance cameras in its urban areas. The police maintain these cameras on city streets, at intersections, and on highways. The purpose of this controversial policy is to monitor suspicious activities, such as abandoned packages or vehicles.

Modern infrastructure security and target hardening recommendations typically include the following procedures:

- Design buildings with an underlying goal of increasing security. For example, dense building clusters allow planners to concentrate and simplify security options. Dispersed building clusters spread out and complicate security options.
- Install recommended "mitigation features" in new building designs to reduce the effects of explosions. In existing buildings, the installation of new mitigation features is recommended to reduce explosive effects.
- Create distance between an infrastructure target and a possible blast. This refers to creating "standoff" distance between a target and a terrorist threat. For example, place buildings back and away from where traffic passes, and at a distance from where terrorists may launch an assault.
- Install building designs in anticipation of terrorist attacks that are also effective against non–domestic security incidents. For example, design ventilation systems that expel intentional and accidental releases of chemical, biological, and radiological hazards. Also, install windows that resist flying debris from explosions as well as from natural events such as hurricanes.
- Design road access to buildings and parking facilities with the purpose of minimizing velocity and "calming" traffic. This can be accomplished using uncomplicated measures such as speed bumps, winding roads, and barriers.

These and other options harden structural targets against terrorist attacks. They cannot completely *prevent* attacks, but they can deter and minimize possible attacks.

Two examples of target hardening on a grand scale involved the building of extensive security walls around entire regions:

### Morocco's Desert Wall

The region now known as Western Sahara in northwest Africa was called Spanish Sahara until 1975, when Spain agreed to withdraw from this last imperial outpost in Africa. After Spain's withdrawal

---

[21]See Anderson, Nick. "More Ports of Entry to Use Digital Screening." *Los Angeles Times,* January 4, 2005. See also Shenon, Philip. "New Devices to Recognize Bodily Features on Entry Into the U.S." *New York Times,* April 30, 2003.

in 1976, the territory was divided between Mauritania and Morocco. Saharan nationalists, called **Polisario**, fought a guerrilla war against the division, eventually forcing Mauritania to withdraw its claim. Morocco then occupied the entire Western Sahara, and Polisario began a protracted guerrilla war against the Moroccans' claim. To defend its occupied territory, Morocco began building a long fortified sand and earthen wall in 1981. The wall stretched for more than 1,200 miles, encircled most of the Western Sahara, and included strong points and electronic sensors. Polisario was unable to effectively breach the wall. The parties began a long period of negotiations after a 1991 cease-fire agreement.

### Israel's Walls on the Border

During the initial stages of its conflict with the PLO, Israel built a network of fences and surveillance posts along its border with Jordan to prevent Palestinian fighters from infiltrating into Israel. Later, during the *intifada,* Israel adapted this concept to its border with the West Bank after scores of bombings and other attacks killed hundreds of Israelis. A long fence was constructed to seal off the West Bank, which had become the main infiltration route for suicide bombers. The Police Border Guards had primary operational jurisdiction. Both the Jordanian and West Bank fences used mounds of razor wire, electronic sensors, patrol roads, and high electronic fences. There were also strips of soft sand to aid in the detection of footprints. The idea of "walling off" the West Bank became a literal goal when the Israelis began construction of a 410-mile wall as a barrier between the West Bank and Israel proper. In March 2005, Israeli officials finalized plans for the eventual route of the wall, which winds along Israel's border with the West Bank.[22]

## Long-Term Coercion: Economic Sanctions

Although counterterrorist policy is largely aimed at terrorist organizations, the problem of terrorist states must also be addressed. It is agreed that counterterrorism policy must take into account states that "support, facilitate, or practice terrorism, or whose help is needed in combating it."[23] Economic sanctions are a precedented counterterrorist method directed against governments. *Economic sanctions* arc defined as trade restrictions and controls that are imposed to pressure sanctioned governments to moderate their behavior. Used as a counterterrorist option, sanctions serve several purposes:

- Sanctions symbolically demonstrate strong condemnation of the behavior of the sanctioned regime.
- Sanctions are an exercise of the power of the sanctioning body.
- Sanctions potentially bring to bear considerable pressure on the sanctioned regime.

Unlike many other counterterrorist options, sanctions inherently require sanctioning nations to commit to a long time line to ensure success. The reason for this commitment is easily understood: Economic pressure is never felt immediately by nations, unless they are already in dire economic condition. Trade restrictions require time to be felt in a domestic market, particularly if the nation produces a commodity that is desired on the international market. For example, economic sanctions were imposed against Iraq during the 1990s, but Iraq is a major producer of oil, and this caused trade "leaks" to occur.

### Conditions for Success of Economic Sanctions

For economic sanctions to be effective, they must be imposed in an environment of long-term cooperation. Examples of these conditions for success include the following requirements:

---

[22]See Associated Press. "Israel Finalizes Route of Barrier." *Los Angeles Times,* March 15, 2005.

[23]Pillar, *Terrorism,* p. 157.

- International cooperation must remain firm.
- Trade leaks in the economic sanctions must be controlled.
- The sanctioned *regime* must be made to suffer.

When evaluating these conditions, one can readily ascertain several fundamental problems inherent in using economic sanctions as a counterterrorist option. These problems include the following:

- **Sanctioned regimes rarely suffer—it is their people who suffer.** Because these regimes are often violently authoritarian, there is no mechanism for the people to petition for changes in policy. Sanctions against Iraq did not appreciably diminish the government's authority or its ability to suppress dissension.
- **Sanctioning coalitions do not always remain firm.** In fact, economic sanctions sometimes become nothing more than symbolic condemnation because the sanctioning nation or nations are alone in their demonstrations of disapproval. U.S. sanctions against Cuba were not strongly coalitional, so trade and tourism kept the Cuban economy from completely destabilizing.
- **Leaks in trade embargoes are difficult to control, and sanctioning policies sometimes become quite porous.** The attempted cultural and trade embargoes against South Africa during the apartheid (racial separation) era failed because there was never broad support from the world community or private industry.

An example of a successful policy of economic sanctions is found in the case of Libya. Economic sanctions imposed on Libya were led by Great Britain and the United States in the aftermath of Libyan sponsorship of international terrorism during the 1980s, including the 1988 bombing of Pan Am Flight 103 over Lockerbie, Scotland. When Libya refused to extradite two men suspected of having planned the Lockerbie bombing, the United Nations Security Council imposed economic sanctions. In March 1982, the United States prohibited importation of Libyan oil and controlled U.S. exports to Libya; these sanctions were expanded in January 1986 and were gradually lifted as Libya renounced terrorism and other interventions. In May 2002, Muammar el-Qaddafi offered to pay $10 million in compensation for each victim of the bombing, provided that all economic sanctions were lifted. By 2004, most United Nations and U.S. sanctions were lifted after Libya dismantled its weapons of mass destruction program and opened itself to international inspections. Unfortunately, Qaddafi again became an international pariah when he ordered Libyan security forces and mercenaries to violently quash a rebellion inspired by the 2011 Arab Spring uprisings. In this case, the international community responded with diplomatic pressure and NATO military intervention, which directly degraded the fighting capability of pro-Qaddafi forces.

Table 13.3 summarizes the conditions for success, as well as problems that commonly arise, when attempting to impose economic sanctions. Table 13.4 summarizes the activity profile of repressive counterterrorist options other than war.

## ❖ Operations Other Than War: Conciliatory Options

Conciliatory responses are soft-line approaches for ending terrorist environments. They apply policies designed to resolve underlying problems that cause people to resort to political violence. Diplomatic options such as negotiations and social reform are typical policy options and can sometimes be very effective. There are also concessionary options, but these are more problematic.

## Table 13.3   Economic Sanctions: Conditions for Success and Problems

Economic sanctions can theoretically pressure state sponsors of terrorism to moderate their behavior. However, successful sanctions require certain conditions to be in place and to remain firm during the sanctioning process.

    The following table summarizes several conditions, problems, and case studies.

| Conditions for Success | Common Problems | Cases |
|---|---|---|
| Bring pressure to bear on sanctioned regime. | Economic pressure is passed on to a politically powerless population. | Sanctions against Iraq beginning in the early 1990s; regime remained strong |
| Maintain strong international cooperation. | International cooperation can weaken or dissolve. | U.S. sanctions against Cuba; perceived by world community to be a relic of the Cold War |
| Control leaks in the sanctioning policy. | When leaks occur, they cannot be controlled. | Uncoordinated sanctions movement against South Africa during apartheid era; failed to affect South African policy |

## Table 13.4   Operations Other Than War: Repressive Options

The purpose of repressive responses other than war is to degrade the operational capabilities of terrorists. The following table summarizes basic elements of repressive options.

| Counterterrorist Option | Activity Profile | | |
|---|---|---|---|
| | Rationale | Practical Objectives | Typical Resources Used |
| **Nonviolent covert operations** | Deterrence<br><br>Destabilization<br><br>Prediction | Deterrent effect on potential terrorists<br><br>Disruption of the terrorists | Covert operatives<br><br>Technology |
| **Intelligence** | Prediction | Calculating the activity profiles of terrorists | Technology<br><br>Covert operatives |
| **Enhanced security** | Deterrence | Hardening of targets | Security personnel<br><br>Security barriers<br><br>Security technology |
| **Economic sanctions** | Deterrence<br><br>Destabilization | Long-term destabilization and deterrence of sanctioned states | National economic resources<br><br>Coalitional diplomacy |

❖ **Photo 13.4**

Hostages return to Israel after the successful Entebbe operation.

Keystone/Hulton Archive/Getty Images

❖ **Photo 13.5**

A lost chance for peace? U.S. President Bill Clinton with Israeli Prime Minister Benjamin Netanyahu and PLO chair Yasir Arafat. Clinton had hoped to establish a framework for an ongoing peace process, but it collapsed amid the fighting of the Palestinian *intifada*.

Ron Sachs/Hulton Archive/Getty Images

# Reasoned Dialogue: Diplomatic Options

Diplomatic options refer to the use of "channels of communication" to secure a counterterrorist objective. These channels range in degree from direct talks with dissidents to formal diplomatic overtures with nations that can influence the behavior of terrorist groups. The characteristics of these overtures are case specific, so the style of interaction and communication between the parties is unique to each example. Peace processes and negotiations are typical diplomatic options used to establish channels of communication.

## Peace Processes

In regions with ongoing communal violence, long-term diplomatic intervention has sought to construct mutually acceptable terms for a cease-fire. **Peace processes** often involve long, arduous, and frustrating proceedings. Contending parties are always suspicious of one another, and they do not always represent all of the factions within their camps. For example, the peace process between Israel and the Palestinian Authority (governing body) during the 1990s was condemned by hard-liners on both sides. Hamas tried repeatedly to violently derail the process. The same was true of the Northern Ireland peace process of the late 1990s and early 2000s, when the Real Irish Republican Army and Continuity Irish Republican Army factions rejected the peace process.

A comparison of the cases of the Israeli–Palestinian and Northern Ireland peace processes is instructive.

***Israeli–Palestinian Peace Process.*** The Israeli–Palestinian peace process began to fall apart in 2000, and it completely collapsed during the escalating violence of 2001 and 2002. The cycle of suicide bombings and Israeli reprisals during subsequent years led to hundreds of deaths and made the peace process an irrelevant consideration for most people on both sides. As civilians on both sides bore the brunt of the violence, distrust and hatred became generalized in both communities. Nevertheless, a February 2005 cease-fire agreement was reached between Israeli and Palestinian leaders at a summit conference in Egypt. However, the cease-fire proved to be difficult to maintain when Hamas fired repeated rounds of rockets and mortar shells in Gaza. The attacks illustrated the fact that hard-line factions have been quite successful in exploiting and exacerbating tensions between the two communities.

***Northern Ireland Peace Process.*** In contrast to the Middle East, the peace process in Northern Ireland enjoyed a significant turning point when the so-called **Good Friday Agreement** of April 10, 1998 (also known as the Belfast Agreement), was overwhelmingly approved by voters in the Irish Republic and Northern Ireland in May 1998. It signaled the mutual acceptance of a Northern Ireland assembly and the disarmament, or **decommissioning**, of all paramilitaries. Despite the fact that groups emerged that tried to derail the peace process—the Real Irish Republican Army killed 29 and injured scores in the August 1998 Omagh bombing—the Good Friday Agreement began a long-term process of building a nonviolent political framework in the troubled North. In July 2002, the Irish Republican Army surprised all parties in the peace process by issuing a formal apology for all of the people it killed during "the Troubles."[24] Although the IRA and paramilitaries failed to disarm by the May 2000 deadline, the scale of violence markedly decreased. Nevertheless, in May 2005, the Independent Monitoring

---

[24]See Reid, T. R. "IRA Issues Apology for All Deaths It Caused." *Washington Post*, July 17, 2002.

Commission—a watchdog group established by the British and Irish governments—reported that the Irish Republican Army and Protestant paramilitaries continued to maintain weapons caches and recruit members. These caches, which contained tons of weapons, became a major hindrance to the peace process. The peace process did not collapse, however, because the IRA maintained as its official position a shift from violence to political struggle.[25] In July 2005, the leadership of the IRA announced an end to armed struggle and ordered its paramilitary units to cease engaging in political violence. For the first time in 3 decades and after more than 3,000 deaths, the Troubles were officially declared ended.[26]

### Negotiations

Conventional wisdom in the United States and Israel holds that one should never negotiate with terrorists, never consider their grievances as long as they engage in violence, and never concede to any of their demands. The rationale for this hard-line approach is that perceived concessionary behavior on the part of a targeted interest will simply encourage terrorists to commit further acts of violence. Nevertheless, history has shown that case-specific negotiations can resolve immediate crises. Not all negotiations end in complete success for either side, but they sometimes do provide a measure of closure to terrorist crises. These crises include hostage situations and manhunts for fugitive terrorists.

The following familiar cases are examples of negotiations between states, terrorists, and third parties that successfully secured the release of hostages:

- *The Organization of Petroleum Exporting Countries (OPEC) hostage crisis of December 1975 in Vienna, Austria,* was resolved when the terrorists were permitted to fly to Algiers, Algeria, with a few hostages in tow. The hostages were released when a $5 million ransom was paid for Palestinian causes, and the terrorists were permitted to escape.

- *The odyssey of TWA Flight 847 in June 1985* ended with the release of the remaining hostages after negotiations were conducted through a series of intermediaries. The Lebanese Shi'a hijackers used the media and the Lebanese Shi'a Amal militia as intermediaries to broadcast their demands. The hostages were freed after the United States negotiated with Israel for the release of more than 700 Shi'a prisoners.

The following cases are examples of negotiations (and bribery) between states that successfully secured the capture of terrorist suspects:

- *Ilich Ramírez Sánchez ("Carlos the Jackal")* was "purchased" by the French government from the government of Sudan in August 1994. When the French learned that the Sudanese had given Sánchez refuge, they secretly negotiated a bounty for permission to capture him, which they did from a Khartoum hospital room. Sánchez was eventually sentenced to life imprisonment for murdering two French *gendarmes.*

- **Johannes Weinrich**, a former West German terrorist, was also purchased—this time by the German government from the government of Yemen. Weinrich was sent to Germany in June 1995 to stand trial for the 1983 bombing of a French cultural center in Berlin, in which 1 person was killed and 23 others were wounded. Weinrich, who had been a very close associate of Sánchez, was convicted in January 2000 and sentenced to life imprisonment. The bounty paid for his capture was presumed to be $1 million.

- *Abdel Basset al-Megrahi and Lamen Khalifa Fhima,* alleged members of Libya's state security agency, were suspected by Great Britain and the United States of being responsible for the bombing of Pan Am Flight 103. After years of negotiations and United Nations sanctions, an agreement was signed in 1998 between Libya, the United States, and Great Britain to try

[25]Dwyer, Jim, and Brian Lavery. "I.R.A. to Renounce Violence in Favor of Political Struggle." *New York Times,* July 27, 2005.

[26]Frankel, Glenn, and William Branigin. "IRA Announces End to Armed Campaign." *Washington Post,* July 28, 2005.

al-Megrahi and Fhima. The two men were tried under Scottish law before a three-judge Scottish court at Camp Zeist near the Hague, Netherlands. In January 2001, al-Megrahi was sentenced to life imprisonment, and Fhima was acquitted.

## Responding to Grievances: Social Reform

Under the assumption that the causes of terrorism lie in political conflict between contending ideologies, ethnonational groups, and religions, it is logical to conclude that solutions to terrorism lie in resolving these political conflicts. A reduction in sources of tensions that lead to intergroup violence would seem to be a long-term solution to political violence. Thus, social reforms attempt to undercut the precipitating causes of national and regional conflicts. Reforms can include the improvement of economic conditions, increased political rights, government recognition of ethnonationalist sentiment, and public recognition of the validity of grievances.

It should be noted that social reforms are rarely the only stratagem used by states to end terrorist campaigns. They are usually used in conjunction with other counterterrorist responses, including violent options. The following cases are examples of social reforms that successfully reduced the severity of terrorist environments.

### Case in Point: Peru and Shining Path

Social reform was one element in the government's response to Shining Path's terrorist campaign. When Shining Path's leader, Abimael Guzmán, was captured in 1992, he subsequently renounced violence, and thousands of his followers accepted the terms of a government amnesty. The Peruvian government also began a social reform campaign in the countryside. Programs included land reforms, political rights, and rural improvements. These new programs successfully undercut peasant support for Shining Path.

### Case in Point: Spain and ETA

Ethnonational sentiment in the Basque region had been repressed during the regime of Francisco Franco.[27] After his death in 1975, Spanish democracy was restored, and Basque semi-autonomy was granted. Nationalism was permitted to be openly discussed, political groups were recognized, labor organizations became independent, and civil liberties were protected. ETA's political party was legalized. Nevertheless, ETA's most violent period occurred immediately following the restoration of democracy. ETA has since continued to strike from time to time, but Basque sentiment turned against the group during the 1980s. In addition, many ETA members returned to civilian life after accepting the terms of a reintegration program during the mid-1980s. Over time, Spanish commitment to social reforms undercut Basque support for ETA. In May 2006, ETA formally declared a permanent cease-fire after 40 years of seeking independence from Spain. More than 800 people had died during their campaign.[28]

## Giving Them What They Want: Concessionary Options

Granting concessions to terrorists is widely viewed as a marginally optimal counterterrorist response. The reason for this is obvious: Giving terrorists what they want is likely to encourage them to replicate their successful operation or perhaps to increase the stakes in future incidents. In other words, many extremists and those in the general population should be expected to conclude that concessions simply *reward* extremist behavior. Concessions include the following policy decisions:

---

[27]See Chapter 7 for a discussion of the Falangist code of self-sacrifice.

[28]See McLean, Renwick. "After 40 Years, Separatists in Spain Declare Cease-Fire." *New York Times,* March 22, 2006.

- Payment of ransoms
- Releases of imprisoned comrades
- Broadcasts or other publications of extremist propaganda
- Political amnesty for dissidents

Table 13.5 summarizes the activity profile of the conciliatory counterterrorist options just discussed.

| Table 13.5 | Operations Other Than War: Conciliatory Options | | |
|---|---|---|---|
| The purpose of conciliatory options is to resolve the underlying grievances of the terrorists. This can be done by addressing immediate or long-term threats. The following table summarizes basic elements of conciliatory options. | | | |
| | Activity Profile | | |
| Counterterrorist Option | Rationale | Practical Objectives | Typical Resources Used |
| **Diplomatic options** | Resolve terrorist crises | Negotiate case-specific agreements<br><br>Negotiate long-term agreements | Direct contacts<br><br>Intermediary contacts |
| **Social reform** | Degrade terrorist environments | Win support from potential terrorist supporters<br><br>Decrease effectiveness of terrorist propaganda | Targeted economic programs<br><br>Intensive political involvement |
| **Concessionary options** | Resolve terrorist crises<br><br>Degrade terrorist environments | Satisfy the demands that motivate the terrorists | Negotiators<br><br>Economic concessions<br><br>Political concessions |

# ❖ Applying the Rule of Law: Legalistic Options

Legalistic responses are law enforcement and law-related approaches for ending terrorist environments. These apply policies designed to use norms of criminal justice and legal procedures to investigate and punish those who commit acts of political violence. Legislation, criminal prosecutions, and incarceration are typical policy measures.

The "law enforcement" approach to combating terrorism has had some success in disrupting conspiratorial networks, and it has brought closure to criminal cases arising out of terrorist attacks. For example, law enforcement investigations in the United States quickly and effectively brought to justice the key perpetrators of the 1993 World Trade Center bombing, the 1995 Oklahoma City attack, and the 1998 bombings of the American embassies in Tanzania and Kenya. In another investigation, the FBI used an informant to break up a *jihadi* conspiracy to bomb landmarks in New York City in 1993. International cooperation between law enforcement officials has also proven to be effective. For example, in the aftermath of the September 11, 2001, attacks, European and Southeast Asian police uncovered a number of Al-Qa'ida and other *jihadi* cells in Spain, Germany, Singapore, and elsewhere.

# Law Enforcement and Counterterrorism: The Global Perspective

Because acts of terrorism are considered inherently criminal behaviors under the laws of most nations, law enforcement agencies often play a major role in counterterrorist operations. The organizational profiles of these agencies vary from country to country, with some countries having large national police establishments and others relying more on local police.

### The Police and Terrorist Environments

Prior to the formation of terrorist environments, the primary mission of police agencies is to serve in a *law enforcement* capacity. After terrorist environments become established, the law enforcement mission of the police is transformed into an *internal security* mission. In these cases, the police become responsible for day-to-day civil protection operations. Internal security missions require law enforcement units to be stationed at strategic locations and to perform security-focused (rather than crime-focused) patrols. These responsibilities are sometimes threat specific and mirror the terrorist environment of the times. For example, because of the threat of airline hijackings, many nations commonly place law enforcement officers aboard aircraft to act as **sky marshals**; Great Britain began placing undercover armed marshals aboard aircraft in December 2002. Other security duties include promoting airport security, securing borders, tracking illegal immigrants, looking out for fugitives and other suspects, and conducting surveillance of groups and people who fit **terrorist profiles**.

In many environments, police officers are the front line in the war on terrorism because they are the first officials to respond to terrorist incidents. This role has become quite common in the terrorist environments that exist in Italy, Germany, the United Kingdom, Israel, and many other countries. In the United States, 60 New York City police officers died during the September 11, 2001, homeland attacks when they were deployed to the World Trade Center site.[29] The police are also the first to stabilize the immediate vicinity around attack sites and are responsible for maintaining long-term order in cities suffering under terrorist campaigns. Thus, the role of law enforcement agencies varies in scale and mission, depending on the characteristics of their environment, and can include the following:

- Traditional police work, in which criminal investigations are carried out by detective bureaus
- Specialized services, in which duties require special training (e.g., defusing and removing explosive ordnance by bomb disposal units)
- Order maintenance (e.g., securing attack sites and stabilizing terrorist environments with large and visible deployments of police personnel)
- Paramilitary deployment using highly trained units that include hostage rescue units and SWAT teams

Chapter Perspective 13.4 provides perspective on the concept of an international police force for combating terrorism.

### Police Repression

Ideally, the security role of the police will be carried out professionally, within the context of constitutional constraints and with respect for human rights. However, the reality is that many police agencies around the world are highly aggressive and sometimes abusive—particularly those in authoritarian and weakly democratic countries. They are less concerned about *human rights* than about *order maintenance*. This is a key distinction because policies protecting human rights also constrain the behavior of the police, whereas policies of order maintenance are more concerned with protecting the integrity of the state.

---

[29]New York Police Memorial website: http://www.cire.com/nypd.

## CHAPTER PERSPECTIVE 13.4: The Role of the "International Police"

Internationally, there is no enforcement mechanism for violations of international criminal law, other than treaties and other voluntary agreements between nations. Nevertheless, many nations have become members of the **International Criminal Police Organization**, more commonly known as **INTERPOL**. INTERPOL is an international association of more than 140 nations that agree to share intelligence and provide assistance in the effort to suppress international crime. The association is based in Saint-Cloud, France, and each member nation has a bureau that serves as a liaison with INTERPOL. INTERPOL is more of an investigative consortium than a law enforcement agency. Its value lies in the cooperative sharing of information among members, as well as the coordination of counterterrorist and criminal investigations. Similarly, the **European Police Office (EUROPOL)** is a cooperative investigative consortium of members of the European Union.

The consequences of ideologies of order maintenance are that police agencies operating in authoritarian environments perform a very different mission compared with the professionalized police forces found in most stable democracies. For example, police in Brazil and Colombia have been implicated in practicing "social cleansing" against undesirables. Social cleansing involves the intimidation of a range of defined social undesirables, including political dissidents, supporters of political dissidents, morals criminals (such as prostitutes and drug users), and marginal demographic groups (such as homeless children). Deaths and physical abuse have been documented during social cleansing campaigns.

## Domestic Laws and Counterterrorism

An important challenge for lawmakers in democracies is balancing the need for counterterrorist legislation against the protection of constitutional rights. In severely strained terrorist environments, it is not uncommon for nations—including democracies—to pass authoritarian laws that promote social order at the expense of human rights. Policy makers usually justify these measures by using a balancing argument in which the greater good is held to outweigh the suspension of civil liberties. Severe threats to the state are sometimes counteracted by severe laws.

### Counterterrorist Courts in Algeria

During the 1990s, several Islamic terrorist movements waged a campaign of terror against the Algerian government. By the time the most severe fighting ended in 1999 (when an amnesty was offered), about 150,000 Algerians had died. During the emergency, special courts were established by the government to prosecute suspected Islamic terrorists and their supporters. The purpose of these courts was to establish a nonmilitary option in their war against terrorism. During a 2-year period from October 1992 to October 1994,

13,770 persons had been judged by the special courts and 3,661 of them, or 25 per cent of those appearing, had been acquitted. There had been 1,551 sentences of death, 1,463 of which had been passed *in absentia,* and 8,448 sentences of imprisonment.[30]

The special courts and special prosecutions were used in conjunction with a brutal suppression campaign. It can be argued that the Islamic rebels had been forced into an untenable no-win situation

[30]United Nations General Assembly. *Report of the Panel Appointed by the Secretary-General to Gather Information on the Situation in Algeria* [ . . . ] (report of the Eminent Panel). July–August 1998. Quoted in Whittaker, *The Terrorism Reader,* p. 148.

by the time the 1999 amnesty was offered. In March 2006, the Algerian government freed a group of Islamic militants as part of a program to pardon or end legal processing for more than 2,000 convicted or suspected terrorists.

### Qualified Amnesty in Italy

Italy suffered thousands of terrorist attacks during the heyday of the Red Brigades terrorist campaign in the 1970s and 1980s. As part of its effort to combat the Red Brigades, the Italian government adopted a two-pronged strategy:

1. The first prong required the Italian law enforcement establishment to continue to root out terrorist cells.

2. The second prong offered Red Brigades cadres terms and conditions for reductions in their sentences; all that was required of them was that they "repent" their terrorist past.

The latter prong—the so-called **repentance laws**—offered Red Brigades members qualified amnesty for demonstrations of repentance for their crimes. Repentance could be established by cooperating within a sliding scale of collaboration. Thus, those who collaborated most generously had a proportionally large amount of time removed from their sentences, whereas those whose information was less useful had less time removed. A significant number of the roughly 2,000 imprisoned Red Brigades terrorists accepted repentance reductions in their sentences.

### Case in Point: The Capture and Arrest of Mir Aimal Kansi

On the morning of January 25, 1993, a man armed with an AK-47 assault rifle began firing on employees of the Central Intelligence Agency who were waiting in their cars to enter the CIA's headquarters in Langley, Virginia. Two people were killed and three were wounded.

The person responsible was **Mir Aimal Kansi**, a Pakistani who had been a resident of the United States since 1991. After the shootings, he immediately fled for sanctuary in Pakistan and Afghanistan. He apparently traveled between the two countries, though he found refuge among relatives and local Pakistanis in Quetta.

The United States posted a $2 million reward for Kansi's capture and distributed wanted posters throughout the region. His photograph was distributed on thousands of matchbooks, printed in newspapers, and placed on posters. The hunt was successful, because still-unidentified individuals contacted U.S. authorities in Pakistan and arranged Kansi's capture. In June 1997, Kansi was arrested by a paramilitary FBI team and, with the permission of the Pakistani government, flown to the United States to stand trial in a Virginia state court.

At his trial, prosecutors argued that Kansi had committed the attack in retaliation for U.S. bombings of Iraq. He was convicted of murder on November 10, 1997. Kansi was executed by lethal injection at the Greensville Correctional Center in Virginia on November 14, 2002.

### Case in Point: Outcome of the Achille Lauro Incident in Italy

American warplanes had intercepted an Egyptian aircraft that was transporting Palestine Liberation Front terrorists to safety, and the aircraft was diverted to an airport in Sicily. In Sicily, U.S. counterterrorist troops were flown in to take control of the plane and its passengers.

After the Egyptian plane landed, an American special operations unit disembarked from its aircraft and rushed toward the Egyptian craft. Italian troops and security officers on the ground positioned themselves between the U.S. troops and their target. The Italians refused to permit American special operations troops to take control of the airliner or its passengers. Tensions ran high during the standoff. The terrorists were eventually placed in Italian custody and tried before an Italian court. Their leader, Abu Abbas, successfully claimed diplomatic immunity and was permitted to leave Italy for Yugoslavia. Three of the hijackers received long sentences, and Abu Abbas was sentenced to five life terms in absentia in 1986. When one of the terrorists (who had been sentenced to 30 years' imprisonment) was later released on parole for good behavior, he promptly fled the country.

An Italian judge made sympathetic comments in open court about the plight of the Palestinian defendants. He essentially said that their behavior was understandable because they had been forced to grow up in harsh conditions in the Palestinian refugee camps. He also noted that they had no prior criminal records. The judge's comments and Abu Abbas's release occurred within the context of a political environment in Italy that granted the PLO diplomatic status. Technically, Abbas's release was legal (and even mandated) under Italian law, and the terrorists' criminal culpability was considered to be a matter for Italian courts to resolve. The Italian government's refusal to transfer the prisoners into American custody was fully within their legal purview, regardless of whether the decision angered the Americans.

Abu Abbas was finally captured in April 2003 near Baghdad by American forces. Italy immediately sought his extradition to serve his sentence for the *Achille Lauro* incident. Abbas died in March 2004 while in U.S. military custody in Iraq.

# International Law: Legalistic Responses by the World Community

International law is based on tradition, custom, and formal agreements between nations. It is essentially a cooperative concept because there is no international enforcement mechanism that is comparable to domestic courts, law enforcement agencies, or crimes codes. All of these institutions exist in some form at the international level, but it should be remembered that nations voluntarily recognize their authority. They do this through formal agreements. Bilateral (two-party) and multilateral (multiple-party) agreements are used to create an environment that is conducive to legalistic order maintenance. These formal agreements include treaties, which are defined as

> contracts or bargains which derive all their force and obligation from mutual consent and agreement; and consequently, when once fairly made and properly concluded, cannot be altered or annulled by one of the parties, without the consent and concurrence of the other.[31]

Nations enter into treaties to create predictability and consistency in international relations. When threats to international order arise—such as hijackings, kidnappings, and havens for wanted extremists—the international community often enters into multilateral agreements to manage the threat. The following examples illustrate the nature of multilateral counterterrorist agreements.

### International Conventions on Hijacking Offenses

In response to the spate of airline hijackings that occurred in the late 1960s and early 1970s, the world community enacted a number of international treaties to promote cooperation in combating international terrorism directed against international travel services. These treaties included the following:

***Tokyo Convention on Offences and Certain Other Acts Committed on Board Aircraft.*** Enacted in 1963 as the first airline crimes' treaty, it required all signatories to "make every effort to restore control of the aircraft to its lawful commander and to ensure the prompt onward

[31]Franck, Thomas M. *Foreign Relations and National Security Law: Cases, Materials, and Simulations.* St. Paul, MN: West, 1987, p. 97.

passage or return of the hijacked aircraft together with its passengers, crew, and cargo."[32]
***Hague Convention of 1970.*** This treaty required signatories to extradite "hijackers to their country of origin or to prosecute them under the judicial code of the recipient state."[33]
***Montreal Convention of 1971.*** This treaty extended international law to cover "sabotage and attacks on airports and grounded aircraft, and laid down the principle that all such offenses must be subject to severe penalties."[34]

### Protecting Diplomats

In reply to the spate of attacks on embassies and assaults on diplomats in the late 1960s and early 1970s, several international treaties were enacted to promote cooperation in combating international terrorism against diplomatic missions. These treaties include the following:

***Convention to Prevent and Punish Acts of Terrorism Taking the Form of Crimes Against Persons and Related Extortion That Are of International Significance.*** This was a treaty among members of the Organization of American States that "sought to define attacks against internationally protected persons as common crimes, regardless of motives."[35] The purpose of the agreement was to establish common ground for recognizing the absolute inviolability of diplomatic missions.

***Prevention and Punishment of Crimes Against Internationally Protected Persons, Including Diplomatic Agents.*** This was a multilateral treaty adopted by the United Nations in 1973.[36] It sought to establish a common international framework for suppressing extremist attacks against those who are protected by internationally recognized status.

### Extradition Treaties

Nations frequently enter into treaties that allow law enforcement agencies to share intelligence and operational information that can be used to track and capture terrorists. Examples of this collaboration are INTERPOL and EUROPOL, discussed in Chapter Perspective 13.3. Another example is *extradition treaties*, which require parties to bind over terrorist suspects at the request of fellow signatories. Strong extradition treaties and other criminal cooperation agreements are powerful tools in the war on terrorism.

When properly implemented, extradition agreements can be quite effective. However, these treaties are collaborative and are not easily enforceable when one party declines to bind over a suspect or is otherwise uncooperative. When this happens, there is little recourse other than to try to convince the offending party to comply with the terms of the treaty. For example, when FALN leader William Morales was captured by Mexican authorities, the government refused to extradite him to the United States. Morales was allowed to seek asylum in Cuba.

### International Courts and Tribunals

The United Nations has established several institutions to address the problems of terrorism, genocide, torture, and international crime. The purpose of these institutions is to bring the

---

[32]Wilkinson, Paul. "Fighting the Hydra: Terrorism and the Rule of Law." In *International Terrorism: Characteristics, Causes, Controls,* edited by Charles W. Kegley. New York: St. Martin's, 1990, p. 255.

[33]Ibid.

[34]Ibid.

[35]Ibid.

[36]Ibid.

perpetrators of crimes against humanity to justice. They are international courts, and their impact can be significant when nations agree to recognize their authority. Examples of United Nations authority include the following institutions:

***International Court of Justice.*** The **International Court of Justice** is the principal judicial arm of the United Nations. Its 15 judges are elected from among member states and sit for 9-year terms. The court hears disputes between nations and gives advisory opinions to recognized international organizations.

***International Criminal Court.*** The **International Criminal Court (ICC)** was established to prosecute crimes against humanity, such as genocide. Its motivating principle is to promote human rights and justice. In practice, this has meant that the ICC has issued arrest warrants for the prosecution of war criminals.

***International Criminal Tribunal for the Former Yugoslavia.*** The International Criminal Tribunal for the Former Yugoslavia (ICTY) has investigated allegations of war crimes and genocide arising out of the wars that broke out after the fragmentation of Yugoslavia during the 1990s. The fighting among Croats, Muslims, and Serbs was exceptionally brutal and occasionally genocidal. Several alleged war criminals, including former Yugoslavian president Slobodan Milošević, have been brought before the court. Others remain at large but under indictment.

***International Criminal Tribunal for Rwanda.*** The International Criminal Tribunal for Rwanda (ICTR) has investigated allegations of war crimes and genocide that resulted from the breakdown of

---

**Table 13.6  Counterterrorist Options: Legalistic Responses**

The purpose of legalistic responses is to provide protection to the general public, protect the interests of the state, and criminalize the behavior of the terrorists. The following table summarizes basic elements of legalistic responses.

| Counterterrorist Option | Activity Profile | | |
|---|---|---|---|
| | Rationale | Practical Objectives | Typical Resources Used |
| **Law enforcement** | Enhancement of security apparatus<br><br>Demilitarization of counterterrorist campaign | Day-to-day counterterrorist operations<br><br>Bringing terrorists into the criminal justice system | Police personnel<br><br>Specialized personnel |
| **Domestic laws** | Criminalization of terrorist behavior | Enhancement of criminal penalties for terrorist behavior<br><br>Bringing terrorists into the criminal justice system | Criminal justice system<br><br>Legislative involvement |
| **International law** | International consensus and cooperation | Coalitional response to terrorism | International organizations<br><br>State resources |

order in Rwanda during the 1990s. Hundreds of thousands died during the campaign of terror waged by mobs and paramilitaries. The indictments against suspected war criminals detail what can only be described as genocide on a massive scale.

Table 13.6 summarizes the activity profile of legalistic counterterrorist options.

# Chapter Summary

This chapter discussed options for responding to terrorism within the context of several categories and subcategories. The decision-making process for selecting counterterrorist options is predicated on several key factors:

- The characteristics of the terrorist movement
- The nature of the overall terrorist environment
- The political goals of the counterterrorist actor

When assessing the practical utility of resorting to the use of force, it must be understood that many of these responses are inconsistently effective against determined terrorists in the long term. Successes have been won against domestic terrorists—especially when governments have been unconstrained in their use of force and coercion—but this is not a universal outcome. Internationally, short-term successes have resulted in the resolution of specific terrorist incidents. However, long-term successes have sometimes been difficult to achieve. Nevertheless, the use of force has produced some success in disrupting terrorist groups and reducing the intensity of terrorist environments.

Repressive operations other than war include a number of options. Intelligence collection and analysis are extremely useful for building activity profiles of terrorist groups and for understanding the dynamics of terrorist environments. Intelligence is also useful for generalized prediction but is less useful for predicting the precise location and timing of specific terrorist attacks. Regarding enhanced security, because target hardening usually involves the erection of fixed barriers, surveillance technologies, and security posts, determined terrorists can design

methods to circumvent these precautions. Nevertheless, there is an increased potential for failure from the terrorists' perspective, and it should be presumed that enhanced security deters less determined and less resourceful terrorists.

Conciliatory responses have achieved both short-term and long-term success in ending terrorist environments. There have also been a number of failed conciliatory operations. Diplomatic options have enjoyed marked success in some cases but have been frustrated by entrenched hostilities and uncooperative parties in other cases. Social reforms have enjoyed long-term success when reforms are gradually accepted as legitimate by target populations. Concessionary options are risky because of the perception of appeasement of the terrorists, but these options are sometimes successful.

Legalistic responses are in many ways the front line for counterterrorist policies. Law enforcement agencies are usually the first responders to incidents, and they are responsible for ongoing civil security and investigations. Problems arise when repression or miscarriages of justice discredit police agencies. Nevertheless, security-oriented police duties have successfully resolved or controlled terrorist environments. Domestic laws are adaptations of legal systems to domestic terrorist crises. Some of these adaptations—both authoritarian and democratic—have been quite successful. International laws and institutions have likewise enjoyed some success, but because they are inherently cooperative in nature, parties to treaties and other agreements must comply with their terms. Otherwise, international laws and institutions have very little enforcement authority.

In Chapter 14, readers will explore the concept of U.S. homeland security and associated civil liberties considerations.

# Key Terms and Concepts

The following topics are discussed in this chapter and can be found in the glossary:

*Achille Lauro*

antiterrorism

biometric technology

Bureau for the Protection of the Constitution

Central Intelligence Agency (CIA)

coercive covert operations

concessionary options

conciliatory responses

Convention to Prevent and Punish Acts of Terrorism Taking the Form of Crimes Against Persons and Related Extortion That Are of International Significance

counterterrorism

covert operations

cyberwar

decommissioning

Delta Force (1st Special Forces Operational Detachment—Delta)

diplomacy

Duvdedan

Echelon

economic sanctions

11th Parachute Division (Paras)

Emergency Search Team

enhanced security

European Police Office (EUROPOL)

Executive Order 12333

extradition treaties

1st Marine Parachute Infantry Regiment

Federal Bureau of Investigation (FBI)

Force 777

Foreign Legion

French Navy Special Assault Units

GEO (Grupo Especial de Operaciones)

GIGN (Groupe d'Intervention Gendarmerie Nationale)

Golani Brigade

Good Friday Agreement

Green Berets (Special Forces Groups)

Green Police

GSG-9 (Grenzschutzgruppe 9)

Hague Convention of 1970

Hostage Rescue Team (HRT)

human intelligence

intelligence

intelligence community

International Court of Justice

International Criminal Court (ICC)

International Criminal Police Organization (INTERPOL)

international law

Kansi, Mir Aimal

law enforcement

legalistic responses

MI-5

MI-6

Military Intelligence Service

Montreal Convention of 1971

Mossad

nonmilitary repressive options

nonviolent covert operations

Operation El Dorado Canyon

Operation Enduring Freedom

Operation Infinite Justice

Operation Peace for Galilee

Parachute Sayaret

paramilitary repressive options

peace processes

Police Border Guards

Polisario

preemptive strikes

punitive strikes

RAPAS

repentance laws

repressive responses

Royal Marine Commandos

Sayaret

Sayaret Matkal

Sea, Air, Land Forces (SEALs)

signal intelligence

sky marshals

social reform

Special Air Service (SAS)

Special Boat Service (SBS)

Special Operations Command

## Discussion Box: The Utility of Elite Counterterrorist Units

*This chapter's Discussion Box is intended to stimulate critical debate about the purpose of elite antiterrorism units.*

Elite military and police counterterrorism units have been mustered into the security establishments of many nations. Many of these units include highly trained professionals who can operate in a number of environments under extremely hazardous conditions. Their missions include hostage rescues, punitive strikes, abductions, and reconnaissance operations.

When elite units perform well, the outcomes include rescued hostages, resolved crises, and disrupted terrorist environments. However, these units sometimes find themselves involved in ambiguous political situations or tenuous operational conditions. In other words, special operations are often high-risk, high-gain situations.

Nevertheless, proponents of elite counterterrorist units argue that conventional forces are not trained or configured to fight "shadow wars"—only special operations forces can do so. Critics of these units argue that conventional forces can accomplish the same objectives and goals and that, aside from the very good special operations units, other elite units have not proven themselves to be very effective.

Historical examples suggest that the deployment of special operations forces is a high-risk and high-gain option.

### Discussion Questions

- How necessary are elite counterterrorism units? Why?

- How effective do you think these elite units are?

- What other counterterrorist options do you think can be effective without resorting to the deployment of elite units?

- Which counterterrorist options work most efficiently in conjunction with elite units? Which options work least efficiently?

- In the long term, what impact will elite units have in the war against international terrorism?

## On Your Own

The open-access Student Study Site at **http://study.sagepub.com/martin5e** has a variety of useful study aids, including eFlashcards, quizzes, audio resources, and journal articles. The websites, exercises, and recommended readings listed below are easily accessed on this site as well.

# Recommended Websites

The following websites provide information and data about counterterrorist policies and options:

Diplomatic Security Service, Rewards for Justice: http://www.rewardsforjustice.net/

iCasualties.org, Iraq Coalition Casualty Count: http://icasualties.org/

International Rescue Committee: http://www.rescue.org/

Long War Journal, The: http://www.longwarjournal.org/

Office of Counterterrorism, U.S. Department of State: http://www.state.gov/s/ct/

United Nations International Court of Justice: http://www.icj-cij.org/

# Web Exercise

Using this chapter's recommended websites, conduct an online investigation of counterterrorism.

1. Compare and contrast the services described online by the referenced organizations. How do their services differ?

2. How important are the services provided by organizations that monitor terrorist behavior and fugitives? Why?

3. In what ways do you think the Internet will contribute to the counterterrorist effort in the future?

For an online search of counterterrorism, readers should activate the search engine on their Web browser and enter the following keywords:

"Antiterrorism"

"Terrorism and Counterterrorism"

# Recommended Readings

The following publications provide information about counterterrorist units and intelligence agencies:

Andrew, Christopher. *Her Majesty's Secret Service: The Making of the British Intelligence Community.* New York: Penguin, 1987.

Bamford, James. *Body of Secrets: Anatomy of the Ultra-Secret National Security Agency, From the Cold War Through the Dawn of a New Century.* New York: Doubleday, 2001.

Begg, Moazzam, and Victoria Brittain. *Enemy Combatant: My Imprisonment at Guantánamo, Bagram, and Kandahar.* New York: New Press, 2006.

Berentsen, Gary. *Human Intelligence, Counterterrorism, and National Leadership: A Practical Guide.* Dulles, VA: Potomac Books, 2008.

Betancourt, Ingrid. *Even Silence Has an End: My Six Years of Captivity in the Colombian Jungle.* New York: Penguin, 2010.

Beyer, Cornelia, and Michael Bauer, eds. *Effectively Countering Terrorism: The Challenges, Prevention, Preparedness, and Response.* Eastbourne, East Sussex, UK: Sussex Academic Press, 2009.

Biersteker, Thomas J., and Sue E. Eckert, eds. *Countering the Financing of Terrorism.* London: Routledge, 2008.

Bowden, Mark. *The Finish: The Killing of Osama Bin Laden.* New York: Atlantic Monthly Press, 2012.

Coulson, Danny O., and Elaine Shannon. *No Heroes: Inside the FBI's Secret Counter-Terror Force.* New York: Pocket, 1999.

Crank, John P., and Patricia E. Gregor. *Counter-Terrorism After 9/11: Justice, Security, and Ethics Reconsidered.* New York, Anderson, 2005.

Daalder, Ivo H., ed. *Beyond Preemption: Force and Legitimacy in a Changing World.* Washington, DC: Brookings Institution Press, 2007.

Dolnik, Adam, and Keith M. Fitzgerald. *Negotiating Hostage Crises With the New Terrorists.* Westport, CT: Praeger, 2007.

Donahue, Laura K. *The Cost of Counterterrorism: Power, Politics, and Liberty.* Cambridge, UK: Cambridge University Press, 2008.

Gardner, Hall. *American Global Strategy and the "War on Terrorism."* Aldershot, UK: Ashgate, 2007.

Ginbar, V. *Why Not Torture Terrorists?* Oxford: Oxford University Press, 2008.

Grey, Stephen. *Ghost Plane: The Inside Story of the CIA's Secret Rendition Programme.* New York: St. Martin's, 2006.

Harclerode, Peter. *Secret Soldiers: Special Forces in the War Against Terrorism.* London: Cassel, 2000.

Howard, Russell D., and Reid L. Sawyer. *Defeating Terrorism: Shaping the New Security Environment.* New York: McGraw-Hill, 2004.

Klein, Aaron J. *Striking Back: The 1972 Munich Olympics Massacre and Israel's Deadly Response.* New York: Random House, 2007.

Maras, Marie-Helen. *Counterterrorism.* Burlington, MA: Jones & Bartlett Learning, 2013.

Mazzetti, Mark. *The Way of the Knife: The CIA, a Secret Army, and a War at the Ends of the Earth.* New York. Penguin Press, 2013.

Pedahzur, Ami. *The Israeli Secret Services and the Struggle Against Terrorism.* New York: Columbia University Press, 2009.

Reeve, Simon. *One Day in September: The Full Story of the 1972 Munich Olympics Massacre and the Israeli Revenge Operation "Wrath of God."* New York: Arcade, 2000.

Rich, Paul B., and Isabelle Duyvesteyn, eds. *The Routledge Handbook of Insurgency and Counterinsurgency.* New York: Routledge, 2012.

Rid, Thomas, and Thomas Keaney, eds. *Understanding Counterinsurgency: Doctrine, Operations, and Challenges.* New York: Routledge, 2010.

Shah, Niaz A. *Self-Defense in Islamic and International Law.* New York: Palgrave Macmillan, 2008.

Suskind, Ron. *The One Percent Doctrine: Deep Inside America's Pursuit of Its Enemies Since 9/11.* New York: Simon & Schuster, 2006.

Thomas, Gordon. *Gideon's Spies: The Secret History of the Mossad.* 5th ed. New York: St. Martin's Press, 2009.

Tophoven, Rolf. *GSG 9: German Response to Terrorism.* Koblenz, Germany: Bernard and Graefe, 1984.

Warrick, Joby. *The Triple Agent: The Al-Qaeda Mole Who Infiltrated the CIA.* New York: Doubleday, 2011.

# A New Era

## Homeland Security

## CHAPTER 14

OPENING VIEWPOINT: DATA MINING BY THE U.S. NATIONAL SECURITY AGENCY

In June and July 2013, the British newspaper *The Guardian* published a series of articles reporting covert surveillance operations coordinated by the U.S. National Security Agency (NSA). These operations involved the acquisition of European and U.S. telephone metadata and Internet surveillance. First reports indicated that the operations were code-named **Tempora** (apparently a British operation cooperating with the NSA) and **PRISM**.[1] **Edward Snowden**, a former Central Intelligence Agency employee and NSA contractor, had leaked details of these operations to the media prior to becoming an international fugitive. The information was apparently delivered to *The Guardian*, *The Washington Post*, and a documentary filmmaker. Subsequent articles in *The Guardian* detailed another NSA operation, code-named **XKeyscore**, which apparently deployed a much more robust ability to collect online data.[2] According to the reports, XKeyscore was capable of collecting real-time data on chat rooms, browsing history, social networking media, and e-mail. These revelations began a vigorous debate in the United States and Europe about privacy, espionage, and whether the programs were justifiable.

Civil libertarians questioned the legality of the extensive data-mining operations. In defense of the surveillance, intelligence officials commented that the NSA's program had thwarted approximately 50 terrorist plots in 20 countries, including at least 10 plots directed against the United States.[3]

### Notes

1. See Greenwald, Glenn. "NSA PRISM Program Taps Into User Data of Apple, Google, and Others." *The Guardian*, June 6, 2013.
2. See Greenwald, Glenn. "XKeyscore: NSA Tool Collects 'Nearly Everything a User Does on the Internet.'" *The Guardian*, July 31, 2013.
3. Lardner, Richard. "NSA Leak Details Citizen Records." *Boston Globe*, July 21, 2013.

The term *homeland security* is common to the modern political lexicon and security environment. Although the term is relatively new, and originated within the context of the September 11, 2001, attacks and American policy adaptations, the underlying concept has been periodically applied during historical periods of national security and political crises. In order to understand the modern conceptualization of homeland security, it is necessary to evaluate this concept within the context of several historical, administrative, and theoretical perspectives.

The discussion in this chapter will review the following subjects:

- Homeland Security in Perspective
- The American Case: Homeland Security in the United States
- Civil Liberties and Securing the Homeland

## ❖ Homeland Security in Perspective

On October 8, 2001, President George W. Bush issued **Executive Order 13228**, entitled "Establishing the Office of Homeland Security and the Homeland Security Council." The executive order stated, "The functions of the Office [of Homeland Security] shall be to coordinate the executive branch's efforts to detect, prepare for, prevent, protect against, respond to, and recover from terrorist attacks within the United States."[1] This statement of purpose by the United States was the first to result from the September 11 crisis and continues to guide the implementation of the concept of homeland security in relation to counterterrorist policies. Post-9/11 homeland security has been adapted conceptually to the unique domestic environments of Western democracies. In the European context, the concept has historically been understood according to the framework of security and (recently) "interoperability" among partners in the European Union. Nevertheless, and regardless of adopted phraseology in the West, the homeland security concept expanded considerably during the post–September 11 era.

**Homeland security** is a dynamic concept that constantly evolves with the emergence of new terrorist threats. This evolution is necessary because counterterrorist policies must adapt to ever-changing political environments and new threat scenarios. Factors that influence the conceptualization and implementation of homeland security include changes in political leadership, demands from the public, and the discovery of serious terrorist plots (both successful and thwarted). Keeping this in mind, the following statement by the U.S. Department of Homeland Security exemplifies the conceptual framework for homeland security in the United States:

> Protecting the American people from terrorist threats is the founding purpose of the Department and our highest priority. The Department's efforts to battle terrorism include detecting explosives in public spaces and transportation networks, helping protect critical infrastructure and cyber networks from attack, detecting agents of biological warfare, and building information-sharing partnerships with state and local law enforcement that can enable law enforcement to mitigate threats.[2]

The discussion in this section will review homeland security from the following perspectives:

- The Threat From Homegrown *Jihadis*
- Crisis and Homeland Security: The European and American Contexts

---

[1] Executive Order 13228 was amended by Executive Order 12656, which clarified that policies enacted in reply to terrorist events outside of the United States would remain within the authority of the National Security Council.

[2] United States Department of Homeland Security website: http://www.dhs.gov/files/counterterrorism.shtm (accessed July 22, 2009).

# The Threat From Homegrown *Jihadis*

A significant threat to homeland security in Europe and the United States arose from an unanticipated source: homegrown sympathizers of the international *jihadi* movement. Domestic security became increasingly challenged in the aftermath of high-casualty terrorist incidents carried out by extremists who resided in Western democracies. Such incidents are particularly problematic because many of the perpetrators are seamlessly woven into the fabric of mainstream society. Also of concern is the fact that thousands of European and American sympathizers of the Islamist cause volunteered to fight alongside *mujahideen* in Syria, Iraq, and elsewhere—often with the stated purpose of returning home to wage *jihad*.

© Sergio Barrenechea/epa/Corbis

❖ **Photo 14.1**

The wreckage of a commuter train sits at the Madrid station of Atocha after a bomb exploded. At least three bombs exploded at the same time at the Atocha, Santa Eugenia, and El Pozo stations.

The following incidents from Spain, the United Kingdom, and the United States are instructive case studies of this phenomenon.

### The Madrid Train Bombings

Spain suffered its worst terrorist incident on March 11, 2004, when terrorists detonated 10 bombs on several commuter trains in Madrid. Terrorists had delivered the explosives in backpacks, which they dropped at key locations. The explosions were synchronized, occurring within a span of 20 minutes, at the height of rush hour when the trains were certain to be crowded with commuters. Casualties were high: 191 people were killed and more than 1,500 were injured. Casualties could have been more severe, but fortunately three additional bombs (also in backpacks) failed to explode and were later detonated by Spanish authorities.

A group calling itself the **Abu Hafs al-Masri Brigades** claimed credit for the attack. In a statement faxed to the Reuters press agency, the group said, "We have succeeded in infiltrating the heart of crusader Europe and struck one of the bases of the crusader alliance," and referred to the attack as **Operation Death Trains**.[3] The Abu Hafs al-Masri Brigades also were implicated in the August 2003 bombing of the United Nations headquarters in Baghdad, Iraq, and the November 2003 bombings of two synagogues in Istanbul, Turkey.

The operation is an excellent example of how terrorist attacks can be carried out with considerable effect. Prior to the attack, Spain had been a staunch partner in the U.S.-led invasion of Iraq. Along with the United States and the United Kingdom, Spain committed a sizable contingent of combat forces—1,300 Spanish troops actively participated in Operation Iraqi Freedom. The government of Prime Minister José María Aznar had strongly advocated a central role for Spain, even though many Spaniards had opposed such participation, particularly the deployment to Iraq. The bombings occurred 3 days before national elections in Spain, and Spanish officials initially blamed the Basque terrorist group ETA for the attack. When this allegation proved to be false, and it was shown that the attacks were linked to Aznar's policies, his government was voted out of power. Spain quickly withdrew all 1,300 soldiers from Iraq.

The Abu Hafs al-Masri Brigades are an example of how Al-Qa'ida–affiliated cells operate as pre-positioned "sleepers" in foreign countries. It was estimated that 12 to 30 terrorists may have participated in the delivery of the bombs.[4] Fifteen suspects, 11 of them Moroccans, were arrested within several weeks of the attack. It was believed that some of the suspects were members of the Moroccan Islamic Combatant Group, another Al-Qa'ida–affiliated faction. When Spanish police prepared to storm an apartment in the town of Leganés, near Madrid, three terrorists and a police officer were killed when the suspects detonated explosives and blew themselves up.

---

[3]Richburg, Keith B., and Fred Barbash. "Madrid Bombings Kill at Least 190." *Washington Post,* March 11, 2004.

[4]Carvajal, Doreen. "Spaniards Turn Out in Huge Numbers to Mourn Blast Victims." *New York Times,* March 12, 2004.

In October 2007, three men were convicted of the attack and received maximum 40-year sentences. Eighteen others were sentenced for lesser charges, and seven others were acquitted of charges.[5]

### The London Transportation System Attacks

On July 7, 2005, four bombs exploded in London, three simultaneously aboard London Underground trains and one aboard a double-decker bus. The attacks, carried out by suicide bombers, killed more than 50 people and injured more than 700. They were well synchronized by suicide bombers, so that the three Underground bombs exploded within 50 seconds of one another. Several days later, on July 21, an identical attack was attempted but failed when the explosives misfired. Four bombs—three aboard Underground trains and one aboard a bus—failed to detonate because the explosives had degraded over time. Investigators quickly identified four suspects from video surveillance cameras, all of whom were residents of London. A fifth bomb was found in a London park on July 23, abandoned by a fifth bomber. Authorities were acutely concerned because British-based cells—sympathizers of Al-Qa'ida—were responsible for both attacks.

Other plots were later uncovered in the United Kingdom. In August 2006, British police thwarted a plot to blow up several transatlantic airliners using liquid explosives. In June 2007, authorities discovered two car bombs in London. One day later, an attempted car-bombing plot went awry when two men crashed a vehicle into the departure doors of Glasgow Airport; the vehicle caught on fire but did not explode.

Politically and in terms of policy, the London case is a counterpoint to the March 2004 attacks in Madrid. Unlike the case of the Madrid attacks, which led to significant political turmoil, Britons rallied around the slogan of "we are not afraid" and supported the government of Prime Minister Tony Blair. Blair's popularity rose, and the three main British political parties (the Labour, Conservative, and Liberal Democratic Parties) agreed to collaborate on passing stricter **antiterrorism** laws.[6]

### The Fort Hood Incident

On November 5, 2009, a gunman opened fire in the sprawling military base at Fort Hood, Texas, killing 13 people and wounding 29. The attack occurred inside a Fort Hood medical center, and the victims were four officers, eight enlisted soldiers, and one civilian. The shooter was Army Major Nidal Malik Hasan, a psychiatrist at the base who treated returning veterans for combat stress.

Hasan is an interesting profile in how someone born and raised in the West can eventually adopt an ideology that advocates violent resistance to Western governments and policies. He was born in Virginia to Palestinian parents. He received an undergraduate degree from Virginia Tech University and graduated from medical school with a specialization in psychiatry. Hasan was a devout Muslim who eventually became outspoken about his opposition to the wars in Afghanistan and Iraq. He also had a history of expressing himself provocatively. For example, at a public health seminar, he presented a PowerPoint presentation entitled "Why the War on Terrorism Is a War on Islam." At another presentation to medical colleagues, Hasan detailed the torments awaiting non-Muslims in hell. On other occasions, he proselytized to his patients about Islam, argued that he believed Islamic law (*shari'a*) is paramount to the U.S. Constitution, and publicly identified himself as a Muslim first and an army officer second. During his trial in 2013, Hasan represented himself and refused to cross-examine witnesses called by the prosecution, thus essentially refusing to mount a defense on his own behalf. Hasan was found guilty as charged.

After the Fort Hood attack, investigators uncovered connections between Hasan and an openly radical cleric named Anwar al-Awlaki. Like Hasan, Awlaki grew up in the United States, having been born in New Mexico. He eventually became a dedicated *jihadi* who specialized in recruiting English-speaking Muslims and Muslims who were raised in the West, the rationale being that such recruits would be able to blend in more easily. Awlaki also became known as a propagandist who maintained a website with his writings about how to wage *jihad*. He was believed to operate from Yemen. In September 2011, Awlaki was killed in Yemen by an American airstrike.

[5]Burnett, Victoria. "7 Are Acquitted in Madrid Bombings." *New York Times*, November 1, 2007; Frankel, Glenn. "London Subway Blasts Almost Simultaneous, Investigators Conclude." *Washington Post*, July 10, 2005.

[6]Lyall, Sarah. "3 Main British Parties to Back Tougher Antiterrorism Laws." *New York Times*, July 27, 2005.

The cases of Major Hasan and Anwar al-Awlaki are two examples of an increasing pattern of homegrown *jihadis* in Western countries. In the United States, for example, federal prosecutors in December 2009 charged David Coleman Headley from Chicago with conspiring to assist the Pakistani terrorist group Lashkar-e-Taiba with planning the November 2008 assault in Mumbai, India, as well as another planned attack in Denmark. There are also cases of Americans leaving the country to join radical *jihadi* groups, including Somali Americans recruited to fight with Al-Qa'ida–affiliated groups in Somalia, and five Americans arrested by Pakistani authorities who proudly proclaimed their dedication to waging holy war.

### The Boston Marathon Bombing

On April 15, 2013, two bombs were detonated at the crowded finish line of the Boston Marathon. Three people were killed and more than 260 were wounded, many severely. The devices were constructed from pressure cookers and were detonated 13 seconds apart within approximately 210 yards of each other. They were packed with nails, ball bearings, and possibly other metal shards. Emergency response occurred swiftly, in part because medical personnel and emergency vehicles were already on hand to assist runners at the finish line. Law enforcement officers were also present as members of the race's security detail.

Two brothers, Dzhokhar and Tamerlan Tsarnaev, were responsible for the attack. The Tsarnaevs were young immigrants from Chechnya who had resided in the United States since about 2002. Tamerlan, the elder brother, became radicalized during a visit to Chechnya when he became a committed Islamist. His and Dzhokhar's underlying motive for the attack was to condemn the United States' interventions in the Middle East. It was reported that they downloaded instructions on how to construct pressure cooker bombs from the online Al-Qa'ida magazine *Inspire*.

FBI analysis of video and photographic evidence from the scene of the attack eventually focused on images of two men whose behavior and demeanor differed from that of others in the crowd. Images of the men, one wearing a black baseball cap (Tamerlan) and the other wearing a white cap backward (Dzhokhar), were disseminated to law enforcement officials, the media, and the public. During the manhunt, the Tsarnaevs shot and killed a Massachusetts Institute of Technology police officer. They also carjacked a vehicle and forced its occupant to withdraw money from an ATM machine. The victim escaped when the pair stopped at a gas station, ran to another station, and notified the authorities. The victim left his cell phone in the car, which was used by the authorities to track the Tsarnaevs. They were later observed driving a stolen sport utility vehicle and were confronted by the police. An intense gunfight ensued, and Tamerlan Tsarnaev was killed when he was run over by the SUV driven by his brother. Dzhokhar Tsarnaev temporarily evaded the police, but he was eventually captured after an intense door-to-door manhunt while hiding in a boat parked in a backyard.

❖ **Photo 14.2**

Dzhokhar Tsarnaev, wearing the reversed white hat on the right, before he and his brother Tamerlan detonated two bombs during the 2013 Boston Marathon.

The Boston Globe Exclusive/Getty Images

## Crisis and Homeland Security: The European and American Contexts

### The European Context

Western European countries have not established centralized ministries or agencies similar to the U.S. **Department of Homeland Security**. Most homeland security and counterterrorism functions are designed to be administered across multiple ministries and agencies. This approach is derived from Europe's historical experience with terrorism in the modern era. As discussed previously, modern terrorist activity in Europe was characterized by ideological, nationalist, and international spillover political violence. The intensity of this violence was often rather high and sustained over several decades. In essence, the European approach to the homeland security concept has evolved in a unique manner during decades of security challenges from organizations such as the IRA, Red Brigade, Red Army Faction, ETA, Action Direct, individuals like Carlos the Jackal, and nationalist spillovers from around the globe.

Most European nations allocated increased resources to counterterrorist law enforcement and intelligence efforts in response to the September 11 attacks in the United States and the transportation system attacks in Spain and the UK. However, the primary focus has been on counterterrorist law enforcement and multi-agency cooperative approaches. This is in contrast to the drastic reorganization and nearly total centralization of federal homeland security bureaucracies in the United States. Thus, although the American approach has been to create a sweeping homeland security apparatus, the European approach has been to operate from within existing bureaucracies.

### The American Context

Strong proposals were made to revamp the American homeland security community within 9 months of the September 11, 2001, attacks. This occurred because of the apparent failure of the pre–September 11 domestic security community to adapt to the new terrorist environment, as well as because of highly publicized operational problems.

Prior to the domestic attacks of September 11, the United States had relied on administratively separated federal law enforcement and service agencies to provide homeland security. These agencies are defined as follows:

***Law Enforcement Agencies.*** These are bureaus within large Cabinet agencies charged with enforcing federal criminal laws. The Federal Bureau of Investigation (FBI), Drug Enforcement Administration, and Bureau of Alcohol, Tobacco, Firearms, and Explosives are examples of federal law enforcement agencies. Prior to the September 11, 2001, attacks, these agencies investigated security threats in the same manner that they investigated crimes—by working cases and making arrests.

| Figure 14.1 | The U.S. Department of Homeland Security Advisory System |
| --- | --- |

The U.S. Department of Homeland Security Advisory System that was developed after the September 11, 2001, attacks. This system was replaced in 2011 with the National Threat Advisory System, a more nuanced warning system that indicates whether threats are Elevated or Imminent.

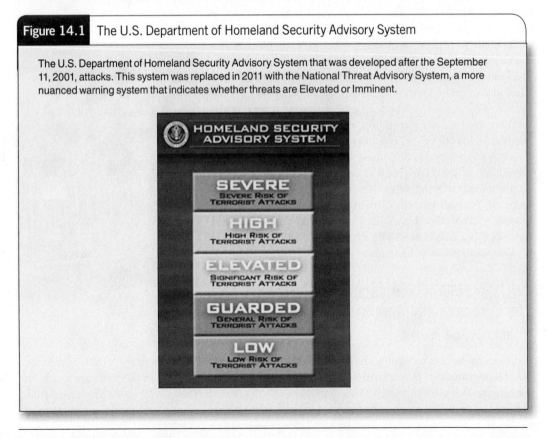

*Source*: U.S. Department of Homeland Security.

***Service Agencies.*** These agencies regulate and manage services for the general population. Service agencies include large Cabinet agencies, regulatory agencies, and independent agencies. The departments of Health and Human Services, Energy, Defense, and the Central Intelligence Agency (CIA) are examples of service agencies. Prior to the September 11 attacks, these agencies had a variety of missions, including regulating immigration, inspecting nuclear facilities, and responding to emergencies.

***Interagency Challenges.*** Among law enforcement agencies, the FBI was one of the few agencies that performed a quasi-security mission, explicitly adopting as one of its primary missions the protection of the United States from foreign intelligence and terrorist threats. The FBI did this through one of its five functional areas, the Foreign Counterintelligence functional area. The FBI also established missions in several U.S. embassies to coordinate its investigations of cases with international links. Among the service agencies, several bureaus performed a variety of security missions. For example, the Secret Service (part of the Department of the Treasury) protected the president, and the Federal Emergency Management Agency responded to natural and human-made disasters.

An ideal policy framework would have required the FBI and CIA to coordinate and share counterterrorist intelligence in a spirit of absolute cooperation. In theory, the FBI would focus on investigating possible domestic security threats, and the CIA would pass along foreign intelligence that might affect domestic security. Table 14.1 summarizes the pre–September 11, 2001, security duties of several U.S. federal agencies.

## Table 14.1   Federal Agencies and Homeland Security: Before the September 11, 2001, Organizational Crisis

Prior to the September 11, 2001, organizational crisis, homeland security was the responsibility of a number of federal agencies. These agencies were not centrally coordinated, and they answered to different centers of authority. Cooperation was theoretically ensured by liaison protocols, special task forces, and oversight. In reality, there was a great deal of functional overlap and bureaucratic "turf" issues.

The following table summarizes the activity profiles of several bureaus prior to the September 11 organizational crisis.

| Agency | Activity Profile | | |
| --- | --- | --- | --- |
| | Parent Organization | Mission | Enforcement Authority |
| Central Intelligence Agency | Independent agency | Collection and analysis of foreign intelligence | No domestic authority |
| Coast Guard | Department of Transportation | Protection of U.S. waterways | Domestic law enforcement authority |
| Customs | Department of the Treasury | Examination of people and goods entering the United States | Domestic inspection, entry, and law enforcement authority |
| Federal Bureau of Investigation | Department of Justice | Investigating and monitoring criminal and national security threats | Domestic law enforcement authority |
| Federal Emergency Management Agency | Independent agency | Responding to natural and human-made disasters | Coordination of domestic emergency responses |
| Immigration and Naturalization Service | Department of Justice | Managing the entry and naturalization of foreign nationals | Domestic inspection, monitoring, and law enforcement authority |
| Secret Service | Department of the Treasury | Establishing security protocols for president, vice president, and special events | Domestic protection of president and vice president and special law enforcement authority (including counterfeiting) |

One problem that became quite clear during the year following the September 11, 2001, homeland attacks was that the old organizational model did not adapt well to the new security crisis. This failure to adapt proved to be operationally damaging; it was politically embarrassing, and it projected an image of disarray. A series of revelations and allegations called into question previous assertions by the FBI and CIA that neither agency had prior intelligence about the September 11 homeland attacks. For example, it was discovered that

- the FBI had been aware for years prior to September 2001 that foreign nationals were enrolling in flight schools, and
- the CIA had compiled intelligence data about some members of the Al-Qa'ida cell that carried out the attacks.

These allegations were compounded by a leak to the press of a memorandum from an FBI field agent that strongly condemned the FBI directors' and headquarters' handling of field intelligence reports about **Zacarias Moussaoui**. Moussaoui was alleged to have been a member of the September 11, 2001, Al-Qa'ida cell; he had been jailed prior to the attacks. Moussaoui had tried to enroll in flying classes, in which he was apparently interested only in how to *fly* airplanes and uninterested in the *landing* portion of the classes.

Policy makers and elected leaders wanted to know why neither the FBI nor the CIA had "connected the dots" to create a single intelligence profile. Serious interagency and internal problems became publicly apparent when a cycle of recriminations, press leaks, and congressional interventions damaged the "united front" image projected by the White House. Policy makers determined that problems in the homeland security community included the following:

- Long-standing interagency rivalries
- Entrenched and cumbersome bureaucratic cultures and procedures
- No central coordination of homeland security programs
- Fragmentation of counterterrorist operations
- Poor coordination of counterterrorist intelligence collection and analysis
- Disconnect between field offices and Washington headquarters
- "Turf"-based conflict between the FBI and CIA

Table 14.2 summarizes the security duties of several U.S. federal agencies immediately after the creation of the new department.

To remedy the highly publicized political and operational disarray of the domestic security effort, President George W. Bush in June 2002 initiated a process that completely reorganized the American homeland security community. The process led to the enactment of the **Department of Homeland Security Act of 2002**, which was signed into law by President Bush on November 25, 2002. The new law created a large, Cabinet-level Department of Homeland Security. Because of the operational fragmentation of homeland intelligence and security—and the important fact that the original Office of Homeland Security had no administrative authority over other federal agencies—the new department absorbed the functions of several large federal agencies.[7] The result of this massive reorganization was the creation of the third-largest federal agency, behind only the Department of Veterans Affairs and the Department of Defense in size.

---

[7] The Department of Homeland Security absorbed the Immigration and Naturalization Service, the Coast Guard, the Customs Service, the Federal Emergency Management Agency, and many other smaller bureaus.

**Table 14.2**  Federal Agencies and Homeland Security: After the September 11, 2001, Organizational Crisis

In the wake of the September 11 organizational crisis, the Bush administration subsumed the homeland security duties of several federal agencies under the jurisdiction of a new Department of Homeland Security. The goal was to coordinate operations and to end overlapping duties.

The following table is a good snapshot of a nation's reorganization of national security in response to a significant shift in a terrorist environment. It is also an example of how two security agencies that arguably precipitated the organizational crisis—the FBI and CIA—were able to maintain their independence.

| Agency | Activity Profile | | |
|---|---|---|---|
| | New Parent Organization | New Directorate | New Directorate's Duties |
| **Central Intelligence Agency** | No change; independent agency | No change | No change; collection and analysis of foreign intelligence |
| **Coast Guard** | Department of Homeland Security | Border and Transportation Security | Coordination of all national entry points |
| **Customs** | Department of Homeland Security | Border and Transportation Security | Coordination of all national entry points |
| **Federal Bureau of Investigation** | No change: Department of Justice | No change | No change; investigating and monitoring criminal and national security threats |
| **Federal Emergency Management Agency** | Department of Homeland Security | Emergency Preparedness and Response | Coordination of national responses to terrorist incidents |
| **Immigration and Naturalization Service (some functions)** | Department of Homeland Security | Border and Transportation Security | Coordination of all national entry points |
| **Secret Service** | Department of Homeland Security | Secret Service | Establishing security protocols for president and special events |

Figure 14.2 shows the organization chart of the U.S. Department of Homeland Security.

Subsequent commission reports led to sweeping changes in the U.S. intelligence community. These reports included the following:

- In July 2004, the National Commission on Terrorist Attacks on the United States, also known as the 9/11 Commission, issued a detailed report on the September 11, 2001, attacks.[8]
- In March 2005, the Commission on the Intelligence Capabilities of the United States Regarding Weapons of Mass Destruction issued a detailed report on intelligence failures regarding the possession and proliferation of weapons of mass destruction.

[8]National Commission on Terrorist Attacks on the United States. *The 9/11 Commission Report: Final Report of the National Commission on Terrorist Attacks Upon the United States.* New York: Norton, 2004.

**Figure 14.2** Organization Chart of the U.S. Department of Homeland Security

Organization chart showing the structure of the U.S. Department of Homeland Security:

- Secretary / Deputy Secretary
  - Executive Secretariat
  - Military Advisor
  - Chief of Staff

Offices reporting to the Secretary:
- Management Directorate
- Chief Financial Officer
- Science and Technology Directorate
- National Protection and Programs Directorate
- Policy
- General Counsel
- Legislative Affairs
- Public Affairs
- Inspector General
- Health Affairs
- Inter-governmental Affairs
- Intelligence and Analysis
- Operations Coordination and Planning
- Citizenship and Immigration Services Ombudsman
- Chief Privacy Officer
- Civil Rights and Civil Liberties
- Domestic Nuclear Detection Office
- Federal Law Enforcement Training Center

Operational components:
- U.S. Customs and Border Protection
- U.S. Citizenship and Immigration Services
- U.S. Coast Guard
- Federal Emergency Management Agency
- U.S. Immigration and Customs Enforcement
- U.S. Secret Service
- Transportation Security Administration

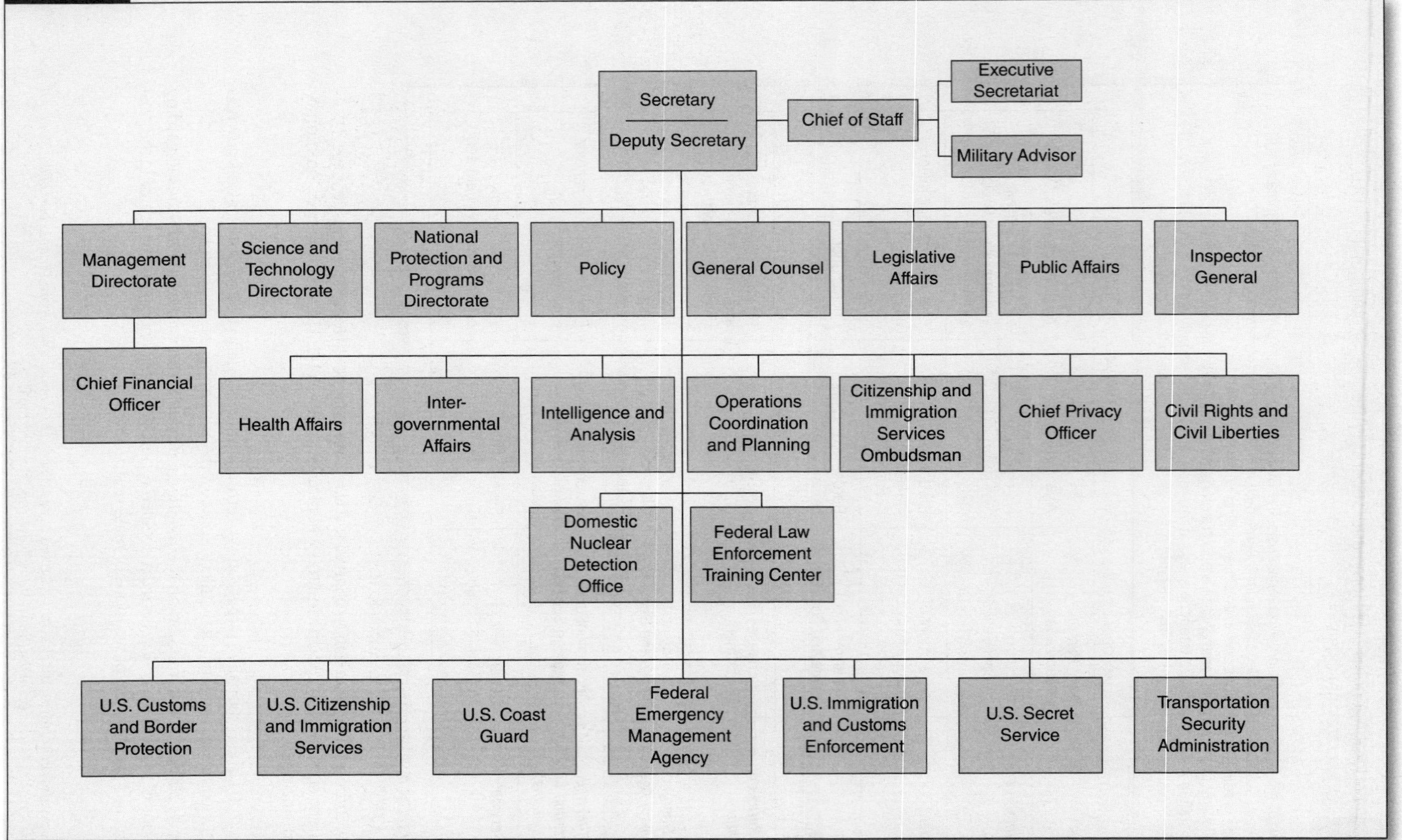

*Source:* U.S. Department of Homeland Security, April 10, 2013.

A **National Counterterrorism Center** (NCTC) was established to integrate the counterterrorism efforts of the intelligence community. Although some jurisdictional tension existed between the NCTC and the CIA's Counter-Terrorism Center, the NCTC became an important component of the new homeland security culture in the United States. Clearly, the attacks of September 11, 2001, were the catalyst for a broad and long-standing reconfiguration of the American security environment.[9]

## ❖ The American Case: Homeland Security in the United States

The discussion in this section will review the following components of the homeland security environment in the United States:

- Counterterrorism Laws in the United States
- Renewed Security in the United States: The Homeland Security Enterprise
- The U.S. Intelligence Community: Mission and Challenges

### Counterterrorism Laws in the United States

The United States designed and adopted counterterrorism laws and law enforcement policies as adaptations to the modern terrorist environment. These laws and policies serve as broad, law-related approaches for controlling emerging terrorist environments. Norms of criminal justice and legal procedures are used to investigate and punish those who commit acts of political violence. Legislation, criminal prosecutions, and incarceration are typical policy measures.

#### *The USA PATRIOT Act*

In the aftermath of the September 11, 2001, homeland attacks, the U.S. Congress quickly passed legislation with the intent to address the new security threat. On October 26, 2001, President George W. Bush signed this legislation into law. It was labeled the Uniting and Strengthening America by Providing Appropriate Tools Required to Intercept and Obstruct Terrorism Act of 2001, commonly known as the USA PATRIOT Act. Examples of USA **PATRIOT Act** provisions include the following:

❖ **Photo 14.3**

The aftermath of September 11, 2001. Rescue workers amid the smoke and debris of the World Trade Center in New York City.

U.S. Department of Justice

- Revisions of the standards for government surveillance, including federal law enforcement access to private records
- Enhancement of electronic surveillance authority, such as tapping into e-mail, electronic address books, and computers
- The use of "roving wiretaps" by investigators, which permit surveillance of an individual's telephone conversations on any phone anywhere in the country

- Requiring banks to identify sources of money deposited in some private accounts and ordering foreign banks to report on suspicious transactions
- The use of nationwide search warrants

---

[9]Commission on the Intelligence Capabilities of the United States Regarding Weapons of Mass Destruction. *Report to the President of the United States.* Washington, DC: U.S. Government Printing Office, 2005.

- Deportation of immigrants who raise money for terrorist organizations
- The detention of immigrants without charge for up to 1 week on suspicion of supporting terrorism

Debate about these and other provisions came from across the ideological spectrum. Civil liberties watchdog organizations questioned whether these provisions would erode constitutional protections. At the same time, conservatives questioned the possibility of government intrusion into individuals' privacy. To address some of these concerns, lawmakers included a sunset provision mandating that the USA PATRIOT Act's major provisions would automatically expire unless periodically extended. Lawmakers also required the Department of Justice to submit reports on the impact of the act on civil liberties. In early 2005, the House of Representatives and U.S. Department of Justice advocated restricting the act's ability to access certain personal records without a warrant.

When the act was renewed in March 2006 (after passage of the **USA PATRIOT Improvement and Reauthorization Act** in 2005), it incorporated compromise provisions that included the following:

- Restrictions on federal agents' access to library records
- Enhanced penalties for financial support of terrorism
- Improved organizational coordination of criminal prosecutions against accused terrorists by creating a new position of assistant attorney general for national security within the U.S. Department of Justice
- Enhanced standards for the protection of mass transportation
- Improved information flow between law enforcement and intelligence officers

### The 1996 Anti-Terrorism and Effective Death Penalty Act

In 1996, during the administration of President Bill Clinton, the United States passed its first comprehensive counterterrorism legislation, entitled the **Anti-Terrorism and Effective Death Penalty Act**. The purpose of the Anti-Terrorism Act was to regulate activity that could be used to mount a terrorist attack, provide resources for counterterrorist programs, and punish terrorism. The act included the following provisions:

- A federal death penalty for deaths that result from acts of terrorism
- The inclusion of so-called taggant agents in plastic explosives, which mark the time and place of their manufacture
- The ability to prosecute crimes against federal employees while on duty as federal (rather than state) offenses
- Funding for terrorism prevention, counterterrorism, and counterintelligence
- Stronger procedural controls on asylum, deportation, and entry into the country
- A prohibition on government and private business financial transactions with terrorist states
- Authority for the secretary of state to designate private groups as terrorist organizations and forbid them from raising funds in the United States

The Anti-Terrorism and Effective Death Penalty Act was passed after the terrorist attack at Centennial Park during the Atlanta Olympics and the explosion of TWA Flight 800 over Long Island, New York. Although the Flight 800 disaster was later concluded not to be an act of terrorism, officials considered the Anti-Terrorism Act to be a milestone in responding to domestic terrorism.

### In Perspective: Homeland Security, Counterterrorism, and the Law

The Anti-Terrorism and Effective Death Penalty Act, USA PATRIOT Act, and Department of Homeland Security Act effectively expanded executive power in the national effort to counter the threat of terrorism. Unlike previous legislation, the sweeping scope of these laws conferred enhanced powers to regulatory, security, and law enforcement agencies, and sought to coordinate this authority within newly established and integrated administrative umbrellas. For example, executive agencies such as the Federal Bureau of Investigation and local law enforcement officers were granted enhanced surveillance and detention authority.

A "watchdog" role was also conferred to the legislative branch of government over provisions of the USA PATRIOT Act through the incorporation of sunset provisions and reauthorization procedures. Congressional oversight counterbalances the enhanced executive authority contained in recent counterterrorist legislation. This process was deemed necessary because of concerns that the executive branch would be conferred unchecked authority absent periodic legislative review. Several judicial decisions have also been rendered that have checked executive authority, as indicated in the following holdings:

- 2004. Enemy combatants have a right to challenge their detentions.
- 2006. U.S. citizens arrested in the United States must be tried in the criminal court system. Also, a military tribunal system created in Guantánamo Bay, Cuba, was declared unconstitutional because it was established without approval by Congress.
- 2013. Customs officials must establish "reasonable suspicion" before conducting forensic examinations of laptops, cell phones, cameras, and other devices owned by U.S. citizens.

Enhanced authority is deemed necessary by supporters of homeland security legislation, and at the same time criticized as too far-reaching by critics. Increased government authority is often viewed with skepticism and concern, usually within a political and social context where such authority is seen as being used to curtail civil liberties. However, the underlying policy rationale is that demonstrable threats posed by terrorists require coordinated action from national security agencies and criminal justice institutions. During the administrative crisis following the September 11 terrorist attacks, comprehensive legislation such as the Homeland Security Act was passed to strengthen the nation's capacity to prepare for, respond to, and recover from terrorist incidents. In the post-9/11 domestic security environment, statutory initiatives moved toward policy and administrative consolidation out of perceived necessity.

Thus, the modern era of homeland security was inaugurated by, and initially defined by, statutory responses to domestic security crises. Nevertheless, privacy and civil liberties considerations underlie many of the debates on, and policy analyses of, homeland security legislation.

## Renewed Security in the United States: The Homeland Security Enterprise

The federal homeland security enterprise is a network of specialized agencies that contribute to the overall mission of securing the United States from terrorist threats. Many of these agencies are subsumed under the direction of the secretary of homeland security, while others are directed by Cabinet-level or independent officials. The *National Strategy for Homeland Security* established priorities for coordinating the protection of domestic critical infrastructures.

### Law Enforcement and Bureaucracy: The Federal Context

***The Law Enforcement Context.*** Law enforcement agencies often take the lead in investigating incidents of domestic terrorism, with other agencies performing support roles to assist in resolving cases. There is no national police force in the United States similar to the French *gendarmerie*, but many federal agencies are charged with law enforcement jurisdictions that concur with their specified missions.

At the federal level, the FBI has primary jurisdiction over domestic counterintelligence and counterterrorist surveillance and investigations. The CIA is not a law enforcement agency and therefore officially performs a supportive role in domestic counterterrorist investigations. Other federal agencies, such as the U.S. **Diplomatic Security Service**, also assist in tracking suspects wanted for acts of terrorism. The Diplomatic Security Service is a security bureau within the U.S. Department of State that manages an international bounty program called the **Rewards for Justice Program**. The program offers cash rewards for information leading to the arrest of wanted terrorists. These bounty programs are sometimes successful. For example, a cash bounty led to the capture and arrest of Mir Aimal Kansi, the Pakistani terrorist who attacked CIA employees in 1993 outside the CIA's headquarters in northern Virginia (discussed in Chapter 13).

***The Bureaucratic Context.*** Ideally, governments act rationally and efficiently to resolve problems. In order to do so, government functions are organized in operational arrangements known as a **bureaucracy**. **Max Weber** used the term to describe and explain rationality and efficiency in managing governments—a field of public administration known as **organizational theory**. It should be obvious that many functions of government require professional bureaucracies and trained managers to ensure social stability and the delivery of critical services. For example, efficiency in regulating interstate commerce permits the delivery of essential commodities throughout the nation. Many of these bureaucratic functions are literally life-and-death missions, such as emergency preparedness and disaster response. In terrorist environments, the consequences can be quite dire if homeland security bureaucracies are not flexible, efficient, and collaborative.

Homeland security's counterterrorist bureaucracy is conceptually an amalgamation of many functions of law enforcement and intelligence agencies, as well as branches of the military. The bureaucratic ideal of rationality and efficiency requires that these sectors of the government coordinate their counterterrorist missions to promote homeland security. For example, domestic law enforcement agencies must be kept apprised of terrorist threats that may be discovered abroad by intelligence agencies or the military—the challenge is how to implement this policy in these and other scenarios.

The U.S. Department of Homeland Security and several sector-specific agencies carry out homeland security-related bureaucratic duties assigned to them.

### The Department of Homeland Security (DHS)

DHS is an extensive department in the federal government whose secretary holds Cabinet-level authority. The major components of the department are a result of the consolidation of agencies with critical domestic missions in the aftermath of the September 11, 2001, attacks. Homeland security is a new concept and a new mission of the federal government. DHS is by far the largest and most mission-diverse department in the homeland security bureaucracy. Broadly defined, its mission is "to secure the nation from the many threats we face. This requires the dedication of more than 225,000 employees in jobs that range from aviation and border security to emergency response, from cybersecurity analyst to chemical facility inspector. [Its] duties are wide-ranging, but [its] goal is clear—keeping America safe."[10] The multivariate missions of DHS's components include the following:[11]

- The *Directorate for National Protection and Programs* works to advance the department's risk-reduction mission. Reducing risk requires an integrated approach that encompasses both physical and virtual threats and their associated human elements.

- The *Directorate for Science and Technology* is the primary research and development arm of the department. It provides federal, state, and local officials with the technology and capabilities to protect the homeland.

- The *Directorate for Management* is responsible for department budgets and appropriations, expenditure of funds, accounting and finance, procurement, human resources, information technology systems, facilities and equipment, and the identification and tracking of performance measurements.

---

[10]Department of Homeland Security website: http://www.dhs.gov/xabout/index.shtm (accessed July 26, 2009).

[11]Department of Homeland Security website: http://www.dhs.gov/xabout/structure/ (accessed July 26, 2009).

- The *Office of Policy* is the primary policy formulation and coordination component for the Department of Homeland Security. It provides a centralized, coordinated focus to the development of department-wide, long-range planning to protect the United States.

- The *Office of Health Affairs* coordinates all medical activities of the Department of Homeland Security to ensure appropriate preparation for and response to incidents having medical significance.

- The *Office of Intelligence and Analysis* is responsible for using information and intelligence from multiple sources to identify and assess current and future threats to the United States.

- The *Office of Operations Coordination* is responsible for monitoring the security of the United States on a daily basis and coordinating activities within the department and with governors, homeland security advisors, law enforcement partners, and critical infrastructure operators in all 50 states and more than 50 major urban areas nationwide.

- The *Federal Law Enforcement Training Center* provides career-long training to law enforcement professionals to help them fulfill their responsibilities safely and proficiently.

- The *Domestic Nuclear Detection Office* works to enhance the nuclear detection efforts of federal, state, territorial, tribal, and local governments and the private sector and to ensure a coordinated response to such threats.

- The *Transportation Security Administration (TSA)* protects the nation's transportation systems to ensure freedom of movement for people and commerce.

- *United States Customs and Border Protection (CBP)* is responsible for protecting the nation's borders in order to prevent terrorists and terrorist weapons from entering the United States, while facilitating the flow of legitimate trade and travel.

- *United States Citizenship and Immigration Services* is responsible for the administration of immigration and naturalization adjudication functions and establishing immigration services policies and priorities.

- *United States Immigration and Customs Enforcement (ICE)*, the largest investigative arm of the Department of Homeland Security, is responsible for identifying and shutting down vulnerabilities in the nation's border, economic, transportation, and infrastructure security.

- The *United States Coast Guard* protects the public, the environment, and U.S. economic interests—in the nation's ports and waterways, along the coast, on international waters, or in any maritime region as required to support national security.

- The *Federal Emergency Management Agency (FEMA)* prepares the nation for hazards, manages federal response and recovery efforts following any national incident, and administers the National Flood Insurance Program.

- The *United States Secret Service* protects the president and other high-level officials and investigates counterfeiting and other financial crimes, including financial institution fraud; identity theft; computer fraud; and computer-based attacks on our nation's financial, banking, and telecommunications infrastructure.

### Sector-Specific Agencies

In order to ensure the implementation of protective priorities, sector-specific homeland security missions were identified for federal agencies in addition to establishing the Department of Homeland Security. These agencies are known as *sector-specific agencies*. These federal agencies have been tasked to protect critical infrastructure in the United States from terrorist attacks. Key U.S. government responsibilities for critical infrastructure are summarized as follows:

***Department of Agriculture (USDA).*** Agricultural and food security are critical to the nation. The primary mission of the USDA is to ensure a "safe, sustainable, sufficient and nutritious food supply for all Americans."[12] USDA's critical infrastructure responsibility is to secure the nation's food supply and agricultural infrastructure.

***Department of Defense (DOD).*** Defending the homeland from foreign threats is paramount to the overall security of the nation. The mission of DOD "is to provide the military forces needed to deter war and protect the security" of the United States.[13] Its critical infrastructure responsibility is to secure DOD installations, military personnel, and defense industries.

***Department of Energy (DOE).*** Securing energy resources, transportation, and markets requires an overarching national agenda. DOE's "overarching mission is to advance the national, economic, and energy security of the United States; to promote scientific and technological innovation in support of that mission; and to ensure the environmental cleanup of the national nuclear weapons complex."[14] Within this context, DOE's critical infrastructure responsibility is to secure power plants, weapons production facilities, oil and gas, and research laboratories.

***Department of Health and Human Services (HHS).*** Protecting and monitoring the health of the nation is a fundamental mission of the department. HHS is "the United States government's principal agency for protecting the health of all Americans and providing essential human services."[15] The agency's critical infrastructure responsibility is to secure the nation's health care and public health system.

***Department of the Interior.*** The primary mission of the Department of the Interior "is to protect and provide access to our Nation's natural and cultural heritage and honor our trust responsibilities to Indian Tribes and our commitments to island communities."[16] Interior's critical infrastructure responsibility is to protect national monuments and lands under its jurisdiction.

***Department of the Treasury.*** The nation's wealth and treasure are hallmarks of the United States. The overarching mission of the Department of the Treasury is to "[s]erve the American people and strengthen national security by managing the U.S. Government's finances effectively, promoting economic growth and stability, and ensuring the safety, soundness, and security of the U.S. and international financial systems."[17] Its critical infrastructure mission is to secure the U.S. financial and banking system.

***Environmental Protection Agency (EPA).*** Securing and preserving the nation's environment and resources is a critical component of homeland security. The overarching mission of the EPA is to lead "the nation's environmental science, research, education and assessment efforts . . . [and] protect human health and the environment."[18] EPA's critical infrastructure responsibility is to secure the nation's drinking water and water treatment infrastructure.

## The U.S. Intelligence Community: Mission and Challenges

Intelligence collection and analysis are important components of the homeland security mission. The intelligence mission is unique in the sense that it is responsible for securing the American homeland

---

[12] Department of Agriculture website: http://www.usda.gov/wps/portal/!ut/p/_s.7_0_A/7_0_10B?contentidonly=true&content id=bios_vilsack.xml (accessed July 26, 2009).

[13] Department of Defense website: http://www.defenselink.mil/admin/about.html (accessed July 26, 2009).

[14] Department of Energy website: http://www.energy.gov/about/index.htm (accessed July 26, 2009).

[15] Department of Health and Human Services website: http://www.hhs.gov/about/ (accessed July 26, 2009).

[16] Department of the Interior website: http://www.doi.gov/whoweare/interior.cfm (accessed July 26, 2009).

[17] Department of the Treasury website: http://www.ustreas.gov/education/duties/ (accessed July 26, 2009).

[18] Environmental Protection Agency website: http://www.epa.gov/epahome/aboutepa.htm (accessed July 26, 2009).

from external threats. That is, although intelligence operations have a significant effect on domestic security, their scope of operations is also outside the borders of the nation.

Chapter Perspective 14.1 discusses the subject of waging war in the era of the New Terrorism.

## CHAPTER PERSPECTIVE 14.1: Waging War in the Era of the New Terrorism

A war on terrorism was declared in the aftermath of the September 11, 2001, attacks on the United States. This is a new kind of conflict against a new form of enemy. From the outset, policy makers understood that this war would be fought in an unconventional manner, primarily against shadowy terrorist cells and elusive leaders. It is not a war against a nation, but rather against ideas and behavior.

The mobilization of resources in this war necessitated the coordination of law enforcement, intelligence, and military assets in many nations across the globe. Covert operations by special military and intelligence units became the norm rather than the exception. Suspected terrorist cells were identified and dismantled by law enforcement agencies in many countries, and covert operatives worked secretly in other countries. Although many suspects were detained at the U.S. military base in Guantánamo Bay, Cuba, other secret detention facilities were also established.

However, the war has not been fought solely in the shadows. In contrast to the deployment of small law enforcement and covert military or intelligence assets, the U.S.-led invasions of Afghanistan and Iraq involved the commitment of large conventional military forces. In Afghanistan, reasons given for the invasion included the need to eliminate state-sponsored safe havens for Al-Qa'ida and other international *mujahideen* (holy warriors). In Iraq, reasons given for the invasion included the need to eliminate alleged stockpiles of weapons of mass destruction and alleged links between the regime of Saddam Hussein and terrorist networks. The U.S.-led operation in Iraq was symbolically named **Operation Iraqi Freedom**.

One significant challenge for waging war against extremist behavior—in this case, against terrorism—is that victory is not an easily definable condition. For example, on May 1, 2003, U.S. President George W. Bush landed on the aircraft carrier *Abraham Lincoln* to deliver a speech in which he officially declared that the military phase of the Iraqi invasion had ended, and that the overthrow of the Hussein government was "one victory in a war on terror that began on September 11, 2001, and still goes on."[a] Unfortunately, President Bush's declaration was premature. A widespread insurgency took root in Iraq, with the resistance employing both classic hit-and-run guerrilla tactics and terrorism. Common cause was found between remnants of the Hussein regime and non-Iraqi Islamist fighters. Thousands of Iraqis and occupation troops became casualties during the insurgency. In particular, the insurgents targeted foreign soldiers, government institutions, and Iraqi "collaborators" such as soldiers, police officers, election workers, and interpreters. Sectarian violence also spread, with Sunni and Shi'a religious extremists killing many civilians.

Is the war on terrorism being won? How can victory reasonably be measured? Assuming that the New Terrorism will continue for a period of time, perhaps the best measure for progress in the war is to assess the degree to which terrorist behavior is being successfully *managed*—in much the same manner that progress against crime is assessed. As the global community continues to be challenged by violent extremists during the new era of terrorism, the definition of victory is likely to continue to be refined and redefined by nations and leaders.

### Note

a. Sanger, David E. "In Speech, Bush Focuses on Conflicts Beyond Iraq." *New York Times*, May 1, 2003

### *U.S. Intelligence Community: Mission*

In the United States, intelligence collection is divided between agencies that are separately responsible for domestic and international intelligence collection. This separation is mandated by law.

For example, the **Federal Bureau of Investigation (FBI)** performs domestic intelligence collection, and the **Central Intelligence Agency (CIA)** operates internationally. This separation of missions is similar to the distinctive roles of the United Kingdom's MI-5 (domestic intelligence) and MI-6 (international collection).

The United States has attempted to coordinate intelligence collection and analysis by creating a cooperative **intelligence community**. This philosophy of cooperation is the primary conceptual goal of the American counterterrorist intelligence effort. In practice, of course, there have been very serious bureaucratic rivalries. To reduce the incidence of these rivalries, in December 2004, the intelligence community was reorganized with the passage of the Intelligence Reform and Terrorism Prevention Act. Members of the community were subsumed under the direction of a new Office of the Director of National Intelligence (ODNI). President George W. Bush appointed John Negroponte, former U.S. ambassador to Iraq, as the United States' first director of national intelligence (DNI). Officially confirmed by the Senate in April 2005, the DNI is responsible for coordinating the various components of the intelligence community. Members of the American intelligence community include the following agencies:

***National Security Agency.*** The **National Security Agency (NSA)** is the technological arm of the U.S. intelligence community. Using state-of-the-art computer and satellite technologies, the NSA's primary mission is to collect communications and other signal intelligence. It also devotes a significant portion of its technological expertise to code-making and code-breaking activities. Much of this work is done covertly from secret surveillance facilities positioned around the globe.

***Central Intelligence Agency.*** The CIA is an independent federal agency. It is the theoretical coordinator of the intelligence community. The agency is charged with collecting intelligence outside of the borders of the United States, which is done covertly using human and technological assets. The CIA is legally prohibited from collecting intelligence inside the United States.

***Defense Intelligence Agency.*** The **Defense Intelligence Agency (DIA)** is a bureau within the Department of Defense. It is the central intelligence bureau for the U.S. military. Each branch of the military coordinates its intelligence collection and analysis with the other branches through the DIA.

***Federal Bureau of Investigation.*** The FBI is a bureau within the Department of Justice. It is a law enforcement agency that is charged, in part, with conducting domestic surveillance of suspected spies and terrorists. The agency also engages in domestic intelligence collection and has been deployed to American embassies around the world. Foreign counterintelligence investigations have included an FBI presence at the sites of the 1998 bombings of the U.S. embassies in Kenya and Tanzania.

### U.S. Intelligence Community: Challenges

***Problems of Intelligence Coordination.*** The collection and analysis of intelligence are covert processes that do not lend themselves easily to absolute cooperation and coordination between countries or between members of domestic intelligence communities. National intelligence agencies do not readily share intelligence with allied countries; they usually do so only after careful deliberation. The same is true of intelligence communities within countries. For example, prior to the September 11, 2001, homeland attacks, dozens of federal agencies were involved in the collection of intelligence about terrorism. This led to overlapping and competing interests. A case in point is the apparent failure by the FBI and CIA to collaboratively process, share, and evaluate important intelligence between their agencies. In the case of the FBI, there was also an apparent failure of coordination between the agency's field and national offices. These problems precipitated a proposal in June 2002 by President George W. Bush to completely reorganize the American homeland security community.

An example of successful international intelligence cooperation occurred in May 2002 between American and Moroccan intelligence agencies. In February 2002, Moroccan intelligence officers interrogated Moroccan Al-Qa'ida prisoners held by the Americans at their naval base in Guantánamo Bay, Cuba. They received information from one of the prisoners about an Al-Qa'ida operative in Morocco and also received information about the operative's relatives. Moroccan officials obtained a sketched description of the man from the relatives and showed the sketch to the Guantánamo prisoner, who confirmed his likeness. The Moroccans located the suspect (a Saudi), followed him for a month, and eventually arrested him and two Saudi accomplices. The suspects eventually told the Moroccans that they were Al-Qa'ida operatives trained in Afghanistan and that they had escaped during the anti-Taliban campaign after receiving orders to engage in suicide attacks against maritime targets in Gibraltar. They had begun the process of inquiring about speedboats, and their ultimate targets were to be U.S. Navy ships passing through Gibraltar.[19]

***Problems of Collection and Analysis.*** Intelligence collection and analysis are not always exact or low-risk sciences. They can reflect only the quality and amount of data that are available. Because of the nature of counterterrorist intelligence collection and analysis, some experts in the United States have concluded that

> the inherent difficulties in both collection and analysis of intelligence on terrorism mean that there will never be tactical warning of most attempted terrorist attacks, or even most major attempted attacks against U.S. targets.[20]

This observation became controversially apparent on July 7, 2004, when the U.S. Select Committee on Intelligence issued an extensive report, titled *Report on the U.S. Intelligence Community's Prewar Intelligence Assessments on Iraq.*[21] The 521-page report's findings were a scathing critique of intelligence failures regarding Iraq. For example, its first conclusion found the following:

> Most of the major key judgments in the Intelligence Community's October 2002 National Intelligence Estimate (NIE), *Iraq's Continuing Programs for Weapons of Mass Destruction,* either overstated, or were not supported by, the underlying intelligence reporting. A series of failures, particularly in analytic trade craft, led to mischaracterization of the intelligence.[22]

In another highly critical report, a presidential commission known as the Commission on the Intelligence Capabilities of the United States Regarding Weapons of Mass Destruction essentially labeled the American intelligence community as being dysfunctional.[23] It also said that the causes for the failure in the Iraq case continued to hinder intelligence on other potential threats, such as the nuclear programs of adversaries. The commission's 601-page report was delivered in March 2005.

## ❖ Civil Liberties and Securing the Homeland

The discussion in this section addresses the difficult balance between securing the homeland and protecting civil liberties in liberal democracies. When examining how democracies respond when challenged by perceived threats to national security, the following viewpoints are instructive:

---

[19]Finn, Peter. "Arrests Reveal Al Qaeda Plans." *Washington Post,* June 16, 2002.

[20]Pillar, Paul R. *Terrorism and U.S. Foreign Policy.* Washington, DC: Brookings Institution Press, 2001, p. 115.

[21]United States Select Committee on Intelligence. *Report on the U.S. Intelligence Community's Prewar Intelligence Assessments on Iraq.* Washington, DC: United States Senate, July 7, 2004.

[22]Ibid., p. 14.

[23]See Schot, Shane, and David E. Sanger. "Bush Panel Finds Big Flaws Remain in U.S. Spy Efforts." *New York Times,* April 1, 2005.

- Security and Liberty: Historical Perspectives
- Balancing Civil Liberties and Homeland Security
- Achieving Security

## Security and Liberty: Historical Perspectives

This discussion presents several illustrative cases of civil liberties quandaries from the United Kingdom and the United States.

### Wrongful Prosecution in the United Kingdom

In the United Kingdom, where factions of the Irish Republican Army were highly active in London and other cities, the British police were considered to be the front line against IRA terrorism. They usually displayed a high degree of professionalism without resorting to repressive tactics and consequently enjoyed widespread popular support. For example, London's Metropolitan Police (also known as "The Met") became experts in counterterrorist operations when the Irish Republican Army waged a terrorist campaign during the 1970s. The Met's criminal investigations bureau generally used high-quality detective work rather than authoritarian techniques to investigate terrorist incidents. The British criminal justice system also generally protected the rights of the accused during trials of IRA suspects. However, in the rush to stop the IRA's terrorist campaign (especially during the 1970s), miscarriages of criminal justice did occur. Examples of these miscarriages include the following examples:

***Guildford Four.*** Four people were wrongfully convicted of an October 1974 bombing in Guildford, England. Two of them were also wrongfully sentenced for a bombing attack in Woolwich. The **Guildford Four** served 15 years in prison before being released in 1989, when their convictions were overturned on appeal. The group received a formal apology from Prime Minister Tony Blair in June 2000 and received monetary awards as compensation. The case was made famous by the American film *In the Name of the Father.*

***Birmingham Six.*** Six men were convicted of the November 1974 bombings of two pubs in Birmingham, England, that killed 21 people and injured 168. On appeal, the court ordered the release of the Birmingham Six after it ruled that the police had used fabricated evidence. The men were released in 1991 after serving 16 years in prison.

### Suspending Civil Liberties in Northern Ireland

After the British army was deployed to Northern Ireland, it became severely pressed by an IRA terrorist campaign. In response to repeated intimidation of jurors by paramilitaries, the government in Northern Ireland established special courts without jury trial. These **Diplock Courts**—so-named after Lord Diplock, who reported to Parliament on the problem—held trials before a single judge without recourse to jury trial. In such cases, all defendants were tried as criminals under the same laws, rather than differentiating between political and criminal suspects.

Another program aimed at prosecuting and imprisoning Irish terrorists was implemented during the 1980s. This was the **supergrass** program, which was a policy of convincing Provos and members of the Irish National Liberation Army (INLA) to defect from their movements and inform on their former comrades (*supergrass* is a slang term for an informer). Many decided to participate in supergrass. With these informants, British-led authorities were able to successfully prosecute and imprison a number of Provos and INLA members. However, many of these dissidents were released in the late 1980s, when cases taken up on appeal successfully challenged the admissibility of supergrass testimony. In the end, supergrass disrupted Irish militant groups during the 1980s (particularly the INLA) but did not have a long-term impact on Northern Ireland's terrorist environment.

The **Northern Ireland Act**, passed in 1993, created conditions of quasi–martial law. The act suspended several civil liberties. It empowered the British military to engage in warrantless searches of civilian homes, temporarily detain people without charge, and question suspects. The military could also intern (remove from society) suspected terrorists and turn over for prosecution those for whom enough evidence had been seized. Nearly a quarter of a million warrantless searches were conducted by the army, which resulted in the seizure of thousands of arms and the internment or imprisonment of hundreds of suspects.

Buyenlarge/Getty Images

❖ **Photo 14.4**

A Japanese American family in San Francisco being evacuated to an internment camp during the Second World War. The relocation program targeted Americans of Japanese ancestry in the aftermath of the attack on Pearl Harbor by the Empire of Japan.

### Red Scares and Internment Camps in the United States

The United States has experienced several periods of crisis in which the American public and political leaders perceived a need for enacting legally based guidelines for managing the crisis. Laws were passed because of fear and uncertainty precipitated by domestic or foreign threats. At the time, these measures were deemed necessary and were therefore often quite popular. However, the constitutionality and ethics of these laws were frequently called into question during reflection in postcrisis years. Examples of these laws and crises include the following:

***Red Scares.*** In the United States, periodic anticommunist **"Red Scares"** occurred when national leaders reacted to the perceived threat of communist subversion. Government officials reacted by adopting authoritarian measures to end the perceived threats. Red Scares occurred during three periods in American history: first in the aftermath of the Bolshevik Revolution in Russia, again during the 1930s, and finally during the height of the Cold War.

The first Red Scare occurred after the founding of the Communist Party–USA in 1919, when a series of letter bombs were intercepted. Other bombs were detonated in several cities, including one directed against Attorney General **A. Mitchell Palmer**. President Woodrow Wilson allowed Palmer to conduct a series of raids—the so-called Palmer Raids—against labor unions, socialists, Communists, and other leftist and labor groups. Offices of many organizations were searched without warrants and shut down; thousands were arrested. Leaders were arrested and put on trial, and hundreds of people were deported. The legal foundations for the law enforcement crackdown against leftists were the Espionage Act of 1917 and the Sedition Act of 1918. An interesting postscript is that A. Mitchell Palmer was eventually prosecuted and convicted for misappropriation of government funds.

The second Red Scare began during the 1930s at the height of the Great Depression. Communists and socialists enjoyed a measure of popularity during this period of crisis, and fears grew that the uncertainty of the Depression would lead to mass subversive unrest. Congress reacted by establishing the House Un-American Activities Committee and with the passage of the Smith Act in 1940, which made advocacy of the violent overthrow of the government a federal crime. In the late 1940s, high-profile investigations, such as that of Alger Hiss, an American government official who was involved in establishing the United Nations and the U.S. Department of State, were common. Hiss was accused of being a Communist, and a number of other alleged Communists were prosecuted.

The third Red Scare occurred during the 1950s, when Senator Joseph McCarthy of Wisconsin held a series of hearings to counter fears of spying by Communist regimes (China and the Soviet Union) and a general fear that Communists were poised to overthrow the government and otherwise subvert the "American way of life." McCarthy sought to expose communist infiltration and conspiracies in government, private industry, and the entertainment industry. McCarthy publicly interrogated people from these sectors in a way that had never been done before—on television. Hundreds of careers were ruined and many people were blacklisted—that is, barred from employment. McCarthy was later criticized for overstepping the bounds of propriety, and the term **McCarthyism** has come to mean a political and ideological witch hunt.

***Wartime Internment Camps.*** The attack on Pearl Harbor on December 7, 1941, by the Empire of Japan created a climate of fear in the United States against ethnic Japanese. Conspiracy scenarios held that sympathizers would begin a campaign of sabotage and subversion on behalf of Japan. This would, in theory, be done in preparation for a Japanese invasion of the West Coast. Unfortunately, a prewar backdrop of prejudice against Asians in general became a focused animosity toward Asians of Japanese heritage. The administration of President Franklin Delano Roosevelt established a War Relocation Authority, and the U.S. Army was tasked to move ethnic Japanese to internment camps on the West Coast and elsewhere. More than 100,000 ethnic Japanese, most of whom were American citizens, were forced to relocate to the camps. Internment camps were operational until 1945, with most internees losing their property and businesses. In 1988, the U.S. government passed the Civil Liberties Act, which formally apologized for the internments, declared the internment program unjust, and disbursed reparation payments.

## Balancing Civil Liberties and Homeland Security

### Terrorist Profiling

European approaches to domestic counterterrorism were security focused long prior to September 11, 2001. These approaches reflected European experience with domestic extremists such as the Red Brigade, IRA, and Red Army Faction, as well as many incidents of international terrorism. In contrast, the American approach to domestic counterterrorism prior to the September 11 attacks was a law enforcement approach; after the attacks, the new terrorist environment called for a more security-focused approach. The FBI and other agencies created a **terrorist profile** that was similar to standard **criminal profiles** used in law enforcement investigations. Criminal profiles are descriptive composites that include the personal characteristics of suspects, such as their height, weight, race, gender, hair color, eye color, and clothing. Suspects who match these criminal profiles can be detained for questioning. The composite of the new terrorist profile included the following characteristics: Middle Eastern heritage, temporary visa status, Muslim faith, male gender, and young adult age. Based on these criteria—and during a serious security crisis—the FBI and Immigration and Naturalization Service administratively detained hundreds of men fitting this description. Material witness warrants were used from the outset to detain many of these men for questioning.

As the investigations continued, and in the wake of several warnings about possible terrorist threats, the U.S. Department of Justice expanded the FBI's surveillance authority. New guidelines were promulgated in May 2002 that permitted field offices to conduct surveillance of religious institutions, websites, libraries, and organizations without an *a priori* (before the fact) finding of criminal suspicion.

These detentions and guidelines were criticized. Critics argued that the detentions were improper because the vast majority of the detainees had not been charged with violating the law. Critics of the surveillance guidelines contended that they gave too much power to the state to investigate innocent civilians. Many also maintained that there was a danger that these investigations could become discriminatory **racial profiling**, involving the detention of people because of their ethnonational or racial heritage. Nevertheless, the new security policies continued to use administrative detentions and enhanced surveillance as counterterrorist methods.

### The Problem of Labeling the Enemy

When formulating counterterrorist policies, Western homeland security experts are challenged by two problems: first, the problem of defining terrorism, and second, the problem of labeling individual suspects. Although defining terrorism can be an exercise in semantics and is often shaped by subjective political or cultural biases, certain fundamental elements are objective. In comparison, official designations (labels) used to confer special status on captured suspects have become controversial.

After September 11, it became clear to Western experts and the public that official designations and labels of individual suspected terrorists are central legal, political, and security issues. The question of a suspect's official status when he or she is taken prisoner is central. It determines whether certain recognized legal or political protections are or are not observed.

When enemy soldiers are taken prisoner, they are traditionally afforded legal protections as *prisoners of war*. This is well recognized under international law. During the war on terrorism, many suspected terrorists were designated by the United States as *enemy combatants* and were not afforded the same legal status as prisoners of war. Such practices have been hotly debated among proponents and opponents.

According to the protocols of the third Geneva Convention, prisoners who are designated as prisoners of war and who are brought to trial must be afforded the same legal rights in the same courts as soldiers from the country holding them prisoner. Thus, prisoners of war held by the United States would be brought to trial in standard military courts under the Uniform Code of Military Justice and would have the same rights and protections (such as the right to appeal) as all soldiers.

Suspected terrorists have not been designated as prisoners of war. Official and unofficial designations such as enemy combatants, unlawful combatants, and battlefield detainees have been used by American authorities to differentiate them from prisoners of war. The rationale is that suspected terrorists are not soldiers fighting for a sovereign nation and are therefore not eligible for prisoner-of-war status. When hundreds of prisoners were detained by the United States at facilities such as the American base in Guantánamo Bay, Cuba, the United States argued that persons designated as enemy combatants were not subject to the Geneva Convention. Thus, such individuals could be held indefinitely, detained in secret, transferred at will, and sent to allied countries for more coercive interrogations. Under enemy combatant status, conditions of confinement in Guantánamo Bay included open-air cells with wooden roofs and chain-link walls. In theory, each case was to be reviewed by special military tribunals, and innocent prisoners would be reclassified as non–enemy combatants and released. Civil liberties and human rights groups disagreed with the special status conferred by the labeling system on prisoners. They argued that basic legal and humanitarian protections should be granted to prisoners regardless of their designation.

### Extraordinary Renditions

In many ways, the war on terrorism is a "shadow war" that is fought covertly and beyond the attention of the public. It is also a war that employs unconventional tactics and uses resources that were hitherto either uncommon or unacceptable. One unconventional tactic involves rendering, or kidnapping, suspects and transporting them to custodial facilities. This tactic is known as an **"extraordinary rendition"** in the United States and it has been adopted as a method to covertly abduct and detain suspected terrorists or affiliated operatives.

In the United States, extraordinary renditions were initially sanctioned during the Reagan administration in about 1987 as a measure to capture drug traffickers, terrorists, and other wanted persons. It involves an uncomplicated procedure: Find suspects anywhere in the world, seize them, transport them to the United States, and force their appearance before a state or federal court. Such compulsory appearances before U.S. courts (after forcible abductions) have long been accepted as procedurally valid and do not violate constitutional rights. The doctrine that permits these abductions and appearances is an old one, and it has come to be known as the **Ker-Frisbie Rule**.[24]

This practice was significantly expanded after the September 11, 2001, terrorist attacks. It became highly controversial because, unlike previous renditions in which suspects were seized and brought into the U.S. legal system, most antiterrorist abductions placed suspects in covert detention. Many abductions have been carried out by Central Intelligence Agency (CIA) operatives, who transported a number of abductees to allied countries for interrogation. The CIA also established secret detention facilities and maintained custody of suspects for extended periods of time.[25] Allegations have arisen that these suspects were tortured, often alleging the use of the "warterboarding" technique depicted in Figure 14.3.

---

[24]See *Frisbie v. Collins*. 342 U.S. 519, 522 (1954). See also *Ker v. Illinois*. 119 U.S. 436, 444 (1886).

[25]See Whitlock, Craig. "From CIA Jails, Inmates Fade Into Obscurity." *Washington Post*, October 27, 2007.

### Figure 14.3   Waterboarding

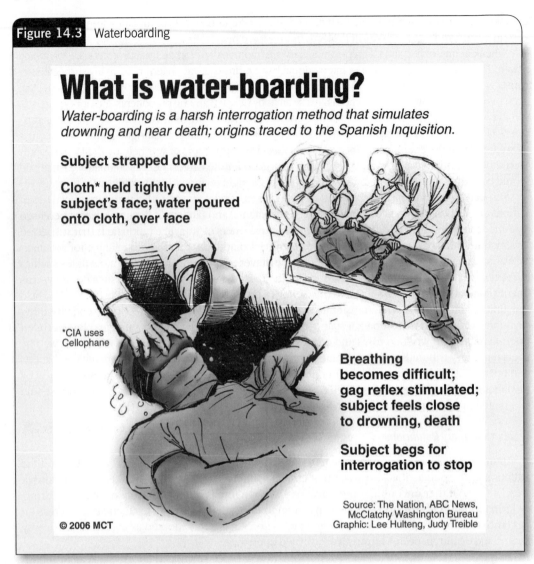

# What is water-boarding?

*Water-boarding is a harsh interrogation method that simulates drowning and near death; origins traced to the Spanish Inquisition.*

**Subject strapped down**

**Cloth\* held tightly over subject's face; water poured onto cloth, over face**

\*CIA uses Cellophane

**Breathing becomes difficult; gag reflex stimulated; subject feels close to drowning, death**

**Subject begs for interrogation to stop**

Source: The Nation, ABC News, McClatchy Washington Bureau
Graphic: Lee Hulteng, Judy Treible

© 2006 MCT

A depiction of the waterboarding procedure. So-designated "enhanced interrogation" methods have been both condemned as unethical torture and supported as a hard necessity in the war on terrorism

❖ **Photo 14.5**

Torture or not? An Iraqi detainee is forced by American captors to stand in a "stress position" in Abu Ghraib prison in Iraq.

www.antiwar.com

Extraordinary renditions are a controversial option. Western governments such as Italy, Sweden, and Germany launched investigations into alleged CIA-coordinated extraordinary renditions from their countries. In June 2005, Italy went so far as to order the arrests of 13 alleged CIA operatives for kidnapping an Egyptian cleric from the streets of Milan.[26]

### The Torture Debate

Few counterterrorist methods garner such passionate debate as the issue of inflicting physical and psychological pressure on terrorist suspects. In the United States, the debate

---

[26]See Wilkinson, Tracy. "Italy Orders Arrest of 13 CIA Operatives." *Los Angeles Times*, June 25, 2005.

was joined in the aftermath of the invasion of Iraq. From October through December 2003, Iraqi detainees held at the U.S.-controlled Abu Ghraib prison near Baghdad were abused by American guards. The abuse included sexual degradation, intimidation with dogs, stripping prisoners naked, forcing them into "human pyramids," and making them stand in extended poses in so-called stress positions. The U.S. Congress and global community became aware of these practices in April 2004 when graphic photographs were published in the media, posted on the Internet, and eventually shown to Congress. Criminal courts-martial were convened, and several guards were convicted and sentenced to prison.

Unfortunately for the United States, not only was its image tarnished, but further revelations about additional incidents raised serious questions about these and other practices. For example, in March 2005, U.S. Army and Navy investigators alleged that 26 prisoners in American custody had possibly been the victims of homicide. A debate about the definition and propriety of torture ensued.

Torture is a practice that is officially eschewed by the United States, both morally and as a legitimate interrogation technique. Morally, such practices are officially held to be inhumane and unacceptable. As an interrogation method, American officials have long argued that torture produces bad intelligence because victims are likely to admit whatever the interrogator wishes to hear. However, during the war on terrorism, a fresh debate began about how to define torture and whether physical and psychological stress methods that fall outside of this definition are acceptable.

Assuming that the application of coercion is justifiable to some degree in order to break the resistance of a suspect, the question becomes whether physical and extreme psychological coercion are also justifiable. For instance, do the following techniques constitute torture?

- Waterboarding, in which prisoners believe that they will drown
- Sexual degradation, whereby prisoners are humiliated by stripping them or forcing them to perform sex acts
- Stress positions, whereby prisoners are forced to pose in painful positions for extended periods
- Creating a chronic state of fear
- Environmental stress, accomplished by adjusting a detention cell's temperature
- Sleep deprivation
- Disorientation about one's whereabouts or the time of day
- Sensory deprivation, such as depriving suspects of sound or light

When images such as those from Abu Ghraib became public, the political consequences were serious. Nevertheless, policy makers continued their debate on which practices constitute torture and whether some circumstances warrant the imposition of as much stress as possible on suspects—up to the brink of torture. In May 2008, the U.S. Department of Justice's inspector general released an extensive report that revealed that FBI agents had complained repeatedly since 2002 about harsh interrogations conducted by military and CIA interrogators.

## Achieving Security

### Government Responses

Homeland security experts must concentrate on achieving several counterterrorist objectives. These objectives can realistically only minimize rather than eliminate terrorist threats, but they must be actively pursued. Objectives include the following:

- Disrupting and preventing domestic terrorist conspiracies from operationalizing their plans
- Deterring would-be activists from crossing the line between extremist activism and political violence

- Implementing laws and task forces to create a cooperative counterterrorist environment
- Minimizing physical destruction and human casualties

It is clear that no single model or method for achieving security will apply across different scenarios or terrorist environments. Because of this reality, the process for projecting counterterrorist models must include a longitudinal framework based on both theory and practical necessity. The *theoretical* models used must reflect respect for human rights protections and balance this against options that may include the use of force and law enforcement. The *practicality* of these models requires them to be continually updated and adapted to emerging terrorist threats. With these adaptations, perhaps terrorism can be controlled to some degree by keeping extremists and violent dissidents off balance—thereby preventing them from having an unobstructed hand in planning and carrying out attacks or other types of political violence.

Assuming that homeland security policy makers grasp the constitutional and practical parameters of counterterrorist options, it is clear that there must be a balance between coercive methods and preventive options. The latter options may provide long-term solutions to future extremism and terrorism. If skillfully applied, adaptations of these options present potential (or actual) domestic extremists with options other than political violence. This would also have the effect of protecting civil liberties.

### Countering Extremism Through Reform

Extremist ideologies and beliefs are the fertile soil for politically violent behavior. Ethnocentrism, nationalism, ideological intolerance, racism, and religious fanaticism are core motivations for terrorism. History has shown that coercive measures used to counter these tendencies are often only marginally successful. The reason is uncomplicated: A great deal of extremist behavior is rooted in passionate ideas, recent historical memories of conflict, and cultural tensions. It is difficult to forcibly reverse these tendencies, and although coercion can eliminate cadres and destroy extremist organizations, sheer repression is a risky long-term solution. Because extremism has historically originated primarily from domestic conflict (sometimes from national traumas such as invasions), efforts to counter domestic extremism must incorporate societal and cultural responses. A central factor is that new societal and cultural norms often reflect demographic changes and political shifts. Dissent can certainly be repressed, but it is rarely a long-term solution absent preventive measures such as social reforms, political inclusion, and protecting constitutional rights.

The United States is a good subject for evaluating these concepts. In the aftermath of the political turmoil of the 1960s and 1970s, the United States underwent a slow cultural and ideological shift that began to promote concepts such as *multiculturalism* and *diversity*. These concepts were adaptations to the fact that the United States has gradually become a country in which no single demographic group will be a majority of the population in the near future, probably by the mid–21st century. This is a significant shift from the "melting pot" ideology of previous generations, when new immigrants, racial minorities, and religious minorities were expected to accept the cultural values of the American mainstream.

In the United Kingdom, the United States, and elsewhere, grassroots efforts to promote inclusion became common features of the social and political environment (although not without political opposition). For example, private "watchdog" organizations monitor extremist tendencies such as right-wing and neofascist movements. Some of these organizations, such as the Southern Poverty Law Center and the Anti-Defamation League in the United States, have implemented programs to promote community inclusiveness. In the public sector, government agencies have long been required to monitor and promote inclusion of demographic minorities and women in government-funded programs. Also in the public sector, the trend among local police forces shifted toward practicing variants of community-oriented policing, which in practice means that the police operationally integrate themselves as much as possible within local communities.

The theoretical outcome of these cultural tendencies would be an erosion of the root causes for extremist sentiment.

# Chapter Summary

This chapter discussed homeland security within the contexts of its conceptual foundation, the need to reorganize security and law enforcement agencies in the aftermath of the September 11 attacks, the homeland security bureaucracy in the United States, the role of intelligence agencies and special operations forces, and the problem of balancing civil liberties and domestic security during periods of crisis.

Because of revelations about bureaucratic inefficiency in the aftermath of the September 11 attacks, the United States implemented a restructuring of its homeland security community. When examining homeland security agencies and missions, it is important to consider that they operate within the context of counterterrorist and antiterrorist options. Many federal agencies are participants in the overall homeland security network, with the Department of Homeland Security the largest and most mission diverse of them all. Intelligence agencies and the military perform a critical international role that helps to secure the domestic homeland security environment. The intersection of their missions with those of domestic agencies creates a large and intricate establishment for combating terrorism domestically and internationally.

There is often a natural tension between preserving human rights and securing the homeland. This tension is reflected in political and philosophical debates about how to accomplish both goals. Nevertheless, during historical periods when threats to national security existed, sweeping measures were undertaken as a matter of perceived necessity. The implementation of these measures was often politically popular at the time but questioned in later years. The modern homeland security environment exists because of the attacks of September 11, 2001, and has resulted in the creation of bureaucracies, the passage of new security-related laws, and the implementation of controversial counterterrorist measures.

An underlying theme throughout this discussion has been that homeland security is an evolving concept. Organizational cooperation and coordination are certainly desirable, but it must be remembered that these can only occur if political and policy responses are able to adapt to changes in the terrorist environment. Homeland security in the post–September 11 era has adapted to new and emerging threats. These threats reflect the creativity and determination of those who wage terrorist campaigns against the United States and its allies. Disruption of terrorist operations requires broad cooperation and commitment to protecting the homeland from these adversaries.

# Key Terms and Concepts

The following topics were discussed in this chapter and can be found in the glossary:

Abu Hafs al-Masri Brigades

antiterrorism

Anti-Terrorism and Effective Death Penalty Act

bureaucracy

Central Intelligence Agency (CIA)

criminal profiles

Defense Intelligence Agency (DIA)

Department of Homeland Security

Department of Homeland Security Act of 2002

Diplock Courts

Diplomatic Security Service

Executive Order 13228

"extraordinary rendition"

Federal Bureau of Investigation (FBI)

Guildford Four

homeland security

intelligence community

Ker-Frisbie Rule

McCarthyism

Moussaoui, Zacarias

National Counterterrorism Center (NCTC)

National Security Agency (NSA)

Northern Ireland Act

Operation Death Trains

Operation Iraqi Freedom

organizational theory

Palmer, A. Mitchell

PRISM

racial profiling

"Red Scares"

Rewards for Justice Program

Snowden, Eric

supergrass

Tempora

terrorist profile

USA PATRIOT Act

USA PATRIOT Improvement and Reauthorization Act

Weber, Max

XKeyscore

## Discussion Box : After the Next 9/11

*This chapter's Discussion Box is intended to stimulate critical debate about the aftermath of another catastrophic terrorist attack on the American homeland.*

The September 11, 2001, attacks on the U.S. homeland produced the most sweeping reorganization of the American security culture in history. The fear that arose following the attacks was matched by concerns that the United States was ill prepared to prevent or adequately respond to determined terrorists. Homeland security became a part of everyday life and culture because of 9/11. Although some degree of terrorist violence is likely to occur domestically, the possibility of another catastrophic attack leaves open the question of what impact such an event would have on society.

### Discussion Questions

1. How serious is the threat of catastrophic terrorism?

2. Can catastrophic attacks be prevented?

3. How would a catastrophic terrorist attack affect American homeland security culture?

4. How will society in general be affected by a catastrophic attack?

5. What is the likelihood that homeland security authority will be expanded in the future?

## On Your Own

The open-access Student Study Site at **http://study.sagepub.com/martin5e** has a variety of useful study aids, including eFlashcards, quizzes, audio resources, and journal articles. The websites, exercises, and recommended readings listed below are easily accessed on this site as well.

# Recommended Websites

The following websites provide information about civil liberties and human rights:

American Civil Liberties Union: http://www.aclu.org/

Central Intelligence Agency: https://www.cia.gov/

Department of Agriculture: http://www.usda.gov/

Department of Defense: http://www.defense.gov/

Department of Energy: http://www.energy.gov/

Department of Health and Human Services: http://www.hhs.gov/

Department of Homeland Security: http://www.dhs.gov/index.shtm

Department of the Interior: http://www.doi.gov/

Department of the Treasury: http://www.ustreas.gov/

Diplomatic Security Service, Rewards for Justice: http://www.rewardsforjustice.net/

Environmental Protection Agency: http://www.epa.gov/

Office of Counterterrorism, U.S. Department of State: http://www.state.gov/s/ct/

Office of the Director of National Intelligence: http://www.dni.gov/

United Nations International Court of Justice: http://www.icj-cij.org/

# Web Exercise

Using this chapter's recommended websites, conduct an online investigation of the missions of homeland security agencies and organizations. Compare and contrast these agencies' organizations.

1. What are the primary missions of these organizations?
2. How would you describe the differences between sector-specific agencies?
3. In your opinion, are any of these organizations more effective than other organizations? Less effective?

For an online search of research and monitoring organizations, readers should activate the search engine on their Web browser and enter the following keywords:

"Homeland Security Agencies"

"Homeland Security Threats"

# Recommended Readings

The following publications are good analyses of the concept of homeland security and the homeland security bureaucracy:

Aronowitz, Stanley, and Heather Gautney, eds. *Implicating Empire: Globalization and Resistance in the 21st Century World Order*. New York: Basic Books, 2003.

Beckman, James. *Comparative Legal Approaches to Homeland Security and Anti-Terrorism*. Aldershot, UK: Ashgate, 2007.

Booth, Ken, and Tim Dunne, eds. *Worlds in Collision: Terror and the Future of Global Order*. New York: Palgrave MacMillan, 2002.

Borrelli, J. V. *Bioterrorism: Prevention, Preparedness, and Protection*. New York: Nova Science Publishers, 2007.

Clark, Robert M. *Intelligence Collection*. Washington, DC: CQ Press, 2014.

Coen, Bob, and Eric Nadler. *Dead Silence: Fear and Terror on the Anthrax Trail*. Berkeley, CA: Counterpoint, 2009.

CQ Researcher. *Issues in Terrorism and Homeland Security: Selections From CQ Researcher*. 2nd ed. Washington, DC: CQ Press, 2011.

Elias, Bartholomew. *Airport and Aviation Security: U.S. Policy and Strategy in the Age of Global Terrorism*. Boca Raton, FL: Auerbach Publications/Taylor & Francis, 2010.

Graff, Garrett M. *The Threat Matrix: The FBI at War in the Age of Global Terror*. New York: Little, Brown, 2011.

Kamien, David G. *The McGraw-Hill Homeland Security Handbook*. New York: McGraw-Hill, 2006.

Monje, Scott C. *The Central Intelligence Agency: A Documentary History*. Westport, CT: Greenwood, 2008.

Purpura, Philip P. *Terrorism and Homeland Security: An Introduction With Applications*. New York: Butterworth-Heinemann, 2007.

Pushies, Fred J. *Deadly Blue: Battle Stories of the U.S. Air Force Special Operations Command*. New York: American Management Association, 2009.

Sauter, Mark A., and James Jay Carafano. *Homeland Security: A Complete Guide to Understanding, Preventing, and Surviving Terrorism*. New York: McGraw-Hill, 2005.

Schawb, Stephen Irving Max. *Guantánamo, USA: The Untold History of America's Cuban Outpost*. Lawrence: University Press of Kansas, 2009.

Smith, Cary Stacy. *The Patriot Act: Issues and Controversies*. Springfield, IL: Charles C. Thomas, 2010.

Tsang, Steve. *Intelligence and Human Rights in the Era of Global Terrorism*. Westport, CT: Praeger Security International, 2007.

Walker, Clive. *The Law and Terrorism*. Oxford, UK: Oxford University Press, 2011.

Wilson, Richard Ashby, ed. *Human Rights in the War on Terror*. New York: Cambridge University Press, 2005.

Worthington, Andy. *The Guantánamo Files*. Ann Arbor, MI: Pluto Press, 2007.

# What Next?

## The Future of Terrorism

## CHAPTER 15

## OPENING VIEWPOINT: CARNIVORE

In July 2000, it was widely reported that the FBI possessed a surveillance system that could monitor Internet communications. Called **Carnivore**, the system was said to be able to read Internet traffic moving through cooperating Internet service providers. All that was required was for Carnivore to be installed on an Internet provider's network at its facilities. Under law, the FBI could not use Carnivore without a specific court order under specific guidelines, much like other criminal surveillance orders.

The FBI received a great deal of negative publicity, especially after it was reported that the agency had evaded demands for documents under a Freedom of Information Act (FOIA) request filed by the Electronic Privacy Information Center (EPIC), a privacy rights group. Concern was also raised by critics when it was reported in November 2000 that Carnivore had been very successfully tested and that it had exceeded expectations. This report was not entirely accurate. In fact, Carnivore did not operate properly when it was used in March 2000 to monitor a criminal suspect's e-mail; it had inadvertently intercepted the e-mail of innocent Internet users. This glitch embarrassed the Department of Justice (DOJ) and angered the DOJ's Office of Intelligence Policy and Review.

By early 2001, the FBI gave Carnivore a less ominous-sounding new name, re-designating the system DCS-1000. Despite the political row, which continued well into 2002 (in part because of the continued FOIA litigation), Carnivore was cited as a potentially powerful tool in the new war on terrorism. The use of DCS-1000 after 2003 was apparently reduced markedly, allegedly because Internet surveillance was outsourced to private companies' tools. The program reportedly ended in 2005 because of the prevalence of significantly improved surveillance software.

**R**eaders have been provided with a great deal of information about the causes of terrorism, the motives behind political violence, terrorist environments, and counterterrorist responses. Many examples of postwar terrorist movements and environments were presented to illustrate theoretical concepts and trends. The discussion in this chapter synthesizes many of these concepts and trends, and it projects emerging trends that are likely to characterize terrorist environments in the near future.

There is one concept that must be understood at the outset: Projecting future trends is not synonymous with predicting specific events, and the two should be differentiated as follows:

- *Projections* involve theoretical constructs of trends based on available data.
- *Predictions* are practical applications of data (that is, intelligence) to anticipate specific behaviors by extremists.

❖ **Photo 15.1**

A U.S. Marine fights to pacify an insurgent stronghold in the city of Fallujah, Iraq.

U.S. Department of Defense

Predicting terrorist threats is the rather difficult work of intelligence agencies. Making accurate predictions is problematic because most uncovered threats involve generalized rather than specific forewarnings. Thus, intelligence agencies can learn about real threats to specific interests or in specific cities, but they often do not have details about the timing or location of attacks. For example, the U.S. Department of Justice issued many threat warnings after the September 11, 2001, attacks, but very few described specific threats against specific targets.

One must develop a logical longitudinal framework to evaluate the future of political violence. A *longitudinal framework* uses past history, trends, and cycles to project future trends. It allows scholars, students, and practitioners to "stand back" from immediate crises and contemporary terrorist environments to try to construct a reasonable picture of the near future. These projections must be made with the understanding that the more near-term a forecast is, the more likely it is to be a realistic projection. Conversely, far-term forecasts are less likely to be realistic because projections must be consistently updated using contemporary data.

The discussion in this chapter will review the future of political violence from the following perspectives:

- An Overview of Near-Term Projections
- The Future of Terrorism: New Threats
- Controlling Terrorism: New Challenges
- Threats to the Homeland: Prospects for Terrorism in the United States

## ❖ An Overview of Near-Term Projections

Professor David C. Rapoport designed a theory that holds that modern terrorism has progressed through three cycles or "waves" that lasted for roughly 40 years each and that we now live in a fourth wave. His four waves are as follows:[1]

- The Anarchist wave: 1880s to the end of World War I
- The Anticolonial wave: end of World War I to the late 1960s

---

[1]See Ehrman, Mark. "Terrorism From a Scholarly Perspective." *Los Angeles Times Magazine,* May 4, 2003.

- The New Left wave: late 1960s to the near present
- The Religious wave: about 1980 until the present

If Professor Rapoport's theory is correct, the current terrorist environment will be characterized by the New Terrorism for the immediate future. Having made this observation, it can also be argued that the sources of extremist behavior in the modern era will generally remain unchanged in the near future. The modern era of terrorism will likely continue to occur for the following reasons:

- People who have been relegated to the social and political margins—or who perceive that they have been so relegated—often form factions that resort to violence.
- Movements and nations sometimes adopt religious or ethnonational supremacist doctrines that they use to justify aggressive political behavior.
- Many states continue to value the "utility" of domestic and foreign terrorism.

These factors are not, of course, the only sources of terrorism and extremist sentiment, but they are certainly among the most enduring ones. These enduring sources have precipitated new trends in terrorist behavior that began to spread during the 1990s, and continued well into the 2000s and 2010s. These new trends include the following:

- Increasing use of communications and information technologies by extremists
- Adaptations of cell-based organizational and operational strategies by global revolutionary movements
- The use of relatively low-tech improvised tactics such as suicide bombers
- Efforts to construct or obtain relatively high-tech weapons of mass destruction or, alternatively, to convert existing technologies into high-yield weapons

**Figure 15.1** | Tactics Used in Terrorist Attacks in the United States, 1970–2011

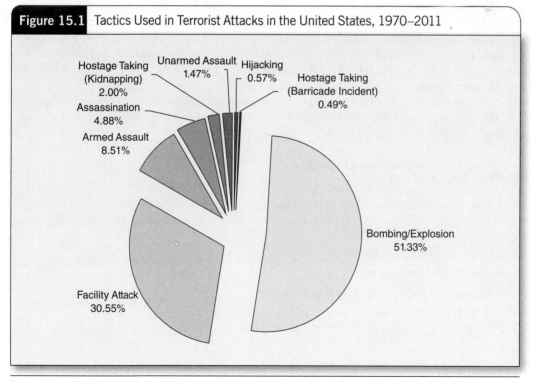

Source: Plumer, Brad. "Eight Facts About Terrorism in the United States." *Washington Post,* April 16, 2013.

## Terrorism by States and Dissidents

The death of Osama bin Laden in May 2011 was a victory in the war on terrorism, but dissident terrorism will continue to be a problem as long as violent dissidents find safe haven in supportive environments such as in Pakistan's semi-autonomous regions, Islamist insurgent strongholds in regions such as Yemen and East and West Africa, and ethnonational regions such as Gaza and the West Bank during Palestinian *intifada*s. There is also a distinct probability that stateless revolutionaries and other independent internationalist movements will continue to engage in terrorist violence on behalf of a variety of vague causes, such as Al-Qa'ida–inspired religious terrorism. Terrorism will also be used as a violent option in countries in which ethnonational and religious conflicts remain unresolved.

State terrorism is always a possibility when regimes are threatened from within by dissident movements or from without by perceived adversaries, or when regimes conclude that their foreign policy will benefit from covert aggression. Authoritarian regimes have historically emphasized the maintenance of order over human rights, and this is unlikely to change in the near future. The use of proxies is likely to continue in areas where states believe that they can destabilize neighboring rivals, such as in the Middle East and along the India–Pakistan border region. One issue that became prominent during the 2000s was nuclear proliferation among activist or authoritarian regimes. The West became particularly concerned about nuclear weapons development in Iran and North Korea, especially after Iran aggressively pursued a nuclear enrichment program. North Korea made an unverified claim in February 2005 that it had manufactured nuclear weapons,[2] and subsequently conducted several tests of ballistic missiles. In the near future, states will continue to conclude that domestic or foreign terrorism serves their interests.

Nevertheless, counterpoints exist to the continuation of dissident political violence in the near future. First, the 2011 Arab Spring uprisings demonstrated that one counterpoint is that support for— and the momentum of—domestic terrorist movements can be undercut by genuine social reform. Early examples of post–Arab Spring reforms suggested that reforms may reduce and possibly end political violence, as long as they are pursued with determination despite setbacks and sabotage. However, subsequent political divisions and Islamist ascension challenged this potential outcome. A second counterpoint is the utility of international counterterrorist cooperation. Several terrorist conspiracies were thwarted in the Middle East and Europe—and a number of terrorists were captured or kept on the run—as a direct result of cooperation among intelligence, law enforcement, and security agencies. A third counterpoint is that there is no single binding or common ideological foundation for political violence. Unlike during the heyday of ideological terrorism, there is no modern equivalent to revolutionary Marxism. Religious extremism is self-isolating, and there is no longer an international "solidarity movement" in the West for ethnonationalist (or religious) violence. It remains to be seen what the long-term impact will be on religious terrorist violence, but it is unlikely that there will be an ideological "glue" to bind together extremist sentiment in the near future.

## Whither the "Old Terrorism"?

The "old terrorism" was characterized by the terrorist environments, organizational profiles, and tactics developed during the postwar era. These characteristics included the following commonalities:

- Leftist ethnonationalist motives
- Leftist ideological motives
- Surgical and symbolic selection of targets
- Deliberate media manipulation and publicized incidents
- Relatively low casualty rates

---

[2]See Faiola, Anthony. "N. Korea Says It Has Manufactured Nuclear Weapons." *Washington Post,* February 10, 2005.

- Identifiable organizational profile
- Hierarchical organizational profile
- Full-time professional cadres

Although this model of terrorism did not become a relic of the past during the 1990s, it ceased to be the primary model for terrorist movements and environments in the 2000s. The relatively clear objectives and motives of the old terrorism certainly continued to fuel many conflicts, but many modern terrorists began to promote vaguely articulated objectives and motives. The new terrorists also became cell-based, stateless revolutionaries, unlike earlier terrorists, who tended to organize themselves hierarchically and had state sponsors. Even though the number of international incidents declined during the era of the New Terrorism, the casualty rates were higher in comparison with the past. This is not to say that the old terrorism has disappeared from the world scene or will do so in the near future. It will continue alongside a growing—and more aggressive—threat from the New Terrorism.

Table 15.1 compares several key characteristics of the old and new terrorism.

| Table 15.1 | Supplanting the Old With the New |
| --- | --- |

The "old" terrorism was, in many ways, symmetrical and predictable. It was not characterized by terrorist environments exhibiting massive casualty rates or indiscriminate attacks. Its organizational profile was also characterized by traditional organizational configurations.

The following table contrasts selected attributes of the activity profiles for the "old" terrorism and the New Terrorism.

| Terrorist Environment | Activity Profile | | | | |
| --- | --- | --- | --- | --- | --- |
| | Target Selection | Casualty Rates | Organizational Profile | Tactical/ Weapons Selection | Typical Motives |
| **"Old" terrorism** | Surgical and symbolic | Low and selective | Hierarchical and identifiable | Conventional and low to medium yield | Leftist and ethnocentric |
| **New Terrorism** | Indiscriminate and symbolic | High and indiscriminate | Cellular | Unconventional and high yield | Sectarian |

# ❖ The Future of Terrorism: New Threats

Despite hopeful examples such as the 2011 Arab Spring, traditional sources of extremist behavior have not been eliminated and will not be in the near future. As in the recent past, intense expressions of intolerance and resentment are likely to motivate many extremists to blame entire systems, societies, and groups of people for their problems. Under these conditions, political violence will continue to be seen by many people as a justifiable option. The likelihood of political violence will remain high as long as intolerance and blaming are motivated by passionate feelings of national identity, racial supremacy, religious dogma, or ideological beliefs. Both state and dissident terrorists will continue to exploit these tendencies for their own purposes.

Many characteristics of terrorism from the past will remain relevant well beyond the immediate future. For example, it is likely that future terrorism will exhibit the same moralist characteristics discussed in previous chapters. At the core of terrorist moralism are conceptual perspectives, which are summed up by the following familiar axioms:

- "One person's terrorist is another person's freedom fighter." (Unknown)
- "One man willing to throw away his life is enough to terrorize a thousand." (Wu Ch'i)
- "Extremism in defense of liberty is no vice." (Senator Barry Goldwater)
- "It became necessary to destroy the town to save it." (allegedly an American officer in Vietnam)

These perspectives, as well as other behavioral attributes such as codes of self-sacrifice, are central and enduring features of modern terrorism.

## Terrorist Environments in the 21st Century

### State-Sponsored Terrorism

State-sponsored terrorism will not soon disappear and will remain a feature of future terrorist environments. Authoritarian states will continue to use terrorism as domestic policy, and aggressive states will continue to foment acts of international terrorism as foreign policy. Domestically, political repression is—and long has been—a common practice by regimes more interested in protecting the authority of the state than in human rights.

❖ **Photo 15.2**

Pakistani demonstrators burn United States flags.

Mazhar Abid/Gamma-Rapho/Getty Images

Domestically, the old instruments of repression will continue to be common tools of authoritarian government. These instruments include security institutions such as police, military, and paramilitary forces. One should expect the pervasiveness of security institutions to be augmented by the continued improvement of surveillance and communications technologies. One should also expect that some of the world's more ruthless regimes will occasionally deploy weapons of mass destruction against dissident ethnonational groups, as the regime of Saddam Hussein did against Iraqi Kurds and the regime of Bashar Al-Assad did against civilian opponents.

Internationally, aggressive regimes in the postwar era frequently supported sympathetic proxies to indirectly confront their adversaries. This practice was often a safe and low-cost alternative to overt conflict. It is reasonable to assume that some regimes will continue this practice in the near future, especially in regions where highly active proxies have the opportunity to severely press their sponsoring regime's rivals. For example, in early 2002, a ship bearing Iranian arms was intercepted by Israeli security forces before it could offload the arms. The weapons, which were bound for Palestinian nationalist fighters, were almost certainly part of a proxy operation by the Iranian government.

❖ **Photo 15.3**

Photographs that shocked the world. An American soldier pulls an Iraqi detainee with a leash in Abu Ghraib prison in Baghdad in late 2003. Such images served to rally opposition to the U.S.-led occupation.

www.antiwar.com

### Dissident Terrorism

Patterns of dissident terrorism during the 1990s and 2000s were decreasingly ideological and increasingly "cultural." Ethnonationalist terrorism continued to occur on a sometimes grand scale, and religious terrorism spread among radical Islamist groups. In addition, stateless international terrorism began to emerge as the predominant model in the global arena. These trends are likely to continue, as vestiges of the East–West ideological competition give way to patterns of religious extremism and seemingly interminable communal conflicts. This "clash of civilizations" scenario has been extensively debated since it was theorized by Professor Samuel Huntington.[3]

---

[3]Huntington, Samuel P. *The Clash of Civilizations and the Remaking of World Order.* New York: Touchstone, 1996.

### Religious Terrorism

The death of Osama bin Laden did not signal the end of the modern terrorist environment, and terrorism motivated by religion continues to be a global problem. Religious terrorism spread during the 1980s and grew to challenge international and domestic political stability during the 1990s, and well into the 2000s. The frequency of and casualties from sectarian attacks grew quickly during this period. Religious terrorists also became adept at recruiting new members and organizing themselves as semi-autonomous cells across national boundaries.

The trends that developed toward the end of the 20th century suggest that religious violence will continue to be a central aspect of terrorism in the 21st century. *Internationally,* religious terrorists of many nationalities have consistently attacked targets that symbolize enemy interests. Unlike the relatively surgical strikes of secular leftists in previous years, religious terrorists such as ISIS and others have proven to be particularly homicidal. For example, Al-Qa'ida was responsible in April 2002 for the explosion of a fuel tanker truck at a synagogue in Tunisia, killing 17 people—12 of them German tourists. This kind of lethality is now a central element of international religious terrorism. *Domestically,* terrorist movements in Pakistan, Israel, Malaysia, the Philippines, and elsewhere have actively sought to overthrow or destabilize their governments and damage symbols representing foreign interests. For example, Western civilians were taken as hostages by radical Islamist antigovernment Abu Sayyaf terrorists in the Philippines during 2001 and 2002 as a calculated—and successful—tactic to garner international attention.

### Ideological Terrorism

Few ideologically motivated insurgencies survived into the new millennium, primarily because most ideological terrorist environments and wars of national liberation were resolved during the 1980s and 1990s. Nevertheless, a few Marxist insurgencies persisted during the 2000s, and Western democracies witnessed the growth of newly activist neofascist and anarchistic movements. Violence from neofascists tended to consist of relatively low-intensity hate crimes, mob brawls, and occasional low-yield bombings. Violence from the new anarchists usually involved brawls with the police at international conferences or occasional confrontations with racist skinheads. Right-wing movements and groups are likely to persist and grow in the near term. With the growth of aboveground neofascist parties in Europe, they could become a vanguard or "armed wing" of a renewed fascist movement.

### Criminal Dissident Terrorism

Traditional criminal enterprises such as the Russian Mafia, La Cosa Nostra, Sicilian Mafia, Colombian gangs, and Mexican drug cartels will continue to ply their trades as long as there is a market for their services. Drugs, arms, and other goods will be illegally transported and sold in the international market regardless of attempts by governments to suppress these transactions. Because of the versatility of these enterprises, it is unlikely that there will soon be an end to criminal dissident terrorist violence directed against law enforcement personnel who challenge them.

Terrorist violence from criminal-political enterprises is also unlikely to end in the near future. With the reduction in support from sympathetic states and the concomitant viability of the drug trade, it is quite possible that more extremist movements will attempt to become self-sustaining through transnational crime. For example, during the 1990s and early 2000s, Colombian, Southeast Asian, and South Asian groups continued to involve themselves in the opium-heroin trade and, to a lesser degree, the arms trade. Thus, it is logical to presume that past trends linking political extremism to transnational crime will continue for the foreseeable future.

## The World in Conflict: Future Sources of Terrorism

During the 20th century, seemingly unmanageable regional and internal conflicts raged for years and often decades before the warring parties made peace with one another. An enormous amount of carnage occurred during communal conflicts, and millions of people died. Terrorism on a massive scale was not uncommon during this period. It was also during this period that high-profile acts of international terrorism became a familiar feature of the international political environment.

During the 1990s and 2000s, contending nations and communities continued to engage in significant levels of violence. Terrorism and violent repression were used by many adversaries, who claimed them as necessary methodologies to resolve the problems of their political environments. This trend is unlikely to abate in the near future, and it is reasonable to project that some conflicts may increase in intensity.

The following cases are projected sources and targets of terrorist violence in the near future.

### The Middle East

The 2011 Arab Spring demonstrations revealed widespread popular dissatisfaction with long-standing authoritarian regimes. Whether such dissatisfaction will produce long-term stability is an open question because several of the uprisings led to chronic discord, primarily in Syria, Libya, and Egypt. Political, religious, and ethnonationalist conflicts continued to be endemic to the Middle East after decades of instability. Many of these conflicts are long-standing and seemingly intractable, at least for the near future. Fundamentalist movements have captured the imaginations of many young Arabs who have become disenchanted with the perceived failures of Arab nationalism and socialism. Large numbers of foreign fighters found their call to action after the U.S.-led invasion of Iraq and rallied to the side of the Iraqi insurgents, and foreign volunteers continued to travel to Iraq after the Western withdrawal. This trend continued in Syria, where foreign fighters included volunteers from Western nations. As a result, many international targets were attacked throughout the Middle East, a trend that will likely continue. For example, in August 2003, Iraqi insurgents bombed the United Nations headquarters in Iraq, killing UN High Commissioner for Human Rights Sérgio Vieira de Mello. Religious tensions between Shi'a and Sunni Muslims also increased after sectarian violence erupted in Iraq and Syria. At the same time, Al-Qa'ida morphed into a model for other Islamists, including insurgents in Africa, a phenomenon that is likely to continue to be replicated by other movements and cells. In a sense, the *organization* of Al-Qa'ida has become an *ideology* of Al-Qa'ida. Al-Qa'ida's evolution engendered new Islamist movements and organizations that proved to be extremely proficient in recruiting dedicated fighters, funding their cause, and effectively waging war. The Islamic State of Iraq and the Levant is typical of this new generation of Islamist insurgencies.

### Palestine and Israel

Palestinian nationalism entered its second generation during the first *intifada,* which became a war fought by young gunmen, terrorists, and suicide bombers who grew up amid the turmoil of the 1960s, 1970s, and 1980s. Black September, the Palestine Liberation Organization's (PLO's) expulsion from Lebanon, the airline hijackings, and many other incidents occurred when members of the new generation were children and teenagers. The new generation unhesitatingly began a new round of violence against Israel, one that was to prove more lethal and more pervasive.

Aside from violence growing out of the first *intifada,* the state of Israel has long been a unifying target for secular nationalists and religious extremists throughout the Middle East. Extremist movements and regimes have used the existence of Israel to attract and motivate prospective supporters. This pattern continued into the era of the New Terrorism, and with a new generation born in the 1990s, as radical Islamist movements cited Western support for Israel as a rallying issue. For example, Osama bin Laden's initial grievances were the supposed "desecrations" of Islam's holy sites by the Saudi government and the deployment of foreign troops to Saudi Arabia. His symbolic concepts of Christian "Crusaderism" and the royal Saud family as enemies were later augmented by a newly professed concern for the plight of the Palestinians. Thus, Al-Qa'ida found common cause with Hamas, Hezbollah, Iran, and other movements and countries that considered Israel to be an implacable enemy.

### Latin America

Most of the communal and ideological conflicts in Central and South America were resolved by the late 1990s. Violent leftist dissidents and repressive rightist regimes were no longer prominent features of the Latin American political environment. However, some conflicts remained unresolved in the early 2000s. The worst scenario for near-term terrorism is found in Colombia, where a weak central government has long exercised minimal control over a society beset by leftist rebels, rightist paramilitaries, and unchecked *narcotraficantes*. In Peru, the Marxist Tupac Amaru Revolutionary Movement (MRTA) and Shining Path were largely dismantled by the early 2000s, but some vestiges of these groups continued to engage in low-intensity political violence. Aside from these pockets of political violence, near-term *indigenous* terrorist violence (as opposed to *international* threats) will likely be sporadic and on a lower scale of intensity than during the period from the end of World War II to the early 1990s.

### Europe

International terrorists have long used Europe as a battleground, as proven by the attacks in Madrid on March 11, 2004, and London on July 7, 2005. This is unlikely to change, particularly in light of the discovery of Islamist cells and arrests of suspected Al-Qa'ida operatives in several Western European countries. European volunteers have also been recruited to fight with Islamist insurgencies in Syria, Iraq, and elsewhere.

Domestically, there is a possibility that followers of neofascist movements may target immigrant workers or other people they define as undesirables. There are also pockets of ethnonationalist conflict remaining in Spain and the United Kingdom, although there is virtually no likelihood that these conflicts will escalate. The Balkans remains the most unstable region in Europe, and sporadic violence is likely to occur from time to time. However, the large-scale communal conflicts and genocidal behavior that resulted from the breakup of Yugoslavia have been suppressed by North Atlantic Treaty Organization (NATO) and UN intervention. Russia's conflict in Chechnya will continue to be a source of terrorism, as well as a possible source of radical Islamist activism.

### Africa

Ethnonational communal conflict has been a recurring feature in Africa. In East Africa, periodic outbreaks of ethnonational violence have claimed hundreds of thousands of lives. Similar outbreaks have occurred in West Africa.

Another pattern of conflict in sub-Saharan Africa has been the use of state-sponsored domestic terrorism by authoritarian regimes to suppress dissident ethnonationalist and political sentiment. Some internal conflicts—such as in Sudan, Somalia, Liberia, and Sierra Leone—are likely to flare up periodically in the near future. These conflicts have been characterized by many examples of terrorism on a large scale.

In North Africa, radical Islamist movements have proven themselves motivated to commit acts of terrorism, and they are very capable of doing so. Algerian, Moroccan, and Egyptian affiliates of Al-Qa'ida and other fundamentalist movements have attacked foreign interests, religious sites, and government officials as part of a vaguely defined international *jihad*. Armed Islamist movements such as Boko Haram in Nigeria pose a particularly troublesome model for future Islamist insurgencies. Libya, a former sponsor of international terrorism, is unlikely to become a reinvigorated state sponsor of terrorism, but Islamist insurgents will challenge the stability of the North African nation.

### Asia

Past patterns of ethnonational conflict and domestic terrorism suggest that some Asian nations and regions will continue to experience outbreaks of political violence. These outbreaks are likely to range from small-scale attacks to large-scale conflicts. Ethnonational groups continue to wage war in Sri Lanka, Kashmir, the Caucasus, and elsewhere. Terrorism is an accepted method of armed conflict among many of these groups. Ideological rebellions are less common than during the postwar era, but pockets of Marxist rebellion are still to be found, such as in Nepal and the Philippines. These leftist remnants have occasionally used terrorist tactics rather effectively. Radical Islamist movements, inspired in part by Al-Qa'ida internationalism, have appeared in several Asian countries, including Indonesia, the Philippines, Malaysia, India, Pakistan, and the Central Asian republics. Some of these movements have demonstrated their willingness to engage in terrorism.

Typical of the remnant ideological movements in Asia is the **New People's Army (NPA),** a Marxist guerrilla group in the Philippines that was founded in 1969.[4] Its ideology is Maoist, and its strategy has been to wage a protracted guerrilla insurgency from the countryside with the goal of overthrowing the government and building a communist society. It engages in urban terrorism, such as bombings, shootings, extortion, and assassinations. The NPA has approximately 6,000 to 8,000 fighters and targets Filipino security forces.

### Case in Point: The United States and the West

During the Cold War, the United States and its Western allies were frequent targets of leftist terrorism. The reasons for this were rather uncomplicated: In the ideological conflict between the Marxist East and democratic West, as well as in the anticolonial wars of national liberation, revolutionaries associated the West with repression and exploitation. In the modern era, the United States and the West have become targets of the practitioners of the New Terrorism. International terrorists still associate them with international exploitation, but they add other dimensions to

---

**Table 15.2**    A World Still in Conflict: Projected Sources of Political Violence

Regional and domestic conflicts are certain to engender terrorist movements in the near future. Some of these conflicts are long-term disputes that have been ongoing for decades and that are often characterized by international spillovers.

    The following table summarizes several long-term conflicts that have increased and diminished in scale and intensity during decades of confrontation.

| Conflict | Activity Profile | | |
| --- | --- | --- | --- |
| | *Opposing Parties* | *Contending Issues* | *Duration* |
| ***Palestinians/Israelis*** | Palestinian nationalists, Palestinian fundamentalists, Israelis | Palestinian state, Israeli security | Decades, from late 1940s and Israeli Independence |
| ***Northern Ireland*** | Catholic Unionists, Protestant Loyalists, British administration | Union with Irish Republic, loyalty to United Kingdom | Decades, from late 1960s and first Provo campaign |
| ***India/Pakistan*** | Kashmiri *jihadis*, India, Pakistan | Status of Kashmir, *jihadi* terrorism, border disputes | Decades, from late 1940s and end of British Empire |
| ***Colombia*** | Marxist rebels, *narcotraficantes*, paramilitaries, Colombian government | Social revolution, drug trade, state authority | Decades, from 1960s |
| ***Stateless "New Terrorism"*** | Internationalist terrorists, targeted interests | Vague goals, international stability | New model, from 1990s |

---

[4]For further information, see "New People's Army (NPA)." In *Terrorist Group Profiles*. Dudley Knox Library, Naval War College. Website: http://www.nps.edu/library/ (accessed October 15, 2002).

the new terrorist environment, such as fundamentalist religion, anti-Semitism, and a willingness to use new technologies and weapons of mass destruction. Symbolic targets have been attacked worldwide, and these include embassies, military installations, religious sites, tourists, and business visitors to foreign countries. In the 1990s and 2000s, attacks against Western interests were symbolic, high profile, and very lethal. In the modern era, attacks became highly destructive and caused a significant number of casualties.

Table 15.2 summarizes several examples of ongoing conflicts that are likely to result in terrorist violence in the near future.

## High-Tech Terrorism

New technologies allow terrorists to communicate efficiently, broaden their message, and wield unconventional weapons in unexpected ways. This is a central characteristic of asymmetrical warfare. Because of incremental improvements in communications and computer technologies, it is reasonable to conclude that the trend among terrorists and their supporters will be to use them extensively. This is also true of the increasing availability of weapons components for weapons of mass destruction, as well as the continuing softening of terrorists' reluctance to use them.

### Information Technologies

**Cyberterrorism** may very well become a central facet of the terrorist environment in the near future. As one possible scenario suggests,

> a variation on [the] theme of terrorism as an asymmetric strategy goes further to suggest that unconventional modes of conflict will stem . . . from a shift in the nature of conflict itself. In this paradigm, unconventional terrorist attacks on the sinews of modern, information-intensive societies will become the norm, replacing conventional conflicts over the control of territory or people.[5]

The Internet and social networking media provide opportunities for commercial, private, and political interests to spread their message and communicate with outsiders. The use of the Internet and social networking media by extremists has already become a common feature of the modern era. Information technologies are being invented and refined constantly and continue to be central to the New Terrorism. These technologies facilitate networking among groups and cells and will permit propaganda to be spread widely and efficiently. The Internet and other communications technologies are certain to be used to send instructions about overall goals, specific tactics, new bomb-making techniques, and other facets of the terrorist trade. Both overt and covert information networks permit widely dispersed cells to exist and communicate covertly.

Information and computer technologies can also be used offensively. The adoption of cyberwar techniques by extremists is quite possible, in which new technologies are used by terrorists to destroy information and communications systems.

### Weapons of Mass Destruction

The scenario of terrorists acquiring **weapons of mass destruction** is no longer the stuff of novels and films; nor is the very real possibility that terrorists may use such weapons on a previously unimaginable scale:

---

[5]Lesser, Ian O. "Countering the New Terrorism: Implications for Strategy." In *Countering the New Terrorism,* edited by Ian O. Lesser, Bruce Hoffman, John Arquilla, David Ronfeldt, and Michele Zanini. Santa Monica, CA: RAND, 1999, p. 95.

In the near future it will be technologically possible to kill thousands, perhaps hundreds of thousands, not to mention the toll the panic that is likely to ensue may take.[6]

There are incentives for international terrorists to construct and use weapons of mass destruction in lieu of conventional weapons. The psychological and economic impact of such devices can easily outweigh the destructive effect of the initial attack (which might be relatively small). For example, regarding terrorists' use of radiological weapons,

> such a bomb would cause very few deaths from cancer. But the economic and psychological costs would be formidable. If a bomb with some six pounds of plutonium exploded in Washington, D.C., 45,000 people might have to stay indoors for an undefined period afterward to avoid being exposed to fallout.[7]

Experts have argued that terrorists are making concerted efforts to acquire the requisite components for constructing weapons of mass destruction and that the acquisition of these components and the assembly of effective weapons are probably just a matter of time. Terrorists who are motivated by race or religion (or both) are likely to have little compunction about using chemical, biological, or radiological weapons against what they define as "subhumans" or nonbelievers. It will be recalled that the Japanese "doomsday" cult Aum Shinrikyō acquired and used Sarin nerve gas in Tokyo's subway system to hasten its vision of the Apocalypse. Aum also apparently attempted to obtain samples of the deadly Ebola virus, which has a very high fatality rate during outbreaks, as occurred in West Africa in 2014. A member of Aryan Nations in the United States tried to obtain bubonic plague bacteria via mail order; fortunately, his behavior was amateurish, and the sample was not delivered to committed racial supremacist terrorists. These examples from the 1990s should be interpreted as precursors to terrorist efforts in the very near future. For example, the anthrax attack in the United States in late 2001 illustrates how toxins or chemicals can be delivered to intended targets.

❖ **Photo 15.4**

A Predator drone aircraft departs on a mission.

U.S. Air Force/Getty Images News/Getty Images

As an alternative to the construction of weapons of mass destruction, terrorists have demonstrated their ability to convert available technologies into high-yield weapons. The destructive and psychological consequences of turning a nation's technology into a high-yield weapon have not been lost on modern terrorists. A case in point is the fact that modern airliners were used as ballistic missiles during the September 11, 2001, attacks. In another case in December 1994, elite French GIGN counterterrorist police thwarted Algerian terrorists from using an airliner as a missile over Paris.

### Case in Point: Exotic Technologies

Some technologies can theoretically be converted into weapons by terrorists who have a high degree of scientific knowledge and training. These exotic technologies include the following:

***Electromagnetic Pulse Technologies.*** **Electromagnetic pulse (EMP) technologies** use an electromagnetic burst from a generator that can disable electronic components such as microchips. If used on a sizable scale, EMP could destroy large quantities of military or financial information. High-energy radio frequency devices are another type of generator that can disable electronic components.

---

[6]Laqueur, Walter. *The New Terrorism: Fanaticism and the Arms of Mass Destruction.* New York: Oxford University Press, 1999, p. 4.

[7]Stern, Jessica. *The Ultimate Terrorists.* Cambridge, MA: Harvard University Press, 1999, p. 3.

***Plastics.*** Weapons constructed from plastics and other materials such as ceramics could possibly thwart detection by metal detectors. Handguns, rifles, and bullets can be constructed from these materials.

***Liquid Metal Embrittlement.*** Some chemicals can theoretically weaken metals when applied. They can *embrittle,* or make rigid, various metals. Should **liquid metal embrittlement** technology be obtained by motivated extremists, it would be easily transportable and could conceivably be applied to vehicles and aircraft.

### Tech-Terror: Feasibility and Likelihood

The *feasibility* of terrorists acquiring and using emerging technologies must be calculated by addressing the availability of these technologies. New and exotic technologies frequently require specialized access and knowledge to acquire, and hence not all technologies are readily available. Having said this, the old adage that "where there is a will there is a way" is very relevant because some practitioners of the New Terrorism (such as Al-Qa'ida) have exhibited great patience and resourcefulness. They have also proven to be meticulous in their planning.

Technical instructions for manipulating new information technologies are readily available. In fact, a great deal of useful information is available for terrorists on the Internet, including instructions for bomb assembly, poisoning, weapons construction, and mixing lethal chemicals. Extremists who wish to use computer and Internet technologies to attack political adversaries can also obtain the technical knowledge to do so. For example, information about how to engage in computer hacking is easy to acquire—instructions have been published in print and posted on the Internet. There is also an underground of people who create computer viruses for reasons that range from personal entertainment to anarchistic sentiment.

The feasibility of obtaining weapons of mass destruction has increased in recent years. This has occurred in part because the scientific knowledge needed for assembling these weapons is available from a number of sources, including the Internet. Some weapons assembly requires expertise, but not necessarily extensive scientific training; an example would be radiological weapons, which are relatively unsophisticated devices because they simply require toxic radioactive materials and a dispersion device. Other devices, such as nuclear weapons components, have so far been exceedingly difficult to assemble or steal. Nevertheless, the feasibility of obtaining weapons of mass destruction has increased not only because of the dissemination of technical know-how but also because terrorists do not necessarily need to acquire new or exotic technologies. Older technologies and materials—such as pesticides, carbon monoxide, and ammonium nitrate and fuel oil (ANFO)—can be used to construct high-yield weapons. Aerosols and other devices can also be used as relatively unsophisticated delivery systems.

The *likelihood* that new technologies will be acquired and used is perhaps a moot consideration because modern terrorists have already acquired and used many of these technologies. For example, apparently apolitical and anarchistic hackers—some of them teenagers—have vandalized information and communications systems, thus demonstrating that cyberwar is no longer an abstract concept. There is little reason to presume that this trend will diminish and many good reasons to presume that it will increase. The increasing availability of new technologies, when combined with the motivations and morality of the New Terrorism, suggests very strongly that technology will be an increasingly potent weapon in the arsenals of terrorists.

## Soft Targets and Terrorist Symbolism

Terrorists throughout the postwar era tended to select targets that were both symbolic and "soft." **Soft targets** include civilians and passive military targets, which are unlikely to offer resistance until after the terrorists have inflicted casualties or other destruction. This tactic was sometimes quite effective in the short term and occasionally forced targeted interests to grant concessions.

This trend continued unabated into the 2000s, even as new movements and the New Terrorism supplanted the previous terrorist environment. Those who practice the New Terrorism have regularly selected soft targets that symbolize enemy interests. These targets are chosen in part because of their symbolic value but also because they are likely to result in significant casualties. Suicide bombers have become particularly adept at maximizing casualties. Fourteen people (11 of them French workers), for example, in May 2002 were killed by a suicide bomber outside a hotel in downtown Karachi, Pakistan. In Iraq, hundreds of people have been killed by suicide bombers in dozens of attacks.

Thus, regardless of terrorist motives or environments, it is highly likely that violent extremists will continue to attack passive symbolic targets.

## ❖   Controlling Terrorism: New Challenges

Counterterrorist experts in the modern era will be required to concentrate on achieving several traditional counterterrorist objectives. These objectives can only minimize rather than eliminate the terrorist threats of the near future. Objectives include the following:

- Disrupting and preventing terrorist conspiracies from operationalizing their plans
- Deterring would-be terrorist cadres from crossing the line between extremist activism and political violence
- Implementing formal and informal international treaties, laws, and task forces to create a cooperative counterterrorist environment
- Minimizing physical destruction and human casualties

It is clear that no single model or method for controlling terrorism will apply across different time lines or terrorist environments. Because of this reality, the process for projecting counterterrorist models must include a longitudinal framework based on both theory and practical necessity. The *theoretical* models used in the near future will continue to reflect the same categories of responses seen in the recent past. These include the use of force, operations other than war, and legalistic responses. The *practicality* of these models will require them to be continually updated and adapted to emerging terrorist threats. With these adaptations, perhaps terrorism will be controlled to some degree by keeping dissident terrorists off balance and state terrorists isolated—thereby preventing them from having an unobstructed hand in planning and carrying out attacks or other types of political violence.

### Government Responses

Assuming that policy makers grasp the limitations of exclusive reliance on coercive methods, it is likely that alternative measures will be developed. Operations other than war include conciliatory options. These options may provide long-term solutions to future extremism. Past reliance on conciliatory options such as peace processes, negotiations, and social reforms had some success in resolving both immediate and long-standing terrorist crises. If skillfully applied, future adaptations of these options could present extremists with options other than political violence. In the past, these options were usually undertaken with the presumption that some degree of coercion would be kept available should the conciliatory options fail; this is a pragmatic consideration that is likely to continue.

### Societal Responses

Societal responses must be adapted to the idiosyncrasies of each nation and region. This is difficult in many cases—and seemingly nothing more than impossibly idealistic in other cases—because a great many regimes and contending groups have little interest in reducing social tensions and often try to manipulate these tensions to their benefit.

# Countering Extremism

Extremist ideologies and beliefs are the fertile soil for politically violent behavior. Ethnocentrism, nationalism, ideological intolerance, racism, and religious fanaticism are core motivations for terrorism. History has shown that coercive measures used to counter these tendencies are often only marginally successful. The reason is uncomplicated: A great deal of extremist behavior is rooted in passionate ideas, long histories of conflict, and codes of self-sacrifice (explored in Chapter 3). It is difficult to forcibly reverse these tendencies, and although coercion can eliminate cadres and destroy extremist organizations, sheer repression is a risky long-term solution.

# New Fronts in a New War

Counterterrorism must adapt to the fact that terrorist environments in the 2000s will reflect the ability of extremists to operate within emerging political environments. During this adaptation process, it is important to remember that

> [counterterrorist] instruments are complementary, and the value of using them should be—and generally are—more than just the sum of the parts. If the process is not properly managed, the value may be less than the sum of the parts, because of the possibility of different instruments working at cross purposes.[8]

Thus, as some terrorist environments continue to be characterized by the New Terrorism, one projection for near-term counterterrorism stands out: Models must be flexible enough to respond to new environments and must avoid stubborn reliance on methods that "fight the last war." This reality is particularly pertinent to the war on terrorism. Unlike previous wars, the new war was declared against *behavior* as much as against terrorist groups and revolutionary cadres. The "fronts" in the new war are amorphous and include the following:

### Covert "Shadow Wars"

These are fought outside of public scrutiny, using unconventional methods. **Shadow wars** require the deployment of military, paramilitary, and coercive covert assets to far regions of the world.

### Homeland Security Measures

These are required to harden targets, deter attacks, and thwart conspiracies. Internal security requires the extensive use of nonmilitary security personnel, such as customs officials, law enforcement agencies, and immigration authorities.

### Counterterrorist Financial Operations

These operations are directed against bank accounts, private foundations, businesses, and other potential sources of revenue for terrorist networks. Intelligence agencies can certainly hack into financial databases, but a broad-based coalition of government and private financial institutions is necessary for this task.

### Global Surveillance of Communications Technologies

This requires surveillance of technologies including telephones, cell phones, and e-mail. Agencies specializing in electronic surveillance, such as the U.S. National Security Agency, are the most capable institutions to carry out this mission.

---

[8]Pillar, Paul R. *Terrorism and U.S. Foreign Policy.* Washington, DC: Brookings Institution Press, 2001, p. 123.

**Identifying and Disrupting Transnational Terrorist Cells and Support Networks**

This requires international cooperation to track extremist operatives and "connect the dots" on a global scale. Primary responsibility for this task lies with intelligence communities and law enforcement agencies.

The new fronts in the new war clearly highlight the need to continuously upgrade physical, organizational, and operational counterterrorist measures; flexibility and creativity are essential. Failure to do so is likely to hinder adaptation to the terrorist environment of the 2000s. Thus, for example, the inability to control and redress long-standing bureaucratic and international rivalries could be disastrous in the new environment.

## The Continued Utility of Force

Violent coercion will continue to be a viable counterterrorist option. The dismantling of terrorist cells, especially in disputed regions where they enjoy popular support, cannot be accomplished solely by the use of law enforcement, intelligence, or nonmilitary assets. Situations sometimes require a warlike response by military assets ranging in scale from small special operations units to large deployments of significant air, naval, and ground forces. The stark use of force, when successfully used against terrorists, has a demonstrated record that is relevant for coercive counterterrorist policies in the near future. This record includes the following successes:

- *Elimination of terrorist threats.* This occurred, for example, in the successful hostage rescue operations by West German and Israeli special forces in Mogadishu and Entebbe, respectively, in 1977.
- ***General deterrence*** *by creating a generalized climate in which the risks of political violence outweigh the benefits.* An example is Saddam Hussein's use of the Iraqi military to suppress armed opposition from Iraqi Kurds in the north and the so-called Marsh Arabs in the south—this sent an unmistakable message to other would-be opponents.
- ***Specific deterrence*** *against a specific adversary that communicates the high risks of further acts of political violence.* One example is the American air raids against Libya during Operation El Dorado Canyon in 1986.
- *Demonstrations of national will.* We saw this, for example, in the deployment of hundreds of thousands of Indian troops to Kashmir in 2002 after a series of terrorist attacks and provocations by Kashmiri extremists, some of whom acted as Pakistani proxies.

History has shown, of course, that military and paramilitary operations are not always successful. Some of these operations have ended in outright disaster; others have been marginally successful. It is therefore likely that future uses of force will likewise fail on occasion. Nevertheless, the past utility of this option and its symbolic value are certain to encourage its continued use throughout the modern counterterrorist era. Absent a viable threat of force, states are highly unlikely to dissuade committed revolutionaries or aggressive states from committing acts of political violence.

## Countering Terrorist Financial Operations

Mohammed Atta, the leader of the September 11 cell, was closely affiliated with Al-Qa'ida members operating in several countries. He apparently received wire transfers of money in Florida from operatives in Egypt and was in close contact with Syrians who managed financial resources in Hamburg, Germany.[9] Estimates suggest that the total cost of the attack was $300,000, which is a small sum for the

---

[9]Cohen, Adam. "Following the Money." *Time,* October 8, 2001.

amount of destruction and disruption that resulted.[10] Very few if any of these funds came from state sponsors. They instead came from private accounts run by Al-Qa'ida operatives.

It is very clear from the Atta example that Al-Qa'ida—and, logically, other practitioners of the New Terrorism—have successfully established themselves as "stateless revolutionaries." Stateless revolutionaries are minimally dependent on the largesse of state sponsors. Some financial support does, of course, covertly emanate from state sponsors, but the modern terrorist environment exhibits less *dependency* than previous environments on state sponsorship. Stateless revolutionaries have, in fact, demonstrated that the world's financial systems and profits from transnational crime provide resources that can ensure their financial (and hence, operational) independence. This profile is unlikely to change in the near future.

### Finding Hidden Fortunes

Terrorists and their extremist supporters have amassed sizable amounts of money from a variety of sources, as illustrated from the following cases:

- Transnational crime—for example, the trafficking and smuggling activities of Colombian and Sri Lankan groups
- Personal fortunes—for example, Osama bin Laden's personal financial resources
- Extortion—for example, the criminal profits of Abu Sayyaf
- Private charities and foundations—for example, front organizations that support Hezbollah and Hamas[11]

Large portions of these assets were deposited in anonymous bank accounts, thus allowing funds to be electronically transferred between banking institutions and other accounts internationally in mere minutes. During the months following the September 11, 2001, attacks, government agencies from a number of countries made a concerted effort to identify and trace the terrorists' banking accounts. Law enforcement and security agencies also began to closely scrutinize the activities of private charities and foundations in an attempt to determine whether they were "front groups" secretly funneling money to supporters of terrorist organizations. Since September 11, 2001, government agencies such as the U.S. Treasury Department have covertly tracked global bank data to monitor transfers of money and other banking activities.[12]

These investigative practices have not been without controversy, and they will continue to provoke serious debate in the immediate future. For example, one problem encountered in the United States came from local coordinators of private charities and foundations, who argued vehemently that their groups were not fronts for terrorist support groups. Another problem encountered on a global scale involved the tradition and policy of **customer anonymity** found in some banking systems, such as those of the Cayman Islands and Switzerland. Many mainstream executives and policy makers were very hesitant to endorse an abrogation of the sanctity of customer anonymity. Their rationale was straightforward: Individual privacy and liberty could be jeopardized if security officers were permitted to peruse the details of hundreds of thousands of bank accounts looking for a few terrorist accounts that might or might not exist. From a practical business perspective, customers could reconsider doing business with financial institutions that could no longer guarantee their anonymity, thus causing these institutions to lose customers. These tensions will not abate in the near future and will require that a balance be developed between the need for international security and the need to preserve the sanctity of long-standing banking practices.

---

[10]One Hamas leader bragged that suicide bombings were cheap—costing approximately $1,500 each in 2001 dollars.

[11]For a report on charities, see Ottaway, David B. "U.S. Eyes Money Trails of Saudi-Backed Charities." *Washington Post,* August 19, 2004.

[12]Meyer, Josh, and Greg Miller. "U.S. Secretly Tracks Global Bank Data." *Los Angeles Times,* June 23, 2006.

### A Resilient Adversary: Terrorist Adaptations

Terrorists adapted quickly to the new focus on financial counterterrorist measures. Implementing a process that apparently began during the global crackdown after September 11, 2001, terrorists and their supporters began to transfer their assets out of international financial institutions, where they were vulnerable to seizure. This is an adaptation that serves as a strong indicator for terrorist behavior in the near future.

Operatives removed assets from financial institutions and began investing in valuable commodities such as gold, diamonds, and other precious metals and gems.[13] From the perspective of counterterrorist officials, this tactic can potentially cripple the global effort to electronically monitor, track, and disrupt terrorist finances. From the perspective of terrorists and their supporters, the chief encumbrance of this adaptation is the fact that they could become literally burdened with transporting heavy suitcases filled with precious commodities. However, this is an acceptable encumbrance because it is very difficult for counterterrorist agents to identify and interdict couriers or to locate and raid repositories. It is likely that this adaptation will continue to be made as circumstances require, perhaps making it virtually impossible to trace terrorists' assets that have been skillfully hidden.

Another adaptation used by terrorists is through an ancient practice known as **hawala**. Hawala is a transnational system of brokers who know and trust one another. Persons wishing to transfer money approach hawala brokers and, for a fee, ask the broker to transfer money to another person. Using the name and location of the recipient, the initial broker will contact a broker in the recipient's country. The recipient of the money contacts the local hawala broker, who delivers the money. To prevent fraud, the sending broker gives the recipient broker a code number (such as the string of numbers on a $20 bill). The recipient (who receives the code from the sender) must give the broker this code number in order to pick up his or her funds. No records are kept of the transaction, thus ensuring anonymity. This is a useful system because it relies on an "honor system" to succeed, and money is never physically moved.

## The Case for International Cooperation

Cooperation between nations has always been essential to counterterrorist operations. International treaties, laws, and informal agreements were enacted during the postwar era to create a semblance of formality and consistency to global counterterrorist efforts. However, cooperation at the operational level was not always consistent or mutually beneficial, as illustrated by the case of the prosecution of the *Achille Lauro* terrorists. In the era of the New Terrorism and international counterterrorist warfare, international cooperation at the operational level has become a central priority for policy makers. A good example of this priority is found in the new front-line missions of intelligence and criminal justice agencies.

### Intelligence and Law Enforcement

The world's intelligence communities and criminal justice systems have always been important counterterrorist instruments. After the September 11 attacks, these institutions were tasked with increased responsibilities in the global war on terrorism—largely because of their demonstrated ability to incapacitate and punish terrorists. These institutions, perhaps more so than military institutions, are also able to apply steady and long-term pressure on terrorist networks. Intelligence and law enforcement agencies are in many cases more adept than military assets at keeping terrorists "on the run" over time. This is not to say that these institutions are a panacea for future terrorism, but international cooperation between intelligence and law enforcement agencies does provide the means to track operatives, identify networks, and interdict other assets on a global scale.

International law enforcement cooperation in particular provides worldwide access to extensive criminal justice systems that have well-established **terminal institutions** (such as prisons) for use

---

[13]DeYoung, Karen, and Douglas Farah. "Al Qaeda Shifts Assets to Gold." *Washington Post*, June 18, 2002.

against terrorists. Counterterrorist terminal institutions—under the jurisdiction of criminal justice and military justice systems—provide final resolution to individual terrorists' careers after they have been captured, prosecuted, convicted, and imprisoned. Applying a concept familiar to students of the administration of justice, these institutions can effectively incapacitate terrorists by ending their ability to engage in political violence or propaganda. When faced with the prospect of lifelong incarceration, terrorists are likely to become susceptible to manipulation wherein, for example, favors can be exchanged for intelligence information. In a cooperative environment, these intelligence data may be shared among allied governments.

Several important objectives are attainable through enhanced international cooperation between intelligence, law enforcement, and security institutions. These objectives—which are certain to be central considerations for counterterrorist policy makers and analysts well into the near future—include the following:

- Destabilization of terrorist networks
- Disruption of terrorist conspiracies
- Collection of intelligence from captured terrorist operatives
- Incapacitation of imprisoned operatives

An example from early 2002 illustrates how international intelligence and security cooperation can achieve these objectives.[14] Mohammed Haydar Zammar, a Hamburg-based Syrian German, was held by Syrian authorities after his capture in Morocco. Zammar had been part of the Hamburg cell that recruited Mohammed Atta, the leader of the September 11 hijackers' cell. Zammar had legally left Germany in October 2001 and traveled to Morocco, allegedly to divorce his Moroccan wife. He was captured and detained by Moroccan authorities, who deported him to Syria with the knowledge of American authorities. During his interrogation in Syria, Zammar provided very useful information about the Hamburg cell; the planning of the September 11, 2001, attacks; and details about Al-Qa'ida. The Germans lodged mild protests against Morocco and Syria, arguing that under international law and extradition treaties, Germany should have at a minimum been notified about Zammar's detention, deportation, and imprisonment. Nevertheless, the operation was successful.

# ❖ Threats to the Homeland: Prospects for Terrorism in the United States

The threat of terrorism in the United States emanates from domestic and international sources. Domestic sources of terrorism include threats from right-wing racial supremacist groups and movements that have succeeded the Patriots. Potential threats from left-wing sources come primarily from single-issue groups, such as radical environmentalists. International sources of terrorism emanate primarily from cell-based religious extremist networks that replicate the Al-Qa'ida model.

## The Future of International Terrorism

During the years immediately preceding and following the turn of the 21st century, it has become very clear that the near future of international terrorism in the United States will be considerably threatening. Trends suggest that the United States will be a preferred target for international terrorists both domestically and abroad. Although this is not a new phenomenon, the modern terrorist environment has made the American homeland vulnerable to attack for the first time in its history. International terrorism has, of course, occurred in the United States—many of these incidents were presented in

---

[14]From Finn, Peter. "Key Figure in Sept. 11 Plot Held in Secret Detention in Syria." *Washington Post,* June 18, 2002.

previous discussions. However, the asymmetrical nature of new threats and the destructive magnitude of newly obtainable weapons are unlike the threats inherent in previous terrorist environments. The existence of pre-positioned "sleeper" agents has proven to be a real possibility. For example, an alleged Hezbollah cell was broken up in July 2000 when 18 people were arrested in Atlanta, Georgia.

Violence emanating from international sources will continue to come from Middle Eastern spillovers during the beginning of the 21st century. It is unlikely that the previous activity profile in the United States—threats from groups such as Omega 7, the Provos, and the Jewish Defense League—will reemerge on the same scale. The most significant spillover threat of the early 21st century comes from religious extremists. It is also conceivable that spillover activity from nationalists with an anti-American agenda will occur in the American homeland; these would likely be cases of the contagion effect, with newcomers imitating previous homeland incidents committed by other terrorists. Regardless of the source of international terrorism, the activity profile is almost certain to be that of the New Terrorism.

❖ **Photo 15.5**
The war on terrorism continues.

U.S. Department of Defense

## The Future of the Violent Left

The future of the terrorist left in the United States is not encouraging for would-be violent extremists. The modern political and social environment does not exhibit the same mass fervor as existed during the era that spawned the New Left, civil rights, and Black Power movements. Nor is there strong nationalism within American ethnonational communities. Perhaps most important, radical Marxism and its contemporary applications are no longer relevant to the American activist community.

Single-issue extremism is certain to be a feature of the radical left. Radical environmentalists have attracted a small but loyal constituency. New movements have also shown themselves to be adept at attracting new followers. For example, a nascent anarchist movement has taken root in the United States and other Western democracies. This movement is loosely rooted in an antiglobalist ideology that opposes alleged exploitation by prosperous nations of poorer nations in the new global economy. It remains to be seen whether violent tendencies will develop within this trend. Sporadic incidents from single-issue terrorists are likely to occur from time to time.

## The Future of the Violent Right

Trends found in the recent past suggest that extremists on the fringe and far right will continue to promulgate conspiracy theories and attract a few true believers to their causes. Reactionary activists continued to attract a number of people to their causes during the 1990s and 2000s. For example, extremist anti-abortion activism continued sporadically, sustained by a core of dedicated true believers.

The future of the politically violent right comes from a potential weak network/weak sponsor scenario. By advocating leaderless resistance, the violent Patriot and neo-Nazi right learned the lessons of 1980s cases of terrorist groups such as the Order. Thus, conspiracies that were uncovered by law enforcement authorities beginning in the mid-1990s exhibited a covert and cell-based organizational philosophy. Possible threats also exist from religious extremists who could reinvigorate the violent moralist movement. An extremist pool still resides within the remnant Patriot movement, racial supremacist communities, and newer movements such as the neo-Confederate movement. There has also been a continued proliferation of antigovernment and racial conspiracy theories. Publications such as *The Turner Diaries*[15] and *The Myth of the Six Million*[16] continue to spread racial and anti-Semitic extremism. The promulgation of these theories keeps reactionary tendencies alive on the right, illustrating the conspiracy mythology that continues to be characteristic of racial supremacist extremism.

---

[15]MacDonald, Andrew [William Pierce]. *The Turner Diaries*. New York: Barricade Books, 1996.

[16]Anderson, E. L. [David L. Hoggan]. *The Myth of the Six Million*. Newport Beach, CA: Noontide, 1969.

## Chapter Summary

This chapter explored trends that suggest the near-term future of terrorism. An underlying theme throughout this discussion was that the near future will reflect the emerging profile of the New Terrorism. Traditional terrorism is certainly still a factor, but it is no longer an exclusive or predominant model. These trends can be analyzed within the context of past terrorist environments, with the caveat that these environments will continue to adapt to emerging political environments. The near future of terrorism will be shaped by ongoing regional conflicts, new technologies, and renewed attacks against symbolic soft targets.

Counterterrorism in the post–September 11, 2001, era will have to adapt to new fronts in the war on terrorism. These new fronts require creative use of overt and covert operations, homeland security measures, intelligence, and cooperation among counterterrorist agencies. Disruption of terrorist financial operations will prove to be one of the most important and challenging priorities in the new war. Regarding prospects for terrorism in the United States, most threats in the near future may come from international religious extremists, domestic rightists, and single-issue leftists.

## A Final Thought

There is one final perspective that is worth contemplating. Throughout history, violent dissidents have claimed the lives of countless innocent people whom they labeled as enemies. Among these "enemies" have been reformers, defined as those who genuinely tried to resolve the problems and grievances that gave rise to extremist sentiment in the first place. Many of these reformers have sympathized with the plight of the groups championed by the dissidents, especially when the championed group has been in fact exploited or otherwise oppressed.

Some terrorist movements have made special work of killing and terrorizing reformers, labeling them pejoratively as *collaborators* or some other term. Why do terrorists harm these people? What possible threat can emanate from those who try to better the conditions of extremists' championed groups? The answers to these questions are straightforwardly addressed in the following quotation:

The best defense against terrorism is a government which has the broad popular support to control terrorist activities through normal channels of law enforcement without resorting to counter-terror. Terrorists often correctly perceive that their greatest enemy is the moderate who attempts to remedy whatever perceived injustices form the basis for terrorist strength. It is often these moderates who are targets of assassinations.[17]

Thus, the true terrorist *wants* to "enrage the beast" within the state and is encouraged when the enemy becomes a genuine instrument of repression. In contrast, the true reformer understands that terrorists will not long survive when—to paraphrase Mao Zedong—the state successfully dries up the sea of the people's support for the extremists. This is a perspective that is worth remembering, but one that is too frequently forgotten when nations must reestablish stability and normalcy after terrorists strike.

---

[17]Hurwood, Bernhardt J. *Society and the Assassin: A Background Book on Political Murder.* New York: Parents' Magazine Press, 1970, p. 146. Quoting Kirkham, James F., Sheldon Levy, and William J. Crotty. *Assassination and Political Violence.* Staff Report to the National Commission on the Causes and Prevention of Violence, vol. 8, Supplement F; Leiden, Carl. *Assassination in the Middle East, Part 3.* Washington, DC: Government Printing Office, 1969, p. 4.

## Key Terms and Concepts

The following topics are discussed in this chapter and can be found in the glossary:

| | | |
|---|---|---|
| Carnivore (DCS-1000) | general deterrence | soft targets |
| customer anonymity | *hawala* | specific deterrence |
| cyberterrorism | liquid metal embrittlement | terminal institutions |
| electromagnetic pulse (EMP) technologies | New People's Army (NPA) | weapons of mass destruction |
| | shadow wars | |

## Discussion Box: Toward Big Brother?

*This chapter's Discussion Box is intended to stimulate critical debate about the possible use, by democracies and authoritarian regimes, of antiterrorist technologies to engage in surveillance.*

Electronic surveillance has become a controversial practice in the United States and elsewhere. The fear is that civil liberties can be jeopardized by unregulated interception of telephone conversations, e-mail, and fax transmissions. Detractors argue that government use of these technologies can conceivably move well beyond legitimate application against threats from crime, espionage, and terrorism. Absent strict protocols to rein in these technologies, a worst-case scenario envisions state intrusions into the everyday activities of innocent civilians. Should this happen, critics foresee a time when privacy, liberty, and personal security become values of the past.

### Discussion Questions

1. How serious is the threat from abuses in the use of new technologies?

2. How should new technologies be regulated? Can they be regulated?

3. Is it sometimes necessary to sacrifice a few freedoms to protect national security and to ensure the long-term viability of civil liberty?

4. Should the same protocols be used for domestic electronic surveillance and foreign surveillance? Why?

5. What is the likelihood that new surveillance technologies will be used as tools of repression by authoritarian regimes in the near future?

## On Your Own

The open-access Student Study Site at **http://study.sagepub.com/martin5e** has a variety of useful study aids, including eFlashcards, quizzes, audio resources, and journal articles. The websites, exercises, and recommended readings listed below are easily accessed on this site as well.

# Recommended Readings

The following publications project challenges facing the world community in the present and in the near future:

Heiberg, Marianne, Prendan O'Leary, and John Tirman, eds. *Terror, Insurgency, and the State: Ending Protracted Conflicts.* Philadelphia: University of Pennsylvania Press, 2007.

Holmes, Jennifer S. *Terrorism and Democratic Stability Revisited.* Manchester, UK: Manchester University Press, 2008.

The following publications are an eclectic assortment of recommendations that provide classic—and arguably timeless—insight into the nature of dissident resistance, ideologies of liberty, state manipulation, and revolution.

Hamilton, Alexander, John Jay, and James Madison. *The Federalist: A Commentary on the Constitution of the United States.* New York: Modern Library, 1937.

Koestler, Arthur. *Darkness at Noon.* New York: Macmillan, 1963.

Mill, John Stuart. *On Liberty.* Edited by David Spitz. New York: Norton, 1975.

Moore, Barrington, Jr. *Social Origins of Dictatorship and Democracy: Lord and Peasant in the Making of the Modern World.* Boston: Beacon, 1966.

Orwell, George. *Animal Farm.* New York: Harcourt Brace Jovanovich, 1946.

# Appendix

## Map References

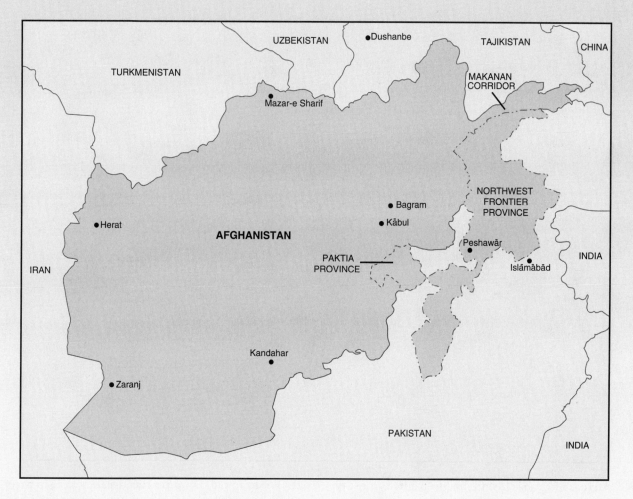

**Afghanistan.** After the invasion of the country by the Soviet Union, a jihad was waged to drive out the Soviet army. Muslims from throughout the world joined the fight, forming prototypical revolutionary movements that culminated in the creation of organizations such as Al-Qa'ida. Following the war against the Soviets, the Taliban seized control in most of the country. Intervention by the United States and NATO began a new phase in which the coalition and new Afghan government vied with the Taliban for control of the country. Al-Qa'ida remained active in the region bordered by Pakistan's Northwest Frontier province and along the border in Afghanistan's Paktia region.

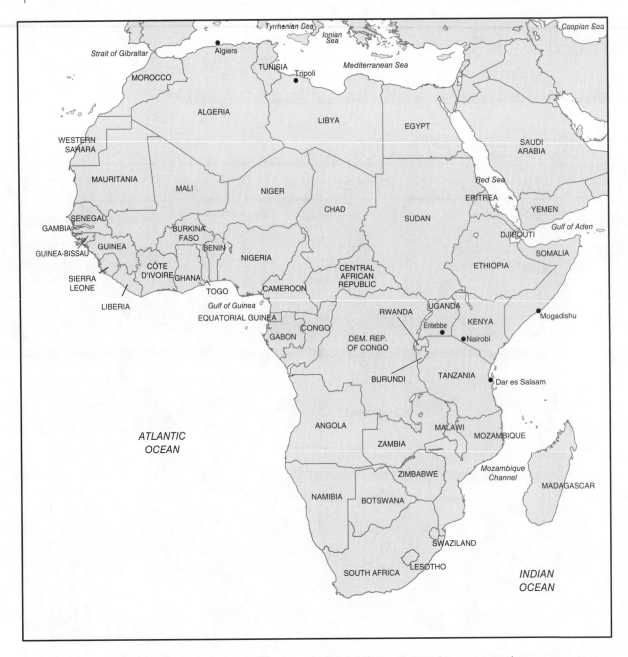

**Africa.** Africa has been home to many terrorist typologies. For example, Libya practiced state terrorism as foreign policy, and the apartheid government in South Africa practiced state terrorism as domestic policy. Religious dissident terrorism occurred in Algeria. Communal terrorism broke out in Rwanda, Somalia, Liberia, and Sierra Leone after the breakdown of government authority. International terrorist attacks occurred in Kenya, Tanzania, and elsewhere.

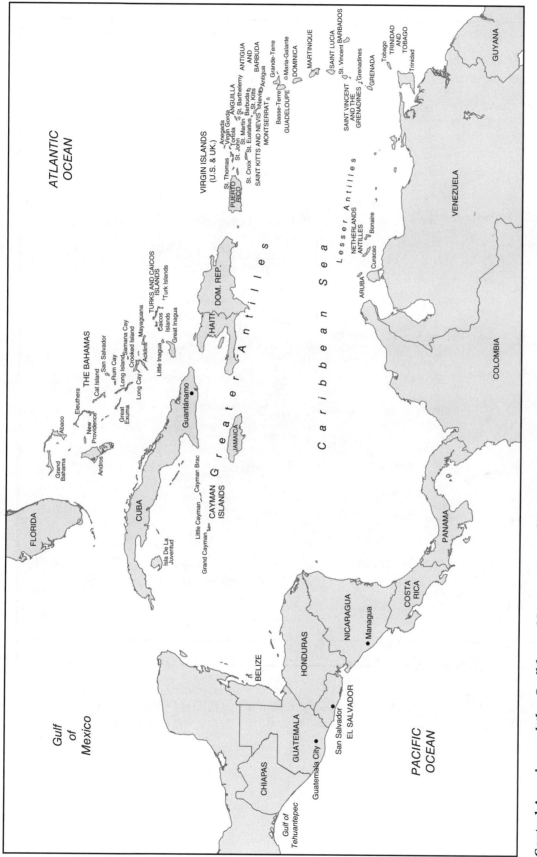

**Central America and the Caribbean.** Most terrorist violence originated in Cold War proxy conflicts and was waged by rebels, paramilitaries, and state security forces. Civil wars in El Salvador and Guatemala were markedly brutal, as was the Contra insurgency in Nicaragua. The Zapatista insurgency in Mexico championed the Chiapas Indians. Cuba was an active partner with the Soviet Union, fomenting and participating in conflicts in Africa and Latin America. The American base at Guantánamo Bay, Cuba, became the primary venue of detention by the United States of suspected members of Islamic terrorist groups.

**Europe.** Terrorist violence in Europe originated from ideological, ethnonationalist, and Middle Eastern sources. The Balkans, Northern Ireland, and the Basque region of Spain have been sources of ethnonationalist terrorism. Ideological terrorism peaked in Germany and Italy during the 1970s, while Middle Eastern spillovers continued into the 21st century.

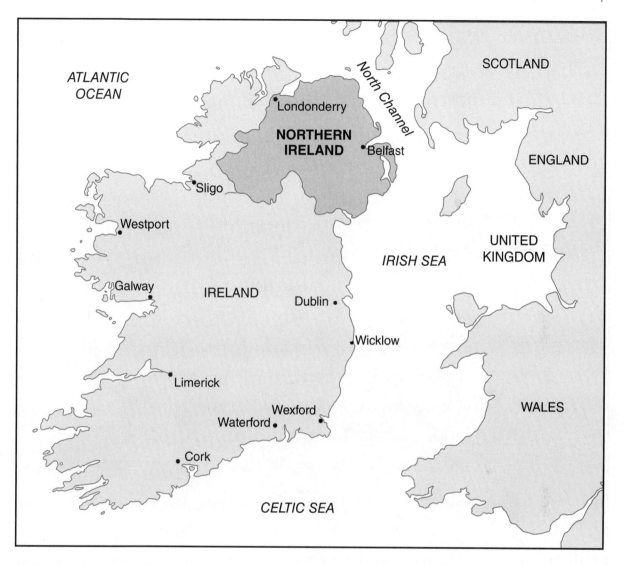

**Ireland.** When the Irish Free State was declared in 1921, six northern counties remained under British rule. The modern politics of these counties, known as Northern Ireland, were marked by violent conflict between Protestant unionists and Catholic nationalists. This conflict was termed *the Troubles*.

**Israel, the West Bank, and Gaza.** Although a geographically small region, the area has been a center for communal and religious conflict that has frequently spilled over into the international domain and brought nations to the brink of war.

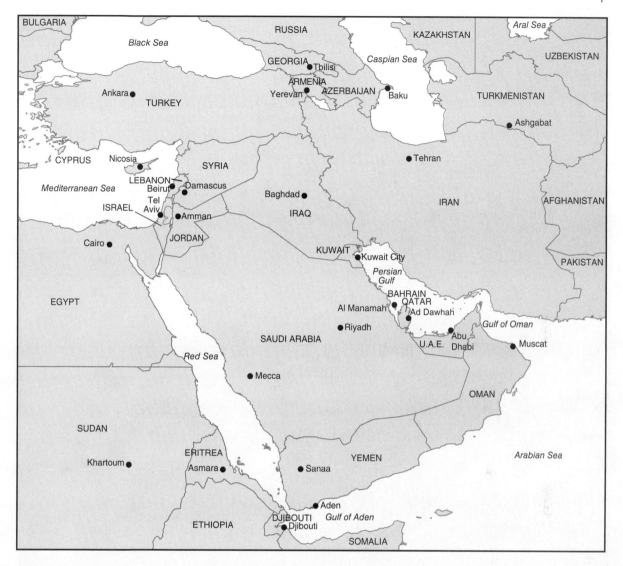

**Middle East.** Religious, ethnonationalist, and state terrorism have occurred frequently.

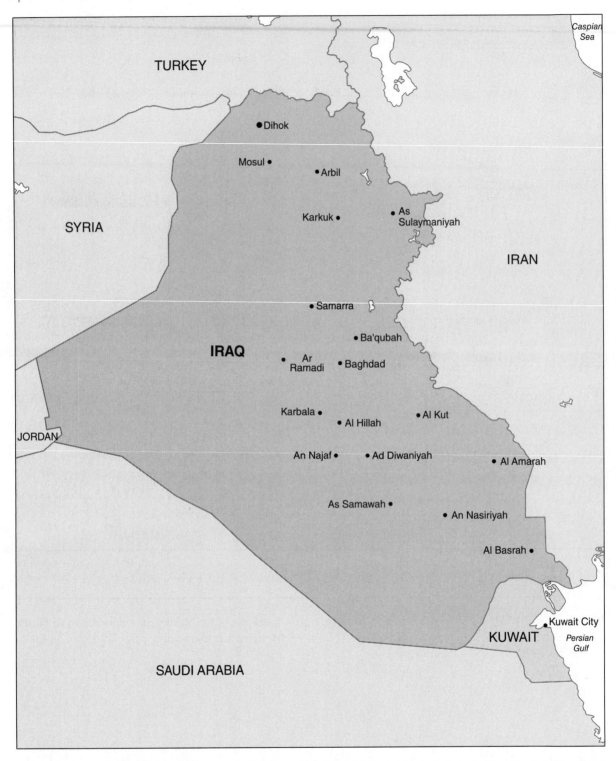

**Iraq.** The regime of Saddam Hussein used terror as a regular instrument of state policy. During the Anfal campaign against ethnic Kurds in northern Iraq, the Iraqi army used chemical weapons against civilians. Iraq also invaded Iran and Kuwait and provided safe haven for secular terrorist operatives. However, the 2003 invasion of Iraq discovered no arsenals of weapons of mass destruction and no links to international Islamist terrorist networks such as Al-Qa'ida. The post-invasion insurgency was comprised Sunni and Shi'a movements including Al-Qa'ida in Iraq. Remanants of Al-Qa'ida in Iraq eventually evolved into the independent Islamic State of Iraq and the Levant.

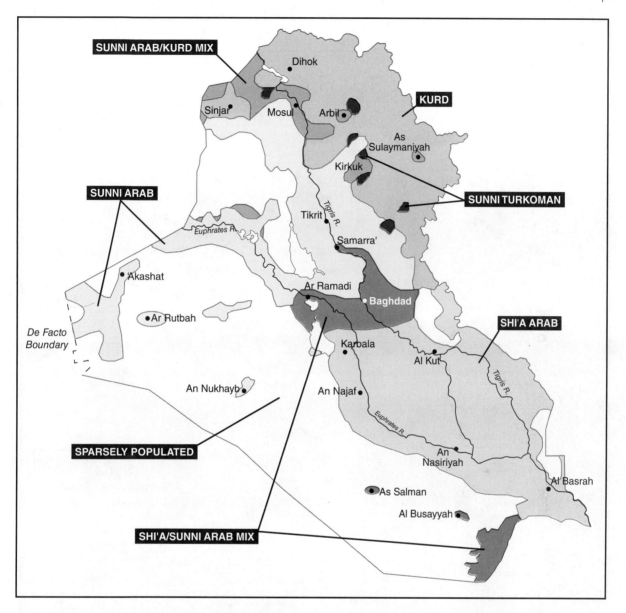

**Distribution of Ethnoreligious Groups in Iraq.** Iraq is a diverse nation of several ethnicities and faiths. Although the predominant groups are Shi'a and Sunni Arabs, there are also sizable populations of Kurdish, Turkoman, Assyrian, and Christian Iraqis.

**Syria.** The al-Assad regime has used terror as a regular instrument of state policy, first under the father Hafez, and then his son Bashar. During the civil war that ensued after the 2011 Arab Spring, Syrian government forces used barrel bombs and chemical weapons against civilians, and engaged in widespread human rights violations. The antigovernment insurgency included Islamist factions such as the pro -Al-Qa'ida Al Nusra Front. It also led to the rise of the independent Islamic State of Iraq and the Levant, which became a viable movement in both Syria and Iraq.

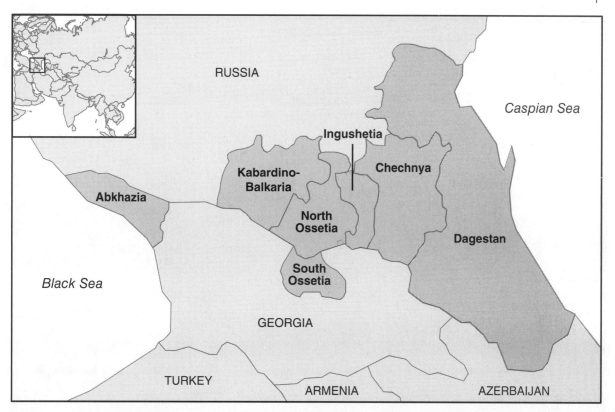

**The Caucasus.** Strong nationalist sentiment grew in the Caucasus with the collapse of the Soviet Union, leading to ethnonationalist violence in regions such as Nagorno-Karabakh. The war in Chechnya became particularly violent, often spilling across its borders. Chechen terrorist incidents in Russia were highly destructive.

**Central Asia.** The five countries of Central Asia gained their independence after the collapse of the Soviet Union. The region is predominantly Muslim. It became an important focus during the U.S.-led war on terrorism.

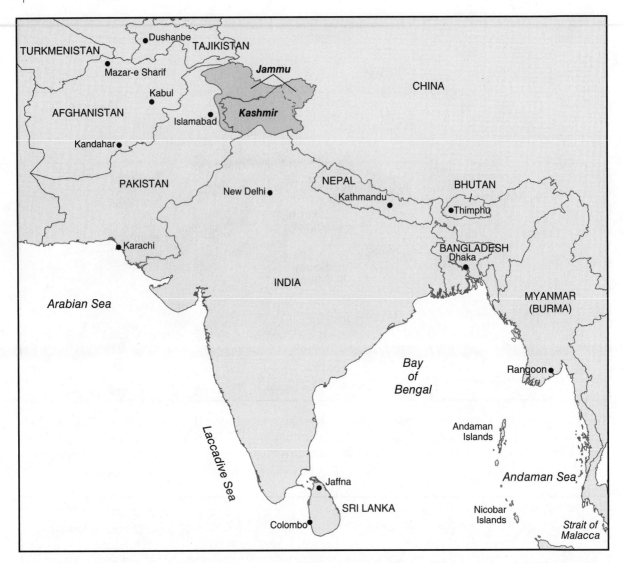

**Indian Subcontinent.** Several areas of confrontation resulted in terrorist violence. Conflicts in Sri Lanka, Kashmir, and Afghanistan became particularly active, with ethnic and religious violence taking many thousands of lives.

**Southeast Asia.** Terrorism typically originated from ethnonationalist, ideological, state, and religious sources. Significant cases of dissident and state conflict occurred during and after the Cold War era. Religious terrorism became prominent in the Philippines and Indonesia in the aftermath of the September 11, 2001, attacks. The killing fields of Cambodia are a special case of exceptional state-sponsored violence.

**South America**. Latin America has been a source for many case studies on terrorist environments. Cases include urban guerrillas in Montevideo and Buenos Aires; state repression in Chile, Argentina, and Uruguay; dissident terrorism in Peru; and criminal dissident terrorism in Colombia. The tri-border region became a center of suspected radical Islamist activism.

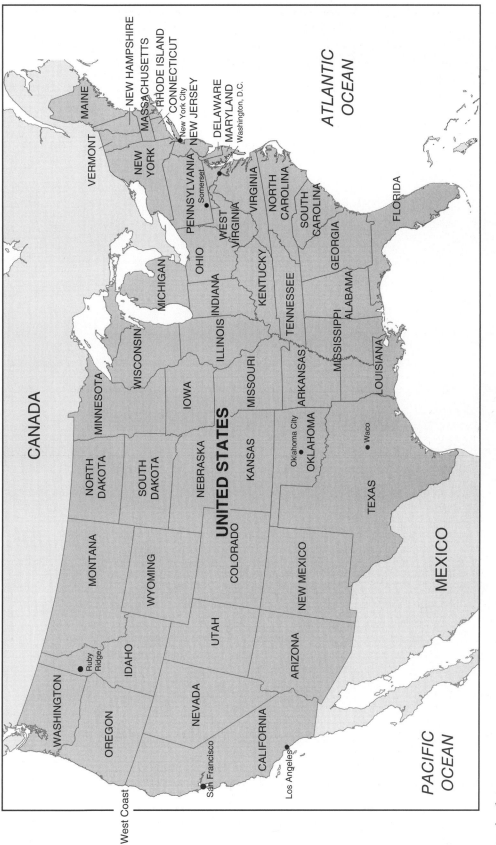

**United States.** Most terrorism in the United States has been characterized by low-intensity ideological and racial violence. Significant incidents occurred during the Oklahoma City bombing and the September 11, 2001, attacks.

# Glossary

The glossary summarizes terms that were used in this textbook. Readers should refer to the glossary to refresh their knowledge of discussions and case studies explored in chapters, tables, and chapter perspectives.

**Abbas, Abu.** The leader of the Palestine Liberation Front.

**Absolute deprivation.** A sociological term that indicates the lack of basic human needs for survival.

**Abu Hafs Al-Masri Brigades.** An Al-Qa'ida–affiliated group that claimed responsibility for several significant terrorist attacks. These included the August 2003 bombing of the United Nations headquarters in Baghdad, Iraq; the November 2003 bombings of two synagogues in Turkey; and the March 11, 2004, attack on commuter trains in Madrid, Spain (so-called Operation Death Trains).

**Abu Nidal Organization (ANO).** The designation given to Abu Nidal's movement.

**Abu Sayyaf.** A Muslim insurgency on the island of Basilan in the Philippines; the group has ideological and other links to Al-Qa'ida. Founded by Abdurajak Janjalani, who was killed by Filipino police in 1998.

**Achille Lauro.** A cruise ship that was hijacked by members of the Palestine Liberation Front. During the incident, the terrorists murdered a wheelchair-bound Jewish American.

**Act of political will.** The notion that one can force change by an absolute commitment to a cause. All that is required is complete and uncompromising dedication to achieving one's goals.

**"Afghan Arabs."** A term given to foreign volunteers, mostly Arabs, who fought as *mujahideen* during the war against the occupation of Afghanistan by the Soviet army.

**African National Congress (ANC).** The principal anti-apartheid movement in pre-democracy South Africa.

**Afrikaner Resistance Movement.** A rightist ethnonationalist movement in South Africa that promoted the interests of Afrikaners.

**Agca, Mehmet Ali.** A former member of the Grey Wolves, a right-wing Turkish paramilitary organization, who was convicted of attempting to assassinate Pope John Paul II.

**Air France Flight 8969.** An airliner hijacked in December 1994 by the Algerian Armed Islamic Group. After the hijackers killed three passengers, the plane was permitted to depart the Algerian airfield and made a refueling stop in Marseilles. Intending to fly to Paris, the hijackers demanded three times the amount of fuel needed to make the journey. The reason for this demand was that they planned to blow up the aircraft over Paris or possibly crash it into the Eiffel Tower. French GIGN *gendarme* police commandos disguised as caterers stormed the plane in Marseilles, thus bringing the incident to an end.

**AK-47.** A durable assault rifle designed by Mikhail Kalashnikov in the Soviet Union in 1947. It became a common weapon among conventional and irregular forces around the world.

**Al-Aqsa Martyr Brigades.** A Palestinian nationalist movement affiliated with the Palestine Liberation Organization. Noted for its use of suicide bombers, it has committed terrorist violence against Israelis.

**Al Fatah.** The largest and most influential organization within the Palestine Liberation Organization. It formed the political foundation for PLO leader Yasir Arafat.

**Al Jazeera.** An independent news service based in the Persian Gulf state of Qatar.

**Al-Qa'ida.** An international network of Islamic *mujahideen* organized by Osama bin Laden in the aftermath of the anti-Soviet *jihad* in Afghanistan. Responsible for many acts of international and domestic terrorism.

**Al-Qa'ida Organization for Holy War in Iraq.** A movement led by Abu Musab al-Zarqawi that waged holy war in Iraq against foreign interests, Shi'a organizations, and "apostate" Iraqis.

**al-Megrahi, Abdel Basset.** An alleged agent of Libya's security service who was convicted and sentenced to life imprisonment by a Scottish court sitting near the Hague, Netherlands, for his participation in the bombing of Pan Am Flight 103 over Lockerbie, Scotland.

**Al-Zarqawi, Abu Musab.** A Jordanian who led the al-Qa'ida Organization for Holy War in Iraq.

**Amal.** A pro-Syrian Lebanese Shi'a paramilitary movement.

**Amir, Yigal.** A Jewish extremist who assassinated Israeli Prime Minister Yitzhak Rabin on November 4, 1995.

**Ammonium nitrate and fuel oil (ANFO) explosives.** A powerful explosive compound made from ingredients easily obtained from fertilizers and common gasoline.

**Amnesty International.** An international watchdog organization that monitors human rights issues around the world, focusing on the status of political prisoners.

**Anarchism.** A political ideology developed during the 19th century that championed the working class and opposed central control by governments.

**Anfal Campaign.** A genocidal campaign waged by the Iraqi army in 1988 against its Kurdish population. Mustard gas and nerve agents were used against civilians.

**Animal Liberation Front.** An American-based, single-issue movement that protests animal abuse. Responsible for committing acts of violence such as arson and vandalism.

**Ansar Allah.** A group that claimed credit in July 1994 for the bombing at the Argentine–Israeli Mutual Association in Buenos Aires, Argentina, where about 100 were killed and 200 were injured.

**Anthrax.** A disease afflicting farm animals that can also be contracted by humans. A possible ingredient for biological weapons.

**Antistate terrorism.** Dissident terrorism directed against a particular government or group of governments.

**Antiterrorism.** Official measures that seek to deter or prevent terrorist attacks. These measures include target hardening and enhanced security.

**Anti-Terrorism and Effective Death Penalty Act.** An act passed by the U.S. Congress in 1996. It was the first comprehensive American counterterrorism law. The purpose of the Anti-Terrorism Act was to regulate activity that can be used to mount a terrorist attack, provide resources for counterterrorist programs, and punish terrorism.

**Apartheid.** The former policy of racial separation and white supremacy in South Africa.

**Arafat, Yasir.** The founder and leader of the Palestine Liberation Organization until his death on November 11, 2004.

**Arellano-Félix Cartel.** A drug-smuggling cartel based in Tijuana, Mexico. Responsible for terrorist violence against government officials.

**Argentine Anticommunist Alliance (Triple-A).** An Argentine death squad active in the early 1970s. It was responsible for numerous acts of violence against leftists, human rights organizers, students, and others. Some of its clandestine operatives were members of the Argentine security apparatus. After the 1976 coup, Triple-A was integrated into the Argentine state terrorist apparatus.

**Armed Forces for National Liberation (Fuerzas Armadas de Liberación Nacional, or FALN).** A Puerto Rican *independencista* terrorist group active during the 1970s and 1980s. Responsible for more bombings than any other single terrorist group in American history.

**Armed Forces of Popular Resistance.** A Puerto Rican *independencista* terrorist organization.

**Armed Forces Revolutionary Council (AFRC).** A rebel movement that arose in Sierre Leone during the 1990s. AFRC forces were responsible for widespread human rights abuses and atrocities.

**Armed Islamic Group.** An Algerian Islamic resistance movement responsible for terrorist violence in Algeria and France.

**Armed Islamic Movement.** An Algerian Islamic resistance movement responsible for terrorist violence in Algeria and France.

**Armed propaganda.** The use of symbolic violence to spread propaganda about an extremist movement.

**Armed Revolutionary Nuclei.** An Italian neofascist terrorist group. Its most notorious act was the bombing of the main train station in Bologna, which killed 85 people and injured 180.

**Armenian Revolutionary Army.** One of several Armenian terrorist groups active in the postwar era that targeted Turkish interests to avenge the Turkish genocide of Armenians.

**Armenian Secret Army for the Liberation of Armenia (ASALA).** One of several Armenian terrorist groups active in the postwar era that targeted Turkish interests to avenge the Turkish genocide of Armenians.

**Army of God.** A shadowy and violent Christian fundamentalist movement in the United States that has attacked moralistic targets, such as abortion providers.

**Arocena, Eduardo.** The founder of the anti-Castro Cuban terrorist group Omega 7.

**Aryan Nations.** A racial supremacist hate group founded in the mid-1970s by Richard Butler. Originally based in Idaho, the group is organized around Christian Identity mysticism.

**Aryan Republican Army (ARA).** A neo-Nazi terrorist group that operated in the midwestern United States from 1994 to 1996. Inspired by the example of the Irish Republican Army, the ARA robbed 22 banks in seven states before its members were captured. Its purpose had been to finance racial supremacist causes and to hasten the overthrow of the "Zionist Occupation Government." Some members also considered themselves to be Christian Identity fundamentalist Phineas Priests.

**Asahara, Shoko.** The spiritual leader of the Aum Shinrikyō cult.

**Ásatrú.** A mystical belief in the ancient Norse gods' pantheon. Some Ásatrú believers are racial supremacists.

**Askaris.** Government-supported death squads in South Africa that assassinated members of the African National Congress and their supporters prior to the end of apartheid.

**Assassination.** The act of killing a symbolic victim in a sudden and premeditated attack. Many assassinations are politically motivated.

**Assault rifles.** Automatic military weapons that use rifle ammunition.

**Asymmetrical warfare.** A term used to describe tactics, organizational configurations, and methods of conflict that do not use previously accepted or predictable rules of engagement.

**Aum Shinrikyō.** A cult based in Japan and led by Shoko Asahara. Responsible for releasing nerve gas into the Tokyo subway system, injuring 5,000 people.

**Ausländer.** Literally, "foreigner" in German. It is a derogatory term given by German rightists to unwelcome ethnonational immigrants.

**Authoritarian regimes.** Governments that practice strict control over public and political institutions and emphasize public order. The media and other public information outlets are regulated and censored by the government. Some authoritarian regimes have democratic institutions.

**Auto-genocide.** Self-genocide. When members of the same ethnic or religious group commit genocide against fellow members.

**Avengers of the Martyrs.** A government-sponsored death squad in Chile during the 1970s that operated under the direction of the security forces.

**"Axis of evil."** In January 2002, U.S. President George W. Bush identified Iraq, Iran, and North Korea as the "axis of evil." In that speech, he promised that the United States "will not permit the world's most dangerous regimes to threaten us with the world's most destructive weapons."

**Ayyash, Yehiya (the Engineer).** A Palestinian terrorist bomb maker affiliated with Hamas. He was responsible for scores of Israeli casualties and was eventually assassinated by a remotely controlled explosive device hidden in his cell phone.

**Baader, Andreas.** A founder and leader of the Red Army Faction/Baader-Meinhof Gang in West Germany. He committed suicide in prison in October 1977 along with

Gudrun Ensslin and Jan-Carl Raspe. The incident became known as Death Night.

**Baader-Meinhof Gang.** A leftist terrorist movement active in West Germany during the 1970s and 1980s. Also referred to as the Red Army Faction.

**Ba'ath Party.** A pan-Arab nationalist party.

**Bakunin, Mikhail.** An early philosophical proponent of anarchism in Russia.

**Balkan Route.** A drug-smuggling route through the Balkans. Political dissidents are involved with the drug trade, using the profits to fund their activities.

**Basque Fatherland and Liberty (Euskadi Ta Azkatasuna, or ETA).** Founded in 1959 to promote the independence of the Basque region in northern Spain. Although ETA adopted terrorism as a tactic in reply to the Franco government's violent repression of Basque nationalism, its campaign of violence escalated in the post-Franco era. At least six ETA factions and subfactions have been formed.

**Battalion 3-16.** A government-sponsored death squad active in Honduras in the 1980s.

**Baumhammers, Richard.** An American racial supremacist influenced by neo-Nazi ideology who shot to death six people near Pittsburgh, Pennsylvania, in April 2000. A case study in politically motivated lone wolf attacks. Also a case study of a minimal degree of criminal skill.

**Begin, Menachem.** A leader of the Irgun. Eventually rose to become the prime minister of Israel.

**Berri, Nabih.** A leader of the Shi'a Amal paramilitary, prominent during the Lebanese Civil War during the 1970s and 1980s, as well as during the TWA Flight 847 incident.

**bin Laden, Osama.** Founder and leader of the terrorist Al-Qa'ida network.

**Biological agents.** A term used to refer to potential ingredients in biological weapons.

**Biometric technology.** Digital technologies that allow digital photographs of faces to be matched against wanted suspects. Biometrics was used at American football's 2001 Super Bowl championship, when cameras scanned the faces of sports fans as they entered the stadium and compared their digital images with those of criminal fugitives and terrorists. The game became derisively known as the "Snooperbowl."

**Birmingham Six.** Six men who were wrongfully convicted of a 1974 bombing of two pubs in Birmingham, England. They were released in 1991 after an appellate court ruled that the police had used fabricated evidence.

**Black helicopters.** Referenced by right-wing conspiracy theorists as evidence of an impending takeover by agents of the New World Order.

**Black Hundreds.** An anti-Semitic movement in czarist Russia that was responsible for pogroms and other violence against Russian Jews during the late 19th and early 20th centuries.

**Black Liberation Army (BLA).** An African American terrorist group active during the 1970s. The BLA was cell-based and tended to target police officers and banks.

**Black Panther Party for Self-Defense.** An African American nationalist organization founded in 1966 in Oakland, California. The Black Panthers eventually became a national movement. It was not a terrorist movement, but some members eventually engaged in terrorist violence.

**Black Power.** An African American nationalist ideology developed during the 1960s that stressed self-help, political empowerment, cultural chauvinism, and self-defense.

**Black September.** A campaign waged by the Jordanian army in September 1970 to suppress what was perceived to be a threat to Jordanian sovereignty from Palestinian fighters and leaders based in Jordan.

**Black Widows.** The term given by the Russian media and authorities to Chechen women who participated in terrorist attacks against Russian interests. Many Black Widows engaged in suicide operations, and such women either volunteered, were manipulated, or were coerced to enlist. They were allegedly the relatives of Chechen men who have been killed in the conflict.

**"Blacklisting."** A policy of prohibiting political activists from obtaining employment in certain industries.

**Bloody Sunday.** An incident on January 30, 1972, in Londonderry, Northern Ireland, when British paratroopers fired on demonstrators, killing 13 people.

**Boland Amendment.** A bill passed by Congress in December 1982 that forbade the expenditure of U.S. funds to overthrow the Sandinista government.

**Botulinum toxin (botulism).** A rather common form of food poisoning. It is a bacterium rather than a virus or fungus, and can be deadly if inhaled or ingested even in small quantities.

**Bourgeoisie.** A term frequently used by Marxists to describe the middle class.

**Breivik, Anders.** A Norwegian right-wing extremist who detonated a lethal bomb in Oslo and went on a killing spree at a nearby youth camp in July 2011.

**Bubonic Plague.** Known as the Black Death in medieval Europe, this disease was spread by bacteria-infected fleas that infected hosts when bitten. The disease was highly infectious and often fatal.

**Bureau for the Protection of the Constitution.** A government agency in Germany responsible for domestic security and intelligence.

**Bureaucracy.** Operational arrangements of government. Max Weber used the term to describe and explain rationality and efficiency in managing governments—a field of public administration known as organizational theory.

**Burke, Edmund.** The British "father" of conservatism. An 18th-century intellectual who denounced the excesses of the French Revolution and other challenges to the traditional European order.

**Bushido.** The Japanese code of self-sacrifice adopted before and during the Second World War. Derived from the ancient code of the samurai.

**Butler, Richard.** The founder and leader of the Aryan Nations organization. Also a promulgator of Christian Identity mysticism.

**Cadre.** Politically indoctrinated and motivated activists. Frequently the core of a revolutionary movement.

**Camorra.** A Neapolitan secret society that became an organized crime enterprise.

**"Carlos The Jackal."** The *nom de guerre* for Ilich Ramírez Sánchez, a Venezuelan revolutionary who became an international terrorist. He acted primarily on behalf of the Popular Front for the Liberation of Palestine.

**Carnivore.** A surveillance technology developed for use by the Federal Bureau of Investigation (FBI) that could reportedly monitor Internet communications. Under law, the FBI could not use Carnivore without a specific court order under specific guidelines, much like other criminal surveillance orders. The FBI eventually redesignated the system DCS-1000.

**Castro, Fidel.** The leader of the Cuban Revolution.

**Cell-based terrorist environment.** A terrorist environment in which terrorists have organized themselves into small, semi-autonomous units rather than in traditionally hierarchical configurations. Difficult to combat because there is no central organization.

**Cells.** Autonomous groups of terrorists who may be loosely affiliated with a larger movement but who are largely independent of hierarchical control.

**Central Intelligence Agency (CIA).** The principal intelligence agency in the United States. The theoretical coordinator of American foreign intelligence collection.

**Chemical agents.** Chemicals that can potentially be converted into weapons. Some chemical agents, such as pesticides, are commercially available. Other chemical agents can be manufactured by terrorists using commonly available instruction guides.

**Chesimard, JoAnne.** *See* Shakur, Assata.

**Child soldiers.** Children who have been pressed into military service.

**Chlorine gas.** A chemical agent that destroys the cells that line the respiratory tract.

**Christian Identity.** The American adaptation of Anglo-Israelism. A racial supremacist mystical belief that holds that Aryans are the chosen people of God, the United States is the Aryan "Promised Land," nonwhites are soulless beasts, and Jews are biologically descended from the devil.

**Christian Right.** A mostly Protestant fundamentalist movement in the United States that links strict evangelical Christian values to political agendas.

**Cinque.** *See* DeFreeze, Donald.

**Classical ideological continuum.** Symbolic political designations derived from the French Revolution. The concepts of *left, center,* and *right* have become part of modern political culture.

**Codes of self-sacrifice.** Philosophical, ideological, or religious doctrines that create a warrior ethic in followers of the doctrine. Codes of self-sacrifice instill a sense of a "higher calling" that allows for the adoption of a superior morality. Acts of violence carried out in the name of the code are considered by followers to be completely justifiable.

**Coercive covert operations.** Covert counterterrorist measures that seek to resolve terrorist crises by disrupting and destroying terrorist groups.

**"Collateral damage."** A term used to describe unintended casualties. Usually applied to civilians who have been mistakenly killed.

**Collective nonviolence.** An activist philosophy of the civil rights movement in the American South that advocated peaceful civil disobedience.

**"Comfort women."** Women from territories conquered by the Japanese army during the Second World War who were forced into sexual slavery.

**Communal terrorism.** Group-against-group terrorism, in which rival demographic groups engage in political violence against one another.

**Composite-4 (C-4).** A powerful military-grade plastic explosive.

**Concessionary options.** Conciliatory counterterrorist measures that seek to resolve terrorist crises by acceding to the terrorists' demands.

**Conciliatory responses.** Counterterrorist measures that seek to resolve terrorist crises by addressing the underlying conditions that cause extremist violence.

**Conservatism.** A political ideology that seeks to preserve traditional values.

**Contagion effect.** "Copycat terrorism" in which terrorists imitate one another's behavior and tactics. This theory is still debated.

**Contras.** Rightist Nicaraguan counterrevolutionaries trained and supported by the United States during the 1980s.

**Convention to Prevent and Punish Acts of Terrorism Taking the Form of Crimes Against Persons and Related Extortion That Are of International Significance.** A treaty among members of the Organization of American States that defined attacks against internationally protected persons as common crimes. The purpose of the agreement was to establish common ground for recognizing the absolute inviolability of diplomatic missions.

**Counterculture.** A youth-centered movement in the United States and other Western countries during the 1960s and 1970s. It questioned status quo social and political values.

**Counterterrorism.** Proactive policies that specifically seek to eliminate terrorist environments and groups. There are a number of possible categories of counterterrorist response, including counterterrorist laws, which specifically criminalize terrorist behavior and supportive operations.

**Covenant, the Sword, and the Arm of the Lord, The (CSA).** An American apocalyptic religious and racial supremacist survivalist community in the Ozark Mountains of Arkansas. The group was effectively disbanded in 1985 after prosecutions by federal authorities for, among other charges, possessing a large quantity of poisonous potassium cyanide. CSA had intended to use the toxin to poison water supplies in U.S. cities.

**Covert operations.** Counterterrorist measures that seek to resolve terrorist crises by secretly disrupting or destroying terrorist groups, movements, and support networks.

**Crazy states.** States whose behavior is not rational, in which the people live at the whim of the regime or a dominant group. Some crazy states have little or no central authority and are ravaged by warlords or militias. Other crazy states have capricious, impulsive, and violent regimes in power that act out with impunity.

**Creativity.** A mystical belief practiced by the racial supremacist World Church of the Creator in the United States. Creativity is premised on a rejection of the white race's reliance on Christianity, which is held to have been created by the Jews as a conspiracy to enslave whites. According to Creativity, the white race itself should be worshipped.

**Criminal cartels.** Cooperative groups of illegal drug enterprises. Involved in the manufacture and smuggling of drugs.

**Criminal dissident terrorism.** Political violence perpetrated by dissidents who also engage in criminal enterprises to fund their movements.

**Criminal-political enterprises.** Political dissident groups that engage in criminal enterprises, such as smuggling drugs or arms, to fund their movements.

**Criminal profiles.** Descriptive profiles of criminal suspects developed by law enforcement agencies to assist in the apprehension of the suspects.

**Crucifixion.** A form of public execution during the time of the Roman Empire. It involved affixing condemned persons to a cross or other wooden platform. The condemned were either nailed through the wrist or hand, or tied upon the platform; they died by suffocation as their bodies sagged.

**Crusades.** A series of Christian military campaigns during the Middle Ages instigated by the Pope and Western Christian rulers. Most of these campaigns were invasions of Muslim territories, although the Crusaders also attacked Orthodox Christians, conducted pogroms against Jews, and suppressed "heresies."

**Cult of personality.** The glorification of a single strong national leader and political regime.

**Customer anonymity.** A policy adopted in some countries that allows national banks to guarantee customer privacy.

**Cyberterrorism.** The term given to the use of technology by terrorists to disrupt information systems.

**Cyberwar.** The targeting of terrorists' electronic activities by counterterrorist agencies. Bank accounts, personal records, and other data stored in digital databases can theoretically be intercepted and compromised.

**"Days of Rage."** Four days of rioting and vandalism committed by the Weathermen in Chicago in October 1969.

**Death Night.** The term given to an incident that occurred in West Germany on October 18, 1977, when three imprisoned leaders of the Red Army Faction committed suicide with weapons that were smuggled into a high-security prison. Many Germans have never believed the West German government's official explanation for the events of Death Night, and some have suggested that the government was responsible for the deaths.

**Death squads.** Rightist paramilitaries and groups of people who have committed numerous human rights violations. Many death squads in Latin America and elsewhere have been supported by the government and the upper classes.

**Decommissioning.** The process of disarmament by the Irish Republican Army that was set as a condition for the Good Friday Agreement peace accords.

**Defense Intelligence Agency (DIA).** The central agency for military intelligence of the U.S. armed forces.

**DeFreeze, Donald.** The leader of the Symbionese Liberation Army, a California-based American terrorist group active during the 1970s. DeFreeze adopted the *nom de guerre* Cinque.

**Degenerate workers' state.** A term used by Trotskyites to describe the Soviet Union.

**Delta Force (1st Special Forces Operational Detachment–Delta).** A secretive American special operations unit that operates in small, covert teams. Its mission is similar to that of the British Special Air Service and French 1st Marine Parachute Infantry Regiment. Delta Force operations probably include abductions, reconnaissance, and punitive operations.

**Democratic Front for the Liberation of Palestine (DFLP).** A faction of the Palestine Liberation Organization, which split from the Popular Front for the Liberation of Palestine in 1969 and further split into two factions in 1991. It is a Marxist organization that believes in ultimate victory through mass revolution, and it has committed small bombings and assaults against Israel, including border raids.

**Department of Homeland Security.** A department of the U.S. government created to coordinate homeland security in the aftermath of the September 11, 2001, homeland attacks.

**Department of Homeland Security Act of 2002.** Statutory authorization for the creation of the Department of Homeland Security in the United States.

**Dictatorship of the proletariat.** The Marxist belief that the communist revolution will result in the establishment of a working class–centered government.

**Diplock courts.** Special courts created in Northern Ireland in response to repeated intimidation of jurors by paramilitaries. Named after Lord Diplock, who reported to Parliament on the problem, they held trials before a single judge without recourse to jury trial.

**Diplomacy.** Conciliatory counterterrorist measures that seek to resolve terrorist crises by negotiating with terrorists or their supporters.

**Diplomatic Security Service.** A security bureau within the U.S. Department of State that protects diplomats and other officials.

**Direct action.** A philosophy of direct confrontation adopted by the Students for a Democratic Society and other members of the American New Left movement.

**Directorate for Inter-Services Intelligence (ISI).** The chief Pakistani security service.

**"Dirty bomb."** A highly toxic bomb that contains conventional bomb components and toxic substances such as radioactive materials or toxic chemicals. The conventional bomb sends out a cloud of radioactive or chemical toxins.

**Dirty War.** A term given to a campaign of state-sponsored terror waged in Argentina during the 1970s. Tens of thousands of people were tortured, made to "disappear," or killed.

**"Disinformation."** Counterterrorist measures that seek to resolve terrorist crises by disseminating damaging information, thus perhaps causing internal dissension and distrust among the terrorists and their supporters.

**Dissident terrorism.** "Bottom-up" terrorism perpetrated by individuals, groups, or movements in opposition to an existing political or social order.

**Dohrn, Bernardine.** A founder and leader of the Weatherman faction of Students for a Democratic Society. She eventually went underground with other Weathermen to form the Weather Underground Organization.

**Drug cartel.** A criminal cartel that is formed to regulate prices and output of illicit drugs. Many Colombian and Mexican traditional organized crime groups have been drug cartels.

**Drug-related violence.** Nonpolitical crime-related violence stemming from the illicit drug trade, when violence is directed against those who interfere with the operations of a drug trafficking organization. This is in contradistinction to *narco-terrorism.*

**Duvdevan.** An elite unit in the Israel Defense Forces that specializes in urban covert operations disguised as Arabs.

**Dynamite.** A commercially available high explosive that has nitroglycerin as its principal chemical ingredient.

**Earth Liberation Front.** A single-issue movement that protests environmental degradation and pollution. A splinter group from the environmentalist group Earthfirst!, the ELF is potentially more radical than the Animal Liberation Front.

**Echelon.** A satellite surveillance network maintained by the U.S. National Security Agency. It is a kind of global "wiretap" that filters through communications using antennae, satellite, and other technologies. Internet transfers, telephone conversations, and data transmissions are the types of communications that can reportedly be intercepted.

**Economic sanctions.** Counterterrorist measures that seek to influence the behavior of terrorist states by pressuring their national economies.

**Eco-Terrorism.** Political violence committed by sef-styled defenders of the environment. Typical targets include laboratories, housing developments, vehicles, and infrastructure.

**Electromagnetic pulse (EMP) technologies.** Technologies using an electromagnetic burst from a generator that can disable electronic components such as microchips. If used on a sizable scale, EMP could destroy large quantities of military or financial information.

**Electronic triggers.** Remotely controlled bombs are commonly employed by terrorists. The trigger is activated by a remote electronic or radio signal.

**11th Parachute Division (Paras).** An elite French army unit that can deploy as a quick-reaction force to deal with terrorist threats.

**el-Qaddafi, Muammar.** The ruler of Libya who became a prominent figure in state sponsorship of international terrorism during the 1980s. His regime collapsed when rebels inspired by the 2011 Arab Spring uprisings seized control of the capital city of Tripoli after a bloody civil war. Qaddafi was killed when his last stronghold fell in October 2011.

**Emergency Search Team.** A paramilitary unit within the U.S. Department of Energy that has counterterrorist capabilities.

**End justifies the means.** A concept wherein the desired goal is so just that the methods used to obtain the goal are acceptable regardless of their immediate consequences.

**Engels, Friedrich.** Karl Marx's colleague and compatriot during the genesis of what was to become communist ideology.

**Enhanced security.** Counterterrorist measures that "harden" targets to deter or otherwise reduce the severity of terrorist attacks.

**Ensslin, Gudrun.** A founder and leader of the Red Army Faction/Baader-Meinhof Gang in West Germany. She committed suicide in prison in October 1977 along with Andreas Baader and Jan-Carl Raspe. The incident became known as Death Night.

**Episode-specific sponsorship.** State-sponsored terrorism limited to a single episode or campaign.

**Establishment, The.** A designation coined by the New Left in the United States during the 1960s. It referred to mainstream American political and social institutions.

**Ethnic cleansing.** A term created by Serb nationalists during the wars following the breakup of Yugoslavia. It described the suppression and removal of non-Serbs from regions claimed for Serb settlement. A euphemism for genocide.

**Ethnonationalist communal terrorism.** Violence involving conflict between populations that have distinct histories, customs, ethnic traits, religious traditions, or other cultural idiosyncrasies.

**Euphemistic language.** Code words used by participants in a terrorist environment to describe other participants and their behavior.

**European Police Office (EUROPOL).** A cooperative investigative consortium of members of the European Union. It has a mission similar to INTERPOL.

**Executive Order 12333.** An executive order by President Ronald Reagan issued in December 1981. It expressly prohibited employees of the United States from assassinating adversaries. The order also forbade U.S. personnel from using anyone hired as an agent to commit assassinations.

**Executive Order 13228.** An order issued on October 8, 2001, by President George W. Bush, entitled Establishing the Office of Homeland Security and the Homeland Security Council.

**Extradition treaties.** International agreements to turn over criminal fugitives to the law enforcement agencies of fellow signatories.

**Extremism.** Political opinions that are intolerant toward opposing interests and divergent opinions. Extremism forms the ideological foundation for political violence. Radical and reactionary extremists often rationalize and justify acts of violence committed on behalf of their cause.

**"Extremism in defense of liberty is no vice."** An uncompromising belief in the absolute righteousness of a cause. A moralistic concept that clearly defines good and evil. The statement was made by Senator Barry Goldwater during the 1964 presidential election in the United States.

**"Extraordinary rendition."** A practice initially sanctioned during the Reagan administration in about 1987 as a measure to capture drug traffickers, terrorists, and other wanted persons. It involves an uncomplicated procedure: Find the suspects anywhere in the world, seize them, transport them to the United States, and force their appearance before a federal court.

**Fallout.** Dangerous radioactive debris emitted into the atmosphere by a nuclear explosion that descends to Earth as toxic material.

**Far-left ideology.** The extremist, but not necessarily violent, ideology of the left wing. Usually strongly influenced by Marxist ideology. Radical in political orientation.

**Far-right ideology.** The extremist, but not necessarily violent, ideology of the right wing. Reactionary in political orientation.

***Fasces.*** A symbolic bundle of sticks with an axe in the center, originally symbolizing the power of the Roman Empire. Modern states also use the symbolism of the *fasces,* and the term *fascist* is derived from the word.

**Fascism.** An ideology developed during the mid–20th century that emphasized strong state-centered authority, extreme law and order, militarism, and nationalism. Variants of fascism were applied during the 1930s in Italy, Germany, and Spain, as well as in Latin America during the postwar era.

**Federal Bureau of Investigation (FBI).** An investigative bureau within the U.S. Department of Justice. It is the largest federal law enforcement agency, and among its duties are domestic counterterrorism and intelligence collection.

**Female genital mutilation (FGM).** In some countries, mainly in traditional African societies, girls are subjected to ritualized genital mutilation (usually clitorectomies) when they reach puberty. Amnesty International reports that approximately 135 million women have undergone the procedure, at a rate of perhaps 6,000 per day.

**Fhima, Lamen Khalifa.** An alleged agent of Libya's security service who was acquitted by a Scottish court sitting near the Hague, Netherlands, of charges that he participated in the bombing of Pan Am Flight 103 over Lockerbie, Scotland.

**1st Marine Parachute Infantry Regiment.** An elite French unit that is similar to the British Special Air Service and the American Delta Force. It deploys small intelligence and special operations squads that are trained to operate in desert, urban, and tropical environments. They are part of the core of French counterterrorist special operations forces.

*Foquismo.* Ernesto "Che" Guevara's theory of continent-wide revolution in Latin America, in which a revolutionary cadre group would instigate and lead the international revolution.

**Force 17.** An elite security unit within Fatah, founded in 1970. It has engaged in paramilitary and terrorist attacks and has served as Yasir Arafat's guard force.

**Force 777.** An elite Egyptian counterterrorist unit that has had mixed success in resolving terrorist crises.

**Foreign Legion.** A branch of the French armed forces that has historically been composed of foreign nationals. The Legion is able to deploy commando and parachute units to resolve terrorist crises.

**Fountain Valley Massacre.** The execution-style slayings of seven whites and one African American employee at the Fountain Valley Golf Club on the island of St. Croix by Virgin Islands nationalists seeking independence from the United States.

**Four Olds.** During the Great Proletarian Cultural Revolution in China, Maoists waged an ideological struggle to eliminate what they termed the *Four Olds:* old ideas, old culture, old customs, and old habits.

**Fourteen Words.** A rallying slogan for the racial supremacist right wing in the United States. Originally coined by a convicted member of the terrorist group the Order, the Fourteen Words are: "We must secure the existence of our people and a future for White children."

**Franco, Francisco.** The leader of the right-wing rebellion in Spain against the leftist republic during the Civil War of the 1930s. He became the dictator of postwar Spain.

**Free press.** A media environment wherein few official restrictions are placed on the reporting of the news. The free press relies on ethical and professional standards of behavior to regulate reporting practices.

**Freedom Birds.** A term given to female combatants in the Liberation Tigers of Tamil Eelam.

**"Freedom fighter."** One who fights on behalf of an oppressed group. A very contextual term.

**French Navy Special Assault Units.** Elite units of the French Navy who are trained for operations against seaborne targets, coastlines, and harbors. Their mission is similar to those of the British Special Boat Service and the U.S. Navy SEALs.

**Fringe-left ideology.** Ideology of the revolutionary left. Often violent.

**Fringe-right ideology.** Ideology of the revolutionary right. Often violent.

**Fund for the Martyrs.** An Iranian fund established for the benefit of Palestinian victims of the *intifada* against Israel.

**Furrow, Buford O'Neal.** A former member of Aryan Nations who went on a shooting spree in Los Angeles, California, in August 1999. His spree included an attack at a Jewish community center in which five people were wounded, and the murder of an Asian mail carrier.

**"Gasoline bomb."** A simple explosive consisting of a gasoline-filled container with a detonator. Perhaps the most common gasoline bomb is the Molotov Cocktail.

**Gender communal terrorism.** A conceptual designation describing political violence directed against the women of an ethnonational, religious, or political group.

**General deterrence.** The creation of an environment by governments and counterterrorist agencies in which the risks of political violence outweigh the benefits.

**Genocidal state terrorism.** State-initiated genocide. The state either involves itself directly in the genocidal campaign or deploys proxies to carry out the genocide.

**Genocide.** The suppression of a targeted demographic group with the goal of repressing or eliminating its cultural or physical distinctiveness. The group is usually an ethnonational, religious, or ideological group.

**GEO (Grupo Especial de Operaciones).** A counterterrorist and hostage rescue force organized by the Spanish National Police.

GEO's training has allowed it to be used in both law enforcement and counterterrorist operations. Most of the latter have been directed against the Basque ETA terrorist movement.

**GIGN (Groupe d'Intervention Gendarmerie Nationale).** An elite paramilitary unit recruited from the French *gendarmerie*, or military police. GIGN is a counterterrorist unit with international operational duties.

**Golani Brigade.** An elite unit within the Israel Defense Forces that normally operates in conventionally organized military units. It has been deployed frequently for suppression campaigns against Hezbollah in South Lebanon.

**Golden Crescent.** The opium- and heroin-producing area of Southwest Asia.

**Golden Temple.** The most sacred temple of the Sikh religion, located in Amritsar, India. Indian troops stormed the temple in June 1984 to retake it from Sikhs who had occupied it, killing hundreds.

**Golden Triangle.** The opium- and heroin-producing area of Southeast Asia.

**Goldstein, Baruch.** A "lone wolf" terrorist who fired on worshippers inside the Ibrahim Mosque at the Cave of the Patriarch's holy site in the city of Hebron, Israel. According to official government estimates, he killed 29 people and wounded another 125. In reprisal for the Hebron massacre, the Palestinian Islamic fundamentalist movement Hamas launched a bombing campaign that included the first wave of human suicide bombers.

**Good Friday Agreement.** A significant outcome of the Northern Ireland peace process. The agreement was overwhelmingly approved by voters on April 10, 1998, in the Irish Republic and Northern Ireland. It signaled the mutual acceptance of a Northern Ireland assembly and the disarmament, or "decommissioning," of all paramilitaries.

**Grail.** A designation for the Soviet-made SA-7 surface-to-air missile.

**Great Proletarian Cultural Revolution.** A period from 1965 to 1969 in China during which the Communist Party instigated a mass movement to mobilize the young postrevolution generation. Its purpose was to eliminate "revisionist" tendencies in society and to create a newly indoctrinated revolutionary generation.

**Greater *jihad*.** In Muslim belief, an individual struggle to do what is right in accordance with God's wishes. All people of faith are required to do what is right and good.

**Green Berets (Special Forces Groups).** A special operations unit of the U.S. Army. Green Berets usually operate in units called A Teams, comprising specialists whose skills include languages, intelligence, medicine, and demolitions. The traditional mission of the A Team is force multiplication.

**Green Police.** The popular name for Israel's Police Border Guards.

**Grey Wolves.** A rightist ultranationalist movement in Turkey that promotes the establishment of a Greater Turkey called Turan, which would unite all Turkish people in a single nation. Responsible for numerous acts of terrorism.

**"Ground Zero."** The location in New York City of the September 11, 2001, terrorist attacks. It is the site of the World Trade Center's destroyed Twin Towers and Building 7.

**GSG-9 (Grenzschutzgruppe 9).** An elite German paramilitary unit that was organized after the disastrous failed attempt to rescue Israeli hostages taken by Black September at the 1972 Munich Olympics. It is a paramilitary force that has been used domestically and internationally as a counterterrorist and hostage rescue unit.

**Guerrilla.** A term first used during Spanish resistance against French occupation troops during the Napoleonic Wars. It refers to irregular hit-and-run tactics.

**Guevara, Ernesto "Che."** An Argentine revolutionary and intellectual who was instrumental in the success of the Cuban Revolution. Eventually killed in Bolivia, he developed his own philosophy of a continent-wide revolution in Latin America.

**Guildford Four.** Four people who were wrongfully convicted of an October 1974 bombing in Guildford, England. They served 15 years in prison before being released in 1989 when their convictions were overturned on appeal.

**Hague Convention of 1970.** A treaty requiring the extradition or prosecution of hijackers.

**Hague Conventions.** A series of international agreements that tried to establish rules for conflict.

**Hale, Matthew.** Leader of the World Church of the Creator in the United States until his conviction in 2004 on charges of conspiring to assassinate a federal judge in Illinois.

**Hamas (Islamic Resistance Movement).** A Palestinian Islamic movement that waged a protracted terrorist campaign against Israel.

**Harkat-ul-Ansar.** A Pakistan-supported movement in Kashmir that has engaged in terrorism.

**Hate crimes.** Crimes motivated by hatred against protected groups of people. They are prosecuted as aggravated offenses rather than as acts of terrorism.

*Hawala.* An ancient transnational trust-based system used to transfer money via brokers.

**Hezbollah.** A Lebanese Shi'a movement that promotes Islamic revolution. It was prominent in the resistance against the Israeli presence in South Lebanon and frequently engaged in terrorism.

**Hitler, Adolf.** The leader of the National Socialist German Workers, or Nazi, Party in Germany during the 1930s and 1940s.

**Ho Chi Minh.** The communist leader of Vietnam in the resistance against the French colonial presence. He later became the ruler of North Vietnam and continued his war by fighting the South Vietnamese government and the American military presence in the South.

**Holy Spirit Mobile Force.** A cultic insurgency in Uganda inspired and led by Alice Lakwena. In late 1987, she led thousands of her followers against the Ugandan army. To protect themselves from death, the fighters anointed themselves with holy oil, which they believed would ward off bullets. Thousands of Lakwena's followers were slaughtered in 1987 in the face of automatic weapons and artillery fire.

**Homeland security.** A dynamic concept first articulated to address threats to the American homeland after the September 11, 2001, terrorist attacks. It was later expanded to include domestic preparedness to respond to natural and human disasters, including terrorist attacks.

**Honor killings.** Murders of women or girls who are perceived to have dishonored a family, clan, or tribe by their behavior. Such killings are meted out by members of the same family, clan, or tribe.

**Hostage Rescue Team (HRT).** A paramilitary group organized under the authority of the U.S. Federal Bureau of Investigation. The HRT is typical of American paramilitary units in that it operates under the administrative supervision of federal agencies that perform traditional law enforcement work.

**House Un-American Activities Committee.** A congressional committee created in the aftermath of a Red Scare during the 1930s to investigate Communist threats to American security.

**Human intelligence.** Intelligence that has been collected by human operatives rather than through technological resources. Also referred to as HUMINT.

**Human Rights Watch.** An international watchdog organization that monitors human rights issues around the world.

**Hussein, Saddam.** The ruler of Iraq who became a prominent figure in state sponsorship of international terrorism and the development of weapons of mass destruction during the 1980s and 1990s. He also attempted to annex Kuwait during the early 1990s, causing the Gulf War.

**Ideological communal terrorism.** Communal violence in the postwar era that usually reflected the global ideological rivalry between the United States and the Soviet Union.

**Ideologies.** Systems of belief.

**Imperialism.** A term used to describe the doctrine of national expansion and exploitation.

**Improvised explosive devices (IEDs).** So-called "roadside bombs" that were constructed and deployed by Iraqi insurgents during the U.S.-led occupation.

**Information is power.** A political and popular concept that the control of the dissemination of information, especially through media outlets, enhances the power of the controlling interest.

**Inkatha Freedom Party.** A Zulu-based movement in South Africa.

**Intelligence.** The collection of data for the purpose of creating an informational database about terrorist movements and predicting their behavior.

**Intelligence community.** The greater network of intelligence agencies. In the United States, the Central Intelligence Agency is the theoretical coordinator of intelligence collection.

**International Court of Justice.** The principal judicial arm of the United Nations. Its 15 judges are elected from among member states, and each sits for a 9-year term. The court hears disputes between nations and gives advisory opinions to recognized international organizations.

**International Criminal Court (ICC).** A court established to prosecute crimes against humanity, such as genocide. Its motivating principle is to promote human rights and justice. In practice, this has meant that the ICC has issued arrest warrants for the prosecution of war criminals.

**International Criminal Police Organization (INTERPOL).** An international network of law enforcement that cooperates in the investigation of crimes. It is based in Saint-Cloud, France.

**International Criminal Tribunal for the Former Yugoslavia.** A tribunal that has investigated allegations of war crimes and genocide arising out of the wars that broke out after the fragmentation of Yugoslavia during the 1990s. Several alleged war criminals, including former Yugoslavian president Slobodan Milošević, have been brought before the court. Others remain at large but under indictment.

**International Criminal Tribunal for Rwanda (ICTR).** A tribunal that has investigated allegations of war crimes and genocide resulting from the breakdown of order in Rwanda during the 1990s. The indictments against suspected war criminals detail what can only be described as genocide on a massive scale.

**International law.** Multinational laws agreed to by governments and enforceable under international agreements.

**International *mujahideen*.** Islamic revolutionaries who have adopted a pan-Islamic ideology.

**International terrorism.** Terrorism that is directed against targets symbolizing international interests. These attacks can occur against domestic targets that have international symbolism or against targets in the international arena.

*Intifada*. The protracted Palestinian uprising against Israel. Literally, "shaking off."

**Iran-Contra scandal.** The term given to an operation in 1985 and 1986, in which American Lt. Colonel Oliver North of the National Security Council illegally sent arms to Iran in an effort to win the release of American hostages held in Lebanon. Profits from the sales were used to support Nicaraguan Contra insurgents.

**Irgun.** A Jewish terrorist group active in Palestine prior to the formation of the state of Israel. Its most infamous attack was the 1946 bombing of the King David Hotel.

**Irish National Liberation Army (INLA).** The INLA grew out of the split in the IRA during the 1970s. The group adopted Marxist theory as its guiding ideology and fought to reunite Northern Ireland with Ireland. The INLA considered itself to be fighting in unity with other terrorist groups that championed oppressed groups around the world. Its heyday was during the 1970s and mid-1980s.

**Islamic Jihad.** A label adopted by some Islamic terrorists seeking to establish an Islamic state. Groups known as Islamic Jihad exist in Lebanon, Palestine, and Egypt.

**"It became necessary to destroy the town to save it."** An extremist goal to destroy an existing order without developing a clear vision for the aftermath. A moral concept used to justify terrorist behavior. The statement was allegedly made by an American officer during the war in Vietnam.

**Izzedine al-Qassam Brigade.** A militant movement within the overarching Hamas movement of Palestinian Islamic revolutionaries.

**Jabotinsky, Vladimir.** A leader of the Jewish terrorist group Irgun. He was killed in 1940.

**Jamahiriya Security Organization.** The Libyan state security agency during the reign of Muammar el-Qaddafi. Apparently responsible for promoting Libya's policy of state-sponsored terrorism.

**Jammu and Kashmir Islamic Front.** A revolutionary proxy supported by Pakistan's Directorate for Inter-Services Intelligence.

**Jammu Kashmir Liberation Front.** An ethnonational and Islamic dissident movement in Kashmir. The movement has waged an irregular war against Indian occupation of part of Kashmir.

**Janjaweed.** An alliance of Arab militias in Darfur, Sudan. When a rebellion broke out among African residents of Darfur in early 2003, the Sudanese government armed and provided air support for a Janjaweed campaign of ethnic cleansing. About 2 million Africans became refugees when they were forced from the land, and about 50,000 were killed. The Janjaweed systematically sexually assaulted African women and girls.

**Japanese Red Army.** A nihilistic terrorist group active during the 1970s and 1980s. Responsible for many attacks, including the May 1972 attack in Lod Airport in Israel on behalf of the Popular Front for the Liberation of Palestine.

**Jewish Defense League (JDL).** A militant Jewish organization founded in the United States by Rabbi Meir Kahane.

*Jihad.* A central tenet in Islam that literally means a sacred "struggle" or "effort." Although Islamic extremists have interpreted *jihad* to mean waging holy war, it is not synonymous with the Christian concept of a crusade.

*Jihadi*. One who wages *jihad*.

**Joint operations.** State-sponsored terrorism in which state personnel participate in the terrorist enterprise.

**Journalistic self-regulation.** The theoretical practice of ethical reporting among members of the press.

**June 2nd Movement.** Founded in West Berlin in 1971, the June 2nd Movement was anarchistic in its ideology. It was known for bombing property targets in West Berlin. The June 2nd Movement's most famous action was the 1975 kidnapping of Peter Lorenz, a Berlin mayoral candidate. He was released in 1 day after four June 2nd comrades were released and flown to Yemen. After disbanding in the 1980s, many members joined the Red Army Faction.

*Jus ad bellum*. Correct conditions for waging war. An element of the Just War Doctrine.

*Jus in bello*. One's correct behavior while waging war. An element of the Just War Doctrine.

**Just War doctrine.** A moral and ethical doctrine that raises the questions of whether one can ethically attack an opponent, how one can justifiably defend oneself, and what types of force are morally acceptable in either context. The doctrine also addresses who can morally be defined as an enemy and what kinds of targets may be morally attacked.

**Justice Commandos of the Armenian Genocide.** One of several Armenian terrorist groups active in the postwar era that targeted Turkish interests to avenge the Turkish genocide of Armenians.

**Kach (Kahane Chai).** Militant movements in Israel that carried on after Rabbi Meir Kahane was assassinated. They advocate the expulsion of Arabs from territories claimed as historically Jewish land. *Kach* means "only thus." *Kahane Chai* means "Kahane lives."

**Kaczynski, Theodore "Ted."** The Unabomber in the United States, who sent bombs hidden in letters and packages to protest technological society. A case study in politically motivated lone wolf attacks. Also a case study of a medium degree of criminal skill.

**Kahane, Rabbi Meir.** Founder and leader of the Jewish Defense League.

**Kalashnikov, Mikhail.** The inventor of the famous AK-47 assault rifle.

**Kamikaze.** Literally, "divine wind" in Japanese. During the Second World War, the Japanese military sent suicide planes against American warships. These were called kamikazes.

**Kansi, Mir Amal.** A terrorist who used an AK-47 assault rifle against employees of the Central Intelligence Agency who were waiting in their cars to enter the CIA's headquarters in Langley, Virginia. Two people were killed, and three were wounded. He was later captured in Pakistan, was sent to the United States for prosecution, and was convicted of murder.

**Ker-Frisbie Rule.** A legal doctrine in the United States named for two cases: *Frisbie v. Collins,* 342 U.S. 519, 522 (1954) and *Ker v. Illinois,* 119 U.S. 436, 444 (1886). The doctrine permits authorities to identify suspects anywhere in the world, seize them, transport them to the United States, and force their appearance before a U.S. court.

**Kerner Commission.** A term given to the presidentially appointed National Advisory Commission on Civil Disorders, which released a report in 1968 on civil disturbances in the United States.

**Khaled, Leila.** A Palestinian nationalist who successfully hijacked one airliner and failed in an attempt to hijack another. She acted on behalf of the Popular Front for the Liberation of Palestine.

**Khmer Rouge.** A Cambodian Marxist insurgency that seized power in 1975. During its reign, between 1 and 2 million Cambodians died, many of them in the infamous Killing Fields.

**Khomeini, Ayatollah Ruhollah.** An Iranian religious leader who led the Iranian Revolution, which eventually ousted Shah Mohammad Reza Pahlavi.

**Kidnapping/hostage taking.** A method of propaganda by the deed in which symbolic individuals or small groups are taken captive as a way to publicize the terrorists' cause.

**"Kill one man, terrorize a thousand."** A paraphrasing of a quotation by the Chinese military philosopher Wu Ch'i. Variously ascribed to the Chinese military philosopher Sun Tzu and Chinese communist leader Mao Zedong.

**King David Hotel Bombing.** The bombing of a hotel in Jerusalem that housed the headquarters of the British military and the government secretariat before the founding of the state of Israel. On July 22, 1946, the Irgun bombed the hotel, killing 91 persons and wounding 45 others.

**Klassen, Ben.** The founder of the racial supremacist World Church of the Creator in the United States.

**"Kneecapping."** A signature method of violence used by combatants in Northern Ireland and by Italy's Red Brigades. The technique involved shooting a victim in the back of the knee joint, thus shooting off the kneecap.

*Komiteh.* Revolutionary tribunals established after the Islamic revolution in Iran.

**Korean Airlines Flight 858.** An airliner that exploded over Myanmar (Burma) in November 1987, apparently after sabotage by North Korean operatives.

**Kosovo Liberation Army (KLA).** An ethnic Albanian dissident movement seeking independence for the Kosovo region of the former Yugoslavia. The group has used terrorism against Serb civilians and security forces.

**Kropotkin, Petr.** An early philosophical proponent of anarchism in Russia.

**Ku Klux Klan (KKK).** A racial supremacist organization founded in 1866 in Pulaski, Tennessee. During its five eras, the KKK was responsible for thousands of acts of terrorism.

*Kuclos.* A symbol adopted by the Ku Klux Klan consisting of a cross and a teardrop-like symbol enclosed by a circle. Literally, Greek for "circle."

**Kurds.** An ethnonational group in the Middle East. Several nationalist movements fought protracted wars on behalf of Kurdish independence.

**La Cosa Nostra.** The American version of the Italian Mafia. Traditionally organized into family networks. Literally, "this thing of ours."

**Labeling.** The attaching of euphemistic terms to the participants in a terrorist environment.

**Lashkar e Taiba.** A Kashmiri Pakistani proxy based in Pakistan.

**Laskar Jihad (Militia of the Holy War).** An armed Islamic group organized in April 2000 in Indonesia. Under the leadership of Ja'afar Umar Thalib, the group waged a communal holy war in Indonesia, primarily against Christians on Indonesia's Molucca Islands.

**Law enforcement.** The use of law enforcement agencies and criminal investigative techniques in the prosecution of suspected terrorists.

**Leaderless resistance.** A cell-based strategy of the Patriot and neo-Nazi movements in the United States requiring the formation of "phantom cells" to wage war against the government and enemy interests. Dedicated Patriots and neo-Nazis believe that this strategy will prevent infiltration from federal agencies.

*Lebensraum.* The Nazi concept that Aryans should colonize Eastern Europe at the expense of indigenous Slavs and other supposedly inferior ethnonational groups.

**Left, center, right.** Designations on the classical ideological continuum. The left tends to promote social change. The center tends to favor incremental change and the status quo. The right tends to favor traditional values.

**Legalistic responses.** Counterterrorist measures that use the law to criminalize specific acts as terrorist behaviors and that use law enforcement agencies to investigate, arrest, and prosecute suspected terrorists.

**Lenin, Vladimir Ilich.** The Russian revolutionary leader and theorist who was the principal leader of the Russian Revolution of 1917. He became the first leader of the Soviet Union and was also the author of several books that were very influential in the international communist movement throughout the 20th century.

*Les événéments.* Literally, "the Events" during May and June 1968 in France. Centered in Paris and sparked by massive student protests, *les événéments* nearly toppled the government of Charles de Gaulle.

**Lesser *jihad.*** The defense of Islam against threats to the faith. This includes military defense and is undertaken when the Muslim community is under attack.

**Liberalism.** A political ideology that seeks incremental and democratic change.

**Liberation Tigers of Tamil Eelam (LTTE).** A nationalist group in Sri Lanka that champions the independence of the Tamil people. Responsible for many acts of terrorism.

**Liquid metal embrittlement.** The process of using chemicals to weaken metals. Such chemicals can *embrittle*, or make rigid, various metals.

**Logistically supportive sponsorship.** State-sponsored terrorism in which the state provides a great deal of logistical support to the terrorists but stops short of directly participating in the terrorist incident or campaign.

**Lone wolf model.** A designation describing political violence committed by individuals who are motivated by an ideology but who have no membership in a terrorist organization.

**Long hot summer.** A term used during the 1960s to describe urban racial tensions that sometimes led to rioting.

**Lord's Resistance Army.** Josef Kony reorganized Uganda's cultic Holy Spirit Mobile Force into the Lord's Resistance Army. He blended together Christianity, Islam, and witchcraft into a bizarre mystical foundation for his movement. The group was exceptionally brutal and waged near-genocidal terrorist campaigns—largely against the Acholi people, whom it claimed to champion.

**Luddites.** A movement of English workers during the early 1800s; the Luddites objected to the social and economic transformations of the Industrial Revolution. They targeted the machinery of the new textile factories, and textile mills and weaving machinery were disrupted and sabotaged. After 17 Luddites were executed in 1813, the movement gradually died out.

**Lumpenproletariat.** Karl Marx's designation of the nonproletarian lower classes. Considered by him to be incapable of leading the revolution against capitalism.

**Lumumba, Patrice.** A Congolese nationalist who became a martyred national hero. The first prime minister of Congo, he was executed by a rebel faction when he fled a military coup in 1961 that was instigated by Mobutu Sese Seko. He was declared a national hero in 1966 and became a nationalist hero in the pan-Africanist movement.

**Lynch mobs.** Groups of white American vigilantes who murdered their victims by hanging, burning, or shooting them to death. Most victims of lynching were African Americans. Lynchings were sometimes carried out in a festive atmosphere.

**M-16.** The standard assault rifle for the U.S. military; first introduced in the mid-1960s.

**MacDonald, Andrew.** *See* Pierce, William.

**Macheteros.** A Puerto Rican *independencista* terrorist group active during the 1970s and 1980s.

*Mala in se*. An act designated as a crime that is fundamentally evil, such as murder or rape.

*Mala prohibita*. An act designated as a crime that is not fundamentally evil, such as prostitution or gambling.

*Manifesto of the Communist Party.* The seminal document of communism, written by Karl Marx and Friedrich Engels.

**Mao Zedong.** The leader of the Chinese Revolution. His tactical and strategic doctrine of People's War was practiced by a number of insurgencies in the developing world. Mao's interpretation of Marxism was also very influential among communist revolutionaries.

**Marighella, Carlos.** A Brazilian Marxist revolutionary and theorist who developed an influential theory for waging dissident terrorist warfare in urban environments.

**Martyr nation.** A theoretical construct arguing that an entire ethnonational people is willing to endure any sacrifice to promote its liberation.

**Martyrdom.** Martyrdom is achieved by dying on behalf of a religious faith or for some other greater cause. A common concept among religious movements.

**Marx, Karl.** A mid-19th-century philosopher who, along with Friedrich Engels, developed the ideology of class struggle.

**Marxism.** An ideology that believes in the historical inevitability of class conflict, culminating in the final conflict that will establish the dictatorship of the proletariat.

**Mass communications.** The technological ability to convey information to a large number of people. It includes technologies that allow considerable amounts of information to be communicated through printed material, audio broadcasts, video broadcasts, and expanding technologies such as the Internet.

**Mathews, Robert Jay.** The founder and leader of the American neo-Nazi terrorist group the Order, which was founded in 1983.

**May 19 Communist Organization (M19CO).** An American Marxist terrorist group that was active in the late 1970s and early 1980s. It was composed of remnants of the Republic of New Africa (described elsewhere in the glossary), the Black Liberation Army, the Weather Underground, and the Black Panthers. M19CO derived its name from the birthdays of Malcolm X and Vietnamese leader Ho Chi Minh.

**McCarthy, Senator Joseph.** A Wisconsin senator who initiated a purge of suspected communists in the United States during the early 1950s.

**McCarthyism.** The term used to describe procedures and the underlying policy applied by Senator Joseph McCarthy in the United States during the purge of suspected communists in the early 1950s.

**McVeigh, Timothy.** A member of the Patriot movement in the United States and probably a racial supremacist. Responsible for constructing and detonating an ANFO bomb that destroyed the Alfred P. Murrah Federal Building in Oklahoma City, Oklahoma, on April 19, 1995. One hundred sixty-eight people were killed.

**Means of production.** A Marxist concept describing the primary source of economic production and activity during the stages of human social evolution.

**"Media as a weapon."** For terrorists and other extremists, information can be wielded as a weapon of war. Because symbolism is at the center of most terrorist incidents, the media are explicitly identified by terrorists as potential supplements to their arsenal.

**Media gatekeeping.** Similar to journalistic self-regulation. The theoretical practice of ethical self-regulation by members of the free press.

**Media scooping.** The obtaining and reporting of exclusive news by a media outlet. An outcome of the race to be the first to report breaking news.

**Media spin.** The media's inclusion of subjective and opinionated interpretations when reporting the facts.

**Media-oriented terrorism.** Terrorism that is purposely carried out to attract attention from the media and, consequently, the general public. Methods and targets are selected because they are likely to be given high priority by news outlets.

**Meinhof, Ulrike.** A founder and leader of the Red Army Faction/Baader-Meinhof Gang in West Germany. Meinhof hanged herself in prison on May 9, 1976.

**MI-5.** An intelligence agency in Great Britain responsible for domestic intelligence collection.

**MI-6.** An intelligence agency in Great Britain responsible for international intelligence collection.

**Military Intelligence Service.** A government agency in Germany responsible for international intelligence collection.

**Military-industrial complex.** A term first used by President Dwight Eisenhower to describe the potential threat of economic and political dominance by corporate interests.

**Militias.** Organized groups of armed citizens who commonly exhibit antigovernment tendencies and subscribe to conspiracy theories. The armed manifestation of the Patriot movement.

**Mines.** Military-grade explosives that are buried in the soil or rigged to be detonated as booby traps. Antipersonnel mines are designed to kill people, and antitank mines are designed to destroy vehicles. Many millions of mines have been manufactured and are available on the international market.

*Mini-Manual of the Urban Guerrilla.* An influential essay written by Carlos Marighella that outlined his theory of urban dissident terrorist warfare.

**Mitchell, Hulon, Jr.** Also known as Yahweh Ben Yahweh (God, Son of God). Founder and leader of a Miami branch of the Black Hebrew Israelites. He taught that whites are descendants of the devil and worthy of death. Followers who did not practice complete obedience were dealt with harshly, and some were beaten or beheaded. Mitchell and some of his followers were imprisoned. Mitchell's group was implicated in 14 murders during the 1980s.

**Moderate center.** The central stabilizing political grouping in democracies.

**"Molotov cocktails."** Simple gasoline bombs consisting of a gasoline-filled bottle with a rag inserted as a wick.

**Monolithic terrorist environment.** A terrorist environment in which a single

national sponsor supports and directs international terrorism. Combating this environment is relatively uncomplicated, because attention can theoretically be directed against a single adversary.

**Montoneros.** A terrorist movement in Argentina during the 1970s. Members espoused radical Catholic principles of justice, Peronist populism, and leftist nationalism. The Montoneros became skillful kidnappers and extorted an estimated $60 million in ransom payments. Shootings, bombings, and assassinations were also pervasive. When the military seized control in March 1976, all political opposition was crushed, including the terrorist campaign.

**Montreal Convention of 1971.** A treaty that extended international law to terrorist attacks on airports and grounded aircraft.

**Mossad.** An Israeli agency charged with carrying out intelligence collection and covert operations.

**Moussaoui, Zacarias.** A suspected member of the cell that carried out the September 11, 2001, attacks. He was being held in custody on other charges at the time of the attacks and was later prosecuted in federal court.

*Movimiento Nacional.* Francisco Franco's movement, which consolidated his power and established the model for Spanish fascism.

**"Mud People."** A derogatory term given to non-Aryans by followers of the Christian Identity movement. Mud People are considered to be nonhuman, soulless beasts who dwelt outside the Garden of Eden.

*Mujahideen.* Individuals who wage war in defense of Islam. Literally, "holy warriors."

**Multinational corporations.** Large corporations that conduct business on a global scale. They are usually centered in several countries.

**Muslim Brotherhood.** A transnational Sunni Islamic fundamentalist movement that is very active in several North African and Middle Eastern countries. It has been implicated in terrorist violence committed in Egypt, Syria, and elsewhere.

**Mussolini, Benito.** The Italian dictator who led the first successful fascist seizure of power during the 1920s.

**Mustard gas.** A chemical agent that is a mist rather than a gas. It is a blistering agent that affects skin, eyes, and the nose,

and it can severely damage the lungs if inhaled.

*Mutaween.* A religious police force in Saudi Arabia, officially known as the Authority for the Promotion of Virtue and Prevention of Vice. In 2002, the *Mutaween* were the focus of a public outcry when 15 girls died in a fire because they tried to escape the blaze without proper head coverings. The *Mutaween* had forced them to remain inside the burning building.

**Narco-terrorism.** Political violence committed by dissident drug traffickers who are primarily concerned with protecting their criminal enterprise. This is in contradistinction to *drug-related violence*.

*Narcotraficantes.* Latin American drug traffickers.

**National Alliance.** An overtly Nazi organization based in West Virginia that was founded in 1970 by William Pierce, a former member of the American Nazi Party.

**National Counterterrorism Center (NCTC).** An agency established in the United States to integrate the counterterrorism efforts of the intelligence community.

**National Liberation Army (Ejercito de Liberacion Nacional, or ELN).** A Marxist insurgency founded in the 1960s that has operated primarily in the countryside of Colombia. Its ideological icons are Fidel Castro and Ernesto "Che" Guevara. The ELN has engaged in bombings, extortion, and kidnappings. Targets have included foreign businesses and oil pipelines. The ELN has also participated in the drug trade.

**National Movement Party (MHP).** An ultranationalist political movement in Turkey that wishes to unite all Turkic people and to create Turan, or the Great Turkish Empire. MHP has links to the clandestine paramilitary known as the Grey Wolves.

**National Security Agency (NSA).** An American intelligence agency charged with signal intelligence collection, code making, and code breaking.

**Nationalist dissident terrorism.** Political violence committed by members of ethnonational groups that seek greater political rights or autonomy.

**Nativism.** American cultural nationalism. A cornerstone of Ku Klux Klan ideology.

**Nazi Holocaust.** The genocide waged against European Jews by Germany before and during the Second World War. The first significant anti-Semitic racial decree promulgated by the Nazis was the Law for the Protection of German Blood and German Honor, passed in September 1935. In the end, approximately 6 million Jews were murdered.

**N'drangheta.** A secret society in Calabria, Italy, that became a criminal society.

**Nechayev, Sergei.** An early philosophical proponent of anarchism in Russia. Author of *Revolutionary Catechism.*

**Neocolonialism.** A postwar Marxist concept describing Western economic exploitation of the developing world.

**Neoconservatism.** A conservative movement in the United States that eschews the lack of activism among traditional conservatives. Neoconservatives advocate strong international intervention. The core trait of neoconservative ideology is the aggressive promotion of democracy among allies and adversaries alike.

**Nerve gases.** Chemical agents, such as Sarin, Tabun, and VX, that block (or "short-circuit") nerve messages in the body. A single drop of a nerve agent, whether inhaled or absorbed through the skin, can shut down the body's neurotransmitters.

**Netwar.** An emerging method of conflict that uses network forms of organization and information-age strategies, doctrines, and technologies. Participants in these networks are dispersed small groups that operate as a "flat" organizational network rather than under chains of command.

**New African Freedom Fighters.** The self-defined "military wing" of an African American nationalist organization called the Republic of New Africa. Composed of former members of the Black Liberation Army and Black Panthers, the group operated in collaboration with other members of the revolutionary underground. It was eventually broken up in 1985 after members were arrested for conspiring to free an imprisoned comrade, bomb the courthouse, and commit other acts of political violence.

**New Left.** A movement of young leftists during the 1960s who rejected orthodox Marxism and took on the revolutionary theories of Frantz Fanon, Herbert Marcuse, Carlos Marighella, and other new theorists.

**New Media.** The use of existing technologies and alternative broadcasting formats to analyze and disseminate information. These formats include talk-show models, tabloid styles, celebrity status for hosts, and blatant entertainment spins. Strong and opinionated political or social commentary also makes up a significant portion of New Media content.

**New Order.** An Italian neofascist terrorist group. The group carried out several attacks in the late 1960s and early 1970s, including a bombing on December 12, 1969, of the famous Piazza Fontana in Milan, causing 16 deaths and 90 injuries.

**New Order, The.** An American neo-Nazi group that was broken up by federal agents in March 1998 in East St. Louis, Illinois. Members had modeled themselves after the Order and were charged with planning to bomb the Anti-Defamation League's New York headquarters; the headquarters of the Southern Poverty Law Center in Birmingham, Alabama; and the Simon Wiesenthal Center in Los Angeles.

**New People's Army (NPA).** A Filipino Marxist guerrilla group founded in 1969. Its ideology is Maoist, and it engages in urban terrorism such as bombings, shootings, extortion, and assassinations.

**New Terrorism.** A typology of terrorism characterized by a loose cell-based organizational structure, asymmetrical tactics, the threatened use of weapons of mass destruction, potentially high casualty rates, and usually a religious or mystical motivation.

**New World Liberation Front.** The name of an American terrorist group active during the mid-1970s. Organized as a "reborn" manifestation of the Symbionese Liberation Army by former SLA members and new recruits.

**New World Order.** A conspiracy theory common among American neo-Nazis and members of the Patriot movement. It holds that non-American interests are threatening to take over—or have already taken over—key governmental centers of authority. This takeover is part of an international plot to create a one-world government.

**News Triage.** The decision-making process within the media that decides what news to report and how to report it.

**Nidal, Abu.** The *nom de guerre* for Sabri al-Banna, a Palestinian terrorist for hire, whose organization was responsible for terrorist attacks in approximately 20 countries.

**Nihilism.** A 19th-century Russian philosophical movement of young dissenters who believed that only scientific truth could end ignorance. Nihilists had no vision for a future society; they asserted only that the existing society was intolerable. Modern nihilist dissidents exhibit a similar disdain for the existing social order but offer no clear alternative for after its destruction.

**Nihilist dissident terrorism.** The practice of political violence with the goal of destroying an existing order, committed with little or no regard for the aftermath of the revolution.

**Nihilist dissidents.** Antistate dissidents whose goal is to destroy the existing social order, with little consideration given for the aftermath of the revolution. They practice "revolution for revolution's sake."

**9/11.** A symbolic acronym for the September 11, 2001, terrorist attacks in the United States.

**Nonmilitary repressive options.** Counterterrorist measures that seek to resolve terrorist crises by using nonmilitary assets to disrupt and destroy terrorist groups and movements.

**Nonviolent covert operations.** Counterterrorist options that include infiltration, disinformation, cyberwar, intelligence, economic sanctions, and target hardening.

**Northern Ireland.** A northern region on the island of Ireland that has been under the jurisdiction of the United Kingdom since 1921. It consists of six counties of the Irish province of Ulster. The region has historically been a center of sectarian and nationalist violence between Catholics, Protestants, and British security forces.

**Northern Ireland Act.** A law passed in Northern Ireland in 1993 that created conditions of quasi–martial law. The act suspended several civil liberties and empowered the British military to engage in warrantless searches of civilian homes, temporarily detain people without charge, and question suspects. The military could also intern suspected terrorists and turn over for prosecution those for whom enough evidence had been seized.

**Nosair, El-Sayyid.** An Egyptian radical Islamic revolutionary who assassinated Rabbi Meir Kahane, the founder of the Jewish Defense League, in New York City in 1990.

**Nuclear weapons.** High-explosive military weapons using weapons-grade plutonium and uranium. Nuclear explosions devastate the area within their blast zone and irradiate an area outside the blast zone and are capable of sending dangerous radioactive debris into the atmosphere that descends to Earth as toxic fallout.

**"Off the grid."** A tactic used by hard-core members of the Patriot movement who believe in the New World Order conspiracy theory. Believers typically refuse to use credit cards, drivers' licenses, and Social Security numbers, as a way to lower their visibility from the government, banks, and other potential agents of the New World Order.

**Official Irish Republican Army.** The predominant organization of the IRA until the late 1960s, when the Provisional Irish Republican Army split to independently wage an armed struggle.

**Official Secrets Act.** An act in Great Britain that permitted the prosecution of individuals for the reporting of information that was deemed to endanger the security of the British government.

**Official state terrorism.** State terrorism that is undertaken as a matter of official government policy.

**Okhrana.** The secret police of czarist Russia. Responsible for writing the anti-Semitic *Protocols of the Learned Elders of Zion.*

**Omega 7.** An anticommunist Cuban American terrorist group that targeted Cuban interests.

**One-Dimensional Man.** German existentialist writer Herbert Marcuse's book that influenced the ideological orientation of the New Left.

**"One man willing to throw away his life is enough to terrorize a thousand."** The symbolic power of a precise application of force by an individual who is willing to sacrifice himself or herself can terrorize many other people. A moral concept that illustrates how a weak adversary can influence a strong adversary. The statement was made by the Chinese military philosopher Wu Ch'i.

**"One person's terrorist is another person's freedom fighter."** The importance of perspective in the use of violence to achieve political goals. Championed groups view violent rebels as freedom fighters, whereas their adversaries consider them to be terrorists.

**One-Seedline Christian Identity.** A Christian Identity mystical belief that argues that all humans, regardless of race, are descended from Adam. However, only Aryans (defined as certain northern Europeans) are the true elect of God. They are the Chosen People whom God has favored and who are destined to rule over the rest of humanity. In the modern era, those who call themselves the Jews are actually descended from a minor Black Sea ethnic group and therefore have no claim to Israel.

**Operation Death Trains.** The term given by terrorists to the attack against the Madrid transportation system in March 2004.

**Operation Eagle Claw.** An operation in April 1980 launched by the United States to rescue Americans held hostage by Iran at the U.S. embassy in Tehran. The operation failed on the ground in Iran when a helicopter flew into an airplane, and both exploded. Eight soldiers were killed, and the mission was aborted.

**Operation El Dorado Canyon.** On April 14, 1986, the United States bombed targets in Libya using Air Force bombers based in Great Britain and Navy carrier–borne aircraft based in the Mediterranean. The strike was in retaliation for terrorist attacks against American personnel in Europe.

**Operation Enduring Freedom.** The designation given to the counterterrorist war waged in the aftermath of the September 11, 2001, homeland attacks.

**Operation Infinite Justice.** The original designation given to the counterterrorist war waged in the aftermath of the September 11, 2001, attacks. The designation was changed after protests among Muslims stated that only God is capable of infinite justice.

**Operation Iraqi Freedom.** The designation given to the U.S.-led invasion of Iraq in March 2003.

**Operation Peace for Galilee.** An invasion of Lebanon by the Israeli army in June 1982, with the goal of rooting out PLO bases of operation. It was launched in reply to ongoing PLO attacks from its Lebanese bases.

**ORDEN.** A right-wing Salvadoran paramilitary that engaged in death squad activity.

**Order, The.** An American neo-Nazi terrorist group founded by Robert Jay Mathews in 1983. Centered in the Pacific Northwest, The Order's methods for fighting its war against what it termed the Zionist Occupation Government were counterfeiting, bank robberies, armored car robberies, and murder. The Order had been suppressed by December 1985.

**Order of Assassins.** A religious movement established in the Middle East during the 11th century. It sought to purge the Islamic faith and resist the Crusader invasions. The Assassins were noted for using stealth to kill their opponents.

**Organization of the Oppressed.** An adopted alias of Lebanon's Hezbollah.

**Organization of Volunteers for the Puerto Rican Revolution.** A Puerto Rican *independencista* terrorist organization.

**Organizational theory.** A term used in the field of public administration to describe the study of bureaucracy.

**Osawatomie.** An underground periodical published by the Weather Underground Organization during the 1970s.

**Padilla, Jose.** An American convert to Islam who was arrested at Chicago's O'Hare International Airport in May 2002. He was suspected of participating in a plan to construct and detonate a radiological weapon in the United States.

**Pahlavi, Shah Mohammad Reza.** The last Shah of Iran, who was ousted in an Islamic revolution led by the Ayatollah Ruhollah Khomeini.

**Palestine Islamic Jihad (PIJ).** The PIJ is not a single organization but a loose affiliation of factions. It is an Islamic fundamentalist revolutionary movement that seeks to promote *jihad,* or holy war, and to form a Palestinian state; it is responsible for assassinations and suicide bombings.

**Palestine Liberation Front (PLF).** The PLF split from the Popular Front for the Liberation of Palestine–General Command in the mid-1970s and further split into pro-PLO, pro-Syrian, and pro-Libyan factions. The pro-PLO faction was led by Abu Abbas, who committed a number of attacks against Israel.

**Palestine Liberation Organization (PLO).** An umbrella Palestinian nationalist organization. It is made up of numerous activist factions, many of which engage in political violence.

**Palmer, Alexander Mitchell.** U.S. attorney general from 1919 to 1921, during the administration of President Woodrow Wilson. He implemented the Palmer Raids in 1919 after two failed assassination attempts against him by anarchists.

**Palmer Raids.** A series of raids in the United States during the administration of U.S. President Woodrow Wilson, targeting communist and other leftist radical groups. Named for U.S. Attorney General A. Mitchell Palmer.

**Pan Am Flight 103.** An airliner that exploded over Lockerbie, Scotland, on December 21, 1988. In the explosion, 270 people were killed, including all 259 passengers and crew and 11 persons on the ground. Libya was implicated in the incident.

**Pan-Africanism.** An intellectual movement among Africans and descendents of Africans in the Western Hemisphere that sought to develop political, intellectual, and cultural ties among all African people.

**Pan-Arabism.** An international Arab nationalist movement that gained momentum after the Second World War.

**Pan-Arabist.** An ideological conceptualization of Arab unity, historically promoted by Arab nationalists.

**Parachute Sayaret.** An elite reconnaissance unit within the Israel Defense Forces. It has been deployed in small and large units, relying on high mobility to penetrate deep into hostile territory. It participated in the Entebbe rescue and was used against Hezbollah in South Lebanon.

**Paradigm.** A logically developed model or framework that represents a concept.

**Paramilitaries.** A term used to describe rightist irregular units and groups that are frequently supported by governments or progovernment interests. Many paramilitaries have been responsible for human rights violations.

**Paramilitary repressive options.** Counterterrorist measures that seek to resolve terrorist crises by deploying armed nonmilitary personnel. These personnel can include covert operatives, localized militia units, or large armed units.

**Participants in a terrorist environment.** People who participate in, or are affected by, terrorist incidents, and who are likely to have very different interpretations of the incident. These include the roles of terrorist, supporter, victim, target, onlooker, and analyst.

**Patrice Lumumba Peoples' Friendship University.** A Soviet-sponsored university in Moscow that attracted students from around the world, particularly the developing world.

**Peace processes.** Ongoing processes of negotiations between warring parties with the goal of addressing their underlying grievances and ending armed conflict.

**People Against Gangsterism and Drugs.** A moralistic Islamic terrorist group in South Africa.

**People Persecuted by Pablo Escobar ("Pepes").** A Colombian paramilitary that waged a terrorist campaign against the Medellin cartel and its leader, Pablo Escobar. Pepes assassinated at least 50 cartel members and targeted Escobar's family for assassination. It was apparently a death squad made up of former Medellin operatives and backers with a history of supporting paramilitaries.

**People's Liberation Army.** The Chinese communist national army, founded by Mao Zedong.

**People's Revolutionary Army.** A Maoist movement active in Argentina during the 1970s that engaged in urban terrorism along with the Montoneros.

**People's war.** A concept in irregular warfare in which the guerrilla fighters and the populace are theoretically indistinguishable.

**People's Will (Narodnaya Volya).** A 19th-century terrorist group in Russia.

**Permanent revolution.** One side of a debate within the international communist movement after the founding of the Soviet Union. It posited that the proletarian revolution should be waged internationally, rather than consolidated in only one country. The theoretical counterpart to socialism in one country.

**Phalangist.** A Lebanese Christian paramilitary movement.

*Phansi.* A rope used by the Thuggees of India to ritualistically strangle their victims.

**Phantom cells.** An organizational concept articulated by former Klansman Louis Beam in the early 1990s. Rightist dissidents were encouraged to organize themselves into autonomous subversive cells that would be undetectable by the enemy U.S. government or agents of the New World Order.

**Phineas Actions.** Acts of violence committed by individuals who are "called" to become Phineas Priests. Adherents believe that Phineas Actions will hasten the ascendancy of the Aryan race.

**Phineas Priesthood.** A shadowy movement of Christian Identity fundamentalists in the United States who believe that they are called by God to purify their race and Christianity. They are opposed to abortion, homosexuality, interracial mixing, and whites who "degrade" white

racial supremacy. It is a calling for men only, so no women can become Phineas Priests. The name is taken from the Bible at chapter 25, verse 6, of the Book of Numbers, which tells the story of a Hebrew man named Phineas who killed an Israelite man and his Midianite wife in the temple.

**Phoenix Program.** A 3-year campaign conducted during the Vietnam War to disrupt and eliminate the administrative effectiveness of the communist Viet Cong.

**Phosgene gas.** A chemical agent that causes the lungs to fill with water, choking the victim.

**Pierce, William.** The founder and leader of the neo-Nazi National Alliance in the United States. Also author of *The Turner Diaries,* under the *nom de plume* of Andrew MacDonald.

**Plan Victoria 82.** A government-sponsored campaign in Guatemala during the early 1980s that was responsible for thousands of deaths.

**Plastic explosives.** Malleable explosive compounds commonly used by terrorists.

**Pogroms.** Anti-Semitic massacres in Europe that occurred periodically from the time of the First Crusade through the Nazi Holocaust. Usually centered in Central and Eastern Europe.

**Pol Pot.** The principal leader of Cambodia's Khmer Rouge during its insurgency and consolidation of power.

**Police Border Guards.** An elite Israeli paramilitary force that is frequently deployed as a counterterrorist force. Known as the Green Police, it operates in two subgroups: YAMAS is a covert group that has been used extensively during the Palestinian *intifada,* and YAMAM was specifically created to engage in counterterrorist and hostage rescue operations.

**Polisario.** An insurgent group that resisted the Moroccan occupation of Western Sahara.

**Political Violence Matrix:** A framework for classifying and conceptualizing political violence. This classification framework is predicated on two factors: force and intended target.

**Politically sympathetic sponsorship.** State-sponsored terrorism that does not progress beyond ideological and moral support.

**Popular Front for the Liberation of Palestine (PFLP).** The PFLP was founded in 1967 by George Habash. It is a Marxist organization that advocates a multinational Arab revolution, and it has been responsible for dramatic international terrorist attacks. Its hijacking campaign in 1969 and 1970, its collaboration with Western European terrorists, and its mentorship of Carlos the Jackal arguably established the model for modern international terrorism.

**Popular Front for the Liberation of Palestine–General Command (PFLP-GC).** Ahmed Jibril formed the PFLP-GC in 1968 when he split from the Popular Front for the Liberation of Palestine (PFLP) because he considered the PFLP to be too involved in politics and not sufficiently committed to the armed struggle against Israel. The PFLP-GC was probably directed by Syria and has been responsible for many cross-border attacks against Israel.

**Port Huron Statement.** A document crafted in the United States in 1962 by members of Students for a Democratic Society. It harshly criticized mainstream American values and called for the establishment of a "new left" movement in the United States.

**Potassium cyanide.** A poisonous chemical agent.

*Prairie Fire.* An underground manifesto published by the Weather Underground Organization during the 1970s.

**Prairie Fire Organizing Committee.** An aboveground network of supporters for the Weather Underground Organization, organized into collectives.

**Precision-guided munitions (PGM).** Technologically advanced weapons that can be remotely guided to targets. Some PGMs are referred to as "smart bombs."

**Preemptive strikes.** Counterterrorist measures that proactively seek out and attack terrorist centers prior to a terrorist incident.

**Pressure triggers.** Weapons such as mines are detonated when physical pressure is applied to a trigger. A variation on physical pressure triggers are trip-wire booby traps. More sophisticated pressure triggers react to atmospheric (barometric) pressure, such as changes in pressure when an airliner ascends or descends.

**Print media.** Media outlets that publish newspapers, magazines, and other products that are intended to be read by customers.

**Progressive Labor Party.** A Maoist faction of the Students for a Democratic Society in the United States. Active during the late 1960s and 1970s.

**Proletariat.** A Marxist term for the working class.

**Propaganda.** The manipulation of information for political advantage. It includes the skillful reporting and spinning of the truth, half-truths, and lies.

**Propaganda by the deed.** The notion that revolutionaries must violently act upon their beliefs to promote the ideals of the revolution. Originally promoted by the anarchists.

**Property is theft.** The anarchist philosopher Pierre-Joseph Proudhon's belief that systems based on the acquisition of private property are inherently exploitative.

***Protocols of the Learned Elders of Zion, The.*** A forgery written under the direction of the czarist secret police in the late 19th century. It purports to be the proceedings of a secret international society of Jewish elders who are plotting to rule the world.

**Proudhon, Pierre-Joseph.** Nineteenth-century philosopher and father of anarchism.

**Provisional Irish Republican Army (Provos).** A terrorist organization in Northern Ireland that champions the rights of Northern Irish Catholics. The PIRA was formed with the goal of uniting Northern Ireland with the Irish Republic. Also known as the Provos.

**Provos.** The popular name given to the Provisional Irish Republican Army.

**Publicize their cause.** The practice by terrorists of disseminating information about their grievances and championed groups. This can be done through symbolic violence and the manipulation of the media.

**Punitive strikes.** Counterterrorist measures that seek out and attack terrorist centers to damage the terrorist organization. Frequently conducted as retribution for a terrorist incident.

**Qassam rocket.** A relatively unsophisticated surface to surface missile developed by the military arm of Hamas in Gaza. Thousands of Qassams have been fired into Israel. Newer designs of the rocket are more sophisticated.

**Qods (Jerusalem) Force.** A unit of Iran's Revolutionary Guards Corps that promotes the "liberation" of Jerusalem from non-Muslims.

**Racial holy war (Rahowa).** A term given by racial supremacists to a future race war that they believe will inevitably occur in the United States.

**Racial profiling.** Similar to criminal profiling, but it uses race or ethnicity as the overriding descriptor to assist in the apprehension of suspects. Race is a legitimate element for criminal profiling, but it cannot be the principal element. Unfortunately, incidents of racial profiling have been documented for some time in the United States.

**Radical.** A term used to describe members of the far left and fringe left.

**Radiological agents.** Materials that emit radiation that can harm living organisms when inhaled or otherwise ingested. Non–weapons-grade radiological agents could theoretically be used to construct a toxic "dirty bomb."

**RAPAS.** Small intelligence and special operations squads within France's 1st Marine Parachute Infantry Regiment (1RPIMa). RAPAS are trained to operate in desert, urban, and tropical environments.

**Rape of Nanking.** During a 6-week campaign in 1937 to 1938, the Japanese army killed between 200,000 and 300,000 Chinese in the Chinese capital of Nanking. Many thousands were bayoneted, beheaded, or tortured. An estimated 20,000 to 80,000 Chinese women and girls were raped by Japanese soldiers, and thousands of women were either forced into sexual slavery as "comfort women" or were made to perform in perverse sex shows to entertain Japanese troops.

**Raziel, David.** A leader of the Irgun, killed in 1941.

**RDX.** The central component of most plastic explosives.

**Reactionary.** A term given to far-right and fringe-right political tendencies.

**Red Army Faction (RAF).** A leftist terrorist movement active in West Germany during the 1970s and 1980s. Also referred to as the Baader-Meinhof Gang.

**Red Brigades.** A leftist terrorist movement active in Italy during the 1970s and 1980s.

**Red Cells (Rote Zelles).** A shadowy Marxist organization that was founded in Frankfurt, West Germany, probably in 1972 or 1973. Members adopted an underground cell-based strategy and disappeared into the middle class by holding jobs, owning homes, and raising families. Their terrorist activity included bombings and other criminal activities.

**Red Guards.** Groups of young Communist radicals who sought to purge Chinese society during the Great Proletarian Cultural Revolution.

**"Red Scares."** Periodic anticommunist security crises in the United States, when national leaders reacted to the perceived threat of communist subversion.

**Red Zora (Rote Zora).** The women's "auxiliary" of the West German terrorist group Red Cells. Red Zora eventually became independent of Red Cells.

**Regicide.** The killing of kings.

**Reid, Richard C.** A British citizen who attempted to detonate explosives on December 2, 2001, aboard an American Airlines flight from Paris to Miami. The explosives were hidden in his shoe. He was a self-professed member of Al-Qa'ida.

**Reign of Terror (Régime de la Terreur).** A period during the French Revolution when the new republic violently purged those who were thought to be a threat to the prevailing ideals of the revolution. "Terrorism" was considered to be a necessary and progressive revolutionary tactic.

**Relative deprivation theory.** A sociological term that indicates the lack of human needs vis-à-vis other members of a particular society.

**Religious communal terrorism.** Conflict between religious groups involving terrorist violence.

**Repentance laws.** An offer of qualified amnesty by the Italian government to Red Brigades members, requiring them to demonstrate repentance for their crimes. Repentance was established by cooperating within a sliding scale of collaboration. A significant number of imprisoned Red Brigades terrorists accepted repentance reductions in their sentences.

**Repressive responses.** Counterterrorist measures that seek to resolve terrorist crises by disrupting or destroying terrorist groups and movements. These responses include military and nonmilitary options.

**Ressem, Ahmed.** An Algerian who was arrested as he tried to cross the Canadian border into the United States with bomb-making components. He and others planned to detonate a bomb at Los Angeles International Airport around the time of the 2000 millennial celebrations.

**Revolutionary Armed Forces of Colombia (Fuerzas Armados Revolucionarios de Colombia, or FARC).** An enduring Marxist insurgent movement in Colombia that has engaged in guerrilla warfare and terrorism since its inception during the 1960s.

***Revolutionary Catechism.*** A revolutionary manifesto written by the Russian anarchist Sergei Nechayev.

**Revolutionary dissident terrorism.** The practice of political violence with the goal of destroying an existing order, committed with a plan for the aftermath of the revolution.

**Revolutionary Guards Corps.** Iranian Islamic revolutionaries who have been deployed abroad, mainly to Lebanon, to promote Islamic revolution.

**Revolutionary Justice Organization.** An adopted alias of Lebanon's Hezbollah.

**Revolutionary Organization November 17.** A Greek Marxist terrorist movement.

**Revolutionary Tribunal.** The revolutionary court established during the French Revolution.

**Revolutionary United Front (RUF).** A rebel movement that arose in Sierre Leone in 1991. Led by Foday Sankoh, RUF forces were responsible for widespread human rights abuses and atrocities.

**Revolutionary Youth Movement II (RYM II).** A faction of Students for a Democratic Society in the United States. RYM II adapted its ideological motivations to the political and social context of the 1960s by tailoring the ideologies of orthodox Marxism to the political environment of the 1960s.

**Rewards for Justice Program.** An international bounty program managed by the U.S. Diplomatic Security Service. The program offered cash rewards for information leading to the arrest of wanted terrorists.

**"Roadside bombs."** Improvised explosive devices (IEDs) constructed and deployed by Iraqi insurgents against U.S.-led occupation forces.

**Rocket-propelled grenades (RPGs).** Handheld military weapons that use a propellant to fire a rocket-like explosive.

**Royal Marine Commandos.** British rapid-reaction troops that deploy in larger numbers than the Special Air Service and Special Boat Service. They are organized around units called commandos that are roughly equivalent to a conventional battalion.

**RPG-7.** A rocket-propelled grenade weapon manufactured in large quantities by the Soviet bloc.

**Ruby Ridge.** An August 1992 incident in Idaho when racial supremacist Randy Weaver and his family were besieged by federal agents for failure to reply to an illegal weapons charge. Weaver's wife and son were killed during the incident, as was a U.S. Marshal. Members of the Patriot movement and other right-wing extremists cite Ruby Ridge as evidence of a broad government conspiracy to deprive freedom-loving "true" Americans of their right to bear arms and other liberties.

**Rudolph, Eric Robert.** An apparent affiliate of the Army of God in the United States who became a fugitive after he was named as a suspect in bombings in Birmingham, Alabama, and Atlanta, Georgia. Rudolph was also suspected of involvement in the July 1996 bombing at Centennial Olympic Park in Atlanta during the Summer Olympic Games. He was linked to a militia group in North Carolina.

**Russian Mafia.** A term given to the criminal gangs that proliferated in Russia after the collapse of the Soviet Union.

**SA-7.** An infrared-targeted Soviet-made surface-to-air missile, also known as the Grail.

**Saint Augustine.** A Christian philosopher who developed the concept of the just war.

**Sam Melville–Jonathan Jackson Unit.** A group that took credit for bombing the Boston State House in Boston, Massachusetts, in 1975. It was a term used by the leftist United Freedom Front.

**Samurai.** A member of the medieval Japanese warrior class.

**Sandinistas.** A Marxist movement in Nicaragua that seized power after a successful insurgency against the regime of Anastasio Somoza Debayle. The Sandinista regime became the object of an American-supported insurgency.

**Sarin nerve gas.** A potent nerve gas. The Aum Shinrikyō cult released Sarin gas into the Tokyo subway system in March 1995, killing 12 and injuring thousands.

**SAVAK.** The secret police during the regime of Shah Mohammad Reza Pahlavi.

Notorious for its brutal suppression of dissent.

**Sayaret.** Elite Israeli reconnaissance units that engage in counterterrorist operations. Sayaret have been attached to General Headquarters (Sayaret Matkal) and the Golani Brigade. There is also a Parachute Sayaret.

**Sayaret Matkal.** An elite reconnaissance unit within the Israel Defense Forces, attached to the IDF General Headquarters. It is a highly secretive formation that operates in small units and is regularly used for counterterrorist operations.

**Scapegoating.** A process of political blaming to rally a championed group against a scapegoated group. Usually directed against an ethnonational, religious, or ideological group.

**Schutzstaffel.** The Nazi SS. Traditionally composed of racially pure Aryans, although the SS also became a kind of German foreign legion toward the end of the Second World War.

**Sea, Air, Land Forces (SEALs).** Similar to the British Special Boat Service and French Navy special assault units, the U.S. Navy SEALs' primary mission is to conduct seaborne, riverine, and harbor operations. They have also been used extensively on land.

**Sectarian violence.** Religious communal violence.

**Semtex.** A high-grade and high-yield plastic explosive originally manufactured in Czechoslovakia when it was a member of the Soviet bloc.

**75th Ranger Regiment.** An elite combat unit of the U.S. Army that can deploy large formations for counterterrorist missions.

**Shadow wars.** Covert campaigns to suppress terrorism.

**Shakur, Assata.** The symbolic leader of the Black Liberation Army (BLA) in the United States, formerly known as JoAnne Chesimard. A former Black Panther, she was described by admirers as the "heart and soul" of the BLA.

**Shining Path (Sendero Luminoso).** A Marxist insurgent movement in Peru. Founded and led by former philosophy professor Abimael Guzmán, the group regularly engaged in terrorism.

**"Shoe bomber."** Richard Reid, a British citizen who attempted to detonate explosives on December 2, 2001, aboard an American Airlines flight from Paris to Miami. The explosives were hidden in his shoe. He was a self-professed member of Al-Qa'ida.

*Sic semper tyrannis.* "Thus be it ever to tyrants." Shouted by Confederate assassin John Wilkes Booth after shooting President Abraham Lincoln.

*Sicarii.* The Zealot rebels who opposed Roman rule. Named for the curved dagger, or *sica,* that was a preferred weapon.

**Sicilian Mafia.** A traditional criminal society in Sicily.

**Signal intelligence.** Intelligence that has been collected by technological resources. Also referred to as SIGINT.

**Signature method.** Methods that become closely affiliated with the operational activities of specific extremist groups.

**Single-issue terrorism.** Terrorism that is motivated by a single grievance.

**Sinn Féin.** An aboveground political party in Northern Ireland that champions Catholic rights and union with the Irish Republic.

**Skinheads.** A countercultural youth movement that began in England in the late 1960s. An international racist skinhead movement eventually developed in Europe and the United States. The term *skinhead* refers to the members' practice of shaving their heads.

**Skinheads Against Racial Prejudice (SHARP).** An antiracist tendency within the skinhead youth movement.

**Skinzines (or zines).** Publications directed to the skinhead movement. Frequently racist literature.

**Sky marshals.** Armed law enforcement officers stationed aboard aircraft.

**Sleeper cells.** A tactic used by international terrorist movements in which operatives theoretically establish residence in another country to await a time when they will be activated by orders to carry out a terrorist attack.

**Smallpox.** A formerly epidemic disease that has been eradicated in nature but that has been preserved in research laboratories. A possible ingredient for biological weapons.

**Social cleansing.** The practice of eliminating defined undesirables from society. These "undesirables" can include those who practice defined morals crimes or who engage in denounced political and social behaviors.

**Social reform.** Conciliatory counterterrorist measures that seek to resolve terrorist crises by resolving political and social problems that are the focus of the terrorists' grievances.

**Social Revolutionary Party.** A Russian revolutionary movement during the late 19th and early 20th centuries. The group adopted terrorism as a revolutionary method.

**Socialism in one country.** One side of a debate within the international communist movement after the founding of the Soviet Union. It posited that the proletarian revolution could be consolidated in the Soviet Union prior to waging an international struggle. The theoretical counterpart to the Permanent Revolution.

**Sodium cyanide.** A poisonous chemical agent.

**Soft targets.** Civilian and other undefended targets that are easily victimized by terrorists.

**Solntsevskaya Gang.** A prominent Russian Mafia gang.

**Somoza Debayle, Anastasio.** The United States–supported Nicaraguan dictator overthrown by the Sandinista-led insurgency.

**Special Air Service (SAS).** A secretive organization in the British army that has been used repeatedly in counterterrorist operations. Organized at a regimental level but operating in very small teams, the SAS is similar to the French 1st Marine Parachute Infantry Regiment and the American Delta Force.

**Special Boat Service (SBS).** A special unit under the command of the British Royal Navy. The SBS specializes in operations against seaborne targets and along coastlines and harbors. It is similar to the French Navy's Special Assault Units and the American SEALs.

**Special Operations Command.** The general headquarters for U.S. Special Operations Forces.

**Special operations forces.** Elite military and paramilitary units deployed by many armed forces. They are highly trained and are capable of operating in large or small formations, both overtly and covertly.

**Specific deterrence.** The creation of an environment by governments and counterterrorist agencies against a specific adversary that communicates the high risks of further acts of political violence.

**Spillover effect.** Terrorist violence that occurs beyond the borders of the countries that are the targets of such violence.

**Stalinists.** Followers of Soviet dictator Joseph Stalin. They advocated socialism in one country and practiced totalitarianism. Stalinists also brutally consolidated central power in a single leader of the party. The movement counterpoint to the Trotskyites.

**State assistance for terrorism.** Tacit state participation in and encouragement of extremist behavior. Its basic characteristic is that the state, through sympathetic proxies and agents, implicitly takes part in repression, violence, and terrorism.

**State patronage of terrorism.** Active state participation in and encouragement of extremist behavior. Its basic characteristic is that the state, through its agencies and personnel, actively takes part in repression, violence, and terrorism.

**Stateless revolutionaries.** International terrorists who are not sponsored by or based in a particular country.

**State-regulated press.** State-regulated media exist in environments in which the state routinely intervenes in the reporting of information by the press. This can occur in societies that otherwise have a measure of democratic freedoms, as well as in totalitarian societies.

**Stern Gang.** A Jewish terrorist group active prior to the independence of Israel.

**Stinger.** A technologically advanced handheld anti-aircraft missile manufactured by the United States.

**Stockholm syndrome.** A psychological condition in which hostages begin to identify and sympathize with their captors.

**Strong multipolar terrorist environment.** A terrorist environment that presumes that state sponsorship guides terrorist behavior but that several governments support their favored groups. It also presumes that there are few truly autonomous international terrorist movements; they all have a link to a state sponsor.

**Structural theory.** A theory used in many disciplines to identify social conditions ("structures") that affect group access to services, equal rights, civil protections, freedom, or other quality-of-life measures.

**"Struggle meetings."** Revolutionary rallies held during the Chinese Revolution. Denunciations were often made against those thought to be a threat to the revolution.

**Student Soviet.** The section of Paris temporarily ceded to students during the 1968 uprising centered at the Sorbonne.

**Students for a Democratic Society (SDS).** A leftist student movement founded in 1962 in the United States. It rose to become the preeminent activist organization on American campuses throughout the 1960s. Its factions—the Progressive Labor Party, Revolutionary Youth Movement II, and the Weathermen—were highly active during the 1960s and early 1970s.

**Submachine guns.** Light automatic weapons that fire pistol ammunition.

**Suicide bombing.** A tactic used by combatants in which an assailant laden with explosives detonates the explosives with the purpose of inflicting death or other damage on the intended target. The assailant intentionally dies during the attack.

**Sun Tzu.** Chinese military philosopher whose book *The Art of War* has been a significant influence on military theory.

**Supergrass.** A policy in Northern Ireland during the 1980s of convincing Provos and members of the Irish National Liberation Army to defect from their movements and inform on their former comrades.

**Suppression campaigns.** Counterterrorist measures that seek to resolve terrorist crises by waging an ongoing campaign to destroy the terrorists' capacity to strike.

**Survivalism.** A philosophy of complete self-sufficiency. Sometimes adopted by those who practice the tactic of going "off the grid."

**Symbolism, role of.** The symbolic value represented by a victim is a fundamental consideration in the selection of targets by terrorists.

**Terminal institutions.** Institutions under the jurisdiction of criminal justice and military justice systems that provide final resolution to individual terrorists' careers after they have been captured, prosecuted, convicted, and imprisoned.

**Terrorism.** Elements from the American definitional model define terrorism as a premeditated and unlawful act in which groups or agents of some principle engage in a threatened or actual use of force or violence against human or property targets. These groups or agents engage in this behavior intending the purposeful intimidation of governments or people to affect policy or behavior with an underlying political objective. There are more than 100 definitions of terrorism.

**Terrorist.** One who practices terrorism. Often a highly contextual term.

**Terrorist cells.** Relatively small associations of violent extremists who operate independently from central command and control authority.

**Terrorist profiles.** Descriptive profiles of terrorist suspects developed by law enforcement agencies to assist in the apprehension of terrorist suspects. Similar to criminal profiling.

**Third World.** A postwar term created to describe the developing world.

**Thody, Walter Eliyah.** A self-proclaimed Phineas Priest who was arrested in 1991 in Oklahoma after a shootout and chase. Thody stated that fellow believers would also commit acts of violence against Jews and others.

**Thuggee.** Member of a mystical movement that existed for centuries in India. Thugees ritualistically murdered travelers to honor the goddess Kali.

**Tiananmen Square.** A central square in Beijing. The Chinese army was dispatched to suppress pro-democracy protests in June 1989. Thousands of protesters were killed or wounded.

**TNT.** A commercially available explosive.

**Tokyo Convention on Offences and Certain Other Acts Committed on Board Aircraft.** A treaty enacted in 1963 as the first airline crimes treaty.

**Torture.** Physical and psychological pressure and degradation.

**Total war.** The unrestrained use of force against a broad selection of targets to utterly defeat an enemy.

**Totalitarian regimes.** Governments that practice total control over public and political institutions. The media and other public information outlets are completely controlled.

**Traditional criminal enterprises.** Criminal enterprises that are interested in maximizing their profits. They tend to become politically active only to protect their criminal interests.

**Transnational organized crime.** Globalized organized crime in which criminal trades (such as drugs) have developed into multinational enterprises.

**Trotskyites.** Followers of Bolshevik leader Leon Trotsky. They advocated the permanent revolution and argued that the working class must develop an international revolutionary consciousness. The movement counterpoint to the Stalinists.

**Troubles, The.** The term given to sectarian violence between Catholics and Protestants in Northern Ireland.

**"Truther" Movement.** A conspiracy-based movement in the United States that rejects the official account of the events of September 11, 2001.

**Tupac Amaru Revolutionary Movement (Movimento Revolucionario Tupac Amaru, or MRTA).** A Marxist terrorist movement in Peru, primarily active during the 1980s and early 1990s.

**Tupamaros.** A Marxist urban terrorist movement active during the early 1970s in Uruguay. After a number of dramatic attacks, the Tupamaros were eventually annihilated when the Uruguayan military used authoritarian methods, and the general Uruguayan population rejected the movement.

**Turan.** A mythical pan-Turkish nation, the establishment of which is a goal for many Turkish ultranationalists.

**Turner Diaries, The.** A short novel written by National Alliance founder William Pierce under the pseudonym Andrew MacDonald. It depicts an Aryan revolution in the United States and is considered by many neo-Nazis to be a blueprint for the eventual racial holy war.

**TWA Flight 847.** In June 1985, hijackers belonging to Lebanon's Hezbollah hijacked a TWA airliner, taking it on a high-profile and media-intensive odyssey around the Mediterranean.

**25:6.** The symbol of the racial supremacist Phineas Priesthood in the United States. It refers to chapter 25, verse 6, of the Book of Numbers in the Bible.

**Two-Seedline Christian Identity.** A Christian Identity mystical belief that rejects the notion that all humans are descended from Adam (see One-Seedline Christian Identity). According to this belief, Eve bore Abel as Adam's son but bore Cain as the son of the Serpent. Outside of the Garden of Eden lived nonwhite, soulless beasts who were a separate species from humans. When Cain slew Abel, he was cast out of the Garden to live among the soulless beasts. Those who became the descendants of Cain are the modern Jews. They are biologically descended from the devil and are a demonic people worthy of extermination.

**Tyrannicide.** The assassination of tyrants for the greater good of society.

**Ulster Volunteer Force (UVF).** A Protestant paramilitary in Northern Ireland. Responsible for numerous acts of terrorism.

**UNABOM.** The FBI's case designation for their investigation into bombings perpetrated by Theodore Kaczynski. "Un" was short for university, and "a" referred to airlines.

**United Freedom Front (UFF).** A leftist terrorist group in the United States that was active from the mid-1970s through the mid-1980s.

**United Jewish Underground.** A shadowy group in the United States that was responsible for several acts of terrorism. These attacks were primarily directed against Soviet targets, such as the offices of the Soviet national airline Aeroflot. These attacks were conducted to protest the USSR's treatment of Soviet Jews.

**United Self-Defense Forces of Colombia (AUC).** A large rightist paramilitary in Colombia. Unofficially supported by the government and officially supported by progovernment members of the upper classes. It was responsible for numerous human rights violations.

**USA PATRIOT Act.** The Uniting and Strengthening America by Providing Appropriate Tools Required to Intercept and Obstruct Terrorism Act of 2001. Passed by the U.S. Congress on October 26, 2001. Its provisions are designed to authorize homeland security–related measures to combat terrorist threats to the U.S. homeland.

**USA PATRIOT Improvement and Reauthorization Act.** Legislation mandating the periodic review and reauthorization of the provisions of the USA PATRIOT Act.

**USS Cole.** An American destroyer that was severely damaged on October 12, 2000, while berthed in the port of Aden, Yemen. Two suicide bombers detonated a boat bomb next to the *Cole,* killing themselves and 17 crew members and wounding 39 other Navy personnel.

**Utopia.** The title of a book written in the 16th century by Sir Thomas More depicting an ideal society.

**Vanguard of the proletariat.** In Marxist theory, a well-indoctrinated and motivated elite that would lead the working-class revolution. In practice, this referred to the Communist Party.

**Vanguard strategy.** In Marxist and non-Marxist theory, the strategy of using a well-indoctrinated and motivated elite to lead the working-class revolution. In practice, this strategy was adopted in the postwar era by terrorist organizations and extremist movements.

**Vehicular bombs.** Ground vehicles that have been wired with explosives. Car bombs and truck bombs are common vehicular bombs.

**Viet Cong.** The name given by the United States and its noncommunist South Vietnamese allies to South Vietnamese communist insurgents.

**Viet Minh.** An organization founded by the Vietnamese leader Ho Chi Minh. The Vietnam Independence Brotherhood League began fighting first against the Japanese conquerors of French Indochina and then against the French colonial forces.

**Vigilante state terrorism.** Unofficial state terrorism in which state personnel engage in nonsanctioned political violence. It can include the use of death squads.

**Waco.** An April 1993 incident in which federal agents besieged the Branch Davidian cult's compound after a failed attempt in February to serve a search warrant for illegal firearms had ended in the deaths of four federal agents and several cult members. During an assault on April 19, 1993, led by the FBI, about 80 Branch Davidians—including more than 20 children—died in a blaze that leveled the compound. Patriots and other rightists consider this tragedy to be evidence of government power run amok.

**Waffen SS.** The "armed SS" of Nazi Germany. Elite military units of the SS, composed of racially selected Germans and fascist recruits from occupied territories.

**Warfare.** The making of war against an enemy. In the modern era, it usually refers to conventional and guerrilla conflicts.

**Wars of national liberation.** A series of wars fought in the developing world in the postwar era. These conflicts frequently pitted indigenous guerrilla fighters against European colonial powers or governments perceived to be pro-Western. Insurgents were frequently supported by the Soviet bloc or China.

**Weak multipolar terrorist environment.** A terrorist environment that presupposes that state sponsorship exists, but that the terrorist groups are more autonomous. Under this scenario, several governments support their favored groups, but many of these groups are relatively independent international terrorist movements.

**Weapons of mass destruction.** High-yield weapons that can potentially cause a large number of casualties when used by terrorists. Examples of these weapons include chemical, biological, radiological, and nuclear weapons. They can also be constructed from less exotic compounds, such as ANFO.

**Weather Bureau.** The designation adopted by the leaders of the Weatherman faction of Students for a Democratic Society.

**Weather Collectives.** Groups of supporters of the Weather Underground Organization.

**Weather Underground Organization.** The adopted name of the Weathermen after they moved underground.

**Weathermen.** A militant faction of Students for a Democratic Society that advocated, and engaged in, violent confrontation with the authorities. Some Weathermen engaged in terrorist violence.

**Weber, Max.** A German sociologist who was a founder of modern sociology and organizational theory.

**Weinrich, Johannes.** A former West German terrorist who was "purchased" by the German government from the government of Yemen. He stood trial in Germany for the 1983 bombing of a French cultural center in Berlin in which 1 person was killed and 23 others were wounded. Weinrich had also been a very close associate of Carlos the Jackal.

**White Aryan Resistance.** A California-based racial supremacist hate group founded by former Klansman Tom Metzger in the early 1980s.

**World Church of the Creator (WCOTC).** An organization founded in the United States by Ben Klassen in 1973 and later led by Matthew Hale. It practices racial supremacist mysticism called Creativity and led the Creativity Movement until Hale's conviction in 2004 on charges of conspiring to assassinate a federal judge in Illinois.

**Wrath of God.** A counterterrorist unit created by the Israelis to eliminate Palestinian operatives who had participated in the massacre of Israeli athletes at the 1972 Munich Olympics. Also called Mivtza Za'am Ha'el.

***Wretched of the Earth, The.*** Frantz Fanon's influential book that championed and sought to justify revolutionary violence in the developing world.

**Wu Ch'i.** Chinese military philosopher who is usually associated with Sun Tzu.

**Xenophobia.** The fear of foreigners, frequently exhibited by ultranationalists.

**YAMAM.** One of two operational subgroups deployed by Israel's Police Border Guards (the other subgroup is YAMAS). It engages in counterterrorist and hostage rescue operations.

**YAMAS.** One of two operational subgroups deployed by Israel's Police Border Guards (the other subgroup is YAMAM). It is a covert unit that has been used to neutralize terrorist cells in conjunction with covert Israel Defense Forces operatives.

**Year Zero.** The ideological designation given by the Khmer Rouge to the beginning of its genocidal consolidation of power.

**Years of Lead.** The politically violent years of the 1970s and 1980s in Italy, during which the Red Brigades were exceptionally active. They waged a campaign of violence that included shootings, bombings, kidnappings, and other criminal acts.

**Yousef, Ramzi.** The mastermind behind the 1993 bombing of the World Trade Center. Also a case study of a high degree of criminal skill.

**Zapatista National Liberation Front.** Leftist rebels who were originally centered in Chiapas, Mexico. During the late 1990s, they engaged in guerrilla fighting that ended when they were integrated into the Mexican political process.

**Zealots.** Hebrew rebels who uncompromisingly opposed Roman rule in ancient Palestine.

**Zetas, Los.** An elite antidrug unit formed within the Mexican military. Many Zetas became rogue enforcers for the so-called Gulf Cartel in Mexico, and were responsible for assassinations and murders.

**Zionism.** An intellectual movement within the Jewish community describing the conditions for the settlement of Jews in Israel.

# Index

Gompers, Samuel, 329

Good Friday Agreement, 398–399

Governments

authoritarian, 92, 323–324, 402–403, 448

legitimacy, 91–93

propaganda, 323–324

regulation of media, 320–323, 325

relations with media, 305, 320

totalitarian, 92

*See also* Democracies; State terrorism

Grail. *See* SA-7

Grand Mosque, Mecca, 148

Great Britain. *See* Britain

Great Proletarian Cultural Revolution, 84

Greece

civil war, 124

death of Socrates, 10

Revolutionary Organization November 17, 292

Green Berets (Special Forces Groups), 387

Green Police, 387

Greenpeace, 86

Grenades, rocket-propelled. *See* Rocket-propelled grenades

Grenzschutzgruppe 9 (GSG-9), 387, 389

Grey Wolves, 196

Ground Zero site, New York, 366

Groupe d'Intervention Gendarmerie Nationale (GIGN), 230, 387, 454

Groupe Islamique Armé. *See* Armed Islamic Group

Grupo Especial de Operaciones (GEO), 387

GSG-9 (Grenzschutzgruppe 9), 387, 389

Guantánamo Bay detainees, 30–31, 227, 305, 425, 429, 435

*Guardian, The*, 413

Guatemala

death squads, 76

Indians, 76, 121

Guerrilla warfare

in Chiapas, Mexico, 109–110

in developing countries, 177–178

distinction from terrorism, 27–28

examples, 28

Mao's doctrine, 61–62

in Spain, 27

*See also* Dissident terrorism; Urban guerrilla warfare

Guevara, Ernesto "Che," 42, 55, 111, 180, 182, 184

Guildford Four, 432

Guillotine, 11, 11 (n24)

Gulf War (1991), 85, 151, 325

Guns. *See* Firearms

Gurr, Ted Robert, 28

Gusmao, Xanana, 78

Guzmán, Abimael, 182–183, 400

Guzman, Joaquin "El Chapo," 252

Habash, George, 118

Haddad, Wadi, 384

Hague Conventions, 8, 406

Hale, Matthew, 352

Hamadi, Mohammed Ali, 319

Hamas (Islamic Resistance Movement)

assassinations of leaders, 88

bombings, 148, 149, 266, 271, 285, 292, 379

competition with PLO, 117, 118

funding, 364

goals, 37–38

history, 117–118

Israeli counterterrorism and, 379

Izzedine al-Qassam Brigade, 118, 285

justification of methods, 8–9

leaders, 379, 384

seen as freedom fighters, 37–38

state supporters, 87, 145

weapons, 281–282, 398

*See also Intifada*

Hariri, Rafik, 88, 281

Harkat-ul-Ansar, 146

Harmoduius, 10

Harris, Kevin, 349

Hasan, Nidal Malik, 416–417

Hate crimes, 22, 331, 352

*Hawala*, 460

Hawi, George, 88

Headley, David Coleman, 417

Hearst, Patricia, 54, 340, 340 (photo)

Hebron mosque massacre, 148–149, 285

Heinzen, Karl, 12

Henry VIII, King of England, 12

Hezbollah (Party of God)

bases, 145, 381

battles with Israeli troops, 380

cell in United States, 462

drug trafficking, 247, 249

funding, 364

goals, 111

leaders, 384

social services, 144

state supporters, 87, 88, 101, 144, 247

television station, 311

terrorist acts, 144, 213, 214, 250, 285, 300–301

use of media, 303, 318–319

website, 303

HHS. *See* U.S. Department of Health and Human Services

High-yield weapons, 366, 454, 455

Hijackings

*Achille Lauro*, 316, 382–383, 390, 404–405

by Algerian terrorists, 229–230

international conventions on, 405–406

as international spillovers, 216

media coverage, 318–319

by Palestinian groups, 56, 186, 210, 389

by Popular Front for the Liberation of Palestine, 55, 71, 216, 278, 292, 390

prevention, 402

purposes, 277

TWA Flight 847, 295, 307–308, 318–319, 399

*See also* September 11, 2001 terrorist attacks

Hill, Paul, 361

Hinduism, 122, 130, 141, 145

Hipparchus, 10

Hiss, Alger, 433

History of terrorism, 6, 9–13, 444–445

Hitler, Adolf, 67, 138, 172, 173 (photo), 190

Ho Chi Minh, 113, 171, 177, 204, 345

Hoffman, Bruce, 28, 31

Holy Spirit Mobile Force, 142

Homeland security

civil liberties and, 434

definition of, 414

European context, 414, 417–418

future of, 457

objectives, 437–438

threats, 415–417

*See also* Counterterrorism

Homeland Security, Department of. *See* Department of Homeland Security

Homeland security organization, U.S.

bureaucracy, 426

conceptual framework, 414

intelligence community, 421–423, 428–431

law enforcement agencies, 425–426

laws, 423–425

reorganization, 366, 420–423, 421 (table)

sector-specific agencies, 427–428

before September 11, 366, 418–420, 419 (table)

*See also* Department of Homeland Security

# ⑤SAGE research**methods**

The essential online tool for researchers from the world's leading methods publisher

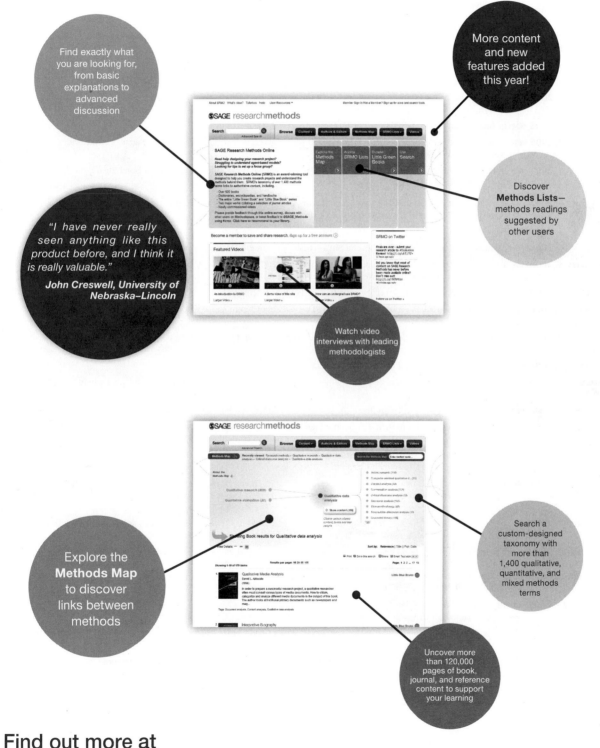

Find exactly what you are looking for, from basic explanations to advanced discussion

More content and new features added this year!

*"I have never really seen anything like this product before, and I think it is really valuable."*

**John Creswell, University of Nebraska–Lincoln**

Discover **Methods Lists**— methods readings suggested by other users

Watch video interviews with leading methodologists

Explore the **Methods Map** to discover links between methods

Search a custom-designed taxonomy with more than 1,400 qualitative, quantitative, and mixed methods terms

Uncover more than 120,000 pages of book, journal, and reference content to support your learning

# Find out more at
# www.sageresearchmethods.com

|  |  |
|---|---|
| **February 14, 2005** | Rafiq Hariri, former prime minister of Lebanon, was assassinated by a car bomb; 20 other people were killed. Syrian agents were suspected. |
| **July 2005** | On July 7, 2005, four bombs exploded in London. The attacks killed more than 50 people and injured more than 700. Several days later, on July 21, an identical attack was attempted but failed when the explosives misfired. British-based cells—sympathizers of Al Qaeda—were responsible. |
| **November 9, 2005** | Three hotels were bombed in Amman, Jordan, killing 59 people, including more than 20 people at a wedding reception. Al Qaeda in Iraq claimed credit for the attacks via an Internet posting. The group stated that all were carried out by suicide bombers—including a husband-and-wife team. |
| **February 22, 2006** | In Iraq, a bombing at the Al Askari Mosque exacerbated sectarian conflict. |
| **April 11, 2006** | More than 50 Sunni worshippers were killed by a suicide bomber in Karachi, Pakistan. |
| **June 15, 2006** | In Sri Lanka, the Tamil Tigers bombed a bus, killing nearly 70 people. |
| **July 31, 2006** | Two unexploded suitcase bombs were deactivated on trains near Dortmund and Koblenz, Germany. |
| **August 10, 2006** | British police broke up an apparent plot to bomb several airliners traveling to the United States via Heathrow Airport. |
| **November 21, 2006** | In Beirut, Lebanon, anti-Syrian politician Pierre Gemayel was assassinated. |
| **November 23, 2006** | More than 200 people were killed and over 250 were injured by car bombs and mortar attacks in the Sadr City neighborhood of Beirut. |
| **March, 2007** | In Iraq, more than 300 people were killed and nearly 600 were wounded in a series of bombings. |
| **May 15, 2007** | Hamas fired 28 rockets into Israel. |
| **June 29 and 30, 2007** | An automobile burst into flames after ramming into the main terminal at Glasgow International Airport. Two car bombs were discovered in the West End area of London. |
| **December 24, 2007** | Four French tourists were shot in Mauritania. |
| **January 16, 2008** | A female suicide bomber killed several Shi'a worshippers in the Diyala province of Iraq. |
| **February 1, 2008** | Two mentally disabled female suicide bombers killed nearly 100 people and wounded more than 200 others in markets in Beirut. Their bombs were detonated remotely. |
| **March 6, 2008** | A man armed with an assault rifle shot and killed eight students in a library at a Yeshiva in Jerusalem. |
| **March 10, 2008** | In Iraq, a female suicide bomber assassinated a prominent Sunni sheik who had allied himself against al Qaeda. |
| **July 2, 2008** | A Palestinian man in Jerusalem used a bulldozer to ram cars and busses, killing three people and injuring more than 50. |
| **July 21, 2008** | Two busses were bombed in Kunming, China. |
| **August 19, 2008** | Nearly 70 people were killed or injured when a suicide bomber detonated outside of a hospital where Shiite mourners congregated. |
| **September 13, 2008** | Five bombs detonated in Delhi, India. At least 30 were killed and 90 were injured. |
| **October 10, 2008** | In Orakzai, Pakistan, more than 200 people were killed and wounded by a suicide vehicular bomb directed against a meeting of leaders discussing mustering a militia to battle the local Taliban. |
| **November 26–29, 2008** | In Mumbai, India, well-trained terrorists assaulted eight locations. They attacked a train station, hotels, restaurants, a police station, and a hospital. More than 500 people were killed or wounded. |
| **February 9, 2009** | In Vishvamadu, Sri Lanka suicide bomber from the Tamil Tigers' Black Tigers detonated explosives among Sri Lankan soldiers and fleeing Tamil refugees. Nearly 30 people were killed and 90 wounded by the female bomber. |
| **March 7, 2009** | In Northern Ireland, the Real Irish Republican Army shot and killed two unarmed British soldiers. Two soldiers and two civilians were wounded in the attack. |
| **May 12, 2009** | Twenty Taliban suicide bombers in Afghanistan detonated explosive belts at a provincial government building. |
| **June 1, 2009** | In Little Rock, Arkansas, Abdulhakim Mujahid Muhammad, opened fire at an armed forces recruiting office, killing Army Private William Long wounding Private Quinton Ezeagwula. |
| **July 29, 2009** | In northern Spain, car bomb containing 200 kilogram of explosives exploded at a *Guardia Civil* barracks. The attack, blamed on ETA, was one of many during a spike in violence by the Basque group. |
| **November 5, 2009** | At the Fort Hood military base in Killeen Texas, Army Major Nidal Malik Hasan, shot and killed 13 people and wounded at least 30. He was an army psychiatrist. |
| **December 25, 2009** | Umar Farouk Abdulmutallab, a Nigerian national, attempted to detonate an explosive compound hidden in his underwear aboard an aircraft flying from Amsterdam to Detroit. |
| **January 2, 2010** | In Aarhus, Denmark, a Somali man affiliated with the al-Shabaab militia in Somalia entered the home of Danish cartoonist Kurt Westergaard's and threatened to kill him with an axe. Westergaard locked himself in a panic room and called the police, who shot and killed the man. |
| **January 7, 2010** | Muslim gunmen shot and killed at least eleven Coptic Christians at a church in Nag Hammadi, Egypt. |